D0016523

In Time

Pacesetter Press
A Division of Gulf Publishing Company
Houston, Texas

In Time

An Anecdotal History of the First Fifty Years of the University of Houston

Patrick J. Nicholson

In Time

ISBN 0-88415-371-1

Library of Congress Catalog Card Number 77-071492

Contents

Acknowledgments

There are a number of acknowledgments within the text, but more are due:

To my beloved wife and son for their forbearance and encouragement during many months when family weekends had to be sacrificed to demanding schedules of research and writing.

To my talented, understanding, and noncomputational editor, B.J. Lowe; his boss, Clayton Umbach; and Gulf Publishing Company and Pacesetter Press.

To the dozens of persons who graciously granted interviews or supplied missing facts or background information; especially to Professor Charles F. Hiller.

To the Writers' Project of the Federal Works Agency and Works Progress Administration for their 1942 guide to Houston's first century, produced with the cooperation and under sponsorship of the Harris County Historical Society.

To my dear sister-in-law, Valerie Harvey of "Long Meadow," Littleton, Surrey, by whose elegantly restored Elizabethan fireplace I outlined two pivotal chapters of this book.

To the research staff of the great library of the British Museum.

To the Houston *Post* and Houston *Chronicle* for permission to use editorial material.

To Leta Gilbert, my guide to the Minute Book of HISD and of the Board of Regents.

To President E.E. Oberholtzer and Professor J. Chester Cochran for their invaluable May 20, 1950 report on the first 23 years of the University.

To Farris Block and Barbara Chrisman for editorial assistance.

And to the Celtic good fortune that placed me in the time and setting to know all six of the presidents of the University of Houston and the events and circumstances that shaped them and their institution.

Patrick J. Nicholson
Houston, Texas
Memorial Day, 1977

For Barbara
and
Michael Patrick James

El tiempo y yo
Contra qualquier dos

(Time and I against any two)

—Spanish proverb

Chapter One

1923-1927

The prelude and earliest beginnings . . . The Board of Education goes on a manhunt . . . Houston and a tenacious Hoosier obsessed with the need for more education find one another . . . A junior college in less than three years, for a city desperately lacking one

How did the University of Houston begin? Certainly, a large public university was a corollary to the city's own magnificent growth. Houston had to have such a facility—one capable of fulfilling the city's need for higher education and committed to serving the community with quality instruction. The institution had to be cut to the city's own great dimensions; it had to be responsive to change and challenge—to reflect the city's tradition of sound, vigorous growth and ever-expanding accomplishment.

In human terms, the University probably began with the interest of some leading Houstonians in Edison E. Oberholtzer, the notable superintendent of schools in Tulsa, Oklahoma. Reacting to remarkable growth stimulated by World War I (between 1920 and 1930 Houston's population was to mushroom from 138,276 to 292,351—or 111%), members of the Board of Education and others in the community power structure saw as early as 1922 the need for a major reorganization and expansion of the public school system under vigorous new leadership.

The first step—a most significant one —was taken in 1923, when the school system was reconstituted as an independent entity apart from city government. Next, a search committee was formed. Its members began looking for a man with fundamentally sound concepts of education combined with energy and vision. He had to have specific experience in coping with a continuing sharp escalation in enrollments as well as the variety of problems to be expected in a rapidly developing city. The committee kept coming across the name of Edison E. Oberholtzer.

Dr. Oberholtzer had become superintendent of schools in Tulsa in 1913. He had arrived there only six years after Oklahoma was admitted to the Union, amid still-fresh recountings of how the Sooners galloped into the Cherokee Strip to stake out two million acres of land at high noon on April 22, 1889.

Tulsa, already a small city in 1913, was plagued with all the difficulties incident to burgeoning growth and was soon to be plunged into further expansion resulting from World War I. As the hub of an oil boom of worldwide significance, and as the major city in a relatively new state, Tulsa's population had soared from 500 to 22,000, overnight.

The new superintendent, noting the short tenure of many of his predecessors, immediately implemented a program emphasizing sound expansion. It is well that he did, for by 1923 Tulsa's population was to explode almost six-fold again, to 125,000. Oil companies were on every corner. The landscape was strewn with supply houses, pipe yards, and tool companies to service the petroleum giant—the ugly infrastructure of a boom city. And everywhere Oklahomans were demanding a good education for their children.

Dr. Oberholtzer met the challenge, partly through innovations in the design and construction of classrooms (the Tulsa "Unit System"), but largely through the introduction and development of new teaching concepts and an unflagging perseverance sometimes misidentified as mulish stubbornness. In 11 years he opened 14 "ward," or primary and secondary, schools and two new high schools. More importantly, he raised the educational standards of the Tulsa system constantly while building and retaining sound relationships with virtually every element of the community.

Many high school graduates during Oberholtzer's years in Tulsa went on to college, establishing what has become a tradition in Oklahoma: an unusually high percentage of the state's public high school graduates pursue higher education. And some of them brought the Sooner State an honor of which few are aware: the University of Oklahoma is exceeded only by Harvard College in the number of its graduates who have become Rhodes Scholars.

There were dozens of candidates for the Houston superintendency in 1924, but the final selection came down to Dr. Oberholtzer and candidates from Savannah; San Francisco; Saint

Joseph, Missouri; and Ardmore, Oklahoma. Almost until the final decision, the California applicant was the leading candidate, but his support vanished when it was learned that he would demand the then-unheard of salary of $12,500 per annum.

Dr. Oberholtzer was elected unanimously, on the first ballot, at the Board of Education meeting of Monday evening, April 7, 1924. His salary was set at $9,000 for 1924-1925, with an automatic increase to $10,000 the ensuing year.

The unanimous vote on the first ballot was of considerable significance. The Board of Education for the Houston public schools was known for its close votes and contentious sessions long before, and long after, 1924. Even as Dr. Oberholtzer was selected, the storm warnings were up again: three trustees were being replaced; a recount that very day had reversed the apparent election of Oscar Lang (as a trustee) over A.C. Finn; and the touchy subject of 1924-1925 teacher contracts was under discussion. So, the unanimous support accorded the new superintendent was somewhat surprising. And it was to continue for a considerable time, even though the honeymoon, as we shall see, finally went into eclipse with earthly as well as celestial fireworks.

More that 25 years later, I asked Dr. Oberholtzer if he remembered the evening of April 7, 1924: where he was, how he reacted to the news of his election, what action he took in anticipation of his new responsibilities.

He had been in Dallas, addressing one of the regional organizations of educational administrators. He could almost recall the telephone number of his hotel, which he had given to C.H. Hurlock, president of the Board of Education, in the hope of receiving good news.

His first reaction, he recalled, was elation over a new and formidable challenge, one laced with opportunity. Tulsa had been a most satisfying experience, but he felt that he had reached a critical point in his career (a month short of his forty-fourth birthday), where he had to decide to stay where he was or move on. I can remember some of Dr. Oberholtzer's words: Houston, to him, was a "can-do" town, with "high-calibre, can-do people." It was a "fresh, energetic, new city," even though he was aware Houston dated back to the days of the Texas Republic.

And what did he say to Mr. Hurlock? He thanked him, of course, and told him that the Board of Education's trust was not misplaced. Then, he did a typical thing that provides some insight into the Oberholtzer personality while affirming his foresight and good judgment: He asked if it would be possible for him to address the June graduating classes of Heights Senior High School and of Central High School, even though he would not be able to report for duty until a week or so after graduation day. And he indicated several alternate dates in May on which he would want to meet with the Board of Education, plus the man he would succeed, Superintendent R.B. Cousins, and key members of the Cousins staff.

Dr. Oberholtzer knew instinctively that he should (1) move energetically into a situation where energy and initiative would be required and expected; (2) make himself and his educational philosophy, policies and plans widely known in Houston as soon as possible; and (3) begin to assess his new colleagues in more depth, and to build his own administrative structure, before the instability of impending but still-unannounced change began to take its toll in morale and organizational effectiveness.

The texts of Superintendent Oberholtzer's addresses to 112 graduates of Heights High and 351 graduates of the much larger Central High are still available. They provide a valuable overview of the speaker's educational philosophy and reveal the degree to which Dr. Oberholtzer was committed to "creative" schools rather than to overemphasis upon "training for work"; to the proper relationship between a democracy, its citizenry and education; and to widely available public higher education.

Years later, the Heights High and Central High addresses were to provide a possible answer to basic conflicts within the emerging University of Houston. In 1924, they told the listener, or reader, that Houston's new superintendent of schools was strongly in favor of basic, old-fashioned education: "The public schools are obliged to give to their students a better command of the fundamentals, the 'three R's,' by habits of study and investigation . . . (public education) . . . seeks to fix upon (the child) responsibility, a sense of things that must be done. Self-realization and self-responsibility (are) great fundamental(s) in learning . . . . The burden of helping to solve economic and industrial problems rests in a measure on the schools, in that they must help the child to become acquainted with the work to be done and must assist him to find himself in this work."

The speeches highlight Dr. Oberholtzer's frugality, that he was conscious of the sacred nature of the tax dollar, of the need to get as large a percentage of that dollar back, in time, as possible: " . . . public education is an important business. There is the large investment in physical property, building and equipment. There is the enormous cost for maintenance. (We do not) tax the people for any individual or selfish purpose. (Instead,) public education seeks to prepare the child for a large participation in the work of the world."

The speeches also reveal that he was in favor of developing the individual in an appropriately organized society that trains its members broadly, and even throughout life, for a constructive existence that recognizes and discharges the obligations of citizenship: "The ideal of a democracy is that the individual and society may find fulfillment each in the other. The purpose of a democracy is so to organize society that each member may develop his personality, primarily through activities designed for the well-being of his fellow members and of society as a whole . . . . It follows that education in a democracy . . . should develop in each individual knowledge, interests, ideals and habits whereby he will find his place, and use that place to shape both himself and society to nobler ends. Therefore, public education in a democracy must tend to clarify public opinion . . . dispel local sectional prejudice, and strengthen the common ties which bind the country together."

Especially in the Central High School address (which began with H.G. Wells' oft-quoted observation: "Civilization is a race between education and catastrophe"), Dr. Oberholtzer emphasized changes in post-World War I society that "are forcing major shifts in curricula and in educational organization. In the progress of public education," he asserted, "the schools have not always kept pace with the general forward movement of society." He then went on to describe his first innovation for the Board of Education—a system of junior high schools:

> . . . a new type of institution known as the intermediate or junior high school, which has for its purpose the organization of curriculum activities (so as) to make a special appeal to children of the adolescent period . . . . It offers an enriched curriculum, a wider range of activities and more special attention to individual needs.

Because he did not want to make too strident a plea for something as innovative as a junior high school before he had even settled into his new job, Dr. Oberholtzer stipulated that " . . . each community must come to know its needs, and to provide for them in terms of its abilities and its desires."

But he had already sounded the cry for keeping up with a changing society while simultaneously praising the "three R's," prudent handling of the tax dollar, and the appropriate relation between a democracy, its citizens and their educational institutions. Now, he reasoned, came the plug for junior high schools, a key element in the greatly-expanded system of public education which he already envisioned for his new home town.

I was unable to find any of the diminishing number of those Central High seniors who heard Dr. Oberholtzer speak at the old City Auditorium on that hot, muggy, un-air conditioned night 53 years ago who could still remember anything about his address. Gordon Turrentine, the long-time Chamber of Commerce official who was president of the Class of 1924, did remember that the ceremony was at the City Auditorium (now the site of Jones Hall) and that he, the other class officers, the valedictorian, and salutatorian sat on the stage with the members of the Board of Education and other officials and speakers.

Mr. Turrentine can hardly be faulted for this, since all that I can remember of possibly 100 visits to the old Auditorium are the night that a noted prima donna came out to open the second act of *Tosca* with the touring Metropolitan Opera, opened her mouth and soundlessly keeled over in 90-degree heat and 95 percent humidity; another time that some of the city's leading matrons, attending a Houston Symphony Society concert, found themselves scratching unidentified bites under their ermine capes (after the Auditorium had been left open the night before for some infested knights of the road threatened with freezing to death during a blue norther); and the morning that John T. Jones, Jr., presented some of us with tiny pieces of the stage to which Edna W. Saunders, the *impresaria* of Levy's elegant old department store, had brought Enrico Caruso, Ignace Jan Padrewski, and most of the world's great masters of the performing arts for more than a generation.

I still have my memento of City Auditorium, and it is likely to outlast us all: a piece of premium, half-inch, quarter-sawn oak. Immanuel Olshan's wrecking crews took the rest the morning of

June 10, 1963, and another landmark was gone. This one, happily, was replaced by a masterpiece of beauty and utility, through Jesse H. Jones' splendid generosity and what is reputed to have been his dying admonishment of his nephew: "Build a new Opera House, and make it a fine one."

Dr. Oberholtzer returned to Houston on June 12, 1924, to assume the post of superintendent of schools officially under a new president of the Board of Education, R.H. Fonville (who was later to become mayor of Houston). The new superintendent was to remain in this post for 21 years, surviving slowly-crescent opposition and, finally, a management consultant's nightmare in which he and H.L. Mills, the business manager of the school system, had "co-equal authority" in overlapping areas of operation.

The possibility of this cardinal sin of administration, with its inevitable and open conflicts, had been lurking about for almost a decade. It was finally committed in 1939, even though the members of the Board of Education must have realized that they were flouting a fundamental concept of management by naming two captains for a single ship. A party to the crime told me that the trustees "had two good men at the top who would never accept orders from another employee of the school system. So we decided to split things up between them."

Wanting to keep both men, the Board of Education took what appeared on the surface to be the easy way out. But even the most skilled of surgeons could not divide the vital organs and winnow out the veins and arteries of the Siamese twins involved. As a result, the trustees confirmed the existence of a two-headed monster that had been pawing around just under the surface. The discovered banshee was to haunt the school system and the nascent University of Houston increasingly until 1945, when H.L. Mills finally put together the compromise that forced Dr. Oberholtzer to resign as superintendent. By that time, as we shall see, the tough and canny Hoosier had put his stamp on the Houston public schools forever, and was probably more than ready to move on to become the University of Houston's first full-time president.

"H.L.," who had a deserved reputation for running roughshod over superintendents, as well as an occasional trustee, circled warily in the middle and late 1920's before tangling openly with the new man. He recognized a new breed of cat, suspected of harboring that final malediction of expensive ideas[1], but still resplendent in the shining armor of a national reputation and a 7-0 vote of appointment. As entrenched as the Rock of Gibraltar because of his long tenure, innate ability, close and valuable ties throughout the city and state, and the degree to which successive Boards of Education had wisely come to depend upon his fiscal knowledge and experience, Mills did not press his advantage for a considerable time. Instead, he apparently sent out the word to his numerous kin (literally dozens of whom were employed in the school system), to step up the gathering and reporting of information while he surveyed the field and probed for an opening.

The business manager had correctly gauged the opposition, which was formidable indeed. Superintendent Oberholtzer survived not only his first 3-4 vote but far more pronounced defeats as he evolved a *modus vivendi* from a beginning *modus non moriendi.* The Oberholtzer policies, although often under attack by Mills as well as by various trustees, were based upon sound research and a farsighted yet reasonably conservative approach. They were also being put forward by a tenacious, resilient man who simply would not give up when he knew that he was right.

The first six years under President Fonville were relatively peaceful ones for Superintendent Oberholtzer, and lucky for him that they were, since this made it possible for him to lay the foundations for 25 years of extraordinary progress within the school system and the fledgling Houston Junior College and University of Houston. "There was no squabbling during the Fonville years," a close observer of this 1924-1930 era told me. "The Board of Education held a luncheon meeting, usually every other Tuesday, at Sam Houston High. We worked until 2:00 or 2:30 p.m., and things went smoothly enough in those days."

Although they continued to constitute an effective team, a running battle between Dr. Oberholtzer and Business Manager Mills began to surface in the early 1930's. Mills' ever-ascendant power, bulwarked by his high-level ties with the State Legislature and long friendship with key members of the teaching corps, was solidified further in 1934. At that time he was listed with the actual trustees as something of a quasi-member of the Board of Education, and highly praised for his successful efforts to increase state appropriations to the public school system while confirming the legality of the Houston Junior College and helping to advance it to four-year status.

The Board of Education had already discovered, however, the many positive attributes of H.L. Mills' rival in the impending struggles for control. Superintendent Oberholtzer was increasingly popular in the community, his national reputation continued on the rise, and he was careful never to become involved in head-on collisions with the business manager. Of singular importance to the Board of Education, he was predicting Houston's extraordinary growth patterns with uncanny success and was providing for them within budgetary limitations (although there were anxious years throughout the Great Depression). Further, his chief deputy, Walter W. Kemmerer, was more and more valuable even though he could occasionally ruffle up a trustee or even the surface calm of Superintendent Oberholtzer.

Colonel W.B. Bates (more about both him and Dr. Kemmerer later) was able to judge Dr. Oberholtzer's contributions to the development of Houston's present-day public school system from a unique vantage point: He was elected to the Board of Education in 1928, served five years as secretary, and assumed the presidency in 1933, when he replaced his good friend Judge K.C. Barkley.

Colonel Bates then remained in close touch with the Board of Education during the remaining 12 years of Superintendent Oberholtzer's incumbency and watched the accelerating expansion of the local primary and secondary schools during the remainder of a long life. He told me this during a series of interviews in 1973, seated in his office or at his favorite luncheon table in the Coronado Club:

"Dr. Oberholtzer took a system that had grown a good bit like Topsy, developed research methods and people to discover which way the town was really going, showed the Board of Education what was required and then pestered us into providing it.

"It's still pretty much the system he laid out," Colonel Bates summarized, "even though the Doctor's been gone from it almost 30 years. He added something like eight junior high schools, and we had none before his time, plus I think four senior high schools and many more grammar schools. And he did it all with good common sense and workable procedures. We owe a lot to him, and even more to his foresight."

It is vital to realize that Dr. Oberholtzer, busy though he was with the current and future problems of the mushrooming public school system, opened the Houston Junior College (HJC), forerunner of the University of Houston, less than three years after taking over as superintendent of schools. He was actually hard at work on this project by the late fall of 1926, and probably earlier, by his own account.

In tracing the genesis of HJC, Dr. Oberholtzer placed great emphasis upon a meeting in his office in November 1926. This was attended by a dozen or so seniors from the Houston high schools who had requested an audience with the superintendent to discuss what their spokesman described as "an urgent matter." All of these youngsters, Dr. Oberholtzer recalled later in various speeches, came from families of modest means, and most of them were working part-time while attending high school. They made average grades but stood far enough down in their graduating classes to eliminate them as successful candidates for matriculation at Rice Institute; nor could they afford to go out of the city to continue their education.

Dr. Oberholtzer encouraged each of his visitors to tell his or her own story to him and to the group. As he went around the room, he was more and more impressed with the need for a junior college, and began to seek a way of establishing one as soon as possible. There are those who intimate that the superintendent had come to this decision even earlier, and might have had a hand in stimulating the meeting with the graduating seniors. In any case, the testimony of his visitors constituted powerful ammunition.

There were obviously many problems to launching a junior college, among them winning over the Board of Education, money, physical plant, accreditation, faculty and administrative staff. The obdurate optimist, Dr. Oberholtzer tackled these quickly and effectively, without any thought of failure.

The junior college idea had a considerable amount of support among the trustees, although several pointed out that the project could not be successful without tax support. Superintendent Oberholtzer countered with proposed budgets in which what he termed modest tuition charges ($150 for 30 semester hours, or $6 per hour for a partial enrollment) would provide very modest faculty salaries. He did ask for a $2,000 loan from the Board of Education with which to open a bank account and pay certain advance costs.

As for physical plant, the HJC would simply use San Jacinto High School in the evening hours, when it was empty anyhow;

this also took care of maintenance, utilities and janitorial services.

Dr. Oberholtzer insisted that the proposed faculty emphasize teaching ability, plus the minimum degree of master of arts. Many of its members, he felt, could be drawn from the ranks of senior instructors in the Houston public schools and paid a modest salary of $40 or $50 per month in addition to their principal income from the school district. Full-time members of the faculty, he proposed, would receive salaries in the $1,800 to $2,800 per annum range.

The administrative staff would depend heavily upon what Superintendent Oberholtzer liked to call the "two-hat theory." Most administrators would simply don another hat when they left for the new HJC operation from their public school system office, although there would be a few full-time appointees.

Accreditation was a somewhat thorny problem, but Dr. Oberholtzer found a solution. He went to Dr. T.H. Shelby, director of extension services for the University of Texas, and to President H.F. Estill of Sam Houston State Teachers College at Huntsville, with this proposition: the University of Texas and Sam Houston State would open and staff an Extension Center for the training of teachers at San Jacinto High School in the summer of 1927; would provide some key members of the first faculty of the HJC; and would agree to accept HJC credits so long as they approved all HJC faculty members and were given continuing assurance that the new junior college was being operated in accordance with standards of the State Department of Education and the Texas Association of Colleges.

The proposition was accepted in principle, clearing the way for the historic resolution of the Board of Education on March 7, 1927, in which the trustees unanimously authorized the "founding, establishment and operation of a junior college."[2] Superintendent Oberholtzer was "instructed to proceed at once to set up definite plans" for the new institution. As he had proposed, HJC would use "public school buildings of the Houston Independent School District (HISD)," specifically San Jacinto High School, with "instruction service" supported by tuition and other fees, and "library and laboratory facilities, light, heat and janitorial service" provided by HISD.

The superintendent was of course far ahead of the Board of Education in the matter of "definite plans." He signed the agreement with the University of Texas and Sam Houston State Teachers on March 11, had it affirmed by the trustees on March 14, and set about immediately to publicize a first summer session, beginning June 5, to hire faculty members for HJC, to determine which of his administrators would join him (as president) in wearing two hats, and to meet with the principal of San Jacinto High School on the impending invasion of that institution. He also drew and banked HJC's $2,000 loan from the Board of Education.

Registration for the first summer session began on schedule on June 5, 1927, with an enrollment of 232 and a faculty of 12, four of them on loan from the University of Texas or Sam Houston State. A "formal opening assembly" was held on the morning of June 7, with principal speeches by President Fonville of the Board of Education and Dr. Oberholtzer. Most classes began on June 6, but a few were held June 5.

Since the 1927 summer session excluded freshmen, and emphasized education courses for teachers in the temporary "Extension Center" manned to a considerable degree by "borrowed" professors, the more accurate opening date for the Houston Junior College may be September 19, 1927, when the first fall semester was launched. In any event, HJC was under way. Dr. Oberholtzer had grave new responsibilities which he relished from the moment he assumed them until he laid them down 23 years later, and Houston and the State of Texas had what would become an enormous new asset.

Who can say with any certainty that Dr. Oberholtzer did not foresee the early development of a junior college within the Houston public school system even before he applied for the superintendency here?

Certainly his main emphasis was, and had to be, on the expansion of the primary and secondary system that was to grow so solidly for the next two decades under his direction. But he obviously carried out a penetrating analysis of both existing and indicated problems and opportunities within Houston's schools and the overall community before the decision to leave Tulsa, the major determination of his career to that point.

Did the analysis make clear to Dr. Oberholtzer, well before it was perceived by his future superiors and peers, the need for a public junior college in Houston? It must have, for a number of reasons:

(1) He was not only an expert on secondary education in rapidly-growing cities, but a rising authority on other related matters, including the strong post-World War I trend to junior colleges, already clearly evident in California.

(2) The junior college trend was threatening to become a fullfledged movement in Texas by the mid-1920's, with more than a dozen of these institutions in operation, some of them in cities and towns with only a fraction of the population of Houston (Clarendon, Hillsboro, Paris, Ranger and Victoria, for example).

(3) How could Houston provide for the post-secondary education of its high school graduates, numbering almost 2,000 in 1924 with every indication of substantial annual increases, without a junior college? (The Rice Institute had already limited its enrollment of these hometown graduates to 200 annually, or 10% of the total output, and would continue to decrease the percentage with each succeeding year).

This hypothesis of a benevolent plot on behalf of Houston's young men and women, as well as the more mature seeking further training, holds up well also in terms of Dr. Oberholtzer's early life, his personality traits and his experience. They reveal a near-obsession for additional education, both for himself and for America's changing society.

Edison Ellsworth Oberholtzer was born May 6, 1880[3] in Patricksburg, Owen County, Indiana. He was the tenth of the 11 children of Augustus and Mary Anne (Collins) Oberholtzer, and one of four sons.

Patricksburg, with a population that has shrunk a bit since the count of 265 in the 1970 census, is about 30 miles south and east of Terre Haute, near the Illinois border. Isolated from the freeways that link Indianapolis, Terre Haute, Vincennes and Evansville, it appears much as it must have in the 1880's, except for the television antennas.

I paid one of the few traffic fines of my law-abiding career to a friendly justice of the peace in an adjoining county, racing up the twisty, black-topped, narrow roads from New Harmony to be on time for a lecture date at Bloomington. As recompense, I saw some of middle America's most beautiful countryside, among rolling, fertile hills where winter wheat thrives, where soybeans are grown to fatten hogs for the food-processing plants in Terre Haute.

When Dr. Oberholtzer was a boy in Patricksburg, there was much more emphasis upon corn and rye. Many farmers worked part-time in nearby coal and clay mines, although Augustus Oberholtzer was not one of them. He listed his occupation as lumberman, farmer, and contractor.

Schooling was hard to come by in Owen County, Indiana in the 1880's and 1890's, although the Three R's were taught in tiny classrooms when children were not needed on the farm, and there was a grammar school at Spencer, the county seat on the White River. This is somewhat ironic, since the county bears the name of Robert Dale Owen, the famed social experimenter who had brought his English savants and their "Boatland of Knowledge" to nearby New Harmony[4] in the first years of the nineteenth century. From New Harmony, less than 100 miles from Patricksburg, had come the concepts of free public libraries, kindergartens, and a Utopia based upon widely-diffused knowledge coupled with social reform.

Fortunately, there was both a larger grammar school and a high school at Clay City, in the next county. Young Ed Oberholtzer was sent there, and he graduated from Clay City High School (the rough equivalent of our ninth grade today) in 1895. To put that date in perspective, the Panic of 1893 was in full force, although beginning to abate, and Adlai Stevenson III's grandfather was the little-known vice president under Grover Cleveland.

Though barely 15 years old, our future educator was at a crossroads as he received his high school diploma. From later statements and speeches, however, it appears that he had chosen a career even in early adolescence, along with clearly-defined lifetime goals.

Edison Ellsworth Oberholtzer would become a teacher as soon as he could earn his temporary certificate; with certificate in hand, he would launch himself upon a long-term program of obtaining the best possible education and helping other young people to do the same.

Young Oberholtzer put his plan into immediate effect, with four significant developments between 1895 and 1899. He found whatever work he could, saved his money for a year, and entered Westfield College (immediately across the Wabash River in

Illinois) in the fall of 1896. In the spring of 1897 he had his temporary teaching certificate and a job in a village school. "My teaching experience," he said later, "began at the grass roots . . . a type of invaluable training which very few people have the opportunity to receive."

The future Dr. Oberholtzer must have been a success at "grass-roots" teaching, for by the spring of 1899 he had a considerably more lucrative contract at another rural school, and a 16-year-old wife, Myrtle Barr.[5] Little did they know that it would be 30 years before the young bridegroom could complete his formal education, in what was to become a saga of determination and perseverance.

It was to be eight years (six of them spent in a variety of Indiana schools, the remainder as a beginning administrator in charge of the school system at Clinton, Indiana) before our young scholar obtained his permanent teaching certificate at Indiana State Normal (now Indiana State University) in Terre Haute. The year was 1907, a full decade since his graduation from Westfield College. His motivation was not diminished, but the responsibilities of heading a young family on a rural schoolteacher's salary made it increasingly difficult to continue his education. The post at Clinton, with the differential paid an administrator, made things a bit easier.

In his early career, Dr. Oberholtzer's contracts were for a maximum of 10 months, even after he departed classroom teaching for administration. This classic pattern, which of course still exists for teachers today, allowed a prudent man to put aside enough to finance his further education, though the nest egg might be slow in accumulating. And in the summer of 1908 the Oberholtzer family, including at first young Kenneth Edison, then later his brother E.E., Jr., and sister Myrtle Esther, began spending vacation months at the University of Chicago. This was to extend through the summer of 1915, when our determined candidate received the master of arts degree.

John Dewey had departed the University of Chicago in a celebrated 1904 row with President William Rainey Harper[6] over the operation of his famed Laboratory School, in which educational theories evolved from philosophy and psychology were being rigorously examined. Dewey was to stay at his next post, Columbia University, for almost a half-century, expounding his "progressive" concept of the child as a living organism, shaped by heredity and environment. But his ideas remained at Chicago, as did opposing theories, in a yeasty, stimulating intellectual climate that made the Chicago institution a Mecca for students of pedagogy and educational systems.

Dr. Oberholtzer had read Dewey's wide-ranging publications for years, including the classic 1899 book, *The School and Society.* He was also acquainted with the work of Francis W. Parker, the legendary superintendent of schools from Quincy, Massachusetts who helped turn Dewey toward the idea of "child-centered" education, wherein one fits the school to the young student rather than the child to the school. Parker had established the so-called "Quincy Method" at his Cook County Normal School in Chicago, which added to the attractiveness of the nearby University of Chicago as a center for graduate study in education.

Moving on to positions of growing scope and responsibilities as superintendent of schools at Evansville, Indiana and at Tulsa, Dr. Oberholtzer found additional motivation for, and value from, his summer studies. Apparently neither a strong champion of the "progressive" nor of the "traditional" schools of thought, the maturing educator read widely in both camps, though his personal convictions leaned toward the latter. He concentrated on courses in the surging field of educational administration to keep well abreast of current developments; but he also took time to co-author what he always called "The Blue-Backed Speller." This volume, the correct title of which was *The Cardinal Speller,* spoke to his life-long interest in the fundamentals of education, as well as ongoing evolvement and progress.

In 1910 our determined candidate received the Ph. B. degree (bachelor of philosophy) from the University of Chicago, shortly after his thirtieth birthday. Five years later, in 1915, he was awarded the masters of arts degree by the University of Chicago, a major step in a campaign nearing its second decade. He returned to Chicago the next summer for additional courses, but soon found that the pressure of his duties at Tulsa, and the impending crises of World War I, would force a moratorium on the Oberholtzer Plan.

In 1921 Dr. Oberholtzer was awarded the degree of doctor of law, *honoris causa,* by the University of Tulsa. This was in recognition of his widely acclaimed accomplishments as superintendent of schools at Tulsa, which were to bring him to the attention of the Board of Education in Houston. The degree also paid tribute to his prominent role in many World War I drives in Tulsa, where he headed campaigns for Liberty Loans, War Savings Stamps, and the American Red Cross. He returned to formal graduate studies in the summer of 1922, at Columbia University's Teachers College, where John Dewey would be active for almost another generation. And seven years later, 30 years after his professional educational project was originally launched in 1899, Columbia University awarded him the Ph.D.

It was a triumph of perseverance, and a model for many another youngster across the land, when Dr. Oberholtzer unrolled that genuine sheepskin signed by the great Nicholas Murray Butler. Little wonder that the graduating seniors who came to his Houston office in 1926, frustrated in their determination to obtain more education, found a sympathetic and effective champion in Edison Ellsworth Oberholtzer. He had travelled that difficult but rewarding road and was determined to make it easier for the next pilgrims embarking upon it.

Notes to Chapter One

[1]Mr. Mills once told a visitor to his rather moth-eaten office in an old school on Washington Avenue that he appreciated the visitor's remarks about the public school system being "an economical operation." "I want you to understand, though," H.L. pointed out, "we don't just run things economically, we run 'em *cheap*."

[2]See actual resolution in Appendix.

[3]Often listed as 1882, but reliable records and the testimony of his peers indicate that Dr. Oberholtzer's birth year was 1880.

[4]New Harmony, of course, has close and increasingly significant ties to Houston. Kenneth Dale Owen, internationally known as a geologist as well as a breeder of fine Hereford cattle and some of the world's greatest trotting horses, is a direct descendant of Robert Dale Owen.

Jane Blaffer (Mrs. Kenneth Dale) Owen, a remarkable woman of wide interests and superb abilities, is the driving force in a careful reconstruction of New Harmony as it was. The project has drawn international notice and acclaim.

[5]Dr. Oberholtzer often said that he was 17 and Mrs. Oberholtzer was 16 when they were married on March 26, 1899. She was 16, but her bridegroom was actually 18, and almost 19. The important thing is that the marriage, marked by obvious tenderness, love and respect, lasted more than a half century.

[6]Dr. Oberholtzer told Colonel Bates this story about President Harper, after Colonel Bates had tactfully suggested that Dr. Oberholtzer was not only persistent, but perhaps overly so, in seeking funds for the University of Houston in its earlier years: John D. Rockefeller had been attracted to the University of Chicago by President Harper's obvious skills in building a brilliant faculty and a firm foundation for an increasingly prestigious institution. Mr. Rockefeller made a series of contributions to the University which finally totalled many millions. But he continued to be besieged by President Harper, who had an apparently endless list of needs for his institution.

After an especially eloquent appeal, Mr. Rockefeller told the minister-educator that he would provide the needed funds on one condition: that President Harper never ask him for another dollar. This was agreed, and Dr. Harper thanked the philanthropist profusely, extracting from him a promise to visit the presidential office from time to time and to keep in touch with the University , even though his splendid gifts were at an end.

In due course, Mr. Rockefeller responded to an invitation for a visit. After an interesting report on the current status of the University, including some emphasis on one of his favorite areas, the Department of Theology, President Harper thanked Mr. Rockefeller for coming to see him and suggested that they conclude with a moment of prayer in a nearby chapel. In the chapel, President Harper spoke eloquently to the Lord concerning Mr. Rockefeller's past generosities, thanking them both. He then mentioned two or three particularly pressing needs, concluding with the fervent hope that the Lord might see fit to bring these somehow to Mr. Rockefeller's attention. The philanthropist was so impressed by President Harper's ingenuity, and by the fervor of his prayer, that he again became the University of Chicago's principal benefactor.

Chapter Two

1927-1934

Life in a far different Houston—and world . . . The first years at San Jacinto High School . . . New principals among the dramatis personae . . . *Validation by the State legislature and quick emergence as a four-year institution*

Houston was different in that long-ago summer of 1927—far more different than an intervening half-century of even such transcendent change might indicate. So was the world changed, in that already legendary era of Charles Augustus Lindbergh's landing at Le Bourget; of Al Jolson's part-talkie, *The Jazz Singer*; of the U.S. Marine Corps landing in Nicaragua and again in China within a three-month period, long before brinkmanship, the Cold War and detente.

What we see now, across the penumbra of 50 years, are those fundamental shifts in the fabric of life that have altered our city and our existence so dramatically. These changes have, of course, been enormously accelerated by more tangible factors: the incessant, sometimes spectacular growth in population; vigorous economic health interrupted only rarely by recession or depression; and always the driving personalities who have been the central source of civic pride, dedication and effectiveness as well as power, who have traditionally shaped Houston.

The spectacular growth was already there in 1927, and to a degree that constituted a major force in the decision to establish the Houston Junior College. As noted earlier, the city gained 111% in population between 1920 and 1930, a rate of increase not exceeded since, even in the boom years of World War II and in the splurge of the 1970's. Nor will this rate be matched in the future, since the laws of mathematics are immutable: the base against which decennial census gains for Houston are calculated has become too large to support anything resembling another 10-year doubling.[1]

Underlying the city's remarkable expansion of population was a relatively short period of halcyon years that rivaled the great boom between the end of Reconstruction in 1872 and the financial panic of 1893. During those two decades, railroads, cotton and lumber brought the Yankee tycoons here in droves, after Governor Richard Hubbard had excited their speculative interest in a widely publicized speech about Texas at Philadelphia's Centennial Exposition of 1876.

Many things brought new residents to Houston between 1920 and 1930. Among them were the recognition of the city, a generation after Spindletop, as the center not only of the petroleum industry but of its bustling offspring—petrochemicals; an astounding total of building permits that approached the $50 million level in 1927; and a half-billion-dollar volume of combined exports and imports at Port Houston.

The year 1927 was a watershed year in more ways than one, as Edison E. Oberholtzer prepared for the opening of the Houston Junior College. Houston surpassed both San Antonio and upstart Dallas in population, to become Texas' largest city; a rash of downtown skyscrapers (among them the still-incredible Italian Renaissance elegance of the Niels Esperson Building, with its gold-plated cupola and chimes) arose scant blocks from the last of the great homes of the inner city; and three new high schools (Jefferson Davis, John H. Reagan and Jack Yates), four junior high schools (Albert Sidney Johnston, Stonewall Jackson, Sidney Lanier and James Stephen Hogg,[2] to name a quartet of proper Southern, Texas and Houston heroes) and accompanying primary schools and other facilities were in planning, construction or final completion stages due to the passage of bond issues totalling $7 million, for which students harangued the voters on downtown streets.

It was significant that when the bubble burst for the remainder of the United States with the stock market crash of October, 1929, and the country plunged into the Great Depression, Houston's economy was strong and stable enough to withstand the worst of the financial and economic storms that rocked the nation and the world.

The city's bustling prosperity in 1927-1930, and its relative insulation from the more pronounced effects of the Depression, were fortunate indeed for the infant Houston Junior College (HJC), where two-thirds of the student body were employed either part- or full-time. During burgeoning prosperity, HJC was able to surge to a beginning enrollment of 460 in 1927, with very substantial increases to 637 in 1928, 730 in 1929, and 858 in 1930. The first downturn (to 743 students) did not occur until 1931, when the institution was well underway with a fairly substantial cash reserve in hand. Further, the upward pattern in enrollment resumed in 1933, when most of the nation was still in a terrible economic slump.

Much of this happy circumstance came about through (1) the innate stability and growing strength of the major oil companies headquartered in Houston; (2) the diversity that has always characterized our economy, even though most non-Texans are convinced that it is based 98% upon petroleum; and (3) the ability, courage, foresight and determination of the uniquely effective group of men who formed the city's power structure in the 1920's and 1930's, and the resources available to them.

Humble Oil & Refining Company ("The Humble"), now the major subsidiary of Exxon/USA, had been organized in Houston on January 20, 1911. There was nothing "humble," of course, about either the company or its founders, who were members of leading families already in the oil industry or quite aware of its potential. The name comes from what was the tiny hamlet of Humble (population 48 in 1900), some 20 miles northeast of downtown Houston. Here, on November 6, 1904, the Sharp Brothers well #1 ("Old Moonshine") came roaring in to confirm a major field and to open a new phase of expansion for our area. It all began because a curious farmer-rancher named J.H. Slaughter wondered about the "shows" of bubbling oil and gas in his water well. The Sharp brothers and other drillers were pumping 20 million barrels a year by late 1905.

"The Humble," with excellent guidance from top-flight executives (and the good fortune of finding geologists such as the fabled Wallace Pratt), moved quickly into a dominant position in the growing number of Gulf Coast oil fields and then strongly into the maelstrom of East Texas. Here, phenomenal gushers lowered the price of crude to a dime a barrel temporarily, but performed a memorable service by forcing proration and appropriate controls upon the industry. Well before this development, however, Humble had gathered the strength that enabled the company to form the core of an industrial Houston capable of remaining reasonably prosperous even in the midst of the Great Depression.

The Texas Company, first chartered in Beaumont,[3] transferred its headquarters to Houston soon after, by expanding a branch office opened in 1902. "The Texaco," along with Gulf Refining Company (although Andrew Mellon kept central operations of "The Gulf" in Pittsburgh as the J.M. Guffey Petroleum Company), also provided stable employment for thousands in this immediate area and stable income for literally hundreds of other companies, and tens of thousands of individuals, dependent upon the petroleum industry for the sale of products or services.

The diversity of the economy, meanwhile, further heightened the positive impact of steady growth and dependable income from the major oil companies. This city has simply never been a one-ring circus such as Detroit, susceptible to even minor fluctuations within a single industry.

Thus, Houston kept its eggs in many baskets from 1927-1934, as was its custom. The city remained a leading world cotton market and center,[4] even though the depression years played havoc with the level of exports. Harris County continued to lead the state in cattle population and in the gross volume of ranching operations, suffering only minor downturns in the production and/or processing of rice, grains and other agricultural products. Sulphur, carbon black, and a long list of other chemicals were in diminished demand; but they are so basic to so many industrial operations that total output remained reasonably constant through 1930 and then recovered well in the Houston area before an upturn was evident in other major U.S. cities. The lumber industry had hit its peak in Harris County well before the Great Depression, but it continued to bring substantial business and some new income, especially in pulping operations associated with papermaking.

Then there was the wealth of other resources and products in the area: shell, cement, fertilizers, scrap iron, metals for fabrication by the oil tool manufacturers. Natural gas, widely "flared" and wasted until World War II, was being piped in from Refugio County for industry and for homes as early as 1926, adding yet another dimension to the 1927-1934 economy with vast significance for the future development of petrochemical plants along the Ship Channel. And 18 railroads and 42 steamship lines, the pride of the Chamber of Commerce, kept Houston's diversified economy literally underway, even though sometimes at a reduced rate, through the Great Depression and on through the recession of 1937-1938. This latter downslide also had a limited impact in the area.

The driving personalities and civic leaders who have always shaped the city were here in 1927, and most of them, fortunately, for a generation more. These were the men who saw Houston through what were also chancy times for the fledgling Houston Junior College.

They included Jesse H. Jones, already a tycoon on the national as well as the local scene; John H. Kirby, the lumberman and real estate investor; Colonel J.W. Evans, in a sense the father of the Port of Houston; Captain (of the Light Guards) James A. Baker, who saved the William Marsh Rice bequest and thereby The Rice Institute; Ross S. Sterling, governor of the State of Texas and first president of the Humble Oil & Refining Company; Oscar Holcombe, perennial mayor and Old Gray Fox; Marcellus E. (Mefo) Foster, editor; W.P. Hobby, publisher and former governor; John T. Scott, banker; and a rising host of other new leaders in the spectacular world of the wildcatting oilmen, including Hugh Roy Cullen, James S. (Jim) Abercrombie and Big Jim West.

Several of these men were to have a material impact upon the University of Houston, although none would have the telling effect of Hugh Roy Cullen's involvement with the institution. They will reappear in our account, but it is important to say something of them and of their times now, if we are to comprehend what they and their city meant to the developing University.

If you had to single out one leader in the decade 1929-1939, when Houston moved so strongly to preëminence in the South and Southwest against an ebbtide of economic debacles elsewhere, it would probably be Jesse Holman Jones. And indeed, he was a towering giant, literally and in terms of his pervasive influence, until his death in 1956. This in spite of the fact that he spent most of the time from 1933 to 1945 in Washington, D.C., and had little or no role in the ever more consequential oil industry, after a brief term as an early director of "The Humble." This ended when he sold an original block of stock (which William Stamps Farish had urged him to buy) to Edgar E. Townes, Sr., doubling his money in a short period of time.[5]

Jesse Jones was born April 6, 1874 in Robertson County, Tennessee, in tobacco-growing country on the Kentucky border, about 30 miles north of Nashville. He came to Houston in the 1890's to work in the lumberyard of his uncle, M.T. Jones. Standing well over six feet, with good, strong features and fine eyes, young Jones combined physical attractiveness with a natural flair for business, plenty of energy, and a manner that seemed to indicate unusual maturity and judgment for his years. By 1902 he was King Nottoc IV in the annual Notsuoh Carnival and a rising young man by any measure. In 1904 he opened his own lumberyard. It was indicative of his nascent political power and connections that he was awarded the contract to supply the lumber for the Texas Building at the St. Louis Louisiana Purchase Exposition as one of his first big sales.

The lumber business was still of great importance to Houston at the turn of the century, and Jesse Jones apparently liked those he dealt with in the trade, such as James M. Rockwell and his boys Jim (later a regent of both the University of Houston and the University of Texas) and Henry. But he was quick to expand his operations into other ventures, primarily downtown real estate (with emphasis upon well-located office buildings and hotels) and commercial and mortgage banking. Later he added newspapers and radio stations. To the end of his days, Jesse Jones was always pleased to be identified as a publisher. This to him was a high calling of special significance and responsibility, and it was one of the many pursuits for which he had an instinctive feeling and obvious ability.

By 1927, the Jones Interests included the National Bank of Commerce, the Houston *Chronicle*, a new 37-story structure just coming out of the ground (the Gulf Building, first identified as the Jones Building, then renamed for its principal tenant), the Rice Hotel, and a thickly-woven lattice of lesser but also profitable buildings and enterprises concentrated in the heart of the downtown area.

The *Chronicle* was acquired in the summer of 1926 from "Mefo" Foster, who had invested a small fortune amassed in Spindletop leases, plus money from Camille Pillot and Sterling Meyer, to launch the new evening newspaper 25 years before. Mr. Jones had always been fascinated with newspapers, and by "Mefo," one of the scintillating personalities of early twentieth century Houston. Mefo had been the correspondent for the old Houston *Post* in Huntsville. He came here in 1893 to join the *Post* staff, where he worked with such brilliant writers and editors as O. Henry, Renzi M. Johnston and Judd Mortimer Lewis. After selling the *Chroni-*

cle to Mr. Jones, he stayed on as a special editor for a year, but was soon champing at the bit for his own operation again. He became editor of the new Houston *Press* in 1927 and completed 50 years in newspapering before he retired as editor emeritus in 1937.

Mefo once claimed that a watermelon had an important influence on American literature. O. Henry, he said, left the *Post* one night and took the train back to Austin to face embezzlement charges. But at Hempstead, he saw watermelons on ice, got off to buy one, missed the train while he ate it, caught a later connection back to Houston and continued on to Honduras, where he wrote some of his best stories. O. Henry (Sidney Porter) later returned to Austin and was convicted.

There is a story, possibly apocryphal, about why Jesse Jones became obsessed with buying the Rice Hotel. It is said that he liked the 25-cent luncheon special at the Rice dining room, and showed up one summer noon in 1900 in a fashionable new shirt designed to be worn without a coat. The proprieties being much more strictly enforced in 1900, the young lumberman was ignored as he waited for a table, and finally asked to leave. Leave he did, but not without telling the head waiter that he would return one day as the owner and straighten out matters.

This could well have happened, since there is virtually a separate literature of such stories; but it seems more likely that Mr. Jones bought the Rice Hotel because the corner of Main Street and Texas Avenue was clearly the hub of Houston when he acquired it, and for almost a generation thereafter. The price was right, the location superb, and the property formed both an anchor and a centerpiece for Mr. Jones' expanding holdings downtown.

Yet another version claims that Mr. Jones acquired the Rice Hotel so that he could have the thick porterhouse steaks that he came to relish in later life delivered by special waiter direct to his nearby office while he worked on through the luncheon hour. Jack Harris, the broadcasting tycoon, tells a different story. He says that attendance was unusually high at a Downtown Rotary Club luncheon at the Rice Hotel one noon, stimulated by the knowledge that Mr. Jones would be at the head table and the hope that Headwaiter Ben Coren's economical and somewhat mediocre menu would be stepped up in honor of the distinguished guest and owner of the joint. The headwaiter played it cagily, however; he served minimal slices of pot roast and a rice pudding dessert as Mr. Jones nodded approval, and furnished the great man a magnificent fruit platter.

Jesse Jones' contributions to Houston were so numerous that it is difficult to single out any one as being the most significant. It would be equally difficult, however, to underestimate his role in preventing the failure of at least two downtown banks, in October of 1931.

The autumn of 1931 was obviously a critical time in the city, as it was to be at the new Houston Junior College. Emergency relief supplies were being distributed at the old Hampshaw Building, and Mayor Walter Monteith had a special committee studying growing unemployment, which was being countered somewhat with temporary jobs on the public payroll.

Still, Harris County was able to sell a $3 million bond issue, Houston had been confirmed officially as Texas' largest city, and building permits were holding up reasonably well. The oil business continued as a major stabilizing factor, and much of a near-record Texas cotton crop of 5.3 million bales was headed for compresses, warehouses and the Port of Houston.

Then, just as it seemed that the city would weather the Great Depression far better than had been hoped, rumors of the impending failure of one, and possibly two, downtown banks began to spread. Fortunately, the banks closed Saturday, October 24, 1931 at noon for the weekend before runs by depositors could develop. Jesse Jones, of course, had been watching the situation for some time with increasing concern. Depositor panic, with ensuing runs on banks, he was well aware, was the financial counterpart to the "Spanish influenza" which had spread with such deadly effect at the end of World War I. He set up the command post in his office on the thirty-third floor of the new Gulf Building.

First, he held an all-night conference with the officers and directors of what he considered to be the key problem: one of the medium-sized banks, rumored to be mismanaged, with a large supply of "slow" notes secured by inadequate collateral. There was little or no progress, but he got a far better grasp of the magnitude of the crisis as well as a plan of action.

Soon after dawn, he telephoned an assistant and told him to come down immediately. His assignment was to call the principals of all downtown banks to a highly secret Sunday afternoon meeting which would go on until some real progress was evident, and as long thereafter as necessary.

The Sunday meeting went on until 5 a.m. Monday. It was agreed that the strong would support the weak throughout Monday's banking hours, while selected officers with tough, realistic experience in shaky loans would obtain new data for another all-night session Monday. A few community leaders from outside the banking profession would be invited to this second meeting.

All banks survived until closing time Monday, and the second emergency session began soon thereafter in Mr. Jones' office. After reported threats of suicide and a call or two from Jesse Jones himself to principal stockholders capable of swaying a stubborn bank president's decision, the bitter but necessary prescription was announced: one of the two sickly banks would have to have its deposits guaranteed, and would then be merged into the National Bank of Commerce; the other would have to be sold after the refinancing of most of its questionable notes.

The price was high for the sounder financial institutions (many of which were having lesser problems of their own), and for a few key companies which underwrote part of the bailing-out process: $1.25 million to guarantee deposits of the first bank and thereby to merge it into the National Bank of Commerce; and an additional $800,000 to refinance inadequately secured paper at the second.

The sound and long-established First National Bank, as W.A. Kirkland, grandson of its founder and a banking and civic leader in Houston for more than 50 years has detailed in his history of the First National, had to undergo some refinancing of its own 18 months after payment of these heavy but necessary assessments. But potential disaster had been averted, and Houston sailed on through the Great Depression without a single bank failure—to a considerable extent because of the indomitable will of Jesse Jones, and of others' respect for his judgment and leadership.

These, then, were the tangible factors accelerating metamorphosis in our city a half-century ago: a rate of population increase that can never be surpassed; a uniquely healthy economy exhibiting both stability and strong, even propulsive motion forward; and proud, dedicated, effective civic leadership of a high order. And we saw how these determining circumstances affected the decision to establish the Houston Junior College (HJC) as well as its early enfoldment.

What are more difficult to understand are the far less tangible, yet innate changes that turned an inchoate metropolis-to-be, with many of the attributes of a small town, into the sophisticated world center we know today. This far-reaching transmutation from town to megalopolis would also affect the evolvement of the HJC and of the University of Houston.

Perhaps such changes are best exemplified by some of the more startling differences between the happenings of the 1920's and those of the past two decades—especially in terms of what they tell us about the real characteristics of our city today, and its ability to assume and maintain the role of a true metropolis.

Contrast, for instance, 2,000 white-hooded men being sworn into the Ku Klux Klan on a cold December night in 1921 in the midst of a cow pasture south of Bellaire[6] against Roman Catholic John Fitzgerald Kennedy's dramatic debate with Protestant ministers here in October, 1960, which probably turned the presidential tide for him against Richard Milhous Nixon.

Or consider William Jennings Bryan fulminating against "infidels, modernists and biological (sic) professors teaching . . . Darwin(ism)" in a February 3, 1923, speech at the City Auditorium, in contrast to the reaction of (later Sir) Julian Huxley, then an assistant professor of biology at The Rice Institute. Professor Huxley, already destined for greatness, reportedly went to hear Bryan excoriate his grandfather Thomas Henry Huxley's close friend and colleague. What must he have thought of Houston's intellectual climate, remembering that Charles Darwin sought the counsel of his grandfather, founder of the Royal College of Science and perhaps the greatest scientist of his own generation, before publishing the *Origin of Species* in 1859? A pity that Sir Julian is not here today to see directly across from his old campus home the Texas Medical Center, site of some of the world's most intriguing and productive research in medicine, biology and their interrelated subdisciplines.

There is also enormous contrast between the race riot of August 23, 1917 (stemming from the U.S. Army's decision to station a black battalion of the 24th Infantry at Camp Logan), which resulted in martial law plus the hanging of 13 black soldiers later at Fort Sam Houston, and the proud moments when Congresswoman Barbara Jordan inspired the 1976 Democratic national convention with a great keynote address.

Yet the city was still in its cocoon in 1927, as Dr. Oberholtzer hurried to complete arrangements for the opening of the new Houston Junior College—and indeed almost until Pearl Harbor, in terms of our cosmopolitan pace today. By 1977 standards, Houston would have seemed somnolent and languid in the time of Light Guard cotillions, yellow fever,[7] Quality Hill and Sunday tea-musicales at the home of the Misses Louise, Adele and Camille Waggaman.

There were many reasons for that different Houston, and for its persisting so long. One, obviously, was the vast difference in transportation and in communications. Even a generation ago, you went down to Grand Central Station with a basket of fresh fruit and plenty of reading material, boarded the northbound train and arrived in New York City the second morning. Today, the jaded folk Maxine Mesinger is always writing about are awakened at noon by a directly-dialled summons to another radical chic party in the East Sixties, check the New York weather on their bathroom television, and are on location before nightfall. And many Houston companies have private jets capable of flying to London non-stop, and on to Riyadh after re-fueling at Heathrow.

Another prime reason for the persistence of the "old" Houston of earlier generations was the tradition of the leisurely life of the Old South that countless colonels (some of them self-appointed in non-existent regiments) brought here after the War Between the States.

On Quality Hill, the River Oaks of the Victorian era, wealthy bankers and merchants recreated an ante-bellum world of spacious gardens, plenty of black servants, and big, colonnaded homes painted dazzling white every other spring. Quality Hill, just northeast of the downtown area and south of Buffalo Bayou, was only 10 to 15 minutes by carriage from the business offices on Main, Commerce or Franklin. The master of the house would be driven down in splendor for a few hours of work, top-hatted and chomping on a fresh cheroot.

This pleasant style of life, adapted somewhat from the more prosperous parts of Georgia, Alabama and Mississippi with a dash of New Orleans thrown in, died hard in a city that practically went into mourning over the 1860 election of Abraham Lincoln, raised more than a dozen companies of volunteers for the Confederacy, and drummed Old Sam Houston out of their hearts for opposing secession.

Thus, with a far more leisurely pace of transportation and communications, there was also a considerable remaining tradition of Old South gentility mixed with the open cordiality and friendliness of the Southwest in our city a half-century ago. Fortunately, many of these qualities have survived, along with a disinclination to hurry along every waking moment, even with the hectic pace and pressures that life in a large city seems to require everywhere else.

I cannot recall seeing a native Houstonian walking up an ascending escalator to this day, a phenomenon that appalled and amazed me when I first encountered it as a student in New York City and Boston long ago. And there are yet those in Houston who would qualify under John Butler Yeats' definition of a true gentleman, or a man not wholly occupied with getting on (materially) in this world.

Similarly, this is the city where a saleslady in Sakowitz's downtown emporium took her own car and her own lunch hour to transport a customer (the wife of one of the 50,000 delegates to the gigantic Homebuilders' convention) out to the Sakowitz Galleria branch to try on and buy the correct size in a gown that was not available downtown. Bernard Sakowitz always thought that this incident, which spread instantaneously through the convention grapevine, was a major factor in the homebuilders' decision to return to Houston. I thought it was Judge Roy Hofheinz' slightly unethical but brilliant idea of flashing weather bulletins on the giant Astrodome screen that did the trick: "Chicago, 12 degrees with snow flurries, high of 16 with sleet tonight; Houston, 58 degrees with sunshine and high of 68." Both approaches undoubtedly helped.

The celluloid kewpie doll still bounced to and fro in 1927. A unique, remaining symbol of the more leisurely Houston of the past, it shot from side to side in the huge popcorn machine at the marvelously spicy, redolent Henke store in the City Market portion of Old City Hall. But Joe Weingarten already had a miniature chain of prototype supermarkets, Henke & Pillot's chain (Kroger today) was in the offing and the grandiose architecture of Old City Hall would soon be sacrificed to a truncated, super-ugly Bus Center.

The opening of Houston Junior College (HJC) for the first summer session on June 5, 1927, and for the first fall semester on September 19, 1927, was destined to accelerate the transformation from inchoate city to world metropolis in many ways. The Houston we know today, however, would have to await many significant advances on a broad front. Among these, some of which we have examined in varying detail, were the opening of a municipal airport, the boom of the late 1920's and following the depression and recession, World War II, enormous increases in oil production and in the output of a vast range of processed and manufactured goods, the constant deepening of the Houston Ship Channel, significant advances in many aspects of the cultural life of the city, the stationing of more and more consuls and consuls general here (as international trade and relationships widened and prospered), and finally, climactic developments such as the Texas Medical Center, NASA's Manned Space Center (now renamed for Lyndon B. Johnson) and the transfer of hundreds of corporate headquarters to Houston in what has almost been a domino effect of the enormous concentration of the petroleum and petrochemical industries in the city and area.

We are fortunate to have many accounts of those earliest days and years at San Jacinto High School from these principal sources: interviews with key administrators and members of the teaching staff; press clippings; interviews with students who attended in the 1927-1934 era; records of the Houston Independent School District; and a valuable thesis, by a Miss Eleanor Sophia Mohr.

Miss Mohr traced the history of the Houston Junior College as part of her work for the master of arts degree awarded to her by the University of Texas in August, 1936. In doing so, she concentrated upon a comparison of HJC with existing other Texas junior colleges, and was apparently not able to obtain any great number of interviews with principal members of the early faculty and staff, or with students; but the Mohr thesis contains invaluable data nevertheless, especially when combined with present-day interviews and the valuable perspective of the years.

In spite of his keen and abiding interest in the Houston Junior College (HJC), Dr. Oberholtzer knew that he would have little time to devote to the details of administering the new institution. As a matter of fact, he was hard pressed, calendar-wise, to work out the original acceptance of the concept of HJC by the Board of Education, and the negotiations with the University of Texas and Sam Houston State Teachers College leading to early approval of HJC credits and acceptance by the State Department of Education and Texas Association of Colleges.

The reason, of course, was that the superintendent was in the midst of the largest expansion of the Houston Independent School District (HISD) to date, with its concomitant, numerous and complex problems, and indications of incessant growth for school district and city alike. Early in the strenuous year of 1926-1927 he saw that he would have to devise a method of operating the HJC that would limit his personal involvement as much as possible. A further complication, one that Edison Ellsworth Oberholtzer either did not understand or was unwilling to admit, was the fact that he was simply not psychologically capable of anything approaching real delegation of authority.

As was often to be the case, Dr. Oberholtzer turned to a carefully considered compromise as the solution to his dilemma of how to be superintendent of HISD and president of HJC simultaneously, without sacrificing either his own concepts of responsibility or overall efficiency and economy.

He chose an administrative team composed exclusively of trusted, full-time HISD employees and a faculty judiciously salted with members of the HISD teaching staff in order to achieve continuity, an efficient, low-cost operation and psychological reassurance. But common sense, sound judgment and his ability to look well into the future told Dr. Oberholtzer that he would need a virtually full-time administrator with specific experience in newly launched junior colleges, and a "mix" of non-HISD instructors.

The latter contingent would have a vital assignment: to prevent undue "inbreeding"; to provide varying viewpoints, backgrounds and approaches to instruction; and to serve as a prime source of the intangible yet invaluable learning that occurs outside the classroom. After all, an HISD teacher completing his HJC class at 9:30 p.m. or even earlier had to think about driving home (often to a distant part of the spreading city) and being back in a school district classroom at 8:00 a.m. Even the best-motivated were reluctant to stay after class for further questions or interaction with students, and understandably left this responsibility pretty well with the full-time teaching staff or administrators. The non-HISD instructors had yet another important function: They dampened down, at least for a time, the feeling that HJC was to a considerable degree a parasite sucking manpower and tax dollars out of the HISD, even though it was constituted as a break-even proposition financially.

The compromise was a workable one. Superintendent Oberholtzer could remain in his HISD offices, or elsewhere on HISD business, about 95 percent of the time, after several well-chosen appearances at San Jacinto High School, mainly at the beginning of the term. He was able to carry out this absentee landlord operation through trusted lieutenants from whom he seems to have demanded—and received—detailed reports of day-to-day goings-on plus hurried telephone calls if a decision of any particular significance at all became necessary. There was something of a gamble involved in naming an untried member of the administrative team to the crucial operational post at HJC, but as we shall see, Dr. Oberholtzer handled this at minimum risk while preserving his extremely conservative standards on the delegation of authority.

The original HJC administrative staff on September 19, 1927 included Dr. Oberholtzer as president; F.M. Black, HISD's director of secondary education, who held the unusual title of "supervising dean" (awarded after careful thought by President Oberholtzer, but never revived here or elsewhere after Dean Black's death in 1932); Horace Walter South, who occupied a similar post in the HISD staff structure, registrar and bursar; and Mrs. Hannah Shearer, an assistant librarian for HISD, librarian.

The key member of the original administrative team at HJC, and throughout the institution's seven-year existence, was Naason K. Dupre, a lanky, newly arrived, prematurely balding World War I flyer of Scandinavian descent. He was to be the on-the-ground operating executive at HJC, in spite of some deliberate obfuscation in titles.

President Oberholtzer had some reservations about naming a rookie on the HISD staff to such a sensitive post, and was constitutionally opposed to any yielding up of administrative power that could possibly be avoided. Yet Mr. Dupre came highly recommended, and someone had to do the job.

Actually, President Oberholtzer had come to a recurring problem that would haunt the University of Houston down the years: how could the chief executive attract highly qualified colleagues in administration, develop them and then retain them against the threats of growing internal rivalries and competition from other institutions? He found the solution this time in titles, but some of his successors would not be so fortunate. Mr. Dupre was named assistant dean and was ostensibly to be subservient to "Supervising Dean" Black, or at least until he had earned his letter under Head Coach Oberholtzer.

As it was, Dean Black was in the last years of his career, with plenty to do helping Dr. Oberholtzer organize and operate an essentially new system of junior high schools and additional high schools. He was perfectly willing to let Assistant Dean Dupre (whom he had checked out thoroughly via Southwestern University at Georgetown, their common alma mater; the University of Texas; and colleagues at San Antonio and Brownsville) run the show at San Jacinto High School.

There is evidence that Assistant Dean Dupre, a quietly effective man who was able to muster growing respect but few close friends, was somewhat amused by all this maneuvering about, content in his job and title and able to tell them all to go to hell at any given moment because his specialized talents were in demand elsewhere and he had the inestimable advantage of an independent income.

Naason K. Dupre, still in his early thirties in 1927, was probably as knowledgeable about junior colleges as anyone available to Dr. Oberholtzer and the HJC. Stationed at Kelly Field as a pilot trainee in the earliest days of the Army Air Corps,[8] he returned to San Antonio after receiving the baccalaureate degree from Southwestern University, taught in the public school system for three years, and helped to organize the San Antonio Junior College in 1925. In the interim, he completed the master of arts degree at the University of Texas, and entered the doctoral program in educational administration at Austin, as a summer student under Dr. Frederick Eby, who would have a major role in organizing the first HJC summer sessions, in cooperation with Dr. J.O. Marberry.

The school board in Brownsville, with their colleagues at the other end of the Rio Grande Valley, in Edinburg, were interested in a junior college in the early 1920's. They heard of Dean Dupre's work in San Antonio, sought his services as a consultant in organizing a junior college for their border city, and named him as its first executive officer in 1926. It was from this post that Dr. Oberholtzer, with some assistance from F.M. Black, called Mr. Dupre to duty with the HISD. It is significant to note, however, that Naason K. Dupre's primary assignment with the Houston school district was as principal of the Montrose Elementary School, where he was engaged for a $2,500 contract. He was paid the magnificent sum of $1,000 additional for his extra assignment as assistant dean and quasi-chief operating officer of HJC.

The 12 original full-time, non-HISD appointees to the first HJC faculty constituted a remarkable group in terms of their academic backgrounds, especially for a junior college in the process of organization. Reports to the State Department of Education indicate the following data, including title, colleges or universities attended, degrees and nine-month salary for the 1927-1928 academic year (everyone but the three teaching assistants, all students from The Rice Institute, was given the title and rank of instructor, regardless of full- or part-time status, degrees, numbers of classes taught, subjects assigned or whatever; Dr. Oberholtzer would have preferred an even further dilution under which all faculty members were simply called "teacher," and all students, "student," in the style of Mark Hopkins):

H.F. Ander, instructor in biology; Texas A&M College, Theological Seminary of Basle and The Rice Institute, B.A., 1923; M.A., 1924; $2,850.

John R. Bender, instructor in physical education and coach; A.B., Nebraska University; M.A., Washington State College; LL.B., Saint Louis Institute; LL.M., University of Tennessee; M.S., Texas A&M College; graduate, University of Illinois School of Athletics; $2,700. Coach Bender, a man with an extraordinarily broad education plus teaching and coaching experience at Washington State College, Saint Louis University, the University of Tennessee, and Texas A&M College, was a great favorite with the students and with his colleagues. He could have had a considerable effect upon HJC and on the University of Houston as well, but unfortunately died suddenly on July 24, 1928. His widow, Mrs. Pearl Bender, became dean of women after his death and served many years in this post. She was also registrar of HJC in 1932-1933 and in the final year of the institution, 1933-1934. A plaque on the original flagpole at Central Campus, dedicated to Mrs. Bender, has been relocated in Cullen Family Plaza.

Samuel Leon Bishkin, instructor in chemistry and physics; The Rice Institute, B.S. in chemical engineering; $1,800. Mr. Bishkin was apparently employed by the Humble Oil & Refining Company, but it is not clear whether or not he continued with The Humble after joining the HJC faculty. He probably did, since he was provided with two teaching assistants who were full-time students at The Rice Institute and was paid substantially less than all but one other instructor. In any case, he was a great investment: Instructor Bishkin is shown as having taught a total of 111 students, 21 hours a week in the classroom plus 24 hours in the laboratory. Enough to make an Association of American University Professors chapter disband![9]

S.W. Henderson, instructor in education; B.A., North Texas State Teachers College, M.A., University of Texas; $2,400.

May Bess Huberich, instructor in English; B.A., University of Texas, 1924; M.A., 1927; $2,000.

Alva Lee Kerbow, instructor in education, B.L., East Texas State Teachers College; B.S., University of Oklahoma, 1925; M.S., 1926; $2,500.

Mr. Kerbow, the first person actually engaged for the HJC faculty, came from the Houston school district to teach in the opening summer session of June, 1927 which was primarily an extension operation of the University of Texas and Sam Houston State Teachers College. He became an early mainstay of the HJC and later of the University of Houston faculty, from which he retired June 1, 1959, in his seventieth year.

Dr. Oberholtzer had known Dr. Kerbow as a faculty member of East Central State Teachers College in Ada, Oklahoma and at the University of Oklahoma, where he was a graduate student. While Dr. Oberholtzer was 10 years older, the two men shared many common interests and views along with a determination to complete their formal education in spite of professional and personal delays and the inexorable march of time. Dr. Kerbow easily won this competition, since he was 50 when he was awarded the Ph.D. at Colorado State in 1940. But he had almost two more decades of distinguished service at the University of Houston, and remained active, alert and a great favorite of former students and colleagues until his death in 1970.

Dr. Kerbow had a major role, along with another well-known member of the College of Education faculty at the University, Dr. Chester Cochran, in preparing the special report on the institution's history from 1927 to 1950 which Dr. Oberholtzer presented to the Board of Regents after he became president emeritus.

J.H. Ledlow, instructor in business administration and economics, B.A., University of Texas, 1923; B.B.A., 1924; M.B.A., 1927. Mr. Ledlow, later a well-known certified public accountant, became HJC registrar for 1930-1931; was auditor and registrar in 1931-1932; and became auditor in 1932-1933, when he was succeeded as registrar by Mrs. Pearl Bender; $1,800.

Murray A. Miller, instructor in history and English; B.A., University of South Carolina, 1908; M.A., 1916; $2,400.

Wallace E. Miner, instructor in history and government; B.A., Allegheny College; B.D., Drew Theological Seminary; M.A., Columbia University; $2,700.

Walter L. Porter, instructor in mathematics; A.B., Howard College; M.S., Texas A&M College; $2,700.

Mrs. Floy DeVore Soule, instructor in Spanish; B.A., University of Texas; M.A., Southern Methodist University; $2,400.

Miss Laura Topham, instructor in French; B.A., University of Kansas; Certificate d'Etudes Françaises, University of Grenoble, 1924; Alliance Française de Paris, 1925 and University of Paris, 1926; $2,200.

Additionally, five of the "Original Twelve" had completed substantial work on their Ph.D. degrees; Ander and Porter at The Rice Institute, Miner and Mrs. Soule at Columbia University, and Miller at the University of Chicago. All of them, with a number of their part-time colleagues, had practical teaching experience at the college or university level, some of it extensive and at well-known institutions.

Dr. Oberholtzer took justifiable pride in this, and he wrote the following copy for Bulletin Number 1 of the HJC: "Without exception, the men and women selected to give instruction in the Houston Junior College have the unqualified endorsement of The Rice Institute, the University of Texas, or other outstanding colleges; and no instructor has had less than master of arts preparation in addition to years of successful college teaching." This was stretching things a bit, in the case of some of the part-time instructors, but not much. Dr. Oberholtzer's determination to emphasize the master of arts level and actual college teaching experience was adhered to in the main, and it was undoubtedly a major factor in the success of HJC.

Early records indicate, incidentally, that Dr. Oberholtzer had Kerbow and Miller doing some serious moonlighting on the side, but it does not appear to have diminished their effectiveness as members of the HJC teaching staff. Although both men were engaged as full-time instructors at HJC, Kerbow had many responsibilities in the downtown HISD offices in 1928-1929 and 1930-1932, when he was relieved of all teaching duties at HJC. Miller taught 15 hours of high school classes in his first two years at HJC.

Another member of the full-time instructional staff, Miss Topham, taught an incredible total of 32 hours in French, 20 hours in high school, and 12 hours at the Junior College. But she resigned after the opening 1927-1928 session to rejoin HISD.

The six part-time instructors on the original HJC faculty, all employed full-time by HISD, were:

L.B. Fields, instructor in engineering; B.S. in electrical engineering, Purdue University; $40 per month. Mr. Fields was supervisor of industrial arts for HISD.

Russell A. Herrington, instructor in engineering; certificate in technical engineering, Cardiff University. Mr. Herrington, a rather remarkable Welshman who taught in the HISD industrial arts department, was actually a naval architect who had served an apprenticeship with a drydocking firm in Wales, and had been headmaster of a nautical academy in Cardiff. He was paid $400 a year for his assignment with HJC, which primarily involved teaching engineering drafting.

Dorothy Mackey, instructor in physical training; diploma from the New Haven Normal School of Gymnastics, an institution just down the road from Yale University, albeit a little less distinguished academically than Old Eli. Miss Mackey was employed full-time by HISD, and also had a part-time position with the Houston YWCA. HJC paid her $50 a month.

Miss Nell Morris, instructor in Spanish; National University of Mexico, University of Colorado, B.A., University of Texas. Miss

Morris taught only one class at HJC, but 25 hours at HISD. She was paid $25 per month by HJC.

Miss Pearl Rucker, instructor in art; Prang Art School (Chicago), New York University, Columbia University, diploma in art, Baylor University. Miss Rucker had been director of art instruction for HISD since 1912. She was paid $35 per month by HJC.

Miss Lulu M. Stevens, instructor in music; Iowa State Teachers College, American Conservatory (Chicago), Buena Vista College, diploma in public school music, Chicago and American Institute of Normal Methods (Evanston, Illinois). Director of music instruction in HISD, Miss Stevens was paid $35 a month by HJC.

Rounding out the original HJC faculty were three students from Rice Institute: Elton F. Reid, assistant in chemistry, was only a sophomore, but showed promise of a brilliant career as early as high school, where he won five scholarships; James M. Whitley, also an assistant in chemistry, was a senior at Rice enrolled in the honors course in chemistry there under Dean Harry Boyer Weiser; William J. Rust, assistant in physics, was also a senior at Rice, where he was a candidate for honors in mathematics. Reid and Whitley helped Mr. Bishkin carry a tremendous load in chemistry, and Rust was an assistant to Mr. Fields in mathematics.

There were a number of changes in the HJC faculty during the institution's seven years of existence, but not as many as might have been expected in such a period of start-up and transition. A number of these changes related to substantial shifts in enrollment,[10] which fortunately climbed strongly from opening day in 1927 through 1930-1931 before dropping some 13% in 1931-1932 and another 5% the following year. Enrollment then resumed a steady upward trend in 1933-1934, with a small but significant gain of 5%.

Additions to teaching staff resulted primarily from rising enrollment, and from the expansion of curricular offerings. Losses in staff usually came about through completion of a temporary assignment, resignations due to personal reasons and some adjustments that became necessary when the student body dropped from 858 to 596 between 1931 and 1933.

Of the 21 members of the original faculty (12 full-time, nine part-time and three student assistants), there were six resignations (Mr. Ander, Miss Huberich, Miss Mackey, Miss Topham, Miss Morris and Mr. Porter) and two deaths (Mr. Bender and Mr. Miner). Mr. Herrington's contract was not renewed when enrollments in engineering drafting fell substantially in the fall of 1932. The three student assistants completed their assignments upon graduation from The Rice Institute.

Twenty-three persons were added to the HJC instructional staff between 1927 and 1934, three in 1928-1929, eight in 1929-1930, five in 1930-1931, two in 1931-1932, a single person (Miss Irene C. Spiess, one of the first graduates of HJC, with an Associate in Arts diploma in physical training) in the depression year of 1932-1933, and four in 1933-1934.

Among those in this "second wave" who took prominent roles in the early years of HJC were Fred R. Birney, instructor in journalism and sponsor of both the *Cougar*, the student newspaper and the yearbook, the *Houstonian;* Miss Kathleen W. Rucker (later Rucker-Duggan), assistant registrar and later registrar, whose son Lee Duggan, a former state legislator, is now a prominent judge and University of Houston alumnus; Miss Julia Ideson, librarian of the Houston Public Library (now the Julia Ideson Building, principally for children's books, other special holdings and a metropolitan archive under the joint aegis of the City of Houston, the University of Houston and Rice University); Warren A. Rees, instructor in mathematics; E.W. Schuhmann, instructor in physics and mathematics; Mrs. Bessie Monroe Ebaugh, instructor in English; Louis Kestenberg, instructor in German; and L. Standlee Mitchell, instructor in English.

Birney, a graduate of Pomona College, was extremely popular with the students and typical of the HJC faculty members who helped to build a strong and lasting rapport with the student body. He contracted pneumonia before the days of antibiotics and died within a few days, on April 26, 1936.

Rees continued with the HJC and later with the University of Houston until his retirement almost four decades later. Schuhmann also had a very long career, serving as chairman of the Department of Physics through the first years of the 1950's. His son, Dr. Robert E. Schuhmann, is dean of science and technology at the University of Houston at Clear Lake City.

Mrs. Ebaugh, a graduate of Sophie Newcomb College (Tulane University) and Columbia University, came to HJC in the fall of

1930 because English sections being taught by her friend Sue Goree Thomason had become too large. She stayed through a distinguished career of more than 40 years during which she rose to the academic rank of full professor and became almost a legend as dean of women.

Kestenberg, primarily a historian, although his first appointment and much of his career was also intertwined with the teaching of the German language, literature and culture, also served on to retirement at the University of Houston. He held many key appointments within the Faculty Association and was a recognized leader of the teaching staff and champion of the rights of his colleagues throughout his many years with the institution.

L. Standlee (Chief) Mitchell really had four careers at HJC and at the University, where he served continuously until retirement. A skilled student and teacher of English, he also spent many years in the Drama Department and as a sponsor of the Red Masque players and other dramatic groups. He is even better remembered as a dean of student life and as the one person most closely connected with the famous and infamous Frontier Fiesta (which we will examine in a later chapter). A fraternity brother of Arlington Brugh (Robert Taylor), "The Chief" did not make it to Hollywood with the reigning matinee idol, but he may be the best known and most popular member of the faculty and student life staff in the first half-century of the University of Houston.

The location of the Houston Junior College in San Jacinto High School was obviously a major factor in the early evolvement of HJC, and one that remained stubbornly in the psychological background of the institution long after it achieved university status and moved to its own campus.[11]

San Jacinto was a first-line addition to the roster of HISD high schools when it opened in 1913 in response to the rapid expansion of residential areas in the so-called South End. It was intended to balance somewhat the preponderance of high schools within the downtown core, in the Heights and in the East End, and was a very large structure with more than 50 classrooms, nine laboratories, a library, auditorium, vocational and technical shop, a handsome suite of administrative offices and, under the protest of some taxpayers, a swimming pool. Perhaps the most unique features of San Jacinto High School were its 13-acre campus, eight acres of which had been reserved for athletic fields, and its total cost. High schools in the past had been placed on cramped tracts of a few acres in Houston, and had not nearly approached the more than $1.2 million cost of San Jacinto (divided approximately $600,000 for plant; $500,000, equipment; $100,000, land).

The comparatively large campus at San Jacinto High School (SJHS), however, involved some basic problems for HJC and its students. Dr. Oberholtzer's predecessors had provided a handsome and functional plant at SJHS, plus room for a wide range of athletic and physical training programs and for future expansion. But land prices, even in 1911 and 1912, had forced HISD to locate their big new high school somewhat farther south and east than might have been wished; and while this problem was ameliorated as the area population continued to provide an increasing number of high school students in the years preceding and following World War I, SJHS was far from an ideal location for a junior college drawing from the entire metropolitan area.

HJC's location, for example, was a good 20 blocks south of the central downtown area. It was only five blocks east of Main Street, but miles from the new developments in the southwest quadrant, and much farther from the West End, Harrisburg, the Heights or the industrial areas along the Ship Channel. There were serious matters in 1927, when automobiles were a rarity for students, and the zero- or one-car garage was standard for their parents. There were plenty of streetcars, of course, but their schedules diminished the moment they left the heavily-traveled main thoroughfares.

Consider the testimony of Birch Blalock, for instance, the man reputed to have been the first student to enroll at HJC on September 13, 1927. He worked from 4 a.m. until noon as a "Phenix Phil" delivering milk for the Phenix Dairy in the downtown area, from a horse-drawn wagon; but this day he finished his route early and hurried to the nearest streetcar line. After a wait, a ride to Fannin and Calhoun, and a wait for the transfer car to the end of the line at Holman and Main, he walked the remaining five blocks to SJHS, on Holman between Austin and Caroline Streets, where the blocks are 80 feet broad[12] and interminably long on a broiling noon in mid-September. Total estimated time, about one hour, on the main line in broad daylight.

Luckily, the line for registration had not formed yet, and "Phenix Phil" Blalock was at its head when the staff returned from lunch. He signed up for mathematics, English, physics, Spanish "and baseball," the latter being a local mania at the time, with the Houston Buffs fielding Dixie Championship teams that included "Dizzy" and "Daffy" Dean and many another future star of the St. Louis Cardinals.

Forty-four years later, Blalock, a landscape specialist with his own business in the Dallas exurb of Garland, came back to the University of Houston for the first time. He was literally astounded by the campus, the enrollment, the faculty of almost 2,000 against the beginning 21 he had known, the splendid new buildings, the landscaping and outdoor sculpture. "Listen to that water," he said, as he looked over the Cullen Family Plaza and its "Waterfall, River and Stele" by the American sculptor Leo Kelley; "this is the happiest day of my life," he exclaimed as he exulted over the indoor splendor of the Hofheinz Pavilion. "Imagine," he added, "having 366 acres and 46 buildings. We had to scramble for a classroom at old San Jac. They moved us all over the place."

Mrs. Ebaugh, a native Houstonian who still lives at 401 Emerson Street in an elegant old neighborhood from which she set forth to find HJC before her interview with Dean Bender and Dean Dupre in 1930, told me that one of her many recollections of those days was about "how hard it was to find the Junior College." "I asked various people, but they didn't seem to know much about it or where it was." HJC was indeed off the beaten track, but they managed to find it.

The atmosphere at HJC was generally one of informal amiability, although some imported members of the faculty were regarded as stand-offish until they identified more with Houston's affable ambience. But there was soon a nucleus of faculty and staff members whom the student body recognized as the best sources of guidance and friendship, as well as of sound and sometimes inspired instruction.

Among this group were Assistant Dean Dupre (who was not promoted to dean until HJC became the University of Houston in 1934, although Supervising Dean Black died November 13, 1932), Mrs. Bender, Mr. Bishkin, Dr. Kerbow, Mr. Miller and Mrs. Soule among the "Original Twelve," and Mr. Birney, Mrs. Ebaugh, Dr. Kestenberg and "Chief" Mitchell among the second wave.

Alumni of the 1927-1934 era speak often of how these teachers "liked young people very much," and "were dedicated persons."

These positive views, especially of Dean Dupre and of Mrs. Bender, were echoed in interviews with their colleagues. Dean Dupre apparently had a heavy administrative load at Montrose Elementary School, which demanded his attention until the middle of the afternoon. He would then drive to San Jacinto High School, meet with the principal there on any common problems or conflicts and plunge into whatever needed to be done: registration in the basement, helping Mrs. Kerbow for a time with bookstore sales, a conference with Mrs. Shearer in the library (or with her successor Mrs. Ruth Wikoff, who arrived in the fall of 1933 as the first professional librarian and remained four decades), a look-see and quick 27-cent meal in the cafeteria, and always, short meetings with individual students—in the hallways, coming in or out of classrooms, in his office, as they arrived or departed.

Mrs. Bender's duties and activities were much less encompassing, but she was constantly busy, in or out of her primary assignments as dean of women and (later) as registrar. Much of her time was spent as a sponsor for student organizations and in personal counseling of women students. She and Dean Dupre were the principal members of a Discipline Committee. This body included four members of the faculty, but there was apparently little reference to *Robert's Rules of Order* when a meeting became necessary, and a quorum might well consist of the two principals, or for that matter of Dean Dupre or Dean Bender alone, if summary discipline was indicated.

These procedures were in accordance with the HJC Handbook, which did not contain any specific regulations on discipline, this being a generation before district judges began to recite such caveats from the bench to a battery of college or university lawyers and an assemblage of legal talent from the American Civil Liberties Union. The handbook did state that it was assumed HJC students were "familiar enough with the ordinary rules of society governing the proper conduct of ladies and gentlemen to need no definite discipline regulations." It also added, in very clear language, that "the College reserves the right to dismiss any student at any time for misconduct."

Actually, there were few disciplinary problems aside from chronic difficulties with students who absented themselves from compulsory assembly on Wednesday evenings or those who rolled up a high percentage of class absences or "tardies."

Dean Dupre brought about a drastic improvement in absences through a simple albeit somewhat Draconian rule: Three unexcused absences in any semester, and you were automatically out of the class involved, subject to reinstatement if you took and passed a special examination within three days, after paying a $1.00 reinstatement fee. There was also a rising scale of penalties under which you could lose up to 100% of credit for a course by failure to attend classes.

Three unexcused absences from assembly and you were out until readmitted after a personal interview. Three "tardies" or early departures from assembly were the equivalent of one absence, but this regulation was reportedly difficult to enforce, and winked at by many faculty members assigned as keepers of the gate.

The curriculum at HJC could be succinctly described as "good standard junior college." In point of fact, it was well above the average quality of curricular offerings at Texas junior colleges in the 1927-1934 era, and in conformity with the goals of the College set forth in HJC Bulletin Number 1 of 1927:

> To give to Houston and vicinity an institution which shall serve to the very best advantage the needs of the citizens of this section of Texas under conditions which shall make it available to all, and organized and conducted on such a basis as to assure every student two years of high grade standard college training.

In the social, moral and legal climate of 1927, the emphasis was on the words "high grade." The phrase "under conditions which shall make it available to all" simply could not mean 50 years ago that black students would be admitted. When a later issue of the Bulletin spoke of the HJC student body being imbued with a "wholesome democratic spirit," and "not divided into social groups," the publication was praising socioeconomic, not racial, equality. Accepting a black student at HJC was inconceivable.

One of the least-known facts about the Houston Junior College, however, is that the Houston College for Negroes was established even before HJC, after special sessions for the training of black teachers had been held at Jack Yates Junior-Senior High School. Dr. Oberholtzer always insisted that "the colored college," as it was called, be given equal pro-rata support; and he encouraged HJC faculty members to help their HCN colleagues in every way. HJC staff members assisted by setting up financial, registration, grading and other administrative systems, and Charles F. Hiller, who will appear frequently in following chapters, tells of meeting with an administrator at HCN who looked quite familiar. He was a Harvard classmate, the Cantabridgians being considerably farther along with integration at the time.

The Houston College for Negroes was finally ceded to the State of Texas in 1947, and became Texas Southern University. Colonel W.B. Bates, then vice-chairman of the Board of Regents of the University of Houston, played a considerable role in obtaining an appreciable part of the present Texas Southern University campus as a gift. The institution has made remarkable strides, especially under Presidents Samuel N. Nabrit (later a member of the Atomic Energy Commission) and Granville M. Sawyer.

The quality of the HJC curriculum was based upon reasonably broad offerings, the caliber of the faculty, and the fact that the $500,000 or so invested by the HISD in San Jacinto High School laboratories and equipment provided facilities that were miles ahead of anything in other Texas junior colleges. The curriculum included offerings in English, education, mathematics (the three most popular areas), basic engineering, the physical sciences, foreign languages, the social sciences and physical training. The 24 courses offered included modern rarities such as Latin (the disappearance of which may explain much of today's epidemic inability to speak or write the English language clearly or correctly) and penmanship. Heavy emphasis remained on courses in education because of enrollments by HISD teachers, especially in the summer sessions—a tradition that persists.

Careful attention to class size and teaching loads, with very few exceptions, was also an important consideration in HJC's academic standards and in the institution's being accredited by the State Department of Education and the Texas Association of Junior Colleges within a year of its establishment.

In general, classes were held to a maximum of 20-25 students, and another section was begun when enrollment hit 30, by splitting the class into two segments of 15 each. Mrs. Ebaugh recalled, for instance, that she joined the staff when her friend Sue Goree Thomason's English classes reached the upward limit of 30. This meant, Mrs. Ebaugh recalled, that you "got to know each student by name, a great contrast over later years at the University." Some of her students from HJC days, she added, became life-long friends and acquaintances: "We still remember one another across the years and recall those days. It was such a friendly, family sort of a school at the beginning."

Under this system, full-time instructors normally taught five classes, or 15 clock hours (two 90-minute sessions, or three one-hour meetings), per week and had a total of somewhere between 75 and 150 students. There were a few large lecture courses in history and government, college algebra and public speaking, but these were exceptions (as was the inimitable Mr. Bishkin, who will be remembered for his 45 hours per week in classroom plus laboratory, along with his research activities for The Humble; but this was with the help of two exceptional assistants). It is significant that in the entire history of HJC, only 10 instructors ever exceeded the maximum standard of 21 hours of teaching per week recommended by the Association of Texas Colleges.

What was the student body like in those early years at HJC? First of all, a surprising percentage of the freshmen were from high schools outside the HISD, especially from the metropolitan area and from small communities within a 50- to 100-mile radius. This percentage began at 12 in 1927, rose steadily until it hit 60 in 1931-1932, then declined to 44 in 1932-1933 and to 37 the following fall. Overall, during the seven years of HJC, just under 40% of incoming freshmen were non-HISD graduates.

Next, an extraordinary percentage of the students were "specials," a category admitted only after detailed interview, and including (1) those with one or more degrees; (2) others having completed the junior college, but not the baccalaureate, level; and (3) those taking courses on a "no credit" basis, either for professional advancement or for the sheer pursuit of knowledge.

These "special" students represented 36 percent of the 1927-1928 enrollment, and 63, 54 and 68 percent, respectively, of the HJC student body in the next three years. Their number then fell drastically to 29 and 33 percent in 1931-1932 and 1932-1933 as the limited effects of the Great Depression were felt in Houston and Harris County; but there was a rise again, to 36 percent as overall enrollment started back on an upward trend in 1933-1934.

The above statistics were apparently available from Dean Dupre's annual reports to the State Department of Education, but they drew little comment at the time. In retrospect, they seem to have indicated several significant things:

(1) Dr. Oberholtzer and the HISD had created not only a junior college for the graduates of HISD high schools, but a major metropolitan and regional resource as well. Talented youngsters from all over the area were apparently coming to Houston, finding a job, and then beginning the post-high school education they could obtain in no other way.

(2) The adult and continuing education aspects of HJC, put forward prominently in the earliest HISD resolutions regarding the institution, and in other documents delineating its basis missions and philosophy, were even more important than had been assumed.

(3) There was obviously a pool of unmet demands for education beyond the junior college in the area served by HJC that would force a reconsideration of its role and scope.

Enrollment statistics also indicated two other very positive aspects of HJC enrollment:

(1) The College was in a sense insulated from the financial difficulties associated with the economic distress of the early 1930's. When special student enrollment fell so precipitately in 1931-1932 and 1932-1933 because of unemployment and wage cuts, the total of freshman and sophomore students ran up sharply to offset any loss in tuition income (from 276 to 528 in 1931-1932, dropping to only 402 in the following year, when overall enrollment shrank to its lowest level since the HJC opening in 1927).

(2) The vital number of freshman students returning as sophomores grew steadily from 31 to 43 to 68 to 94 to 139 to 145.

Only in the number of graduates were HJC officials somewhat disappointed, but on closer inspection, this appeared to be related to "stretch-out": cases where students, hard-pressed financially, took fewer courses and delayed the year of their graduation with the Associate in Arts diploma. The number of graduates from 1928 through 1934 was actually remarkably steady: 34, 39, 47, 41, 44 and 45. The relatively small numbers must be perceived in terms of the relatively limited number of HJC students who were actually candidates for graduation.

While hard data on the average age of HJC students is lacking, we know that this was 19 for entering freshmen in 1927. Remembering that the older special students comprised almost 40 percent of the overall student body between 1927-1934, it is reasonable to assume that the average age must have risen to the low and even to the mid-20's.

There was no one to rival John M. Carley, who walked across the stage in his eighty-first year (to tremendous applause) to receive his earned Ed.D. at the University of Houston's summer Commencement Convocation in 1976. But members of the early instructional and administrative staffs can recall many individual students who were well past their teens, some of them in their thirties, at San Jacinto High School; and an inspection of class and graduation lists reveals well-known Houstonians, many of them still alive, who would have pushed the median well past 19 when they were at HJC.[13]

Males outnumbered females in each of the freshman classes from 1927 through 1933, and by an overall total of 1149 to 747. This statistic probably reflects how much higher education for women was still suffering from the low matriculation levels of the early 1900's—and generally higher rates of employability for men, since 65% of the HJC student body had to earn all or part of their support.

Yet women outnumbered men in five of the seven sophomore classes at HJC, and were far more widely represented than the males in the special student category (the totals here were 1,373 against 816, with females in the lead for each of the seven years from 1927-1934).

A questionnaire from Dean Dupre, distributed in 1927 to 376 students (82 percent of those enrolled) and answered by 218 (47 percent of those enrolled) reveals some information about the respondents and, since the sample was quite large, about the student body in general. Unfortunately, the questionnaire was not distributed in later years; nor are we certain that it was anonymous, which would obviously have a major effect upon answers. In any event, it sheds some valuable light. Here are the questions and answers, by principal category:

1. Age: Median age of 19 years.

2. Have you chosen a vocation, and if so, what is it? 78 percent expressed a preference, which is somewhat meaningful in a 19-year-old population. The seven leading career choices were all in the professions: teacher (47), dentist (22), electrical engineer (the Houston *Post* had recently established KPRC as the first major radio station in the city after purchasing its predecessor from Will Horwitz, the theater magnate, and students were fascinated with the new medium of communication (which they identified

with electrical engineering), although few of them or their parents could afford the early expensive receivers), (13), business-man (13), lawyer (11), physician (10), architect (7). The remaining choices were scattered from chemist (3) through librarian, social worker, and journalist (2) to commercial artist, physicist, geologist, garageman and other single selections.

3. Why are you attending HJC rather than a four-year college? (There are some apparent possibilities of psychological skewing of this question, and of the following one.) The leading answers by far were: convenient location as compared to four-year college (70), can work in day and attend classes at night (55), and less expensive (31).

4. If there were no junior college here, would you be in school at all? Yes, 113 (52 percent); No, 89 (41 percent). No answer, 16 (7 percent). These responses seem open to question, in view of the high percentage of HJC students who were employed, the difficulty of entering The Rice Institute, and other factors. In terms of the psychological dynamics involved, it would be difficult for a reasonably well-motivated person to admit, especially to another person, that he did not have some alternative means of obtaining education beyond the high school.

5. Why are you attending college? To gain an education (79), to prepare for a vocation (the word "vocation" was used much more interchangably with "career" 50 years ago) (59), to obtain a degree (28), to prepare for life (12), and for self-improvement (7) were the leading responses.

6. In choosing a college, which would attract you most, outstanding activities or outstanding instruction? Instruction (87 percent) far outdistanced activities (13 percent). Even though HJC had some excellent student organizations and extracurricular activities, the tradition of a high percentage of more mature, working students with little time for, and limited interest in, anything out of the classroom or laboratory has persisted at the University of Houston—to the chagrin of two generations of deans of student life and the frustration of many others in the administration and student body. The tradition may yet change, if the average age of matriculants and the number of employed students should turn downward again, as it did after the University joined the state system of higher education.

7. Are you earning your own way? Yes, completely (93, or 43 percent); Yes, in part (50, or 23 percent); No (74, or 34 percent). It

is interesting that the percentage of those earning all or part of their expenses at HJC in 1927 is clearly less than that for any year at the University of Houston for which we have records. This is probably explained by the fact that the median age of questionnaire respondents was 19. The older special students, many of them employed, appeared in far greater numbers after 1927, but not in the opening session at HJC.

8. How many courses are you carrying? Almost half of the freshmen (42 percent) were carrying a full load of five courses, or 15 hours. Of the remainder, 21 percent were enrolled in four courses, 13 percent in three courses, another 13 percent in two courses and the remaining 11 percent were taking only one course. The average student credit hours for these 1927 freshmen was remarkably close to the average for today's overall University of Houston student body: 11.1.

Sophomores took a considerably smaller number of courses, averaging 9.9 student credit hours. The special students, none of whom registered for a full load, and virtually all for one or, at best, two courses, averaged only 4.1 student credit hours.

A vital characteristic of any student body is the ability of its individual members to perform the academic work required of them in their own institution, and in other institutions to which they transfer. The variables here are many, including intelligence, aptitudes, high school preparation, teaching staff, time available for study, personal problems, course load, major field of study, degree of motivation, and grading standards.[14]

Formal records indicate that academic performance at HJC was reasonably good, especially in comparison to other junior colleges in the state, and in view of sometimes severe financial problems for HJC students (most of whom paid only the required one-third of tuition plus mandatory fees at registration and signed a note for the balance). Students passed an average of 83 percent of all courses attempted from 1927-1934, after a rocky beginning in 1927-1928, when there was a 32 percent rate of failures.

One concrete indication of both academic standards and performance lies in a special report prepared by Dean Dupre in 1932. This concerned 40 former students at HJC who transferred to The Rice Institute between 1928 and 1931. Of this group, one "busted out" because of the academic deficiencies (reportedly revolving around the fearsome Math 100, a combination of college algebra, trigonometry and beginning calculus that is still required for virtually all Rice degrees) and another withdrew voluntarily. The remaining HJC transfers averaged slightly better than a 3 on the 1=A, 2=B, 3=C, 4=D and 5=F scale that President Edgar Odell Lovett brought to Rice from the Ivy League. A 3 would translate roughly to a "C" at HJC, where the transfer students had averaged a weak C+.

One distinguished former student at HJC, Judge Roy Hofheinz, gave me what I interpreted as a minority report on scholarship at the College. He said that it was "too damned friendly out there," the inference to me being that emphasis on academic performance by the student body was sometimes lacking. Judge Hofheinz, it must be remembered, has exhibited a mind like a steel trap since the days when he first came to prominence as a "boy wonder" public speaker, debater, state legislator and county judge. This intellectual yet quick brilliance survived political and business ups-and-downs reminiscent of the Astroworld roller coaster, plus a stroke that put him in a wheel chair. Further, within the Hofheinz clan the competition has always been fierce where grades are concerned: One son (Roy Mark, Jr.) was a full professor of Oriental languages in Edwin Oldfather Reischauer's Yenching Institute at Harvard while most scholars his age were still quibbling over a topic for their dissertation. Mayor Fred Hofheinz, no slouch from the podium himself, has a law degree, an earned doctorate in economics, and a Phi Beta Kappa key.

A good project in oral history would have preserved far more of the flavor and actual details of the 1927-1934 era at HJC, but, as indicated earlier, much of it can be reconstructed from interviews with key surviving members of the instructional and administrative staff and student body, from press clippings, the *Cougar* and *Houstonian* (although the first issue of the yearbook did not appear until May, 1934), HISD records and reports, and other sources.

Another very successful former HJC student is a well-known physician, surgeon and investor in Houston, Dr. Hampton C. Robinson. He walked to classes from the family home on nearby San Jacinto, and has vivid memories of the high quality of instruction in biology and chemistry. He remembers especially Mr. Bishkin, "the fine chemistry teacher from the Humble Company," and L.T. Hooker, an instructor in biology who had taken the M.A. at the University of Texas before joining the HJC faculty in the fall of 1931.

Mr. Hooker, with whom he worked as a student assistant, might well have inspired Dr. Robinson to attend the Baylor College of Medicine, where he completed the M.D. degree in 1940. Dr. Robinson became the first tenant in the new Hermann Professional Building when this central facility, which did much to concentrate a wide range of specialists in the Texas Medical Center, opened after World War II.

Dr. Robinson transferred to the University of Texas from HJC, and "found that place just too big." He made an A in analytical chemistry (often the bugaboo of pre-medical students) at Texas, but found that he would not be allowed to transfer the grade unless he took a prerequisite which to him appeared to duplicate a course taken earlier under Mr. Bishkin. Luckily, the professor knew him and was aware that he had made the highest grade awarded by Mr. Bishkin. "What are you doing in here, Robinson?" the professor asked. Dr. Robinson told him, and after class they went together to see the registrar, who immediately absolved him of having to repeat work he had already passed with honors.

"Those kids at HJC were dedicated," Dr. Robinson says of his contemporaries. "They were tired and sleepy sometimes in those evening classes, but there was no 'goofing around.' They knew that they must take advantage of the opportunity they had."

There were still so few automobiles at HJC in 1933-1934, Dr. Robinson recalls, "that they were all parked in the big U-shaped driveway in front, including one huge Cadillac that took up two spaces." Some students who wearied of taking the streetcar to Holman, or the Austin Street bus that had begun running in 1931, did pool their meagre funds to buy old jalopies in which they carpooled before anyone even dreamed of 60-cent gasoline or Arab oil embargoes. Judge Hofheinz, as a budding entrepreneur, had to have his own weather-beaten Model "T" back in 1929-1930. He was promoting dances on the side or doing whatever else he could to turn an honest buck that could be put aside for law school.

Classes at HJC began at 4 p.m. and continued until 9 p.m., with a "supper intermission" from 6 until 6:30 p.m., when most of the faculty and many of the students gathered in the cafeteria. This was opened at 5:30 p.m. and served as something of an auxiliary library or study hall for students preparing belatedly for a class or completing an assignment. The food lines shut down rather promptly at 7:30 p.m. so that the cafeteria could be cleaned and readied for its high school trade the next day, but coffee, milk and soft drinks were usually available in a separate area until 9 p.m. Prices were quite low, especially compared to today's. Refills could bring the real cost of a nickel cup of coffee down unbelievably low.

Faculty meetings were sometimes scheduled in the 6 to 6:30 p.m. period, and Mrs. Ebaugh recalls that this gave the more high-spirited students a chance to enlarge upon some rivalries that had arisen between the freshman and sophomore classes. One night, what she described as "sort of a free-for-all" developed outside, requiring the peacemaking and disciplinary talents of Dean Dupre. After things settled down and classes resumed, she noticed one of her male students was unusually quiet, with his head down on the uncomfortably small desk into which the larger and taller students had to squeeze themselves.[15] On closer inspection, the student was obviously unconscious, and the multi-talented Dean Dupre was called to the scene. He found evidence of a mild concussion, administered first aid and had the young man driven to Saint Joseph Hospital. He had been in the middle of the freshman-sophomore fracas and had been hit in the head by a falling gate. Recovery was complete, but there is an unauthenticated story that the victim was presented a bill for replacing one large gate, by order of H.L. Mills.

One of Dean Dupre's other peacemaking assignments was the more frequent one of adjudicating misunderstandings between his own instructors and SJHS teachers. These occurred when the high school teachers needed a classroom or some other facility after 4 p.m. for a rehearsal, a temporary detention hall or the meeting of some SJHS student organization, and found it in use by HJC. Such conflicts were supposedly prevented by channeling requests for rooms through the SJHS principal, who then met daily with Dean Dupre on any resulting problems. But there were breakdowns before the system was finally worked out, and the SJHS teachers were often unhappy to see the arrival of the 4 p.m. HJC shift, their briefcases, hats and coats jamming the cloak closets as they prepared for another evening of instruction.

Dr. Oberholtzer, as noted, spent little time at San Jacinto High School other than during registration periods or for an occasional surprise visit. Once he saw the abilities of Dean Dupre in full display, he was content to stay in touch by telephone, through written reports, and via the eyes and ears of his secretary, Miss

Virginia Stone (who, in time, was to become a major source of controversy with H.L. Mills and some of the members of the Board of Education).

His interest in registration was understandable, since HJC had to be self-supporting, and tuition income was all-important. Things had gone quite well financially (as an analysis in the next chapter will reveal), except for some concern over the summer session of 1928;[16] but Dr. Oberholtzer not only ran a tight fiscal ship, he also wanted to run up a surplus in order to convince the Board of Education of the next big step forward: the expansion of HJC to four-year status. There was talk of this as early as 1929, and it became a sounder proposition every time another student enrolled.

Mrs. Ebaugh had an opportunity to see Superintendent Oberholtzer's fiscal control policies from up close one evening, when spring rains and an early heat wave had brought an invasion of the big mosquitoes the students called "gallinippers" to her English class.

She used all the insect spray that was available, and then went down the hall to ask Dean Dupre's secretary to get some money out of the Revolving Fund[17] petty cash and to go over to a nearby drugstore for reinforcements. Dr. Oberholtzer happened to be in the office, and he asked what the problem was, his interest heightened by the threat of spending ready cash. He asked Mrs. Ebaugh to show him the mosquitoes, but when they got to the classroom, he maintained that he couldn't see any. Mrs. Ebaugh then pointed out a few dozen insect carcasses on the floor, and won the day. The Flit was purchased and the invaders repelled.

When the 41st Legislature opened on January 5, 1929, HJC (which was not even in existence as the previous legislative session adjourned) was well established as the largest junior college in the state. H.L. Mills, whose abilities as a lobbyist have been previously noted, had been working behind the scene to bring about official validation of HJC. This was accomplished by including in a new statute governing junior colleges (Chapter 29, Acts of the 41st Legislature) a Section 16 which validated "all public junior colleges then organized and actually in operation on January 1, 1929." On February 10, 1930, the Board of Education accepted the provisions of Section 16, Chapter 29, by a formal resolution which had the immediate effect of full validation, and was to cause the University of Houston to retain at least the organizational structure of a junior college within its various components until the institution went into the state system of higher education at midnight on August 31, 1963.[18]

Student organizations played a considerable role in the overall educational process at HJC, in spite of the difficulties of finding time for meetings and activities, of having facilities available, and of stretching already-taut student budgets for even the most modest dues and fees.

The interest in extracurricular activities was certainly there, as evidenced by the response when Captain Archie French sent out the call for football players. The only time for practice was from 9:30 p.m. until midnight, but enough men for three teams showed up regularly until it became apparent that a man simply could not work, attend classes until 9:00 p.m., scrimmage two-and-a-half hours under inadequate lighting, and do anything effective on the job, in the classroom, or on the football field.

Captain French, an M.A. from Columbia University who taught government and physical education, had replaced Cecil B. Smith, an instructor in history, government and athletics who also carried the titles of dean of men and coach, when Mr. Smith resigned in 1930 after a stay of two years at HJC.

In spite of the understandable demise of the football team at HJC, however, there remained a surprising range of activities, among them a girls' basketball team, an ice hockey team,[19] the Student Council, the John R. Bender Dramatic Club, the HJC Oratorical Association, the Cougar Collegians, the Girls' Outdoor Club, the Guild Savant, the Student Association, the Speakers' Club, the *Cougar*, and the *Houstonian.*

A remarkable publication, the 1934 *Houstonian* (which was produced from start to finish in two weeks and sold for 75 cents as the "First Official Annual") tells us in some detail about typical student activities during 1933-1934.

The girls' basketball team, coached by Miss Irene Spiess, played only two games but was honored by the Cougar Collegians at a banquet which included awarding gold medals to all eight members of the team: Winnie Allen, Avis Carks, Edith Carlton, Lou Gaines, Alice Claire Luckel, Maizie Lyle, Jo Meda Parks, and Jen E. Wait (earlier rosters showed a ninth team member,

Mildred Blair). The young ladies batted .500, devastating Southern Pacific 52-21, but losing a close one to the W.T. Grant Department Store, 16-19. You obviously played whatever teams you could schedule in girls' basketball, back there in 1933-1934. Coach Spiess, incidentally, will be remembered as the sole addition to the HJC instructional staff in 1932-1933. She was paid $300 as an assistant instructor in girls' physical education, and apparently threw in her coaching duties on the side.

The ice hockey team was remarkable. Led by Ed Chernosky, they were undefeated, and they outscored the opposition three to one. But they had to forfeit the city championship because of an incomplete schedule, even though they played Rettig's (Ice Cream Parlor) in attempting to get in the minimum number of games. Stars other than Captain (and Manager) Chernosky included Bill Irwin (high scorer for the season), Paul Franks, and John Burns. Other men on the team were Nelson Hinton, Bob Swor, Lawrence Sauer, Donald Aitken, Gus Heiss, Erwin Barrow, John Staples, and Bill Goggan. Harry Gray was assistant manager.

The Student Council, sponsored by Dean Dupre, consisted of the presidents of the major student groups. Its principal functions were to facilitate communication between faculty, administration, and student body, and to help with key campus projects such as the freshman and sophomore dances.

The John R. Bender Dramatic Club, sponsored by L. Standlee (Chief) Mitchell, was the forerunner of the Red Masque Players. The Club honored the memory of Coach Bender, whose untimely death in 1928, as noted earlier, deprived HJC and the University of Houston of a potentially fine leader.[20] The 1933-1934 productions of the Bender Club were a bit difficult to locate on any list of the world's greater plays: "Apple Blossom Time," "Ghost Parade" and "Children of the Moon." The club's president was Bill Stanford; the vice president, Marjorie Willke; and the secretary, June Learned.

The Oratorical Association, which had featured Judge Roy Hofheinz, in earlier years, had one of its best debate seasons in 1933-1934, losing only two of eight matches. Sponsored by Harvey W. Harris, the Association featured two lady debaters, our basketball player Edith Carlton (Mrs. Edith Lord Carlton, one of the relatively few married students in the freshman and sophomore classes), and Josephine Fastenrath, in addition to Tommy Cooksey, Louis Ehlers, Allen Marshall, and William Stanford.

The Cougar Collegians was perhaps the leading women's organization in the first years of HJC and the University. Sponsored jointly by Miss Mildred Hubbard, a part-time instructor in French; Mrs. Ebaugh and Mrs. Bender, the principal activities for 1933-1934 included a formal tea in Mrs. Ebaugh's home, a Vice-Versa Dance in the gymnasium, and the banquet for the girls' basketball team. Officers for the Collegians were Lou Gaines, president; Nelda Eaves, vice president; Margie Cheek Goggan, secretary; and Lucy Grady, treasurer.

The Girls' Outdoor Club, sponsored by Miss Spiess, claimed that its members "strive for good health by spending a large part of their spare time out of doors (where it is) easier to really study." They got all the way to Casa Del Mar on Galveston Bay for a weekend party in late April planned by president Dorothy Golden and secretary-treasurer Evelyn Lewis.

The Guild Savant included many of the more active and popular student leaders. Their principal objective as to "attain a better relationship between students and faculty," and a traditional project was the reception for graduating seniors, held every May since 1928. This highly successful undertaking was credited with attracting a goodly number of students to HJC, primarily boys who were struck by the comely high school girls who entered a beauty contest held in conjunction with the reception. This competition was won six years in a row by girls from Sam Houston High School, the old Central High downtown where future President Lyndon B. Johnson was a teacher for a brief time in 1930-1931.

The Student Association meant just that at HJC, with each student holding membership and the organization active in assisting the various campus organizations. James Coulson was president; another well-known student, Marjorie Willke, was secretary; and the other two posts were held by members of the popular ice hockey team: Harry Gray, vice president, and Donald Aitken, treasurer.

The HJC Speakers Club, allied with the Oratorical Association and also sponsored by Mr. Harris, trained its members in extemporaneous speech on current topics of interest. There were two presidents in 1933-1934, Reo King in the fall and Lynn Davis in the spring. The ever-present members of the ice hockey team scored yet another point: Bob Swor was vice president in the fall and parliamentarian in the spring.

The *Cougar* was actually the first extracurricular activity at HJC, pre-dating the original classes in journalism (which began in 1928-1929 under Fred R. Birney) by a full year. It was both a laboratory for journalism students and a student activity (the *Cougar* appeared only semi-monthly from 1927 to 1935, when it became a weekly), and served as a valuable communications device and source of information throughout the history of HJC. The 1933-1934 staff was headed by Mary Elizabeth Horan, editor; Jane Nevill, associate editor; and Carolyn Rosenberg, news editor.[21]

As noted earlier, the 1934 *Houstonian* was a remarkable publication. The staff was organized (to a considerable extent from the *Cougar's* key personnel) soon after the Easter holiday of 1934. Within two weeks, the 32-page "First Official Annual" was on sale for 75 cents. Six pictures were left out, but these were tucked in neatly on page 21, and the entire project was a speedy triumph for Jane Neville, editor-in-chief; Carolyn Rosenberg, associate editor; the remainder of the staff; and Mr. Birney, the sponsor of both campus newspaper and annual.

Among the spear-carriers for the *Houstonian* was a mainstay of the current Houston *Post*, and veteran of newspapering for more years than he might want to admit: C.W. Skipper. He was art editor for the 1934 yearbook.

The 1934 *Houstonian* was dedicated to Dr. Oberholtzer. The text of the dedication bespeaks both the respect and admiration that the staff had for him, and how far 1934 was from the student unrest of the late 1960's and the brief era in which many yearbooks were temporarily discontinued or drastically altered:

VISION FOR THE FUTURE

Inspired by the boundless energy and buoyancy of the spirit of youth coupled with the abiding belief that youth, if educated, will care for the future, Doctor Oberholtzer visualized a great educational system for Houston.

> The University of Houston rises today to provide and to extend practical training for the youth of the city, from kindergarten through the necessary period for thorough training in life pursuits.
>
> Such a plan, long a dream but gradually becoming a reality, is today reaching fruition with the establishment of the University of Houston.
>
> Years hence, when the University has thoroughly established itself as a pioneering institution in newly marked fields, founded upon the practical wisdom of one of America's truly inspired educators of this age, this day will be marked as one to be commemorated as Founder's Day.[22]
>
> But today, looking into the future with steadfast confidence and courage, we admire and respect our beloved president and therefore
>
> We dedicate this, the first *Houstonian*
> to
> DOCTOR E.E. OBERHOLTZER
> President, The University of Houston
> Superintendent, Houston Public Schools
> President, Department of Superintendence, 1934-1935
> The National Education Association

The 1934 *Houstonian* also had two other significant and prophetic statements within its pages: (1) A Message of Greeting to the Student Body and Prospective Students of the University of Houston, by Dr. Oberholtzer; and (2) Descriptive Statements of the General College of the University of Houston.

"The University of Houston," the Message of Greeting began, "extends a cordial invitation to all students who are interested in broadening their outlook on life to enroll . . . June 4, 1934 . . . (or) for the first regular year's work, beginning September 17." Other excerpts are also of interest:

> The University of Houston is a service institution for the metropolitan area . . . . (It) desires to grow in service and (to) become the center of culture, as well as the center of practical learning in professional, business, and industrial pursuits. This University will become great if the citizenship of this area desires to make it great. The University, under the control of the Board of Education, is dedicated to community service, to the development of that kind of education which will render each individual better able to perform well some definite service and to receive from such service a lasting satisfaction in his life pursuit.

> If you desire to grow in usefulness, to keep your mind alert and your eyes turned toward the better things of life, the University covets an opportunity to assist you . . . Houston wants the University to grow and to share in . . . building not only a fine city industrially and professionally, but a city noted for its outstanding citizenship and (for) its emphasis on the cultural aspects of life.

If you compare the above with excerpts from Dr. Oberholtzer's 1924 addresses to the graduating classes of old Central High and Heights High School, there are some remarkable, and meaningful, parallels. Now he had the system closed, from kindergarten to University.

Statements concerning the General College were written by Walter W. Kemmerer, whose crucial role from 1934 to his controversial resignation in 1953 as president of the University we will begin to examine in the next chapter. The General College of the University of Houston, with its considerable effect on the further evolvement of the institution, will be analyzed next.

First we must go back for a moment to consider the role of another new principal in our unfolding story, Colonel William Bartholomew Bates. Colonel Bates was to have a major impact upon the HJC and the University of Houston from the day in 1928 when he was appointed to the Board of Education until August, 1971, when he refused to be considered for another term on the Board of Regents "because I would be pushing 90 at the end of another six-year appointment."

Colonel Bates, as indicated in the opening chapter, had a deep and lasting admiration for Dr. Oberholtzer, probably stemming from the similarities in their early backgrounds and in their approaches to life. Both men were philosophically and financially dyed-in-the-wool conservatives, yet they were willing to innovate, to look far into the future, to take even dangerous chances if the odds for success were reasonably sound and the potential for public gain and betterment high. Both were also what the British call "unflappables"; neither man "lost his cool," when the going got rough. This admirable quality probably stemmed from early and lasting psychological maturity: "Bill" Bates and "Eddie" Oberholtzer believed in themselves and found it difficult to believe they could lose.[23]

Colonel Bates had met Dr. Oberholtzer a few weeks before the latter had actually assumed office as superintendent of schools. The colonel recalled often that he uncovered what he called the

"Oberholtzer Plan" very soon after joining the Board of Education in 1928. It was to revamp the primary and secondary public school system with the aid of research and advanced planning, to get the Houston Junior College underway and to convert it as soon as practicable to a four-year institution.

Two of these three goals had been reached (although the revision and expansion of the public school system was to continue for many years), when Colonel Bates became one of Dr. Oberholtzer's "bosses" in May, 1928. The superintendent's plan was to bring the third goal into the picture just as soon as he could prove the HJC was fiscally sound and that there was enough demand for a University of Houston. In this high undertaking he had a working partner in W.B. Bates, who knew that Houston could not continue its rate of expansion without readily available, university-level training for increasingly large numbers of students.

Everything went swimmingly at HJC through 1930-1931, insofar as fiscal health and increasing demand for courses was concerned. Enrollment was at 858, a gain of 87 percent over 1927, with an operating surplus for each of the past three years. But the crucial time for a decision on the overall Oberholtzer Plan was to come for the Board of Education in the fall of 1933. Would the enrollment trend, in reverse for two years, continue downward, or would it reverse itself?

Everyone could understand the drop in enrollment to 743 in 1931-1932, but things turned a bit queasy when there was another, and substantially greater, loss of students in 1932-1933, all the way down to 596. Still, budgets remained in the black, after salaries and other elements of expense were cut, and Dr. Oberholtzer (noting an upturn in some area economic indicators) began to make a few optimistic statements. Although these sounded a little like whistling past the graveyard, he was a prophet with honor: the student body increased from 596 to 624 in September, 1933, and moved on strongly from there.

In the meantime, Colonel Bates became increasingly involved as a member (and secretary) of the Board of Education. He was also approaching a time of decision regarding the division of his time between his young family (which always came first), his law practice, and his civic responsibilities, especially on the Board of Education. There was also his new assignment as a director of the State National Bank, which would lead to a second, and most significant, career in banking.

It was now Fulbright, Crooker, Freeman and Bates (since January 1, 1928, exactly five years after he had first reported for work in a driving wet norther on New Year's Day, a holiday far less observed in those days). As a partner in what was to become one of the great law firms of the country, he was more and more involved with a growing list of clients. Moreover, his primary assignment was to the Anderson, Clayton and Company account. He had done an excellent piece of work for both Ben Clayton and Will Clayton in his first years with the firm, and he had become close also to Monroe D. Anderson, who was soon to establish the M.D. Anderson Foundation with Colonel Bates as one of three charter trustees.[24]

Colonel Bates told me one summer day in 1973, while a thunderstorm fierce enough to drive us from his accustomed table by the big glass windows of the Coronado Club roared through the city, how he resolved these conflicts without prejudicing his strong and growing interest in what was still the Houston Junior College; his conviction of its enormous potential for the future, as a four-year institution; and his personal admiration for Dr. Oberholtzer, for H.L. Mills and for his colleagues on the Board of Education.[25]

The matter of a decision on the distribution of Colonel Bates' time, especially in regard to the Board of Education, became crucial in the early months of 1933. At that time, he was asked to succeed his friend Judge K.C. Barkley as president of the Board. This would mean, of course, a considerably greater involvement, at a time when he had received some preliminary inquiries about the possibility of his accepting the first vacancy on the Board of Regents of the State Teachers' Colleges, representing his alma mater, Sam Houston Teachers' College at Huntsville, where he was awarded a diploma and teaching certificate in 1911.

Colonel Bates needed some key pieces of information before coming to a decision. First, he asked about the possibility of the Houston Junior College reversing its downward trend in enrollment and was told that the chances seemed reasonable for a reversal, even though the final answer would not be available until early in September. Next, he went over the situation with H.L. Mills and Palmer Hutcheson, an old friend who was serving as principal attorney for the Board of Education. They both felt, as did almost all of his colleagues on the Board of Education, that if the fiscal picture at HJC brightened, the institution should definitely go on to four-year status. The demand was there, the community need was clearly present, and unless unforeseen opposition developed in Austin, it was believed that legislative approval of a University of Houston, under the aegis of the Houston Independent School District, could be obtained.

Next, he asked Dr. Oberholtzer to come by his office in the State National Bank Building in the late afternoon; to be prepared to go on over to the old Houston Club, in the Houston *Chronicle* Building, for continued discussions over dinner if this became necessary.

He told Dr. Oberholtzer that he must make a decision soon on whether or not to succeed Judge Barkley, and of the other growing demands on his time. He also outlined his findings regarding the feasibility of four-year status and reinforced his previous statements regarding his continuing interest in HJC and—if it developed—in a University of Houston.

Then, the proposition: Colonel Bates would take the presidency of the Board of Education, but only for two years, from 1933-1935. During this time his principal objective would be to obtain four-year status for HJC and to set the University of Houston as firmly as possible on its hopefully ascendant new path of service to the community and area. In 1935 he would step down from the Board of Education, after seven years, but he would continue to do anything he could for the University of Houston and for Dr. Oberholtzer. He hinted at the time that he might be capable of locating some major contributions for it in the future, if the plans of one of his friends came to fruition. Although he did not identify the friend, or reveal any confidences, he was thinking of Monroe D. Anderson. Mr. Anderson had formed a habit of coming by Colonel Bates' office each morning before he went on to the old Anderson, Clayton and Company headquarters on Main and Rusk, and they were far along with discussions regarding the establishment of the M.D. Anderson Foundation, which was to come into being in 1936 with a tremendous endowment of Anderson, Clayton and Company stock.

Dr. Oberholtzer was of course most grateful for the proposal that Colonel Bates outlined to him, although he realized what a loss it would be to have the Colonel step down from the Board of Education in two years.

Colonel Bates moved to carry out his part of the bargain as soon as possible. On September 11, 1933 (after favorable reports on an increase in registration for the first time since 1930-1931 were available), the Board of Education unanimously adopted a resolution[26] extending the "scope and services" of the Houston Junior College "to include at least two additional years of college work," referring to "said proposed institution" hereafter as "The University of Houston" and affirming that the Board of Education was negotiating with the federal government for a loan to assist in the conversion to four-year status and to provide "proper and suitable buildings and grounds."[27]

Palmer Hutcheson and H.L. Mills, with assistance from Colonel Bates and others, then went into action on the Austin scene. House Bill 194 of the 43rd Legislature, which became law on October 16, 1933, adopted the September 11, 1933, Board of Education resolution, and specifically authorized the Houston Independent School District to operate the University of Houston.

Finally, on April 30, 1934, detailed resolutions prepared by Dr. Oberholtzer acknowledged and accepted the provisions of House Bill 194 and outlined the "emergency in public education" requiring the establishment of a "self-supporting" University of Houston "at this opportune time"; the five major fields of its services (foundational [sic] to professions and vocations, arts and industries, science as applied to technical and vocational pursuits, liberal arts and culture, and extension and adult education); the officers of the University, by title; the University's authority to use "public school buildings when not otherwise in regular use, at the actual additional cash expenditure which may be incurred by such use"; and the authority of the President of the University, with his Executive Committee, to organize for the opening of the University in June, 1934.

The University of Houston began its first session, a six-week summer school, on June 4, 1934, at San Jacinto High School. The charter of the University was formally presented to President Oberholtzer and to the faculty by Colonel Bates at a luncheon in the SJHS cafeteria, on June 9, 1934.[28] Dr. Oberholtzer spoke of the great faith he had in the new institution, especially if it pursued its first objective: to be of service. He praised Colonel Bates and the Board of Education, and thanked the faculty and staff for their dedicated work that had brought the institution so quickly to this significant point. He then announced summer enrollment at 682 and told everybody to get back to work.

Thus the seven crucial years from 1927-1934 came not only to a triumphant end but to a new beginning at the same time. Since 1927, the city that had to have a University of Houston had gone through unprecedented prosperity, the 1928 Democratic national convention, a reasonably mild version of the Great Depression, a great downtown flood, the continued deepening of the Ship Channel that helped to spark a new wave of prosperity, and such bizarre events as 300,000 people gathered at Bellaire Speedway to watch a balloon race.

Now the city had housed in a high school one of its most significant new resources: The University of Houston.

Notes to Chapter Two

[1]See Appendix data on rates of population growth in Houston and Harris County between 1850 and 1977, 1980 (estimated). The remarkable patterns revealed are significant to any understanding of how and why the University of Houston developed as it did.

[2]The names are all felicitously chosen, but particularly that of Governor "Jim" Hogg, who personally slowed down the granting of enormous chunks of Texas' public lands to the railroads and thereby preserved billions of dollars in future income for our schoolchildren. Governor Hogg hated pretense and "airs." When a fawning young reporter asked soon after his election if he pronounced his name "Hay-ogg" or "Hagg," he responded: "It's Hogg, son; just like a rootin' hog."

[3]Beaumont, with a deepwater port, nearby Spindletop, the locally-chartered Paraffin Oil Company, wealthy and ambitious citizens and the headquarters of the Texas Company, whose incorporators included John W. (Bet-A-Million) Gates and Walter T. Campbell (whose son-in-law, R.L. Blaffer, helped to organize Humble Oil) could have sidetracked Houston as the "oil capital of the world" had it not been for some of Houston's attributes and her leaders, mentioned here and later.

[4]It took well over a century for Houston to reach its pinnacle as a center for the marketing and processing of cotton, primarily through the vast importance of this fiber to Texas, the Port of Houston's favorable location and facilities, and the location here of the great cotton factors, Anderson, Clayton & Company, with branches scat-

tered from the principal U.S. cities to Tokyo, Sao Paolo, Bombay, Cairo, Rome, London, Manchester and half the remaining mercantile centers of the world.

The beginning was in 1821, when Jared E. Groce, a Stephen F. Austin colonist, brought cotton seed to his plantation along the fertile bottoms of the Brazos River. The next year, he raised his first crop, and by 1825 he had installed a crude gin. Before Houston was founded, the Groce wagons pulled by seven-yoked oxen fought their way through the mud and swamps, snakes and mosquitoes to Harrisburg. Here he transferred more than 100 bales a year for transportation by barge and ship to New Orleans.

In a later era, wealthy planters from the Brazos Bottoms left their plantations and thousands of slaves to come up to Houston in foppish pantaloons and waistcoats of figured French silk. They bargained with the more than two dozen cotton merchants here in the 1850's and 1860's, including blockade runners who would pay almost any price during the War Between The States' early phases. One of the first important businesses to open here after Reconstruction was a textile mill. The city had six cotton compresses plus storage facilities for two million bales in the 1890's, and a dozen compresses and storage for three million bales when World War II broke out.

But it took only a few years of government intervention to destroy the cotton market as a meaningful component of the free enterprise system. And although the Port of Houston remains a major factor in the exportation of cotton, there are fewer cotton merchants here than a century ago, the Houston Cotton Exchange is fearfully diminished, and Anderson, Clayton & Company has left the field to become a billion-dollar conglomerate in cotton oil, specialty foods and insurance. There is obviously a lesson here in government, history and resiliency.

[5]Mr. Jones had assisted both Mr. Farish and R.L. Blaffer, Humble Oil's treasurer, in some crucial early financing for the company, and remained a close friend of both and of many of their associates.

Reminded years later of the millions he could have made by keeping his stock in "The Humble," Mr. Jones reportedly replied that he "never looked back on a deal that made me money," and "liked to look at his chips on the table" (as with high-quality real estate), "not under the ground" (as in wildcatting).

[6]Schoolchildren saw the humor in the otherwise tragic and shameful event, and chanted endlessly: "Oh, the night was dark and dreary, the air was full of sleet, Papa joined the Ku Klux Klan and took our best sheet." Many Houstonians fought the Klan, including my great-uncle, Monsignor John T. Nicholson, who blasted its members and supporters regularly from the pulpit of what is now Sacred Heart

Co-Cathedral. But at their peak, in 1924, the Klansmen saw their gubernatorial candidate Felix D. Robertson lead the first Democratic primary. He was defeated by Miriam A. (Ma) Ferguson, still our only woman governor. She ran on a strong anti-KKK platform, and won 4-3 in the second primary. In those days, when children were likely grown before they saw a real live Republican, she had no difficulty in the general election.

[7]Houston was plagued by malaria and by the far more dangerous yellow fever in the last century, primarily because only the central business district was properly drained until the early 1900's, in a sub-tropical climate with 50 inches of rain in a normal year, 100 in abnormal times, and literally billions of mosquitoes. The two worst outbreaks were in 1848 and in 1867, when one of the victims was the hero of Sabine Pass, Richard W. (Dick) Dowling of the Davis (Irish) Guards and the Bank of Bacchus Saloon. It became traditional for the Sisters of Charity of the Incarnate Word to nurse afflicted Houstonians through recurring sieges of yellow fever, before and after a half-dozen members of the order established the original St. Joseph's Infirmary on Franklin and Caroline in 1887. The sisters were awarded free transportation on city streetcars in recognition of their heroic work, a reward that lasted from the era of mule-drawn cars to modern days.

A letter in the Sound-Off column of the Houston *Post* of November 1, 1972, tells the story of the Sisters of the Incarnate Word:

Mary Augustine
McKeever

In this hurrying, infelicitous time when most news is negative in fact as well as in shading, it is regrettable that the news media did not record in any detail the sad but happy death and last rites of Mary Augustine McKeever, who would have been 93 years old on Nov. 1.

Mother Augustine (and finally, in the humble tradition of the great order to which she belonged, Sister Augustine) was for many years the superior general of the Sisters of the Incarnate Word. These self-sacrificing and noble women were in Houston almost a century ago, helping to stem a yellow fever epidemic. They are known to most of us, and especially to the native Houstonians, as the founders and operators of Saint Joseph Hospital; but they serve God and country in many other ways as well.

Mother Augustine spent her final years in a wheel chair, with her hearing at minimum, but Irish wit, courage and faith totally undiminished. There was everywhere in evidence as her funeral mass was said in a medieval-like chapel, love and respect and memories of long service and signal achievement, but no tears. Then the mourners walked quietly through the grounds of the Villa de Matel, in sound if not in sight of Wayside Drive traffic, and Mary Augustine McKeever was laid simply to rest among her own.

The debt owed this woman by our city is great indeed, although she would be the last to have mentioned it in any way.

[8]Dean Dupre told a student flying class at the University of Houston many years later than his hero was the legendary Lieutenant Benjamin D. Foulois, who was assigned to Fort Sam Houston in February, 1910 (just seven years after the Wright Brothers' flight at Kitty Hawk) with orders to teach himself to fly, did so, and helped to lay the groundwork for Kelly Field, a vital link in the early and ongoing history of military aviation.

[9]Samuel Leon Bishkin, a handsome, black-haired man of enormous energy, was also a gifted high school teacher before joining the HJC faculty. Mrs. Esther (Aaron J.) Farfel remembers across 50 years his ability as a chemistry instructor at Sam Houston High School, his patience with students and his willingness to stay with small groups who were having difficulty with formulae after class, for special tuition.

[10]HJC's official enrollment figures (summer enrollments in parentheses): 1927-1928, 460 (232); 1928-1929, 637 (223); 1929-1930, 730 (300); 1930-1931, 858 (383); 1931-1932, 743 (418); 1932-1933, 596 (232); 1933-1934, 624 (193).

[11]There was nothing unique in this sharing of facilities. Of the 16 junior colleges in Texas in 1927, only five had their own buildings; two of these were ancient edifices accepted as gifts, and actually were more suitable to the State Antiquities Commission than to an institution of higher education.

[12]Houston streets were originally laid out 80 feet from curb to curb, this being the distance required for a fully-loaded wagon of logs to make a U-turn. Unbelievably, there were campaigns as late as the 1940's to reduce the 80 feet to a "more practical" 60 feet or less. What some cities would give to have 80-foot streets!

[13]One of the more reliable means of checking the age of prominent female Houstonians of senior years is now far less available than it was. Dowagers and matrons once proudly listed such venerable institutions as Kidd Key, with year of graduation, in the Social Directory of Houston. They failed to realize that this is tantamount to listing their age, give or take a year or two. The word got out several editions ago, however, and there was a rash of confidential communications, both oral and written, asking that the year of graduation be omitted henceforth.

[14]Grading standards were considerably harsher in the first years at HJC, according to some members of the early staff and students themselves. Certainly there was no tendency to pass out A's "like a candidate's wife handing out his election cards in front of the polling place," as one former instructor expressed it. Or the leniency on grades in many institutions in the late 1960's and early 1970's, which

still persists to some degree. I once idly looked over a grading sheet outside a dean's office while waiting for an appointment with him during the student unrest over Vietnam and the draft. I was struck by the fact that one class of 26 persons had all been awarded A's by a young assistant. I told the dean that I did not know whether to congratulate him on the uniformly scintillating brilliance of his students or to report a new statistical miracle to the Guinness Book of World Records. The dean checked the grade sheet, made a careful note of the assistant's name, and muttered something about "arranging a conference with this fellow."

[15]Many of the desks at San Jacinto High School had been originally purchased for 12- to 14-year-old junior high students.

[16]There was considerable concern when summer session enrollment fell slightly from 232 to 223 in 1928, since summer classes attracted primarily teachers (an excellent source of students for the long semesters), and provided both extra income for key instructors and a small but useful surplus. Enrollment was up substantially to 300 in 1929, however, reached 383 the following summer, and went on to a peak of 418 in 1931 before falling, understandably, in the depression years of 1932 and 1933, when tuition was hard to come by for teachers faced with salary cuts.

[17]The Revolving Fund, authorized in 1930, consisted of the grand sum of $500 derived from small fees charged the students (one-time matriculation fee, $5.00; library, $4.00; blanket tax, $5.00; and various laboratory fees ranging from 50 cents in education to $10.00 in biology). Small portions of the Revolving Fund, which was replenished as needed, could be obtained by an instructor through a complex six-step disbursing procedure roughly similar to amending the federal budget.

[18]See Appendix.

[19]Those who believe that athletic competition between the University of Houston and Rice University began in 1971 with a classic football game should know that the Cougars and Owls played ice hockey 40 years ago in the old Polar Wave rink on McGowen Avenue.

[20]John R. Bender lives in University of Houston memory for another and unusual reason: He named the athletic teams "Cougars" because he liked the mountain lion as a symbol of courage and tenacity and had coached the Washington State Cougars early in his career,

[21]In later years both the *Cougar* and the Rice *Thresher*, plus a bewildering array of junior high and senior high school newspapers, were printed by (and their editors were taught by) John L. Scardino of 4312 Garrow, the Grand Old East Side Printer, for more than four decades. John Sr. retired in the early 1970's, but John L., Jr., John L., III, and Tommy carry on the much-expanded operation.

[22]Ironically, the only Founder's Day celebrated thus far at the University of Houston came on May 2, 1950, when the Board of Regents, faculty, staff and other friends gathered to honor Dr. and Mrs. Oberholtzer soon before his retirement from the presidency of the University. The evening went well enough, although Dr. Oberholtzer always felt that he was maneuvered into resigning to a considerable extent. And he was, as we shall see; but he was only four days short of his seventieth birthday, the time had come for new leadership (even under the cloud of an "acting" presidency), Dr. Oberholtzer was treated generously, and the steaks were of the uniformly superb quality served by Ernest Coker at the old College Inn.

[23]Dr. Kemmerer told me that Dr. Oberholtzer, with whom he often played golf, would invariably be a few dollars behind on the final tee. He would always press "double or nothing," and Dr. Kemmerer cannot recall Dr. Oberholtzer ever losing.

[24]Colonel Bates, Ben Clayton, and M.D. Anderson were fishing pals. Although Mr. Anderson died in 1939, the Colonel was still going deep-sea fishing with Ben Clayton when he was 80—and Mr. Clayton was nearly 90.

[25]The Colonel had a tremendous memory for important details, for faces and for names, even after many years (although for some reason he always called Dean Dupre "Roebuck" when we were discussing him). Looking around the Coronado Club, he suddenly said: "There's Logan Wilson's senator, that water lawyer we could never get a vote out of. But we beat him once; 18-8 I think it was." He then nodded courteously to and identified Charles Herring, the former state senator from Austin, whom he had not seen since 1961. The "water lawyer" threw me for a moment, but I recalled that Senator Herring, who understandably was very close to President Logan Wilson and to the University of Texas, had become the chief executive of the Lower Colorado River Authority. Colonel Bates was remembering with great accuracy a turning point in the desperate legislative battles to get the University of Houston into the state system of higher education, and an important luncheon at the Austin Club at which he, President A.D. Bruce of the University of Houston and I were the guests of President Wilson. We were on a fishing expedition to determine if by some chance the University of Texas might support our legislative campaign, and I believe that under the appropriate circumstances we might even have agreed to join the University of Texas System. But there was only splendid hospitality and light conversation, and, eventually, Senator Herring's gentlemanly but skilled opposition. Colonel Bates had also remembered that our Senator Robert W. Baker had watched his historic Senate Bill 2 become the subject of one of the Senate's longest and bitterest filibusters while he remained short one vote of the minimum two-to-one margin required to bring it up for floor action. Senator Baker

discovered, however, that Senator Herring would be absent until at least 10:30 a.m. on the morning of May 12, 1961. After checking and rechecking, this made it possible for us to gamble on the two-to-one margin, which was voted 18-8 when both Senator Herring and the only lady member of the Senate, Mrs. Neville Colson, were absent. Senator Herring arrived about 20 minutes later, realizing that if he had been present, he could have brought the count to the barest minimum, and possibly have won 17-9 by switching a single vote. But all he could do now was to watch Senator Baker survive a parliamentary maneuver 14-12 and pass his bill by voice vote. Now, 12 years later, Colonel Bates could recall virtually all of this, and even remind me where Senator Herring was when the fateful 18-8 vote was taken (which distressed me somewhat until I remembered the harsh realities of life in the State Capitol). He was attending the funeral of his lifelong friend, Commodore W.P. Perry.

[26]See Appendix.

[27]Mrs. Ray K. Daily, M.D., of whom considerably more later, made the actual motion for passage of the September 11, 1933 resolution.

[28]The entire text of the charter will be found in the Appendix.

Chapter Three

1934-1939

Key reinforcements for a full-university operation . . . Enter W.W. Kemmerer, the Innovator, and the General College . . . Sound fiscal policy through the Great Depression and beyond . . . The intensifying search for a seperate campus . . . Memorial Park is out, but the Settegast-Taub tract is in . . . Power structure, alternate financing schemes, publicity, and low-level lobbying . . . Dr. Oberholtzer and friends find a man with a great heart, Hugh Roy Cullen . . . The 1938 fund drive and the Roy Gustav Cullen Memorial Building, after a 3 a.m. decision . . . Reorganization by the Board of Education and the move to the new campus . . . Safe harbor, in a pine and oak swamp with great potential, but fresh and alarming challenges in a world going to war.

Edison Ellsworth Oberholtzer was usually a little ahead of the game—through foresight and an ability to balance good planning and sound operations with a reasonable level of chance-taking.

He must have felt real satisfaction as he accepted the institutional charter from Colonel Bates at that historic luncheon on June 9, 1934 (ten years, to the day, since he had assumed the post of superintendent of schools). Now he had his four-year University of Houston; a competent faculty and staff (including a remarkable innovator who would leave his lasting and controversial stamp upon the institution) to help shoulder the burden of full-university status; a small but commendable surplus in spite of the fiscal threats and pitfalls of the Great Depression; and a university with the clear prospect of a sharply climbing enrollment, broader role and scope, and growing community support. But Dr. Oberholtzer also faced some formidable problems as he prepared for the first fall semester of the new University, which was to begin formally with the opening of classes on September 19, 1934.

He recognized that a resumption of the upward trend in enrollment would bring back, and intensify, overcrowding at San Jacinto High School, along with understandable demands for a new campus. Houston Junior College had been forced to turn to temporary classrooms ("the shacks") as early as 1930, and the handwriting was on the wall: summer school enrollment had jumped to 682 for opening classes on June 4, 1934; Houston's rapidly convalescing economy was on the move again; and there were literally hundreds of inquiries about junior- and senior-level courses.

As a practical and efficient planner, President Oberholtzer had foreseen many of these difficulties. Actually, he had made a major step toward their resolution as early as 1929, when he hired Walter W. Kemmerer, a fellow graduate student at Columbia University, as director of curriculum for the Houston Independent School District (HISD) and an unofficial counselor, assistant, and trouble-shooter.

Dr. Kemmerer had enough to do in his primary assignment, with the ongoing expansion of the HISD and the need to devise and apply research methodologies that would keep curricular development abreast of the remarkable growth in the physical plant. But President Oberholtzer knew that he had in Dr. Kemmerer a rare resource for the future, as the Houston Junior College went through its 1929-1932 expansion and the concept of a future University of Houston began to take shape.

For example, "Bill" Kemmerer was very knowledgable in the application of machine accounting methods to educational management, at a time when the state of the art was generally comparable to the abacus. In fact, he had done his doctoral dissertation at Columbia University on this subject, attracting attention from pioneering companies such as National Cash Register. President Oberholtzer was aware of these talents, as was H.L. Mills, with whom Dr. Kemmerer was to form an alliance of considerable importance to the future of the University.

Moreover, HISD's promising director of curriculum was a progressive thinker and an innovator in areas of education and administration that complemented and strengthened his superior's own formidable talents. And President Oberholtzer, ever wary of anything that even hinted of a budget deficit, was comforted to find that he and his associate had in common a good measure of frugality stemming from their similar backgrounds.

The upshot of all this was that Dr. Oberholtzer began to lean increasingly upon Dr. Kemmerer as a sounding-board and sometime advisor for his problems at HJC, even though Bill Kemmerer was very seldom at San Jacinto High School during the 1929-1934 era. He also, consciously or unconsciously, began to assign his director of curriculum another significant role: that of ambassador—and sometimes whipping boy—to the Board of Education. Colonel Bates told me, for example, that Dr. Kemmerer "was an able fellow, but we certainly began to get into a lot of squabbles with him on the Board of Education, from about the last years of Judge Barkley's presidency (1931-1932). Nothing like the smooth going in the Fonville administration."

Colonel Bates, as we shall see, was detecting some growing and inevitable pressures upon the Board of Education. These stemmed primarily from fundamental differences in philosophy; but they were being exacerbated by the half-hidden presence of that needy orphan—the Houston Junior College soon to become the University of Houston—within the tightly-budgeted HISD family.

Dr. Kemmerer had completed his doctorate at Columbia University in 1929, but he continued an intensive study of contemporary problems in higher education, and approaches toward their solution. He was drawn inevitably to the University of Chicago, where the vigorous tradition of John Dewey and Francis W. Parker, together with their disciples and detractors, preserved another authentic fountainhead of seminal thought and theory in education. At an earlier stage in its evolvement, this deserved reputation for scholarly leadership and challenging innovation at the University of Chicago had brought Edison Ellsworth Oberholtzer to the great Midwest institution in the 1908-1915 era, when he was stubbornly and successfully pursuing his further education under the legendary William Rainey Harper.

Now in the years between 1929 and 1934 there was a new guru in residence at Chicago—the brilliant Robert Maynard Hutchins, humanist, super-intellect and former dean of the Yale Law School. It is ironic that Bill Kemmerer, opposed to some of President Hutchins' most cherished tenets, learned in a University of Chicago workshop related concepts that would have a major impact upon the early history of the University of Houston.

Dr. Hutchins had zeroed in on what he termed "vocationalism" and "anti-intellectualism," as typified by Bennington College in Vermont, which was in his judgment enormously overemphasizing the role of the student in course selection and self-expression. This, he maintained with demonstrable correctness, led to a reduced interest in mathematics, grammar, philosophy and what he termed the "never-changing first principles." (Having once had a girl friend of impeccable Boston Brahmin background whose main concern at Bennington was actually the management of the communal compost heap, I can understand some of President Hutchins' concern.)

Anyone at all familiar with the evolvement of the University of Houston in its first two decades can comprehend the probability of sharp philosophical clashes between Robert Maynard Hutchins and W.W. Kemmerer. There were obviously strong strains of "vocationalism" and what Dr. Hutchins would term the "debasement of pure learning" in the original and developing concepts of both HJC and the University of Houston. These more practical approaches to higher education, however, were in appropriate balance with the less tangible stuff; and they were consonant with the needs and circumstances which brought the Junior College and the University into being.

Bill Kemmerer, therefore, did not attempt to oppose President Hutchins' surging crusade against "vocationalism"; nor, apparently, did he feel that opposition was necessary. He knew instinctively that what came to be known as the Great Books approach was not suited to a struggling new institution in Houston, Texas in the early 1930's—especially one described, among other things, as the "center of practical learning" for its metropolitan area.

Yet Dr. Kemmerer, stimulated by lively discussions at a University of Chicago workshop, devised an educational component for the new University of Houston that would certainly have been applauded by Robert Maynard Hutchins. This was the General College, a blend of ideas from Chicago, an extensive experiment at Harvard University, and the subject of discussions within the Association of Texas Colleges.

"It was a simple approach," Dr. Kemmerer told me more than 40 years later. "I was convinced that we must teach students to think more logically and effectively, and thereby to become better citizens, capable of identifying and understanding problems in broad overview—and of resolving them, either as professional practitioners or as perceptive, intelligent adults."

He felt that the soundest method would be to train the student to solve simple problems and then to confront him with progressively more complex and difficult ones. But what was the training curriculum to be?

In the University of Chicago workshop Dr. Kemmerer's colleagues discussed his idea with him and turned naturally to Robert Maynard Hutchins' "first principles" as the best preparation for specific training in the recognition and resolution of a wide range of problems. Dr. Kemmerer did not accept the authentic Great Books "Oxford don" approach, but he saw that a curriculum "providing a comprehensive survey or overview of the activities and problems of mankind" for the freshman and sophomore years might be a logical compromise. It would have to be offered primarily to full-time students, in a separate location, on an experimental basis.

Back in Houston Dr. Kemmerer found support for what he described to me as the "Experimental College" in several quarters. He had kept in touch with his long-time friend and classmate, Charles Francis (Charlie) Hiller,[2] who had gone on to Harvard from their old campus, Lehigh. Charlie was very positive on a long-range experiment in general education at Cambridge. This program (formally unveiled in the highly significant *General Education in a Free Society*, in 1945) seemed to be the Hutchins prescription in far more palatable form. It called for a return to fundamentals, but through a mandatory curriculum of mathematics, English language and literature, the physical sciences, and the social sciences in the first two years at Harvard College. Specialization would them follow on a solid foundation and sensitivity to, the traditions and values of our Western civilization.

The Harvard program was of course attracting wide attention in educational circles, and Dr. Kemmerer was probably part of a group who placed it on the agenda for discussion at meetings of the Association of Texas Colleges. As a result, at the 1934 annual meeting of the Association there was every indication that experimental programs in general education would be approved within the year.

Finally, to get downright practical, Dr. Kemmerer found that President Oberholtzer, who had already offered him the post of vice president at the University of Houston, liked the idea of a

General College. It was experimental yet seemed increasingly acceptable; tentative budgets indicated that it would be self-supporting; and Dr. Oberholtzer believed that he could find a separate location for the College, rent-free, thereby relieving some of the fierce pressure for classrooms and related facilities.

Dr. Kemmerer was therefore instructed to begin drawing up specific plans for the General College forthwith and to be ready to launch it under his supervision with the fall term of 1934.

The *Houstonian* of 1934, which was to some extent a well-written advertisement for Dr. Oberholtzer, the University of Houston's fall semester, and the General College, had this to say about Dr. Kemmerer's brainchild:

> . . . (The) General College . . . will provide . . . opportunities for cultural advancement and general self-improvement desired by individuals who are frequently barred from such opportunities by technical prerequisites . . . (and will) provide higher education for high school graduates who for various reasons cannot leave home.
>
> The General College is being planned as a day college introducing . . . a new type of college curriculum providing a comprehensive survey . . . of the activities and problems of mankind. It is being designed not as a school to transmit and advance knowledge alone but to utilize knowledge of facts, principles, laws and essential human attitudes related to the study and possible solution of problems of modern life.

With "college work of this broader type" replacing the "usual fragmentary specialization courses," specialization would be postponed "almost to the last two years of college," although one elective would be allowed freshman and sophomore students.

Four "general fields of study" were provided in the General College, their purpose to train "intelligent citizens,"not simply "specialists."

The fields were the social sciences (economics, history, government, sociology, philosophy, and psychology), the biological sciences, the physical sciences (mathematics, chemistry, physics, and descriptive astonomy), and the (English) language and other fine arts.

So far, we have recognized the considerable dependence of the General College upon the emerging Harvard College model for general education, even though the stated purposes of the General College bespeak Dr. Kemmerer's emphasis upon the student's ability to learn how to cope with the problems of everyday life.

But within the customary disciplines listed under the four fields of study we find unique sub-disciplines that reflect a different educational philosophy and approach. Kemmerer the Innovator was definitely at work, and, typically, a generation or so ahead of his time.

For example: economics included the preservation of natural resources (while billions of cubic feet of natural gas were being flared and wasted throughout most of Texas); history and government included lectures on the problems of other races, and the use of propaganda (particularly via the new medium of radio) in political campaigning.

Students in other social sciences would study such unusual problems as how to be a better parent (the subject of an excellent television series produced by the University of Houston-affiliated Gulf Region Educational Television Affiliates 42 years later), the effect of divorce, or how to furnish a home. Human biology was extended to encompass the economical purchasing of foods, consumer fraud, and a critical appraisal of synthetics and substitutes. The physical sciences included "mathematics needed in life activities" and "practical" chemistry such as a study of the composition of the more common medicinal remedies. In the areas of the English language and the fine arts, composition was studied intensively in small laboratory groups, and there would be instruction in the appreciation of the motion picture, now clearly recognized as an art form.

Long after World War II had swept aside the General College, some of its influence was still felt at the evolving University of Houston. Dr. Kemmerer told me many years later of some other goals he had hoped to reach through this innovative component. He wanted to provide as broad an intellectual experience as possible for those who could devote only two years, or less, to college; he wanted as well to give an opportunity to the student whose aptitudes were simply outside highly specialized, technical fields of knowledge, at least until his intellectual horizons could be expanded in two years of a broad, general education.

We need to know more about Walter William Kemmerer, who was moving strongly to the center of the stage as the University of Houston prepared to open its first fall semester in that long-ago September of 1934. Actually, his background and early history were remarkably similar to Edison Ellsworth Oberholtzer's, who was 23 years his senior.

Born in 1903 on a farm in Wind Gap, Pennsylvania (a community less than 10 miles from the new Jersey border in Northampton County, in the northeastern quadrant of the state half-way between Scranton and Philadelphia), he was one of six children and the only child to receive more than an elementary education, even though his father was a rural schoolteacher with a great respect for the advantages of academic training.

Bill Kemmerer seems to have had a special admiration for his father, who instilled in him pride in the family name and a dogged determination to give everyone his just due, and more.[3] A Frederick Kemmerer had received a land grant of 150 acres in Bushkill Township as early as 1742, and the name can be traced to one Hugh Johann von Kemmerer, who went to the Holy Land on the first Crusade, in 1096.

The word "kemmerer," incidentally, has some intriguing connotations. It probably derives from "die kimme," the triangular notch in a gunsight. A masculine form could be "der kemmer" or "der kemmerer," a marksman or target-or goal-oriented person.

Bill Kemmerer was goal-oriented, all right; otherwise, he might still be farming his ancestral acres, his world encompassed by the neighboring towns of Pen Argyl, Kunkletown, and Walnutport. Instead, he was determined to obtain a college education in preparation for a career in the professions.

In rural Pennsylvania in the years immediately preceding and following World War I, the professions were pretty well limited to medicine, law, engineering, and theology. Colleges or schools of education were beginning to arise, but they were to be centered for some time yet at Chicago and at Columbia. Most teachers sought two-year certificates and were prepared in normal schools rather than in a university setting.

For some reason, Dr. Kemmerer first chose civil engineering as his field. When we discussed this more than a half-century later, he was not certain of all the factors involved in his choice; but they seemed to include disinclination toward medicine, law or theology; the unique challenge that civil engineering might provide; and the fact that Lehigh College (now Lehigh University) was only 20 miles from home.

Lehigh, an independent institution dating to 1865, was located in the Allentown-Easton-Bethlehem industrial triangle, on the outskirts of Bethlehem. It had already established itself as one of the better engineering schools in the East, and was increasingly recognized as a center for quality training in the liberal arts and fine arts.

Luckily, by the time Bill Kemmerer was ready for college in 1920 he had some second thoughts about engineering. A serious, intent teen-ager, he engaged in a procedure that might be recommended for today's restless youth: introspection. Apparently, he came to two basic conclusions: (1) his primary objective in life was "doing something for others that will be appreciated"; and (2) this objective could be reached more quickly and effectively though a broader education that would equip him for working more directly with people. Soon after, Lehigh College offered him a scholarship in art, one of several awards made to promising graduates of high schools in the area.

Bill Kemmerer accepted the scholarship, but the overall financing of his college education remained a considerable problem. There were two choices open to him; he could work his way through, taking perhaps an additional year, or even two; or he could borrow the additional funds required, obtain his degree as soon as possible, and start repaying the loan once he had found employment. Typically, he selected the latter course. "I think," he said many years later, "that any young man who wants to succeed should have the courage of his convictions and the faith in his ability to borrow money to invest in his future."

Dr. Kemmerer received an excellent, far-ranging education in the liberal arts at Lehigh; he also took advantage of a strong faculty in mathematics and in what was then termed "commerce" to sharpen a natural aptitude for new procedures in machine accounting. He graduated in 1924 with high honors and a Phi Beta Kappa key, having formed a lasting friendship with another fine scholar and member of Phi Beta Kappa, Charles Francis Hiller. ("Charlie" Hiller will reappear in this chronicle shortly, since he was invited to the young University of Houston by Dr. Kemmerer in 1935, after a decade of managing a lumber and coal business in Michigan, studying and teaching at Harvard, and completing part of the work toward his Harvard doctorate while a Leverett B. Saltonstall Scholar at the University of Paris.)

For the next five years, Dr. Kemmerer taught in the public schools of nearby Nesquehoning and then at Williamsport, Pennsylvania before moving on to New Rochelle, the beautiful exurb of

New York City's northern limits. In Williamsport he met Helen Eckhenstein, a pretty and intelligent young lady, one of many children in a well-known Williamsport family, who had been educated at the local Dickinson Seminary for Young Ladies. Their mutual interests were rather unusual, but they augured well for what has been a fine marriage of almost 50 years' duration. Helen worked for a business machine agency (thus being conversant with one of Bill Kemmerer's underlying concerns), and ran into her future husband on a committee selling tickets for a Girls' Guild benefit, one of the principal projects for the Williamsport public school system.

Dr. Kemmerer was a good teacher, and he was moved into assignments requiring administrative ability as well, both at Williamsport and at New Rochelle. From the beginning of his career, however, he had been struck by the degree to which most educational administrators were committed to "strait-laced" curricula, policies, regulations, and interpretations. Excess devotion to this sort of red tape, he believed, hampered good teaching and creative education and would in time produce robots instead of individuals capable of sound yet innovative thinking. These concerns were heightened as he continued his graduate studies at Columbia University in the summers, concentrating on new methodology including the use of machine accounting and analysis in both secondary and tertiary (higher) education.

Then came one of those career-shaping encounters that most of us experience, even though we may not recognize more than a fraction of their total impact when they occur. As Bill Kemmerer related it a generation later: "I was at Columbia in the summer of 1929, my doctoral dissertation completed and accepted, my oral examination somehow passed. I was helping a friend with some statistical concepts[4] when my principal professor, Nickolaus L. Englehardt, called me into his office, 'Dr. Oberholtzer is here from Houston,' he said. 'He is looking for a director of curriculum. Would you be interested in the position?' "

"Well," Dr. Kemmerer recalled, "I thought possibly I could survive in Texas—a dumb Pennsylvania Dutch boy like myself—and besides, I did not care what part of the country I worked in; I figured I was a citizen of the United States.

"Dr. Engelhardt said that it would be an excellent system in which I could get excellent experience under an excellent administrator; that latter appealed to me frankly and seriously. One thing I needed was experience."

Dr. Oberholtzer left Columbia University and New York City without coming to any decision about Bill Kemmerer, impressed though he was with his qualifications and how they could fit into the expanding situation at the Houston Independent School District (and later at the University of Houston). Several interviews with the young teacher-administrator-student convinced the normally over-cautious superintendent of schools, nevertheless, that Dr. Kemmerer would be a hot item on the market, and that he must act with far more than his usual deliberate speed or run the clear risk of losing him.

Consequently, when his south-bound train reached Harrisburg, Pennsylvania that evening, Dr. Oberholtzer got off long enough to send a telegram to Dr. Kemmerer offering him the position of director of curriculum and research with HISD.

Dr. Kemmerer recalled the telegram, which he kept for many years, "The next morning I had a telegram from Harrisburg. It told me to get ready to come on to Houston. So I figured, well, he got on the train and got relaxed, thought the matter over, and picked the best man—me. I got ready and went on to Houston."

No undue modesty there, nor any unjustified braggadocio. But it was quite a move for a 26-year-old, brand-new Ph. D. with a young wife expecting their first child. Bill Kemmerer had a high and justified opinion of himself and believed that he could do a good job in Houston. Still, the Houston Ship Channel was pretty far south and west of the Delaware Water Gap, and he would have to fill a position for which he had little or no actual experience.

As expected, however, the new hand fitted well into Superintendent Oberholtzer's HISD team, and into developing plans for him. Dr. Oberholtzer told me once that "Kemmerer tended to be a little rambunctious, at least in the early stages." Dr. Kemmerer, ever frank and honest, confirmed this soon after he became acting president of the University of Houston in 1950. He recounted a time when Dr. Oberholtzer ". . . evidently felt that I was stepping a bit too lively, and he quietly called me . . . and gave me the nicest dressing down I ever received . . . I (was) fresh out of graduate school and was feeling my oats, unaware that I was . . . no longer in graduate school (but) in the hard, everyday world where I had to face facts . . . I appreciated deeply . . . the fact that he came into my office, closed the door, and privately told me what I had done wrong. I profited by it." And there were similar anecdotes.

In retrospect, the most unusual thing about Bill Kemmerer's career from 1929 to 1934 may be the fact that he was almost never at the Houston Junior College during his first five years in Houston. This seems inconsistent with his usual curiosity about anything even remotely within his field of view and his high energy level. Dr. Kemmerer indicated to me that he was simply too busy with the specific duties assigned him at the downtown HISD offices, at a time of ongoing expansion of the school system when the director of curriculum and research was producing data of fundamental importance.

This was a reason, and a salient one, for Bill Kemmerer to have little contact with HJC. He was needed downtown, in the front lines. Dr. Oberholtzer depended heavily upon sound and continuing research to keep Colonel Bates and the other key trustees of HISD sold on his policies. These policies usually stressed future growth patterns and sometimes received withering criticism during the Depression years of 1931-33, when taxpayers could see little merit in planning and providing for the 1940's and 1950's—much less for the decades beyond. The data resulting from Dr. Kemmerer's research into demographic patterns and curricular modifications often provided the margin of victory in close HISD votes, and he could not produce this ammunition while poking around HJC.

There were other reasons for Dr. Kemmerer's not being around HJC too often before 1934. These had to do with Superintendent Oberholtzer (who, it will be remembered, was seldom around San Jacinto High School himself when the HJC was in session): Dr. Oberholtzer was quite impressed with Dr. Kemmerer, but he was always loath to spread the authority around—at least until there had been a reasonably long testing period.[5] Naason K. Dupre was a prime example. He was running things quite well at HJC, as he had done since coming aboard at the very beginning in 1927 as assistant dean. He checked in regularly with Dr. Oberholtzer (or at least with Virginia Stone, the ever-present secretary and alter ego at Taylor School headquarters) without bothering anyone with details, was a good disciplinarian, and a close man with a budget. But when HJC was completing its five years of existence in 1934, almost two full years after F.M. Black (who carried the nominal title of dean) had died, it was still Assistant Dean Dupre. Why complicate things, and even incur the risk of some additional salary payments, by sending Bill Kemmerer out to HJC? His day would come a little later, as would a belated promotion for Naason K. Dupre, who was named dean of the new University of Houston at the same time that Dr. Kemmerer was appointed vice-president in June 1934.

Bill Kemmerer's appearance as the number two man at the University of Houston was inevitable in terms of Edison Ellsworth Oberholtzer's foresight and careful attention to timing. Comforted though he was by the younger educator's primary assignment to the complex and never-ending problems of HISD and the Board of Education, Dr. Oberholtzer knew by the time of the resolution of September 11, 1933[6], that Bill Kemmerer would have to be given a considerably wider scope of authority (galling though any ceding of authority might be), and be brought into king's row as preparations for the University of Houston accelerated.

Dr. Oberholtzer had to have someone capable of discussing in depth the concept of the new and expanded institution's role and scope, and how this might relate both to HJC and to current ideas in higher education. Dr. Kemmerer's quick and facile mind was full of ideas, including as noted earlier that of a General College. President Oberholtzer also saw in Dr. Kemmerer the ideal person to tackle, objectively and immediately, two pressing problems that would confront the University of Houston even before it began its first full semester of operations on September 17, 1934.

The next move was obvious. Dr. Oberholtzer went to Dr. Kemmerer in the fall of 1933 and told him that he proposed to name him vice-president of the University of Houston as soon as he was authorized to do so. He asked him to accelerate planning for the General College, to begin a detailed consideration of two key problems already clouding the future, and, of course, to continue full tilt in his current post and responsibilities.

The first problem facing President Oberholtzer and his new chief lieutenant *im pecto* was space. The University of Houston, as a four-year institution, would inevitably draw higher enrollments from HJC graduates continuing on for the baccalaureate degree, from others seeking either the baccalaureate or more specialized training, from "practical" and extension course enrollments, and from the normal, ongoing expansion of 4 p.m. to 10 p.m. classes at San Jacinto High School. But there was absolutely no more room at SJHS before 4 p.m.; a new or alternate location, possibly an entire new approach, would have to be found.

A second problem could be generally described as a lack of controls and reports, including projections as well as actual data. True, HJC had done surprisingly well financially; there was not even the hint of fiscal irregularities, but the days of part-time payments on tuition (the overwhelming source of HJC income[7]), of informal debits and credits on tally sheets, and of minimal budgetary and accounting procedures would have to come to an end.

There were particular reasons for shoring up procedures in the counting house. The books showed a cumulative surplus of $58,950.09[8] as HJC became the University of Houston, but as an analyst pointed out "... (where) physical equipment was used, either in whole or in part, with another institution; where teaching and administrative personnel had duties in the school system other than those connected with the (Junior) College; and where some persons served in double capacities as administrator and as instructor, accurate data concerning the distribution of ... costs and of operating expenses were unobtainable." The problem was further exacerbated, of course, because HJC was a non-paying tenant at San Jacinto High School, under the fiscal control of men who knew how to channel true costs elsewhere.

Dr. Oberholtzer was not losing any sleep over the question of true costs versus what the books indicated. The healthy HJC surplus at August 31, 1933 (now increased by another $2,951.60) had been a potent factor in selling Colonel Bates and the other HISD trustees on advancing HJC to four-year status. Earlier operating results had obviously helped to bring the Junior College through some difficult beginning years. It was all in a good cause, after all, and although he was a staunch Methodist[9], Jesuitical theories of how the end justifies the means seemed to impress Edison Ellsworth Oberholtzer.

But he could tell which way the wind was blowing. The trustees were asking more and more questions, as was H.L. Mills, about a more accurate determination of administrative salaries, pro rata sharing of maintenance and additional operating costs, space requirements, one- to five-year projections, and firmer controls in general. The time had come to put Bill Kemmerer's specialized knowledge of budgeting, accounting, and fiscal controls in higher education into use.

Even more pressing, however, was the problem of space. HJC counselors had asked students during fall 1933 registration about the possible effects on enrollment of advancing from junior college to four-year status, and the results indicated a possible 50 percent increase. The volume of mail and telephone inquiries (many called after the September 11, 1933, HISD resolution, thinking that the transition to the University of Houston was in immediate prospect) reinforced the upward projections: it appeared that fall 1934 enrollment would be approximately one-half again that of fall 1933—or somewhere between 900 and 950.

Edison Ellsworth Oberholtzer saw that the real solution to the fortunate but growing problem posed by an escalating demand for higher education in the Houston area was a separate campus and physical plant for the infant University of Houston. In the meantime, a temporary resolution must be found—specifically, a location for daytime classes, preferably one reasonably accessible and available for little or no rent.

It was not difficult to discover a location meeting these specifications. A downtown church was the obvious answer.

Dr. Oberholtzer had been fairly active in the First Methodist Church, and now, luckily for the University of Houston, he called upon John Thaddeus Scott, Sr., the leading Methodist layman of the area, and chairman of the board of the First National Bank, and one of the city's most respected business and civic leaders. He remembered that he had first met Mr. Scott at an interdenominational meeting organized by the banker, shortly before assuming the office of superintendent of schools. And he reasoned that Mr. Scott would have a considerable number of contacts and significant influence within various denominations.

Mr. Scott was sympathetic to the problem, and played a leading role in obtaining the use of the Second Baptist Church, through its pastor the Reverend Doctor F.B. Thorn, as the site for the General College and first daytime classes of the University of Houston. Second Baptist, at Milam and McGowen, was well located and the rent was nominal, only a small fee to help provide extra janitorial service.

The University of Houston had accomplished its first expansion; but of even more importance for the future, Dr. Oberholtzer had brought John T. Scott, Sr., a direct link to Hugh Roy Cullen and F.M. Law, into the picture.

The link to Mr. Scott, who was to some extent Mr. Cullen's personal banker, was to prove crucial in the next few years. What Dr. Oberholtzer did not realize for a time, however, was the advantage of the additional tie to Francis Marion Law.

F.M. Law had come from Beaumont to join the First National as a vice-president in 1915, the year after John T. Scott, Sr., had completed a steady progression of 21 years from bookkeeper to president. The two men formed a friendship and professional relationship that was to continue four decades, until Mr. Scott's death in 1955.

W.A. Kirkland, the grandson of the founder of the First National and a most distinguished banker and civic leader in his own right, tells in a history of the bank how Mr. Law acted quickly to establish himself at "Shepherd's Bank." He was barely settled behind his desk when the receptionist announced three oil men: R.L. Blaffer, William Stamps Farish, and Ed Prather. They wanted to borrow $50,000, a hefty sum in those days, and they needed it before the end of the business day to close a hot "lease deal" in East Texas.

Mr. Law looked the trio over. He had heard their names, but knew nothing in detail about them; further, it was something of an insult in those days to ask a man of substance for a personal financial statement. Matters were complicated by the fact that John T. Scott, Sr., and W.S. Cochran, the senior vice-president, were out of the city.

Mr. Law asked for an hour to consider the matter. Preliminary investigation and available bank records confirmed the stability and good reputation of the loan applicants, who certainly looked to be men of substance. He decided to contact E.A. Peden, a prominent director of the First National, who urged him to make the loan and agreed to accept joint responsibility for it. Mr. Law then called Robert Lee Blaffer, later a founder and long-time treasurer of Humble Oil & Refining Company, told him that the loan was approved, transferred the money to the appropriate correspondent bank in East Texas, and telephoned confirmation back to Mr. Blaffer—all within the hour.

This obviously impressed Messrs. Blaffer, Farish, and Prather and helped to establish F.M. Law in the higher circles of the business and banking community—all the more since the lease obtained with the $50,000 loan turned out to be fabulously profitable, and a mainstay of "The Humble" after its holders signed it over to the newly-organized company two years later.

When Dr. Oberholtzer came to John T. Scott, Sr. for help in finding a daytime home for the University of Houston in late 1933, F.M. Law had just been made president of the First National Bank and was serving as president of the American Bankers' Association. He was also active in alumni affairs at Texas A&M College and in the problems of higher education in general, a field of interest that would bring him to the post of chairman of the board of his alma mater during some rocky years at College Station.

It was natural, therefore, for John T. Scott, Sr., to discuss his growing involvement with the fledgling University of Houston with his colleague Mr. Law, and to counsel with him before and after the 1938 appointment, during which Mr. Scott and Dr. Oberholtzer obtained Mr. Cullen's agreement to serve as chairman of the University's first fund drive.

Mr. Law became a regent of the University of Houston in 1948, and served until 1961, when he accepted appointment as a member of the Board of Governors. Mr. Cullen, who was a great one for experience, turned to Mr. Law often when difficult decisions were before the Board of Regents, especially when the answer had to be "no." Francis Marion Law lived until June 2, 1970, when he went down, full of honors, in his ninety-third year.

It was fortunate that the Second Baptist Church was available for daytime classes of the University of Houston that fall of 1934. Early indications of a strong upward trend in enrollment were correct, but seriously understated. The actual overall figure was 909, or 46 percent over fall 1933.

Ironically, the University of Houston was to use the Second Baptist Church for only one year. The precedent had been set, however, and Dr. Oberholtzer was able to move the General College two miles south and west, to the South Main Baptist Church on Main between Richmond and Eagle in the fall of 1935. It was an excellent location, on the principal bus routes and next to the terminus and transfer point for one of the few remaining street-car lines, on Eagle at Fannin.

Many years later, I asked Dr. Kemmerer why the General College was moved from Second Baptist after a single year. "Simple," he replied; "they found too many decks of cards in the temporary student lounge. Those Second Baptist folks are fine people, but they hewed pretty close to the fundamentalist position."

South Main Baptist was increasingly needed for daytime classes, since both General College and overall University of Houston enrollment continued to grow substantially through 1938-1939, when the new campus along what was then Saint Bernard was ready.

The figures were 948 for the fall of 1935, 1,249 for 1936, 1,285 for 1937, and 1,563 for 1938. Enrollment had almost doubled since 1934.

What was the University of Houston like in those first five years of operation as a four-year institution? The overall impression, confirmed by the dwindling number of students, faculty members, and administrators still available for interviews and by press clippings, minutes, and other data, is of a bustling, crowded friendly institution with a dedicated and surprisingly competent faculty, hard-working and reasonably effective administrators, and earnest, ambitious students existing (as did the University itself) on marginal budgets.

The key figures in the administration were President Oberholtzer (most of the time he could dedicate to the University, apart from the complexities of his duties as superintendent of schools, was spent in conferences with Dr. Kemmerer and on the omnipresent problem of a new campus and physical plant); Vice-President Kemmerer (who concentrated on the General College but began the moment he was installed as vice-president of the University to have a principal role in the overall direction of the institution[10]); the reliable Naason K. Dupre, at long last with the title as well as the responsibility of being dean; and Mrs. Pearl Bender, now registrar.

The faculty had been strengthened by the addition of some especially skilled teachers who were to remain for long periods of time with the University. These included C.F. McElhinney, who had an appointment in education, but was primarily assistant business manager of HISD, under the redoubtable H.L. Mills;

E.W. Schuhmann, physics; Leon G. Halden, government; Charles F. Hiller, languages and fine arts; Louis Kestenberg, German; Warren A. Rees, mathematics; Robert W. Talley, history and art; Jules A. Vern, French; and Joseph S. Werlin, sociology. The total faculty for the 1934-1935 session numbered 39.

Another key appointment during this period was Mrs. Russell (Ruth S.) Wikoff, who was named librarian at HJC in the fall of 1933, in anticipation of a move to four-year status. Mrs. Wikoff, a professionally-trained librarian of marked ability and perseverance, remained with the University 40 years on active duty, retiring as a full professor and associate director of libraries, emerita.

The year that she came aboard, the library had a total of 8,627 books, documents, and periodicals—representing an almost geometric progression from the beginning total of 1,988 in 1927-1928 (which had to be quickly expanded to 3,442 to meet minimum standards). These totals, however, included both HJC library and "usable books of college grade" in the San Jacinto High School library.

Total expenditures for the HJC library had been appallingly low throughout the seven years of HJC's existence, beginning with the sum of $3,614 ($2,250 for books, $56 for magazines, $75 for supplies, $1,233 for salaries, and nothing for binding) in 1927, never reaching even that level again, and ending at the nadir of $2,042 in the depression year of 1933.

Mrs. Wikoff was able to turn the situation around beginning in 1934, although she had continued difficulty in selling Dr. Oberholtzer on the need to expand the library collections to include reference works and collateral materials. In her ladylike manner, Mrs. Wikoff could still criticize gently in an interview almost four decades later. "You have to remember," she told me, "that Dr. Oberholtzer was a very economical, careful person. We had limited sums with which to purchase books directly related to a course, but little or nothing for reference works."

Mrs. Wikoff's main weapons were: patience, perseverance, and the accrediting association, of which Dr. Oberholtzer stood in considerable awe. She made out the annual reports, as required, faithfully and true; then she took the criticism from the association, which I suspect she was sometimes able to have strengthened a bit, back to Dr. Oberholtzer. "The eternal problem," she remembers, "was lack of money. But we were able somehow to meet the standards." This was at least a minor miracle, considering total budgets available, and the crowded, minimal conditions within the library area itself, which was divided to the last square foot between book stacks and jammed-up study tables.

What satisfaction Mrs. Wikoff must have taken from the remarkable progress which the University libraries made after those first difficult years: the opening of the M.D. Anderson Memorial Library in 1950; the amazing growth under Director of Libraries Edward G. Holley, continued under Stephen Salmon; the major expansion of 1965-1967, which provided room for up to one million volumes; the dedication of the new John H. Freeman wing in 1977, with a ceremony the same day marking the acquisition of the one millionth volume barely 15 years after the collection reached 200,000; and the ongoing program of expansion in three additional phases that will provide space for 2,670,000 books by 1985.

As soon as the General College was successfully launched, along with substantial curricular additions and modifications for the partly-reorganized College of Arts and Sciences at San Jacinto High School and the College of Community Service, Dr. Kemmerer turned his attention to the second of President Oberholtzer's pressing problems, which he described as "establish(ing) a complete system of accounts receivable, budgets, and regular monthly and annual financial reports."

Charlie Hiller, man of all parts, had become quite familiar with the lamentable state of fiscal control soon after his arrival in 1935. He took enough time from teaching English and French and his extra assignment as acting bursar to lend some valuable assistance to his old Lehigh classmate in straightening things out.

The system that Vice-President Kemmerer finally devised was based on National Cash Register machine accounting. It must have been effective, at least for the period from 1934-1944, since the University operated without deficits, according to regular reports submitted by Dr. Kemmerer, and at an administrative cost of three percent of total income.

Dr. Hiller claims that the old tally sheets (and perhaps some of those receipts he gave students for two-dollar payments on account) are still somewhere on the third floor of the Ezekiel W. Cullen Building or in the Art Annex. He thinks that the base he built out in his garage for one of the smaller but important file sections is still around the University (perhaps in the new multimillion-dollar computing center across Elgin?).

The obvious need for a separate campus and physical plant, however, began to overshadow most other problems in 1935, or even earlier. Enrollment was escalating; there were not nearly enough classrooms, much less related facilities such as library space, meeting rooms, auditoria, laboratories or adequate cafeteria space; and the entire situation was deteriorating in terms of any real progress toward the University of Houston that President Oberholtzer, and now Vice-President Kemmerer, knew that the city and area must have.

Dr. Oberholtzer decided, apparently sometime in the fall of 1935, that he would have to take personal direction of a planned campaign for a new campus. Morale was usually quite high among the faculty, but a necessary salary cut of 10 percent had created some problems that a strong and heartening announcement could counteract; the *Cougar,* now a weekly, was editorializing regularly on the need to move on from San Jacinto High School.

There are several ways to proceed: externally, through the general public, news media and various private organizations and public agencies; internally, through the Board of Education, faculty members, students, their parents, the *Cougar;* or by some combination of external and internal targets.

After examining all his options, President Oberholtzer leaned toward an internal campaign emphasizing the Board of Education. He decided to go back to Colonel Bates for counsel and guidance. The colonel had completed his term on the Board of Education, but he maintained close relationships with the trustees, especially with his successor as president, E.D. Shepherd. A meeting with Mr. Shepherd revealed that the Board of Education was not at all opposed to a new home for the University of Houston, particularly if this could be a beginning step toward getting such an overgrown foundling off the HISD doorstep.

This was valuable information that President Oberholtzer might have found it difficult, or even embarrassing, to obtain for himself. With it in hand, he could proceed.

The time was ripe, in more ways than one, for a big step forward. A budget crunch announced in the summer of 1935, with concomitant salary cuts of 10 percent,[11] seemed to be safely past.

Dr. Oberholtzer had been present, as usual, for the 4 to 9 p.m. registration periods in the SJHS library, and the results had been encouraging enough to add six faculty members to make a total of 45. Expansion to a total of 151 courses ("in all the regular departments of a four-year, accredited senior college, plus a variety of practical and technical courses") had brought a heartening total of 948 students. The brochures distributed to prospective students were careful to state "accredited" rather than "fully-accredited," for the new University was of course not in any way prepared to apply for full recognition by the regional accrediting agency. However, a "full Class A rating" had been obtained from both the State Department of Education and the Texas Association of Colleges.

Two of Dr. Kemmerer's projects were adding substantially to the growing aura of success in the second year of the University's history as a four-year institution. The General College (Dr. Oberholtzer had experienced a little queasy feeling every time that his colleague continued to call it the "Experimental College" before the Board of Education, which was not exactly an experimental-minded body) was already the fastest-growing component of the University. And Dr. Kemmerer's innovative "special teacher's diploma" was stimulating wide interest with many inquiries. The diploma would be awarded those satisfactorily completing two years of general preparation plus two years of specialized courses and a fifth-year internship that included apprentice teaching within the HISD system under close supervision, with related courses in theory and methodology at the University.

Meanwhile, there were constant reminders of the need for more University of Houston space at SJHS, including a showdown over the University library. There was simply no more room in which to shelve the books that the energetic Mrs. Wikoff and her augmented corps of one full-time plus eight student assistants were bringing in. Their objective was to double the collection as soon as possible, to about 15,000 volumes, in order to meet the needs created by a major expansion in the number of courses and in student enrollment.

Dr. Oberholtzer was sympathetic. He recognized the central importance of the library, and was quite sensitive to criticism by either the professional library associations or the State Department of Education and Texas Association of Colleges. There were naturally negative comments regarding space from these quarters, plus a crescendo of complaints from the student body.

The solution was hardly pleasing to the San Jacinto High School staff, but then Edison Ellsworth Oberholtzer was superintendent of schools. He simply moved the University of Houston library holdings into the SJHS music room after showing Mr. Shepherd, the new HISD Board of Education president, the situation. It is not clear how explicit Dr. Oberholtzer was about the remaining part of the solution, but a new SJHS music room had to be provided.

Mr. Shepherd was becoming more and more interested in the University, and was now a frequent visitor to evening classes at SJHS. This had some fortunate and far-reaching effects; it gave President Oberholtzer and Dr. Kemmerer a new ally, and one increasingly aware of the need to find a new University campus. It also helped with small problems, such as how to justify the new SJHS music room.

A completely new music room was built at SJHS, without any particular attention as to how the need for it arose. This project was apparently just rolled up into a far-ranging $3,821,000 building program for the Houston public school system that was giving employment to almost 1,600 men in the winter and spring of 1936.

President Oberholtzer now turned to Mr. Shepherd and the narrow majority he enjoyed on the Board of Education[12] for much more basic assistance—permission to apply formally, in October of 1935, for a federal loan with which to acquire a "proposed new University of Houston building and campus." The permission was granted, even though Dr.Oberholtzer was well enough acquainted with Washington red tape, and with "Terrible Harold" Ickes' policies at the Public Works Administration to know that the application had little chance of being approved, and no chance whatsoever of being approved quickly. But sensing more the need for a valid application with which to generate continuing publicity and to confirm the official involvement of the Board of Education, President Oberholtzer did not let the odds, or the realities of the situation, bother him too much.

Dr. Oberholtzer told the news media that "(although) plans . . . are still indefinite, . . . I hope that we may be able to announce the exact status of the government loan and the possibility of securing a campus and building for the University within the next week or 10 days." It would be more than 18 months (May 5, 1937) before a complicated partial grant of $86,000 from the Public Works Administration to cover Works Progress Administration labor on a new campus was available, but Edison Ellsworth Oberholtzer, the eternal optimist, was off and running.

Next, with Colonel Bates having paved the way a bit more, President Shepherd was recruited to head up a reconnoitering expedition. The objective was to find 100 to 150 acres of well-located land for a new campus.

A likely target for such expeditions in the mid-1930's, even as today, was Memorial Park, the priceless 1503-acre green belt on the site of old Camp Logan. Provided by members of the Hogg family (whose attorneys, it is increasingly apparent, knew how to draw up an unassailable deed of gift), the beautiful wooded area was partly under the jurisdiction of the Park Board, whose chairman R.W. Franklin was a good friend of E.D. Shepherd.

When contacted, Chairman Franklin felt that 150 acres might be carved out of Memorial Park for such an exemplary purpose as a new home for the University of Houston, especially if some other needed civic projects could be included in the deal. A.C. (Tex) Bayless and Gaylord Johnson,[13] his fellow members on the Park Board, agreed.

Little did Mr. Franklin and his friend E.D. Shepherd know that they were stoking the furnace for the University of Houston's first public controversy, a brouhaha that would involve Mayor Oscar Holcombe, Miss Ima Hogg and her brother, Mike Hogg, civic clubs and organizations without end, early environmentalists, the University student body, and anyone who had a three-cent stamp with which to command the momentary attention of the *Post*, *Chronicle* or *Press*.

Still, the war of words attracted a great deal of attention, and in the end accomplished Dr. Oberholtzer's goal of a new campus.

The Memorial Park proposition looked fairly simple on the surface. Chairman Franklin wrote President Shepherd on March 9, 1936, indicating a willingness to support the donation of a 150-

acre site in the Park as the location for a new University of Houston campus under certain mutually agreeable conditions. The letter suggested a meeting between representatives of the Board of Education, City Council, and the Park Board.

Dr. Oberholtzer asked the next day for a Board of Education committee authorized to confer with councilmen and members of the Park Board, and was placed on such a group headed by President Shepherd. The other members were Mrs. B.F. Coop, A.C. Finn, and W.C. Ragan. The committee reported back on March 18 that it found "certain difficulties" with the City Council position, and Melvin E. Kurth, who had succeeded Palmer Hutcheson as attorney for the Board of Education, was instructed to set down the exact position of the school district. This was summarized, agreed to by the trustees and formally transmitted to City Council within days.

The HISD proposition was that the University would begin work within six months on a $100,000 building, would construct a 12,000-seat stadium as part of a WPA-financed recreation center (or would spend another $50,000 on building(s) if the stadium was not completed by 1939); would never mortgage the donated land in order to obtain a government grant, and would allow the 150 acres to revert to City of Houston ownership if it ever ceased to be used for educational purposes.

Against these substantial guarantees, the Board of Education asked that the City of Houston agree not to develop the contributed tract for oil, even though it would retain the mineral rights. It seemed a reasonable demand, on balance; but the deal was to fall through over the stipulation forbidding exploration and drilling within the 150 acres.

Mayor Holcombe and City Council were greatly influenced by adverse taxpayer reaction to a gift of public property, by the fact that Memorial Park had been recently described as a "hot" area for prospecting for oil, and by opposition from members and representatives of the Hogg family.

Typical of the flak from the public was a statement by Frank W. Meyers, a prominent East End resident and vice-president of the Taxpayers' Association. He threatened a law suit, and rallied his organization with a cry to "keep Memorial Park as a park, not as the donated location for a profit-making university." Mr.

Meyers reminded as many of the public as he could reach through frequent statements to the newspapers that "Oberholtzer and his crowd tried to put Stonewall Jackson Junior High School in Eastwood Park in 1927, but we backed 'em down and we can do it again."

Mr. Meyers thundered on. The Board of Education, he remembered, "bought the old West End park for $100,000, and did little or nothing with it. Then they bought land next to Taylor School (on Louisiana at Bell) for $226,000, and all they did was put a few tennis courts on it. Just one blunder after another."

Dr. Oberholtzer attempted two final compromises in direct contacts with Mayor Holcombe over Memorial Park: the Board of Education would throw in $135,000 for landscaping, and would consider swapping some of the land contiguous to Taylor School (far more valuable than the fulminating Mr. Meyers realized) as right-of-way to open up Smith Street to the south. President Shepherd was actually opposed to any land swaps, but gave approval for a little probing of the Old Gray Fox, who was a canny man on real estate values.

After a continuing barrage of controversial stories and editorials in the downtown press, and a great deal of interest on the University of Houston campus, the newspapers of April 7, 1936, announced "final rejection" of the Memorial Park proposal, primarily, it was stated, because of Board of Education insistence that the 150 acres in contention never be drilled for oil. The news media, which usually sided with the politicos, proclaimed this was unacceptable to Mayor Holcombe and City Council. As we have seen, Mr. Holcombe and the councilmen had other reasons for their opposition, and if anyone were to be accused of intransigence, they, not the members of the Board of Education, were the likelier candidates.

In retrospect, all this was a blessing in disguise when you consider the obvious difficulties of obtaining the 384 acres of today's Central Campus of the University of Houston in Memorial Park. President Oberholtzer did not ever mention the matter to me in our several conversations in 1950 and 1951 (although he urged even then the acquisition of additional land contiguous to what is now the Central Campus). Dr. Kemmerer and virtually all of the early-day administrators I asked about Memorial Park are agreed that the site in question would never have satisfied the longer-range, or even the more immediate, needs of the University. There are still those, however, who maintain that even a circumscribed location in a beautiful setting on the West Side, now contiguous to a system of major freeways, would have had advantages offsetting its small size. Dr. Oberholtzer had lost an engagement, not a campaign, or even a decisive battle. As he regrouped, he quickly perceived substantial gains stemming from the Memorial Park controversy, even though it had stirred up animosities and had caused both the University and the Board of Education some difficulties and temporary embarrassment.

The issue in the first place seemed to unite and inspire the student body, characterized then, as now, by a lack of cohesiveness and minimal interest in most extracurricular matters. As its members gathered in the SJHS cafeteria; in B.J. Thigpen's Almeda Pharmacy; at King's, the "eatery" on the corner of Main and Eagle; or at the nearby Pig'n Whistle; the "Greasy Spoon" (Varsity Cafe); or a cluster of popular little shops in the 1400 block of Holman, the "new campus" was a constant subject of discussion. Several potentially damaging "marches on City Hall" were proposed, and narrowly averted by Dean Dupre, who made it clear that leaders of, and participants in, such operations would be looked upon with marked disfavor upon returning to campus.[14] It was considered inadvisable to be on Dean Dupre's "list," or to be summoned to his office in the little temporary headquarters for University administrators on the east side of San Jacinto High School.

Another major advantage involved in the Memorial Park controversy was the matter of alternate locations for a new campus. Each one announced or even hinted at in the press tended naturally to emphasize and to draw attention to the worsening situation at SJHS.

The Houston Gun Club, for instance, was suggested as the site for the new high school stadium, with additional adjoining acreage to be added as the University of Houston campus. It was an interesting offer, but the site (owned by The Rice Institute) was too far out South Main to be acceptable, even if details could have been negotiated.

The Universal Land Company offered 100 acres south of Foster Place, and Dr. Oberholtzer had what he described as "several other nibbles," usually of small or otherwise unsuitable tracts.

Then, the publicity surrounding Memorial Park and the original announcement concerning an application for federal aid paid off. Julius Settegast of the pioneer land-owning family, representing the J.J. Settegast heirs, told his lawyer John H. Freeman that he might be interested in helping the Board of Education find a new home for the University. The heirs had about 75 acres south and east of old Buff Stadium, in a swampy tract of mixed oaks, pines, and other native trees and shrubs along an extension of St. Bernard.

Lawyer Freeman told his partner Colonel Bates (who had helped to stimulate Mr. Freeman's interest in the first place) that four or five Settegast heirs were involved, but that it might be possible to work out a donation of the land. The good news was relayed immediately to E.D. Shepherd and on to Dr. Oberholtzer and Dr. Kemmerer, who realized that the tract involved was too small.

Then someone remembered that Captain Ben Taub, whose family had amassed large land holdings on the then outskirts of Houston,[15] (in contrast to their friend and patron, Jesse H. Jones, who wanted his real estate downtown) owned 35 acres next to the Settegast land.

Within a surprisingly short time, the Settegast heirs and Ben Taub had agreed to donate separate but adjoining tracts to the University. I sometimes played gin rummy with Mr. Taub, an exceedingly modest and marvelous man who lived near the University of Houston, at the Houston Country Club. This was before his long illness beginning in the mid-1960's (from which he somehow recovered enough to report in at his long-time office—J.N. Taub & Sons, Cigars, 909 Franklin—with considerable regularity in the early 90's). He told me once that the 35 acres he gave was "little enough, considering that the University of Houston educated two of my nephews, and how much it came to mean to Colonel Bates, Lamar Fleming, and Mr. Cullen."

Captain Ben had a deed of gift ready in May 1936, but several months were to elapse while the two tracts were surveyed and Attorney Kurth prepared deeds for approval and for final execution by the donors. On October 12, the deeds were ready, with several modifications.

First of all, the two pieces of property were thought for a time to include only a total of 105 acres (70 acres from the Settegasts and 35 acres from Mr. Taub). A new survey correcting an error in the alignment of St. Bernard, however, raised the combined acreage to 108.875 acres, and the Board of Education purchased another 1.125 acres for $1,800 to "square up the tract." Further, provisions were added stipulating that the University must begin building on the new campus by January 1, 1938; that the property would revert to the City of Houston as a park if used for other than educational purposes; and that the deeds could not be recorded until construction had actually begun. The Settegast deed was then delivered to President Shepherd by Julius Settegast on October 19, 1936, at the regular meeting of the Board of Education; and Captain Ben, with typical reserve, sent his deed over by messenger later in the week.

The January 1, 1938, reversion deadline could have been troublesome to many persons. It was a stimulus and welcome call to action for Dr. Oberholtzer, who sprang to arms on old and new fronts.

One of the first things he did was to ask C.F. McElhinney to "go see what we have out there." His first inspection trip, Mr. Mac recalled, "was none too encouraging." "First of all," he remembered, "there was no direct access to the new campus. From my residence, at 2502 Wentworth (near the intersection of Live Oak, in Riverside), the only way to get there was via a gravel road running east and west along Wheeler, to the old South Side sewage disposal plant.

"I used to go over there the first thing in the morning in my hunting clothes and boots, climb over the barbed-wire fence on the corner of Wheeler and St. Bernard, and take off into a mixture of low-lying, swampy areas of blue gumbo mud; and higher, sandy ground with pretty stands of pine, a variety of oaks, and native shrubs. We had a good bit of trouble surveying the land that summer of 1936, what with the heat, heavy afternoon showers, and mosquitoes everywhere. Some snakes, too."

Luckily, the sewage disposal plant would soon be gone. But the 110 acres would have to be drained in some areas, and filled and landscaped as road and utilities were extended into it. It would be years before the principal connecting streets were all in place: the extension of Wheeler east, and of St. Bernard (Cullen Boulevard) to the south; the opening of other key thoroughfares such as Calhoun, Elgin, Holman, and North MacGregor Drive—much less improving all these access routes to anything approaching current standards. The University of Houston had the nucleus of a good campus of its own, but many years and the expenditure of tens of millions of dollars would be required for its proper development.

President Oberholtzer, ever the realist, decided that his next move was clearly indicated. He had to make certain that a building was under construction on the Settegast-Taub acreage, as agreed, by January 1, 1938. To increase the odds on success, he reasoned, he would move on several alternate, and mutually reinforcing, fronts at once.

He therefore launched campaigns aimed at (1) the power structure of Houston; (2) the possibility of internal financing, perhaps in combination with external grants or loans; (3) expanded publicity; and (4) low-level, but persistent, lobbying in Washington, D.C.

Edison Ellsworth Oberholtzer was, among other things, a percentage player. Just as Willie Sutton,[16] he went where success was most likely. In the early fall of 1936, as he probed into the power structure of a city recovering rapidly from the disastrous flood of December 1935,[17] Dr. Oberholtzer found more and more evidence that he should return to John T. Scott, Sr., who had been so helpful in finding a temporary home for the General College in the Second Baptist Church.

As he went back to Mr. Scott, Dr. Oberholtzer was not perceiving him as the nationally-known Methodist lay leader he had become, but as John Thaddeus Scott, chairman of the board of the First National Bank and an obvious and appropriate channel to the business and civic suzerainty.

John Thad Scott, Jr., a noted labor attorney, remembered many years later something of the crucial relationship that was now established between his father and Dr. Oberholtzer. "I had also met Dr. Oberholtzer through the church (Mr. Scott, Jr., was a steward of the First Methodist Church from 1920 until his death in 1973), and recall that my father liked him at once. He was so earnest, and so convinced of the good that the University of Houston could do."

The younger Scott was off a few years in remembering the interdenominational meeting at which Dr. Oberholtzer had met his father (it was in May, 1924, a month before Dr. Oberholtzer took office as superintendent of schools, not after the Houston Junior

College was already underway). But Mr. Scott, Jr., had in mind many of the details of the October 1936 dinner that John Thaddeus Scott helped President Oberholtzer plan and carry out, and he understood the key role that his father played in this significant yet all-but-forgotten event.

The dinner was an Oberholtzer idea, and a sound one. He realized how badly he needed to explain his concept of the new campus for the expanding University of Houston, and the widening opportunities and benefits it entailed, to the community leadership. But he was aware that apart from the Board of Education, which had brought him into close and valuable contact with Colonel Bates, E.D. Shepherd, R.H. Fonville, and at least one old-line Brahmin (W.A. Kirkland); and his valuable Methodist friendships; he and the University had quite limited access to the fountainheads of economic and social power.[18]

The dinner was staged at the Houston Club, then, as now, a favorite stomping ground for the captains of the town. The invitation list was apparently drawn up with close cooperation from John Thaddeus Scott, who was a prominent member of the distinguished group at the speaker's table. Joining him at the dais were such luminaries as E.D. Shepherd; Bishop A. Frank Smith of the Methodist Church; M.E. (Mefo) Foster, the noted editor; W.L. (Will) Clayton; Julius Settegast; J.W. Neal, co-owner of the Maxwell House (Neal-Cheek) Coffee Company, who was later to gain control of the Second National Bank[19] after selling Maxwell House to General Foods; Sam Bertron, president of the Houston Lighting and Power Company; Colonel Bates; George A. Hill, one of the founders of Houston Natural Gas and a noted authority on Texas history who was instrumental in building the San Jacinto Republic (but in style) and in establishing the San Jacinto Museum of History; Major E.A. Craft, area executive of the Southern Pacific Lines; and Colonel J.W. Evans.

Colonel Evans, considered by many to be the father of the Port of Houston, and a founder of the American General insurance conglomerate, was toastmaster. In the tradition of the Old South, and of prayer meetings, he had most of those at the head table give testimony in support of the new University of Houston. Mr. Shepherd, for example: "The Board of Education is solidly behind you." Similar sentiments were widely expressed in what was really a remarkable endorsement of the University, a full 18 months before the far more celebrated banquet of May 2, 1938—when a $1,000,000 campaign would be launched.

Dr. Oberholtzer told the Houston Club gathering what he thought they would want to hear. The idea of fund-raising, or of major philanthropic contributions, was still in the future. "The University of Houston," he said, "is self-sustaining." He went back to the very beginning to quote from the March 7, 1927, HISD resolution establishing the Houston Junior College those fundamental words: "Whereas, said Board also believes that a Junior College can be operated on a self-sustaining basis on a comparatively low tuition cost . . . ."

Some of this language, and philosophy, would come back to haunt him and those who followed him at the presidential helm; but Dr. Oberholtzer expanded the theme of down-to-earth education to provide maximum efficiency on a non-deficit basis. "What we need," he explained in his not unpleasant Indiana twang, speaking sometimes with more fervor than precision of syntax, "is proper housing and equipment, especially that required to teach vocational courses."[20]

Proper housing, of course, would include that all-important first building. Dr. Oberholtzer had some old sketches dating back to 1933, hastily-devised estimates and elevations by the architect Lamar Q. Cato and some general idea of overall space requirements; but nothing even approaching the detail required for accurate costing. He told his Houston Club audience that the building he must have underway in little more than a year would cost "around $400,000, turnkey and equipped." Against this, he had $85,000 in surpluses, saved somehow since 1927 in a miracle of close budgeting and perseverance, coupled with what H.L. Mills termed a "cheap, not an economical" operation; hope of a $300,000 combined grant and loan from the federal government; and the further hope of a $50,000 loan from local banks.

Dr. Kemmerer spoke of Houston University (the term was used interchangably with University of Houston in the earlier years) as a "practical school of continued education." "It seeks," he stated, "to break down traditional educational requirements for college entrance, in order that it may better provide for the (broad) educational needs of the community."

President Oberholtzer and Vice-President Kemmerer were overemphasizing the fourth and fifth responsibilities of the University of Houston, as set forth in the charter of June 4, 1934:

"To assist modern industry in obtaining more intelligent leaders and workers" and "To encourage the constructive use of leisure time." There was apparently little or no mention in their remarks of the General College and its "return to first principles," of preprofessional courses, or of the many broader aspects of the University. The result, whether intentional or not, was to demean conventional curricula along with established entrance requirements, and probably to identify the University of Houston to a considerable extent as an experimental institution with questionable standards and a curriculum heavily oriented toward vocational training.

The Houston Club dinner was a roaring success in the quality of the company, in terms of the testimonials delivered by outstanding citizens, and as a means of exposing the University and its two top administrators to the king's row of the town.

There is clear evidence, however, that this event had damaging effects—some temporary, some lasting. In the first category, the dinner somehow presented the young institution as more of a quasi-commercial venture with *pro bono publico* overtones than as an essentially eleemosynary proposition, always requiring (and deserving) community support as much because of its worthy, sometimes intangible, objectives as for its vital and more pragmatic services. As a result, the guests passed a resolution urging Franklin Delano Roosevelt, Jesse H. Jones (as head of the Reconstruction Finance Corporation), Harold Ickes, Harry Hopkins, and any other gods in the New Deal pantheon to approve the requested grant to the University of Houston forthwith. John T. Scott, Sr., and others indicated that a $100,000, not a $50,000, local loan might be available if an appropriate balance sheet could be prepared.

The temporary stress on quasi-commercial aspects, on grants and loans, would soon disappear as philanthropy and fund-raising came to the forefront; but the second effect of the Houston Club dinner was to take stubborn root. It would be a generation before the image of overemphasis on vocational and noncredit education, of dedication to experimental curricula, and of challenges to established standards for admission, however undeserved, could be fully eradicated.

The link-up to the power structure had begun, even if on a temporary course that would have to be corrected almost 180 degrees. The possibility of a combination of internal financing, external grants, and bank loans was being explored actively with Dr. Kemmerer preparing an updated financial statement for the consideration of the loan committee at the First National Bank. Now President Oberholtzer turned to another component of his campaign to ensure that construction of the first building on the new campus would begin by the agreed deadline. He approved a plan for substantially expanding publicity regarding the University of Houston. He had the assistance of Ardis Phillips of the Department of English, who had replaced the beloved Fred R. Birney as advisor to the *Cougar* after Mr. Birney died suddenly of pneumonia on April 25, 1936; but President Oberholtzer handled a good bit of the publicity, or at least the engendering of it, himself. He did this by becoming something of a one-man speakers' bureau, by encouraging Vice-President Kemmerer and the more articulate membrs of the faculty to seek speaking engagements, by fostering active, news-making campus organizations, and by placing far more emphasis on baccalaureate and commencement ceremonies.

The newspapers, far more interested in the late 1930's in what would often be disregarded today,[21] and without the never-ending flow of copy available in our age of super-communication, responded.

There was also a considerable amount of radio coverage, as KXYZ and KTRH (which became the *Chronicle* station in 1937, although the Jones Interests had also owned KXYZ since 1932) began to compete more and more actively with the pioneer KPRC. Radio became a considerably more important medium in 1936, when KPRC and KTRH joined forces to share a 375-foot transmitter at Deepwater. This allowed both stations to increase their power to 5,000 watts and greatly encouraged the purchase of radio "sets," even though the omnipresent transistor receivers were still a generation away.

After a spate of stories concerning the controversy over the possible acquisition of 150 acres in Memorial Park, and the actual gift of 110 acres from the Settegast Estate and Ben Taub, the publicity began to roll again.

President Oberholtzer told the public in a series of statements and in speeches before various civic groups that:

> . . . my dream is the establishment of the University of Houston as an institution where the men and women of Houston, and high school

graduates, can obtain a higher education while living at home, and at small cost. . . . We may have to close the day college unless the Public Works Administration (PWA) grant comes through . . . . We may have to close the night school while the new west wing is being built at San Jacinto High School. We don't even have room for the overcrowded "shacks," which are partly on the construction sight. (Actually, Dr. Oberholtzer simply moved the five "shacks," utilized partly as offices, partly as classrooms, to the front of SJHS while expansion was underway in 1936-1937.) We could make a nice start even with $200,000 out at the new campus, if we had to cut it to that, by building an economical but sound structure, probably of reinforced concrete. We will just omit some of the purely decorative effects.

Leon G. Halden, a brilliant lecturer and writer in government and foreign affairs, was the source of excellent publicity in those earlier days. An expert on the Far East, Dr. Halden spoke to dozens of luncheon clubs and women's organizations on the danger posed by rising Japanese militarism. He published three books in 1936-1937: *Japan, Colossus of the Far East; Current Problems in Government;* and *Diplomacy of the Ethiopian Crisis*, the latter sponsored by the Rockefeller Foundation. As a result, Dr. Halden was given a Carnegie Foundation fellowship, the first such major academic award to a University of Houston faculty member. The Houston *Post* pointed out editorially that " . . . the University of Houston was signally honored when Dr. Leon G. Halden received a Carnegie Foundation fellowship . . . Rice Institute has attracted to the city outstanding scholars with worldwide reputation . . . Now the University of Houston is providing new opportunities for study and research which are attracting other brilliant educators."

Dr. Halden, a noted conservative, further distinguished himself by lecturing before the Atlanta Public Forum on "The New Pan-Americanism" in a series sponsored by the United States Department of Education and carried by the National Broadcasting Company. Some of his more liberal colleagues pointed out to the foreign affairs expert that the broadcast went out over the NBC "Red" rather than the NBC "Blue" network. (The terms "red" and "blue" denoted regional components of the network as well as programming differences.)

Others on the early publicity campaigns included Joseph S. Werlin, a sociologist trained at Rice Institute and the University of Chicago, and Robert W. Talley, architect and art historian who was also a product of Rice. Dr. Werlin, a brilliant teacher, was a prolific lecturer before community groups, and he also had a nose for news abetted by his wife, Rosella Horowitz Werlin. Mrs. Werlin, a graduate of the Class of 1936, was a skilled writer who produced for the March 28, 1937 Houston *Post* the first definitive article on some of the background on the new University, and on plans for the new campus. She termed the institution the "Cinderella school."

The Werlins uncovered together, in one of Dr. Werlin's classes, a Mrs. Pearl Strange Weimer, granddaughter of one of the early governors of Alabama, who had taught Dr. Werlin and two of his brothers in a one-room classroom in Pearland in 1912. Mrs. Weimer, pursuing a degree in social science to enhance her abilities as an HISD teacher, was good copy. As were the long accounts of a European tour for students which Dr. Werlin mailed back for publication. Mr. Talley, who held the Mary Alice Elliott Traveling Scholarship in Architecture at Rice Institute in 1936, transmitted enormously detailed comments on the architecture of western Europe back to the Houston *Post*, which published them verbatim.

Society page copy was relatively easy to obtain, and even Sunday afternoon teas for the Faculty Wives Association were newsworthy events in those days. One or two Houston debutantes had enrolled at the University of Houston, and some of their friends transferred from the University of Texas to join them. The least happening involving this group was faithfully reported. The annual reception for high school seniors, combined with a traditional beauty pageant, continued to attract capacity audiences and heavy publicity, as President Oberholtzer and Dr. Kemmerer were pressed into service to crown the Royal Court.

Some of the publicity was not always just what Dr. Oberholtzer might have wanted, but it all mentioned the University of Houston. Mrs. Sadie Streusand, for example, fell through a hole in the floor of the SJHS auditorium dressing room during a Red Masque Players production of "Granny." She was taken to Methodist Hospital in a Perry-Foley ambulance for X-rays, but was apparently never heard of again in the world of footlights and fantasy. Another newspaper story of questionable impact involved Jimmy Brinkley, former president of the University of Houston student body. Mr. Brinkley, a perennial Big Man on Campus during the early days at SJHS, went on to the University of Texas, where he headed the Student Council and was a member of the Athletic Council. BMOC Brinkley, in one of those headlined incidents that seems so all-important at the moment, and so trivial in retrospect, reportedly "leaked" a story that Jack Chevigny, the head football coach at the University of Texas so beloved by team and student body, was to be fired after a longish string of losses. The "leak" went down very badly indeed with the football team, which empowered one Nicholas (Nick) Frankovic, a mainstay of the, 'Horn line and a tough opponent indeed, to remonstrate with Mr. Brinkley. This interview ended in a fist fight, and BMOC Brinkley then tangled, at least verbally, with Clint Small, later a state senator and (subsequently) a noted lobbyist. He lost both matches.

The commencement programs were more reliable sources of positive notice, and after some deliberate changes in emphasis, President Oberholtzer began utilizing them—not only for publicity, but as a further means of establishing bridgeheads into the power structure of the community and area.

The First Annual Commencement Program, as it was proudly titled, was in an earlier pattern. Held at the Miller Memorial Theater on May 30, 1935, it featured a colleague in higher education who was virtually unknown in the Houston area except for occasional forays here to speak to local graduates of Texas Christian University. Dean Colby Hall of the Forth Worth institution delivered an appropriate address to the 80 graduates, but provided little or no access to community support. The invocation and benediction at this historic convocation were given by Reverend Charles B. Mahle, pastor of the South End Christian Church.

Victor Alessandro, Sr., whose son and namesake was to have a long and illustrious career as conductor of the San Antonio Symphony, directed the First Band of the Houston Independent School District in the grand march from *Aida;* the University Glee Club sang "Softly Call The Birds," by Franz Liszt; and Maestro Alessandro closed with a favorite that had the columns in old Miller Memorial Theater[22] shaking, John Philip Sousa's "Stars and Stripes Forever."

The second commencement ceremony, on June 2, 1936, also hewed to the academic line in the choice of a speaker. President A.W. Birdwell of Stephen F. Austin College in Nacogdoches, a close friend of Colonel Bates, delivered the address to what would be the smallest class of graduating seniors in the history of the University of Houston. This was a group of 62 hardy souls who had weathered the city's relatively minor depression without withdrawing from classes for more than a semester or two, but had found that it required five or six, and in a few instances, seven or eight years to complete the baccalaureate degree.

By the University's third commencement convocation, on June 1, 1937, President Oberholtzer had gained a considerably deeper insight into the community, to some extent through the Houston Club dinner of the previous October. He decided upon a new pattern; for the time being at least, he would seek commencement speakers from the area power structure, with special invitations to dozens of their friends, a reception after the ceremony and a step-up in pomp and circumstance throughout.

Dr. Oberholtzer's first choice of a speaker under the new pattern was a natural one—Colonel J.W. Evans, toastmaster for the Houston Club dinner and a fixture in the higher constellations of the conservative business world. However, some portions of the Evans text almost boomeranged.

Joseph W. Evans delivered a thoughtful and provocative message to the 152 graduates of the Class of 1937, which surprisingly struck a theme of the late 1960s and early 1970s rather than the prevailing tone of Houston in 1937. "The days of the great fortunes are over," Colonel Evans proclaimed, to the probable amazement of any podium guest listening at all carefully. "Your goal," he continued, "should be to find an ideal way of life, with a comfortable home, sufficient money to travel and possibly a two-car garage." This was mild heresy in opportunistic Houston 40 years ago, and would be today in many quarters. There are, as a matter of fact, various areas of the city where even Colonel Evans' admonition to "take yourself less seriously" might well be challenged.

The speaker moved to noncontroversial ground by admonishing his audience "to emphasize tolerance and courtesy," but closed with some additional statements that might or might not have passed a Chamber of Commerce censor. After predicting that the University of Houston would take its place "among the highest of our institutions of higher education within 20 years, because it was founded on an idea, not on money" (something that President Oberholtzer surely appreciated when he heard it, but might well ponder later), Colonel Evans proceeded to chide the city fathers. They have taken, he maintained, a lackadaisical attitude toward public health problems. "Houston has a long way to go to take care of our fellowmen," he charged. "We should be spending two dollars a head on public health, not 50 cents per capita."

By great good fortune, one guest President Oberholtzer had particularly wanted to attend the 1937 commencement ceremonies was not present. This was Hugh Roy Cullen, who was to play such a key role in the development of the University from 1937 until his death in 1957. This support has continued throughout the years through the ongoing generosity and assistance of the Cullen Foundation and succeeding generations of the Cullen family. Mr. Cullen respected and admired Colonel Evans, but he might have choked on some of his well-meaning words and admonitions.

Dr. Oberholtzer had met Hugh Roy Cullen a few weeks before the Houston Club dinner, after he had enlisted John T. Scott's support in organizing the event. Actually, the two men had called on Mr. Cullen, still mourning the death of his only son Roy Gustav, to interest the oilman generally in the University of Houston, and specifically in the October 1936 banquet.

Dr. Oberholtzer told me almost 15 years later, when I was helping him in his new post as area director of the Hoover Commission, that he felt an instinctive bond with, and liking for, Mr. Cullen. "I looked at him, chomping on that cigar in his office at the Sterling Building," he recalled, "and I could tell that he and I had some things, deep and lasting things, in common, even though we had traveled different roads."

Mr. Cullen received his visitors gracefully. He was fond of John T. Scott, who always addressed him in private as "Brother Cullen." Mr. Scott introduced Dr. Oberholtzer as a friend who had a problem, "a problem affecting our whole town."

Hugh Roy Cullen was always one to come to the point. He told Dr. Oberholtzer that he would be glad to hear his story, but to keep it short if he could. "I'm trying to help Governor (Alfred M.) Landon beat FDR before that fellow ruins the country," he explained.

Dr. Oberholtzer compressed the entire idea behind the University into two or three minutes, and told Mr. Cullen that he simply had to have some land and some buildings, and needed the support of the business community.

Mr. Cullen's reply was typical. He couldn't do anything right now, but he would think it over. He invited Dr. Oberholtzer to come back to see him, "after the election."

On the way out to the elevators, Dr. Oberholtzer pointed out that Mr. Cullen "at least didn't throw us out." When they were in the lobby, he asked John T. Scott what Mr. Cullen "might be good for," if he really became interested in the University. Mr. Scott thought that he might make a contribution in the $25,000 to $50,000 range, "depending on what he really thinks about the University after he has the time to look into it."

Since the total Cullen contributions to the University of Houston are now some one thousand times the $50,000 upper-range figure, Messrs. Oberholtzer and Scott deserve at least a footnote in the *Guinness Book of World Records,* division of conservative estimates.

Dr. Oberholtzer had too much common sense to return to the Sterling Building immediately after Governor Landon's disastrous loss to Franklin Delano Roosevelt. He waited a decent interval for Mr. Cullen to lick his political wounds and then, preoccupied with other approaches to the resolution of his problem, it was December 1936 before he arranged an appointment. This time, he was accompanied by Dr. Kemmerer.

Hugh Roy Cullen showed immediate interest in the University, "if it gives a chance for an education to youngsters whose fathers have to work for a living." He told his two visitors in his bluntly honest way that his own formal education had ended in the fifth grade, when he went to work for three dollars a week in a San Antonio candy factory.

President Oberholtzer explained that the University of Houston was not only for young men and women without the money to leave home for an education, "the children of working folks." It was also for adults whose high school education had not provided the opportunity to broaden their horizons and reach their true potential. There was as well the vital dimension of vocational and technical training, he added; plus graduate work for teachers, continuing education courses in great variety—a broad mixture of higher education which Houston must provide if the city was to continue its remarkable growth and progress.

"That sounds like my kind of proposition," Mr. Cullen replied. "How much are you short?" On cue, Vice-President Kemmerer pulled out the first preliminary sketches for what was then titled the Liberal Arts Building. He could have given an approximate cost, in the $150,000 to $180,000 range; but something told him to reply that even estimates of the total cost of the project were delayed until the architects were able to proceed further. In the meantime, a brochure was in preparation, and an advance copy would be made available to Mr. Cullen.

Even though it violated some basic precepts of fund-raising, such as having a definite amount in mind when the prospect is interested enough to inquire, the interview with Mr. Cullen was a signal success for President Oberholtzer and Vice-President Kemmerer.

The salient point was that Hugh Roy Cullen understood and accepted the fundamental concept of the fledgling University of Houston. This was an institution where he might have obtained more formal education,[23] something for which his quick mind and intellect must have yearned in earlier years; or where his son Roy Gustav, who left Rice Institute without a degree, could have completed one while working to support his young family. The University would surely provide opportunity for tens of thousands of students otherwise destined to be stranded on the shore of inadequate motivation and education. It was an institution that Mr. Cullen, just as his grandfather Ezeziel Wimberly Cullen, could appreciate.

The idea that the University of Houston would require major financial support, was worthy of it, and should be considered in his own philanthropic plans, had been firmly implanted in Hugh Roy Cullen's mind.

Hugh Roy Cullen's usually accurate biographers, Edward W. (Ed) Kilman and Theon Wright, always referred to Dr. Oberholtzer as "Oberholzer," which was probably the spelling for the family name generations ago in Germany. This is a minor aberration, but they are also incorrect in the important matters of describing the chronology and relationship of the Settegast-Taub gift of land, of Mr. Cullen's first major contribution to the University of Houston, and of his decision to participate in the University's 1938 fund-raising campaign.

Kilman and Wright thought that President Oberholtzer and Vice-President Kemmerer did not have the vital matter of the Settegast-Taub tract resolved when they first called on Mr. Cullen in December of 1936. Actually, they had the final deeds in hand before the presidential election, on October 19, and had been reasonably certain of the consequential 110-acre gift (which obviously placed them in a much stronger position) since May 1936. But it was to be 16 months, not the few weeks inferred by the biographers, between the Oberholtzer-Kemmerer visit to Hugh Roy Cullen and his first splendid gift to the University; and almost that long before the oilman would agree to serve as finance chairman of the $1 million campaign in 1938.

Mr. Cullen decided to do some checking; although he was quite interested in the University of Houston for a number of reasons, he wanted some outside, objective information. He thought naturally of his long-time friend Francis Marion Law, who had loaned him money in the lean days when he was still a cotton broker. He recalled Mr. Law's experience as a member (later chairman) of the governing board of Texas A&M College. Fortunately for the University of Houston, John T. Scott had already told his banking colleague of his own high opinion of the University and its potential value to the community under the leadership of President Oberholtzer. The report to Mr. Cullen was quite positive, and stimulated him to act for the first time on behalf of the University of Houston. He called Julius Settegast and Ben Taub, told them of his interest, and assured them that although it might take a little time to work out the details, he would personally guarantee that the required building would be constructed on the new campus, if not by January 1, 1938, then soon thereafter.

Meanwhile, there had been a series of other promising developments as 1937 began. In January, the Board of Education and the City of Houston signed an agreement providing for the opening of St. Bernard Street (Cullen Boulevard)[24] on the western periphery of the Settegast-Taub tract, the installation of basic water and sewerage connections and the topping of the street with asphalt. Drainage and general landscaping (which included a great deal of filling in low spots) of the new campus began February 15, with

250 part-time National Youth Administration (NYA) workers hired at 50 cents per hour. It was indicated late in February (a month in which the University of Houston spent only $10,864.20 for its entire operation) that local banks were satisfied with the balance sheet prepared by Dr. Kemmerer, and might provide as much as $215,000 in loans to combine with an accumulated $85,000 surplus. This would total $300,000, the minimal sum estimated for the Liberal Arts Building if the facility were trimmed to the bone.

On March 12, 1937, the entire student body was invited to a picnic on the new campus, with members of the Board of Education; W.O. Alexander, Houston area director for NYA; and his project superintendent, C.A. Lawrence, as guests of honor. A classic picture of this event shows President Oberholtzer, wearing his customary gray fedora, perched on one end of a huge pine log and on the other end is a group of students. Dr. Oberholtzer had recalled James A. Garfield's oft-quoted description of higher education in a simpler era: "The ideal college is Mark Hopkins at one end of the log, and the students at the other end." It was the Oberholtzer pattern—keep things as simple as possible for as long as possible.

The first model of the Liberal Arts Building was shown at the picnic, and this stimulated both a splendid editorial in the Houston *Post*[25] and the March 18, 1937, article by Rosella Werlin summarizing progress at the University of Houston in its first decade.

The University, the *Post* proclaimed, "... has already demonstrated its worth. Operating on a makeshift basis in borrowed quarters ... (it has nevertheless) made available to hundreds ... an educational opportunity they could have obtained in no other manner."

The article by Rosella Werlin claimed that "the magic wand has been waved for Houston's Cinderella school." Recounting the University's early difficulties, Mrs. Werlin said that it now "bids fair of blossoming forth into one of the most beautiful and up-to-date institutions of its kind." Dr. Kemmerer was described as "the greatest optimist," a Napoleonesque figure (five feet, five inches tall) who decapitated the hydra-headed dragon of Hercules only to see it sprout nine more problems, most of them centering around the need for building(s), scholarships, and more revenue. Note that Dr. Kemmerer stressed more than the single building required to perfect title to the Settegast-Taub tract.

Mrs. Werlin unveiled a "complete layout of the campus" that reveals, naturally, vast differences between original concept and present status. The plan was by the Kansas City, Missouri landscaping (and city planning, a rare profession in the 1930s) firm of Hare and Hare. Hare & Hare had done several projects earlier for the HISD. The original quadrangle, including the reflection pool bordered by rose bushes, is reasonably recognizable without the Ezekiel W. Cullen Building; but once you leave this central portion of the beginning campus, the changes are major.

The central quadrangle around the reflecting pool was to house the College of Liberal Arts and Sciences, with three facilities to be built in a first phase building program: the north wing of a Science and Vocational Center; an Industrial Training Center; and the west wing of a Liberal Arts and Cultural Center. Scheduled for later construction within this College were four other structures still unnamed, three to the south and one to the northwest. The Science and Vocational Center would have been in the present location of the Ezekiel W. Cullen Building.

A second phase building program was to involve the College of Fine Arts, centering approximately on the present A.D. Bruce Religion Center, the Student Life Building, and the Oberholtzer Quadrangle. Four facilities were proposed for this area: a Student and Faculty Center toward the west, a Dramatic Arts and Music Building to the east, a Physical Education Center adjoining a future stadium and Health and Recreational Center, and a smallish library to the north. There were also to have been four future buildings for the College of Fine Arts, including the museum.

A third component of the original campus plan was a College of Commerce and Industry to the north of the original quadrangle. This included five unnamed buildings, one of them rather similar in design to the current Cullen College of Engineering.

Among the unusual items in the Hare and Hare plan disclosed in Mrs. Werlin's article were a swimming pool, bowling green, sand beach with a bath house, a recreation shelter, and an outdoor theater.

The article, replete with hyperbole, was nevertheless a superb piece of propaganda for the University, and for Dr. Kemmerer, who was now clearly assuming a central role in planning as well as in administration: "We want to show all Houstonians and those at large that (the University) is going to forge ahead. Nothing is going to stop us *now* . . . We believe in *now* . . . We are going to build right *now*."

As landscaping, the installation of basic utilities, drainage and the paving of St. Bernard Street continued at the new campus, there was substantial progress in other quarters. Enrollment, at 1,384 for 1935-1936, jumped to 1,513 and then to 1,701 in the next two years. Extension courses, which were to be significant for more than two decades, expanded into Beaumont, Richmond-Rosenberg, West Columbia and other widely-separated communities in the area. Faculty members were assigned as liaison representatives to industry, in preparation for more "practical training courses to be conducted in shops . . . "

Substantial additions had been made to the curriculum for 1935-1936, in physical chemistry, auditing, income tax procedures, "advanced" geology, French literature, theories of investment, and public health. A nursing certificate was also offered for the first time.

The full significance of these changes was revealed the following summer, when it was announced that baccalaureate degrees would now be available in business administration, chemistry, health and physical education, geology, public health nursing and education. Preprofessional, or "preparatory" curricula were also initiated on a more formal basis for students in law, engineering, medicine and dentistry, although similar training had been offered.

The degree in public health nursing (a degree in nursing education was added in December 1937), and the innovative field of training for "licensed vocational nurses" (a term which apparently originated at the University of Houston) represented strong interests of Dr. Kemmerer. He foresaw critical shortages of nurses years before these occurred. Problems in providing adequate training for nurses without a faculty of medicine, however, plus the burgeoning budgetary and administrative difficulties involved in a College of Nursing, were to plague the Kemmerer administration in the next decade.

The central problem in the crucial year of 1937-1938 was getting a first building underway on the new campus, although Hugh Roy Cullen removed some of the pressure by guaranteeing Julius

Settegast and Ben Taub that the facility would definitely be built, even if dirt actually did not fly by New Year's Day of 1938.

The Oberholtzer-Kemmerer team[26] had experienced varying degrees of success in their multi-front campaign aimed at the power structure; at internal financing, perhaps combined with external loans and/or grants; at expanded publicity; and at low-level lobbying with federal agenices. But after charging up and down the field, they were still scoreless, and perched on the opposing 10-yard line, third and eight, with time running out.

It was decided in the spring of 1937 that Dr. Oberholtzer would go to Washington, D.C. and attempt to get a final "yea" or "nay" from the Public Works Administration on the question of the major grant for the new campus. Because of some sensitivity about such expeditions on the part of the conservative members of the Board of Education, it was announced that the prime purpose of his trip was to examine policies in other large school districts operating relatively new senior high schools.[27]

To his surprise, Dr. Oberholtzer was told by PWA Administrator Harold W. Ickes that the University would receive an unusual $86,000 grant, the first of its type in Texas. This was barely half of the $165,000 that he had hoped for, but the University president had a considerable victory nonetheless. The $86,000, to be reimbursed against the wages of workers hired from Works Progress Administration relief rolls, would be very helpful, especially in combination with assistance from the National Youth Administration in draining and landscaping the campus.

H.L. Mills, ever the one to watch administrative costs, pointed out that the grant included a 15 percent extra reimbursement against overhead. The business manager was so impressed that he worked out the first addition to the Settegast-Taub tract late in June 1937. The Board of Education donated 6,280 square feet at the rear of Taylor School to the City of Houston, thereby opening up Smith Street to the south. In return, the trustees paid a token amount to the city fathers for a small but important strip of land along Wheeler Street.

The PWA grant seemed to bring a succession of minor but significant victories to President Oberholtzer and Dr. Kemmerer as the summer of 1937 lengthened into fall. One of the first University alumni to attain political office, County Judge Roy M. Hofheinz, came forward to help in various ways after upsetting the incumbent W.H. Ward. The so-called "boy wonder," in spite of his youth and clashes with combative groups such as the shell producers, had growing impact throughout the city and county and valuable contacts in Austin, where he had been chosen one of the five most effective legislators in his first term as a member of the House of Representatives.

The flow of positive publicity continued, and the community leadership seemed to take a growing interest in the new institution. Spring and summer inquiries indicated a record 1937-1938 enrollment, stimulated by the many new baccalaureate degrees being added, and the emergence of particularly able and talented new members of the faculty, including Jules Vern, the French scholar and founder of the quarterly *Le Bayou*; Lyle T. Hooker (who taught a course in "Preparation for the Marriage Relationship"); Ruth V. Pennybacker, founder of the *Harvest*, a campus publication for student poets and creative writers; and Raymond W. Baldwin in business administration, who carried the title of field director and was charged with "keeping in constant touch with the commercial, financial, and industrial community."

The architects, Lamar Q. Cato and Victor E. Johnson, had been told to expedite detailed plans for the Liberal Arts Building, now decided upon as the first unit on the new campus. On July 17, 1937, it was announced as the "first completely air-conditioned university facility in the nation—and probably in the world."

But there were errors regarding the cost of this structure that would come back to haunt the University of Houston before being finally, and happily, resolved. The first estimate for the Liberal Arts Building was $180,000 to $185,000, but it was not revealed that this included only the first phase of construction. The second phase of the project would require another $100,000. Further, after some necessary revisions, first phase estimates went up as high as $260,000, then down to $235,000. As a result, a facility understood in the beginning to cost about $185,000 would actually run up another 80 percent, to $335,000.

Regardless of the final price tag, President Oberholtzer and Dr. Kemmerer now had some definite plans to show Mr. Cullen. They had not been able to see him during the summer of 1937, much of which Mr. Cullen had spent on vacation at his two favorite resorts, the Greenbrier in White Sulphur Springs and the Broadmoor Hotel in Colorado Springs,[28] when he was not incommunicado in his office, working on plans to offset the growing power of FDR's New Deal with conservative gains in off-year Congressional elections. There had been one important contact, however. In a remarkable instance of good fortune (and foresight), Vice-President Kemmerer had prepared advance proofs of several sections of a new brochure regarding the University the next day after his original meeting with the oilman. This was "on the off chance," Dr. Kemmerer later recalled, that Mr. Cullen might want more information, specifically about the unique opportunity that the institution could provide for students who could not go elsewhere for an education—a point that seemed to appeal greatly in the Sterling Building interview. Dr. Kemmerer left the proofs at the Quintana Petroleum Company offices, and Mr. Cullen called him early the next day.

The oilman's eye had fallen exactly where Dr. Kemmerer had hoped that it might—on a two-page layout headed, "A Typical Student's Daily Program." The copy surrounding 11 photographs began, "This young man wanted to get ahead. The odds were against him. His friends went away to college, but he had to go to work. The University of Houston helped him turn handicap into opportunity. Now, when his friends with their degrees return looking for jobs, they will find this young man holding a job, with training demanded by the job (plus his University of Houston degree), ahead of them on the road to success. Without the University of Houston, a majority of the students would be deprived of the opportunity to continue their education . . . As facilities are expanded . . . more of Houston's workers can get a fair chance."

The photographs in the layout took the reader through a typical day with a young chemist: arising at 6:45 a.m. in his modest residence; boarding the 7:18 a.m. Southmore bus in dark suit and hat; at the laboratory by 8:00 a.m.; eating the 35-cent luncheon special at a Walgreen's Drug counter; leaving the job at 5:00 p.m.; in classes and studying in the library until 9:30 p.m.; an hour of study at home; and in bed at 11:15 p.m.

It was strong meat for Hugh Roy Cullen, and he told Dr. Kemmerer after looking over the proofs that "this is the kind of person I want to help." Dr. Kemmerer, describing the incident to me almost 40 years later, felt that a very positive and indelible impression had been made upon Mr. Cullen. He also pointed out that it demonstrated again the value of finding out as much as possible concerning a man's likes and dislikes, and the importance of "doing things on time—now; being prepared for an opportunity, or even creating the opportunity yourself."

The University was doubly in luck, because in the intervening months since the first interviews with the oilman, a new and particularly significant matter for discussion with Hugh Roy Cullen had emerged. There had been a definite decision to proceed with a $1 million fund-raising campaign as early in 1938 as possible.

The Board of Education had considered the matter for months, and had almost granted authorization on several occasions after President Oberholtzer had entered into what he sometimes described as "prayerful lobbying" with individual trustees concerning the campaign. Dr.Oberholtzer apparently felt that he had received approval from trustees attending the March 12, 1937, picnic on the new campus, when the need for at least three buildings was discussed along with the possible locations for these structures. Typically, he brought this matter up almost immediately after obtaining ratification of a contract, for their low bid of $5,439.58, with Cagle & Proctor, Inc. for "drainage and excavation of the so-called Settegast-Taub tract." Following the picnic he instructed Dr. Kemmerer to proceed with final copy with a complete layout of the campaign brochure, part of which was still in draft.

There were questions, however, about whether or not the gathering of the trustees on the new campus could actually be considered a formal meeting, and President Oberholtzer decided not to push his luck, impatient though he was to get on with fund-raising. The campaign was discussed again on September 29, 1937, after a summer in partial hiatus, when the Board of Education met as the Board of Trustees of the University; wider questions of budgets, campaign leadership, extent of solicitation, control of contributions, etc., emerged. Finally, on November 24, a one million dollar campaign to be conducted under the close supervision of a committee of "prominent businessmen and other community leaders" was authorized, together with necessary promotional and administrative budgets.

Dr. Oberholtzer recalled in 1950 some of his own basic thoughts about the 1938 drive for funds. "I . . .felt that if the community understands the functions and purposes of the University and is aware of the service it is trying to give, it will be supported . . . the University, if it deserves aid, ought to be its own best salesman." This was of course sound philosophy upon which to base a fund-raising campaign—in 1938, today, and in the future. As usual, Dr. Oberholtzer knew what he was doing.

President Oberholtzer and Dr. Kemmerer, with official authorization for the fund drive in hand, surveyed the situation over the Thanksgiving holiday of 1937, and decided to go back to Hugh Roy Cullen as soon as possible. Next, they arranged to call on John T. Scott, who had already demonstrated his ability to get people in to see the oilman. They proposed to Mr. Scott that the three of them return to Mr. Cullen, ostensibly to review the current situation at the University of Houston with him, and to show him a finished copy of what came to be known as the "blue brochure," which Dr. Kemmerer had now completed.

The real objective, however, would be to obtain Hugh Roy Cullen's agreement to serve as general chairman of the 1938 fund drive. With him to bring together a blue ribbon committee, and it was hoped, to become simultaneously a principal donor, they reasoned, how could the campaign fail?

The appointment with Mr. Cullen was quickly arranged, and the three benevolent conspirators plotted their strategy. There was general agreement that it would be best to gain Mr. Cullen's attention after the opening amenities by a brief report on the overall situation by President Oberholtzer, followed by Dr. Kemmerer's presentation of a copy of the blue brochure, turned to the appropriate page with the photographic layout of "A Typical Student's Daily Program." Mr. Scott would then take over as soon as possible and ask the object of all their attention to accept the general chairmanship. President Oberholtzer emphasized the need to get to the point as soon as possible. He remembered his first interview; after a brief description of the University, Mr. Cullen said to him, "Young man[29], I'm busy; I'll think about it; you'll have to come back." But Mr. Cullen had also said more than once, "I have more money than time." That, President Oberholtzer pointed out, was the encouraging part of the deal.

The historic interview went very well, possibly because Hugh Roy Cullen had already decided, at least subconsciously, that he wanted to help the University of Houston and was willing to do so. There are several versions of what actually happened, but a consensus would be that John T. Scott greeted "Brother Cullen" and presented his two accomplices again, after which President Oberholtzer gave a two-minute progress report emphasizing the fact that preliminary work was actually underway on the Settegast-Taub site.

Dr. Kemmerer then, as agreed, showed Mr. Cullen the photographic layout of the chemist-student's daily program with a few brief words reinforcing the impact of the layout. After a question or two from the oilman, John T. Scott was up to bat.

"Brother Cullen," he said, "we've got a little job, a nominal job that you could do in a short time with no trouble at all. We need your name, your enthusiasm, the wallop you pack in this town, to head up a drive for a million dollars to get the University of Houston on its feet and really rolling. You would be general chairman, but the rest of us will do most of the work."

It was a classic approach that has been used over and over in the fund-raising profession—no general chairmanship is ever anything but a nominal, or "letterhead" position; everyone else will do the work. But Mr. Cullen accepted, for a number of reasons, not the least the high regard he had for John T. Scott and was coming to have for President Oberholtzer—plus the message that he had received loud and clear from Dr. Kemmerer's key layout in the blue brochure.

Dr. Oberholtzer told a meeting a dozen years later that the chairmanship of the fund drive, "which we described to him as a nominal job, something without much work to it," was one of the best things that Mr. Cullen ever did of all his accomplishments for the University of Houston and for other worthy causes in the community and area. "He did it in a relatively brief time," Dr. Oberholtzer continued, "and it was something of lasting significance, something that placed the University in a position to really move forward."

The plan of the campaign was simple. The overall goal of $1 million was broken down into a list of four needs: the Liberal Arts Building, at $350,000 including equipment; a Science Building, $225,000 including equipment for 700 student stations; a College of Commerce and Industry, $275,000 including equipment; and industrial laboratories and shops (actually a beginning phase of the College of Commerce and Industry), at $150,000. With these facilities, the University of Houston, it was estimated, could enroll a total of 3,000 students, split evenly between daytime and evening enrollees.

A high-powered executive committee, with subsidiary units under the ablest leadership available, would be organized. A new publicity campaign would be launched to encompass media coverage, dozens of speeches before a wide variety of community organizations, and specialized publications. Actual solicitation of funds would be carried out during seven intensive days, from May 2-9, although series of advance and follow-up meetings for campaign committees, units, and individual workers would be required.

The executive committee, headed by Mr. Cullen and by Jesse H. Jones as honorary chairman,[39] included Joseph W. Evans and John T. Scott, associate chairmen; Colonel Bates; J.A. Phillips, well-known certified public accountant and civic leader; George W. Strake, the independent oilman who had hit it big at Conroe; and Dr. Oberholtzer. Oveta Culp Hobby, soon to become one of the most powerful and best-known women in the nation, took the leadership of the Women's Division; and Mayor C.A. (Neal) Pickett was chairman of the Downtown Division.

The campaign was actually launched at the Downtown Rotary Club,[31] one of the largest such organizations in the world, on January 20, 1938. The principal speakers were President Oberholtzer, George W. Strake, and John T. Scott.

Dr. Oberholtzer was going through another difficult time with the Board of Education, and curiously enough, he began his address with a few observations about that body: "I don't want to inject anything personal into the meeting," he said, "but some of my fellow Rotarians might want to know that my contract will soon expire. The Board of Education can renew or cancel as they see fit. I am satisfied to step out of the picture, and goodness knows, I might have to at any time."

These remarks, widely reported, may have been a trial balloon. Dr. Oberholtzer, known to be weary of a never-ending succession of 4-3 votes on the Board of Education, might have been seriously considering leaving the trustees with the problems incident to a public school enrollment of 61,843, while he became a full-time president for the University of Houston and the Houston College for Negroes. In any event, his contract was renewed.

What President Oberholtzer really wanted to tell the Rotarians, one of the best audiences in the area, was something of the unique and valuable mission of the University of Houston. "The University was established," he said "to provide practical education for employed adults in cooperation with local business and industrial concerns, higher education for those who must go to work immediately after graduation from high school, opportunity for cultural advancement and general self-improvement for those barred from such opportunities by technical prerequisites, and higher education for those who cannot leave Houston."

As the campaign of publicity and information was expanded, the Association of the University of Houston[32] was formed with such prominent members as W.N. (Bill) Blanton, long-time executive director of the Houston Chamber of Commerce; J.W. Sartwelle, pioneer rancher and meat packer whose packing plant was located just east of Calhoun Road on the boundary of the new campus;[33] Joe Weingarten, founder of the supermarket and realty holding company chain; W.H. Walne, prominent attorney and executive who helped develop the Houston Symphony Society; A. Dee Simpson, banker and charter member of the University Board of Regents; and E.L. Crain, the realtor and appraiser.

The three Houston newspapers carried a series of articles on virtually every aspect of the University of Houston in the early months of 1938, including the campaign leadership, campus organizations, make-up of the student body, where the students were employed, present and future plans for the institution, etc.

Ione Kirkham of the old Houston *Press* spent weeks preparing an especially effective group of features on such students as a minister, a window-washer[34], a foundry worker, a 45-year-old accountant, and four students who spent 10 years, from the earliest days of the old Houston Junior College, to complete their baccalaureate degrees. These students, Christine Liverman, Ruth Whitworth, Smith Garrison and Kathryn Johnson, would have had their 1937 diplomas stamped with General Sam Houston's personal seal—an H in script, set in an amethyst with the motto "Forever Thine"; but they were a year late for this distinction, accorded graduates in Texas' centennial year of 1936.

Editorial support was also strong and helpful. The *Chronicle* of March 22, 1938, read:

> For $1 million the University of Houston can build and equip a plant that will accommodate 3,000 students in day and evening classes. Most of those students would not be able to obtain higher education if the University of Houston were not here. . . . the university, operating under crowded, makeshift conditions in temporary quarters, has 1,650 students. Seventy-five percent of the men and 58 percent of the women attending are employed. Most of the remainder would be unable to go to colleges in other cities . . . The (present) enrollment . . . is only a beginning; the potentialities have only been touched.
>
> If the university had sufficient buildings . . . and facilities to broaden its curriculum, thousands would avail themselves of the opportunity to continue their education, fit themselves for better positions, develop their possibilities along cultural lines . . . The University of Houston is self-sustaining. A million dollars donated for buildings will enable it to accommodate as many students as an $8 million investment . . . does in the average university.

The radio stations were widely used. Mr. Cullen was heard in a series of recorded messages originating over KTRH. Dr. Kemmerer appeared in a novel program over the same station. He spoke to a special meeting of the Houston Advertising Club, sharing the program with one "Doma," who professed to be able to analyze your character through the occult quasi-science of physiognomy.

Vice-President Kemmerer's speech over KTRH was an important one that had considerable impact when quoted later in the campaign. He pointed out that there were 30,000 persons between the normal college-atttending ages of 18 to 25 in the city, "the great majority of which are denied education beyond the high school because of a lack of means or opportunity . . . getting little jobs and drifting along as best they can, often with minimal hopes for advancement." Asking for moral and financial support in the drive for $1 million with which to create "a permanent University of Houston," Dr. Kemmerer used a novel approach. He challenged his audience to "call me up if you are against this proposition, because I just cannot see how anyone in our community could oppose it."

The more articulate faculty members, especially Leon G. Halden, Joseph S. Werlin, Velma K. Soule, Standlee Mitchell, and Charles F. Hiller joined President Oberholtzer, Dr. Kemmerer, and the other campaign leaders on the speechmaking circuit; as did members of the Board of Education, an array of judges and public officials, and leading clubwomen such as Mrs. Allen B. Hannay. Mrs. Oveta Culp Hobby was not only a star of the Speakers' Bureau; she made a movie short in support of the campaign which was shown at the downtown Kirby, Loew's State and Majestic, and throughout the city.

The alumni, under the chairmanship of County Judge Roy M. Hofheinz, accepted a goal of $50,000, and the student body, after a sprited address by Dr. Hiller, agreed to raise $15,000.

Meanwhile, the molding of a campaign organization proceeded well with professional assistance in the background from Dr. J. Howard Hutchinson of New York City, brought here, Mr. Cullen told the executive committeee, "to help us in every way with the drive."

The idea was to have a minimum of 1,000, and preferably 1,500, trained workers fan out over the city from May 2-9 in divisions, groups, and teams. Recruiting posed few real difficulties. The early preparation by President Oberholtzer, Dr. Kemmerer, and John T. Scott; the strong and positive image of Hugh Roy Cullen; the broad and logical appeal of the drive; the fact that Houston was still a tight-knit community capable of responding quickly and affirmatively to such a project—all of these factors helped.[35]

Then, too, the city and area had demonstrated again in late 1937 and early 1938 its ability to run counter to national economic trends. After a short "Roosevelt recession," as Mr. Cullen termed it, building permits in Harris County went to $18 million and then to $25 million in 1938; 12,400 new automobiles were sold; and Houston became the fourth largest port, in terms of tonnage, in the nation. The city, which attracted 26,881 new residents in 1938, had just added the Sam Houston Coliseum and Music Hall, Jefferson Davis Hospital, and the elegant Empire Room of the Rice Hotel (where Cecil Amelia (Titi) Blaffer, now the Princess von und zu Furstenberg, was the one and only Allegro debutante at a memorable presentation ball soon after this facility was opened. It was marred only by the brown bags in which the patrons had to bring their booze under Texas' archaic mixed drinks law).

As evidence of the degree to which the University fund-raising drive was accepted, Mrs. Oveta Culp Hobby recruited more than 700 members for her Women's Division. This especially pleased

Mr. Cullen, who immediately offered to be the host for a luncheon at the River Oaks Country Club honoring Mrs. Hobby and an "advisory committee" within the Division. The advisory committee was of course a time-honored device similar to having Chris Evert endorse a tennis racquet today: If enough prominent women in the community are "advisors," the Women's Division and the cause it espouses must be worthy of support; as Chrissie swings the racquet convincingly and effectively during overlong television commercials, the female viewer becomes convinced that it is the answer to a faltering forehand and nonexistent backhand.

Acceptances for the organizational luncheon came in at a gratifying, and then at an alarming, rate. Extra places had to be set at the last moment in the ballroom, a smaller version of this splendid facility in the remodeled and enlarged River Oaks Country Club of today. (In a triumph of architecture and engineering roughly comparable to building Khufu's Great Pyramid at Giza, the River Oaks Country Club was extensively remodeled and enormously enlarged during the early 1970's while life went on as usual within the undisturbed core structure, the membership understandably swallowing the formidable extra costs and assessments involved rather than giving up use of the club for a year or more. As part of this operation, the ballroom and east wing were substantially increased in size and capacity.)

Many of the more prominent members of the advisory committee in attendance are still in command of Houston's entrenched society today, though most of those surviving have been promoted from matron to dowager. The list included, for example, Mrs. L.S. Bosworth, Mrs. G.E. Cranz (Mrs. H.R. Cullen's sister-in-law), Mrs. Cullen, Miss Nina Cullinan, Mrs. Ray K. Daily, M.D., Mrs. Ray L. Dudley, Mrs. H.M. Garrett, Mrs. Allen B. Hannay, Mrs. George A. Hill, Jr., Miss Ima Hogg, Mrs. Harry Holmes, Mrs. Palmer Hutcheson, Mrs. W.J. Kinkaid, Mrs. Harris Masterson, Mrs. Haywood Nelms, Mrs. H.E. Neuhaus, Mrs. W.B. Sharp, Sr., Mrs. Frank C. Smith, Mrs. J.A. Tennant, Mrs. Walter H. Walne, Mrs. Mike Hogg, Miss Blanche Higginbotham, Mrs. J. Alston Clapp, Jr., Mrs. Herbert Childress, Mrs. Charles J. Koenig, Mrs. J.L. McReynolds, Mrs. A.S. O'Brien, Mrs. J.J. Devoti, and Mrs. S.C. Red.

This was a startling assemblage of the female power structure, and Mr. Cullen found them an attentive audience, even though some of them have not yet set foot on the University of Houston campus.

C.A (Neal) Pickett, later a short-term but popular mayor, told one meeting that it took him only 45 minutes on the telephone to enlist the group chairmen for his Downtown Division. They constituted a formidable lot, including Lewis W. Cutrer, himself to become mayor, sub-chairman for attorneys; Charles G. Heyne, engineers and architects; General Vincent Chiodo, finance and commercial; and H. Dick Golding, merchandising and manufacturing.

As detailed planning and actual organization of the 1938 campaign proceeded, Hugh Roy Cullen found that the project was not the "nominal job" that John T. Scott had asked him to accept. Sometime in late 1937 or early 1938, he must have realized that far more than interest in a civic undertaking, no matter how worthy, was motivating him. Veteran members of his staff at Quintana Petroleum recall that at times he seemed almost obsessed by the campaign.

There was probably a strong psychological reaction, and a healthy one, underway. Mr. Cullen had lost his only son Roy Gustav in May of 1936, after an oil field tragedy that naturally was most difficult to accept. There were harrowing circumstances that even the strongest person would tend to recall again and again. Roy Gustav had gone to Edinburg to check on a well in which pipe had "frozen" at 7,000 feet. Mr. Cullen had a presentiment of tragedy over the use of a rented rig with an insubstantial wooden base, and telephoned down to tell the tool pusher to "get Sonny off that rig."

The message was delivered, and Roy Gustav had started away from the drilling platform floor when it was decided to make one more attempt to free up the stuck pipe in the well. Under tremendous pressure, the derrick collapsed and young Cullen was struck by a falling metal support, then buried under the wreckage. He died two days later in the tiny Edinburg hospital, his parents at his bedside after a punishing 350-mile drive down from Houston.

Hugh Roy Cullen had kept much of this inside him, although he and his beloved Lillie must have grieved for months in private. Now, he seemed to perceive the University of Houston campaign as an antidote to his sorrow, as something to galvanize his tremendous energies into full action again.

He personally recruited the top leadership for the fund drive, bringing to bear the full impact of his name and interconnections, as well as his popularity within the petroleum industry and the developing new society of the city—a combination of Old Houston and newly powerful families from the Oil Patch. Next, he turned his attention to a banquet for campaign leadership groups and Associates of the University of Houston, scheduled for March 24, 1938, at the Rice Hotel. The formal week-long drive for $1 million would not begin until May 2, the date of yet another banquet, this one for 1,000 guests; but advance solicitations were to begin immediately after the March 24 dinner, which Mr. Cullen perceived as the real beginning of the campaign.

As March 24 approached, Hugh Roy Cullen, an impulsive and generous man, did a typically impulsive and generous thing. He called President Oberholtzer at his home early one morning and told the educator that he and Mrs. Cullen had decided to give the Liberal Arts Building (he called it the Fine Arts and Cultural Center, as it was identified in the "blue brochure," with a price tag of $260,000) to the University. It would be a memorial to their son.

Dr. Oberholtzer said later that Mr.Cullen told him of being unable to sleep, and of thinking about the upcoming fund drive, of Roy Gustav, of all that the University of Houston might come to mean to the people of Houston, especially young men and women unable to continue their education. About 3 a.m. he turned on the light, awakened Mrs. Cullen, and told her that he had decided to build the first structure on the University of Houston campus as a memorial to their son.

Dr. Kemmerer added further details to this remarkable predawn conversation in an interview with me almost 40 years later. Realizing its significance, he asked Mr. Cullen to tell him more about the original call to President Oberholtzer. Dr. Kemmerer's recollections, based upon extensive notes and his still-keen memory, seemed clear and positive, just as they were to be on so many other important points in the ongoing history of the University. He said that Mr. Cullen told him, "Mrs. Cullen was real pleased, but she did remind me that Roy Gustav had attended Rice Institute and that we had at least talked about a building over there named for him. I told her that we can do that too, maybe, but later." Mr. Cullen's interests and his sympathies were clearly with the University of Houston, however, and there they remained. There is no indication that Mrs. Cullen, a 1,000-percent supporter of her husband since the day that her friend Annie Schuhmacher had first introduced him to her in Schulenberg, ever mentioned Rice Institute again, worthy though that institution was and remains.

President Oberholtzer was thunderstruck by Mr. Cullen's announcement, and lavish in his appreciation. But his eminently practical mind began reviewing the momentous early-morning call as soon as it was completed. First of all, was the philanthropist thinking of both phases of the Liberal Arts Building, costing up to $100,000 more than the figure of $260,000 quoted in the "blue brochure"? Or phase one only, at $260,000? Or, as a third and worst alternative, did he mean phase one only at a bid of $235,000? Such a bid was already in hand, from a contractor named Nathan Wohlfield, to include equipment but to omit phase two plus eight additional classrooms and design changes in the facade of the structure.

Secondly, when would the magnificent gift from Hugh Roy and Lillie Cranz Cullen be announced? This had not been discussed at all with Mr. Cullen, but Dr. Oberholtzer knew instinctively that it might be wise to hold any such news in reserve—certainly until the formal campaign was officially launched, and perhaps until somewhat later, as a happy and potent stimulus at a crucial moment after the battle was actually joined.

President Oberholtzer called Dr. Kemmerer, gave him the earthshaking report, and arranged for an immediate meeting. His vice-president was of course elated, but he agreed that they must resolve the crucial matters of just how much money Mr. Cullen was talking about, and when the gift was to be announced.

The team of Oberholtzer and Kemmerer batted a little under .500 on these two problems. Torn between the fear that Mr. Cullen would think that they were trying to pressure him into increasing his contribution, and concern lest he find out about the second phase from someone else, Dr. Kemmerer recounted to me, they decided the best policy would be one of complete frankness.

They took the complete plans for the Liberal Arts Building (now the Roy Gustav Cullen Building) to the philanthropist as soon as possible, and explained that the facility was to be built in two stages, one now, the other simultaneously or the moment that additional funds were available. But President Oberholtzer, for some reason, either had not thought the problem through, or his widespread reputation for plain, direct communication failed him for once.

Mr. Cullen, with predictable directness, immediately asked, "How much will the whole thing cost?" Dr. Oberholtzer answered, "Another $100,000," meaning $100,000 atop the figure of $260,000, for a total of $360,000 to cover both phases of construction as well as the additional eight classrooms and a differently-designed facade.

"You can have the other $100,000; I'll build the whole thing," Mr. Cullen replied. "I don't want anyone adding to my son's building." But he had in mind $100,000 plus the bid price of phase one with equipment of $235,000—not $100,000 plus $260,000, as he made clear before the meeting was concluded.

Edison Ellsworth Oberholtzer had just left $25,000 lying on the table, but he wisely didn't blink an eye; and Dr. Kemmerer remembered primarily how exhilarated they both were as they left the Sterling Building offices of Quintana Petroleum that early spring day in 1938. The $25,000 would be as nothing in the total picture of Mr. Cullen's generosity to the University of Houston, even though it was to cause the temporary loss of eight classrooms and the deletion of a more handsome facade. Hugh Roy Cullen, of course, would have been embarrassed to learn that the ante was really $360,000, not $335,000; he would have put up the remainder in a moment[36].

The second problem, that of timing the announcement of the Cullen gift for maximum impact, was pretty well a Mexican stand-off. Mr. Cullen simply could not wait to communicate the enthusiasm he felt for the fund drive, and the pride and satisfaction he and Mrs. Cullen understandably took in having the first building on the University of Houston campus named for their son.

He decided that he would present a check for the Roy Gustav Cullen Building at the March 24 advance dinner for the campaign leadership. On the plus side, the check was for $260,000—not for his total commitment of $335,000, leaving $75,000 for later publicity. Then, Dr. Kemmerer recalled, the University's benefactor asked representatives of the three newspapers and the radio stations to a luncheon at the Houston Club just a few hours before the March 24 dinner, which the Rice Hotel chefs were already preparing.

In today's far stiffer competition for media space, this would probably have resulted in a quickly-written bulletin on the front page of the last edition of the *Chronicle*, a brief, instantaneous report on the radio wire, a mention on the evening television programs, and much-diminished coverage in next day's *Post* and *Chronicle*. The purpose of Mr. Cullen's ill-timed luncheon, to Dr. Kemmerer's consternation, was to provide a convivial forum for the advance announcement of the big news of the fast-approaching dinner—the $260,000 gift.

There werc still "newsboys" in those days before television, mainly weather-toughened, middle-aged men with an iron set of lungs and nodulated vocal cords. The patriarchs of this sub-profession were Charlie and Shorty, who plied their trade from the best location in town, the front door of the Rice Hotel across from George Kelley's restaurant.[37] Dr. Kemmerer must have dreaded driving home to get ready for the 6:30 p.m. dinner, or even walking into the Rice Hotel later. For the shout might already be going up: "Cullen Gives University $260,000," or "Biggest Gift to Education Here Since Rice Institute Founded." But the word had gone out—presumably from on high at the level of Jesse Jones, Governor Hobby and "Mefo" Foster. The Cullen story was a Friday morning story, to be played to the hilt at that time—not to be truncated and diminished in a journalistic competition on Thursday afternoon and evening.

Newspaper coverage of the March 24, 1938, banquet for the campaign leadership was stunning, as it should have been in terms of the involvement of those who ran the city at the time. The Houston *Press*, gadfly and junior member among the three dailies, carried more than 100 column-inches, with the lead story by Harry Johnston; this detailed how the audience "rose and applauded for many minutes" after Mr. Cullen presented a $260,000 check to the toastmaster, Joseph W. Evans.

Coverage in the *Post* and *Chronicle* was substantially greater than that in the *Press*, with all three publications quoting liberally from well over two-and-a-half hours of laudatory speeches. We can learn a good bit concerning the attitude of community leaders toward the University of Houston by reprinting some of their comments during that long evening of four decades ago:

Palmer Hutcheson:

I'm from one of those 'high-falutin' colleges in the East, and I learned that the best of the students were those who made their own way. That's why I'm completely sold on this proposition.

Harry C. Weiss (president of Humble Oil & Refining Company, and later, chairman of the board of trustees of Rice Institute):

I have endorsed the campaign and I have indicated that I will support it.

Mrs. Oveta Culp Hobby:

Of the 725 women I contacted to join this division, I have not one refusal. I did not have to persuade them. They were eager to serve in the campaign.

Judge Roy M. Hofheinz:

. . . the University of Houston is an institution I believe in, and know. The faces of students at this school aren't social faces. Their faces and hearts and minds are serious, intent on bettering themselves at any cost. We as citizens are shirking our responsibility if we tell our children that they must have $700 or $800 a year to go off (somewhere to school) when they finish high school. There would be no more human nor more gracious thing to do than to provide buildings for these youngsters . . . I have never seen a more worthwhile campaign.

W.L. (Bert) Childs, an industrialist representing the expanding oil tool industry:

We're not doing what we should do if we don't provide that our children can at least get an education after working hours.

John T. Scott:

$1 million will provide buildings (for the new campus) for the next 10 years. If we raise the money, we won't have to pass the hat (again) for 10 years. Let's do it.

President Oberholtzer wisely took a back seat as the plaudits from the leaders of the community rolled on. He did speak, rather briefly, on a somewhat obscure point that would not have occurred to anyone in particular. The students, he pointed out, were already paying all that they could in tuition, "It would be unfair to ask the students to pay for the buildings." Indeed it would, but not 25 years later, when tuition was down to $50 a semester in a vastly-inflated economy and there was no other practicable source from which to provide a critically needed expansion of physical plant. Then, the building use fee would become the salvation of an institution bursting at the seams and over-utilizing every square foot of space 15 hours a day.

The main speech of the evening, after a musical interlude by the University glee club and the already-venerable Walter R. Jenkins (leader of one verse of "America" at the Downtown Rotary Club, in true pitch and great style, for more years than anyone can remember) was given by Mr. Cullen. One of the principal themes would have thrown any professional fund-raiser into severe shock, since it recounted how Chancellor John G. Bowman had allegedly gone to the individual citizens of his city to raise much of the necessary $12,000,000 for the great Tower of Learning at the University of Pittsburgh; it is an axiom of the profession that 80 to 85 percent of the contributions to any campaign come from 10 to 15, sometimes only five, percent of the donors; and in spite of Mr. Cullen's natural tendency to embellish things a bit in the telling or re-telling of a good story,[39] the big dollars for Chancellor Bowman came from the coal kings and the Mellons and their cousins, the Scaifes, not from steel puddlers at the Homestead Works or their wives cutting down on purchases of good Polish sausage to save money for a contribution to the University of Pittsburgh.

The Hugh Roy Cullen speech at the March 24, 1938, dinner, however, had other statements that strongly impressed his audience, reinforced his own beliefs and provided a great deal of positive impact and newspaper copy. For example:

> I know a half dozen millionaires in Houston who are planning to use their wealth for the good of humanity. They would give to the University of Houston if they could . . . see the worth of the project. With the limited and wholly insufficient facilities heretofore available, the University has more than met every obligation. When its plan, purposes, and accomplishments are known and understood, it will develop into one of the outstanding universities of the country.

> The millionaires whom I have in mind were poor boys, as I was a poor boy, and they went through the tortures of hell to reach their step on the ladder of success. They work longer hours than any day laborer, for their problems are always with them . . . If (they) could see that by helping the University of Houston, they would materially help many poor boys and girls, they would give freely to our cause, and during their declining years they would be happy in the knowledge they had assisted in initiating an educational program that will never end.

Mr. Cullen gave the first indication of a theme that he and Mrs. Cullen would follow, in the last paragraphs of his remarks:

> Suppose that William Marsh Rice . . . or George Hermann . . . could look back from the world beyond and could live their lives over. Would they have waited . . . to do their great work of giving? Or would they have started giving . . . earlier . . . so that they could bask in the sunshine of their own creations? I am sure they would have started . . . earlier.[40]
> [Mr. Cullen had a particular admiration for the millionaire recluse and philanthropist George Hermann, who was born in a tiny house on the site of the Mellie Esperson Building, had little formal education, but amassed a fortune and left the bulk of it to public charities of great significance to the people.]

To thunderous applause at the Rice Hotel dinner, Mr. Cullen concluded:

> Never again will we have the opportunity to have a part in building the first home of this University of ours. I sincerely and firmly believe that as we see the beautiful buildings of this great institution take shape, we will be exceedingly happy in having had a part in making them possible.

The campaign was underway, with about a month to obtain advance gifts before an estimated 1,500 volunteers set out on the one-week, May 2-9 formal drive for funds.

First, there was the crucial matter of getting the Roy Gustav Cullen Memorial Building actually underway before the extended deadline of April 1, 1938, that Julius Settegast and Ben Taub had agreed to at the request of Hugh Roy Cullen. President Oberholtzer knew that the donors might agree to a further extension, within reason, but there were compelling reasons—legal, psychological, and otherwise—to break ground on the new campus almost immediately.

Dr. Oberholtzer arranged first for the Nathan Wohlfeld bid of $216,769 (plus separate bids for equipment expected to bring the total cost to $235,000) to be accepted at the Monday, March 28 meeting of the Board of Education. Next, he obtained Mr. Cullen's agreement to a groundbreaking ceremony on Thursday, March 31; this was cutting it pretty close, but it was the best he could do.

Beginning a tradition of appalling weather that has since hounded many groundbreaking and building dedication ceremonies at the University of Houston (in contrast to an unbelievable record of bone-dry outdoor commencement convocations before Hofheinz Pavilion was available), ground was broken for the Roy Gustav Cullen Building in a near-monsoon.

President Oberholtzer, ever the realist, had a steam shovel and a crew of slicker-clad workmen standing by just in case the symbolic ceremony was washed out. There was no cover, but plenty of umbrellas for the principals (Mr. and Mrs. Hugh Roy Cullen, Mrs. Roy Gustav Cullen, now Mrs. Edwin Burton; Cornelia Cullen, now Mrs. Meredith Long, the three-year-old daughter of Roy Gustav Cullen who threw her arms around her grandfather's neck and watched proceedings from his left shoulder; Roy Henry Cullen, Cornelia's eight-year-old brother; the trustees of the Board of Education; President Oberholtzer and Dr. Kemmerer and their wives; and the Reverend T.C. Jester, who gave the invocation).

After ground was broken by Mr. Cullen with a short, silver-coated spade (he told one reporter that he "had a lot of experience shoveling blue gumbo mud around, but not much recently"), J. Wilbur Smith, president of the student body, presented Mr. and Mrs. Cullen with a commemorative book bound in red leather. The students present then began a perilous parade around the waterlogged campus, to the accompaniment of Victor Alessandro's First Band and the HISD's ROTC drum and bugle corps.

The advance fund-raising campaign, meanwhile, rolled on beautifully in terms of organization, media coverage, and editorial support; but it was only moderately successful on the bottom line; checks and firm pledges arrived in a trickle at the campaign office at 305 Electric Building (the old Houston Lighting & Power Company headquarters on Walker at Fannin).

Mr. and Mrs. Cullen had planned a 10-day trip to New York, Washington, D.C., and Pittsburgh (to meet again with Chancellor John G. Bowman) before the May 2 kickoff dinner at the Rice Hotel, and Mr. Cullen waited as long as he could before issuing the first report on the drive, on April 18. This showed $102,488 on hand in addition to the original Cullen gift of $260,000, for a total of $362,488. The general chairman termed this "a fine start," but he was in truth somewhat disappointed at the reaction thus far to what he described as "Houston's greatest civic need and opportunity," a new home for what he had begun to call "our democratic University."[41]

There were few additional contributions as the May 2 dinner approached, but the number of reservations indicated a capacity crowd. Such was the case, and the black-tie affair was a roaring success in terms of stimulating new enthusiasm and interest. The newspapers were full of the affair the next day, with many photographs and long quotations from a battery of distinguished speakers.

Mr. Cullen rose to the occasion by promising to be "personally responsible" for $650,000 of the $1 million goal. President Oberholtzer observed that "anything that might be desired could be accomplished by this group of people here tonight, especially if they set their hearts on it."

Mrs. Hobby delivered a particularly effective speech. She pointed out that the American attitude toward higher education thus far is "a fusion of Jeffersonian . . . intellectual aristocracy democracy, and the Jacksonian doctrine of mass education." She deplored the fact that only 11 percent of our young men and women between 18 and 21 are in colleges or universities, urging that the percentage be increased by "building such schools as the University of Houston." "It is no longer true," she said, "that America is the land of opportunity for all. Most of us must seek opportunity."[42]

Judge Hofheinz, chairman of the Alumni Division, termed the University of Houston "an underprivileged institution" which provided "a rare opportunity" to serve the "90 percent of average boys and girls who are not fortunate enough to attain college" by providing a "home" in which they can seek knowledge. "The University already has a fine faculty and a fine student body," he concluded. "They only ask us for buildings. Can we afford to refuse them?"

Dean T.H. Shelby of the extension division of the University of Texas, a staunch friend when Dr. Oberholtzer was getting the Houston Junior College underway in 1927, asked the many Universities of Texas graduates in the audience to stand. Since the legendary Judge E.E. Townes, dean of the Law School at

Austin, had literally dozens of his graduates in the leading firms in Houston (including such luminaries as Colonel Bates, first in the Class of 1915; and Palmer Hutcheson, Class of 1911), there was a considerable stirring. Dean Shelby then admonished the Longhorns, "The eyes of Texas are upon you. Texas University expects you to do your part in this drive."

Part of Mr. Cullen's closing remarks must have been especially gratifying to President Oberholtzer and Dr. Kemmerer. He called for the University to be built along "practical, rather than theoretical, lines." He quoted from a current report of the Carnegie Foundation that could have been made required reading for students of Dr. Kemmerer's General College: "The current practice of the vast majority of American . . . colleges makes no requirement whatsoever that a given body of knowledge shall become the relatively permanent and available equipment of the student."

Typically, Mr. Cullen then concluded the banquet and the evening with his promise to raise $650,000 of the $1 million goal ("including our previous gift") as part of his personal responsiblity as general chairman. It was Monday evening, and report luncheons were scheduled for the next Friday, Tuesday, and Friday.

It looked for a time as if the 1938 fund drive might reach its $1 million goal; or at least get within comfortable striking distance. At the first report meeting, on May 6, the Women's Division had raised $4,075.50; the Alumni Division, $19,335; the Downtown Division, $8,221; the Associates of the University, $31,091; and Special Gifts (including the Cullen contribution of $260,000), $351,920. Faculty members, giving an average of more than $100 per 60 donors, oversubscribed their $5,000 quota handsomely at $6,450. The students reported in with $11,665.44.

A notable gift was the $5,000 contribution by the children of a revered Houstonian who had just died after a long and illustrious career as civic and professional leader. Judge Joseph C. Hutcheson, Jr., Palmer Hutcheson, Dr. Allen Hutcheson, Mrs. L.S. Bosworth, and three other Hutcheson daughters from Dallas, New York City, and Chattanooga gave the $5,000 as a memorial to Captain J.C. Hutcheson.

Volunteer workers went out encouraged for the last days of the drive, with as many as 1,500 continuing solicitation calls.

Relatively small but meaningful contributions, each duly publicized, continued to come in: $100 from Saint Joseph Hospital; $503 from employees of the Houston Electric Company; $50 from the Business and Professional Women; the fifth grade of Lamar Elementary School gave the $100 prize it had won in a Parent-Teachers Association competition; kindergarten and primary grades at the Allen Elementary School gave $9.33 in dimes, nickels, and pennies.

There were already problems, however: the campaign was originally to have ended on May 10, but it had been extended through May 13 (a Friday the thirteenth, at that); the real difficulty was overemphasis on small and medium gifts, and the emerging inability of major divisions to meet their quotas.

The Tuesday, May 10 report luncheon was preceded by a downtown parade of University students flanked by 2,500 members of the Sam Houston Black Battalion, the Milby Co-Ed Cadettes, the Austin Scottish Brigade, the San Jacinto Jacadettes, and assorted high school ROTC units. Before a large crowd of workers, it was announced that a total of $575,106 was in hand. This was $160,574 above the $414,632 of the initial report.

But at the "final" meeting of May 13, the grand total had risen only another $69,345, to $644,451. This was more than $350,000 short of the $1 million goal, and would not support the objective of four buildings on the new campus with equipment.

Upon analysis, the difficulty was fairly obvious. Neither the crucial Special Gifts Division (at $505,620 including the Cullen $260,000) nor the significant Associates of the University Division (at $51,745) had been assigned specific sub-goals, and both were substantially behind expectations. The Women's Division had brought in a very commendable $30,014, but this had been with the use of 700 volunteers. The Downtown Division had only $32,103 of its $100,000 objective, and the Alumni Division only $22,030 of a hoped-for $50,000.

It was announced that the campaign would continue "for a few more weeks." Mr. Cullen thanked everyone involved, and said that he would bring in the minimum of $650,000 for which he had assumed responsibility. W.N. (Bill) Blanton, manager of the Chamber of Commerce, told the final report meeting that "it would be a shame and an outrage, if we failed after Mr. Cullen has so generously set the pace." John T. Scott said that the drive would not be over until $1 million was in hand. Bishop Clinton S.

(Mike) Quin urged that everyone continue quietly but effectively to solicit funds. "If we keep up our spirits," said the good cleric, "we can't be whipped."

Exact records disappeared after the closing of the Electric Building office in the late summer of 1938, but it appears that the campaign finally brought in a total of $660,000, including $335,000 from Mr. and Mrs. Cullen. Dr. Kemmerer, who knew as much as anyone about the fund drive, confirmed that the net amount received by the University was very close to $660,000.

While the 1938 campaign was technically a failure, in spite of heroic efforts by its leaders and by Hugh Roy Cullen in particular, it was a roaring success in terms of getting the University of Houston underway on its new campus, and in obtaining far wider understanding and acceptance of the institution within the community. It also had the obvious benefit of enlisting Mr. Cullen's escalating involvement with the University and—in time—of accelerating some inevitable and fundamental changes in the relationship between the Board of Education and the now-lusty orphan that had been a tiny junior college only a few years ago.

While construction moved rapidly ahead on the Roy Gustav Cullen Building, Hugh Roy Cullen's interest in the University of Houston broadened and deepened. He was the speaker at the fourth commencement convocation on May 30, 1938, held in a beautiful setting, at sunset, in Miller Memorial Theater. One might have expected that Mr. Cullen would turn again to the theme of the need for the developing University, which he had emphasized so many times during the fund drive; this would have been much in point, with new campus construction actually underway. Alternatively, he could have turned naturally to the necessity of bringing in more dollars to close the gap between actual proceeds of the drive, and the $1 million goal; he mentioned this, but indirectly, choosing to reaffirm his pledge to see that a minimum of $650,000 was raised (after President Oberholtzer had warmly praised Mr. and Mrs. Cullen for their help).

Instead, he turned to a philosophical theme, telling the 174 graduates that "truthfulness is the first essential of a truly successful life," and expanding upon this as the only appropriate basis for personal, business, or professional relationships.[43]

When President Oberholtzer and Dr. Kemmerer drove out to the new campus via Wheeler and the extension of St. Bernard,[44] they began to see real progress as the spring of 1938 lengthened into summer. Much of the drainage, requiring 2,000 feet of underground pipe, was complete after the difficult task of digging through hard clay with pick ax and shovel. Filling and general landscaping was also in penultimate stages. These operations had fortunately been begun more than a year before, when it was hoped that a first campus building would be ready by February 1, 1938.

There would have to be additional drainage after the first torrential rains of 1939 (and after an incredible rainstorm of June 15, 1976, looking ahead a generation), but the 110-acre site was vastly improved from the tangled semiswamp that C.F. McElhinney had helped to survey more than a year earlier. And constantly, as the Oberholtzer-Kemmerer team picked their way between mounds of dried blue gumbo mud, their eyes were drawn to the Roy Gustav Cullen Building. Handsome exterior walls of Texas limestone were being set into place there by stonemasons, changing a near-wilderness into the beginnings of a campus. They returned to their tiny, temporary administration offices at San Jacinto High School to work on the interesting problem of a seal for the new University; but not before they watched the rays of the sun, surprisingly warm for March, reflected against the walls of the strikingly clean walls of their first University of Houston building.

There were other reasons for optimism in that long-ago summer of 1938. The Board of Education, eyeing both the $660,000 proceeds of the just-completed fund drive and indications of improving chances for a Public Works Administration grant for the project, told Lamar Q. Cato to expedite final architectural plans for the Science Building. The addition of this second element of the original academic quadrangle, directly across from the Roy Gustav Cullen Building, would be a substantial step toward having at least a minimum physical plant on the new campus. It would also demonstrate to the community that the University of Houston was a viable and expanding entity in its new location and prospect.

Meanwhile, Mr. Cullen, impressed by the growing need for a third element of the $1 million building package upon which the campaign had been based, became very interested in the combination of shops and industrial laboratories originally termed the Industrial Training Center. He asked Stephen Power Farish,[45] a pioneer in the oil tool industry whose older brother William Stamps Farish had been a founder of the Humble Oil & Refining Company, to look into the matter for him, since such a facility would be training potential employees for oil tool manufacturers and service companies.

Mr. Farish responded, characteristically, by having preliminary plans for the Center drawn up at his own expense.

On August 15, 1938, the good news arrived from Washington, D.C., that PWA authorities announced a grant of $125,370, or 45 percent of the estimated total cost of $278,600 for the Science Building. There was only one problem, Hugh Roy Cullen's gift of $335,000 had been of course completely allocated to the building honoring his son, and only $77,875 had come in to date on campaign pledges. This amount would be $75,355 short of the University's $153,320 share of the project, but the matching sum was due within the month.

The solution was to commit the deficit of $75,355 from the General Fund. President Oberholtzer, it will be remembered, had been squirreling away operating surpluses every year since 1928. At his request, after some questioning by H.L. Mills, the trustees appropriated the $75,355 plus $27,749 for equipment, a total of $103,104, from the General Fund.

By the October 3, 1938, meeting of the Board of Education, Architect Cato had received nine bids for the Science Building and could recommend the low bid of $237,000 form Harry B. Friedman of Fort Worth. Ground was broken on October 29, and the University had its second building underway. The construction crew on the half-completed Roy Gustav Cullen Building across the reflection pool worked on throughout the groundbreaking ceremony. They had to have the facility ready for the transfer to the new campus, and the scheduled opening of classes there on June 5, 1939.

Dr. Kemmerer presided as ground was broken for the Science Building, President Oberholtzer having been called away by the death of one of his sisters. Chairman Shepherd was on hand to represent the Board of Education, along with trustees George D. Wilson, Dr. Ray K. Daily, and a most articulate new member of the governing body, Dr. Henry A. Petersen. Captain Ben Taub and Joe Weingarten were among the prominent Houstonians present.

Dr. Kemmerer paraphrased a statement to be engraved later in stone on the Ezekiel W. Cullen Building:

> We rededicate ourselves today to the ideals of education, the only dictator that free men acknowledge. We are grateful to the loyal citizens of Houston who made these buildings possible.

Chairman Shepherd emphasized that the institution, raised to unversity status only four years earlier, had almost tripled its 1934 enrollment, and could now expect a substantially greater influx of students on the new campus.

The University of Houston, then, seemed to have reached a significant new level of present achievement and future potential as it began the academic year of 1938-1939, the last on the old San Jacinto High School campus. Two buildings were underway on the new campus, with a third under at least preliminary consideration. The faculty, now numbering 60, had coalesced into a talented corps of teachers,[46] with an increasingly experienced group of administrators of marked ability and effectiveness.

On another measure, the officers of administration seemed to be reasonably popular with faculty members and students alike, although some of the nicknames and anecdotes attached to them were less flattering.

As noted, the 1934 yearbook, the *Houstonian*, had been rather fulsomely dedicated to Dr. Oberholtzer, and was primarily a selling piece for the new four-year institution. One suspects how much this represented affection and regard for the chief executive, since Dr. Oberholtzer was seldom seen at San Jacinto High School other than at registration periods. The 1935 dedication, however, went to Dean Naason K. Dupre, " . . . because of his faithful service and perseverance in developing our school, and, because we admire and respect him as a man, a dean, and a friend." A year later, Mrs. Pearl C. Bender, former dean of women serving as registrar, was honored as " . . . one . . . characterized by . . . constant cheerfulness; . . . tempered with kind consideration; . . . (in) whom sympathetic understanding is an innate characteristic; . . . one who has made every effort to lighten the burden of the student body." In 1937, the *Houstonian* was dedicated to " . . . the Spirit of the future Great University of Houston," and in 1938, most appropriately, to Mr. and Mrs. Hugh Roy Cullen, "in appreciation of their generous and inspiring gift . . . "

Dr. Kemmerer was honored by the 1939 *Houstonian* with a dedicatory page that President Oberholtzer probably read with raised eyebrows. "In the mind of this man," the plaudit began, "the University of Houston has held first place for years; his dreams were, in no small measure, the beginning from which our Alma Mater has grown . . . His incessant efforts have enabled the school to attain its present heights, and his heartfelt zeal will long serve as a driving force in the continued rise of this university."

The sobriquets hung upon some of the administrators, and the little anecdotes told of them, were both interesting and revealing. President Oberholtzer was "Old Budget" to some of the faculty, especially after he found it necessary to reduce salaries temporarily in the 1935-1936 academic year. He was only Dr. Oberholtzer, or Mr. President to the students, although he sometimes urged them in his infrequent appearances before the student body to "come to see me at any time," or "be certain we get the chance to visit when we meet on campus," or even to "call me Eddie."[47]

Dr. Kemmerer was dubbed "The Dutchman" soon after he became vice-president in 1934, and was thought to like this nickname. It is used to identify him in a picture in the 1939 yearbook, dressed in a natty, vested suit of gray flannel with Phi Beta Kappa key prominently displayed.

Dean Dupre somehow turned up with the nickname of "Death's Head." This was undeserved, but probably related to his sharply-receding hairline and profile, and to his infrequent, thin, and fleeting smile.[48]

Another plus in the 1938-1939 era, as the University prepared to move to its new campus, was the emergence of new leaders, some of them to become well-known citizens of the city and area, within the student body. Among these students were Phillip Allin, J.Q. Baldridge, Josephine Del Barto, Patrick Henry (Pat) Foley, Johnny Goyen, Ed Harris, Foster Montgomery, Stewart Morris, Joe Potter, Bill (then Billy) Roberts, J. Henry Taub and his brother John Ben Taub, and Jack Valenti.

The first alumni were also beginning to make their way: Judge Hofheinz, one of the first of the ex-students to gain a major political office; Congressman-to-be Robert Randolph (Bob) Casey, who was also to hold the county judgeship, and his wife Hazel,[49] Le Roy Melcher, who was to parlay a shipload of peppercorns into the Utotem chain and chairmanship of the great Fairmont Foods conglomerate; and others who emerged early into the spotlight.

There was a final development of consequence on the optimistic side during the 1938-1939 year, as the University prepared to move to its new home. This involved Mr. Cullen and an old friend who had remained an active supporter of the University even though he had left the Board of Education—Colonel Bates. The colonel had been greatly encouraged by the caliber of men and women participating in the 1938 campaign; he was particularly impressed by Hugh Roy Cullen's obvious interest, and decided to call on the oilman as soon as details of the fund drive had been cleaned up in the late summer of 1938.

William B. Bates had learned back in Nat[50] that a man must look ahead. This instinct had brought him to Houston in 1923, and helped constantly to propel him forward in the professional, business, and civic life of his adopted city. As his judgment matured, Colonel Bates became quickly aware that foresight and future planning are even more indispensable to an institution. This awareness was illustrated time and again in his significant roles with the University of Houston, the Texas Medical Center, with what was to become one of the largest law firms in the nation, and with the future Bank of the Southwest.

The subject of his visit to Mr. Cullen, which Colonel Bates recalled vividly even in his eighties, was future planning; specifically, it was the acquisition of two additional tracts of land for the University, to bring total acreage from 110 to the 250 acres that the colonel considered to be the absolute minimum in terms of the projected growth of Houston and the indicated role for the University of Houston.

Colonel Bates proposed that the new Monroe D. Anderson Foundation, which he had helped establish in 1936, and was serving as a trustee, purchase 90 of the 140 acres sought from the Settegast Estate, and then donate it to the University of Houston. In turn, Mr. Cullen would buy up a number of lots, some of them with small residences, along the western boundary of Calhoun Road. The proposed Cullen purchase would add 50 acres.

Hugh Roy Cullen accepted the plan, and the details proceeded expeditiously, since Colonel Bates' law partner John H. Freeman represented the Settegast heirs and the firm was skilled in blocking up small but important tracts such as those Mr. Cullen was being asked to buy and contribute. Early in 1939, the deeds were delivered, and an extremely important forward step had been taken for the University of Houston, increasing its land holdings by 127 percent and obtaining without cost to the institution about two-thirds of the total acreage now constituting the Central Campus. (With his usual discernment, Colonel Bates waited until the University had been formally separated from HISD before presenting the deeds for final acknowledgement and acceptance by the Board of Regents [not the trustees of the School District], almost seven-and-a-half years later, on July 17, 1946.)

Then, just as things seemed to be going well on all fronts, a long-smouldering fire on the Board of Education (whose members also served as a Board of Trustees for the University) burst into flames.

Dr. Oberholtzer, Vice-President Kemmerer recalled in reconstructing events for me many years later, went through four separate phases in his relationships with the trustees and H.L. Mills, the firmly-entrenched business manager, before coming to a decision in the early 1940's. First were the early tests of strength, between 1924 and 1927, when Mr. Mills circled warily while sizing up the new superintendent. Next came a period of relative quiet, and of nascent strength for Dr. Oberholtzer; these were the years from 1927-1935, while Colonel Bates was secretary, and later president, of the Board of Education; there were run-ins with Mr. Mills, and on occasion with individual members of the governing body including Colonel Bates, but no pitched battles.[51]

There was a major shift in the academic year 1936-1937, however, when Judge Norman Atkinson was replaced on the Board of Education by Holger Jeppesen, a tall, physically imposing and articulate Scandinavian who had his own opinions and liked to voice them often. Mr. Jeppesen immediately formed a strong anti-Oberholtzer coalition with Alfred C. Finn and W.C. Ragan. Suddenly, almost every vote of real significance was 4-3, with the pro-Oberholtzer bloc of Mrs. B.F. Coop, Dr. Ray K. Daily, George D. Wilson, and President E. D. Shepherd barely able to win over the Finn-Jeppesen-Ragan triumvirate.

As a result, Dr. Oberholtzer survived so many 4-3 votes between 1936 and early 1940 that he became a surefooted mountain goat, making his way from precipice to precipice, but often with loose rocks, or even a shifting glacier field, underfoot. Even before the move to the new campus, in June, 1939, it was apparent that a final phase had opened. Edison Ellsworth Oberholtzer's days in the dual position of superintendent of schools and president of the University of Houston were numbered, even though how and when the resolution was to come would remain unclear for a time.

The chronic irritation became acute in the summer of 1938, when H.J. Antoine of the West End Improvement Club began to appear at Board of Education meetings as an obviously interested spectator, and sometime speaker. On October 28, Mr. Antoine issued a statement on behalf of 22 civic clubs, protesting high absenteeism, poor maintenance of physical property, and the lack of free lunches in the HISD. The absenteeism, the statement claimed, could be traced to the use of HISD teachers as faculty members at the University of Houston, thus preventing them from doing a good job as public school instructors, and disrupting classroom discipline. There was a further complaint about the "costly" tuition rates at the University, which had been pegged for years at $150 for the two long semesters, the rate decided upon at the very beginning in 1927.[52]

It is significant that President Oberholtzer, in replying to Mr. Antoine, did not even mention the $150 tuition rate. Nor did he respond to charges of a high level of absenteeism (which he regarded as a problem for the parents of the student, not for the school system) or allegations of poor maintenance of physical property. The latter really fell on H.L. Mills' side of the fence, and that crusty old curmudgeon was perfectly capable of defending himself, if he condescended to do so.

"The progress of the public school system since 1924," he told his critics in more general terms, "speaks for itself." Regarding free lunches, "The Community Chest maintains a fund to provide these for needy students." There was still no hue and cry for free breakfasts, although this issue would develop in time.

President Oberholtzer then spoke to what would become a central problem: "Public school faculty members," he asserted, "teach at the University of Houston only on a part-time basis. They are assigned to extra sections where enrollment is not large enough to justify a full-time instructor." This was part of an established, and laudable, practice of limiting the maximum number of students in most classes to 30. And it was how the

HJC, and then the University, acquired some excellent teachers; simultaneously, the quality of instruction was improved through smaller class sections, costs remained low, and HISD faculty members had access to at least some added income.

The attack from H.J. Antoine and friends subsided, but sniping continued from less concentrated positions within the community, and increased steadily in intensity within the Board of Education itself. One curious aspect of all this was how criticism was always leveled against President Oberholtzer, Dr. Kemmerer, and their supporters within the governing body. There was, in contrast, often praise for members of the anti-Oberholtzer bloc, and specifically for Holger Jeppesen. One might suspect that some variety of campaign, deliberately planned and directed, was underway.

Mr. Jeppesen began to criticize President Oberholtzer on a wide range of matters, varying from the piddling to the obviously important. "Why," he questioned, "is Dr. Oberholtzer always chairman of the High School Athletic Association, and of the Luncheon Committee, instead of having a trustee in these posts?" Dr. Oberholtzer, the plain-spoken Hoosier, countered, "Board of Education members have no business in these (administrative) assignments. You might just as well have the members selecting teachers." Mr. Jeppesen replied, "That's not such a bad idea, either; but to return to the matter at hand, why are you the perpetual chairman of these committees?" Dr. Oberholtzer, puzzled said, "Perpetual?" There's nothing perpetual about it; I'm elected each year." Mr. Jeppesen pressed on, "Well, perennial, then."

On matters of far more consequence, Mr. Jeppesen could also be a nonconstructive gadfly. He charged that the Board of Education had met "secretly" to pass "an illegal, improper" motion authorizing an application for a $400,000 grant ($220,000 from the Reconstruction Finance Corporation and $180,000 from the Public Works Administration) with which to construct a heating and cooling plant on the new campus. Investigation showed that the motion, opposed by Mr. Jeppesen, was passed quite legally during his absence from the city, but had to be rushed through because of an impending deadline.

After the Board of Education had thoroughly inspected the new Roy Gustav Cullen Building, including the newly designed seal of the University as a special addition on the first floor,[53] President Oberholtzer patiently answered many questions and finally asked for approval and acceptance of the structure, since only a few weeks remained until the actual move from San Jacinto High School. Mr. Jeppesen's retort was, "This is an inspection trip, not an official meeting." As a result, there was another delay, this of almost two weeks, before even the preliminaries of the complex move could begin.

In April of 1939 things seemed to be back on an even keel as the University prepared to leave the San Jacinto High School campus that had been home for its first dozen years. The Roy Gustav Cullen Building was routinely approved and accepted for occupancy, after the addition of a $5,000 cooling tower for the air conditioning system, and contracts were let on an $80,000 Power House.

At the April 30 meeting of the Board of Education, President Oberholtzer was finally given approval for graduate work, beginning with the master's degree in education. This came after a long and sometimes acrimonious discussion, during which Dr. Oberholtzer revealed that 307 HISD teachers had already been approved for graduate study. Further, "we could have enrolled 600." Mr. Jeppesen pointed out that since the master's degree automatically adds $100 annually to an HISD teacher's salary for the remainder of his or her career with the district, "it's like a dog eating his tail." He explained, somewhat inaccurately and with disregard for some of the less tangible values involved, "We get $100 tuition out of them, one time; and then we pay them $100 more a year, for the rest of the time they're with us."

The Oberholtzer-Kemmerer team found suddenly that April's calm was a short-lived phenomenon. Indeed, a most unusual new member of the Board of Education had been working quietly for months on an explosive report that would have lasting effects upon the University of Houston, and to a lesser extent upon President Oberholtzer and Dr. Kemmerer.

The new trustee was Dr. Henry A. Petersen, an elegant and brilliant surgeon who had gone from the University of Maine to Oxford (as a Rhodes Scholar), and then to Johns Hopkins,[54] for training as a physician and surgeon. The report was by the Committe on Rules and Regulations, and it was approved by the Board of Education on May 5, 1939 with little or no warning, although one must wonder in retrospect if President Oberholtzer, almost never caught by surprise, did not know about the report in advance, and perhaps even welcomed it.

The immediate, and ostensibly major, effect of the report was to abolish the office of vice-president of the University, and to remove Dr. Kemmerer to a new position of director of curriculum and comptroller. President Oberholtzer was specifically assigned authority over the dean of the University, the registrar, the faculty, and the student body. Dr. Kemmerer, together with the auditor, book store operators, accountant, purchasing agent, and the heads of the maintenance and operations departments, was to report directly to business manager H.L. Mills.

To anyone even roughly familiar with the long struggle for power between Dr. Oberholtzer and H.L. Mills, and the classic examples of dual authority that it had engendered and sustained, this reorganization was immediately suspect. The suspicion was confirmed when you read on into a list of certain duties of Dr. Kemmerer, which one might think were in large measure the responsibilities of President Oberholtzer—or of Business Manager Mills. Dr. Kemmerer, for example, would "assign specific duties to the faculty in curriculum matters, direct any necessary studies pertaining to a revision of the University curriculum, and manage all funds."

The Houston *Press* surmised that Dr. Kemmerer's vice-presidency was abolished "largely because the trustees (of the Board of Education) felt that this post carried too much authority." President Oberholtzer was criticized "for turning his power over to the vice-president and acting . . . merely as a representative of the college on public occasions."[55]

The *Press* also carried a statement from Holger Jeppesen, who was always good copy, on his interpretation of the May 5, 1939, reorganization. After a few gratuitous blasts at both members of what he sometimes referred to as the "Oberholtzer-Kemmerer axis," he said that the plan was primarily "a new setup that will make it possible for us to divide up University affairs and public school affairs." One understood "affairs" to mean "business," of course, in that innocent era before leaders of the United States Congress began keeping strippers and highly paid "secretaries" as mistresses.

Mr. Jeppesen was a realist. He knew that the true organizational pattern is that mandated by the principal figures within the organization at any given time. Call Walter W. Kemmerer what you like, executive vice-president, vice-president, or director of curriculum and comptroller; he would still function as the number two, or even the number one-and-a-half man at the University. The remainder of the featured cast also included some well-known performers: Dr. Oberholtzer, H.L. Mills, Dean Dupre, and Charles F. Hiller as a key understudy, currently assigned as registrar. What the institution was probably moving toward, at least unofficially, was some variety of an executive committee, with decreasing input and direction from the Board of Education (a body plagued with its own public school system problems), or an internal executive committee under the control of a powerful advisory board of leading citizens, named and approved by the Board of Education.

The latter plan had already occurred to a number of people, including Colonel Bates. He was well enough established now in his new legal, philanthropic foundation, and banking responsibilities to yearn for more demanding civic assignments. The campaign of 1938 had brought him into contact with the University at the community support level of Hugh Roy Cullen, and had renewed his friendship with President Oberholtzer, at the operational level. Now, he reentered the picture, at a critical juncture. After some preliminary conversations with Dr. Oberholtzer, Colonel Bates broached the idea of an advisory board to Hugh Roy Cullen and to E.D. Shepherd; it found favor in both quarters.

President Shepherd told him not to worry about either Holger Jeppesen or Dr. Petersen, intimating that both were well aware of the primary need to split the University off from the public school system, and the sooner the better—perhaps a year or two after Dr. Oberholtzer and his people had settled in at the new campus. Mr. Mills, it was suggested, could be a problem; but the business manager's first loyalties lay with the public school system, which he knew had been made to give increasing support to the University of Houston. If ever there came a choice between the fiscal health of the schools (beset with their own budgetary difficulties), and the satisfaction of also being a central figure in the power structure of the University, it was fairly clear what H.L. Mills would do.[56]

He had been running HISD for years before anyone ever heard of the University of Houston, and he planned to do so until they put him six feet under, even though that fellow Oberholtzer could be a problem from time to time.

It was clear to Colonel Bates, as early as the spring of 1939, that the idea of an advisory board was a viable one, even though it was perceived quite differently in various quarters. His good East Texas intuition, and common sense, told him also that acceptance was essentially a matter of time, of waiting until the idea could gain enough strength to take hold. He decided, as a final preliminary step, to discuss the plan, separately, with both President Oberholtzer and with Dr. Kemmerer. This was done cautiously, in terms of a beginning concept rather than anything resembling a definite plan; the colonel knew a tangled pathway when he saw one. And he sensed something in the relationship between these two men that he did not fully comprehend.

Was it the beginning of competition for the top position at the University of Houston? Of incipient philosophical and professional differences? Or was it an ambitious yet compassionate younger man, anxious to protect his older and respected colleague but concerned also for the future of the institution they both served and loved, at a crucial stage in its development?

These questions would be unresolved to any real degree for more than a decade, and Dr. Kemmerer himself would have to strip the final cover from them, almost 25 years after he had left the University.

The real, and rapidly emerging, issue of separating the University of Houston from the public school system dominated Board of Education meetings for a time after the reorganization of May 5, 1939. There were several reasons for this: a growing realization of the wisdom of such a policy from various standpoints; the impending move from San Jacinto High School, with its implications in terms of an ideal time for at least beginning severance; the dangers of expanding inroads into public school finances by a University growing by leaps and bounds; and the indications of high-level community support for some variety of separation.

The articulate Mr. Jeppesen, obviously armed with data supplied by H.L. Mills, pointed out during the meeting of May 8 that 17 members of the University of Houston staff "are now drawing most of their salary from the Board of Education, but they devote most of their time to the University." He added, "I just think we need full-time people at the University. There's too much division of time now."

Dr. Oberholtzer countered, "Are we going to be like the man who bought two stoves to save 100 percent on his fuel bill, when he found one of them would save 50 percent?" (Laughter). Mr. Jeppesen replied, "Well, I'll just say that the students in the public schools are freezing to death from an educational standpoint."

Mr. Mills added, "The University of Houston is simply getting too big to be handled by part-time people. You have to have full-time employees out there." Then, curiously, the business manager provided some fiscal projections that were alarming, but substantially incorrect.

After reminding the Board of Education and assembled media representatives that the University of Houston paid only $250 a month for light, heat, and janitorial service (there was no air conditioning at old San Jacinto High School), Mr. Mills claimed that the institution would have only an estimated $140,000 in 1939-1940 income from tuition and fees with which to operate an entire year on the new campus. This, he continued, would have to cover about $130,000 in salaries, with only some $10,000 remaining for utilities, janitorial service, other maintenance, and the additional costs of keeping up the new 110-acre location.

The headlines in the *Chronicle* the next day read:

University As Separate Unit Is Discussed
School Board Plans Full-Time Administration And Faculty
Slim Budget Is Problem

Actually, HISD minutes show that general educational and general income for fiscal 1939-1940 at the University of Houston was not $140,000, but the tidy sum of $296,646, leaving a surplus of $100,091 after expenses of $196,555. Mr. Mills, ever the conservative, probably had no idea that 1939-1940 enrollment would climb so substantially to 2,067 or 504 students more than the 1,563 of the previous year.

The business manager's big mistake in that spring of 1939, however, was his apparent belief that a formal separation of the University from the public school system was imminent. Lasting changes in the governance and control of the institution were underway, thanks to Colonel Bates and others, but it would be

March 12, 1945, before a complete and legal severance was effected. And President Oberholtzer would still be skating along on the thin ice of 4-3 decisions by the Board of Education for several years to come, even dropping to a 3-3 stand-off after the resignation of his long-time friend and supporter, Mrs. B.F. Coop, to accept a position from H.L. Mills. That is another story, however. After a few more tense meetings in the spring of 1939, attention shifted to the dedication of the Roy Gustav Cullen Building, on June 4, 1939, and the opening of the first classes on the new campus, on Monday, June 5, 1939.

Dr. F.B. Thorn, pastor of the Second Baptist Church who had provided the University with a quite temporary home for its first day classes, was the speaker at the dedicatory ceremonies for the Roy Gustav Cullen Building, which attracted an audience of several thousand. Many of those at the dedication had to have their automobiles hauled out of various mudholes by Stephen P. Sakach, landscape architect and grounds superintendent, and the dry-cleaning establishments of the town had a field day refurbishing the long mid-calf-length frocks that were in fashion for lady guests. There was plenty of wet clay and blue gumbo mud between parking areas and the new facility, after a three-inch rain on the preceding Friday that made it necessary to shift the fifth commencement exercises from the Roy Gustav Cullen Building back to San Jacinto High School.[57]

Dr. Thorn spoke at some length, as was appropriate, of Roy Gustav Cullen. He quoted from a Houston *Post* editorial of May 20, 1936, that seemed to catch the spirit of this quiet, hard-working young man of great potential who died at the age of 31: "Roy G. Cullen was a young man but he had made his mark in the oil industry when death cut short a career that promised to be both useful and brilliant. . . . Young Cullen's life was singularly free from the antics and escapades which keep the names of so many American sons of wealth constantly on the front pages. He was . . . hard working. . . . He preferred earning his way . . . to a life of ease. . . . He was a genial man of simple tastes, blessed with a personality that won him many staunch friends."

The Reverend Dr. Thorn also reminded his audience of a significant statement that Hugh Roy Cullen had made when he handed over his contribution of $260,000 (later increased to $335,000) for the construction of the memorial to his only son: "I have only one condition in making this gift. The University of Houston must always be a college for working men and women and their sons and daughters. If it were to be another rich man's college, I wouldn't be interested."

Some of the guests at the dedication went to the wrong building. This happy mistake came about because the Science Building, directly across from the memorial to Roy Gustav Cullen, was also complete. It had been built in a record time of exactly eight months and one week from the award of the contract to Harry B. Friedman, and was formally accepted on June 12, 1939.[58] Nor was this $237,000 structure, still in heavy use today, anything resembling a jerry-built proposition. It contained 14 large, fully-equipped laboratories plus six classrooms and two lecture halls on two floors. The building, also of native Texas limestone (actually a shellstone, with intriguing patterns left by crustacea millions of years before), had aluminum window frames and chromium trim, to match the Roy Gustav Cullen Building across the reflection pool from it.

Either Harry B. Friedman, the general contractor, had discovered some new secret of motivating his workers, or they were simply very productive men. One theory was that they were aware of a $553,284 federal grant to expand campus utilities, and wanted employment on the new project. Whatever, it would probably take a year today to duplicate the Science Building, even with major improvements in technology.

The "Roy Cullen," as it quickly came to be known, swarmed with summer school enrollees the day after it was dedicated. The first summer semester began immediately, and extended through July 17; a second session ran from July 19 through August 25. The building had 21 classrooms, a "temporary" library plus two stack rooms, a large lecture hall and a three-room administrative suite, about half of which was a presidential office for Dr. Oberholtzer. Typically, the 40 "non-science" members of the faculty were packed into two offices; there were, however student lounges on both floors.

The architects had included some little touches which meant a great deal to the University community, after 12 years as a squatter on someone else's property: a beautiful red tile roof worthy of Cuernavaca, or Positano;[59] a public address system; acoustical ceilings; Venetian blinds; polished stone interior decorations; and *mirabile dictu,* air conditioning.

In the lobby was an oil painting of Roy Gustav Cullen, not at all distinguished but a fair likeness, by one Josef de Sigall; on the outside walls were the words of Mirabeau B. Lamar:

> A cultivated mind is the guardian genius of democracy. It is the only dictator that free men acknowledge, and the only security that free men desire.[60]

Roy Gustav Cullen's great-grandfather, Ezekiel Wimberly Cullen, had been Lamar's floor leader in the Third Congress of the Republic of Texas, in 1838-1839, and was a teller in the election in which General Lamar was chosen president. It was a fortunate coincidence that the Roy Gustav Cullen Building was dedicated exactly one hundred years after Ezekiel W. Cullen presented his historic report establishing a system of free schools in the Republic. His report, as chairman of the Committee on Education, became the basis of the Cullen Act, a bill "to appropriate certain lands for the purpose of establishing a general system of Education." (See Appendix)

Hugh Roy Cullen noted the coincidence between 1939 and the dedication of the memorial to his son, and 1839, when his grandfather in effect became the "Knight Errant of Education" in Texas, as one writer identified him. This was to become a powerful impetus toward the contribution of the Ezekiel W. Cullen Building, and many millions of dollars to the University of Houston by Hugh Roy and Lillie Cranz Cullen.

Edison Ellsworth Oberholtzer, as a perennial watchdog of the cash box, was on the new campus counting receipts the evening of June 5, 1939. It must have been an especially sastisfying experience, together in his just completed office with Dr. Kemmerer; Charlie Hiller (who now held the title of bursar); and Robert A. White, soon to be named auditor. (Dean Dupre was busy "troubleshooting," as usual).

Registration for the first summer session, stimulated by new graduate offerings and, some said, by the novelty and attraction of air conditioning, was running above expectations. The Roy Gustav Cullen Building, short by eight classrooms though it might be, was handsome and functional. Across the way, he could see workmen completing final details inside the Science Building, which no one had really expected to have ready so soon. And progress was already evident on the major expansion of utilities centering upon the Power House (he must remember to thank Jesse H. Jones, as head of the Reconstruction Finance Corporation, for his help in obtaining federal assistance for this project).

Everyone on the faculty and staff was hard at work on the fall semester, which looked so promising. With a new total of 334 courses to be available, the dedicated teaching corps had been meeting with prospective students since January, in a series of "career-planning conferences" scheduled from 8:00 to 9:30 p.m. at San Jacinto High School.[61] Even though few of them were on the summer school payroll, many faculty members were spending a good bit of time on the new campus, familiarizing themselves with it.

With many of his friends and colleagues, particularly Dr. Kemmerer, Dean Dupre, Charlie Hiller, Leon Halden, Joe Werlin, and Jules Vern, President Oberholtzer was aware of the growing crisis throughout Europe and, to a lesser degree, of the bloody battles being waged between the Japanese and the Soviets and Mongol irregulars in Manchukuo. But he could not know that Adolf Hitler would invade Poland; that Great Britain and France would declare war against Germany on the same late summer day (September 3, 1939); and that Franklin Delano Roosevelt would proclaim a limited national emergency—all before the fall semester began on Wednesday, September 20, 1939.

The University of Houston had found safe harbor on its new campus, and had thereby completed the first major era in its history; but the next decade, to 1950, was opening with the prospect of fresh, perhaps alarming, challenges.

Notes to Chapter Three

[1]Jubal R. Parten, one of the more interesting, knowledgable and valuable Texans of our time, once told me how he handled the problem of introducing Dr. Hutchins in a few seconds, on a crowded, over-long banquet program, to a somewhat stodgy audience. Knowing that Dr. Hutchins would prefer a brief introduction, yet faced with a lengthy canned biography (including 23 earned and honorary degrees) prepared by some earnest and hard-working publicist, he

thought of Dr. Hutchins' justified reputation as an iconoclast of remarkable ability and memory. The solution: "Ladies and gentlemen, our speaker and my friend, the Great Boobshocker, Bob Hutchins."

[2]Dr. Hiller was to begin a career of almost 40 years with the University in the fall of 1935. Much more of him later.

[3]Dr. Kemmerer once told a reporter that his father was a 'baker's dozen' Dutchman who believed in giving 13 for 12.

[4]At the same time that Dr. Kemmerer was guiding his friend through the statistical forest, another graduate student at Columbia University, Charles F. McElhinney (long-time vice president and business manager and acting president of the University of Houston from 1953-1954) was tutoring yet another graduate student, E.E. Oberholtzer, in statistics at Morningside Heights. The University of Houston owes a great deal to statistical science, Columbia University, chance, or all three, since Dr. Oberholtzer found his two principal assistants while they were paying some of their expenses at Teachers' College with a little tutoring in statistics on the side.

[5]Dr. Oberholtzer was once discussing alternative proposals for the possible administrative reorganization of the University of Houston with C.F. McElhinney, who mentioned the significant role usually accorded deans. "Deans," Dr. Oberholtzer snorted with disgust, "I don't want any deans; they'll figure they're running things. That faculty rank business can cause a lot of problems, too." Mr. McElhinney explained to me that "Dr. Oberholtzer ran a tight ship; his idea of delegating authority was to delegate only to the very minimum degree—just so *you* knew that *he* knew that you were alive!"

[6]See the Appendix for the text of this resolution, in which HJC was first formally designated the University of Houston.

[7]Some now-prominent alumni used to pay Charlie Hiller (who received an additional salary of $25 per month as bursar) two dollars a week on account, when he could catch them.

[8]The supporting data are quite remarkable:

Year	*Total Income*	*Total Expense*	*Profit (Deficit)*
1927-1928	$33,424.00	$36,336.88	($2,962.88)
1928-1929	43,697.25	37,919.90	5,777.35
1929-1930	47,705.91	45,883.97	1,821.94
1930-1931	66,206.35	47,672.13	18,634.22
1931-1932	64,556.66	45,031.79	19,524.87
1932-1933	54,006.15	48,943.61	5,122.54
1933-1934	50,412.37	47,460.77	2,951.60

[9]Dr. Oberholtzer told a meeting at the First Methodist Church in June 1924 that Mrs. Oberholtzer was the daughter of a Baptist preacher, and he a Methodist. Before they were married, however, it was

agreed that the stronger of the two would go with the weaker to his church. Thus Mrs. Oberholtzer came to join her young husband in the tenets of John Wesley.

[10]Dr. Kemmerer always regarded himself as chief operating officer of the University of Houston, from the time that he was named vice-president in 1934, until Dr. Oberholtzer assumed the full-time presidency on April 1, 1945. In 1952, at the request of Mr. Cullen, he wrote Colonel Bates a summary of "my part in the building of the University of Houston as an evaluation of my fitness for the position of top leadership." The summary states in plain English "When the University of Houston was founded in 1934, I was made the vice-president and the chief operating executive of the university." While this would be difficult to maintain solely on the basis of the minutes of the Board of Education, Dr. Kemmerer was certainly perceived as the *de facto* "chief operating executive," and functioned as such.

[11]Charlie Hiller says that some 1935-1936 contracts were reduced 10 percent from the previous year, but with an informal understanding that the cut would be made up "if the income picture perked up." The Hiller contract was for $2,000, he recalls; but the Forum Cafeteria sold a cut of Kansas City roast prime ribs in those days for 21 cents, with two vegetables thrown in; Levy Brothers offered a suit, topcoat or overcoat at $14.80 each; and the list price for a Cadillac was $1,495 (but they could be bought for $1,300 from L.R. Willis' gentleman salesmen, by anyone with minimal bargaining ability).

[12]Mr. Shepherd, a pioneer insurance executive who opened his own agency here in 1904, served almost 20 years on the Board of Education, most of the time as president or vice-president. He was alert and active until his death at the age of 91, in 1967. His son and namesake, E. Dale Shepherd, Jr., recalls his father's detailed knowledge of HISD affairs, and his dedicated and effective work (often in concert with Colonel Bates) on behalf of the public schools and of the young University of Houston.

[13]Dr. Johnson, who earned the first Ph.D. in chemistry awarded by The Rice Institute, owned and operated The Gables, a traditional drug store hangout for both University of Houston and Rice students in the 1920's and early 1930's. He was business manager of athletics at Rice in a time of legendary success for the Owls in football, basketball, and track (earning the undeserved sobriquet of "Red Dog" from the student body for having placed its members on the sunny side of Old Rice Stadium), and then served for many years as a senior vice-president of Sakowitz and distinguished civic leader.

[14]Judge Roy Hofheinz and other student leaders at HJC and in the early days of the University invariably characterized Dean Dupre as "tough but fair." The dean understood instinctively that student marches were capable of prejudicing almost any cause. A battle-

scarred veteran of the Texas Legislature told me once how students at the University of Texas were instrumental in having their tuition raised from $25 to $50 a semester. The legislator watched students march up Congress Avenue and on into a committee room at the Capitol. As they did he spotted a young demonstrator from a prominent family in his district. When the hearing was well underway, with some emphasis upon the great burden that $25 more a semester would represent for students, he greeted the hometown constituent and requested permission to ask him a question. "Tell me, Bob," he said, "did you march over from The Drag with your friends, or drive over in that new red convertible that your mama gave you for Christmas?" The young student was embarrassed no end, but honest enough to reply that he had "driven to the Pi Phi house to get his girl friend, but walked the rest of the way." The hearing broke up shortly thereafter, and $50 a semester tuition was in effect "before the cotton gins shut down."

[15]Henry J.N. Taub once took me to a working ranch the family owned along Chocolate Bayou Road, wholly within the city limits. He wanted to show me a fine Arabian stallion he proposed to cross with one of the huge magnificent jumpers you see at the Dublin Horse Show, if I could find an especially fine mare. Knowing nothing about horses, but something about Dublin and the fascinating people who frequent the Horse Show, I located what outside counsel pronounced a marvelous animal, after an unbelievable two days centering on the Churchill Bar in the Shelburne Hotel and the competition for the Aga Khan Cup (which the United States lost to Italy on the final water hazard). After making a temporary deal with a renowned horse trader in Stillorgan, however, it fell through over the technicalities of quarantines, shipping rates, and the bargaining skills of Irish horse traders, some of whom are at best half-tinker (Gypsy).

[16]Willie Sutton, the legendary bank robber, was brought before a somewhat philosophical judge for sentencing—for the third time. "Tell me," said the jurist, peering down from above, "why do you keep robbing banks?" "Why, Your Honor," Willie replied with some surprise, "banks is where the money is."

[17]Fifteen solid blocks of downtown's principal business area south of Buffalo Bayou were inundated by this terrible flood, which followed a week of incessant rains triggered by a monster wet norther on December 3, 1935. Two-thirds of Harris County was also under water, seven persons died, the National Guard had to be called out, and it was eight months before silt from the bayous could be completely removed from the Ship Channel. The disaster brought lasting relief, however; from it came the impetus for the development of a long-range, county-wide program of flood control. The first phase, straightening out a dangerous bottleneck in Buffalo Bayou just

north of the present Civic Center, began in October 1936. And the Navigation District, ever alert to opportunity, combined the desilting of the Ship Channel with a project to deepen the waterway to a new record level of 34 feet.

[18]Of the faculty and staff, Mrs. Bessie Ebaugh knew many of the leading families, as did Miss Ruth Pennybacker, who was a houseguest of Governor and Mrs. William Pettus Hobby when she first came from Austin to join the faculty in 1935.

[19]No one was able to obtain the 60 percent or so of controlling stock in the Second National Bank from Mrs. Neal after her husband's untimely death a few years later. Colonel Bates, however, had become chairman of the board of the San Jacinto National Bank through a recommendation by his friend Ben Clayton; was interested in the Second National; and was able to obtain options on the Neal stock after long conferences with Randolph Bryan, whom he had known in law school at the University of Texas and as a fellow officer in World War I. The Colonel sold the stock represented by the options to the M.D. Anderson Foundation, Ben Clayton, H.R. Cullen, and a syndicate headed by Glenn McCarthy, the legendary oilman, in his palmier days—after keeping a small percentage to himself. Next, he merged the San Jacinto National into the Second National with himself as chairman of the board and Mr. Bryan as president. The final steps came when Colonel Bates sold the relatively new San Jacinto National Bank Building as part of the site for Foley's Department Store, purchased another location from realtor Ernest Hester (on a handshake, Colonel Bates told me, "reinforced later by well-drawn deeds") and the Esperson Estate. He also broke local tradition for the first time by placing a major bank, the Second National renamed the Bank of the Southwest, off Main Street. All of these complex negotiations, particularly in terms of the ascending influence they gave Colonel Bates, and the opportunity they provided for him to know Mr. Cullen better, were to have an important bearing on the future development of the University of Houston.

[20]W.A. Kirkland, who was closely associated with him for years on the Board of Education, remembers Dr. Oberholtzer as an extremely capable and effective person, enormously blessed with common sense, "but difficult to recognize as a member of the company of scholars, somehow unlettered."

[21]The *Chronicle*, for example, carried annually until 1942 a full page of photographs of the Rice Institute Archi-Arts Ball that the newspaper's Prince Charming, Chief Photographer Jess Gibson and his staff had snapped the evening before at this event, which would be hard-pressed today to merit even a two-column, single picture. One of my indelible memories of the *Chronicle* (where I, as campus correspondent at Rice, may have learned as much as I did at the old In-

stitute itself) is being summoned downtown to discuss the crucial matter of Archi-Arts coverage. In the old city room, where Emmet Walter held sway, drawing endless triangles within circles between bellowed summonses to the talented but unpredictable stable of reporters, I was met by my new boss, Stewart Hatch. He had been given the post of school and church editor after an urgent telephone call from his father, United States Senator Carl Hatch of New Mexico, to none other than Jesse H. Jones. He greeted me cordially, and we went immediately to the crowded office of the septuagenarian society editor, Belle Costello.

Mrs. Costello (nee Donna Belle Murray) was a delightful lady of some 75 summers who had taken her baccalaureate at Albion, the excellent little college in southern Michigan, in 1890. As our conference with her began, Mr. Hatch reached inside his coat, pulled out a half-pint of Crab Orchard, delicately wiped the opened top with a clean handkerchief, and handed it to the society editor. Mrs. Costello nodded her thanks, swallowed a good two-finger jolt without missing a word in her orders on how to cover the ball, dabbed at her lips with an elegant little wisp of a handkerchief and handed the Crab Orchard back. I said nothing, of course, then or later, but my education outside the classroom was progressing.

[22]Henry Rockwell, the long-time Houstonian who often discovered and financed such projects for his city, rescued these columns when the original Miller Theater was pulled down. He had them rearranged around a graceful fountain at the northern entrance to Hermann Park, in what is surely one of the more pleasing monuments to thoughtfulness and good taste in the town.

[23]The University of Pittsburgh awarded Mr. Cullen an honorary doctor of science degree in 1936, for his success in drilling through the "heaving shale" in the old Humble oil field to find new levels of production. This drew the immediate approval of the coffee drinkers at Harry Short's Esperson Drug Store, the center for "Oil Patch" intelligence up and down the Gulf Coast, who considered "H.R." to be "a natural genius" in geology. Both Mr. and Mrs. Cullen were given honorary doctorates of law at the May 30, 1938, commencement ceremonies of the University of Houston.

[24]Ora D. Brown, the first president of what was then termed the Ex-Students Association, went to a recalcitrant member of City Council a year or two later, and asked him to vote for a resolution to change the name of St. Bernard Street to Cullen Boulevard. The councilman said that he was opposed to such changes, "besides," he added, "what did this fellow Cullen ever do for me?" "Well," Brown replied, "what did St. Bernard ever do for you?"

[25]The *Post* editorial, quoted for years, became a prime source for speeches and brochures regarding the University. It went on at

length, but here are some of the more salient points the editorial made: "That (the provision of an educational opportunity not otherwise available) is the great advantage the University of Houston enjoys over conventional colleges and universities. Its principal objective is the dissemination of useful knowledge, rather than the handing out of sheepskin degrees. It does not neglect the arts and sciences, but opens its doors to any person with a desire to learn.

"It is an institution dedicated to the people of the community, specializing in preparing its students for greater earning opportunities and in providing vocational and technical guidance that can be converted into dollars and cents. If more such institutions were in existence, there would be less unemployment, less poverty and less need for government relief.

"The older, formal university has a place in the American scheme of education, of course, but there is a definite need in an intensely practical age for the practical instruction being made available by the University of Houston and similar institutions elsewhere."

The editorial had its uses in 1937, and for years thereafter; but there would come a day when its themes had to be subdued and its praises of practicality in higher education tempered.

[26]Charles F. McElhinney worked closely with both men over a long period of years, and was in a strategic position from which to observe them and their interrelationships with one another and with other key members of the growing University "family" as well as community leaders. He was probably among the first to note what an effective team they made in spite of their differences; knew as much as anyone about their eventual struggle for power; and was Dr. Kemmerer's personal choice (as well as that of the Board of Regents) to become chief executive when Dr. Kemmerer was summarily fired and removed from the presidency in 1953 in what was long alleged to be a "resignation."

In a memorable speech to the faculty on February 5, 1965 Vice-President McElhinney recalled Dr. Oberholtzer, "a considerable paradox . . . capable of remarkable faith and vision, (but) nevertheless incapable of effective delegation of authority . . . frugal in his personal life (and) even more so in his educational administration" and "his extremely capable but often frustrated assistant, Dr. Kemmerer." "Together," he reminisced, "they worked and fought, sometimes with each other, to keep the University abreast of community needs. Kemmerer was the urger, the promoter. Oberholtzer was the brake. Together they made a remarkably effective team."

[27]HISD had Mirabeau B. Lamar High School under construction at the time, after a considerable delay while the value of the four-acre site on Westheimer Road at River Oaks Boulevard was debated. E.L. Crain, Sr., well-known realtor, was named arbitrator, and he ruled

that the price should be $8,000 (which H.L. Mills was willing to pay) rather than the $10,000 or $2,500 per acre which the sellers insisted the tract was worth. Prices in the area have escalated somewhat since 1937.

[28]A Houston matron, entranced by the splendid accomodations of the Broadmoor Hotel and by what she felt was the very elegance of the name, decided to rechristen her Tall Timbers mansion "Broadmoor," and directed her architect to have enormous new gates prepared for the winding front entrance, with "Broadmoor" prominently displayed on them in wrought iron. The architect was fortunately an erstwhile scholar of Elizabethan England, and a man of honor. He was obliged to tell his client that the original Broadmoor was a well-known asylum for criminal lunatics in Berkshire, even more infamous than Bedlam, the sixteenth century madhouse of St. Mary Hospital in Bethlehem.

[29]Actually, Hugh Roy Cullen, born July 3, 1881, had only 10 months on "Young Man" Oberholtzer, who was born May 6, 1882. And at 55, the graying Dr. Oberholtzer, already beginning to stoop slightly and blinking behind his rimless glasses, looked older than Mr. Cullen.

[30]Mr. Jones' acceptance of the honorary chairmanship, although it involved little active participation, was of considerable significance. He had taken few such assignments in the years since removing to Washington, D.C. as head of the Reconstruction Finance Corporation (RFC); also, he and Mr. Cullen had not always seen eye to eye on matters local or national.

[31]Downtown Rotary has a unique tie with higher education in the form of prized scholarships awarded for decades by the Club. Jack Harris said that the scholarships began on a long train trip to a Rotary International meeting in Mexico City. Someone started a crap game with a pretty hefty pot, which went on for days. The Most Reverend Clinton S. (Mike) Quin, irrepressible Bishop of Texas, was an interested spectator from time to time as the Mexican countryside rolled by. When the pot reached a new high, he halted play a moment, dove in, removed around 10 percent and announced that this was a "scholarship tithe." By the time the Rotarians got back to Houston, there was enough in the Bishop's poke to establish a scholarship fund, since Mike Quin came around not once but most hours on the hour.

[32]This was a high-level "booster" group. Organized specifically to help with the forthcoming drive, many of its members became quite interested in the University, and continued to serve and to assist it after the Association became inactive.

[33]There were rumors for years that Mr. Cullen was going to buy the packing plant site, later acquired from J.D. and Robert Sartwelle as a major expansion of the University of Houston campus across what

is now a six-lane Calhoun Boulevard. I asked Mr. J.W. Sartwelle once, as we walked to a meeting iin the Texas Medical Center, why the sale to Mr. Cullen had never gone through. He straightened his Stetson as we strode along, loosed a mighty cud of Beech-Nut, and thought a minute. "Simple," he said, "never made me no offer on my prappity . . . .Good man, but no offer . . . .Like some of those fellers perched on the fence at the calf auction, lot of looking, but no action."

[34]The window washer, Thomas J. Keating, was a hard-working and especially popular civil engineering student. He told in the Kirkham article of a narrow escape when a safety belt slipped far above Main Street. Several months later, he died instantly when a defective bolt snapped and he fell to the street from the twelfth floor of the Medical Arts Building.

[35]In the 1930s and before, aside from building campaigns aimed at the members of a church, raffles, the Community Chest, the Red Cross, Salvation Army Christmas kettles, and an infrequent drive by a hospital, there was relatively little organized fund-raising here. W. Stewart Boyle told me that when a downtown group heard that Rice Institute, its income then deriving principally from three percent bonds and three-and-a-half percent mortgages, might need some financial help, Chairman (Captain) James A. Baker and others of the trustees were invited to a luncheon. The purpose of the meeting was never too clear, but Captain Baker gathered somehow that these were well-meaning folk attempting to be helpful in some manner. He expressed his appreciation for the luncheon in brief remarks after dessert, but told his hosts in a gentlemanly, tactful, and yet plain fashion, that the Institute had made it on its own thus far, and figured to continue to do so.

Today, there are literally dozens of worthy fund-raising projects in the city, where the staggering amount of almost 150 benefit or testimonial dinners, balls, formal balls, galas or whatever are staged each year. Meanwhile, an army of fund-raisers and direct mail specialists from over the nation (and parts of the Western World) eye the area hungrily and flood it regularly.

[36]Years later, I was summoned to Mr. Cullen's office in Judge J.A. Elkins' "new" City National Bank Building to discuss a writing assignment for him. He greeted me, and asked, "Did you see Father Roach when you came in?" (the Reverend John J. Roach, then pastor of Sacred Heart Church and long-time head of Catholic Charities, was to receive the rare papal title of prothonotary apostolic instead of being appointed—as had once been widely expected—Bishop of Galveston-Houston).

"Yes, I saw him in the outer office," I replied. "And how did he look?" Mr. Cullen continued. I told him that Father Roach looked a little down in the mouth, for such a usually cheerful and optimistic person. Mr. Cullen laughed. "We're having a little fun with the good padre," he explained. "He's been around here passing the hat; his boss, the bishop, told him that he had to pay off a note downstairs, but I told him that I was a little short."

Just then, Evelyn Carter, Mr. Cullen's attractive secretary and the wife of Professor John Carter at the University, entered the room and gave Mr. Cullen what seemed to be a promissory note. He handed it to me for a moment, and I saw that it was indeed a note for $25,000, signed by John J. Roach, and freshly stamped "paid." I returned it to Mr. Cullen. He tore the note carefully in two, placed the pieces in an envelope Mrs. Carter had prepared and asked me to mail it when I left. It was addressed, of course, to Father Roach, the happy subject of a $25,000 practical joke that Hugh Roy Cullen devised to mask his innate generosity.

[37]Mr. Kelley, a generous, community-spirited Greek immigrant who chose an Irish ancestry rather than test an immigration official's ability to spell his correct, polysyllabic surname, dispensed cold, delicious Louisiana oysters on the half-shell and a menu ranging from superb 30-cent roast beef sandwiches to porterhouse steak. Until World War II, everything in the house was half price during Mr. Kelley's celebration of his birthday and U.S. citizenship, which coincided. Prudent men, including most of us in my East Hall entrance at Rice, put something by for this high celebration, and ate our way through the Kelley menu once a year, night by night of George Kelley Week.

[38]Palmer Hutcheson was the epitome of old-line Houston families whose scions traditionally attended Harvard, Yale, or Princeton and less frequently, the University of Virginia. It was very important in terms of community ties to have him assume a role in the 1938 campaign at the request of Colonel Bates and Mr. Cullen, and to have him serve as attorney for the Board of Education, which led to his appointment as a charter regent of the University of Houston. Palmer Hutcheson was a graduate of the Class of 1909 at Princeton, and his three sons followed him there (Palmer, Jr., 1935; Thad Thomson, who would have been either Governor of Texas, U.S. Senator or both, had his timing been a little better, 1940; and Edward C., 1942). The Princeton tradition continued with grandsons Thad T., Jr., and Houghton B.

[39]Chancellor Bowman had come to Houston in the mid-1930s on a brave but curious mission: to obtain a major contribution from Mr. Cullen, whom he had heard about primarily through Gulf Oil executives including Ben Belt. Dr. Bowman was a house guest of the Cullens, and from him Mr. Cullen got the idea that large sums might be given by large numbers of "ordinary citizens," if they became interested enough in a cause. From this stemmed a "downtown march" in which students and faculty and staff members of the University of Houston were given a day off to go to various office buildings where

they were escorted from floor to floor to seek cash contributions from executives, secretaries, traveling salesmen, clerks, office boys, or anyone encountered. Whatever the donor gave was placed by him in a hat decorated with the University colors and newly designed seal. "I borrowed a hat to pass around, because I didn't wear one," Dr. Charles F. Hiller recalls. "There were an awful lot of quarters, and even some pennies. We didn't get much, but people seemed to appreciate our spirit, and the willingness of the students, faculty, and staff to do their part in fund-raising."

Mr. Cullen was awarded the honorary Doctor of Science degree mentioned earlier by the University of Pittsburgh, in 1936. This was for his accomplishment in drilling successfully through "heaving shale" in the old Humble oil field, and thereby opening up deeper oil-bearing strata. Mr. Cullen's grandson Roy Henry Cullen says that his father, Roy Gustav, had a major role in perfecting the new drilling technique that made it possible to "pound" through soft, collapsing shale.

[40]Hugh Roy Cullen enlarged upon this in a statement he gave to the media the next morning after he and Mrs. Cullen had been engulfed with various expressions of appreciation: "There is a saying that 'there is nothing new under the sun,' that every thought has been fully digested . . . but . . . I (want) you to understand what prompted me and what, in my opinion, will prompt and induce others . . . not to delay their beneficences. I consider it the first duty of financially successful men to provide for their dependents. When this duty has been performed, the further problem presents itself, What shall I do with my surplus earnings? . . . My first impulse was, and the first impulse of most men similarly situated is, I believe, to accumulate a large fortune and leave it after death to some worthy cause . . . .This is a generous and unselfish impulse. Upon investigation, I found that I had a life expectancy of some 20 years, that intervening time might bring legal restraints (under which) heavy penalties would probably be imposed . . . if accomplished now, all these probabilities would be avoided, the help of a worthy cause would not be deferred, controversy would be eliminated, personal effort and assistance could be exerted . . . and last, but not least, my own selfish pleasure could be gratified. After much meditation and due consideration, I see no reason for delaying beneficences until death, but believe that prompt accomplishment of such beneficences as one can afford, will scatter sunshine to his friends, his loved ones, and his fellow man; and that its lengthening rays will reflect pleasure and happiness upon, and lighten and lengthen the fulness of his years of life expectancy."

[41]"That's democratic with a small 'd,' son," Mr. Cullen reportedly told a reporter. "Got nothing to do with FDR and the Democratic Party he and the New Dealers have wrecked."

[42]With the publicity stage nearing an end, and actual fund-raising on the immediate horizon, Mrs. Hobby had with her at the podium not the excellent "window-dressing" names of her advisory committee, but the front-line troops, the district chairmen of the Women's Division: Miss Blanche Higgingbotham, Mrs. Charles J. Koenig, Mrs. Joe Rabinowitz, Mrs. J. Alston Clapp, Jr., Mrs. A.S. O'Brien, Mrs. Herbert Childress, Mrs. W.J. Roland, Mrs. J.L. McReynolds, and Mrs. J.J. Devoti.

[43]The 1938 graduation ceremonies of the University were the last at which separate baccalaureate and commencement ceremonies were held, possibly because Mr. Cullen misinterpreted the baccalaureate message of Reverend Paul Quillian. Dr. Quillian, a noted preacher and writer, said " . . . character is not dependent upon material circumstances. Wealth and poverty are not the determining factors in - . . . a man's life."

Mr. Cullen apparently thought upon this for a while, and told President Oberholtzer that while he admired the Reverend Doctor and respected his right to his own opinions, it sounded as if Preacher Quillian was saying that poor men tend to have better characters than rich men. "I've been on both sides of that fence," Mr. Cullen pointed out, "and I don't necessarily hold with the Reverend."

[44]Dr. Oberholtzer proposed informally to members of City Council in April, 1938, that St. Bernard Street be renamed University Boulevard forgetting that there already was a principal thoroughfare by this name (running east and west through the periphery of Rice Institute to South Main), and the possibility of a far more appropriate and felicitous name, such as Cullen Boulevard. Council members fortunately took no action on the request.

[45]Steve Farish, a charter member of the governing board of the University of Houston, had a summer job with the firm of Blaffer & Farish as early as 1911. An early leader in both the petroleum and oil tool industries, he served the University for a quarter-century until his death in 1962. Farish Hall on Central Campus is named for him.

[46]Among the better-known and best-remembered faculty members at this time, many of whom were to remain for many years, or until eventual retirement, were: Raymond W. Baldwin, George W. Drake, Bessie Monroe Ebaugh, Leon G. Halden, Harvey W. Harris, James D. Hutchinson, Alva L. Kerbow, C.F. McIlhenny (thus listed, although his correct name was McElhinney), Murray A. Miller, L. Standlee Mitchell, Zelda Osborne (assistant librarian), Ruth Pennybacker, Warren A. Rees, Ewald W. Schuhmann, Jules A. Vern, Lillian L. Warren, Joseph S. Werlin, Ruth S. Wikoff (librarian), and Robert A. White.

[47]Carl Houston, long-time professor and associate dean of the College of Technology who was a student both as SJHS and on the new campus, confirms the "call me Eddie" anecdote; but he adds that it was understood within the student body that anyone with the nerve to try this "would be fired and hitchhiking back to town within the hour."

[48]A colleague on the faculty, expert in Anglo-Irish history of the nineteenth century, was said to have described the good dean's smile as being "like a gleam of wintry sunshine on the brass handles of a coffin." This was actually said of Sir Robert Peel, the British prime minister, by Daniel O'Connell, the brilliant Irish orator (the "Great Liberator"). O'Connell, the first Irish Catholic to sit in Parliament, was often exasperated by Sir Robert's cold, indifferent manner and delaying maneuvers. He helped overthrow the Peel ministry in 1835 after receiving support from Arthur Wellesley, first Duke of Wellington.

[49]Dr. Charles F. Hiller claims that Bob and Hazel Casey spent a substantial part of their time in classes holding hands. If this is true, the teaching profession may have another and highly-recommended approach to learning. Now a member of the Maritime Commission, Robert Randolph Casey had a brilliant career for almost three decades as judge of Harris County and a Member of Congress. In the latter post, he was extremely helpful to his alma mater on many occasions.

And all that Hazel Marian Brann Casey has been able to do is to help Bob raise a marvelous and accomplished family of 10 children, plus devoting increasing time to a growing number of grandchildren, while being one of the most active and best-liked women in Washington.

[50]Colonel Bates, the soul of honesty, once corrected me when I mentioned his birthplace as Nacogdoches. "Born in Nat," he said, smiling almost imperceptibly with his mouth; his big, liquid eyes; and his East Texas voice with its overtones of the Deep South. "Nat's about 16 miles north and west of Nacogdoches, and a good day's journey by wagon in the old days."

[51]The first two issues of the *Houstonian* in 1934 and 1935, did not even carry the names of the members of the Board of Education, a possible clue to the relative freedom and independence that President Oberholtzer must have felt in running the new University with increasing help from Dr. Kemmerer. Beginning in 1936, names and sometimes pictures of the trustees were carried in a very prominent position.

[52]One of the unexplained oddities in the early history of the University of Houston is why there was not more criticism of the $150 annual tuition rate, which would be about $1,500 in unadjusted

(inflationary) 1977 dollars. The answer probably is that need and demand balanced a rate that was a considerable burden upon most students and/or their parents. A 1976 Carnegie Foundation report shows that "the net cost of higher education per student in the family has gone down . . . by about nine percent (since 1929)." During this time, real (adjusted) per capita income in the United States almost tripled, and the cost of virtually anything you can mention is up sharply.

There are those who maintain, however, that low (or as in a few states, free) tuition has turned higher education into a gigantic babysitting operation for our late teen-agers or, at best, a halfway house for millions of unmotivated young adults attempting to decide upon a career. Dr. Oberholtzer, who set the $150 rate himself in 1927 (and did not lower it, even in the worst year of the Great Depression) was content to build up small operating surpluses. He obviously believed that the student must perceive higher education as a major opportunity and advantage, well worth personal sacrifice and automatically involving high levels of motivation. Dr. Kemmerer, you may remember, borrowed the money to complete his first degree as soon as possible, in what he clearly regarded as an investment in himself to be protected by hard work and constant application. He also had no difficulties with building up operating surpluses for special needs or for the rainy day to come, and would recommend the first increase in University of Houston tuition soon after the move to the new campus.

[53]See Appendix for detail and history of the seal, both in its original and redesigned version, including personal research in the library of the British Museum, and further investigation commissioned at the College of Heralds.

[54]Few things could ruffle the brainy but imperturbable Dr. Petersen, but he would bridle at those who misidentified his medical alma mater as "John" rather than the correct "Johns Hopkins." He once gave the press a quick and nonoffensive two-minute lecture on Johns Hopkins (the "Johns" was his mother's maiden surname), the Baltimore banker and philanthropist (and Quaker) who founded Johns Hopkins University.

[55]This statement could be traced in part to knowledge that Dr. Oberholtzer had prepared a plan in opposition to the Committee on Rules and Regulations which proposed an executive vice-presidency for Dr. Kemmerer, with "supervisory responsibility" (whatever that means) for fiscal, student life, and faculty areas.

[56]Nevertheless, Mr. Mills obviously enjoyed his dual powers, as almost anyone would have. Charlie Hiller says that "H.L." came to call on Dean Dupre soon after the move to the new campus, and as they stood outside the dean's office, Mr. Mills lit up a cigar and began puf-

fing away. "Mr. Mills," said Dean Dupre, "smoking is not allowed in this building. As dean of the University, I must ask you to put that cigar out immediately." "Dupre," replied Mr. Mills, "as business manager of this whole outfit, I must tell you to go to hell."

[57]Dean T.D. Brooks of Texas A&M College spoke to 146 graduates. Mr. and Mrs. Cullen were made "honorary members of the faculty," but both were absent because of Mrs. Cullen's illness, from which she fortunately recovered before the dedication two days later.

[58]The eight months and a week included what H.L. Mills called "red tape time," the interval between tabulation of bids and the preparation of a more detailed contract and bond for approval of "The Czar," the state Public Works Administration director.

[59]One of the most difficult decisions for then-President A.D. Bruce, when the academic quadrangle was being expanded almost 20 years later by the addition of the Fred J. Heyne Building (a gift of Jesse H. Jones) was to omit a red tile roof for this structure. The cost of such embellishments had risen astronomically since 1938.

[60]Erroneously attributed to Sam Houston by the editors of the 1940 *Houstonian,* who obviously did not major in Texas history.

[61]The University has apparently come full cycle, after almost 40 years, with far more attention being paid now to career counseling and (by statutory requirement) to maintaining contact with the student after graduation as a means of assessing efficiency in counseling, the educational process, and placement in chosen field.

Chapter Four

1939-1945

Adapting to national emergency, and then to total war, on the new campus . . . Carpe diem, *before and after October 16, 1940, and Selective Service . . . The Navy is fortunately piped aboard . . . The (Manufacturers' Industrial) Shop Building and the round-the-clock construction miracle of the (Student) Recreation Building . . . Casualty lists and full wartime footing . . . Colonel W.B. Bates on center stage again . . . Acceleration toward the separation of the University and the School District . . . The Advisory Board is created, and takes over . . . Three-to-three votes on a badly-split Board of Trustees . . . Senate Bill 207 and establishment of the Board of Regents . . . Aims of the University restated . . . The first wave of returning veterans under the GI Bill, and adjustments for them . . . Enormous fluctuations in enrollment and budgets . . . Hugh Roy Cullen's growing new interest and involvement . . . President Edison Ellsworth Oberholtzer is maneuvered away from downtown and is finally inaugurated after 18 years on the job*

As the University of Houston opened its historic first full semester on the St. Bernard campus on Wednesday, September 20, 1939, a visitor would have been hard pressed to discover any real connection with the impending crisis and tragedy of World War II, even though the nation was in the second week of a limited national emergency and the media overflowed with the frightening prospects of a global conflict.[1]

Certainly until the harsh reality of Selective Service registration on October 16, 1940 (a massive operation involving 77,177 young men in Harris County alone), and to a considerable extent until most of the male student body had departed for the armed services, there was an attitude of *carpe diem* (live for today) on the campus. This was coupled strongly with understandable uncertainty about the future, as life took on a phantasmagorial quality for young men and women unable to discover what the phrase "for the duration" meant, either in terms of the calendar or of their own disrupted lives.

The two men closest to reality at the University, as ever, were Dr. Kemmerer and President Oberholtzer; the prospect of war severely crippling, or even destroying, the institution they had worked so hard to develop to this crucial stage was not lost upon them. Understandably, the emergency brought forward qualities of leadership, initiative, and positive action in Dr. Kemmerer, still only 36, that had begun to diminish somewhat in President Oberholtzer, who would be 61 years old before the actual outbreak of hostilities after Pearl Harbor. The two men continued to function extremely well as a team, and this would be the case for a decade to come; but Dr. Kemmerer began now, at first almost imperceptibly, to assert crescent leadership.

In his modestly furnished office in that fall of 1939, Walter W. Kemmerer pondered often the possibly disastrous effects of war on total enrollment, and thereby on sensitive operating budgets. There had been another major surge in enrollment, this time from 1,563 the previous autumn to 2,067 for 1939-1940—probably stimulated by the addition of graduate courses and the well-publicized move to the St. Bernard campus. A similar increase to 2,488 would occur in 1940-1941, but Dr. Kemmerer's attention was correctly focused on 1941-1942 and beyond—into that segment of time ambiguously identified as "the duration."

Almost four decades later, Dr. Kemmerer could recall many details relating to his grave concern over how to keep the University alive and well in wartime, while simultaneously serving the city, area, and nation to maximum effect. On analysis, the two likeliest avenues of approach were quickly apparent: contract training for the armed services and special courses for war industry employees. At the same time, the principal and long-term missions of the institution could not be neglected. Even if it came to having a class of 15 women and three men (as it did), instead of a more normal 15 women plus 20-25 men, regular instruction must proceed and the faculty must be kept intact, despite the younger male members' vulnerability to military service. It also seemed wise to adapt existing courses such as current history, international relations, marine shipping, and political science to the realities of the day, and to provide instruction in such areas as civilian pilot training programs.

Dr. Kemmerer, with major assistance from President Oberholtzer, quickly discovered a number of logical contacts in pursuit of the new war-footing objectives. He went first to George A. Hill, Jr., chief executive officer and one of the founders of Houston Natural Gas, who was a colonel in the Army reserve and chairman of the Military Affairs Committee of the Houston Chamber of Commerce.[2]

Through the Military Affairs Committee and his own personal contacts, Mr. Hill helped the University to apply for both an Army and a Navy reserve officer training corps (ROTC) unit. The services were supportive; they could see immediately the advantages of being on the campus of an expanding university in a major city; but there were severe financial and personnel problems. Pre-Pearl Harbor military budgets were ridiculously low in an isolationist, Oxford Movement era when the Selective Service Act could only pass the House of Representatives by a single vote. Organizational tables were full of vacancies and even West Point and Annapolis graduates could be frozen in grade for years. A further complication for the Navy involved pressure from the powerful Congressman Albert Thomas (who was to befriend the University of Houston in so many ways later on) to establish an NROTC unit at Rice Institute, his alma mater.

Nevertheless, the University was to be successful in obtaining not one, but three Navy training units at the St. Bernard campus, as well as a small Army Air Corps unit. Meanwhile, progress continued on other fronts designed to accomplish an optimum transition from peacetime to wartime conditions. President Oberholtzer made it clear in a series of speeches in the early fall of 1939 that the University would continue to seek out and assume new responsibilities consonant with the deepening national emergency, but would neglect neither its basic curricula and commitment to serve the high school graduate unable to go elsewhere for a post-secondary education, nor its unique dedication to the needs of the individual rather than to educational tradition.

Here are excerpts from a typical Oberholtzer address of the period: This fall, we will be offering 354 courses in our new home, with three baccalaureate degrees and the master's degree in selected fields including education. We also have available a new certificate for training undertaken on an extension basis.

> Since its founding, the University has tried to do everything possible to enable young people and adults alike to get advance training while they live at home and while they work for a livelihood. Now, as we shift with the nation to a war footing, we will seek new assignments as part of the overall defense effort; but we will not forget either our antecedents, or the long future.
>
> All University of Houston curricula are designed to be vital and significant, and to be presented in relation to the world in which the student must live. We began, and we will continue, as a service institution, undergoing continuous growth and expansion to provide whatever courses are needed. The deciding factor for us is not tradition, but what the individual needs.

President Oberholtzer then announced a new College of Community Services, "to provide industrial training both on site and on the campus." It was being established, he said, "to make possible the organization of needed courses at any time, with or without college credit."

The concept of a College of Community Services had been under consideration for some time, certainly since a 1938 news release in which Dean Dupre announced that Eby Nell McElrath, one of the newest members of the faculty and a brilliant young chemist from Rice Institute who would remain for a long and effective career with the University, would be teaching organic chemistry to nuns and other nursing students at Incarnate Word Academy, the Dominican Novitiate, and at St. Joseph Hospital. "Whenever an institution or agency expresses the desire for such outside classes," Dean Dupre was authorized to state, "the University will cooperate."

The College of Community Services would soon add a wide spectrum of courses, including electricity, diesel engines, machine shop, drafting, shop mathematics, radio, aircraft engines, and even lens-grinding. It became the administrative vehicle for training war industry employees, beginning in May 1940. At the peak in 1943, more than 10,000 trainees were enrolled in war production courses taught by University personnel at the plant location. Another 8,045 industrial employees completed University of Houston technical instruction between 1942 and 1945.

A civilian pilot training (CPT) program, in cooperation with the Civil Aeronautics Administration (CAA), was quickly established in the fall of 1939 with major assistance from Dean Dupre of World War I, Kelly Field fame. Dean Dupre enrolled with the first students and was successful in having his pilot's certificate, dating from 1918, renewed.

Students took their ground training, which included meteorology, navigation, CAA regulations, airplane engine, and beginning aerodynamics, at the University. At the Cliff Hyde Flying Service and other private flying schools they were given eight or more hours of dual instruction. This covered the usual pre-solo flight training, plus stalls and spins. After soloing, the pilot candidate continued with spot and pattern landings, power turns, and "pylon eights." The final examination, a cross-country flight and flight check, then completed the overall course.

Mr. and Mrs. Hyde were extremely popular with the CPT students, as they should have been, because of their close cooperation with and assistance to the program. There was not a single failure in the first class of 30 students, and they received their pilot certificates on May 16, 1940. The graduates included Raymond P. Elledge, Jr. and a Miss Seawillow Long.

The CPT program trained a total of 582 civilian pilots before it was phased out in 1942. It also had a significant role in bringing 704 Navy pilots, 202 Army pilots, and 40 Army flight instructors to the University of Houston for part of their training.

Carpe diem and a seeming dissociation from the reality of national emergency, were clearly in evidence on campus through the 1939-1940 academic year, and on to the arrival of the first students in the United States Naval Reserve Vocational School (USNRVS) on October 28, 1941.

The 1940 *Houstonian* was dedicated " . . . to the campus, present and future . . . with the Roy Gustav Cullen Memorial and Science Building in use . . . a feeling of loyalty, pride, and devotion to the ideology of the founders." The only mention of war, or impending war, in the yearbook is a jocular reference on the page dedicated to the *Cougar* in the activities section: "War! . . . Came a siege . . . ended by a Versailles which placed (P.J.) Sterne at the head of the staff, and straightaway the *Cougar* became a newspaper instead of a warmonger."[3]

Nor can you discover any particular references to the continuing national emergency in the 1941 *Houstonian*, published months after hundreds of University students had registered for the draft, and the opening of a Selective Service Counseling Center in room 104 of the Roy Gustav Cullen Building. The dedication is to a new major project originated by Dr. Kemmerer, and it sounds as if he might have written it, "To the Frontier Fiesta and the school spirit it has helped to create, to the student unity and fellowship it has called into being, and to the closer reality of our goal, the Student Recreational Building."

A half-generation of University of Houston students still recall the Frontier Fiesta more vividly than any of their experiences on campus.

The Fiesta was the brainchild of Dr. Kemmerer, who saw the need to balance strong new emphasis on defense-oriented projects with extracurricular, as well as classroom, innovations for the civilian student body. He also perceived the event as an answer to increasing student unrest over the lack of an intercollegiate sports program (usually a prime and traditional means of engendering and maintaining school spirit), and the failure to provide a student recreation center.

Somehow, there came to be a widespread and erroneous idea that the Frontier Fiesta was the principal, if not the only, extracurricular project at the University between 1939-1945, and for that matter, on into the 1960's. The record shows instead that there was a great deal of extracurricular activity and school spirit in evidence from the first days on the new campus until the end of World War II. This activity was totally apart from the original Frontier Fiesta, which was held only in 1940 and 1941, and it occurred in spite of the gradual disappearance of an overwhelming percentage of the male student body into the Armed Forces.

But as interesting, innovative, and enjoyable as the first two Frontier Fiestas were, and as much as they did contribute to school spirit, they definitely took a back seat to the year-long spectrum of events, programs, and projects on campus between 1939 and the end of hostilities. It was only in 1946, with the revival of the Fiesta by returning veterans, that it assumed a dominant place in University extracurricular life.

The extracurricular menu at the University in wartime included Slop Week, Sadie Hawkins Week, the presentations of the Red Masque Players, the competition for inclusion in the Vanity Fair Section of the *Houstonian*, Varsity Varieties, the sophomore-freshman football game, the all-school picnic, the *Cougar* best-dressed girl of the week competition, the annual High School Senior Reception and May Fête, the complex programs and activities of some 30 student clubs and organizations, and that never-failing diversion, campus politics.

As the war years rolled on, a surprising number of these traditional events were continued, and those that fell by the wayside were often replaced with new projects and undertakings. A principal reason for this appears to be the relatively high percentage of faculty and staff members, many of whom were women or men in their forties and beyond, who remained civilians. These dedicated people, many of them with 10 to 15 years of service at the University, were often the sponsors and advisors for key organizations and activities. They provided stability and continuity for the extracurricular as well as the instructional programs and were constantly active in such new projects as war bond and defense stamp drives, the blood bank, meatless Tuesdays,[4] special assembly programs on second and fourth Wednesdays, and other wartime activities.

The "slops" were the freshman students, male and female, who were subjected to what was then a series of accepted tribal rites. These minor indignities occurred during "Slop Week" at the opening of the fall semester. They had actually begun at San Jacinto High School, where sophomores met incoming freshmen with shoe polish and lipstick on Friday evenings in September, giving them what one victim described in an early issue of the *Cougar* as "a welcome that was sure hard to wash off."

As refinements were added on the new campus, all first-term students were required to wear identifying signs around their necks, showing their name (Slop Smith), address, and (for the girls) home telephone number. The required uniform for men was chopped-off trousers, preferably with ruffled cuffs, no shirt, red suspenders, and a red-and-white UH "beanie" cap.

Make-up for male victims was by sophomore experts, and included mercurochrome in smallpox-like patterns, abstract designs in lipstick on torso and face, and shoe polish applied liberally to the lower legs and feet. Between classes, upperclassmen played tic-tac-toe on the backs of male freshmen, using either mercurochrome or (in the case of a few sadists) orange shellac. This zany diversion was strictly confined to male first-year students.

The young ladies were treated with more consideration, although dresses of hideous design, pigtails tied with toilet tissue, teeth blackened out with shoe polish, high-heeled shoes, and bizarre make-up including green eye shadow utilized as lipstick were in fashion.

"Slops" were required to walk backwards on certain sidewalks and, when the reflection pool was completed, to march endlessly in a giant ellipse around the pool, teetering on the edge of a narrow curb made slippery by someone falling in from time to time.

Freshmen also recited gibberish on the command of their sophomore tormentors during Slop Week, and kept a vigil on their knees around the University seal on the floor of the Roy Gustav Cullen Memorial. Dean Dupre was usually a little more in evidence than usual during Slop Week, watching, "lest anything get out of hand."[5] "We don't mind a little fun," he told a reporter, "but nothing violent, no real hazing."

The dean need not have worried. Slop Week generated a good bit of fun and greater school spirit, even though a large percentage of the student body (the average age of students in 1939-1940 being 28) simply ignored these tribal rites. But any self-respecting Aggie of the good old days when a freshman knew his place at College Station would have looked on in bored disbelief.

Sadie Hawkins Week, a product of the era's nationwide preoccupation with Al Capp's Dogpatch hillbillies (the "Dogpatch craze" has reappeared several times since), was a diversion each November from 1939 through 1942. The first celebration of this notable academic event, in 1939, was a marked success. One student told the *Cougar* that "the empty landscape has certainly improved overnight around here."[6]

Henry J.N. Taub was the first Lil' Abner; he reigned with dozens of Daisy Maes at a ball at the Arabia Temple attended by more than 500 costumed hillbillies. There was a marked shortage of Mammy Yokums, though.

The Red Masque Players are remembered as perhaps the most active campus organization of the 1939-1945 era. They began with an unexplained episode in which Dr. Kemmerer apparently fired some members of the faculty connected with what was then called "dramatics." He immediately brought L. Standlee Mitchell over from the English faculty to administer the drama program. This meant only minimal extra involvement for "Chief" Mitchell, who had been the driving force behind the Red Masque Players since the group was organized in 1932 to supplant the John R. Bender Dramatic Club.

The list of productions by the Red Masque Players is long and distinguished. Among them were *Our Town; You Can't Take It With You; Ah, Wilderness; Smilin' Through; Cry Havoc;* and *Dark Victory.* The organization, which added as many as 190 members in one drive alone, had a unique role in stimulating school spirit and is deservedly remembered. Among the lasting traditions of the Players are the dedication the Red Masquers brought to their roles in well-chosen productions, the marvelous parties they gave on the closing night of each play, and "Chief" Mitchell's great contributions to the organization—mustache and Essex coupe included.

Charles A. Saunders, Jr., was one of the most active members of the Red Masque Players, along with Lela Blount (later a member of the faculty and co-sponsor of the Players with "Chief" Mitchell), Ray Campbell, Rosemary Pellerin, and the three-time business manager, Joe Potter. He confirms the many contributions of the organization, which presented more than 100 productions, and the sense of accomplishment coupled with the enjoyment and feeling of camaraderie that all Masquers seem to remember, including, Charlie Saunders adds, the year-end beach parties at Galveston.

The University had an early reputation for attractive coeds. It probably stemmed from the annual reception for graduating seniors of the HISD high schools, at which the most attractive female graduate was selected to preside over a Royal Court. The reputation was strengthened with the competition for the Vanity Fair Section of the *Houstonian,* in which such forgotten celebrities as Walter Wanger and Perc Westmore picked 10 "Vanity Fair beauties" and an additional 14 "favorites."

Mr. Westmore chose to include a few helpful hints on hair styling and make-up with his selections for the 1945 *Houstonian.* "I would suggest," he said of one winner, "that . . . she dispense with her bangs." Of another, " . . . (she) minimizes her loveliness by a hairstyle that is not at all worthy of her . . . she should wear a simple, sleek coiffure." He complimented another winner on her " . . . lovely forehead, the naturally arched brows, the retroussé nose." It was noted, however, that she "could improve her appearance by not making up her lower lip . . . "

Mr. Westmore only used five words in describing one Vanity Fair winner who went to establish her own modeling school (Mary

Beth Roberts). "Hers," he pronounced, "is a sultry beauty." And it was.

Vanity Fair selections were traditionally announced at an elegant reception and ball, and the January 19, 1940, event at the Houston Club will never be forgotten. Ten inches of snow, the most seen in the city since the previous century, fell between sunrise and the next dawn, when most of those who finally got to the Houston Club for the festivities were still trying to get back home. All of the honorees and guests survived, although there were horror stories of beauties walking for miles in organdy frocks, evening shoes, and thin coats, their escorts trudging along in dinner jacket and pumps after abandoning a stalled automobile.

Varsity Varieties was another highlight of the annual extracurricular calendar in the 1939-1945 era. Drawing much of its talent from Red Masque Players and Vanity Fair candidates, although usually sponsored by student publications, the musical revue was first presented in a unique setting—at a midnight show in the downtown Metropolitan Theater in November 1941. It was moved to the Music Hall in December 1942. The "VV," as the revue was called, became something of a fall Frontier Fiesta, with an ongoing exchange of vocalists, musicians, and other performers between the two events.

The annual high school reception, established by Dr. Oberholtzer in 1928, continued throughout World War II as the University's most durable tradition. The eighteenth reception, on May 10, 1945, drew 4,000 persons to the City Auditorium, where Carole Holtkamp of Austin High School was named "the most beautiful high school senior"; and Gene Padon Robinson, president of the Class of 1945, and Ed Kotch, editor of the 1945 *Houstonian,* were announced as queen and king.

President Oberholtzer, convinced of the value of the reception as a publicity and recruiting device over the years, ordered the next day that the 1945 yearbook, with an eight-page section on the traditional event, be distributed on publication day to all nine participating senior high schools, their counselors, and their representatives in the Reception Court.

There was, in summary, a surprising depth and range of student activities at the University of Houston from 1939-1945. This was all the more remarkable because of the accelerating loss of male students to the military services beginning in 1942, and the increasing shortages, priorities, and unavailability of so many products and services.

The original Frontier Fiesta, as noted, was presented only in 1940 and 1941, and was definitely overshadowed by the total spectrum of campus events. However, it seemed to epitomize the depth and range of student involvement in wartime activities in terms of wide participation by organizations and individuals alike.

The first Fiesta was held April 26, 1940, in conjunction with the long-established annual high school reception, after two postponements caused by rain, an unseasonable norther, and a hailstorm. Dr. Kemmerer, determined to make the Fiesta a success, issued a statement urging " . . . the entire student body (to) take part in Frontier Fiesta, recreating for the people of Houston the good old days when men were men, women loved them for it, and a maverick was an unruly steer instead of an unruly politician."[7]

He then went out to the Fiesta lot and worked day and night with the students knocking together Midway shows, earning the nickname of "Doc" with his enthusiasm and ability as an amateur carpenter. The 1941 *Houstonian* shows him, his mouth apparently full of nails, hammering away on part of a dance floor.

The outstanding shows at the historic first Frontier Fiesta, still remembered at any alumni gathering that includes the authentic oldtimers, included Casino Royale, Pioneer Palace, Scoggins' Scanties, the Bowery Cafe, Dr. John Zell Gaston's magic show (he had been a friend of Houdini), Judge Roy Bean's Court, Latin America, Bank of Roaring Camp, Singapore Spider, Madamoiselle Zola, and the Spanish Casino. Among the stars were Olivia "Chez Paree" Bradford, stunning in a filmy harem costume as she alternated with the Yacht Club Boys and the Harmony Trio at the Casino Royale; the "ta-ra-ra-boom-de-a" girls, with their unique Bowery Cafe version of the can-can; Lela Blount, in the stirring melodramas at the Singapore Spider, at the mercy of a succession of villians but always rescued in the nick of time by a succession of heroes; Alec Murrelle as Judge Roy Bean; Evelyn Taylor as Belle Starr; and Gerald Leinweber as Wild Bill Hickok. Always in the background at the Frontier Fiesta were "Chief" Mitchell, friend, confidante, and troubleshooter; and Joe Potter, general chairman.[8]

The first Frontier Fiesta beard-growing contest was won by Bill Cardiff, even though he would not have made it to the quarter-finals in later years, when beards increased geometrically in length, density, uniqueness of color, and general unattractiveness. This competition, which was to become a feature of post-war Fiestas, was spurred on by constant publicity and by the Ford automobile that Don McMillian traditionally awarded to the contest winner.

At the conclusion of the 1940 Fiesta, Dr. Kemmerer proudly announced that $2,000 had been raised (much of it at the perenially crowded bingo game). This was twice the estimate of $1,000 and every dime was to be contributed toward the building of a student recreation center.

School spirit at the University of Houston in the years between 1939 and 1945 was perhaps reflected most accurately in the myriad activities of the smaller student clubs and organizations—and in that mirror of campus life, political campaigning.

Among the more unusual projects and activities of the less prominent student groups were the following: the first student art exhibition, held in March 1940 to celebrate the expansion of departmental course offerings from two to seven, and of enrollment from 14 to 152, under the guidance of Frederic Browne, artist, teacher, and administrator (reviews by Ione Kirkham of the *Press* and Harry Johnston of the *Post* were quite complimentary); a performance of Henrik Ibsen's difficult, seldom-seen *Rosmersholm* by the Collegiate Dramatic Society in April 1940; a class in creative music, in the summer session of 1940, during which students and faculty members improvised their own instruments and composed their own music; the Engineers' Club devised a plan in the winter of 1939 they were certain would keep Blackstone the Magician locked up in his secret cage at the Metropolitan Theater, and felt so strongly about it that they raised a pot of $100 and bet the great escape artist he could not get free in five minutes (he bounced out on the stage in two minutes flat and walked off with the money).

There are other examples of an almost unique level of enthusiasm and involvement by the student body that has unfortunately been lost to a considerable extent today. To cite some further instances: the Class of 1941, beset as they must have been with personal problems and uncertainties at the time, raised $300 at the Junior Prom as the first contribution toward the Student Recreation Building; members of their various classes gave a series of impromptu parties for the first four members of the University faculty to go into the Armed Forces, in the spring of 1942: Anthony A. Aucoin, Archie W. French, Charles W. Goyen, and Robert W. Talley—the Buckaroos, members of a girls' riding club that met every Saturday afternoon at the Palace Stable on Almeda Road—saddled up on a frosty February morning in 1943 to ride in the Houston Fat Stock Show parade, lassoing prosperous-looking types from the crowd of spectators along the line of march who were then made to buy Stock Show tickets; Student Council members went from class to class on Monday and Tuesday for three years, selling defense stamps.

The Co-Ed-Ettes, organized in February, 1942 with Mr. and Mrs. Cullen as sponsors, gave a dance a month thereafter until 1945, honoring the men in the services;[9] after five successful war loan drives, the Student Assembly raised $46,500 against a quota of $15,000 in a sixth campaign during the dramatic Allied victories in Europe in the spring of 1945; an all-school picnic in 1942 (mistakenly billed as the first such event by *Cougar* reporters who were not present for the truly historic picnic of March 12, 1937) featured a classic faculty-student body baseball game with Charles A. Saunders, Jr. (still suffering at the time from a rheumatic heart condition he later surmounted) as umpire, and some of the most bizarre base-running and hotly disputed decisions in the history of the game.

One of the major outpourings of wartime student energy and interest came in the summer of 1940, when Stephen P. Sakach was in charge of a WPA project to drain and fill the area immediately west of the reflection pool, which had been badly flooded the previous summer. A second phase of the project involved the planting of 1,000 square yards of St. Augustine grass after the installation of a 20-acre underground sprinkling system. Sakach, a veteran of the Engineers' Corps and expert scrounger, knew where he could lay his hands on another 1,000 square yards of grass, plus surplus supplies of petunias, moss roses, and snapdragons. However, his money was running out, and he would have to let the large WPA work crew of 150-200 men go before completing the desperately needed landscaping and beautification of the bare, raw campus. He pondered this, and began looking over the group of student onlookers who often watched the progress of the project between classes. Soon, he had his men, a group of volunteers who knew little about landscaping, but agreed to do anything to improve the scraggly appearance of their campus.

Within 10 days, Sakach and his new, unpaid crew had planted the remainder of the St. Augustine grass and the flowers. The latter were placed in long beds along the two sides of the quadrangle, and in symmetrically-arranged triangular beds.

It would be 25 years before the University had a campus-wide program of landscaping, including the installation of plazas, fountains, and outdoor sculpture by internationally renowned artists, fully under way; but the first step had been taken.

The early war years saw a small but significant revival of varsity sports and an intensification of broad, underlying interest in them. However, by 1943, student athletes were leaving for the armed services, with most of the other males, in a steady stream, and competition was discontinued. The revival was of consequence because it provided a springboard from which the institution was able to mount a major program of intercollegiate athletics in record time, beginning in 1946.

There had been a Cougar ice hockey team dating back to the Houston Junior College days, and C.F. McElhinney, the Nova Scotian of flashing blades, coached the first University of Houston team (described as a "fighting bunch of puck-pushers") in 1934. This historic group included Ed (then Eddie) Chernosky, Harry Girard, Frank Miller, Lake Alexander, Sidney Sampson, Frank Gooch, Bland Williams, Allen Cameron, and Boyd Watkins, manager.

Captain Chernosky and his small band fought the good fight, but the season ran more to heroic stands than to victories in the tough City Amateur League.[10] The 1934 *Houstonian* states diplomatically that a lack of reserve material was a severe drawback, but players were awarded silver watch fobs.

Ice hockey was revived in 1940, and the Cougars, led by Coach Archie W. French and Captain Ferdinand B. (Bubba) Paris, scored a memorable 2-1 victory over Rice Institute. Oldtimers claim a win over the Owls in earlier years at the Polar Wave rink; this would have been an unofficial game, however, since the University team did not play a full schedule in those days and was ineligible to compete for the city title.

There was no taint on the 1940 victory, in any case, as Fred Mauldin, R.J. Fenzl, and Marcus Jones starred for the Cougars on the wings and Jack Busby, together with Harry Girard (brother of Rice's star, Louis Girard) were standouts on defense. Fenzl scored one of the Cougar goals, and Billy Rynd, the other.

The Owls took their revenge in 1941, inflicting the single defeat that prevented the Cougars from having a perfect season. A unique two-game playoff was decided upon, the team scoring the most goals overall to be the city champion. The University of Houston won the first game, but Rice, led by its offensive ace Lee Blocker, ran away with the second and the title. Many of the accounts of these games are by William Gayle (Bill) Roberts, Jr., later the Town Crier and chief gossip-monger in the old *Press*. Roberts began his journalistic and publishing career as a sports writer for the *Cougar*, and was especially skilled in covering ice hockey from 1939-1941.

The University of Houston organized a basketball team in 1940-1941, under Coach E.A. Snapp, instructor in health and physical education. Ironically (and especially so today, with the demand for more emphasis on intercollegiate athletics for women), this was seven years after the first Cougar girls' basketball team took the court against such stellar competition as the W.T. Grant Department Store team.

Coach Snapp presents no threat to the redoubtable Guy V. Lewis, the current and long-time University basketball coach, already immortalized by the unforgettable win over UCLA in January, 1968, before 53,000 fans in a zany but profitable setting in the Astrodome; by his win-loss record over the toughest possible competition; the size of his tailoring bill at Harold's; and his security towel.

The 1940-1941 Cougars did, however, lose only one game, that to Carr-Sweeney's in the City Recreation League. They also anticipated a current, and reprehensible, campus style by appearing in bright red tank tops with striped red-and-white piping, and baggy red shorts. Their captain was James Roderick Morgan, who led a roster that included Burt Bader, Henry Hope, Herman Earlywine, Dudley Vance, Norman Woodruff, Glenn Cornwell, Buddy Toomey, and Bill Sparr.

Coach Snapp kept many of his basketball players with him in the summer of 1941, when they won 10 games and lost two representing the University in the Mason Park night softball league.

It was not possible to organize another basketball team until the season 1944-1945, when returning veterans provided the nucleus for a group capable of intercollegiate competition. These players are considered to constitute the University's first official representatives in basketball, and Coach Snapp did an excellent job with them, running up a very commendable 10-5 record in a good semiprofessional league in the city. The eight-man roster included Bill T. Swanson (Guy V. Lewis' half-brother), who was to carry a crucial bill for the University of Houston while a member of the House of Representatives in later years. As a staff member of the department of athletics, he now plays a key role in providing long-range financial support for intercollegiate athletics programs and in initiating and carrying through special projects for Harry Fouke, director of athletics.

Other members of the 1945 basketball team who helped to get the sport off and running quickly and successfully at the University after World War II were Gerald Plaster, high point man; Irwin Kaplan; Freddie Sanchez; Tony More; Carew Bean; Charles Hooper; and Eddie Faust.

There was no organized department of athletics at the University of Houston in 1945, and the Student Assembly simply took the matter of awarding letters to the basketball team into its own hands. A bill was passed and sent to "Chief" Mitchell requesting that letters be awarded all eight members of the team. There was no precedent, but no objection, either. In due course, the basketball players appeared at the regular assembly program for the student body, and were awarded their letters to tremendous applause.

Emboldened a bit by this, the Student Assembly passed a resolution creating a Student Athletic Association, "to work on student athletic and campus problems." Little came of this move, however, although it was thoroughly discussed with student leaders including Jim Palmer, Student Assembly vice-president.

Palmer, who operated from a wheelchair because of severe physical handicaps, was emerging at the time as an intelligent and articulate spokesman for the student body. He was later to teach for many years in the journalism area and assumed a prominent role in student publications. He would rejoice today in the fact that the University of Houston is in the forefront of providing special facilities and programs for the handicapped student.

Political campaigns livened up the campus a great deal in wartime, or at least until the male population had been decimated. Thereafter, the young ladies began to be elected in overwhelming numbers, dominating the scene until the veterans of World War II returned. By the fall of 1943, all four officers of the junior class, three-quarters of those holding office in the sophomore and senior classes, and half of the elected freshman officials were female. A similar situation was found in most other principal elective posts on campus. The women took all the fun out of campus politics, electing often-unopposed candidates by overwhelming margins in what was more of a caucus than a campaign.

Two students, more than any others, bring to mind campus electioneering from 1939 to 1943: John W. (Johnny) Goyen and Jack Joseph Valenti. Active in student elections from high school days, both were popular, handsome men with many friends, although Johnny Goyen has described himself as a "very timid, very frightened guy" in his early days at the University.[11]

There was nothing shy about Jack Valenti, and he and Goyen quickly formed a winning team. They were elected vice-president and president, respectively, of the freshman class and went on from there.

Johnny Goyen was day vice-president of the sophomore class, and ran for at least one office, sometimes for two, every year that he attended the University of Houston. Valenti was elected to the 1942 day Student Council, which Goyen served as councilman-at-large.

The next year, both men reached the pinnacle of campus politics. Valenti was elected president, and Goyen secretary of the new Student Association. This was an important new body charged with "cooperating with the day and night Student Assembly and Student Council to unify and coordinate the activities of those governing bodies." An administrator of the era translated that for me as follows: "It is a bad, and deteriorating, policy to have separate day and night Student Assemblies and Student Councils, especially as we head full-tilt for World War II. So get in there and cut down on the bickering, rivalry, cross-purposes, duplication and wasted motion."

The Valenti-Goyen team had just sunk its teeth into this job when the Army Air Force Reserve's 17-man campus unit was called to active duty. Valenti ended up as a bomber pilot in the European theater, and Goyen in varying assignments with training squadrons in airfields on the Texas border.

Other politicos of note on the 1939-1943 campus included Sherwood Crane, who was named president of the Texas Student Government Association after serving as vice-chairman of the Student Assembly; Charles Saunders, Weed Peterson, Tommy Yerxa, and Henry J.N. Taub.

Henry Taub was active in a bewildering array of campus assignments. In 1939, as business manager of an unofficial Cougar football team, he attempted to book a game with an all-star eleven at the Huntsville penitentiary after losing a tough one to the Cherryhurst Tigers, 0-20. He then helped organize a short-lived basketball team, also without official sanction. This group had to rally past the Modern Delivery five, 22-19, after dominating the game at the half, 11-5. Its members did have the distinction of playing an intercollegiate team, the Stephen F. Austin Lumberjacks. This was no contest; the Lumberjacks coasted home 54-18.

Henry Taub deserves some sort of unique award as one of the most sportsmanlike political candidates in history. He mounted a spectacular campaign against Weed Peterson in 1940, for the key post of president of the day Student Council, and brought out a swing band plus a midget racing car in a last bid for votes. When his opponent indicated that this was laying it on a bit thick, Taub let Peterson borrow the band for a concert in the Roy Cullen Building. In exchange, Peterson had to agree to make a campaign speech for Taub.

Taub was defeated, which seems to say something about the dangers of being an innovator in political strategy. He was widely applauded for his sportsmanship, however, and had the consolation of being named to a select list of "glamor" boys selected in a *Cougar* poll.[12]

Neither Valenti nor Goyen had enough "glamor boy" votes to count, a fact which some of their contemporaries still bring up at alumni reunions. This is something of a mystery, unless the *Cougar* ballot boxes were stuffed against them, since neither man would qualify at all under the "large, bruising, athletic type" category. There is also the countervailing fact that no one could have attended the University of Houston from 1939-1946 without hearing of both, not once, but many times.

Indeed, the 1942 *Houstonian* proudly called attention to one group picture as "not including Jack Joseph Valenti." J.J. (whose campaign slogan was "You won't get stuck with Cactus Jack") appeared in photographs being sworn in as a cadet in the Army Air Corps Reserve, selling *Houstonians* at registration, tea-dancing at George Kalleen's Hi-Hat,[13] with the *Cougar* and *Houstonian* staffs, in a Student Council meeting, feeding a (nickel) jukebox in a booth at Bill Williams' Chicken House on South Main, and talking to extremely attractive girls, usually a toothsome blonde, small in stature (it was widely proclaimed that Cactus Jack made the minimum Air Force height through the use of cleverly camouflaged double elevator shoes).

Goyen could not compete directly with Valenti's formidable screen credits, but he was very evident in *Houstonians* of the era: at the Frontier Fiesta, at every prom scheduled, lolling on the grass in what the English would term "obscene" four-toned sports shoes, with other members of the Outer Chamber Pre-Law Association (80 percent of whom were never to see a law textbook or darken a courtroom door), or "brown-bagging" his own $1.98 rum into the Empire Room on Tuesday, the cut-rate night.

Both Valenti and Goyen have remained extremely loyal and active alumni, contributing directly and indirectly to their alma mater while pursuing careers in public life and business that have brought them well-deserved acclaim and, in the case of Jack Valenti, national and international recognition.

Goyen has been a perennial member of City Council, where his long experience and ebullient energy have made him a valuable member of a succession of city administrations. He was the first executive director of what was then called the Ex-Students' Association, in 1946, and has held virtually every office, and been given every honor in the Association (now the Alumni Organization).

Councilman Goyen has come to the aid of the University—appropriately, forcefully, and effectively—on numerous occasions at City Hall. One particular instance of this I recall especially because of its significance to the development of what is now the central campus.

In 1958, I had attended a meeting at Tulane University in New Orleans, where I was shown "shotgun"[14] houses. The administration was buying these houses at unbelievable prices in excess of $100,000 each in order to obtain a few more thousand square feet of land adjacent to Tulane. This made quite an impression on me, and caused me to look around our own borders, for it was increasingly apparent that 250 acres of land would not suffice for the central campus of the future.

When I discussed the problem with President A.D. Bruce, he told me to draw up a preliminary plan of action, and to bring it directly to him. Realizing the difficulties, financial and otherwise, of putting such a plan into effect, I nevertheless listed for him what I considered to be four key tracts. These were Settegast Park, an undeveloped 39-acre property of the City of Houston immediately west of Cullen Boulevard, bounded on the north by Elgin (then still a narrow, two-way street), by private property to the west, and to the south by our own acreage running to Holman; the 67-acre Jeppesen Stadium site, owned then by the HISD;[15] the large holdings of the Sartwelle family, which included the Port City stockyards, abattoir, and meat-packing plant; and another major tract extending to the north along Calhoun, owned by Harold Link and other members of his family. The Sartwelle property, immediately east of Calhoun Boulevard across from the University campus, extended south to Brays Bayou, east to a complex of railroad tracks, and north to the Link property.

General Bruce asked me for a recommendation. I told him that the University in my judgment should eventually acquire all of this additional land, even though such acquisitions might involve many years of negotiations and very large sums of money. "How would you begin?" he then asked. I said that I proposed to go to Johnny Goyen and other friends on Council, and then to Mayor Lewis Cutrer, with Settegast Park as our first objective.

General Bruce took the matter to Vice-President C.F. McElhinney, whose sage advice was always valuable, and then to Staff Conference. I was instructed to proceed, with caution.

In some preliminary discussions, primarily with Goyen, I found that it might be possible to purchase Settegast Park, at an appraised price, under three conditions: first, it would have to be shown there were no substantial improvements or equipment in the park, and that little or no use was being made of it; second, that the University had a valid need for it; and finally, the citizens of Houston had to approve the property being offered for sale.

The first point was practically moot, since the City of Houston had invested exactly $12 in Settegast Park over the years, this being the price of one water hydrant. Moreover, the property had never been used as a park, and there was little or no prospect of such use in the future. It was obvious that the University needed the land involved, and could make excellent use of it, specifically for an expansion of our intramural playing fields, practice areas for intercollegiate sports, and the replacement of obsolete tennis courts along Wheeler.

With these matters established, I had to turn to other projects and Johnny Goyen was on his own eternally busy schedule, compounded by a campaign for reelection. Nothing further was done for weeks, until I luckily bought an afternoon *Chronicle* at the old Houston International Airport, enroute to a meeting in Philadelphia. One of the paper's political reporters had noted that only a few days remained for any issues to be decided by the electorate to be placed on the ballot.

The moment I was in my room at the old Bellevue-Stratford (three decades before the outbreak of the "Legionnaire's disease"), I called Johnny Goyen and explained the situation to him. He agreed that it would be best to place Settegast Park on the ballot at once, helped to bring this about, and watched with me as the issue—never at all controversial—passed on election night by a huge margin.

In due course, Settegast Park was appraised at $10,000 per acre. Some months after this, Vice-President McElhinney and I found the opportunity to explain the importance of this acquisition to the University's good and generous friend, Corbin J. Robertson. Upon his recommendation, the Cullen Foundation provided the funds for the purchase.

Johnny Goyen has made another major contribution to the University of Houston over the years; he is the competent and knowledgable announcer for all home football games, and has always refused to accept a fee for this important and taxing assignment.

Jack Valenti has also made some uniquely valuable contributions to his alma mater over the years, including service as a charter regent of the institution from September 1, 1963, until he was called to Washington as assistant to President Lyndon B. Johnson.

As is widely known, President Johnson had come to rely upon Jack Valenti for crucial assignments in the early 1960's, and seldom let him out of his sight in those tragic and dangerous first weeks after the assassination of President John F. Kennedy. I had seen Jack very briefly in Houston the evening before the tragedy in Dallas, watched him on all three networks in the memorable swearing-in ceremony on Air Force One (for which he helped locate Judge Sara T. Hughes), and caught a glimpse of him once or twice during the historic and interminable television coverage of the next three days. I could swear that throughout the ordeal, Valenti wore the same suit he was wearing at the Kennedy dinner in the Coliseum here, which was most unusual for him but probably explained by the fact that LBJ would never let him go change.[16]

Jack Valenti's influence and advice was extremely important to the University during his years with President Johnson, on matters ranging from interrelationships with the National Aeronautics and Space Administration (NASA) to the recruiting of high-level members of the faculty and staff.

I went to see him once in his small but strategically located office near President Johnson at the White House, at the behest of some of our senior departmental heads and deans. They wanted LBJ to be the keynote speaker for a conference and were convinced that Jack Valenti could arrange this without any particular difficulty, if I would simply visit with him in person about the invitation. I was a realist in such matters, but the petitioners were earnest, well-meaning men, and good friends and colleagues. Since I was regularly in Washington, as president at the time of one of the higher education organizations now concentrated at One Dupont Circle, I accepted the assignment.

At the White House, Valenti and I talked a few moments of his beautiful wife and new son, of his upcoming book, and the latest Washington gossip.

"What can I do for you, P.J.?" he asked.

"Some of the senior faculty want to know if there might be any chance of getting your boss down in a few weeks, for a conference they have in mind."

"What's the subject?"

"Well, it's different," I replied, "all about credibility gaps."

I thought for a moment that Jack Valenti, as experienced a cigar smoker as I know, was going to choke on the $2 panatela he had obviously been enjoying to this point in our conversation. He recovered quickly, and responded, "That's a barrel of snakes. What else do you want to talk about?"

The next time I saw Jack Valenti, it was at the University of Houston. As president of the Motion Picture Producers' Association of America (MPAA), he had offered me a campus preview of an outstanding picture, plus a day-long seminar with its distinguished director and himself as principal participants. The picture was "In the Heat of the Night," a Sidney Poitier triumph which was a multiple Oscar winner; the director was Norman Jewison, the brilliant Canadian. The preview and the following seminar were jam-packed with students, faculty, and staff; and the entire project was one of the most successful ever staged on our campus.

It is difficult to pinpoint when the University of Houston went on a full wartime footing, but the way is marked with a succession of clearly visible signposts: the opening of the United States Naval Reserve Vocational School (NRVS) on October 28, 1941, immediately after completion of the Manufacturers' Industrial Shop Building, already renamed the Industrial Building; the inauguration of the far larger United States Navy Electricity and Radio Materiel School (NERMS) on March 12, 1942, in conjunction with the emergency construction of the Recreation Building, needed for support of NERMS; the dedication of the 1942 *Houstonian* to the burgeoning number of students "who have left to serve in the Armed Forces of the United States, in appreciation of their supreme sacrifice for our beliefs" (some wit, writing in the Letters to the Editor section of the *Cougar*, said that he and his friends appreciated the dedication and the spirit in which it was written, would be willing to do what they could, but hoped that their sacrifice "wouldn't necessarily be all that supreme, as they had post-war plans"); and finally, in sorrowful and complete recognition of the transition to war, the lists of students killed or missing in action.

Although President Oberholtzer and the HISD trustees, plus key citizens asked for assistance, helped bring NRVS, NERMS, a Navy V-5 primary flight school, and a small Army Air Corps reserve unit to the University, much of the credit must go to Dr. Kemmerer. As early as the 1938-1939 academic year, he alone saw the dangers confronting the institution in wartime, as well as the many opportunities for national service.

And he was often the gadfly, urging President Oberholtzer to place yet another call to Congressman Albert Thomas, or to meet with George A. Hill, Jr. and the Military Affairs Committee of the hyperactive Houston Chamber of Commerce.

Dr. Kemmerer had even more of a role in the financing and construction (in what were astoundingly short periods of time, especially considering the problems of escalating wartime shortages of materials and labor) of the Industrial Building and the Recreation Building. (He always referred to the former as the "Vocational" Building, and the latter as the "Rec" Building, and these names tended more and more to be adopted within the University).

The objective of NRVS was to bring in specially selected Naval trainees in groups of about 100 for four months of training in drafting, machine shop procedures, electrical installation, testing and maintenance, welding, the operating of diesel and gasoline motors, and sheetmetal working. The trainees, many of them from the Houston and New Orleans areas, were selected by examination at the Corpus Christi Naval Base.

The NRVS trainees were an intelligent, clean-cut, hard-working lot, with the exception of a very few misfits who were quickly weeded out under Naval disciplinary procedures. President Oberholtzer and Dr. Kemmerer worked closely with the ranking officers who came down from Washington, D.C. to get the unit underway[17] and with the permanent staff. There was a great deal of emphasis upon creating a positive impression of the NRVS students from the very beginning, and civilians were invited and urged to attend the unit's formal retreat ceremony in the quadrangle each day at sundown. Student leaders encouraged this, and NRVS representatives were special guests at Student Council and Student Assembly meetings in the tiny library (adorned with pictures of Abraham Lincoln and Robert E. Lee left and right, with a plaster bust of George Washington in between, for balance).

The University had already pocketed one extremely valuable bonus from its new NRVS and would shortly have another. The first bonus was the Industrial Building, under discussion since 1937, but suddenly in the limelight through a combination of the national emergency, Houston's booming population and economy, ongoing negotiations with the Navy for NRVS and a glaring shortage of skilled technicians.[18]

Mr. Cullen had asked Stephen P. Farish to look into the matter of what was originally called the Manufacturers' Shop Building, and had named a committee in 1939 consisting of Mr. Farish, Robert Mueller, Colonel Rudolph C. Kuldell, Edward L. Lorehn, Donald H. Thornbury, W.B. Sharp, Thomas Shartle, Dr. J.V. Pennington, and George O'Leary to raise the necessary funds.

The committee organized itself, met a few times, and began to solicit funds from companies with a need for trained technicians and craftsmen, particularly those in the oil tool manufacturing industry. The leading prospects included Hughes Tool, Reed Roller Bit, Mission Manufacturing, Hunt Tool, Wilson Supply, Houston Oil Field Material Company, Maintenance Engineering, Gray Tool, Gulf Publishing Company, Lane-Wells, Magnolia Airco, Schlumberger Well Surveying, Cameron Iron Works, Mosher Steel, Thornhill-Craver, Mid-Continental Supply, and the Howard F. Smith Company.

There was a very high correlation between committee members and a list of the chief executives of the principal oil tool manufacturing companies at the time, and Quintana Petroleum did a good bit of business with all of them.

The campaign for the Manufacturers' Shop Building lagged, although there was some success; then some of the economic and manpower developments cited above began to emerge. In the meantime, negotiations with the Navy had reached a stage where it was apparent that a facility such as the Manufacturers' Shop Building would be required for NRVS and for NERMS, in addition to trainees from local industry. With these positive developments, there was a greatly renewed interest in contributions, and most of the goal had been pledged by the early days of November 1940.

Mr. Cullen had been following the campaign closely, because of his intense interest in providing the University with badly needed new buildings and with assuring the institution a direct role in the defense effort as soon as possible. He had seen President Oberholtzer at a benefit performance of the Houston Symphony Society just before Thanksgiving, and told him to "stand by for some good news."

The following week, Dr. Oberholtzer was asked to have the trustees of the HISD stand by at their next meeting for the possibility of accepting a gift of the Manufacturers' Shop Building.

The next session was December 3, 1940, and President Oberholtzer hand-carried the following letter, addressed to him and to the trustees from Mr. Cullen to that meeting:

> Some time ago you informed me that the Houston University was seriously in need of a Shop Building, and I agreed to help you raise the necessary funds to build the same. I prevailed upon Steve Farish, Bob Mueller, Colonel Kuldell, Ed Lorehn, Don Thornberry, W.B. Sharp, Tom Shartle, Dr. Pennington, George Oleary (sic) to act as a Committee to raise the necessary funds, and to appoint a Sub-Committee to go into all the details of the matter.
>
> The Committee secured pledges of One Hundred Two Thousand ($102,000) Dollars and made the Second National Bank Depository.
>
> Some of the pledges were to cover a period of five years, while some agreed to pay all cash. I then agreed to underwrite the balance due on pledges, so the construction of a shop building could be started.
>
> Now, I want to compliment Drs. Oberholtzer and Kemmerer and the members of the School Board on the great success they have had in building one of the greatest educational institutions in the United States. Nearly all other institutions of learning are subsidized by taxes, or endowment, while the Houston University has neither of these revenues, but stands on the strong foundation of self-support.
>
> *H.R. Cullen*

This is a remarkable communication, for several reasons: it indicated Mr. Cullen's continuing interest in the University, and his success in having others join with him once more in important support for the institution; it demonstrated his impatience in getting on with the building of additional facilities, particularly since he had exacted a promise from President Oberholtzer and Dr. Ray K. Daily, then president of the trustees of HISD, to accept the gift immediately, adopt a budget on the spot and get on with it;[19] it showed again that he would put up significant sums of money for the University, in cash if necessary. (Records indicate that less than 10 percent of the $102,000 gift had actually been paid in, the remainder being on pledges for as long as five years. Mr. Cullen simply asked for the difference between $102,000 and cash paid in, and issued a check for the remainder, which was paid back to him between 1941 and 1946.)

The letter also indicates Mr. Cullen's pride in the University, and his determination to keep it on a self-supporting basis. He was to violate this resolve, fortunately for the University, by the magnificence of his future gifts, both to physical plant and to operations; but it would be the final year of his life before he was able to admit that the institution must begin to look toward becoming a member of the state system of higher education.

Endowment concerned him so little that I mistook the corpus of the University endowment fund, when I was first offered a position on the staff, for annual income from the fund. I had been asked by Mr. Cullen and General Bruce to discuss any impressions of the institution with them, as part of an interviewing process that preceded my employment. I blithely told them a number of things, concluding with the observation that it appeared there would have to be a serious effort to get the endowment fund up from its present indicated level of $10 million. That level was assumed, I added, since $10 million invested prudently in 1955 should have returned about $400,000, or four percent, this being the amount I had noted in the latest financial report.

Luckily, I was seated on General Bruce's partly deaf side, and I don't think he really heard me. Mr. Cullen did. He hesitated for a moment and then said very clearly, "That four hundred is all we have in endowment, not annual income from money we have salted away. Only those big Eastern schools can do that."

I was shaken, but said nothing. It was the last time I tried to show off my Harvard Business School training. Mr. Cullen changed his views on endowed income somewhat after some substantial gifts in this category were made in the 1950's; but it took a concentrated effort to get the corpus of the University endowment fund up substantially in the mid-1970's. Even at the present level of approximately $15 million, it is far below current, and certainly future, requirements.

Analysis of Mr. Cullen's December 2, 1940, letter also reveals one other important fact. It was addressed to President Oberholtzer as chief executive of the University, not as superintendent of schools, HISD; and to the trustees of HISD in their alternate role as members of the Board of Trustees of the University of Houston, not as members of the Board of Education, HISD.

This was at least technically correct, but it reveals an important change in Hugh Roy Cullen's thinking, probably already stimulated anew by Colonel Bates, who had begun an intensification of his quiet but persevering campaign to obtain legal and complete separation of the University of Houston from the Houston Independent School District.

Regardless of how they were addressed, the trustees of HISD voted unanimously on December 3 to accept the proferred gift of $102,000 for the Manufacturers' Shop Building, and to thank Mr. Cullen for his generosity. Gratitude was also expressed, of course, to the various other donors and to the fund-raising committee.

A total budget of $174,745 was then adopted for the third campus building, with $102,000 from donors (of which $15,000 was escrowed for the purchase of equipment), $52,745 from the WPA, and $20,000 from the University of Houston Building Fund. (Virtually all of the $20,000 was recouped later when additional donations brought total contributions to $127,385.)

Because of the assistance from Dr. Kemmerer and the executive committee of laymen from the original fund-raising group, plus cooperation from WPA officials, it was also possible to have at least preliminary approval of Architect Cato's plans and sketches at the December 3, 1940, meeting. The plans called for a facility of approximately 36,000 square feet—at a cost of less than five dollars per square foot!

This was a highly flexible building, designed in module-like wings adaptable to the total funds available. The $102,000 pledged by donors, and made immediately available through Mr. Cullen's generosity, meant that all three wings in the original plan could now be built.

The interior was quite functional, and essentially plain vanilla, including faced-tile walls in the shop areas and concrete floors. The exterior, however, harmonized well with the Roy Gustav Cullen and Science Buildings, with a slightly-raised central portion, facing limestone, and a handsome dark red tile roof. A steel frame and steel windows added stability to the structure which is in good condition today having recently been remodeled as part of the $12 million plant for the ever-expanding College of Technology.

Under constant prodding from the University administration and Navy officials, the Shop Building was ready for partial occupancy on September 29, 1941, and was completed somehow for the arrival of the NRVS trainees a month later, on October 28, 1941. This was a remarkable achievement, especially in view of intensifying shortages of materials, supplies, and equipment that hampered plumbing, heating, and electrical contractors.

The Shop Building was dedicated December 15, 1941, in brief and solemn ceremonies reflecting the fact that war had been declared less than a week before. Some of the NRVS trainees drawn up in dress uniform for the occasion would help avenge what FDR had so eloquently termed "a day that will live in infamy" at the climactic battles of Midway and the Coral Sea.

Meanwhile, there had been growing pressure for the Recreation Building, long sought by the student body but now a central factor in the University's prospects for a major expansion of relationships with the Navy. Dr. Kemmerer had been told that his institution would be assigned the big NERM School, with the possibility of training as many as 5,000 technicians, if there could be reasonable assurance of occupying the new structure before the end of the government's fiscal year on June 30.

Dr. Kemmerer was uncomfortably perched on the horns of a troubling, and potentially dangerous, dilemma. He wanted NERMS very much; in fact he simply had to have NERMS at the University, he decided, as he pondered the final figures on Fall 1941 enrollment.

The figures were not unexpected, but they were clearly disturbing. After successive increases in enrollment, from 1,285 in the fall of 1937 to 1,563, 2,067, and 2,488 students (representing hefty gains of 22, 32 and 20 percent) from 1938 through 1940, total registration had suddenly stabilized at 2,494 in September, 1941. And the full exodus from the campus to the armed services, or to draft-exempt, high-paying jobs in industry, had not yet begun. All signs pointed unmistakably to a continuing drop in enrollment, and concomitant loss of the tuition income upon which the University of Houston depended so heavily, until the end of the war—or at least until victory was so clearly in sight that substantial numbers of men were being released from active duty.

A steady input of NERMS students, estimated at 1,500 per year, would obviously make a tremendous difference to the University, both in terms of the short-range financial picture and of the ability to retain a solid base from which to launch into the post-war era.

Dr. Kemmerer could obviously go to the Navy, guarantee them occupancy of the "Rec" Building (which they had to have in order to feed large NERMS classes and to provide an all-weather location for mandatory drills and physical education classes) by the June 30 deadline. This would gain a great deal of stability for the University while performing a considerable service for the nation. But normal construction time for the "Rec" was estimated at eight to ten months (plus any delays for rain, extreme cold, or shortages of materials and supplies), and it would be at least mid-January before plans and blueprints could be placed before the trustees of the HISD for approval and issuance of contracts. What if he guaranteed occupancy, and then simply could not deliver?

The solution was a compromise, plus a highly innovative approach to construction. How would it be, Dr. Kemmerer proposed, if the Recreation Building were built in two stages, with guaranteed occupancy of a first unit before June 30, 1942, and the possibility of completing the second unit soon thereafter, certainly by September 1?

The Navy was not completely happy with this, but they had actually reached a point of no return in their negotiations with the University. It would be far better to have reasonable assurance of at least an emergency first unit by the June 30 deadline, with the second unit also being raced to completion, than to go elsewhere. NERMS graduates were desperately needed, and the decision announced to President Oberholtzer and Dr. Kemmerer was, "Yes, but we are really depending upon you to make the deadline."

With close cooperation from H.L. Mills (whose appetite for the project was whetted not only by the prospect of a major and stabilizing increase in operating income, but the revelation that the Navy would pay for any later alterations or change orders), Dr. Kemmerer had determined that it would be feasible, and reasonably efficient, to take the two-stage approach. Moreover, he had located an old-line "boss of the works," reportedly with plenty of experience in emergency construction in Central America, who claimed that the initial unit could be built in 60 days, with the second unit not far behind such a schedule.

Both Dr. Kemmerer and Mr. Mills took this with a grain of salt, but even 90 days would still leave a leeway of almost a month, if the project could be expedited through the maze of WPA paperwork as soon as possible after the approval of final plans and issuance of blueprints. After further discussion with the "boss of the works," they began to believe that he might somehow be able to meet his 60-day schedule, preposterous though this had seemed. There would be some added costs; in particular, the rental of a giant tent to cover the entire building site. The boss also demanded three shifts of men, plenty of lights day and night, and music, and gallons of hot coffee at all times on the job.

With some major misgivings, Dr. Kemmerer went back to the School Board and told them that he believed the Navy deadline of June 30 could be met by going to a two-unit approach and 24-hour shifts. He recommended that he and H.L. Mills be given plenipotentiary powers to deal directly with the WPA (which was to provide about 45 percent of the total project cost) in order to expedite matters as much as possible between meetings of the School Board.

Any such request would have precipitated vociferous and resounding protests a few months, or few weeks, before from Holger Jeppesen and Dr. Henry A. Petersen ("Jepperson" and "Peterson" in the 1942 *Houstonian*, a matter which they brought forcibly to President Oberholtzer's attention). Now, in a post-Pearl Harbor atmosphere plus assurances from their crony, H.L. Mills, there was silence, and acquiescence.

After School Board approval, Dr. Kemmerer announced publicly, in order to keep maximum pressure on the "boss of the works," that he estimated completion of the first unit of the Recreation Building by May 1, 1942, with the second unit to be occupied "during the summer." Lamar Q. Cato somehow had plans and blueprints for the first unit ready for the January 16, 1942, meeting of the HISD trustees. These were approved with little discussion, along with a $70,000 commitment from the University of Houston Building Fund. The total cost for the first unit of the Recreation Building was estimated at $110,000, including an expected grant from the WPA of approximately $40,000.

Now the critical matter became getting WPA approval from the regional office in Fort Worth, a process that normally required a minimum of three to six months, and sometimes considerably longer. WPA officials were ready to cooperate as much as possible, and a few strategically placed telephone calls from Eighth Naval District Headquarters in New Orleans, followed up from the recently opened Pentagon in Washington, D.C., helped to preserve a high level of motivation. Actual work orders were approved in Fort Worth on the morning of March 6, 1942, and were hand-delivered to the campus the same day.

Meanwhile, the boss of the works had recruited three crews of 60 men each, calculated to provide full working strength of 55 men per eight-hour shift at all times. One shift was composed of blacks, one of Latin-Americans, and one of Anglos, in today's terminology. Back in 1942, it was the "black," the "brown," and the "white" shift, and they were never intermixed, although many of the men on the three crews came to know one another as the project and a friendly spirit of competition developed.

The tent was set in place, with plenty of student observers and advisors on hand, and Navy enlisted men were ordered by their NRVS chief petty officers[20] to "keep the coffee pot boiling" at the construction site. Lights were strung throughout the tent and in the surrounding work areas; a turntable was borrowed from one of the local radio stations and wired up by Navy trainees; a plentiful supply of loud, fast records was provided for constant programming by water-boys, often relieved by students volunteering as project disc jockeys.

Charles F. Hiller, the efficient utility outfielder who handled so many assignments so well, had been named University coordinator for Navy activities in 1942, and he and other administrators at the time still remember the surrealistic scenes at the "Rec" construction site, with workmen trotting instead of walking, the shifts competing against one another, the bright glare of lights at night, and the pounding music. And always, midnight, dawn, or dusk, the work went on—often with the sound of winter and early spring rains pounding deafeningly down on the huge protective tent, stretched tautly above like a giant percussion drum.

As work began on the first unit of the Recreation Building, described in the Board of Education's minute book as the East Wing, plans were being expedited for the second unit, which included a two-story central portion of the total structure. The cost of this unit was estimated at $127,685, to be financed with $70,501 from University reserves and an expected $57,184 from the WPA, at the usual 55-45 ratio. Tentative approval was given by the Board of Education at the March 16, 1942 meeting; and in an unusual procedure recognizing again the critical time element, President Oberholtzer and Mr. Mills were authorized not only to negotiate with the WPA, but to sign all necessary documents on behalf of the trustees.

Final approval for the second unit of the Recreation Building was voted April 15, 1942, with separate authorization for a small temporary shop building in which to conduct an aircraft mechanics school for civilians. This project had been put forward earlier by Dr. Kemmerer, who saw the necessity for service schools so clearly, but also wanted to provide some degree of balance in offerings for civilian employees or prospective employees of defense plants.

Things were progressing famously, meanwhile, at the round-the-clock center for construction of the first unit of the Recreation Building. Navy officials, accustomed to months and even years of procedural delays within the bureaus charged with procurement and construction, could hardly believe their eyes when they saw the incredible degree of progress between frequent inspection visits. By mid-April, they decided to move a first class of NERMS trainees onto the campus as soon as possible, sharing NRVS facilities temporarily until the East Wing was ready.

The first contingent of NERMS enrollees, who were to total 4,278 before the unit at the University was phased out three years later on March 31, 1945, arrived on campus March 12, 1942. They occupied the East Wing, unbelievably, in the first week of May. Walter W. Kemmerer watched them march in with great satisfaction and a sigh of relief.

He and the University of Houston owed a lasting debt to the "boss of the works" and his three unflagging crews, who had completed the East Wing in just under eight weeks. They then went on to finish the second unit of the Recreation Building before the end of summer.

There was one unhappy postscript to all this. The "Rec" Building began to show some alarming structural faults as early as the mid-1950's, and the entire structure had to be pulled down in stages between 1965 and 1967, barely surviving until the opening of the $5.8 million University Center in the latter year. By that time, Harry F. Ebert, then in charge of physical plant, was issuing daily bulletins on the width of cracks in certain outside walls. Floors were settling and disintegrating as the foundation subsided, and sizable chunks of limestone facing from the "Rec" had narrowly missed students passing by it.

Nevertheless, the University had marvelous value and use, as did the Navy, from a facility that cost the institution less than $150,000—and provided a 24-hour spectacle while it was being constructed. It was ruled officially that the Navy had 95 percent use of the Recreation Building until it departed the campus in 1945 (civilians, for example, had to eat on the second floor of the central portion, the downstairs being reserved for NERMS and NRVS trainees at mealtime), and the University was accordingly paid an additional $35,655.59 for alterations to the facility.

Once the post-war era was launched, particularly since there was virtually no construction of additional student life facilities for 25 years, the "Rec" became a vital center for such operations as campus snack bar, cafeteria, bridge club and general hangout, medical services, bookstore, placement, counseling, Army Reserve Officer Training Corps (ROTC), intramurals, intercollegiate athletics, student life offices, and the meetings of a vast array of campus organizations.

It is interesting to list just what was required, in additional facilities and in dollars, to absorb what went on in the old "Rec," overcrowded, unsuitable, and unsafe though it became: the previously-mentioned $5.8 million University Center;[21] $2 million for the Athletics Building (now named to honor Harry Fouke, our first and only and great director of athletics) and related facilities; a $1.6 million Student Life complex, since extensively remodeled; parts of the $5 million Hofheinz Pavilion; and the $600,000 Bruce Religion Center.

The arrival of the NERMS trainees gave the campus a considerably more military appearance, especially when the new Navy unit combined with colleagues from NRVS in marching to and from classes or meals, or in parade and retreat formations.

Enlistments and call-ups had increased so drastically by the spring of 1943, that it was becoming difficult to find male civilians in any concentration on campus. Even the annual reception for high school seniors featured a military backdrop and theme from 1942, the participants in the Royal Court looking more and more out of place in their white suits and gowns of tulle and organdy. Moselle Jacobs, the *Cougar* editor, announced the departure of five male members of the staff (Harold Elliott, Johnny Johnson, Bob Matthes, and the omnipresent Jack Valenti and Johnny Goyen) for active duty; but more significantly, this increased the number of stars on the *Cougar* service flag to 28. And the campus newspaper carried a feature story on civilian students facing active duty soon and volunteering to train on the Navy's dreaded obstacle course, with its 20-foot walls to be scaled with a rope.

The Red Masque Players were strongly influenced in their choice of *Our Town* as a featured presentation of the season because it could be cast with seven women to every man.

Then came the most telling signal of the shift to a full-wartime status—the 1942 *Houstonian* carried a full page "...paying tribute to those boys for whom we sing 'Auld Lang Syne.' Their part in America's war effort was far greater than any pictured herein."

On the page appeared the names of Hugh Walker, ensign, USNR; Ferdinand B. Paris ("Bubba" Paris, captain of the ice hockey team and a star of the Red Masque Players, had been one of the best known and most popular men in the student body), second lieutenant, Army Air Corps; and James T. Ferguson, civilian pilot training (program).

The 1943 *Houstonian*, in sharp contrast, is dedicated to "... (the) group of University of Houston students working and fighting upon a larger campus ... the battlefields of World War II. As the *Houstonian* went to press, 762 of these had been listed upon the roll of honor and 15 were known to have died or been lost in action ..."

The former students killed or missing in action are not listed in the 1943 yearbook, but the 1944 edition names 34: J. Mitchell Allemand, AAC; John S. Arant, Jr., AAF; Coleman R. Asher, AAF; William Batchelor, Jr., AAC; William A. Bloom, AAC; Cleve M. Brown, Jr., AAC; Raymond E. Campbell, Jr., USA; J.T. Coleman, AAC; Loren Crouch, USN; William J. Dupree, USN; Ralph M. Edwards, AAC; James Burleigh Fahey, AAF; James T. Ferguson, USA; Joseph D. Fulton, AAC; Waley H. Garrett, AAC; Gustave M. Heiss, Jr., AAF; Harold Helfrich, AAC; Healy J. Mills, USN; Milas A. Mugnier, NAC; Ferdinand B. Paris, AAC; Ralph E. Parlette, NAC; Ivy Rees, AAC; Thomas P. Ridley, AAC; Augustus Payne Rutherford, AAF; Sam Frederick Semo, Jr., AAF; Billy A.

Smith, USN; Durward Sowell, USA; Merlyn C. Vogelsand, AAC; James A. Waddle, USA; Warren Walton, USA; Claude D. Weatherford, MAC; George W. Wells, USA; Marvin Westerfield, AAC; and Gordon M. Young, AAF.

By service or branch, the totals were Army Air Corps or the alternate designation Army Air Forces (AAC or AAF), 21; United States Army (USA), six; United States Navy (USN), four; Navy Air Corps (NAC), two; and Marine Air Corps (MAC), one. Thus, 24 out of the first list of dead or missing were fliers, an extraordinary percentage.

There are apparently no official records to reveal who was the first World War II casualty from the University of Houston student body. It is assumed that James T. Ferguson, "Bubba" Paris, and Hugh Walker were singled out in the 1942 *Houstonian* because they were the first to enlist, or to be called to active duty, rather than as casualties. Otherwise, why does Hugh Walker's name fail to appear on any later casualty list that I have been able to discover? And although Bubba Paris and James T. Ferguson's names were unfortunately on the 1944 list, why is Lieutenant Ferguson shown as a USA loss, rather than being identified again as he was in 1942 (CPT, or civilian pilot training program participant)?

The death of Rice Institute's first alumnus killed in Allied action in World War II, by contrast, was highly publicized, and Lieutenant O.D. Wyatt of the Class of 1939 became something of a symbol of the many students and former students of Rice and of the University of Houston who lost their lives in the long conflict. Lieutenant Wyatt actually died a day before the formal declaration of war. He was killed at Clark Field on Pearl Harbor Day as he attempted to get his fighter plane in the air to contest the "Tora, Tora, Tora" waves of attacking Japanese Zeros.

A high school in Fort Worth, his hometown, is named for Wyatt, although neither Rice (which does have a Memorial Center) nor the University of Houston were to provide World War II memorials named for a specific person or persons. O.D. Wyatt achieved campus fame at Rice Institute in an experiment involving Frank A. Pattie, a brilliant psychologist and the only man I can recall who had earned degrees from Harvard, Yale, and Princeton.

Dr. Pattie put Wyatt into a deep trance during a demonstration of hypnotic behavior, told his subject—a "high suggestible" susceptible to hypnosis—that a half-dollar he would spin on the long Chemistry Lecture Hall table was red-hot (it was actually at room temperature), and ordered him to pick it up. Wyatt did so, only to drop the coin immediately with a cry of pain. He then exhibited what appeared to be definite burn marks on thumb and forefinger. The campus split into believers and skeptics by nightfall, the latter claiming a hoax perpetrated by Professor Pattie and the fun-loving Wyatt. I was a believer, having seen the victim rubbing Unguentine on his thumb later in the day.

A year after the casualty report in the 1944 *Houstonian,* President Oberholtzer spoke proudly but with sorrow of the University's war dead and missing in action. He placed the "unofficial" total at 77 students or former students, out of some 1,200 in the armed services. There were apparently no deaths among the considerable number of faculty who went on active duty.

The moment that the Board of Education saw the Naval Electricity and Radio Materiel School safe in harbor at the Recreation Building, and classes for NERMS and NRVS trainees (as well as civilians) being conducted 15 hours a day in the Shop Building, the HISD trustees turned immediately to another fundamental problem. This was to at least get under way the eventual separation of the University of Houston from the School District. There were problems enough within the public school system; why add the increasingly complex difficulties and responsibilities involved in an outdated relationship with a tiny junior college grown into a bustling university?

This was a conclusion, it will be recalled, that Colonel W. B. Bates had been quietly but adroitly advancing since his confidential talks with E.D. Shepherd on the subject in 1939. The colonel still had not puzzled out some of the intricate equations he saw within the patternings before him, especially the changing interrelationships of President Oberholtzer, Dr. Kemmerer, and H. L. Mills. But he felt that quick action—even if it had to be limited to the naming of a high-level study committee—was in order when he turned his attention to the situation again in the spring of 1942.

The trustees had in a sense learned their lesson about attempting to operate both the public school system and the University of Houston. They had just been through the tense, time-consuming predicament surrounding the emergency completion of the Recreation Building, and were still uneasy about some financial projections at the University through 1945, presented by Dr. Kemmerer. If these were examples of the degree of their expected involvement in the institution's affairs (and of some of the possible fiscal pitfalls out there), they reasoned, a prudent man would be wise to begin to look for a way out.

This reaction was especially prevalent among the business and professional members of the Board of Education, who could already predict an obvious need for more attention to their own affairs in wartime. Scarcities of manpower and materials were cropping up everywhere, yet Houston was booming again; one pivotal economic indicator, bank deposits, was shooting up at a phenomenal rate that would average 28.2 percent per annum throughout the 1940's.

Colonel Bates could see other cogent reasons for moving quickly toward at least the first stages of separation of the University from the School District. Hugh Roy Cullen and other leading citizens had agreed to accept appointment with him on an Advisory Board for the institution, and men of their caliber were not inclined to sit around waiting. It was either move ahead, or see them captured by some other challenge, especially as the community organized itself for citizen support of the war effort.

Further, the full process of separation (which was obviously the true objective) would require a time of adjustment, legislative action, and other possibly complex operations. These were decisive matters that should be accomplished, if at all possible, before the end of the war—and onrushing enrollments for the University of Houston, which were already being predicted.

William B. Bates had done his missionary work well, in the tradition of the circuit-riding Presbyterian preachers who visited Nat and Nacogdoches in his childhood. On May 18, 1942, the Board of Education voted unanimously that a committee "... consisting of the Board as a whole and ... Dr. E.E. Oberholtzer, Dr. (sic) H.L. Mills, Dr. W.W. Kemmerer, and N.K. Dupre study a plan of change or expansion in the control of the University."

This satisfied everyone; the four trustees who still held a majority, paper thin though it was (Dr. Ray K. Daily, president; Mrs B.F. Coop, secretary; George D. Wilson; and E.D. Shepherd, president for so many years but now returned to the back benches), knew that consideration of a different system of governance for the University was long overdue; the minority members (Holger Jeppesen, vice-president; Dr. H.A. Petersen; and Ewing Werlin,[22] who had just replaced long-time member A.C. Finn) saw separation as a means of finally getting rid of "Old Eddie" Oberholtzer as superintendent of schools; H.L. Mills now lived for the day that he could get his nemesis Superintendent/President Oberholtzer relieved of one of his titles, but he was also increasingly enthusiastic about effecting a financial divorcement between the HISD and the University; Dr. Kemmerer, as we shall see, not only approved separation but was heavily involved in some negotiations with Mr. Mills that improved the chances for such action dramatically. Dr. Oberholtzer was an outspoken proponent of separation, but he hoped that it would not involve the loss of his long established position as superintendent of schools. Dean Dupre was on the committee at the insistence of Dr. Daily, who had great respect for his hard work and grasp of details; he would not add substantially to the committee's deliberations and findings, and was somewhat ignored by President Oberholtzer, who looked upon the dean as more of an operations manager than a molder of policy. Nevertheless, Naason K. Dupre was extremely aware of the need for separation, supportive of it, and could cite numberless instances of how HISD domination had hampered the University's development.

President Oberholtzer reported for the study committee at the July 19, 1943, meeting of the Board of Trustees, HISD. An abstract of his report, one of the more significant in the history of the University even though its findings were clearly predictable, follows:

> The time will come, in the course of the next year or two, when the growth of the University will be revived, in the post-war period, and a program of expansion will become necessary, thereby necessitating additional administrative personnel. A planning commission for the University should be provided. A separate Board of Trustees should be provided, which should have full responsibility for control and management of the University. Legislation would be required in order to give such a Board of Trustees full legal status. Many districts of the State now operate with separate boards for junior colleges. Legislation can be provided for such a Board of Trustees to operate the University of Houston in the Houston Independent School District.

> A more complete set of by-laws should be provided to define the powers and duties of the executive and administrative officers, and provide for more participation by members of the faculty in formulating and developing the educational policies of the University.

Dr. Kemmerer, as might have been expected, had a considerable role in urging more faculty particpation in the formulation and development of educational policies for the University. There was no delay on moving ahead with the report, once it had been presented and discussed. A vote on July 19, 1943, stipulated that "... Dr. Oberholtzer be given precedence in presenting his plan ... in full."

One week later, on July 26, 1943, an Advisory Board for the University of Houston was created by the following resolution:

> WHEREAS, the Board of Education of the Houston Independent School District, constituting the Trustees of the University of Houston, recognizes that the growth of the Houston Independent School District and of the University of Houston has greatly increased its responsibilities, its opportunities for service, and the scope of its work to such an extent that in the judgment of the said Board of Education of Houston Independent School District, it is advisable that a Committee or Board be established to act on a voluntary gratuitous basis and to advise with the said Board of Education of Houston Independent School District, from time to time, concerning the policies, functions and operations of the University of Houston, and to make recommendations in regard thereto.
>
> NOW, THEREFORE, BE IT, AND THE SAME IS, HEREBY RESOLVED by the Board of Education of the Houston Independent School District, that:
>
> (a) An Advisory Board be adopted by said Board of Education for the purpose of advising with it, the said Board of Education of Houston Independent School District, acting as the Trustees of the University of Houston, from time to time, and to make recommendations to the said Board of Education of Houston Independent School District concerning the policies, management and functions of said University of Houston, and the planning and safeguarding of its further growth and operation.
>
> (b) Said Advisory Board shall consist of fifteen (15) well-qualified and outstanding citizens who reside within said Houston Independent School District.
>
> (c) That, H.R. Cullen, W.B. Bates, A.D. Simpson, Noah Dietrich, H.O. Clarke, Simon Sakowitz, Palmer Hutcheson, Harry C. Wiess, Lamar Fleming, Mrs. James P. Houstoun, Mrs. Haywood Nelms, James W. Rockwell, S.P. Farish, Mrs. Dudley Sharp, and D.H. Thornbury, be and they and each of them are hereby named and appointed as constituting said Advisory Board. The said members of such Advisory Board shall

determine by lot the term for which they shall respectively serve. The five members drawing numbers 1, 2, 3, 4, and 5 shall serve for two (2) years and/or until their sucessors shall be elected by said Advisory Board, the five members drawing numbers 6, 7, 8, 9, and 10 shall serve for four (4) years and/or until their successors shall be elected by said Advisory Board, and five members drawing numbers 11, 12, 13, 14, and 15 shall serve for six (6) years and/or until their successors shall be elected by said Advisory Board. The said Advisory Board is hereby requested and directed to hold, as soon as possible, an organization meeting at which they shall elect from their number, officers, including a Chairman and Secretary, and they shall draw up suitable by-laws for the organization and operation of such Board, including the annual election of officers, the filling of vacancies, and the election of new members for terms of six years to succeed members, whose terms of office shall, from time to time, expire.

(d) Until such time as the Legislature of the State of Texas shall pass a proper law authorizing and creating a separate Board of Trustees for said University of Houston, said Advisory Board and/or its successor or sucessors shall continue to advise with the said Board of Education of Houston Independent School District and make recommendations to it concerning the policies, management and functions of the said University of Houston. Said Advisory Board is hereby authorized and requested to cause to be drafted, and at the proper time, submitted to the Legislature of the State of Texas, an amendment to the law under which said University of Houston is presently being operated, in order to create a separate Board of Trustees for said University of Houston, but to retain such benefits as teachers' retirement and junior college affiliation so that the said University of Houston may continue to receive the benefit of the funds from the State of Texas, it being the sense of said Board of Education of Houston Independent School District that any such amendment, which may be presented by said Advisory Board to the Legislature of the State of Texas, should provide for the retention of all of the advantages of public school affiliation.

Paragraphs (a) and (b) of the resolution seem to emphasize the advisory nature of the new body, especially in such language as "voluntary, gratuitous basis . . . advise . . . from time to time . . . recommendations . . ."

By paragraph (c), however, we find that leading citizens are to serve for terms up to six years; that the Advisory Board is urged to organize itself as soon as possible and to "draw up suitable bylaws . . . including . . . (provisions for) the election of new members for terms of six years to succeed members whose terms of office, from time to time, expire."

And in the final paragraph (d), the Advisory Board is authorized to submit to the Legislature "at the proper time" an amendment to existing law creating a separate Board of Trustees for the University of Houston. (Mr. Mills characteristically stipulated that the amendment should "retain such benefits as teacher retirement and junior college affiliation." By retaining 1927 or any later year in which employment began as the starting date for calculating retirement benefits for faculty and staff, and by passing junior college appropriations on through to eligible students until August 31, 1963, the canny Mr. Mills saved many millions of dollars for those affected.[23]

As Colonel Bates once correctly pointed out, the Advisory Board "was in no sense a 'window dressing' body," nor did its members consider it to be. They met for the first time on August 3, 1943, at H.R. Cullen's home and named Mr. Cullen chairman; Colonel Bates, vice-chairman; Mrs. James P. Houstoun, secretary; and Mrs. Haywood Nelms, assistant secretary.

Of the 15 members, all except Hiram O. Clarke, Noah Dietrich, Simon Sakowitz, A.D. Simpson, D.H. Thornbury, Harry Carothers Wiess, Mrs. Dudley Sharp, Mrs. James P. Houstoun, and Mrs. Haywood Nelms have been identified earlier.

Hiram Clarke was president of Houston Lighting & Power, which named one of their principal operational centers for him after his untimely death; a main traffic artery in the city also carries his name.[24]

Noah Dietrich was Howard Hughes' right hand at Hughes Tool, Gulf Brewing, and elsewhere. Long a resident of Los Angeles after leaving Houston, he was in the headlines again in 1975 and 1976 as executor of a contested will by Hughes that was claimed to be a forgery. Simon Sakowitz, with his brother Tobias the senior member of Sakowitz Brothers, was the merchant prince of the city in the 1940's and 1950's. A.D. Simpson, a leading banker, held key posts at Jesse H. Jones' Texas Bank of Commerce. D.H. Thornbury, the head of Mid-Continent Supply in this area, served briefly as a regent but resigned in 1946 to move to Fort Worth.

Harry Carothers Wiess, the chief executive officer of Humble Oil & Refining Company and a founder of the firm, could not be active on the Advisory Board because of his other enormous responsibilities during World War II. After discussing this with his friend Mr. Cullen, he resigned on April 25, 1944, and was replaced by James Anderson, a marine engineer and vice-president of Humble who had served in the Corps of Engineers.

Colonel Anderson became a very active and valuable regent of the University.

Mrs. Dudley Sharp (Tina Cleveland) was a prime example of the intermarriages of consequence between "Old Houston" and the families which quickly became dominant in the petroleum and oil tool manufacturing industries of the area. Her father, W.D. Cleveland, was a pioneer tycoon, civic leader, and charter trustee of The Rice Institute. Her brother-in-law was W.A. Kirkland, grandson of the founder of the First National Bank, a trustee of The Rice Institute and of Princeton University, city councilman, and one of the most outstanding citizens of Houston.

The Sharps "hit it big" in the original Humble oil field, and Walter Benona Sharp, Sr., with his sons Bedford and Dudley, controlled Mission Manufacturing Company. Dudley Sharp was later a ranking figure in the Republican party, and Secretary of the Air Force. Tina Cleveland Sharp resigned from the Advisory Board soon after it was organized, and was succeeded by Mrs. Ray L. (Fredrica Gross) Dudley.

Fredrica Gross Dudley, a Baylor alumna and remarkable woman who helped her husband organize the Gulf Publishing and Gulf Printing Companies, was to serve as a charter regent from 1945 to 1963, after which she became chairman of the University of Houston Foundation.

Mrs. Houstoun, a 1913 graduate of the University of Chicago and a lady of unusual intelligence and charm, was one of the three socially prominent Gano sisters who married well-known Houstonians: James Patrick (Pat) Houstoun, Dr. Frederick Rice Lummis, and Howard Hughes, Sr.

Mrs. Nelms (Agnese Carter Nelms), a member of the Carter family so long identified with the lumber industry, was the wife of a prominent business leader. She, too, brought brains, charm, and social position to the distaff side of the Advisory Board.

The members of the Advisory Board obviously constituted the top echelon of community business, professional, and social leadership that Mr. Cullen and Colonel Bates, who selected them personally, wanted. Within the group of 15 were persons with immediate entrée to most of the chief executive suites of leading Houston corporations; to the big law firms, just beginning their huge expansion to national and international recognition and stature; to the most exclusive clubs, such as the Eagle Lake Rod and Gun, Tejas, and Bayou; to Assembly (the senior organization for the local presentation of debutantes, featuring a much smaller and more exclusive list, and often, afternoon teas instead of individual balls for each debutante) rather than to Allegro (the junior member of the industry, a men's club organized in 1925 to present the daughters of members at a resplendent and expensive ball each November, and once known as the Twenty Dollar Club, that being the original rate of annual dues); and to long-established churches.

As the Advisory Board organized itself with such commendable speed in the late summer of 1943, and began to address some of the problems still involved in the University's transition from peace to war, as well as the difficulties envisioned for the post-war period, one might wonder why the study committee took 14 months to prepare the brief, although extremely meaningful, report made by President Oberholtzer on July 19, 1943.

The answer lies in a fierce, year-long struggle for power, conducted in a series of closed meetings of the Board of Education, and in what had to be a most difficult decision for Walter W. Kemmerer. The story was never revealed in full, as it might have been in public meetings, and remains obscure; but the following seems to be a logical reconstruction of what occurred.

Dr. Kemmerer saw as early as 1939, but with growing regularity in 1941 and 1942, that it was unfair to Dr. Oberholtzer (and dangerous for the University of Houston) for the almost stalemated 4-3, pro-Oberholtzer margin on the Board of Education to continue. Dr. Oberholtzer's reply would have been that his colleague did not realize the many times in the very early days (before Dr. Kemmerer's arrival in 1929), and for that matter in the 1929-1942 era, that really significant votes had carried 4-3 (or sometimes, 3-4).

Dr. Kemmerer pondered the razor's edge on which he and President Oberholtzer were so often finding themselves for months. He was torn between his loyalty to President Oberholtzer, for whom he had a real admiration and affection, and growing doubts over whether or not his long-time superior should continue to hold the dual posts of superintendent of schools and of president—especially if at growing danger and cost to the University.

At one stage soon after Dr. Kemmerer lost his vice-presidential title in 1939, Colonel Bates had sensed a new relationship between the long-established team of Oberholtzer and Kemmerer, perhaps involving H.L. Mills in some manner. By the time he returned to deliver the first commencement address on the new campus,[25] however, and could visit with both men for some time, there seemed to be no problems between them. But the intuitive Colonel Bates was not far off; the problem had simply gone underground temporarily. Walter W. Kemmerer still had some severe reservations about his superior's dual role, and what it might be doing to the institution to which they were both so dedicated.

Early in 1942, Dr. Kemmerer made up his mind. He would sell H.L. Mills on the idea of splitting the University away from the School District, with Dr. Oberholtzer as full-time president. Mills was not a difficult convert, and he agreed to go to the minority trustees with the plan. They accepted the plan, with the condition that there would have to be an interim report prepared by the newly formed executive committee of the University (Dr. Oberholtzer, Dr. Kemmerer, Mills, and Dean Dupre) under supervision of the Board of Trustees. This was the motion unanimously passed by the Board of Education on May 18, 1942.

Complications then developed with Dr. Oberholtzer, whose five-year contract as superintendent of schools was coming up for renewal. Central though he was to the developing plot, no one had made it clear to him that there was not to be a renewal of contract, this being the price of separation of University and School District. In truth, no one wanted to bell the cat, and everyone involved had assumed that the job was done.

Mills was furious, although he maintained his usual gruff aplomb, and decided that he would deadlock the Board of Education at 3-3, let pressures continue to build up, and see what happened. He did this by offering Mrs. B.F. Coop, a staunch Oberholtzer supporter, a position with the HISD she could not turn down. Mrs. Coop resigned from the Board to accept the new position and the 3-3 tie votes began.

Another strategic move backfired. Dr. Daily was somehow convinced that a nominee for appointment to Mrs. Coop's unexpired term was pro-Oberholtzer, and arranged for him to be nominated. Dr. Kemmerer discovered the nominee's real loyalties at the last moment, and Dr. Daily voted against her own nominee to prevent his election.

Although Mr. Cullen knew nothing of it, George D. Wilson presented his name at one of a long series of deadlocked votes as a replacement for Mrs. Coop. The motion failed by the usual count of 3-3.

Things rocked along until the regular HISD election in April, 1943, at which the Daily-Wilson-Shepherd bloc had the brilliant idea of running Miss Ima Hogg with Dr. Daily for the two vacant spots. They both won, George D. Wilson was named president of the Board of Education and Dr. Oberholtzer was given a new five-year contract, all of course by a 4-3 vote.

Once he had assuaged his pride by winning a bitter, year-long fight, it appeared that Dr. Oberholtzer did not really want a new five-year contract as superintendent of schools. This would be even more the case if he could be assured of quick agreement on a powerful Advisory Board as a new major step toward separation.

H.L. Mills suspected that this was pretty much the case. After all, he reasoned, how long is a 63-year-old man going to want to hold two big jobs, with a 4-3 sword of Damocles still hanging over one of them? He was a realist, also, not one to sit around licking his wounds; the problem was still how to get Dr. Oberholtzer out of that big downtown office at Taylor School, at any reasonable price. Separation, with its side benefits of insulating the School District from escalating administrative headaches plus the continuing threat of severe financial losses at the University, carried not only a reasonable, but a downright attractive, price tag.

Mills went back to the minority trustees and renewed their enthusiasm for separation, which had diminished somewhat as the 3-3 deadlock persisted. Apparently, he and his old foe Edison Ellsworth Oberholtzer then came to an understanding about the real duration of five-year contracts, because the report of the study committee was made within two months after Miss Hogg was sworn in, and the Advisory Board was created just one week after that, on July 26, 1943.

Amid all this infighting and maneuvering (and just after the crisis over emergency construction of the Recreation Building had kept him on a 16-hour daily work schedule), the indefatigable Dr. Kemmerer announced a comprehensive reorganization of the University's academic operations into six colleges and the Graduate School. The plan was officially promulgated in a 1942-1944 catalogue, issued in biennial form to conserve paper, manpower, and money.

The reorganization indicated again the degree to which Dr. Kemmerer, as both comptroller and director of curriculum, could influence the fundamental structure and operations of the University, with or without the title of vice-president. This was especially true while President Oberholtzer continued to condone, and to approve, apparently, an accelerating transfer of power and authority to his energetic first assistant.

Much of the reorganization plan related directly to Dr. Kemmerer's prediction, in early 1942, of post-World War II enrollments. "We must set the stage," he said, "for the greater University of Houston of the future, with the 10,000-15,000 students envisioned. . . " Actual enrollment, it may be recalled, had stabilized suddenly at 2,494 in the fall of 1941; and Dr. Kemmerer himself was privately predicting a substantial drop for 1942, while working night and day to counteract this by bringing Navy training schools to the campus.

When the registration fees were all paid in late September 1942, Dr. Kemmerer's worst fears were realized: there had been a calamitous decrease of 65.4 percent in non-military enrollment, down to 1,508. This wiped out the substantial gains of the past five years; and another loss, to the nadir of 1,104, was to come in 1943.

The Kemmerer prediction of 10,000-15,000 post-war enrollments, therefore, was ignored even by the ever-ebullient Houston Chamber of Commerce, and was regarded by the more conservative members of the faculty as sheer ranting. But President Oberholtzer, to his credit, did not criticize his colleague. He recognized a fellow optimist and enthusiast, even though his own buoyancy and drive seemed more and more to be on the wane. Nor did he challenge the 1942 academic organization.[26]

The Kemmerer plan, though modified in the 1947-1949 era (primarily by the replacement of colleges by schools and by the addition of new schools), was the substance of the University's academic framework for more than two decades. It was built around Colleges of Arts and Sciences, Business Administration, Education, Engineering and Commercial Service, plus the Junior College and the Graduate School.

The College of Arts and Sciences was divided into a Division of Cultural Arts (general music, piano, chorus, voice, dramatics, art,

English, journalism, public speaking and modern languages, including French, German, Italian, and Spanish); a Division of Sciences (biology, chemistry, geography, geology, mathematics, physics, pre-dental and nursing);[27] and a Division of Social Sciences (history, psychology, political science, sociology, and economics).

The College of Business Administration, encompassing what had always been one of the most active academic areas, added a Downtown Business School (quickly shortened to "Downtown School") in 1942. Located first at 705 Fannin, this component was a strong and continuing new tie to the business community and the genesis of a wide-ranging University program in continuing education. It also brought into the institutional orbit two key administrative figures of later years, James C. Taylor and Jerome M. Peschke.

Taylor, a Baylor-trained lawyer of rare initiative and perseverance, would eventually be responsible in large measure for the construction of a beautiful and extremely functional Continuing Education Center on the Central Campus, and for the establishment of the Conrad N. Hilton School of Hotel and Restaurant Management, which may have already closed the gap between its older rivals in the field, at Cornell and Michigan State Universities.

Peschke was recruited from the Massey Business College, where he had been teaching the use of what were then termed "business machines." He taught downtown and on the St. Bernard campus, left for distinguished war service in the Navy, and returned to become a full professor in business technology and, finally, a competent and extremely helpful assistant to the president in the area of academic affairs (as well as in a wide range of special projects and problems).

The Colleges of Business Administration and Arts and Sciences collaborated during World War II in one of the institution's first interdisciplinary programs, Emergency Science-Management War Training, or ESMWT. Hundreds of civilian trainees were taught on campus and at the Downtown School in this program, which combined instruction in chemistry and business management.

The reorganized College of Education had a vital wartime assignment recruiting and retraining teachers to take the places of the hundreds who left the profession for high-paying jobs in war industry or for the armed services. Former teachers, particularly women, were urged to seek recertification, primarily through a unique Education Workshop.

The College of Engineering was subdivided into civil, electrical, general, and mechanical subdisciplines. There were neither petroleum nor chemical engineering programs at this stage in the development of the College.

The Graduate School had been under way with a small program since 1939, but emphasis in the Kemmerer plan of reorganization was heavily on master's degrees in education.

The College of Community Services continued as a highly flexible unit, providing primarily a wide range of non-credit offerings taught either on campus or in the community. These emphasized training for war industry, as a course list indicated: electricity, machine shop procedures, drafting, diesel and aircraft engines, shop mathematics, radio, and even lens grinding. This College also administered the three Naval training schools and a program of training in pre-nursing conducted in cooperation with five hospitals.

In order to put his reorganization into effect, Dr. Kemmerer needed some administrative reinforcements, especially in two areas where there was increasing activity, as opposed to the severely curtailed enrollments in the College of Arts and Sciences and a status quo situation in the College of Education (being countered, as indicated, with a vigorous program of recruiting and recertification).

Recalling President Oberholtzer's views on "naming a bunch of deans who'll think they're running things," he sought a different title that would carry some ring of authority without raising the hackles of his superior. He also cautiously raised again the touchy subject of some beginning system of faculty ranking (the Board of Trustees had previously approved the granting of the first professorial titles, that of associate professor, to Charles F. Hiller, Robert A. White, and Arvin N. Donner, but Dr. Oberholtzer had simply not got around yet to issuing the necessary papers of appointment).

Both "director" and "supervisor" were already in use at lower echelons, as was "chairman" at the departmental level. Seeking a compromise, Dr. Kemmerer proposed that Charles F. Hiller be named "head" of the College of Community Services; Robert A. White, the auditor, head of the College of Business Administration; and Arvin N. Donner, head of the College of Education. When there was no objection, he decided to press his luck, and asked that all three heads also be affirmed as associate professors.

Surprisingly, this was all accepted, but at a price: President Oberholtzer indicated that he had an appointment of his own. This was an eye-opening designation that would have considerable effect: He named Virginia Stone, his long-time secretary and alter ego, bursar. The appointment apparently stemmed from some further horse-trading between Dr. Oberholtzer and H.L. Mills. Miss Stone was a born troublemaker and old maid with two interests in life: Superintendent Oberholtzer (she always used this title instead of Dr. or President Oberholtzer), and a horde of nieces and nephews whose education she was selflessly providing.

Miss Stone guarded her boss as effectively as the Praetorian guards of the Caesars, and could sit on papers requiring immediate action for weeks. This loyal soul became expert at infuriating anti-Oberholtzer trustees, and Mills was finally told to get her out of the downtown office, or else. The solution became her appointment on the St. Bernard campus.

Virginia Stone, who was to die tragically a few years later in an automobile collision near Conroe, was replaced by Dorothy Shriner, who had been on Dr. Oberholtzer's downtown staff for many years. A more consequential addition to the front office in the Roy Gustav Cullen Building was a new secretary for Dr. Kemmerer. This was Leta Gilbert (then Leta Nutt), a highly competent young widow who had been secretary to Lamar Q. Cato, the architect.

Mrs. Gilbert has since been secretary to each of the succeeding presidents of the University of Houston, and will soon complete 35 years of dedicated service to the institution, 28 of those years to its chief executives. Leta Gilbert has also served as *de facto* secretary of both the Board of Regents and the University of Houston Foundation over the years. Her knowledge of the University since 1943, and of the persons who have shaped and formed it for three-and-a-half decades, is encyclopedic.

Once organized, the Advisory Board was moving strongly ahead under the energetic and able guidance of Hugh Roy Cullen and

Colonel Bates as the 1943-1944 academic year began, with University enrollment suddenly diminished to 1,104.

William Bartholomew Bates was an ideal man to act as the intermediary between the Advisory Board and the trustees of the HISD.[28] As a former president of the Board of Education, he was "family" to all the multiple-term members, several of whom had served with him; the newer trustees perceived him both in this role and as a community leader of impeccable reputation and wide experience whose opinions were sought and respected. The Colonel's very demeanor was another valuable attribute. Never ruffled, he was also never argumentative, although he held and would express very clear-cut opinions.

Colonel Bates had told Mr. Cullen, before it was agreed they would head the Advisory Board, that he detected a strong inclination on the part of the school board to "turn it over to the Advisory Board, unless, of course, there was some real disagreement on fundamental policy."

But the Colonel was always a cautious man in such circumstances, and as he recounted it to me three decades later, he "just felt that he better double-check this thing all the way around." His friend H.L. Mills "just flat told (him)" that the entire Board of Trustees wanted separation. Dr. Daily had her own interesting comment: "Colonel," she said, "the University of Houston needs to kick itself out of the womb." When he found these attitudes clearly affirmed, he arranged for a meeting with the Board of Education, in advance of one of their official sessions in September 1943, at which he and Mr. Cullen asked for "clarification of the powers of the Advisory Board." They were told that the advisory group should set a course headed directly for legal separation and a completely independent Board of Regents, both goals to be achieved as soon as possible and practicable.

The chairman and vice-chairman now had an unequivocal mandate for action. Colonel Bates, however, had a related matter to consider (possibly at the secret behest of his old friend and colleague, Oberholtzer) as the Advisory Board sprang into action. The Colonel respected and admired Dr. Kemmerer for his dedicated and efficacious work on behalf of the University, but to him President Oberholtzer was "the moving force of the University of Houston" and someone "who seemed to be cut from the same pattern as Roy Cullen."

Roy Cullen's views were also involved in this covert matter, which bears on some later developments of consequence. Colonel Bates told me in 1973 that Mr. Cullen (who was known to vacillate in such opinions) made the following remark to him "early in the game": "I like that fellow Oberholtzer—always have, since I first met him. Don't like Kemmerer, although he can get things done. He's the perfect man for the number two job, but the problem is that he doesn't want it. He wants to be president, and I just can't see him as president." There is contrary testimony to this, as we shall see, primarily the fact that, after waiting around in the wings for several years, Dr. Kemmerer was finally named president of the University of Houston—with the approbation of Mr. Cullen.

Whatever the circumstances and motivation involved, Colonel Bates arranged in the early fall for a series of recommendations that seemed to be aimed at clarifying President Oberholtzer's authority, while obscuring at least temporarily the rising prospects of Walter W. Kemmerer.

Four of the recommendations, adopted unanimously by the Board of Education at the request of the Advisory Board on October 18, 1943, were:

That the President of the University of Houston be vested with all the authority commensurate with such office;

That the present Executive Committee consisting of the four officers of the University of Houston be dissolved;[29]

That in the judgment of the Advisory Board, now is not the propitious time to secure a full-time President;

That, for the time being, the office of Vice-President not be created.

It is not difficult to surmise that these recommendations were drafted by Dr. Oberholtzer as the vehicle to accomplish some rat-killing he had in mind and that they were accepted by Colonel Bates and Mr. Cullen as a gesture of friendship and support and as a token of a new partnership. The recommendations certainly clarified Dr. Oberholtzer's authority as president; they also diminished the powers of Dr. Kemmerer (whom he had taken to task on more than one occasion), of Dean Dupre,[30] and, to some extent, of H.L. Mills, while preserving at least temporarily the concept of Dr. Oberholtzer's retaining both the office of superintendent of schools and of president of the University.

Two other recommendations proposed by the Advisory Board were unanimously adopted by the Board of Education on October 18, 1943:

That the President of the University of Houston report directly to the Advisory Board, and that the University of Houston be operated under the supervision and direction of the President (all officers and employees to be under his direction), subject to the approval of the Advisory Board and the approval of the Board of Education on matters of policy that the Board of Education cannot delegate to the Advisory Board;

That Dr. E.E. Oberholtzer remain in office as President at the pleasure of the Advisory Board.

President Oberholtzer may also have drafted the final two recommendations. They obviously extended both the powers of the Advisory Board and his own specific authority. As to his remaining in office only at the pleasure of the Advisory Board (and *not* the Board of Education), this is axiomatic in the highest echelons of university administration: there is no tenure for university presidents, and no union to which they can appeal for job protection. Some chairmen of governing boards maintain that the operation of institutions of higher education would be immensely simplified if the regents or trustees began every meeting with a motion to ask for the resignation of the president; if this fails, a new motion is put: to support the president in every way possible in the discharge of his duties and responsibilities.

With the unanimous approval of these six recommendations, then, the Advisory Board had demonstrated that it did indeed have the full backing of the Board of Education and was ready to press on with the vital matter of obtaining legal separation from the HISD, through a bill to be submitted to the 49th Legislature, which was to convene in Austin on January 9, 1945.

The bill was drafted by M.E. Kurth, Palmer Hutcheson, and Colonel Bates, and was given preliminary approval by the Board of Education on May 29, 1944. At this point, some mild dissension developed on two key provisions: the method by which the original regents would be selected, and the procedure to be followed in the naming of their successors.

Although the matter had never been completely resolved, the understanding Colonel Bates had with Mr. Cullen, and with Holger Jeppesen and Dr. Henry A. Petersen (president and vice-president, respectively, of the Board of Trustees) was that the members of the Advisory Board would simply be nominated as charter regents, and confirmed immediately, by the Board of Education. This procedure was adopted without difficulty.

Dr. Kemmerer maintains that the second point, regarding the naming of successors (or providing an additional term for a regent whose time in office had expired), became a major obstacle that cost the University one-half of the oil royalties from the prolific Thompson oil field in Fort Bend County. He says that a raging controversy over the dismissal of President Homer P. Rainey of the University of Texas caused Senator Weaver Moore "or some other members of the Harris County delegation" to add some "harsh and abrupt" language to the separation bill in an attempt to strengthen the powers of the governing board (and thus prevent a future confrontation between the administration and the regents at the University of Houston). The proposed change, according to Dr. Kemmerer, "would have allowed the Board of Regents to dismiss the president of the University, or any other employee of the University, at its discretion."

The controversial clause was stricken after public hearings; but Dr. Kemmerer still maintained in 1976 that the hearings caused Mr. Cullen to withhold one-half of the Thompson field royalties "if they're going to play politics with our University," and to give them instead to four Houston hospitals.[31]

The naming of successors, or the appointment of regents to additional terms, was fundamental. It involved having a self-perpetuating Board of Regents, as against one dependent upon the Board of Education for the confirmation of its members; or, far worse, regents appointed directly by the Board of Education. It was soon apparent to Colonel Bates that the trustees of HISD were not willing to cut the cord of relationship (and, technically, of control) completely; but he felt that he might be able to sell the trustees on a procedure involving confirmation of regents by the Board of Education, rather than direct appointment. He perceived confirmation as a perfunctory rite, with rubber-stamp endorsement of the Board of Regents' own nominees.

"They had us between a rock and a hard place," as he explained it to me many years later, "and there comes a time when you just have to trust people—or your judgment concerning them."

The compromise over confirmation was unofficially approved by several members of the Board of Education in private conferences, but Colonel Bates was not at all certain how the trustees would vote in a showdown. And there were rumblings within the Advisory Board, where some members were skittish on the compromise involving confirmation, and others simply wanted to hold out for a self-perpetuating Board of Regents, pure and simple.

Further discussion was indicated, and this continued through the summer and, alarmingly, through the fall months as well. The matter was finally resolved at the penultimate moment, at a January 8, 1945, meeting of the Board of Trustees, and in a unique manner that probably made legislative history. Two differing procedures were actually written into the separation bill, and the Board of Education was told to make up its mind between them.

The trustees were instructed to specify, in a formal resolution adopting what became Senate Bill (SB) 207 after its passage, their choice between the two "following methods":

> All future members of the Board of Regents to succeed those whose terms have expired, or to fill vacancies created by the death or resignation of a member, shall be selected or appointed by one (but not more than one) of the following two methods:
>
> 1. Within 30 days after the expiration of the term of any member of any such Board of Regents, or within 30 days after any vacancy occurs on such Board of Regents by death or resignation of any member thereof, it shall be the duty of the remaining members thereof, by not less than a majority vote thereof, to appoint members of such Board of Regents to succeed those whose terms have expired or to fill any such vacancy, subject, however, to the approval and confirmation thereof by a two-thirds majority of the members of the Board of Education or Board of Trustees of any such independent school district included within the terms of this Act.
>
> 2. Within 30 days after the expiration of the term of any member of any such Board of Regents, or within 30 days after any vacancy occurs on such Board of Regents by death or resignation of any member thereof, it shall be the duty of such Board of Trustees or Board of Education of any such independent school district included within the terms of this Act, by not less than a majority vote thereof, to appoint members of such Board of Regents to succeed those whose terms have expired to fill any such vacancies.
>
> The Board of Education or Board of Trustees at the time of divesting itself of management or control of any such junior college or university and vesting the same in the Board of Regents, and as a part of the action of the Board of Education or Board of Trustees of any such independent

> school district adopting the benefits of this Act, shall select, adopt and specify by a resolution adopted by a majority of the Board of Trustees or Board of Education of such independent school district and incorporated in the minutes thereof, one of the two methods set forth above for selecting future Regents, and thereafter all such Regents (other than the first Board of Regents) shall be selected in accordance with the method so specified.

Once SB 207 was actually filed by its sponsor, Senator Weaver Moore, the controversy over a self-perpetuating, confirmed or appointed Board of Regents seemed to vanish. Colonel Bates said that Holger Jeppesen told him: "Well, lots of people wanted to be heard, and we let them all get their two-bits in. Now that the bill actually sets up a choice, I can't see any trouble in getting a unanimous vote for the confirmation procedure." His estimate of the situation, as it turned out, was correct; nor did the confirmation of regents ever present a problem during the 18 years that this arrangement was to prevail, even though a two-thirds vote of the Board of Education was required for affirmation of nominees chosen within the Board of Regents.

There were some minor delays in passing SB 207, primarily because of the relatively high number assigned it, and the fact that Harris County had only one state senator in 1945, compared to six today, and only a handful of state representatives, in contrast to the present delegation of 23.

In mid-February 1945, the student body planned a march on Austin in support of separation. They proposed to flood the Senate and the House of Representatives with circulars, and then to deliver to Governor Coke Stevenson a petition that had been circulating on campus for several weeks. Dozens of posters, on the theme "Liberate the University of Houston" were readied, and the project gained steam as it took on some of the characteristics of an early spring holiday.

H.L. Mills, who was masterminding the overall SB 207 campaign, deflated most of this commendable, but misplaced, enthusiasm with a telephone call to Dr. Kemmerer. The last thing he wanted to do was to stir up attention, and thereby possible opposition, to the separation bill. One also did not rattle the cage of Governor Stevenson with impunity. A super-conservative goat rancher from Junction, the governor had as his prime objective the elimination of a galling deficit in the general fund (inherited from the free spending W. Lee (Pappy) O'Daniel).[32] He looked with suspicion on anything that might directly or indirectly increase state spending, but had been assured that separation of the University from HISD was a necessary, reasonable and non-cost item.

SB 207 was signed into law on March 12, 1945, precipitating a series of quick and historic moves on the part of the Board of Education, the Board of Regents (immediately after it had been constituted from the former Advisory Board), and Edison Ellsworth Oberholtzer. The moment that Holger Jeppesen had official word of the signing of SB 207, he convened a meeting of the trustees of the Board of Education, who had been standing by.

The entire proceeding required a reported seven minutes, virtually all of it for the reading *verbatim* of the resolution. One must ponder to what extent the trustees realized how seven minutes would affect the destiny of the University of Houston, and thereby the future of the community and area it serves, down all the years to come.

The provisions of SB 207 were unanimously adopted by the trustees in the following resolution:

> WHEREAS, Houston Independent School District by and through its Board of Education, pursuant to applicable laws relating to junior colleges and more especially to Chapter 34 of the Acts of the First Called Session of the Forty-Third Legislature of the State of Texas and the general powers conferred on it by the Special Act passed by the Thirty-Eighth Legislature of the State of Texas creating said Houston Independent School District, has heretofore established, managed, controlled and operated the University of Houston, and as a branch thereof, Houston College for Negroes; and
>
> WHEREAS, the members of the Board of Education of said Houston Independent School District deem it to be the best interest of said The University of Houston and said branch thereof known as said Houston College for Negroes, that the management, control and operation of said The University of Houston and its said branch aforesaid to be divested from and out of said Board of Education of said Houston Independent School District and vested in a separate Board of Regents, all as is provided for by Senate Bill No. 207 passed by the Forty-Ninth Legislature of the State of Texas and approved by the Governor of said State on this the 12th day of March, A.D. 1945;
>
> NOW THEREFORE, BE IT AND THE SAME IS HEREBY RESOLVED by the Board of Education of Houston Independent School District as follows:
>
> 1. That the management, control and operation of said The University of Houston and the branch thereof known as the Houston College for

Negroes be and the same is hereby divested out of the Board of Education of Houston Independent School District and invested in a separate Board of Regents to consist of fifteen (15) members to be known as the Board of Regents of the University of Houston.

2. That H.R. Cullen, W.B. Bates, A.D. Simpson, Palmer Hutcheson, James W. Rockwell, Simon Sakowitz, Hiram O. Clarke, Noah Dietrich, Lamar Fleming, S.P. Farish, Don H. Thornbury, James Anderson, Mrs. James P. Houstoun, Mrs. Agnese Carter Nelms and Mrs. Ray L. Dudley, all of whom reside within the Houston Independent School District, be and they are hereby named and appointed as the Board of Regents of said The University of Houston, and they as a Board of Regents, upon their qualifying as such, are to have the complete management, control and operation of said The University of Houston and its branch aforesaid, with all of the powers, and responsibilities, duties and immunities, imposed upon such Board of Regents by the terms of said Senate Bill No. 207 so passed by the Forty-Ninth Legislature of the State of Texas and approved as aforesaid.

3. That all future members of such Board of Regents of the University of Houston to succeed those whose terms expire, or to fill vacancies created by the death or resignation of a member, shall be appointed in the following method:

"Within thirty (30) days after the expiration of the term of any member of any such Board of Regents, or within thirty (30) days after any vacancy occurs on such Board of Regents by death or resignation of any member thereof, it shall be the duty of the remaining members thereof, by not less than a majority vote thereof, to appoint members of such Board of Regents to succeed those whose terms have expired or to fill any such vacancy, subject, however, to the approval and confirmation thereof by a two-thirds majority of the members of the then Board of Education of Houston Independent School District."

4. That when the members of the Board of Regents of said The University of Houston hereinbefore designated and appointed as such shall have duly qualified as such, that the President of the Board of Education of Houston Independent School District and such other officers of said Board of Education as may be necessary, shall cause to be transferred to said Board of Regents of the University of Houston all monies then held by the Board of Education of Houston Independent School District and belonging to said The University of Houston and its said branch, and that all personal property of whatsoever kind or character which may at that time be in use exclusively in the operation and maintenance of said The University of Houston and its branch shall be deemed to be vested in said Board of Regents of The University of Houston, and further that the President of the Board of Education of Houston Independent School District shall be, and is hereby in all things authorized, empowered and directed, in behalf of said Houston Independent School District to make, execute and acknowledge and to have duly attested by the Secretary of said Board of Education and delivered to such Board of Regents of The University of Houston as a proper deed or deeds conveying all lands and buildings

> presently used exclusively in connection with the operation of said The University of Houston and its branch, all as is provided for by the terms of said Senate Bill No. 207, hereinbefore referred to.

Mr. Cullen and Colonel Bates also had their troops standing by for quick deployment and action in that climactic second week of March 1945. It had been too late for the newly constituted Board of Regents to meet on March 12, by the time the members of the Board of Education had completed their own brief but memorable session; but the new governing body of the University gathered the next morning at 11:30 a.m., in Mr. Cullen's office on the thirteenth floor of the Sterling Building, for an organizational meeting.

All of the 15 regents were present except for A.D. Simpson, who was ill at home, and Mr. Cullen had already sent his secretary Miss Nedra M. Pattison, a notary, out to the Simpson residence to administer the oath of office.

Colonel Bates called the meeting to order promptly at 11:30 a.m., and suggested that Mr. Cullen be elected temporary chairman. This was agreed by acclamation, and Mrs. James P. Houstoun was then named temporary secretary.

With the meeting now under way, Mr. Cullen stated for the record that he and Colonel Bates, as presiding officers of the Advisory Board, had been officially informed by President Jeppesen of the formal appointment of the Board of Regents the previous afternoon, under provisions of SB 207, and that Miss Pattison was now ready to administer the oath of office.

This was done, and a premeditated scenario then quickly and efficiently unfolded. Palmer Hutcheson proposed, as the first motion before the Board of Regents, that the new body adopt the by-laws of the Advisory Board, with only such changes deemed necessary to make the by-laws apply to the Board of Regents. The by-laws could then be included in the new Board of Regents Minute Book, and be made part of the minutes of the organizational meeting by reference, he explained. The motion, seconded by Noah Dietrich, passed unanimously and the Board of Regents was a functioning body.

This maneuvering was necessary because the by-laws adopted on the Hutcheson-Dietrich motion provided for permanent, as opposed to temporary, officers. Mr. Hutcheson then nominated Mr. Cullen as chairman; Colonel Bates as vice-chairman; Mrs. Houstoun as secretary; and Mrs. Agnese Carter Nelms as assistant secretary. The nominees were elected by acclamation.

William B. Bates' many interests included history, so he moved that, in order to have a formal record of the historical development of the University of Houston, the secretary be "authorized and directed to transcribe upon the first pages of the Minute Book of the Board of Regents" copies of the following documents:[33]

(a) Resolution of the Board of Education of the Houston Independent School District adopted March 7, 1927, providing for the establishment of the Houston Junior College;

(b) House Bill 194 adopted by the Legislature of the State of Texas on October 13, 1933, and signed by Governor Miriam A. Ferguson on October 16, 1933, authorizing the expansion of a Junior College, such as the Houston Junior College, into a university;

(c) Resolution of the Board of the Houston Independent School District adopted April 30, 1934, providing for the establishment of the University of Houston;

(d) Charter of the University of Houston as adopted by resolution of the Board of Education of the Houston Independent School District on April 30, 1934;

(e) Resolution of the Board of Education of the Houston Independent School District adopted July 26, 1943, creating and establishing the Advisory Board of the University of Houston, consisting of fifteen members;

(f) Senate Bill 207 by Senator Weaver Moore adopted by both houses of the Legislature of Texas and signed by the Governor on March 12, 1945, giving authority to the Board of Education of the Houston Independent School District to divorce the management of the University of Houston from the Public Schools, and to appoint a Board of Regents for the University;

(g) Resolution of the Board of Education of the Houston Independent School District adopted March 12, 1945, separating the management of the University of Houston from the Public Schools and creating a Board of Regents for the University of Houston, and appointing the members thereof.

The meeting then reverted to what was pretty much a prepared script, designed to clear up some long-pending matters as soon as possible in order to get to higher ground. After asking Dr. Oberholtzer to leave the room, Chairman Cullen proposed a discussion that went back to the very first days of the University, and indeed before that to 1924. He requested consideration of the election of a full-time president, and called attention to a likely candidate by reviewing Dr. Oberholtzer's pivotal role in the successful development of the institution during its first 18 years.

After a discussion by the regents, all laudatory of Dr. Oberholtzer, the consensus was that if he was available (there still being three years remaining on his 1943-1948 HISD contract), he should be offered the full-time presidency of the University plus "branches thereof." The latter phrase translates as Houston College for Negroes, which Dr. Oberholtzer had always attempted to help as he could.

This was the substance of a motion offered by Mr. Clarke, and seconded by Mr. Fleming, which specified a contract of five years at a salary of $15,000 per annum. There was no mention of the usual presidential perquisites such as a residence and its maintenance, and an automobile, which are virtually universal today.

As soon as the motion was adopted, Dr. Oberholtzer was asked to return to the meeting. He was told what the regents were offering him. Being what Palmer Hutcheson once called a "nonshillyshallyer," he gave his answer at once. He accepted the offer, to be effective "as soon as he could clear up a few matters pending downtown"; said that he would inform HISD President Jeppesen immediately of his decision; and agreed to resign as superintendent of schools "as soon as possible."

Edison Ellsworth Oberholtzer would probably have enjoyed watching the expression of H.L. Mills, his implacable foe of 21 years, at this moment; but Mr. Mills was absent, as was Dr. Kemmerer. M.E. Kurth was the invited observer for the HISD, as attorney for the District; and Dr. Oberholtzer was the sole representative of University of Houston Administration. This was noted by the press, whose representatives included Moselle Jacobs, the former *Cougar* editor who had survived the simultaneous loss of Jack Valenti and Johnny Goyen as staff writers; and Mary Elizabeth Johnston, member of a talented journalistic family who in time would join her brother Harry on the national journalistic scene.

There was more, at what was obviously one on the most meaningful sessions in the history of the Board of Regents, even though it was only an organizational meeting. Palmer Hutcheson moved that the governing body prepare a statement concerning the purposes and policies of the University under what he termed "new management." A committee consisting of Mr. Hutcheson, Colonel Bates, Mrs. Houstoun, Mrs. Nelms, Mr. Fleming, Mr. Clarke and Dr. Oberholtzer was given the charge. The committee report, filed barely two months later, on June 20, 1945, was of special use and consequence in clarifying and restating institutional aims at the time, and it is significant and valuable now in retrospect. The report read:

Whereas, recently we have been named as a Board of Regents of the Univeristy of Houston, under the provisions of the Senate Bill 207, adopted by the Legislature of Texas and signed by the Governor on March 12, 1945, and it is now desirable for the Board of Regents to make a public declaration of the purposes and policies of the Board of Regents with reference to the University; and

Whereas, the University is a part of the educational system of the State of Texas and the Constitution of the State provides that 'a general diffusion of knowledge is essential to the preservation of the liberties and rights of the people'; and

Whereas, we believe that as said by Mirabeau B. Lamar 'cultivated mind is the guardian genius of democracy';

We hereby adopt the following expression of our permanent aims for the University:

1. The University of Houston will be operated and maintained as a University of the first class.

2. The program of the University will be directed toward developing general knowledge, culture, scientific appreciation of truth, intellectual honesty, independence, tolerance, and capacity for human usefulness among all students, so that their lives may be enriched and their service to humanity enlarged.

3. The courses offered by the University will emphasize the liberal arts and humanities, and the sciences and selected vocational training; and the educational program will be expanded as the future needs of the community may prescribe and in keeping with the growth of learning.

To meet present conditions we desire that as a part of the University program, veterans of World War II and others whose education has been interrupted during the war, be encouraged in the resumption of their education and during the period of readjustment following the war be offered such courses as may be practicable to prepare them for specific gainful occupation as well as to furnish them a general education.

It will always be the policy of the Board to encourage at the University freedom of learning and education, as well as an understanding knowledge of the world's problems in order to promote furtherance of World Peace and Christian Civilization.

Finally, the members of the Board of Regents desire to serve the interests of the citizens of this community and of the Houston Independent School District, and will work to the end that the University of Houston will at all times deserve the good will and understanding and helpful cooperation of the citizenry.

As a final item of business, the first meeting of the Board of Regents got around to drawing lots for original terms of office (expiring on April 1 of 1946, 1948 or 1950), as provided in SB 207. Mr. Cullen, of course, drew a minimum term, although he was to serve continuously as chairman of the Board of Regents until his death on July 4, 1957. He told everybody that he had never won anything in his life, but was obviously unhappy at not having drawn one of the maximum initial five-year terms that went to Mr. Rockwell, Mr. Hutcheson, Mrs. Houstoun, Colonel Anderson and Mrs. Dudley. Then he took everyone—reporters, photographers, and his secretary included—to a splendid luncheon at the Houston Club, preceded by toasts to the "new" University of Houston and its rapidly improving prospects.

A lesser man than Walter W. Kemmerer might have been quite adversely affected by the October 18, 1943, resolution of the Advisory Board (adopted unanimously by the Board of Education) that seemed to be so pro-Oberholtzer and so anti-Kemmerer. The non-vice-president, comptroller, and director of curriculum, however, wasted no time sulking or bemoaning his fate. Instead, he immersed himself in a series of meaningful projects that were to have an immediate and lasting effect on the post-war University of Houston.

He was able to do this for a number of reasons. By nature, Dr. Kemmerer was of an essentially sanguine disposition. Rather than harboring paranoid visions of his being shoved into the outer darkness, he considered the positive aspects of the situation. He had strong support from many faculty members who had come to perceive him as their champion in the difficult battle for even minimal raises in salaries; he alone had detailed knowledge of current budgets and fiscal projections; and—above all—he had the energy and the vision to seek out and to find the post-war opportunities that would become a catapult for launching the University of Houston into an era of unprecedented expansion.

As a beginning, Dr. Kemmerer organized a guidance program that was to be expanded in 1945 into an office of psychological services, with heavy emphasis on student counseling. Then, following a recommendation that representatives of industry had strongly supported within the Advisory Board, he provided for a major strengthening of vocational and technical training.[34]

Under this concept (which would unjustly stigmatize the University in later years as a center of vocational, rather than academic, education), Dr. Kemmerer installed C.A. Hall as director of industrial plant training, added five specially qualified faculty members in vocational and technical fields and broadened curricular offerings substantially in this instructional area.

These changes became the underpinning for what was usually known as the "vocational and terminal (non-degree) curriculum." The Minute Book of the Board of Education termed it "an adequate program of general, pre-professional and technical education."

Dr. Kemmerer's most telling contribution in the crucial 1943-1945 triennium, however, and possibly during his entire career at the University, came in connection with the return of the World War II veterans.

Visiting servicemen on campus through the fall of 1943 were almost always former students, including a surprising number of Naval trainees from the NRVS and NERMS units, and the little-publicized CAA-Naval Air Primary Training Command (V-5) School.[35]

One of the returning Naval cadets told a reporter that "the University was such a friendly place, and those Co-Ed-Ettes (who traditionally gave a farewell dance for graduating Naval trainees) were so cute."

Most of the Navy men wanted to pay a nostalgic visit to the "USS Texan" (Industrial Building), to their barracks or the "Rec" Building, or to one of their great favorites, Commander R.E. Herndon, the veteran medical officer for Naval units who was usually good for a "heat and rest" prescription after a tough fall climbing the 20-foot-high wall on the obstacle course. Commander Herndon doubled as the morale officer, and presided at satiric "Bund" meetings in which cadets who failed examinations, made bumpy landings or committed "other acts of sabotage that aid and abet the Axis" were awarded the "Iron Cross" by "Der Fuhrer."

In the winter of 1943-1944, however, an increasing number of men who were discharged early because of a disabling wound or injury, or being rated "4-F" in a final physical examination, were inquiring about registration. A substantial number of these, it was noted, were not former students; they had heard about the University of Houston from a "buddy" in the service, had been stationed in the area's training camps and stations or were simply attracted by that perennial magnet, Houston's vigorous economy.

Then, suddenly, it was the fall of 1944, and the veterans (usually recognizable because of their mixed garb—half-GI and half-leftover civilian) were all over the campus, helping immediately to boost enrollment back to 2,720 from the low point of 1,104 the previous autumn.

Dr. Kemmerer stimulated a great deal of this, and the mushrooming enrollments in the offing, by his insistence that the University be ready for the returning ex-servicemen (and women: one of the first to inquire about post-war classes was WAVE Ishuan McCutcheon).

In the summer of 1944, he devised a complex program designed to bring back not only those students called to active duty from the campus; but former NRVS, NERMS and CAA-NAPTC trainees; those who seemed to be hearing about the institution through the grapevine of hearsay and rumor; and what he had become convinced might be a major new source of enrollees: mature men and women past the normal 18-24-year-old age span on virtually all pre-World War II campuses, but anxious to utilize the GI Bill to make a completely fresh start in life or to enlarge their horizons and opportunities.

Dr. Kemmerer wanted, in sum, to establish the University of Houston as "Headquarters GI Bill" for this area, and to accomplish his goal, he rushed to complete what could be accurately called "Operation Returning Veteran."

The campaign began with an in-depth study of what the returning ex-serviceman would not only require, but want. Some of this was obvious, and was being pursued on campuses across the land:

adequate curricula; an expanded faculty, staff and physical plant; more equipment and supplies; and additional housing. Dr. Kemmerer quickly isolated these fundamental problems, set into motion various means of combatting them, and raced off into areas requiring a much more innovative approach. He saw the need, for example, of cushioning the veterans as much as possible from the inevitable red tape and future log-jams of an already panicky Veterans Administration; of streamlining the admissions procedure, including the usual bottleneck, the analysis of transcripts, drastically; of very good, broad scope counseling and guidance, handled not only by professionals in the field but by individual faculty members as well.

To these requirements he added a critical need for temporary housing, shortages having been exacerbated in Houston during the war years by a major influx of population while so few new residences were being built. Dr. Kemmerer also pointed to the lack of some innovative manner in which the veteran could begin his education as soon as possible, without waiting for the normal rotation of semesters; and to the importance of providing remedial or refresher courses; of locating temporary loans and part-time jobs as possible; and of assuring a constant flow of reliable information concerning the GI Bill, especially on how its provisions were to be interpreted, and means of expediting payments to veterans.

The plan that Dr. Kemmerer completed before mid-summer addressed each of the needs and requirements enumerated above, and it quickly attracted the attention of the Veterans Administration as well as of increasing thousands of prospective students. In addition to its broad and innovative approach, it was based upon considering "each veteran and his problems on an individual basis," as its principal architect often stated.

The moment the plan was in final draft, Veterans Administration officials were brought to the campus for detailed briefings. They were immediately impressed by many things: the University's war record; Dr. Kemmerer's imaginative yet practical recommendations, so indicative of his ability and readiness to act; his enthusiasm, and that of the faculty and staff; interviews with veterans already enrolled; and Houston itself, apparently protected to a considerable extent against the signs of post-war economic recession that were more apparent with the closing of every wartime production line. By December of 1944, when the University of Houston was selected as the site for a Veterans Administration Advisement Center, enrollment for the spring semester was already projected at 3,500 (it actually hit 3,780—one of only three times in the 50-year history of the institution when spring enrollment, normally three to five percent under the preceding fall, was to be higher).

In the intervening months, Dr. Kemmerer had begun an increase in faculty strength that would take the teaching staff to 100 within the next year, and on to 450 for 1947-1948, when enrollment was to hit the amazing total of 10,882, an increase of ten-fold in four years. This major escalation in instructional personnel included a considerable percentage of part-time faculty members; but there were also substantial additions to permanent staff as courses and related facilities and services mushroomed.

Dr. Kemmerer remained in very close touch with President Oberholtzer during all these significant changes, of course, but he began to find it better to emphasize the need for permanent additions to the physical plant to his superior, and to push on by himself, as best he was able, with curricular changes, negotiations with the Veterans Administration, temporary classrooms and housing, and the other elements of his new plan. As he expressed it to me many years later, it became increasingly difficult to obtain firm, fast decisions and action from President Oberholtzer, who simply could not perceive in the 1943-1945 era the 1,000 percent increase in enrollment (from 1,100 to 11,000) that would soon hit the University and engulf it if preparations were not made almost immediately for the waves of veterans demanding an education.[36]

Implementing other areas of his plan, Dr. Kemmerer obtained 12 temporary classroom buildings from the Federal Works Agency (FWA) after quick inspection trips to Camp Wallace (the old Maco Stewart Ranch at Hitchcock) and Camp Bowie (near Fort Worth) to inspect used but structurally sound barracks and office units that FWA would move and reconstruct on campus. These became temporary classrooms for instruction in art, home economics, band, orchestra, dramatics, business administration, pre-law, radio, and automotive shops. They added 40,000 square feet of immediately available instructional space, and were such a godsend that some of them were still being heavily used in the late 1960's and even into the early 1970's.

Next, he wangled 320 trailers and 350 tiny prefabricated "apartments," providing temporary housing for 1,500 veterans and their families from the Federal Housing Authority. There were the infamous "shacks," on the eastern perimeter of the campus along Calhoun Boulevard; but they were better than having to check with the campus Housing Office three times a day in the hope of finding a rented room miles from the campus, or simply not being able to enroll. (The term "shacks"derived from the name given the temporary classrooms and offices on the east side of San Jacinto high school in the early days of the University. This term distressed President Oberholtzer, who attempted to have it changed to "University Village." But "shacks" it was, and, for the entire area of trailers and prefabricated apartments, "shacks" it remained.)

Usable equipment and supplies were more difficult to come by, but Dr. Kemmerer did find shipments worth about $500,000 at various surplus depots, obtaining these for nominal transportation charges. Invaluable though all these successful excursions were, Dr. Kemmerer proved his unique worth with a series of changes suggested in his original study of how to improve the lot of the ex-serviceman, and thereby the coffers and future prospects of the University.

The beginning guidance program was quickly broadened and fleshed out with the appointment of a chief counselor, R.O. Jonas, and a head of the new office of psychological services, Roy A. Crouch. Faculty members were given courses themselves in counseling within specific fields, and as soon as they could be located, former members of the armed forces were hired in counseling and guidance slots, on the sound theory that they could empathize with most veterans who sought their assistance.

In a major departure from the usual rigamarole, any veteran with an honorable discharge was admitted to classes immediately upon completing his application. The University itself then filled out forms required under the GI Bill, and the applicant began attending classes without the delay of many weeks before full Veterans Administration clearance and processing. This super-streamlining of admissions led to a few problems, and to some instances where eligibility, either academically or under the requirements of the GI Bill, could not be met. But these instances were extremely few, leading some visitors from other institutions to wonder if perhaps they had been purchasing a $100,000 insurance policy for years on what could be a maximum $1,000 loss.

Other major elements of the Kemmerer approach involved remedial and refresher courses, the flow of current information on the GI Bill, intensive testing and guidance for applicants, and personal assistance to enrolled veterans, their wives and dependents.

Special "130" courses were set up for ex-servicemen long away from the college classroom, or never in it, although most sections were on a "refresher" basis. These courses, primarily in mathematics, English and the social sciences, were taught by carefully selected instructors in small classes. Students were allowed to progress at their own rate, and to earn credit if satisfactory progress was made. Otherwise, the class had to be repeated. The "130" courses were uniquely valuable for veterans from 25 to 40 who had found a new career in the services but lacked the fundamental academic preparation necessary to pursue the career in civilian life.

Current information on, and interpretations of, the GI Bill were presented in special assemblies, and mimeographed bulletins were prepared as soon as possible. Intensive testing and guidance, coupled with counseling in depth, was especially valuable in "removing square pegs from round holes," as one 35-year-old, persuaded to shift his entire career plan, put it. A nursery school for working and studying parents with small children, a housing bureau, temporary loans, and the assignment of special maintenance crews to "the shacks," where hastily installed utilities sometimes presented emergency problems, were instances of some of the personal assistance provided veterans. This help often came after regular office hours, even though most members of the faculty and staff were already working extraordinarily long and demanding days.

Walter W. Kemmerer received wide and deserved recognition for his sound and innovative programs for ex-servicemen, designed as he told the campus Veterans Club[37] "to do whatever is necessary to permit and encourage the ex-serviceman (and woman) to obtain as good an education as possible with the least further loss of time."

Difficult though Dr. Kemmerer had found it to impress upon his boss the ascending rate of change at the University in those strenuous years from 1943-1945, the proven Oberholtzer-Kemmerer team was still functioning well as its senior member prepared to become full-time president of the University of Houston on April 1, 1945.

Despite crises of varying degree within the Board of Education, Dr. Oberholtzer had been concentrating for almost a year on finding financial support for major additions to the physical plant. This was a project that Dr. Kemmerer continued to encourage openly. It effectively kept the Office of the President out of some areas where immediate action was often required; it addressed a problem that Dr. Kemmerer knew was growing worse by the day;[38] and it put Dr. Oberholtzer back on an assignment in which he had previously demonstrated special competence. It also kept President Oberholtzer in close touch with Hugh Roy Cullen, who was known to be interested in further substantial contributions to the University he now served as chairman of the Board of Regents.

There was no overt indication that Dr. Oberholtzer suspected his right-hand man of chicanery in the now inevitable loss of his dual position as superintendent of schools—an often trying honor that he was just about to abjure anyhow, if allowed his own schedule of repudiation.

Similarly, the 1943 resolutions that (1) deprived Dr. Kemmerer of some of his new power; (2) made crystal clear President Oberholtzer's indisputable authority, at least insofar as the Advisory Board was concerned; and (3) specified that there was no need to recreate the post of vice-president, had never been discussed in any detail by either of the two men most closely involved, galling though they must have been to Bill Kemmerer.

Whether surface indications reflected either man's true feelings or not, Edison Ellsworth Oberholtzer knew a do-er, a thinker, and an innovator when he saw one. And this was no time to be on the outs with such a paragon. It must have been the early spring of 1944 when Dr. Oberholtzer had a long talk with his chief lieutenant. The first item up for discussion was a bit delicate, but the time had come to broach it. Even though the post of vice-president had to remain on the *verboten* list for now, it might be possible to create the office and title of assistant to the president. This was not ideal, but it would do away with the cumbersome title of comptroller and director of curriculum, and the anomaly of "directors," "heads" and other administrators reporting to a director.

This was agreed upon, and a bargain was apparently struck very soon, for Dr. Kemmerer was named assistant to the president by the Board of Trustees on May 11, 1944, confirming a recommendation by the Advisory Board. At the same meeting, Naason K. Dupre was demoted to director of extension (services), after 17 years of devoted service as dean. President Oberholtzer and Dr. Kemmerer then proceeded through a long and significant agenda, much of it proposed by his chief of staff: the violent fluctuations already evident in enrollments, and prospects for advancing from the nadir of 1,104 reached just a few months earlier; the effect of these fluctuations on cash flow, budgeting, and forward planning, obviously to be severe; building the infrastructure of an expanded post-war administrative team; how to proceed with the crucial matter of expanding curricula, faculty, and support services before the inevitable quantum jump in enrollment; relationships with the new Board of Regents when separation became a reality; and the certain need for major expansion of the physical plant (Bill Kemmerer's favorite item). Dr. Kemmerer had his own sanguine predictions on enrollment, which turned out to be quite reliable, unbelievable though they had appeared. He proposed that existing budgets simply be disregarded, while revisions based on new five-year projections were prepared as soon as possible. And he warned that the University of Houston might run its first deficit since 1927 while preparing for the post-war boom, a situation worsened by the dwindling volume of cash until new funds were in hand from the enrollment of veterans.

This naturally disturbed the more conservative President Oberholtzer, to whom the very word "deficit" was anathema; but he was still enough of an Indiana farm boy to know that you have to plant and tend a crop before you can harvest it. "Do what you have to," he told Dr. Kemmerer, "but watch your overhead ratio; and let's get McElhinney out here as business manager as soon as we're on our own." They both had known and admired Charles F. McElhinney for more than a decade now, and it was obvious that his talents would be needed.

Dr. Oberholtzer especially remembered Dr. Kemmerer's emphasis on the need for new major contributions toward expansion of the physical plant when I asked him, in 1951, about the various steps through which Mr. Cullen had become more and more interested in providing very substantial financial support for the University.[39]

Both Dr. Oberholtzer and the newly titled assistant to the president had their hands full as 1944 progressed, particularly when the Advisory Board spun into high activity, and fall enrollment was up 146 percent over the preceding September (with the prediction that it would double again to the 5,000 range in 1945).

Dr. Kemmerer continued to carry an extraordinary workload as the post-war era rapidly approached, partly because there was no one else yet available to carry out certain complex assignments, but also to leave his superior as free as possible to concentrate on the growing prospect of 10,000 students on a campus with only four permanent buildings. Late in 1944 there was really encouraging news. Dr. Oberholtzer reported in confidence that Mr. Cullen was definitely interested in financing a huge Administration Building, probably as a memorial to his grandfather.

The first tentative plans called for a structure costing about $1,850,000, and Alfred C. Finn (a trustee of the HISD for many years) was already hard at work on preliminary plans. Mr. Cullen thought that the building as projected might be too small, and was also talking of future campus structures: both a temporary and a permanent Engineering Building, a Junior College Building, a gymnasium and swimming pool, and a Religious Activities Center. He had mentioned a $3 million facility to house veterans and their families, and an even larger dormitory complex for unmarried students, probably to be financed by revenue bonds.

Colonel Bates, it was added, was far along in discussions with his fellow trustees of the M.D. Anderson Foundation (John H. Freeman and Horace M. Wilkins, president of the State National Bank) on the possibility of a future major grant for a campus library. This was proposed as a memorial to Monroe D. Anderson, founder of the M.D. Anderson Foundation, who had died in 1939.[40]

Rumors of these possible developments had reached Bill Kemmerer earlier, and he realized that it might take years, or forever, for possibilities to become realities; nevertheless, he was plainly delighted to have even this limited affirmation of the rumors—all the more because of the caliber of the persons reportedly involved.

Dr. Kemmerer saw rumor become reality far more rapidly than even he might have hoped. On March 21, 1945, a committee headed by Stephen Power Farish presented a report on plans for the Administration Building, and a recommendation that this facility be named for Mr. Cullen's grandfather, Ezekiel Wimberly Cullen. The plans and the recommendation were accepted forthwith.

Colonel Bates then announced that Mr. and Mrs. Cullen were contributing oil and gas royalties from the Thompson oil field in Fort Bend County, which would more than finance the new building, now estimated to cost about $5 million.

Mr. Cullen told the Houston *Post* on March 26, 1945, that "(the value of) the overriding royalties in the Thompson and South Thompson fields given to the University of Houston will approach $5 million." He added that an estimate by "The Humble" of 1.5 million barrels of "very fine crude" selling at $1.20 per barrel was "conservative, to say the least." He reasoned correctly that the price of oil would soon be considerably higher, and that "deep sands in this field have already been proved productive on the edge of the structure." Further, "the Thompson hasn't even been drilled yet on the top of the dome where the 'cream' usually is."

These were prophetic words. The various Thompson fields are now on the honor roll of what oilmen call "the big 'uns," which have actually produced or have in proven reserves 100 million barrels or more of crude. This includes fabulous strikes such as Spindletop, Barbers Hill, Conroe, Tomball, East Texas, and the Tom O'Connor bonanza (which Mr. Cullen also got a drill into). The difficulty is that nothing of this size has been hit since 1960, while the costs of a wildcat well go steadily up and the chances of getting back to the bank with anything after running the gauntlet of escalating taxes, the Yankee demagogues in the Congress and the super-environmentalists go steadily down.

On June 20, 1945, the Board of Regents approved an earlier recommendation of the Executive Committee[41] to proceed with plans for the formal inauguration of Edison Ellsworth Oberholtzer as president of the University of Houston. President Oberholtzer immediately named Dr. Kemmerer chairman of the faculty Inaugural Committee, and the dates of October 18-19, 1945, were selected.

After 18 years, three times the average tenure of a university president today, Dr. Oberholtzer had finally made it into the hallowed circle. "At any rate," he told a faculty committee, "I won't have to turn around to see who they're calling when they shout out 'Mr. President.' " And when the curtain rang down on the inaugural proceedings, on October 19, 1945, the University of Houston had both feet in the post-war era, literally as well as figuratively.

Notes to Chapter Four

[1]Rice Institute had announced its first World War II casualty a few days earlier: a lieutenant in the German army who had studied at the Institute a decade before. Called from the reserves to active duty in the Wehrmacht, he had fallen in the very first days of the blitzkrieg against Poland. His death, communicated through diplomatic channels to a faculty member later accused of overweening Nazi sympathies in a sensational trial before Judge Allen B. Hannay, was duly, and appropriately, reported on the front page of the Rice *Thresher.*

[2]George A. Hill, Jr., an expert on Texas history whose key role in establishing the San Jacinto Museum was mentioned earlier, had another unusual connection with the University of Houston, which he had served as a volunteer fund-raiser in the 1938 campaign. When his two sons, George A., III and Raymond fell mysteriously ill while on vacation from The Hill School, it had been very difficult to diagnose their ailment, which seemed to resemble typhoid, or even plague. Dr. Ray K. Daily was asked to have a look, even though she was an ophthalmologist by specialty. As any ophthalmologist, she had a look at the conjunctiva and retinal arteries of the two patients, whose condition had been worsening by the hour. Dr. Daily correctly diagnosed a relatively rare typhoidal form of tularemia (rabbit fever), primarily through the abnormal appearance of the conjunctiva. Upon being treated with tetracycline, the Hill brothers rapidly

This San Jacinto High School graduating class may include many of the students who called on Dr. E. E. Oberholtzer in November 1926, and requested creation of Houston Junior College.

Houston Junior College Pep Club of 1930. This organization later became the Cougar Collegians, under the sponsorship of Mrs. Pearl C. Bender.

The 1931 graduating class poses in hall of San Jacinto High School.

The University of Houston administrative office in temporary building on the east side of the campus of San Jacinto High School, 1935.

Looking at a model of the Roy Gustav Cullen Building during campus visit in March, 1938 (left to right): Dr. Oberholtzer; Mrs. B.F. Coop; E.D. Shepherd and Dr. Ray K. Daily of the Board of Education; and W.O. Alexander, National Youth Administration official.

First facility on campus, the Roy Gustav Cullen Building, is under construction in 1938.

Group picture of the faculty in 1939.

1940 Commencement exercise outside Roy Gustav Cullen Building.

Aerial view of campus in 1940. Shown are the Roy Gustav Cullen Building and the Science Building.

Final phase in construction of Recreation Building, later known as "Cougar Den," after giant tent allowing 24-hour work schedules had been removed, in early May, 1942.

Coeds selling saving stamps during World War II to laborers on campus.

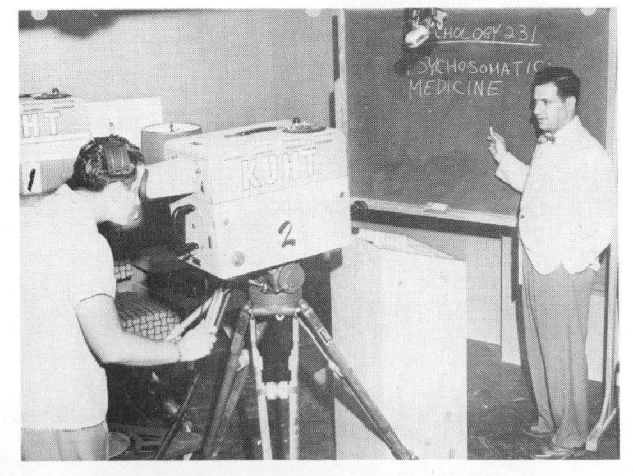

Richard I. Evans teaches an early telecourse in psychology on KUHT, the world's first educational television station.

Naval students attending Electricity and Radio Materiel School on campus during World War II march in front of the Roy Gustav Cullen Building. (1943)

Trailers and "shacks" occupied by World War II veterans and their families from 1945 to 1956.

Board of Regents of the University of Houston at organizational meeting on March 13, 1945. Back row: James W. Rockwell, H.O. Clarke, Stephen P. Farish, Lamar Fleming, Jr., Simon Sakowitz, Palmer Hutcheson, Don Thornbury, Colonel James Anderson, Noah Dietrich. Front row: Mrs. Ray L. Dudley, Mrs. Agnese Carter Nelms, H.R. Cullen, Mrs. James P. Houstoun, and Colonel W.B. Bates. (A.D. Simpson absent because of illness.)

President E.E. Oberholtzer greets members of his administrative team as he becomes full-time president on April 1, 1945. Left to right: (front) Terrel Spencer, registrar; C.F. Hiller, director, College of Arts and Sciences; M.L. Ray, acting director, School of Engineering; Arvin N. Donner, director, School of Education and director, Graduate School (shaking hands); Roy A. Crouch, head, office of psychological services; (back) C.A. Cate, coordinator, office of business and industrial cooperation; Ray Sims, coordinator, industrial service program; Harry Fouke, director, health and physical education; Vernon L. Engberg, coordinator, police training; David W. Knepper, chairman, department of public administration; and J.D. Neal, acting director, School of Business Administration.

University of Houston Tailback Charlie Manichia (scored first touchdown in Cougar history in 1946.)

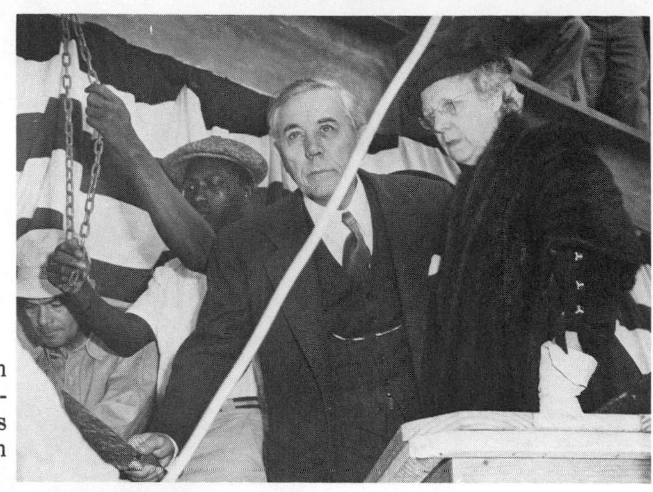

Mr. and Mrs. H.R. Cullen participating in cornerstone-laying ceremonies for Ezekiel W. Cullen Building, March 16, 1949.

Typical scene in Recreation Building, "Cougar Den," in the late 1940's.

Governor William P. Hobby delivers address at laying of cornerstone for Ezekiel W. Cullen Building. Seated at right are William V. Houstoun, president, The Rice Institute; and Herman Brown, founder, with his brother George, of Brown & Root.

A 1950's Frontier Fiesta belle poses with poster.

Dr. Kemmerer at time of appointment as president (1952).

General A.D. Bruce, chancellor; H.R. Cullen, chairman of the Board of Regents; and Dr. Clanton W. Williams, president, as Dr. Williams accepted the presidency in 1956.

First officers of the University of Houston Foundation at organizational meeting in 1960. Seated, left to right: Frank C. Smith, Mrs. Ray L. Dudley, Lamar Fleming, Jr.; standing, Colonel W.B. Bates and Roy Henry Cullen.

Change in administration when General A.D. Bruce is succeeded by President Philip G. Hoffman, September 1, 1961.

Senior Vice President C.F. McElhinney and President Philip G. Hoffman, as the latter assumed office in 1961.

Governor John B. Connally signs the 1963 bill amending the original 1961 statute providing for the admission of the University of Houston into the state system of higher education. Left to right: President Phillip G. Hoffman, Senator Criss Cole, Governor Connally, Representative Wallace H. Miller, and Vice President Patrick J. Nicholson.

First Board of Regents after admission to state system on September 1, 1963. Clockwise: Edward Manion, James Elkins, Mrs. Gus Wortham, James T. Duke, Colonel W.B. Bates, Corbin J. Robertson, A.J. Farfel, Jack Valenti, and George S. Hawn.

President Phillip G. Hoffman speaks at 1963 dinner honoring the 63 governors of the university. Left to right: W. Stewart Boyle, Mrs. W.B. Bates, Governor John B. Connally.

Groundbreaking for Bates College of Law Building. Participants include Dean John B. Neibel, (left); Colonel W.B. Bates; and President Philip G. Hoffman, 1967.

Agnes Arnold Hall is inspected by Architect Kenneth Bentsen and President Philip G. Hoffman, 1967.

The largest paid crowd in basketball history, 52,693, saw the Cougars defeat UCLA 71-69 in the Astrodome on January 20, 1968.

'resident Philip G. Hoff-
ıan and Conrad N. Hilton
t news conference announc-
ıg gift of $1,500,000 by Mr.
Iilton, for the Conrad N.
Iilton School of Hotel and
Restaurant Management,
969.

Iews conference for
nnouncement of
1,500,000 gift from
Roy Hofheinz Foun-
ation. Pictured are
udge Roy Hofheinz
nd President Philip
G. Hoffman, 1969.

Groundbreaking for Continuing Educa-
on Center, July, 1971. Participants in-
lude Regent James Duke, Eric Hilton
nd Barron Hilton; and Dr. Emmett B.
ields, executive vice president and dean
f faculties.

Vice President Patrick J. Nicholson with Senator Claiborne Pell (D-RI) during debate of the Higher Education Act in Washington, D.C., 1971.

Opening of the Sarah Campbell Blaffer Gallery, March 13, 1973.

Left to right: Head Coach Bill Yeoman; tri-captains Val Belcher, Paul Humphreys and Wilson Whitley with Bayou Bucket Trophy after defeating Rice for Bucket championship and clinching Cotton Bowl bid, 1976.

Cougars acknowledge those who helped them get to a Cotton Bowl victory over Maryland, 30-21.

"You fellers sure know how to make a guy feel welcome." Copyright © The Houston *Chronicle*

John H. Freeman, left, at dedication of John H. Freeman Wing of the M.D. Anderson Library during which the library's one-millionth volume was presented by Kenneth Franzheim II, 1977.

The university gets a new mascot: Shasta IV, December 29, 1976, at three weeks of age. The little cougar evidently made short work of the owner of that hat!

recovered. They had been shooting rabbits out at the Cinco Ranch, and had skinned some infected animals. After this incident, the elder Hill always took an added interest in the University, which Dr. Daily supported so faithfully throughout her long tenure on the School Board and recommended unfailingly to her friends.

[3]N.K. Dupre killed an editorial in the February 27, 1940 *Cougar*, a generation before some recent court decisions and the now long-established policy of no censorship for student publications (even though an immature editor or staff member will occasionally overstep the bounds of judgment, journalistic standards, and the laws of libel). The editorial stated that there would be no need for a current drive against honky-tonks "if parents would simply stay home with their children." This innocent bit of satire, coupled with some earlier, and serious, criticism of City Hall for the deplorable condition of streets near the campus, bothered the English instructor who doubled as *Cougar* censor, and Dean Dupre went into action. When the editor, Wellington Abbey, resigned with some staff members, the dean appointed P.J. Sterne editor, and publication of the four-page weekly resumed. Dean Dupre told downtown reporters, "There's nothing to all this. We're not going to let the students take the paper out of the school's hands. If the staff quits, we'll get another; and if we can't, we'll just discontinue the paper. Mrs. (Edith Lord) Carlton will continue to act as censor. If we have any further such upsets, (I will have to take) disciplinary action." Later, Dean Dupre elaborated a bit on his policies vis-à-vis student editors, "Mr. Abbey, I hear, wants to return as editor; I don't think he will." The irrepressible Carl Victor Little of the *Press* pointed out that it should be a pleasure to be censored "by the 'oomphological' Mrs. Carlton."

[4]A *Cougar* reporter was told by one wag that the only difference between meatless Tuesdays and pre-war Tuesdays in the cafeteria was "three ounces of gristle and a dab of gravy."

[5]The ubiquitous dean stood in stark contrast to his scholarly peer at Rice Institute, the distinguished chemist Harry Boyer Weiser. Dr. Weiser carried the title of dean but had virtually no contact with the student body except for a few isolated cases in which he decampused pugnacious residents of the dormitories, expelled extremely stubborn students, such as the chemistry major (later reported to have won endless scholastic honors) who insisted in attending class in Bermuda shorts, or entered final judgment (including one instance involving his own daughter) in honor council cases.

On-the-scene discipline at Rice was handled by John Thomas McCants, bursar and de facto dean of students, but he was little in evidence unless the offense cried to heaven for attention. It took an elephant, borrowed by Vernon (Buzzy) Baird (now a television star and chief executive officer of his grandmother's bakery empire) from Hans Nagel of the Hermann Park zoo for a Sallyport appearance during a campus election, to get Mr. McCants out of his Lovett Hall office on one notable occasion. But he regained fame as a disciplinarian and champion of campus order by appearing *deus ex machina* at a midterm West Hall, high-stakes poker game that was roaring along in its third day. The password was "Johnny McCants," and surely enough, old Johnny burst into the room after giving it. The guard at the end of the hall, who normally fired wet tennis balls at unidentified visitors from a murderous giant slingshot constructed from a truck inner tube, had fallen asleep at his post.

[6]The student was referring both to the appearance of the campus, then totally devoid of landscaping, in 1939, and to the number of coeds who took the opportunity to improve things by appearing in "Daisy Mays," an earlier version of the short short and peek-a-boo (then termed "have a look") blouse. Landscaping had been delayed both by a lack of funds and by a freak flood caused by heavy rains on July 12 and 13, 1939. This left water and ankle-deep mud in low places on campus for weeks, and made it necessary to extend drainage to additional areas before the construction of the reflection pool and related plantings could begin. H.L. Mills reported later to the Board of Trustees that the July flood cost the University $1,882.83, including emergency loads of shell and gravel.

WPA workers built the reflection pool during the winter of 1939-1940, and surrounded its 300-yard circumference with 2,000 rose bushes. Flowering shrubs and small native trees were planted nearby. Unfortunately, there was no underground watering system in those days, and few of the rose bushes survived Houston's blistering hot, interminable summers. Hyacinths placed in the pool itself thrived, along with algae and billions of tadpoles, and finally had to be removed. Although there was some landscaping in conjunction with later buildings, the campus pretty well had to depend upon natural groves of oaks and pines, plus some native shrubs, until an aggressive, long-range landscaping program was undertaken in the mid-1960s.

[7]A reference to Maury Maverick, San Antonio politico who was much in the news at the time because of controversy over FDR's third-term candidacy. Maury Maverick's grandfather, Samuel A., saw his name become a synonym for unbranded cattle because of the hundreds wandering lost on the family's huge, arid ranch in what is now Maverick County.

[8]Experts on the early Frontier Fiestas claim that "De Chief" actually spent most of his time looking for a mysterious and never-ending supply of iced beer that kept showing up in various places on the midway and behind the stage at the most popular attractions, especially in the waning hours near closing time. Painstaking research

indicates that the refreshments were probably kept on ice in false bottoms of Conestoga wagons scattered around the grounds. Joe Potter had borrowed these for a downtown parade (after City Council would not issue a permit to drop circulars advertising the Fiesta from student-flown airplanes borrowed from J.D. Reed) and kept the wagons on loan for atmosphere, quick naps, and general storage. Another theory is that the beer was packed, with ice, into disconnected water mains in the early afternoon before "Chief" came over to the Fiesta lot, and distributed through a courier system using empty costume trunks.

[9]Mr. and Mrs. Cullen set a fine precedent by this generous assistance in entertaining servicemen, an activity to which they were both devoted. Their daughters Margaret and Wilhelmina (a student and president of the Psychology Club in 1944) later met their respective husbands, the handsome Air Force captains Douglas Marshall and Corbin J. Robertson, Jr., at an Ellington Field dance. Weddings, only a week apart, followed in 1945.

[10]Among the organizers and mainstays of the City Amateur Ice Hockey League were some of the good Basilian padres at St. Thomas High School, who had learned their hockey the hard way in Toronto and elsewhere in Canada. St. Thomas was a CAIHL member, and it was common practice to mix high school and university players. The priests taught a fair, but fast and rugged game that toned up the league considerably. It was rumored that they were not above slipping in a "ringer" occasionally, with more muscle and finesse than their high school lads, and more connections in Toronto than in Houston.

[11]Mr. Goyen, hardly a shrinking violet in middle age, credits Harvey W. Harris, a member of the English faculty who also taught public speaking and coached the debate team, with giving him self-confidence, and "Chief" Mitchell with "having learned me English." Councilman Goyen and other freshman public speaking students were required by Harvey Harris to speak extemporaneously for three minutes each Friday afternoon, on any topic they chose. "I would memorize my speech," Goyen recalls, "reel off the first sentence or so, and then struggle along lamely to the end. One afternoon, I announced my topic, drew a complete blank and finally had to say 'I'm sorry; I just can't remember a thing.' When I stumbled back to my seat, with the whole class laughing and some of them really guffawing, I was suffering; my chair looked 10 feet tall, and I had to pole vault into it.

"Professor Harris waited until things quieted down. Then he said something I'll never forget; he said, 'Forget it, Johnny. The first time I had to do this, I couldn't even remember my topic, and now I'm teaching the stuff.' That was a kind thing, instinctively kind; and Harvey Harris continued to encourage me; as I improved in public speaking, and lost what really was a good bit of natural shyness, he told me that I should enter campus politics."

[12]The *Cougar* asked female students in February, 1940 if they preferred the "smooth, social, glamor boy type," or the "large, bruising, athletic type," and to name their ideal representative of the type chosen. Henry J.N. Taub was high on the "glamor boy" list, along with his political nemesis, Weed Peterson; Tommy Yerxa, Jimmy Jordan, Cecil Smith, Gerald Leinweber, Joe Slay, Clem Baldwin, Philip Allin, and Leonard Sehlin.

[13]The Hi-Hat, located just east of where old South Main Street crossed Bellaire (now Holcombe) Boulevard, was the "in" place at the time, especially for a beer and a little cheek-to-cheek dancing in the afternoon, or for jam-packed gatherings on the weekends in the fall. George Kalleen, owner and host, ran what was described as a "good joint," although it was understood that the presence of one non-obtrusive bouncer on crowded nights was both reasonable, and prudent. Further, Kalleen was not above putting a few Grand Prizes on the cuff until payday, and he was a dependable source of short-term, non-interest-bearing loans in real emergencies.

[14]A "shotgun" house is a long, narrow frame residence of one story, with a hallway running directly from the front door to the back door, and separating the house into two halves. It was said that an irate neighbor could fire a shotgun right through such modest homes, without hitting anything or anybody.

[15]HISD bought the original Jeppesen Stadium site from the Settegast Estate in March, 1940 for $75,550.16. The site, later augmented by the acquisition of approximately seven more acres to round out the property, surveyed out in 1940 at 59.7939 acres, which brought the price per acre to slightly over $1,253. Jeppesen Stadium and its subsidiary installations and environs covered the entire area bounded by Cullen Boulevard, and Scott, Wheeler, and Holman Streets. The property simply had to be acquired by the University, as emphasized in a master plan completed in 1966. Otherwise, any expansion of the campus to the west would be blocked. After long and complex negotiations, including three separate appraisals, it was purchased by the University of Houston in 1970 for the only bid offered, the final appraisal of $6,700,000 or $100,000 per acre. Terms were cash on the barrelhead, and HISD was allowed to use the property on a rental basis until 1976, while substitute facilities were constructed for the school district.

The difference between $1,253 and $100,000 per acre represents an increase of almost 8,000 per cent in 30 years; but Jeppesen Stadium and the small Jeppesen Gymnasium (where early Cougar teams played basketball), plus playing fields, and other improvements were of course added by HISD over the years. K.S. (Bud) Adams also made substantial investments in Jeppesen Stadium in upgrading it as the site for home games of the Houston Oilers, in the pre-Astrodome era when the Oilers dominated the American Football League.

[16]Frank "Posh" Oltorf, the sage of Marlin and erstwhile gin rummy partner of Herman Brown on long flights, told me a story about LBJ and suits that demonstrated how well the late President could combine wit, courage, and practicality in an emergency. Oltorf was at a beautiful estate that Brown & Root maintained in the Virginia steeplechase country around Warrenton when LBJ suffered a massive heart attack. Mrs. Johnson rushed to his bedside, and as soon as the attending specialists would permit it, she brought in a few memoranda of special consequence that LBJ had kept insisting he must discuss, even if for only a moment or so. Lady Bird hurried through the papers as soon as possible, noting on each the action to be taken. Then noting an approaching specialist out of the corner of her eye, she prepared to leave, transmit LBJ's instructions to appropriate staff members, and resume her vigil outside. She did ask, however, if there was anything else of particular importance she might do. LBJ reportedly thought a moment and replied, "Yes, there is. I promised that little tailor on Fourteenth Street he would have my decision on those two suits today, without fail." "Well," Lady Bird responded, "What shall I tell him?" "Tell him," said LBJ, "to finish the dark blue one as soon as possible . . . we can use it either way."

[17]Congressman Albert Thomas, already a formidable figure in Washington's appropriations and budgeting jungle, laid it on so thick with the Navy that one of the undersecretaries ordered down a rear admiral and asked the State of Texas to name James R.D. Eddy, head of the newly-created Department for Vocational Defense Training, as NRVS co-sponsor.

[18]The Armed Forces were combing the nation's industrial centers in 1939 and 1940, looking for firms capable of accepting major defense contracts without major changes in equipment or workmen, although additions to production capacity and the size of the work force would obviously be necessary in most cases. Houston attracted early and continuing attention from Army and Navy specialists in procurement, especially because of the relative ease of converting an oil tool manufacturing plant to the production of a military priority item such as machine gun tripods, as was the case at the McEvoy Company.

In the meantime, Houston's population climbed to 384,514 in 1940, an increase of 31.5 percent from 292,352 in a decade that had spanned years of depression and of recession. The county population reached 528,961. Economists, noting many positive indicators in 1940, began to predict another jump, even to the magic number of

500,000 Houstonians, by 1950, with perhaps 750,000 in Harris County. Then, some other factors began to emerge: indications of huge defense contracts; projections of vast demand for the raw and processed agricultural products in the area, especially cotton, grain, sugar, and rice; the demand for petroleum, petrochemicals, and elemental sulphur; the location of major training camps in the immediate area and nearby; the impact of approaching World War II on the Port of Houston; and special projects such as the San Jacinto Ordnance Depot.

Economists began to wonder if even their optimistic predictions were too low, and to warn company executives to prepare for vigorous expansion, including the recruitment of technicians and other industrial workers. Their second guess was more correct, as it turned out. The city population reached 596,163 in 1950, and the Harris County total was 806,701. The decennial increase for the city was a staggering 55 percent.

[19]As a practical matter, President Oberholtzer had gone to Mr. Cullen in the late summer, when the campaign began to pick up, and asked him to name an executive committee to work with him; Dr. Kemmerer; Lamar Q. Cato, the architect; and the trustees on details of the building in order to expedite things as much as possible. Mr. Cullen acquiesced, and named Mr. Mueller, Dr. Pennington, Mr. Lorehn, and Francis Berleth (acting for his boss, Colonel Kuldell, of Hughes Tool Company).

[20]The NRVS unit was commanded by Lieutenant (jg) F.J. Sabathier, but in staunch Navy tradition the outfit was really run by the chief petty officers, F.T. Harrowing and G.S. Beale.

[21]When the University Center was in planning stages in 1963, I suggested that it be given this name instead of the commonly used "Student Center," to reflect what I hoped would be an all-University (and to some extent, a specialized community) use. The name caught on after a year or two, although the facility is usually described as the "UC."

[22]"Werlin" is a misspelling for "Werlein", the correct surname of the distinguished lawyer and jurist who was to complete a long career as a justice of the Court of Civil Appeals before stepping down from the high bench three decades later. The variant spelling appears frequently in HISD records, as it often did in the newspapers, there also being prominent Werlins in the city.

[23]This is the reason that the University continued to have a junior college, at least on paper, from 1945-1963, and was so concerned in the intervening years with the amount of the per capita appropriation provided for junior colleges in Texas. These sizable funds were simply passed on through to eligible students, thus effecting a substantial reduction in the net cost they paid for tuition.

[24]Hiram Clarke suffered from mild insomnia, and would often appear at Harry Short's Esperson Drug Store for early coffee. Harry Short became interested in Mr. Clarke and in his company, put his savings into HL&P stock and amassed enough in time to become a major stockholder and director.

[25]The 1939 address, by Dean T.D. Brooks of Texas A&M College, was scheduled for the new campus, but was rained out and moved to the San Jacinto High School auditorium. This ceremony was attended by Patrick Henry (Pat) Foley, as president of the new University of Houston Ex-Students Association. He announced that the Association had records on 657 graduates, and would sponsor a first Homecoming in the fall. This event was staged around a dinner party at the Carolina Pines which attracted more than 75 couples. Pat Foley and his fellow officers (Charles Shearn, vice-president; and Catherine Berry, secretary-treasurer) told the guests at this November 14, 1939, event that it had been so successful it would be repeated in five years.

Colonel Bates' historic address, on May 26, 1940, was delivered in the Roy Gustav Cullen Building. The *Cougar* had announced that "Mr. Bates would preach to the largest class in history, 194 graduates." The Colonel took this in stride, pointing out that he was not really his friend Dr. Dawson C. Bryan of St. Paul's Methodist Church, "who had delivered such an inspiring baccalaureate sermon." He then gave a very good address of his own on the theme that "opportunities for young men and women have never been greater. If you are to succeed," he continued, "you must cultivate, mature, and develop within you a strong desire and fixed determination to succeed, a self-reliance that will eliminate all thoughts of timidity and self-pity, that will overcome all obstacles, that will make opportunities where none appear to exist." After his address, Reverend E. Hermond Westmoreland gave the benediction.

[26]Walter W. Kemmerer was a prophet of marked distinction. University of Houston enrollment zoomed to 10,028 in the fall of 1946, averaged 12,760 for the next 10 years, and in 1961 began the quick ascent to the present total of some 40,000 in the University of Houston System (1961 was the year that the passage of Senate Bill 2 assured the admission of the institution to the state system of higher education).

[27]There was some difficulty in obtaining admission to medical and dental schools for University of Houston graduates in the early years of the institution. Although it is clear that applicants were well prepared, the fact that the University was not accredited by the Southern Association of Schools and Colleges, the regional accrediting body, was a continuing problem. Professor Catherine Cominsky, who served effectively for many years as coordinator for pre-medical and pre-dental majors, says that the first candidate accepted for medical school was Asa Martin, M.D., who practices in

Alaska; and the first pre-dental candidate was Maxwell Taylor, D.D., who still practices in Houston. Both men were members of the Class of 1943, while George Drake, a long-time mainstay in the Department of Chemistry, was chairman of the Pre-Medical Committee.

[28]Colonel Bates told me that he sat next to his brother, Jesse Watson Bates, in law school at the University of Texas, and "Judge (Dudley) Tarleton would read out your entire name when he called the roll. When I told him that I had no middle name, he said that 'we will have to look into that.' At the next class, he asked me what I thought about William Bartholomew Bates. That sounded fine to me, so that was it."

[29]The Executive Committee had been established without any particular fanfare in the summer of 1941, when the volume of paper work, especially in connection with governmental agencies, was sharply on the rise at the University. It was authorized to act for the entire Board of Trustees in matters affecting the University, subject to later affirmation. In actual practice, there was almost always discreet checking with a key trustee or two before initial action. President Oberholtzer accepted the wisdom of this arrangement, especially when the Board of Education had quorum difficulties or missed a meeting, as in the summer. But he had begun to note increasing instances of action by the other three officers of the University and members of the Executive Committee (Dr. Kemmerer, Dean Dupre and Mr. Mills) in his absence or unavailability.

[30]Leta Gilbert says that Dr. Oberholtzer was "always Dr. Kemmerer's 'brake'; he had held him back just enough, and that's why they made such a good, balanced team." She also believes that President Oberholtzer was in a very tenuous position with the faculty in the summer and fall of 1943, as factions for and against his policies and style of administration began to form. Much of the unrest must have stemmed from consistently low salary schedules, at a time when industry, in spite of war controls, was not only far ahead of the University in compensation for comparable positions (or some skilled hourly jobs), but was also paying cost-of-living adjustments.

Mrs. Gilbert remembers that when Dr. Kemmerer was interviewing her for the position as his secretary she accepted in June, 1943, he asked if she knew anyone on the faculty. "Yes," she replied, "I know Freeman Nixon." There was an immediate chill in the air, as if she had made some fatal admission; the history (and pilot-training) instructor in question was believed to be pro-Oberholtzer. Mrs. Gilbert, sensing that she had indeed struck a nerve, immediately added that she knew Mr. Nixon only casually through church activities. She got the job, and never mentioned Freeman G. Nixon again.

Although evidence on this is difficult to uncover, Leta Gilbert believes that the Faculty Association balloted secretly in the summer of 1943 on a "vote of confidence" for President Oberholtzer, which he carried by the perilous margin of 34-33. Thereafter, she opines, President Oberholtzer took an inordinate interest in just who voted how. And although some faculty opponents complained bitterly about administrators with minimal or no teaching assignments being allowed to vote, the truth was that a number of administrator votes went *against* Dr. Oberholtzer. This, Mrs. Gilbert maintains, is why Naason K. Dupre was demoted from dean to director of extension in 1944, after running the Houston Junior College for the seven years of its existence, and serving since 1927 as the only person with the title of dean (F.M. Black held the title of supervising dean from 1927-1932, while N.K. Dupre was proving himself as "assistant dean"; but Dean Black, HISD's director of secondary education, hardly knew the way out to San Jacinto High School, and the title of supervising dean was abolished after his death in 1932, whereupon it became Dean Dupre in official title as well as in fact.)

[31]This is an interesting conjecture which Dr. Kemmerer said that he based upon Mr. Cullen's direct statements to him in the first few weeks of 1945. Mr. Cullen's biographers, Edward W. Kilman and Theon Wright, have a different version. They stated that Mr. Cullen's interest in major gifts to Houston hospitals had been stimulated early in 1943 by Robert Jolly, then superintendent of Memorial Hospital, an old-time evangelist who used to belt out a few fundamentalist hymns with Mr. Cullen now and then of a convivial evening. This interest was further advanced by Mrs. Cullen, even though she shared her husband's primary interest in the University of Houston. In any event, Mr. and Mrs. Cullen gave $1 million each to Memorial, Methodist, and Hermann Hospitals (advanced in cash from future Thompson oil field royalties) during Christmas week of 1944, and added a million for their old friend Clinton S. (Mike) Quin (a total donation of $4 million). His Episcopal diocese didn't have a Texas Medical Center hospital yet, but he had some plans for what would become St. Luke's Hospital there, and he rushed them down to Mr. Cullen's office as soon as he could locate them in the files.

Almost a decade later, Mr. Cullen asked me to go out to St. Luke's, where his son-in-law Isaac (Ike) Arnold was involved in raising the remainder of the funds required to complete the new hospital, and "help them out with some kind of a dedication Bishop Quin wants to put on." I did so, and found that a feature of the dedication was the belated installation of the cornerstone, with a text from Scripture selected after endless deliberations by a committee of bishops.

At last, the dedication was only 24 hours away, and the cornerstone, long delayed, was being delivered as Bishop Quin and I waited. He kneeled down for a look at the graven stone, and got up slowly, shaking his head. He pointed to the text in his Bible, a most appropriate text from John 10:10, "I am come that they might have life," and then back to the cornerstone. It was apparent that the stonecutter had pondered for a while and had decided that he could improve on Scripture a little; he added the word "so" between "come" and "that." Bishop Quin recovered his never-failing sense of humor after a few charitable observations about stonecutters turned Biblical scholars and his own probable fate at the hands of the distinguished prelates who had so carefully selected the text (this was when holy writ was still intact, not "modernized" to remove flavor, style, and authenticity). "You know anything about erasing granite?" he asked me. "No sir," I replied, "but I'll bet he does," pointing to the representative of the stonecutting firm who was walking toward us. He somehow had a corrected copy back a few hours before the dedication, by working two men straight through night and morning.

[32]One of the unexplained mysteries of Texas politics is how Lyndon B. Johnson, already proclaimed by the Houston *Chronicle* as a surprise winner over W. Lee O'Daniel in a 1941 special election for the United States Senate, lost narrowly to O'Daniel when the final count was in. One theory is that Coke Stevenson may have tipped the scales in the Hill Country, especially in San Saba and surrounding counties, because of his opposition to LBJ's all-out support of FDR's New Deal and an unnatural alliance with O'Daniel forces who controlled much of the rural vote, especially in East Texas.

I was a sort of head office boy in the LBJ campaign, operating out of Rice Hotel campaign headquarters under Judge Roy Hofheinz, whom I had met while editor of the Rice *Thresher*. The summer job was pleasant and enlightening, but we seemed to be running a strong second at best. Then support for LBJ began to multiply, and a week before the election, Judge Hofheinz came in with one of the first political polls I had ever seen. It showed Johnson with a narrow lead. "Find the candidate," he told me. I did, after considerable difficulty, at a rally in Yoakum. The judge quickly explained the findings of the poll to LBJ. "It looks good," he concluded. "That's fine," said the candidate, "what do you want me to do?" "Just put that Stetson hat back on and keep your mouth shut," replied the judge.

At 9 p.m. on election night, O'Daniel forged a narrow lead in rural returns, after LBJ had been ahead for two hours in the official count and in most telephoned reports we were receiving. There was little change at 11 p.m., but a statistician told us that if LBJ could regain the lead at 1 a.m., there would probably not be enough votes out at that stage to beat him. A group of campaign officials, including Judge Hofheinz, Allen Hannay, and Sam D.W. Low were in Editor George Cottingham's office at the *Chronicle* as the midnight returns came in from the Texas Election Bureau in Dallas. LBJ was back in the lead, and after waiting for the 1 a.m. count, which still showed

Johnson ahead, Cottingham ordered up 48-point headlines for the last edition of the *Chronicle's* Sunday edition, proclaiming LBJ's surprise victory.

Judge Hofheinz fired up a fresh cigar, and beckoned to me, Hannay, and Low. "We're going to Austin to see this one through," he said. "You drive," he added, pointing to me. There was a detour at Bastrop, and by the time we got to Austin it was dawn. A perturbed Lyndon Baines Johnson met us at the Stephen F. Austin hotel; he had news that two central West Texas counties, near his own Johnson City, had gone overwhelmingly for "Pappy" O'Daniel. There was talk of a recount, but in the end, O'Daniel was sworn in to replace General Andrew Jackson Houston, the 86-year-old son of the hero of San Jacinto, who had lived only 24 days after being named to the Senate by O'Daniel.

The epilogue to this anecdote, of course, came in 1947. LBJ was elected to the Senate over Coke Stevenson by what was correctly termed a "hairline" margin of 87 votes—all from Box 13 in George Parr's Duval County.

[33]SB 207 and other bills are identified differently in current compilations of state statutes.

[34]Much of this emphasis stemmed from the organization of the successful Hughes Industrial School of the University in 1940-1941. Organized and staffed by faculty members, this unique unit had as many as 660 Hughes Tool Company employees in training at the firm's Harrisburg Boulevard plant at peak levels. The school became a model for as many as a dozen smaller such operations during World War II. These were administered from an office of industrial and business cooperation in the (Chamber of) Commerce Building downtown, and included special classes for the Army Air Force at Ellington Field.

[35]There was apparently some sensitivity about media attention to this third and last of the three Naval training units on campus during World War II, and it received considerably less attention than the NRVS and NERMS operations. Nevertheless, it was a major undertaking. A total of 704 cadets took their first flight training at Cliff Hyde Flying Service, and ground instruction at the University, in the pattern established earlier for civilian (CPT) pilots. They then went on for intermediate and advanced flight training. Two CAA-NAPTC pilots were on the 1944 *Houstonian* list of University students killed or missing in action, as was a Marine Air Corps pilot from the CAA-NAPTC unit.

[36]Dr. Kemmerer said that President Oberholtzer, "or more probably Virginia Stone," at one time had 60 personnel authorization forms stacked up somewhere for several weeks. Many of the new members

of the faculty and staff whose employment was authorized by these documents had already gone to work. They were asking daily about confirmation of their employment, while putting in 12- to 15-hour days admitting, counseling or teaching veterans. Dr. Kemmerer, in desperation, finally recovered all the forms and signed them himself.

[37]The Veterans Club was organized in the fall of 1944, and quickly became one of the most active of the campus groups. Their officers included Dan Kury (who served as president, vice-president, and secretary at different times in 1944 and 1945), Clarence Raver, Mac Word, George Hovey, Jr., Harry Marsalis, Billie Word, Kenneth Urban, Arthur Miller, Ralph Miller, Frank White and Oscar Johnson. The members marched in the Armistice Day parade of 1944 downtown, and worked throughout the year on projects, including a war memorial to the University's World War II dead.

[38]A 1944 study by the Federal Works Agency had shown that the average amount of instructional space available per student in state universities was over 150 square feet. In 1945, this figure for the University of Houston was about 25 square feet, with the immediate prospect of huge increases in enrollment. This is a problem that was at crisis proportions throughout the 1940's and 1950's, began to abate somewhat in the late 1960's, but is still unresolved on Central Campus and especially at the Downtown College as the 1980's approach.

[39]By this time, Dr. Oberholtzer had retired and was helping direct the area activities of the Hoover Commission under the sponsorship of Mr. Cullen. I was working on various projects for the great philanthropist-oilman-citizen, and had been asked by him to assist Dr. Oberholtzer in every way possible. Dr. Oberholtzer was often in my office at 1428 Commerce Building, and I first conceived the idea for *In Time* in our various conversations about the early days with the School District, the University, Mr. Cullen, and my own impressions of teaching at the University, where I had begun to lecture in 1950 in the Colleges of Business Administration and of Arts and Sciences. Dr. Oberholtzer, still a fine-looking man at 71, though he had started to stoop a bit and was bothered increasingly by an inflammation of the iris that was affecting his sight, told his friends that he didn't want anything to do with J. Edgar Hoover, but would go along with Herbert Hoover and the Hoover Commission. Actually, he soon became a bit bored with the Hoover Commission, much as he supported its sound plans for economy in government and appreciated the opportunity it gave him to stay active and to remain in contact with Mr. Cullen and other prominent Houstonians. Mainly, he missed the University of Houston, even though he maintained many friendships there and headquartered occasionally in Charlie Hiller's office.

Dr. Oberholtzer would reminisce about Dr. Kemmerer to me. He had friendship and respect for his successor, but he did not once express to me any opinion about how the presidency was being conducted once he left office; nor did he comment on the question of when or if Dr. Kemmerer would be advanced from acting to full president. It is known, as will appear later, that Dr. Oberholtzer opposed Bill Kemmerer's being named to succeed him in 1950.

[40]There were only three trustees of the M.D. Anderson Foundation until recent years, and there are but four today. When the founding donor passed away in 1939, Colonel Bates and Mr. Freeman elected their friend and client Mr. Wilkins to succeed him. On Mr. Wilkins' death in 1953, they elected Warren S. Bellows, Sr., a leading general contractor and loyal friend of the University of Houston, later a member of the governing board. Mr. Bellows remained an Anderson Foundation trustee until his death in 1967. His sons, Warren, Jr., George and Frank, have maintained the same interest that their father, one of the most respected, able and popular of the great Houstonians of his era, always had for the University.

[41]The regents had authorized an Executive Committee on April 18, 1945. The members were Mr. Cullen, chairman; Colonel Bates, vice chairman; and Mr. Farish, Mr. Dietrich and Mr. Hutcheson. This committee constituted an admirable and effective amalgam of "Old Houston" and the new loci of oil, industrial, and major law firm power. Its appointment and charge created a precedent that would have an immediate and lasting effect upon relationships between the governing board and administrative and executive officers of the University.

Chapter Five

1945-1954

The marathon inauguration of Edison Ellsworth Oberholtzer . . . A Janus-like view back to 1927, and ahead to 1977 and beyond . . . The $12 million expansion of physical plant that could have been much larger . . . Deemphasis of the Junior College Division . . . Four professional schools emerge in less than five years . . . "The Chief" slows down, retires and is blamed for appointment of an "acting" president . . . The rampant Frontier Fiesta on a campus of veterans, University Village, and rising athletics fever . . . Stabilization and the threat of deficits . . . Conflict at high levels . . . The brief administration of President Walter W. Kemmerer, and a "resignation" that was not . . . C.F. McElhinney to the rescue ad interim *. . . General A.D. Bruce changes his uniform as the "public school" era finally ends*

To understand the evolvement of the University of Houston without a clear perception of the nine years between October 19, 1945, and September 1, 1954, would be comparable to comprehending the mysteries of Egyptian hieroglyphics without Jean-François Champollion's unravelling of the Rosetta Stone.

Within this relatively short yet pivotal space of time, the University lost both of the dedicated, opposing yet complementary presidents who had shaped and formed it; added $12 million in physical plant, primarily through the generosity of one donor and his wife; increased enrollment from 5,379 (it had been as low as 1,104 in the fall of 1943) to 13,066; established four professional schools (thereby fulfilling one of the fundamental requirements for a true university), and began the long, convoluted ascent from a stultifying identification as a junior college too closely affiliated with a public school system.

The marathon inauguration of Edison Ellsworth Oberholtzer both closed and opened an era at the University of Houston. His

Janus-like speech on that pleasant fall evening of October 19, 1945, looked back discerningly to 1927 and prophetically forward to 1977 and beyond.[1] The festivities honoring Dr. Oberholtzer were in the heroic mold, extending over two full days of morning, afternoon and evening sessions that were clocked at a little over 13 hours in total time.

It all began at 11 a.m. on Thursday, October 18, 1945, on the lawn between the Roy Gustav Cullen Building and the reflection pool, with Colonel Bates presiding.

(The programs moved inside for the late afternoon and evening sessions. Librarian Ruth Wikoff said that this probably relates to the 1940 baccalaureate service, which began at dusk. The audience sat in chairs around the reflection pool, enjoying a soprano soloist who, when she became aware that she was being accompanied by a chorus of tree frogs in a nearby hedge, sang a bit louder. But the frogs only stepped up their volume. By this time, the audience was enthralled by the contest, which ended with the soprano hitting her highest note, and a giant bull frog giving out with a basso "harrump" exactly in pitch and on cue. The audience roared its approval, but next morning Dr. Oberholtzer sent for the chief of maintenance. He handed him a mason jar and pointed out the window. "There's a giant bull tree frog in that hedge by the pool," he said. "Get him, and throw him in the bayou.")

Mr. Cullen gave a brief word of welcome on behalf of the Board of Regents, and Dr. Peterson, as president of the Board of Education, followed. Dr. Daily, who had made the motion advancing the University to four-year status in 1934, added her own piquant phrases. The University of Houston, she pointed out, "had been established in true Texas tradition. It was Dr. Oberholtzer's 'Lone Star wildcat,' it hit good production, and it will improve in quantity as well as in quality as it goes along." F.M. Law brought greetings from the Chamber of Commerce, and Colonel Bates then introduced Mayor Otis Massey, County Judge Glenn Perry, Mrs. L.E. Ferris, president of the City Federation of Women's Clubs, and the respective presidents of the Kiwanis Club of Houston and of the Downtown Rotary Club, G. Maxfield Taylor and Merrill E. Brown.

Elsie Roberts, stunning photographs of whom were featured in the Vanity Fair section of the *Houstonian* each of the four years she attended the University from 1942 to 1946, enlivened the proceedings when she spoke on behalf of the student body. She was president of the Student Association at the time, and surely one of the best-looking young women to hold such an office anywhere, any time.

The choice of a principal speaker for the opening session of the inaugural ceremonies was significant. The faculty committee recommended, and Dr. Oberholtzer approved, a respected historian, Professor Frederick Eby of the University of Texas.[2] Professor Eby's real fame, however, was associated with the junior college movement, and he had been a consultant to the Houston Junior College as early as 1927. His selection as a principal inaugural speaker was understandable in view of the antecedents of the University of Houston; but the choice was also tied directly to a continuing new emphasis on the junior college aspects of the University, an emphasis that was to become almost an obsession before it was eradicated in 1954.

Professor Eby spoke, with accuracy combined with hyperbole, of "glorious programs," of the fact that "it would take no crystal-gazer to foresee a full future for this infant institution." He emphasized the "fitness of time" surrounding the University, in a world "seething with expectancy" and a new age demanding new institutions of higher education "to take care of new educational needs."

The Board of Regents and invited guests then attended a luncheon in an area next to the Recreation Building which had been fitted-up as a makeshift Board Room (while the by-laws stipulated that the governing board was to meet on campus, there was a loophole under which alternate locations could be indicated in advance; the organizational meeting had been held in Mr. Cullen's office, he liked to meet there, and virtually all meetings were held there or in his home "where we can have a little taste of something after the business is over.")

The opening day program resumed at 3 p.m. in the Roy Gustav Cullen Building, with Mrs. Martha Gano Houstoun presiding over a panel of 12 discussing "The Contributions of Higher Education to the Economic Life of a Community," initiating a theme that would run through a number of the remaining inaugural events.

The distinguished but far too numerous participants were James R.D. Eddy, director of extension and research, C.C. Colvert, junior college consultant, Frederick Eby, professor of history and expert on junior college education, and E.W. Bertner,

M.D., director of the M.D. Anderson Hospital for Cancer Research, all of the University of Texas; E.L. Williams, professor of industrial education, and T.L. McNew, dean of the School of Engineering, both of Texas A&M College; R.A. Mueller, president, Gray Tool Company; Ewing Werlein, attorney and trustee of the Board of Education; R.M. Dyer, personnel director for the Humble Oil & Refining Company; and M.L. Ray, A. Ray Sims and Dr. Kemmerer of the University of Houston. Mr. Ray had recently been named acting director of the School of Engineering, and Mr. Sims, coordinator of the industrial service program.

After a two-hour break for a buffet dinner, the lengthening proceedings resumed with Stephen P. Farish presiding at an evening session. The principal speaker was one of Dr. Oberholtzer's closest colleagues in the Department of Superintendence of the National Education Association (which Dr. Oberholtzer had served as president in 1934-1935). This was Dr. A.J. Stoddard, superintendent of schools in Philadelphia.

Dr. Stoddard said all the things you might expect about his old friend's signal accomplishments in the field of primary and secondary education since 1897—and his sanguine prospects in higher education. He then emphasized a fact that has been somewhat obscured: Dr. Oberholtzer was not only one of the few public school administrators to serve as a university president; he was probably the only chief executive to establish his own institution.

The musical interlude drew almost as much applause as the speaker. Bruce Spencer King had chosen Charles Gounod's superb "Sanctus" from the *St. Cecilia Mass* for his small but well-trained Choral Club, with Gloria Brienza as soloist.[3]

The marathon resumed the following morning at 11. Hiram Ocie Clarke, Jr., presided at a program that began with greetings from local educational institutions and organizations: The Rice Institute (Dean Harry Boyer Weiser), Baylor Medical School (Dean W.H. Moursund), Texas Dental School (Dean Frederick C. Elliott), Houston Independent School District (Superintendent W.E. Moreland, Dr. Oberholtzer's successor), Harris County School District (Superintendent J. Hall Shepherd), Houston Council of Parents and Teachers (Mrs. A.B. Anderson, president) and the parochial schools of the area (Reverend Jacob Schnetzer).

The principal address on this occasion was given by Dean T.D. Brooks of the School of Arts and Sciences, Texas A&M College.

Dean Brooks, a humanist of distinction in an institution then better known for the more pragmatic disciplines, was the choice of several members of the inaugural committee who had heard him deliver the 1939 commencement address. He spoke eloquently on "The Contribution of Higher Education to the Cultural Development of a State," thereby balancing, in subject and scope, the themes of the previous speeches by Drs. Stoddard and Eby.

After a two-hour break for luncheon, Mrs. Agnese Carter Nelms presided at a panel discussion of "The Contribution of Higher Education to the Cultural Life of a Community." This time the number of participants was increased to 13: E. William Doty, dean of the School of Fine Arts and A. Caswell Ellis, director of the Extension Department, University of Texas; Cleanth Brooks, professor of English, Louisiana State University; John McGinnis, professor of English, Southern Methodist University; Charles O. Stewart, professor of English, Sam Houston State Teachers College; Dean Brooks, then introduced as from the School of Liberal Arts at Texas A&M College, rather than the School of Arts and Sciences at that institution; Dean Alfred H. Nolle of Southwest Texas State Teachers College (which had recently graduated a tall, thin and highly motivated fellow by the name of Lyndon Baines Johnson); James Chillman, a professor of architecture at The Rice Institute who was appearing in his other role as director, Houston Museum of Fine Arts; Mrs. Marguerite Palmer, president, Houston Garden Club, representing all similar organizations in the city; Hubert Roussel, critic for the Houston *Post*, "representing the theatrical profession";[4] and Mrs. Ebaugh, then chairman of the Division of Languages and Fine Arts, Dr. Kemmerer, and Dr. Hiller for the University of Houston.

The actual inauguration of Dr. Oberholtzer finally came at 7:30 p.m. on the second day. Colonel James Anderson was master of ceremonies, and the music was by an ensemble from the Houston Symphony Society, conducted by Joseph A. Henkel of the music faculty. For one of the few such times in recorded history, the processional music was not the Triumphal March from *Aida*, but the seldom-heard Coronation March from Meyerbeer's *The Prophet* (presented by the Metropolitan Opera in 1977 for the first time in almost a half-century). There had been some concern about the rather sparse response from robed delegates marching in the processional, but this was pieced out at 81 by dragooning some faculty members to represent their out-of-state *alma maters* and by filling in with representatives of various learned societies, also locals.

At the moment of installation, Mr. Cullen stepped forward. He read from a document prepared by Dr. Kemmerer and Charlie Hiller: "Acting as chairman (of) and in behalf of the Board of Regents of the University of Houston, upon the authority of the State of Texas, I vest in you, Edison Ellsworth Oberholtzer, the presidency of the University, together with all the authorities (sic) necessary to the office, and charge you in the fear of God and (in) the eyes of these men (and women) with the burden of the responsibilities hereof, and I now declare you, Edison Ellsworth Oberholtzer, to be the president of the University of Houston." They then shook hands on the deal, as Mr. Cullen would have said. And the chairman of the board told the audience, "Of all my (civic and philanthropic) activities, I consider the University of Houston the one for which I want to be remembered."

There were five principal themes in President Oberholtzer's inaugural address, all of them interrelated, and most of them will recur later in this history of the University of Houston's first half-century. The themes were: a review of the history to date of the University, including its philosophy and purposes; restating of the fundamental principles set forth in the institutional charter (which were also reminiscent of the educational tenets Dr. Oberholtzer expounded to the graduating classes of Heights High and Central High Schools in 1924); an overview of University organization and curricula at a crucial juncture; a recounting, with understandable pride, of the University's record in World War II, and of its unique programs for returning veterans; and a closing section entitled "A New Era Opens," as indeed it did.

Cogent excerpts from Dr. Oberholtzer's text follow:

> A university is generally distinguished from other institutions of higher learning by the fact that it is made up of several schools or colleges unified under a single administration and having certain objectives in common. Because a university must maintain such a rich and varied program, it must have for the achievement of its purposes a highly trained professional staff, adequate equipment and library facilities, and a variety of laboratories and shops. Generally speaking, the principal functions are teaching, research, and service, but teaching is the first obligation.
>
> In speaking of these general requirements, it should be understood that every university has an individuality of its own. In this respect, the University of Houston is unique in many ways. True, the university must

have a campus and buildings, yet it must have more than its material possessions would indicate. It must have a spirit of learning; it must have students; it must have a scholarly faculty; it must have due regard for the traditions and the ideals of the society which it serves; it must believe in truth; it must protest against error; it must lead by reason rather than by force. A university is not a place for propaganda but rather a place to search for truth, to study, and to reach conclusions. When these processes of thought have been followed, men have been free to express their views because they are thoroughly supported by facts.

Mr. Cullen was observed frequently applauding, and nodding in vigorous agreement with the foregoing. He and the other regents and community leaders present also endorsed wholeheartedly the following section of the Oberholtzer address:

The University of Houston is a public institution created by the State, but it is unique in that the institution is not bound by the traditions of academic rigidity. In its original Charter, which was adopted for the University of Houston in the spring of 1934, there is provided an official statement giving expression to its purposes, social import, and fundamental principles of operation. Although this Charter was enacted more than a decade ago, it is still most adequate and timely for a dynamic program of education designed to inculcate the democratic principles of our American way of life. It is dedicated to the principles of our American government as established by the Constitution of the United States and embodied in the ideals and purposes of the early patriots and founders of this nation. The authorities of this University are pledged to continue these precepts and principles as the patriotic foundations and fundamentals from which its educational objectives shall never waver.

Dr. Oberholtzer's remarks regarding organization and curricula offer an accurate breakdown on how the University was constituted in the watershed year of 1945, and an equally valuable listing of offerings actually available in various fields:

The offerings of the University of Houston, on its campus and at the Downtown School, are made available to those who must combine a work and school program.

In the Senior College School of Business Administration the following courses are offered: accounting, banking and finance, economics, real estate, insurance, merchandising, trade and transportation, aeronautical administration, business research, secretarial training, management and public administration.

In the Division of Public Administration, plans have been completed for co-operation with the city government to offer personnel training in several phases of municipal government, including the police, fire, and health departments. The Business Research Department will meet a long-recognized need and will provide valuable statistics for the use of businessmen of this area.

The School of Education is expanding by offering work toward the degree of Doctor in Education.

The School of Engineering offers a four-year program leading to degrees in general engineering and chemical engineering. The fifth year leads to respective degrees in petroleum, civil, mechanical, and electrical engineering.

The School of Nursing offers a three-year course of college work with one-year credit for those completing the courses as registered nurses. More than six hundred nurses in training now are enrolled regularly in the University. The University sends instructors to five of the large hospitals to give basic science and related work, as well as regular first-year college subjects related to the nursing-education program.

The School of Liberal Arts and Sciences offers courses from the freshman through the graduate year in languages and fine arts, literature, dramatics, home economics, speech, journalism, history, government, sociology, economics, psychology, philosophy, botany, bacteriology, zoology, geology, physics, chemistry, and mathematics.

The School of Technology and Industry offers both short and long courses, known as terminal courses, varying all the way from twelve weeks to two years, which are designed to prepare students for work in industries. The University has enrolled more than eight thousand students in the School of Industry directly related to the war program.

Advanced degrees offered by the University of Houston include the Master of Arts, the Master of Science, the Master in Education, and the Doctor in Education.

The University's record in World War II was indeed impressive. The seeming inconsistency between Dr. Oberholtzer's mention above of "more than eight thousand students in the School of Industry" and higher figures that follow for "employees in training for various phases of war plant production in the year 1943 (alone)," is easily explainable. The University of Houston had thousands of war industry trainees in programs outside what President Oberholtzer termed the School of Industry, the model for which was at Hughes Tool Company. And the Houston area overall had more than $300 million in war contracts at peak production. The changing of shifts at Hughes Tool or Reed Roller

Bit, where huge contracts for airplane engines and parts were concentrated, resembled Times Square on New Year's Eve.

Dr. Oberholtzer added a summary of his own basic educational philosophy: "the greatest hope for the future lies in more practical and complete education for all mankind." He then concluded with a prediction of new successes for the University in a new era, plaudits for the Board of Regents and all segments of the University community, and formal acceptance of the presidency:

> In the year of 1945, no other university so young can look forward with greater prospects of accomplishing the objectives set forth in its original charter.
>
> This year opens a new era in the life of this institution—a new page is written in its history which brings new inspiration and a new vision for service. The citizens of this district have enthusiastically supported this University through its struggles and advancement, not only by giving funds for its buildings but also by showing in many ways their faith in its continued growth and accomplishments. For this, our grateful thanks and appreciation shall ever be recorded.
>
> Now we are thrice blessed with the leadership of a new Board of Control whose services are devoted to the single objective of creating a University to be unexcelled in its field of service.[5]
>
> In accordance with the legislative enactment of March, 1945, a Board of Regents, as a governing board, was created for the control of policies and for the operation of this University. Search far and wide, one cannot conceive of a better selection for membership on this governing body. The membership of this Board is a cross-section of business and professional men and women who have lived as citizens of this community for a long period of years. They know Houston; they love its people; they are devoted to the functions and purposes for which this institution was created. They have added much to the sound structure of this University through their advice, counsel, and judgment.
>
> As the president of the University of Houston, I have been with this institution from its founding. Eighteen years of service [have] made it a part of my life. The success of this institution belongs to many: the Board of Education and its members for years of faithful service; a large group of loyal and efficient faculty members, some of whom are now serving who started with the founding of the institution; an earnest and hard-working student body, from year to year; many members of the alumni who have distinguished themselves in service; many citizens who, through good will and generous gifts, have helped to finance this institution in its years of growth. All of these have warmed the heart and inspired the leaders who bear the responsibility for carrying on. And, finally, this Board of Regents,

first as an Advisory Board, now the governing body, has launched this institution on a broad career of service to the cause of education.

Mr. Chairman and other members of the Board of Regents:

In the presence of these colleagues from other colleges and universities, faculty members, students, and friends of the University of Houston, I accept the honor and the office with which you do now endow me. I accept this office and its responsibilities with due humility and with earnest desire to contribute all that my life can give. I accept because it keeps me in association with

This excellent Board of Regents as governing authority;
This loyal and faithful group of scholars—the Faculty;
This inspiring and enthusiastic community of learners—the Students;
This host of friends and leaders—Our Houston;
This institution than which to me there is none greater.

Mr. Chairman, I pledge to you and this institution in all good faith my full measure of service, commensurate with high and noble functions, of which the president and chief executive of this University may be called upon to perform. With full appreciation and gratitude, I seal this solemn pledge.

The $12 million expansion of physical plant at the University of Houston between 1945 and 1952 was remarkable in a number of ways: its sheer size duly impressed an earlier generation that had not seen One Shell Plaza and Pennzoil Place, or plans for a $40 million Fine Arts Center at the University of Texas in Austin; much of it had been financed by one donor; it had a great psychological impact on students, faculty and staff, and on the community in general; it would be followed not by the continued additions to physical plant expected and required for an institution undergoing a shift to true university status, but by a frustrating time during which only minor facilities would go on-line.

Members of the University of Houston community from 1945 to 1952 will tell you repeatedly how meaningful it was then, under grievously overcrowded conditions, to read of the magnanimous gifts for buildings (which quickly reached a total of almost $6 million and then escalated further); to see architectural plans and continuing publicity on the expansion program, which President Oberholtzer and Dr. Kemmerer wisely emphasized; and, finally, to see huge new buildings actually under construction.

This had a similarly salutary effect on the general public, many of whom had persisted in misidentifying the University as an HISD operation at San Jacinto High School, or as a tiny, friendless institution isolated in the woods between the South Side sewage disposal plant and the Port City stockyards.

Two noteworthy aspects of the seven-year, $12 million construction era, however, have never been fully understood. First, several major projects that would have run the total above $15 million were either abandoned or postponed for many years. Second, virtually all actual construction was compressed into the 36 months from May 1948 to May 1951.

The abandonments and postponements came about largely because Hugh Roy Cullen's heroic generosity outran fiscal reality. With the announcement of the Cullen Foundation ("leaked" to a meeting of the Texas Hospital Association on March 27, 1947),[6] it was widely assumed that there was simply no end to the oilman-philanthropist's largesse. Some 225,000 letters came in from all over the world, asking money for an unbelievable range of causes (some simply pleaded, "Give me some of that money").

Actually, the Cullen Foundation and its donors were hard up for cash after estimates on the enlarged Ezekiel W. Cullen Building (originally budgeted at $3 million) had escalated $2 million; after little-publicized gifts of $150,000 annually toward the retirement of dormitory bonds; after giving $1,299,267 for engineering laboratories and small buildings for architecture and the department of psychology.

Additional gifts to the University in 1949 and 1950 would exacerbate this situation. This led to abandonment of a "Main Junior College" Building and a major facility for engineering (although the latter was completed from newly drawn plans more than a decade later, in 1959), and it helped bring about the postponement of a chapel (Religious Activities Building), a Fine Arts Building, a gymnasium and a swimming pool. There were other reasons for compressing the building program into slightly less than three years, in addition to the obvious problems stemming from delays in the flow of donations. Among these were the lack of an established procedure, and adequate staff for designating, planning, contracting for and supervising the construction of new additions to physical plant; lingering inflation (which the regents kept hoping would diminish); severe shortages in the availability of materials; and mild internal dissension regarding the priority of specific projects. As a result, it was more than three years between announcement of the Ezekiel W. Cullen Building, on

March 21, 1945, and the groundbreaking for this key facility, on May 10, 1948.

Other postponements and abandonments of building projects came cascading down, at a time when record enrollments had brought the University to an incredibly low ratio of instructional space per student. The new Board of Regents had concentrated heavily on the obvious need for additions to physical plant (with constant urging from President Oberholtzer) from almost the moment its members were sworn into office. After the extraordinary news of Mr. Cullen's decision to provide a magnificent memorial to his grandfather, President Oberholtzer spoke at length at the Board of Regents meeting of July 12, 1945, on the need for campus dormitories. A committee of Lamar Fleming, Jr., Mrs. James P. Houstoun, Donald H. Thornbury, Colonel James Anderson, Hiram Clarke, and James W. Rockwell was named to confer with the president on the problem.

It had been previously determined that dormitories should be financed with revenue bonds, and the committee immediately contacted a bonding syndicate. Members of the syndicate presented what was described as an "excellent" bonding plan on April 17, 1946, but the contract contained a provision that final architectural plans must be ready by June 15, 1946—an impossible deadline. The matter was then referred to the Executive Committee, and Colonel Bates reported to that body on September 18, 1946, that "the estimates we are getting on plans are just sky-high." The Committee recommended that the dormitory project be postponed, in the hope that prolonged wartime inflation would abate.

Meanwhile, enrollments were growing at an unprecedented rate, especially in engineering, technology, and education. Dr. Oberholtzer was given an emergency appropriation of $26,700 on December 19, 1945, to provide a foundation for a large temporary engineering and shop building. After the holidays, this was increased by $30,000 in order to place 20 small shop structures on the foundation.

What appeared to be a major new breakthrough in campus construction came on February 20, 1946. Dr. Oberholtzer was authorized to engage Alfred C. Finn as an architectural consultant. Mr. Finn, a fellow of the American Institute of Architects, combined competence and experience in his profession with service on the Board of Education from 1935 through 1939. He would not be disqualified from accepting commissions from the University, and was charged with assisting in the choice of architects and in negotiating contracts with them.

It was carefully noted, however, that President Oberholtzer was limited to commissioning the preparation of preliminary plans, and he had a spending ceiling of $25,000 in 1946 and $25,000 in 1947 for these plans. This severely circumscribed his ability, and that of Mr. Finn, to get the multi-faceted program they really wanted and needed under way. It is difficult to determine why the regents decided to place such restrictions on architectural planning, since they simultaneously approved the major engineering facility and Junior College Building in which Mr. Cullen had expressed specific interest, as well as a library and other construction projects which the chairman of the board had previously called to the attention of the other members of the governing body.

The Main Junior College Building, core of an eventual Junior College Quadrangle in the area north and west of the Industrial Building, could have changed the entire history of the University of Houston. It reflected an institution with two largely incompatible segments, and concepts deemed by many to be alien to the development of a true university: the Junior College (or Community Service) Division and the Advanced and Professional Schools Division.

The Junior College Division, as Dr. Kemmerer explained to Mr. Cullen and Colonel Bates, would provide the entire University program for the first two years, with emphasis upon "a broad general and civic education for all students, pre-professional courses as required, terminal and vocational courses, and an extensive Student Service Center." The Center would encompass educational, vocational, and personal guidance; aptitude testing; reading, writing, and speech clinics; a health clinic; and a student employment service and student loan agency. A fundamental objective was to isolate the estimated 75 percent of students "who do not spend more than two years in college," providing them specialized, far less expensive education and the services to enable them to find their "appropriate field of endeavor" as soon as feasible.

Schools in the far smaller Advanced and Professional Division would offer the final two years of the appropriate baccalaureate program, plus graduate and professional education "for those who have demonstrated abilities to succeed in their chosen professions."

This approach appealed mightily to President Oberholtzer and Dr. Kemmerer. With all their admirable qualities, they were still essentially public school administrators, thoroughly imbued with the idea of extending the underlying public school philosophy—maximum educational opportunities for the maximum number of people—to the college campus. This also involved strong commitments to adult education and to broad concepts of community service . . . as had been clearly (and even boldly) stated in formal resolutions as early as 1927, enunciated again by the Board of Education in 1934 and by the Board of Regents on the very day of its inception.

Further, the central role accorded the Junior College Division echoed portions of President Oberholtzer's inaugural address (and even hearkened back to his 1924 speeches), in terms of institutional responsibility for instilling a high regard for the duties of citizenship. This aspect, just as the provision of broad educational opportunities, drew immediate support from Mr. Cullen and the other members of the Board of Regents, many of whom tended to perceive the University of Houston primarily as a source of employees well trained in vocational and technical pursuits.

A final element of support for the Junior College Division came from a community movement for a new and separate junior college, which surfaced in 1947. The idea gained some backing from those who failed to understand that junior college appropriations were being passed on to eligible University of Houston students, thus effectively reducing their tuition.

Providentially, the Main Junior College Building, and with it the Junior College Quadrangle, was abandoned in 1950, although Mr. Cullen commissioned Alfred C. Finn to prepare plans for the project (along with plans for a $4 million Engineering Building) in November 1948, and Dr. Kemmerer, in 1952, was still strongly urging the Junior College Division and its related facilities as a pivotal part of the future University.

The project also died hard with Mr. Cullen. On January 28, 1949, he and the other regents heard Colonel Bates offer $1.5 million from the M.D. Anderson Foundation for a library. This was enthusiastically accepted as a "magnificent and timely gift."

It was indeed, for the institution's meager holdings of less than 50,000 volumes were then located in a hopelessly inadequate single room of the Roy Gustav Cullen Building. But after the M.D. Anderson Library architects, John F. Staub and Roy L. Rather, had presented perspective drawings of the handsome three-story facility, Chairman Cullen announced that the next structure on campus would be the Main Junior College Building.

In 1950 the "JC," as the students were beginning to call it, went permanently down the drain, and the Engineering Building was postponed for almost 10 years. This was inevitable, for the costs of the Ezekiel W. Cullen Building would exceed $5 million[7] (estimated earlier at $3,621,000 but built on a cost-plus basis with many and expensive changes by the donor as construction proceeded) and someone would have to provide an immediate $676,000 for additions to the Power House, $230,000 for modernizing and air-conditioning desperately needed smaller buildings, $73,000 for a radio station transmitter and tower, and $141,000 for vital lighting, paving and landscaping projects affecting the Ezekiel W. Cullen Building and the new Anderson Library.

Mr. and Mrs. Cullen and the Cullen Foundation, as usual in those days, were left with the check, and a hefty one it was, when added to their earlier benefactions. As a result, it would be seven years before the Cullen Foundation could make major new gifts. And it was clear that the Main Junior College Building, as well as the Engineering Building, would have to be forgotten for the time being. The engineering facility was subsequently resurrected, in 1957; but the "JC" Building was abandoned and the Junior College Division became a paper shell, existing solely to funnel state allocations on to junior college enrollees, until it was removed in 1963 with the shift to membership in the state system of higher education.

The buildings that did go up between 1948 and 1951, and the smaller but significant other additions to physical plant before and after the three-year span of frenetic construction activity on campus,[8] obviously had enormous impact on the institution and on those it served.

As the huge dimensions of the half-built Ezekiel W. Cullen Building began to take shape, the Board of Regents took definitive action on three other major projects at the same meeting, on June 29, 1949. A $1.5 million contract was let on the M.D. Anderson

Library; $4 million in dormitory bonds were sold to the Prudential Insurance Company of America, at a three percent rate that would be unheard of today; and a contract for a $1 million expansion of the Power House was approved. The regents also agreed to accept a low bid of $58,842 for a new cross-campus street connecting Cullen and Calhoun Boulevards (this was closed in 1963 after it had become a short-cut for taxicabs, miscellaneous members of the commuting public, and an occasional truck).

While the campus was being transformed by $12 million in new buildings, there were other developments at the University of Houston that would overshadow this expansion. Predominant among these changes were the establishment of professional schools and the precipitate, yet not wholly unexpected, retirement of President Oberholtzer.

The professional schools evolved much as the Houston Junior College and the University of Houston had—in response to urgent, clearly expressed community and area needs. But the schools came along at a pace that would have been out of the question at a more established university, with its echelons of committees, task forces and councils, and layerings of faculty, administration and governing body response. With streamlined channels of authority and responsibility geared to almost instant action on matters deemed to be of high consequence, the Oberholtzer-Kemmerer team had a standardized response to professional groups seeking to replenish the normal supply of nurses, pharmacists, optometrists and lawyers (and to assure an increased flow of practitioners for the future), in a post-war world severely depleted of these and other specialists. The response was, give us the full backing of your professional group, including financial assistance to get the new school off the ground, and we will undertake it.

Under this philosophy, the Board of Regents approved a School of Pharmacy on October 16, 1946; a School of Law on March 19, 1947; a School of Practical Nursing on September 1, 1948, to be followed by a central College of Nursing which opened September 1, 1949; and a School of Optometry, on April 23, 1951.

More than one president, discussing this phase of the University of Houston's development, shook his head in disbelief at the rapidity with which these schools were set in motion. Much of their astonishment derived from intimate knowledge of the time and cost involved in the birth pangs, care, and feeding of professional schools.

Dr. Kemmerer's specific response, which he recounted to me many years later, was that "the people came to us with an obvious need, promised to help establish the schools, support them and get them accredited; so we went along with them."

Dr. Oberholtzer predictably responded in the same manner, even though he knew that most of the burden involved in repeated meetings with professional groups and accrediting associations, and virtually all of the curricular planning, budgeting, and recruiting of faculty, would fall to the lot of his overworked assistant. And so it did. Only in the case of law, where Colonel Bates was a central figure, with assistance from Palmer Hutcheson and some of the other leaders of the Houston bar, did Dr. Kemmerer fail to accept, and to discharge, heavy responsibilities in the establishment of the professional schools.

Dr. Kemmerer could not know that three of the professional units would find outstanding success, even though it would be from 15 to 30 years before they were all even housed in separate and adequate facilities.

The School of Professional Nursing (later the central College of Nursing) was another story, although I am convinced that Bill Kemmerer would open it again tomorrow given the circumstances under which he brought it into being in 1948, as an extension of a program in nursing education dating back to 1944 and the HISD era.[9]

The School of Pharmacy was organized at the behest of the registered pharmacists of the area, who were working an average of 60 to 70 hours per week throughout World War II, and found that there was even more pressure on them after the return to a peacetime economy. Dr. Kemmerer was faced with severe shortages of faculty, equipment, specialized library holdings and operating funds; but he got the School under way in the Science Building by prevailing upon Dr. Allan Collette, a local physician who also had a degree in pharmacy, to accept a temporary assignment as director and to recruit a beginning teaching staff that drew heavily upon part-time lecturers.

Dr. Kemmerer then began to evidence his usual energy and initiative, by discovering that Western Reserve University in Cleveland was closing its School of Pharmacy. The next summer, on an expedition to Ohio, he bought most of the Case Western pharmacy equipment, and the nucleus of an excellent library, for about twenty-five cents on the dollar. He also hired Noel Moore Ferguson, a research-oriented pharmacognosist, as director of the School of Pharmacy, initiating a career with the University of Houston that was to span the years from 1949 to 1973, when Dean Ferguson retired.[10]

The School of Law (now the Bates College of Law) had to begin life in a converted barracks in September, 1947, but it was blessed from the beginning with solid interest on the part of leading attorneys, including Colonel Bates and Palmer Hutcheson, and by the fortunate selection of A.A. White as director (and later, dean). Director White, a well-established practitioner with a fine reputation among his colleagues, quickly built the nucleus of an excellent faculty and had gained tentative approval by the American Bar Association before the graduation of the first class at the School. Full accreditation came on February 24, 1953, after the move to still temporary, but enormously improved, quarters in the M.D. Anderson Library.

After 10 years, A.A. White turned his deanship over to Newell Blakely to accept a challenging position in corporate practice. Fortunately for the University, he decided after a few years to return to the classroom. When a selection committee was unable to decide upon a successor to John B. Neibel (whose 10 years as dean had seen the move to the new home of the Bates College of Law, in the northeast quadrant of the campus, and the development of what is a law center, rather than a single college), A.A. White accepted the deanship again for 1975-1976, on an *ad interim* basis. Now that George W. Hardy III is the full-time dean, A.A. White continues as a skilled senior professor, although retired from other critical assignments such as chairman of the Athletics Committee and faculty representative to the Southwest Conference.

The School of Optometry followed the general pattern of the School of Pharmacy, in terms of a key role for Dr. Kemmerer and heavy involvement with the profession. This time, however, what would clearly have to be a regional rather than a local component was involved; and beginning enrollment was projected so low that Dr. Kemmerer requested, and was given, a firm pledge of $100,000 from members of the Texas Optometric Association. The pledge was honored and paid in full, and along with it went the enthusiastic and continuing support of leading practitioners in Texas plus nine other states. One of the powerful incentives toward establishment of the School of Optometry at the University of Houston was the fact that the nearest such facility was in Memphis. After that, the student would have to look to the Pacific Coast or to the Middle West for training in this rapidly growing specialty.

One of the senior optometrists of the nation, Nelson Greeman of San Antonio, was particularly helpful in the long series of conferences which led to the new School of Optometry being opened at the University in the fall of 1952. Dr. Greeman, whose son and grandson followed him as members of the optometric profession, was also instrumental in the selection of Charles R. Stewart as the first dean. Dean Stewart guided the new component through its first difficult decade before turning the reins over to the present dean, Chester T. Pheiffer, under whose direction the College of Optometry has evolved into a true regional facility with a $10 million home that trains hundreds of students (including practitioners returning for mandatory refresher courses), and is serving more than 30,000 patients annually in its clinics.[11]

These success stories were crucial to the development of the University of Houston as a true university with a complex of professional schools. Dr. Kemmerer's batting average dropped drastically, however, with the School of Professional Nursing and its successor, the central College of Nursing.

As indicated earlier, the training of nurses during and after World War II represented the highest level of community service to Bill Kemmerer, who was to his eternal credit always a man to respond to community needs, budgets notwithstanding. He understood the desperate need for nurses at a time when many patients saw only untrained "maids" during much of their stay in hospital, and applauded early programs in the late 1930's during which University of Houston instructors were conducting noncredit science courses for separate schools of nursing in various hospitals. Once the war was over, he was appalled to see even worse shortages of nurses.

In the meantime, under a Nursing Education Program approved by the National League for Nursing Education, the hospital schools were admitting and registering their own students, who were then enrolled as freshmen at the University. Upon successful completion of a two-year course, students would be awarded the Associate in Arts diploma. This program was elevated to the status of a School of Nursing on June 26, 1944, and Mrs. Vivian M. Stuart Watkins was named director of the School, which was operated under agreements with Hermann, Jefferson Davis, Memorial, Methodist, and St. Joseph Hospitals.

As the Texas Medical Center began to develop rapidly, there seemed to be a growing need to centralize the training of nurses at one point, and to consider the source and role of "practical," or vocational, nurses. Dr. Kemmerer welcomed a study aimed at these interlocking problems, and such an investigation was completed in 1947. The study recommended a central College of Nursing offering a four-year program leading to the baccalaureate in nursing or the baccalaureate of science with a major in nursing, to replace the five separate hospital schools. It also recommended one or two schools for vocational nurses trained to work under the supervision of registered nurses.

Dr. Kemmerer proposed that the University of Houston operate the central College of Nursing at Hermann Hospital. He also wanted to move the School of Practical Nursing (which the University had been conducting at Memorial Hospital) to Hermann Hospital and to reconstitute it as a department of the College of Nursing. Another Kemmerer proposal was to do away with the term "practical" nurse, and to replace it with "licensed vocational nurse" or LVN, which he seems to have originated.

The offers were accepted, but when the College of Nursing opened on September 1, 1949, only Hermann and Methodist Hospitals were willing to close their own schools and send trainees to the central facility. Then, Methodist Hospital withdrew from the program in 1951, precipitating a five-year struggle during which the University of Houston had to turn to aggressive and sometimes expensive recruiting of nursing students, essentially in competition with four other hospitals. Further complications involved teaching personnel, usually available through the interrelationships between a college of nursing and its affiliated medical college, and growing misunderstandings concerning the possible duplication of facilities. There were shortages of instructors, especially in the medical specialties; and there was a plethora of misunderstandings.

Until the end of his presidency, Dr. Kemmerer thought he could solve the frustrating entanglements that emerged at the College of Nursing, and that this component should and must progress just as the units of pharmacy, law and optometry had. He grappled with the problems involved but was never able to find his way out of the labyrinth.

While he did not fully realize it, the College of Nursing was certainly a major factor in his departing the post of president in 1953. Regents maintained that the College was losing between $60,000 and $90,000 a year, and that it tended to create complicating situations within the Medical Center as well as in other sensitive areas throughout the community. It was not until 1956, however, that then Dean Lillian E. Willetts was finally ordered to close the College of Nursing. Ironically, the University now trains dozens of nurses in three interrelated areas: pre-clinical instruction for those going on to the advanced nursing courses at local campuses of Texas Women's University and the University of Texas (which offer only upper-level work); non-nursing electives in specialized fields for candidates for the master's degree in nursing; and a wide range of other offerings not available in the Texas Medical Center.

As the threat of reidentification as a junior college receded with abandonment of the Main Junior College Building, and as the professional schools began their slow but crescent impact, the really significant area of the University of Houston became that of executive leadership. The institution was caught up for the first time in a veiled yet discernible contest for the post of chief executive officer . . . a pattern that would repeat itself, with variations, in the next decade. Edison Ellsworth Oberholtzer had been blessed with vigorous health throughout his life, but he was after all almost half into his sixty-sixth year when he was inaugurated as president. Within twelve months, he began to slow down perceptibly, although "The Chief" (as he was increasingly known after assuming the full-time presidency) was still in command. This was especially true in terms of relationships with the Board of Regents, and of how he was perceived by the general public.

Within the University, it was a different story. Dr. Kemmerer was the ever-present dynamo who devised innovative plans that attracted enormous enrollments, who recruited faculty and staff, established new professional schools, and prepared and administered budgets. In terms of total impact, he was an All-American quarterback who doubled as a Lombardi Award linebacker. Consequently, Dr. Kemmerer was increasingly perceived as the *de facto* president, perhaps as early as 1946, certainly by the 1947-1948 academic year.

This process was accelerated when Dr. Oberholtzer's beloved "Mame" began to fail physically, and he himself contracted chronic iritis, a troublesome condition which progressively affected his eyesight. Dr. Oberholtzer had a little bed installed next to his office in the Roy Gustav Cullen Building in 1947, so that Mrs. Oberholtzer, who was required to rest for a part of each day, could come to the campus with him. And although the president was still an early riser, it would often be 10 a.m. before he arrived on campus with Mrs. Oberholtzer, her meticulously coiffed hair rivalling the elegance of her long, beautifully manicured fingernails.

Soon, it was even more difficult to obtain a clear-cut decision from Dr. Oberholtzer, who had always been reluctant to delegate authority. Under his instructions, his secretary Dorothy Shriner and Pearl Woodall, the secretary of the Faculty Association who also maintained his calendar, granted fewer and fewer appointments. Even the trusted C.F. McElhinney had difficulty in setting a definite meeting with "The Chief" (a sobriquet, L. Standlee Mitchell pointed out, not to be confused with his own nickname "De Chief," as in "Here Come De Chief").

This pattern of disengagement was not apparent at the Board of Regents level, where President Oberholtzer was busily occupied in the pivotal matter of seeking new buildings. Among the faculty, and even within his own staff, however, the continuing lack of communication and personal contact with the chief executive progressively weakened his power and influence. Incidents such as the summary demotion of Naason K. Dupre to director of extension services, after 17 years as a top administrator, had a further erosive effect on Dr. Oberholtzer's power.[12]

By 1949, it was evident that President Oberholtzer was nearing the end of his active career, after almost a quarter-century with the University, and 50 years in education. He would never tell me, and I did not want to ask directly, who took the initiative in this delicate matter; but there must have been some high-level urging. At any rate, there were discussions with Mr. Cullen and Colonel Bates, in which it was agreed that The Chief would step down at the end of the 1949-1950 academic year. There would be a special Founder's Day program, perhaps on Dr. Oberholtzer's seventieth birthday on May 6, 1950, to honor him; he would be named president emeritus, and the central unit within the new dormitory complex would be named Oberholtzer Hall (the entire complex is now called Oberholtzer Quadrangle).

There was also an agreement, in which it appears certain that Dr. Oberholtzer was closely consulted, concerning Dr. Kemmerer. Much as he had hoped and expected to be offered the presidency, he would instead be requested to accept the consolation prize of acting president, effective June 1, 1950. This was a bitter pill for the man who had completed 20 years of devoted service to President Oberholtzer and 16 years as an effective official of the University of Houston, including the past five years during which he had been the driving force within the institution.

Dr. Kemmerer blamed Dr. Oberholtzer directly for his not being named president, even though Mr. Cullen and Colonel Bates had reservations about him. He told me many years later that Dr. Oberholtzer had discredited him with individual members of the Board of Regents in a 1949 incident wherein Dr. Kemmerer had used University funds to assume what he felt was both a legal, and a moral, obligation of the institution. A student had been allowed to "contract" for odd jobs on campus during a time of marked shortages of labor and materials, under what was assumed to be University of Houston sponsorship. When he defaulted on payrolls, he left many student employees, all of them short of funds, with a financial crisis. Dr. Kemmerer liquidated the little enterprise, and paid its debts, amounting to several thousand dollars.

Dr. Kemmerer was very specific. He wrote regarding his failure to obtain the full presidency in 1950: "I shall always respect the great achievements of a great educator, Dr. Oberholtzer. I can understand why a man of his constant aggressive activity could not accept advancing age, inevitable loss of vitality, and the idea of retirement. After working very closely with him for 20 years, he opposed me as his replacement during our twenty-first year because he was opposed to any replacement."

The acting president-designate was also very frank in giving me his opinion, across the years, of such an appointment: "Generally, an acting president is so appointed to give the governing body time to select someone else as president. In this case, it was a compromise of some sort. Had I been able to evaluate the forces at work then as I can now in retrospect, I would have refused to be considered for the position of president. I would have resigned myself to a life of service in second position, doing the thinking, planning and much of the executing, and letting the credit go to a superior office. The life of an aggressive acting president is not easy. The word acting lessens his influence over staff members and holds down his prestige in the community, a prestige so essential for the financial promotion of the University."

President Oberholtzer's impending retirement, and Dr. Kemmerer's selection as acting president, were announced at a press conference following the Board of Regents meeting of February 21, 1950, ending what the Houston *Chronicle* maintained had been "several weeks of speculation." The media representatives were told that Dr. Oberholtzer would be awarded an honorary doctor of laws degree, but this was apparently overlooked after his actual retirement on June 1, 1950.[13]

President Oberholtzer received a more tangible award from Mr. Cullen. In a typically generous gesture, the chairman of the board personally arranged for the founding chief executive to receive as president emeritus the same $15,560 salary he had received as president.

Plaudits for the retiring Edison Ellsworth Oberholtzer came from every quarter, as was deserved and expected. Fortunately, the program of the May 2, 1950, Founder's Day dinner honoring him was recorded, and verbatim excerpts, seldom free from hyperbole, are available.[14]

L. Standlee Mitchell, president of the Faculty Association, presiding: "Dr. Oberholtzer, you should be very happy to know that you have been the leader in establishing one of the greatest universities of our nation."

Mr. Cullen: "The small acorn . . . has grown into a very large tree. Dr. Oberholtzer, with the able assistance of the faculty and the confidence of the regents, has succeeded in building the greatest university in the world."

Colonel Bates traced in detail much of the earliest history of the University, his first meeting with Dr. Oberholtzer and his long association with him both as superintendent of schools and as president of the University. He concluded, "although Houston owes much to the great philanthropists George Hermann, William Marsh Rice, Monroe D. Anderson and Hugh Roy and

Lillie Cranz Cullen . . . none of them has done more for Houston, for Texas and (for) the nation than this simple educator."

Dr. Kemmerer began by adjusting the microphone downward, explaining: "I'm not a big man, like Oberholtzer or Cullen; I have to cut things down to my size." He then recounted his first meeting with Dr. Oberholtzer, more than two decades ago at Columbia University, and how he decided to come to Houston to work under the man he had known as another graduate student at Morningside Heights. He revealed for the first time how he almost left HISD in 1933 to become assistant superintendent for planning in the giant Los Angeles school system. At the end, he paid tribute to Dr. Oberholtzer's ability to train and mold those who worked with him: "I have the distinction and the privilege of having worked with him longer than anybody else. I appreciate that opportunity of working with a man of his caliber, and of learning from him, frankly without my knowing it in all probability, for one always absorbs and acquires the characteristics of the man he works with, and whom he admires. I appreciate more than I can put into words the opportunity I have had for 21 years."

Arvin N. Donner, the director of the School of Education who had rapidly become an acknowledged faculty leader since his return from three years of service as assistant superintendent of schools at HISD, traced the history of the University in terms of the growth and development of the faculty, student body, component schools, and curricula of the institution. He attributed "the University's greatness" to its location in Houston, the hub of the Gulf Coast; to its emphasis on community service; to a "mature, serious student body which values education"; to a "competent faculty, interested primarily in teaching"; to its friends and donors; to "the very fine philosophy of education reflected in the Board of Regents"; and "to the leadership of our president, who had a vision and was able to combine theory with realism."

Dr. Oberholtzer concluded the program with a rambling but always interesting half-hour address, somewhat tinged with sadness yet relieved throughout with frankness and humor. With typical modesty, he told the audience, "I feel humiliated that you must listen to me, but it gratifies me to hear my good friends, who I know are sincere, saying these things about me. I feel like a flattened-out pancake with a lot of syrup spread over it and nothing much underneath." He had high praise for Mr. Cullen, Colonel Bates, and the other members of the governing board, but did point out that it was one of the few times they felt reasonably certain of having a quorum of the regents. He seemed especially touched by a telegram from Mrs. Ray L. Dudley, who could not be present,[15] and hinted that he knew what might have detained Judge J.A. Elkins (the judge was reportedly en route to Churchill Downs, on a traditional pilgrimage to the Kentucky Derby with his close friends J.S. Abercrombie and W.A. Smith).

Looking to the future, in what was to be his valedictory, President Oberholtzer had some significant things to say about the next decades of the University: "I do not think that there is any stumbling block in the future development of the University of Houston that cannot be overcome. . . . We have reached the stage where there is a stable foundation, a policy well-founded and a determination to go forward." He had little to say about Dr. Kemmerer, but did state, "If my successor makes any mistakes, I am not going to claim them; but if he does some good things, I'll claim them, because I am in some measure responsible for his training," as Dr. Kemmerer had just explained to the audience.

Then he said, "I do hope that I will be able to be of some service in some way to the Board of Regents, the faculty, and the student body of the University. My heart will be here as long as I live, and I trust that I may be privileged to do what I can." He thanked Mr. Cullen, Colonel Bates and the other members of the Board of Regents "for their very great kindnesses," and the Oberholtzer Era at the University of Houston was over, except for the four weeks involved in completing the spring semester and conducting Commencement exercises.

In terms of some very tangible measures, it had been a memorable 23 years:

	1927	*1950*
Estimated value of physical plant and other property	0	$20,000,000
Students	461	13,569
Faculty	16	586
Graduating class	0	1,302
Budget	$36,387	$ 3,459,797
Library holdings	1,988	56,000

The years since 1927 were even more momentous in terms of less tangible but enormously consequential impact upon individual lives and the total community.

Walter W. Kemmerer could not have been an unhappy man on that Thursday morning of June 1, 1950, when he assumed the presidency. True, there was that galling matter about the prefix "acting" before his title, but Mr. Cullen had told him face to face, only last fall at the opening football game: "I'm going to make you president." And informal though that statement had been, in the unlikely setting of Jeppesen Stadium, Dr. Kemmerer realized how much he *was* the president of the University, in terms of acceptance by so many elements of the University community: student body, faculty, staff, and alumni. Only in relationships with the Board of Regents, where President Oberholtzer had carefully, sometimes jealously, asserted his precedence, did he perhaps sometimes feel a bit ill at ease. The student body recognized him as president and, to a considerable extent, as their champion. After all, who had foreseen the precipitate drop in enrollment beginning in 1942, taken the necessary measures to counteract it with trainees from three Navy units and from industry,[16] and then begun in 1944 to provide for staggering increases in the student body (from 1,104 to 13,569 between 1943 and 1949)?

Further, more than half of these post-war students were veterans, well aware of "Doc" Kemmerer's ingenuity and energy having provided a University of Houston program for ex-servicemen that was a nationwide model.

He had accepted the need for a Village Nursery School, for example, as a personal challenge, realizing how many student wives found it necessary to work to help keep their husbands in school, and thus had no place to leave a child during much of the day. A facility charging low rates was set up in a residence belonging to the University along Calhoun Boulevard. Dr. Kemmerer was widely recognized for his vigorous support in two other areas of student life: Frontier Fiesta and a proposed Student Union Building.

Frontier Fiesta was resumed with vigor in 1946 and soon became almost an obsession for hundreds of students between the selection of officials for the event in the fall and the final darkening of the midway lights in April. Analysis of the *Houstonians* in the heyday of the Fiesta, from 1949 through 1953, gives some idea of how this "Greatest College Show in the World," originally conceived by Dr. Kemmerer, came to dominate extracurricular life at the University.

The 1949 yearbook had Shasta on the front cover in gunslinger costume, opened with a Frontier Fiesta frontispiece and was dedicated to the five past chairmen of the spring extravaganza: Joe Potter, 1940; Joe Koppel, 1941; Johnny Goyen, 1947; Bill Sparr, 1948; and Harrey Scott, 1949.[17] Four pages of pictures followed.

The tempo increased until 1953, when the *Houstonian* featured a 28-page Frontier Fiesta section, opening with a four-color cover. This was a 10-page gain over 1952. The established Fiesta shows, dating back to 1940 in most instances, continued to gain acclaim: Wells Fargo, Silver Moon, Stars and Bars, Belle Union, Silver Dollar, Crow's Nest and Bayou Queen, among others. The Top Ten acts, sometimes with stunning girls in early versions of short shorts, or a chorus line as in Powder Puff Revue, drew record crowds. The 1953 Frontier Fiesta attracted some 150,000, triple the total in 1949, and netted $97,300. When you added ancillary events—the opening of the beard-growing contest, building elaborate floats for the downtown Fiesta parade, the pre-Fiesta dance, completion of the first show on the midway, auctions, barbecues, weeks of rehearsals, the original song contest and the seven-day spring holiday during the Frontier Fiesta—you had what was almost a separate industry. The fad spread even to Houston high schools, as talented youngsters from the schools were allowed to participate as Fiesta performers, and the word spread that the midway was the place to be.

The Student Union Building (called "SABUH", or Student Activities Building, University of Houston on campus) was another Kemmerer project that drew wide support within the student body. This facility, which finally opened fifteen years later, was consonant with the new president's innovative yet sound ideas for a major broadening of student services to include a health clinic, a counseling and guidance center, a placement office,[18] an alumni headquarters, a student bank and loan center, offices for the deans of men and women, offices for student organizations, and a religious activities center ("to be in the very center of the maelstrom of student life instead of being set aside and apart from it").

The students had other reasons to regard Dr. Kemmerer as their champion as he assumed the post of acting president. Rapid and evident progress on both the huge Ezekiel W. Cullen Building and the Anderson Library gave promise of an entirely new level of campus facilities. More than 100 student organizations had been approved for the fall, and it had been tentatively agreed that fraternities and sororities would be approved for the first time, at least on a provisional and local basis.

Faculty and staff support for the acting president was also strong and waxing as the 1950-1951 term got under way. Convinced of the need for a more traditional academic organization, Dr. Kemmerer moved quickly to name three vice-presidents (Charles F. Hiller, for university development and public relations; C.F. McElhinney, as business manager; and Terrel Spencer, for student affairs) and seven deans (R. Balfour Daniels, arts and sciences; Eugene H. Hughes, business administration; A.A. White, law; N.M. Ferguson, pharmacy; M.L. Ray, engineering; A. Ray Sims, technology; and Arvin N. Donner, education. Charles R. Stewart, would join this group the following year as the first dean of optometry).

At the same time, Dr. Kemmerer initiated plans for a system of faculty rank from instructor to full professor, and he emphasized the need for salary increases to adjust for inflation. Vice-President McElhinney, however, presented some alarming data in late 1950, based upon the obvious decrease in enrollments by veterans, and thereby the University income, 70 percent of which derived, at the time, from tuition payments for ex-servicemen. There were indications of a $200,000 deficit, the first since a $13,462 loss for fiscal 1945 and the second since 1927, when a deficit of $2,963 was sustained in getting HJC under way.

In this emergency, President Kemmerer called a mass meeting of the student body to discuss the need for a 40 percent jump in tuition, from $25 to $35 per course. Some 500 students showed up, out of almost 14,000, and there was little or no objection when the circumstances were explained (and it was realized that Uncle Sam would be providing a large percentage of the proposed increase).

The increase, with an unexpected influx of Korean War veterans, improved the financial picture enough to allow some long-overdue salary increases, thus further strengthening Dr. Kemmerer's popularity with the faculty and staff. But the relief was only temporary; there were to be new and more serious budget problems. And a new pattern foreshadowing the momentous shift to state support was emerging: higher tuition and fees, stabilizing, slowly decreasing enrollment, the constant need to raise faculty and staff salaries, and a surge in overhead, from three percent to more than ten per cent.

For a time, it seemed as if Dr. Kemmerer might survive the high-level jousting match into which he was being inevitably drawn. His armor, after all, had only one perceptible crack, even though in a vital area, and his lance was barely flawed. Surely his staunch support among students, faculty and staff, to which he had added a close relationship with the Ex-Students' Association, appeared to give the acting president significant strength.[19]

This optimistic view was heightened by the general euphoria surrounding the gala dedication of the Ezekiel W. Cullen Building, on October 31, 1950, and by a statement that Mr. Cullen had given the Houston *Press* shortly before the dedicatory ceremonies. A rumor had spread somehow that Attorney General Howard McGrath, a mainstay of the Harry S. Truman cabinet, was being considered for the presidency of the University of Houston.[20]

Mr. Cullen put the rumor to rest: "I wouldn't have that fellow Howard McGrath in a doghouse . . . he's too radical for me," he explained. "We're not figuring on a new president, except for the man now serving as acting president, as far as I'm concerned. We've never discussed anybody else. We're not hunting at all. The regents are trying to give Dr. Kemmerer a chance to see what he can do out there." Then he thought again about Attorney General McGrath, and snorted: "I'd hate to see any New Dealers or Fair Dealers associated with the University of Houston, or with anything else I'm hooked up with."

One immediately sensed the importance of the dedication of the giant Ezekiel W. Cullen Building on Halloween, 1950, when he saw the line in the special invitation sent to more than 100 special guests packed on the stage: the prescribed dress was white tie and tails.

F.M. Law was master of ceremonies, and the principal speaker was President Francis P. Gaines of Washington and Lee College. The Cullen Guards were on hand from the 827-man University ROTC unit, and Efrem Kurtz, his toy poodle safely in the hands of a trusted student backstage, conducted the Houston Symphony Orchestra in two of Mr. and Mrs. Cullen's favorite selections: *I'll Take You Home Again, Kathleen* and *I Dreamt I Dwelt In Marble Halls.*

President Gaines described the new building as "the finest testimonial to democracy that Houston has ever seen." He paid a beautiful and most appropriate tribute to the donors: "Tomorrow is being born today in the confidence and character of the growth manifested here. Roy and Lillie Cullen are in the fellowship of those who have made a lasting imprint on youth, and have thus brought tomorrow within their grasp, . . . have found a way to reach a hand through time into a tomorrow they will never see."

Appropriate mention was made of Dr. Oberholtzer, but he was not on the program. Among those who mentioned his service to the University were Bishop A. Frank Smith, who gave the invocation. Acting President Kemmerer accepted the memorial to Ezekiel W. Cullen on behalf of the University. Turning to Mr. and Mrs. Cullen, he said, "We offer our humble thanks for this marvelous addition to our physical plant." He then quickly described the building, which was finally to cost $5.5 million before the donor received all the bills.[21]

Wade Wiley, the president of the Student Association, expressed the gratitude of the student body, and was followed by Mr. Cullen.

The dedication of the Ezekiel W. Cullen Building was obviously a high point in Mr. Cullen's life, and he delivered an address that was a landmark in the tangled history of such occasions. After a few brief remarks concerning the pleasure that he and Mrs. Cullen took in providing such a facility "for the deserving students you have here at the University of Houston," he launched a vigorous attack on "a federal government saturated with socialism," in a nation "where Harry Truman and his cabinet are doing everything possible to control education, medical care and the electric utilities, and the Political Action Committee of the Congress of Industrial Organizations (CIO-PAC) is trying to crucify the one great statesman with the courage left to fight them, Senator Robert A. Taft."

Charlie Hiller and I were following Mr. Cullen word for word to this point, from mimeographed copies of the text. But as we looked at one another in growing disbelief, the philanthropist inserted an *ad lib* paragraph excoriating one especially high-ranking member of the Truman brain trust. This comment was either lost to posterity because media representatives depended upon the official text, or because Dr. Hiller took pains to see that it was not reported. In any event, Mr. Cullen's long address was followed by vigorous applause, both within the crowded auditorium and from those listening through loudspeakers rigged up in the lobby and outside the main entrance.

Dr. Kemmerer emphasized to me 25 years later how he was given almost a free hand as acting president, and later as president of the University. "To Mr. Cullen's everlasting credit," he said, "he almost never interfered in administration. Only once did he, and then by inference, suggest that I employ a certain individual."[22]

Dr. Kemmerer's specific ideas and plans regarding the future development of the University of Houston under his leadership, in addition to how he perceived his own accomplishments at the institution from 1934-1950, are spelled out in a remarkable letter, with attachments, which he sent to Colonel Bates in January, 1950, after it had become apparent that Dr. Oberholtzer was in the last months of his long presidency. Mr. Cullen had obviously asked the vice-chairman of the Board of Regents to obtain an actual statement from Dr. Kemmerer "as an evaluation of (his) fitness for the position of top leadership." The letter is frank, honest and unique. It is relatively brief, although some of the attachments do become lengthy, and it is significant enough to reproduce verbatim.[23]

The "attachments" consisted of a "Summary Record of My Participation in the Growth and Development of the University of Houston," followed by "A More Complete Statement, Exhibit A," and a "Summary of My Ideas and Suggestions Concerning the Future of the University of Houston," followed by "A More Complete Statement, Exhibit B."[24]

The important pronouncements by Dr. Kemmerer would have been criticized then and now by many university administrators, as well as regents or trustees, primarily because of the complete omission of research, the third principal function of any major institution of higher education; the failure to stress the need for gaining accreditation by the Southern Association of Colleges and Secondary Schools; and continuing overemphasis on the Junior College Division. They were apparently accepted by both Colonel Bates and Mr. Cullen, however, even though Dr. Kemmerer was limited for the time being to the acting presidency; and the proposals were in consonance with the perception of the University of Houston's mission, role, and scope among the overall Board of Regents, and among the community in general.

This seeming acceptance of his objectives, policies and future plans, with little or no interference in his administering the affairs of the University, may well have lulled Bill Kemmerer into a false sense of security as the first year of his acting presidency came to a close in the spring of 1951. But three fundamental problems were lurking beneath the surface, each of them a grave threat to Dr. Kemmerer's continued leadership.

First was a nationwide epidemic of Joseph R. McCarthy's sensational but unsubstantiated allegations of Communist subversion in government, higher education, and elsewhere; this had unfortunately spread its morbid poisons and paranoid extremisms into some areas of Houston. The second threat was within the governing board itself, where two relatively new regents, Judge J.A. Elkins and Corbin J. Robertson, recognized Bill Kemmerer's many abilities but had deep, frank, and intensifying differences of opinion with him from the moment they took the oath of office.

Judge Elkins, nearing the height of his extraordinary power and influence in banking, politics and legal circles, was simply never convinced that Dr. Kemmerer understood his proper role in the formulation and execution of policy.

Mr. Robertson, Mr. Cullen's son-in-law, and an imaginative, extremely competent executive, believed that the accelerated development of a successful program of intercollegiate athletics was a *sine qua non* for any young university aspiring to greatness. He therefore urged emphasis on the athletics program. Dr. Kemmerer maintained that the Athletics Department had incurred a $250,000 deficit in 1951, at a time when expenditures elsewhere in the University had been severely curtailed, and had eaten up half of an overall operating surplus of $2 million, jealously guarded for a time of need, by the end of 1952. So, he advocated retrenchment, the balancing of income against outgo, and the interdiction of any further deficits in the area of intercollegiate athletics . . . a position that placed him on collision course with Corbin J. Robertson.

A third, and lethal, threat to Dr. Kemmerer's leadership was a subtly hidden time bomb difficult to describe, but perhaps best labeled "fiscal planning and operations." Bill Kemmerer, to his lasting credit, was particularly adept at identifying the challenges and fields of opportunity for the University, particularly those associated with community needs. Yet he could be myopic in detecting true costs and potential problems.

In the years from 1945-1951, when enrollments, income and operating surpluses were constantly on the rise, his natural inclination to move the institution into new programs and activities was heightened by a sense of fiscal security. When warning signs appeared in 1951 and again in 1952, from the deadly combination of stabilized enrollment and the ongoing, obvious need to increase both faculty salaries and inflation-plagued operating accounts, the experience gained in long years of penurious budgeting triggered a yellow caution light; but the temporary relief that arrived in the form of tuition increases and a fresh influx of veterans, this time from the Korean War, encouraged Dr. Kemmerer to resume the search for still broader response to community and area needs.

The encouragement was reinforced when early reports indicated that only one of the new professional schools was experiencing more than normal start-up problems. The isolate was the College of Nursing, the development of which the acting president had described as "the most complicated and difficult task that the University has ever undertaken," but one that would in his judgment soon justify the escalating investments of staff time and hard cash it required.

In sum, Bill Kemmerer felt in the crucial academic year of 1951-1952 that he had surmounted troublesome but temporary fiscal problems, and was free to push on again with further expansion, including an expedition into the *terra incognita* of educational television. In truth, the irreversible dynamics of an enduring conflict between institutional income and outgo had already been set in motion. There would be many effects, ranging from the ability to pursue innovative, yet potentially costly, challenges and opportunities, to the future decision to seek membership in the state system of higher education.

The University of Houston's confrontation with McCarthyism was inevitable, as small but persistent elements in the community began to articulate their own extreme views and psychological difficulties in terms of the Wisconsin senator's demagoguery.

Mr. Cullen became innocently involved in an episode that was probably far more damaging than Dr. Kemmerer realized. The philanthropist had come to the campus on May 11, 1951, to address the third annual Career Conference, at which he and Colonel Bates (then president of the Houston Chamber of Commerce) were guests of honor. Using in part material supplied him by President George S. Benson of Harding College and Dean Clarence Manion of the College of Law at Notre Dame University, Mr. Cullen stressed the importance of a sound knowledge of American history, "if we are to preserve our system of government." At the conclusion of his address, a student stood up for a question, "Was Mr. Cullen aware that American history was not a required course at the University of Houston?" Mr. Cullen indicated that the student was surely mistaken, but the fat was in the fire, since there was indeed no such requirement, the departments having enough trouble as it was sandwiching in legislatively mandated courses in political science.

Elmer Bertelsen, the one-time *Cougar* editor just beginning what has become a lifelong career as the *Chronicle's* expert on education, confirmed his facts with Ramon A. Vitulli, the registrar, obtained some quotes, and turned in what became a front page story, headlined "Cullen Ired At UH Lack of History Study." The *Press* followed with "Cullen Irked At UH?; Silly, Scoffs Kemmerer." Actually, Mr. Cullen was not all that disturbed; but statements by Charles E. Gilbert, state director of the Sons of the American Revolution, and by Mr. Cullen's close friend and attorney, Judge E.E. Townes, kept the controversy alive, even though these were moderate in tone. And a quite reasonable statement by Dr. Kemmerer served to some extent to inflame extremist elements in the community.[25]

In the next published catalogue of the University, American history was listed as a required course, and the earlier controversy had in the meantime subsided. Dr. Kemmerer told me later that he placed far more importance on allegations of communism in the University of Houston classrooms than he did on the brouhaha regarding American history. There are indications, however, that this controversy was disturbing to Colonel Bates, who had close connections to Charles E. Gilbert and the Sons of the American Revolution, and to other members of the Board of Regents. And it helped to attract the attention of John P. Rogge, a prominent arch-conservative and American Legion official, and of Mrs. Ross Biggers, head of the ultra-conservative Minute Women, to the University.

The allegations of communism were in the classic mold, revolving about campus speakers and claims of subversive statements in the classroom. Dr. Kemmerer recalled two instances for me that were not without their humor, distressing though they must have been to a university president. He said that he was in Mr. Cullen's office with Colonel Bates one day when a young woman who maintained that she had evidence of the teaching of communistic theories in a philosophy class at the University was shown in. To Dr. Kemmerer's consternation, she began to read shorthand notes which, she said, "proves that this professor believes in relative truth."

There was no reaction to this, and the young woman explained: "You see, the communists teach four things: that there is no God; that all truth is relative; and . . . I forget the other two." Dr. Kemmerer, knowing that all scientific truth is relative, and deciding that the charade had gone far enough, decided to step in: "Well," he said, "I believe in relative truth." "What," she replied, "do you believe that murder is ever justified?" Kemmerer: "If I came upon someone about to kill my son, and I could stop him by killing him instead, I would, wouldn't you?" Mr. Cullen interrupted at this point: "Just let anyone try to harm my grandchildren, and . . . " Colonel Bates laughed and said: "Mr. Cullen, you believe in relative truth."

The other allegation involved a personal friend of Dr. Kemmerer's who was a professor of educational psychology at Stanford University. He was charged by John P. Rogge and others with having associated in the late 1930's with the California Labor School, an organization later placed on a "subversive" list, and they demanded that his scheduled appearance on a University of Houston panel be cancelled. Dr. Kemmerer of course refused to entertain this, a preposterous proposal that he have all speakers approved by a "group of citizens," or the suggestion that a young Methodist pastor on the panel was "communistically inclined."

Bill Kemmerer had not heard the last of John P. Rogge, nor had the University of Houston. Mr. Rogge and his friends would meet with Jerome M. Peschke, assistant to the president, and correspond with the chairman of the department of communications regarding departmental research, in the summer of 1976.

Dr. Kemmerer felt that his differences with Judge Elkins and Corbin Robertson delayed his elevation from acting chief executive to full president, but he failed to connect this troubling dissonance with more fundamental problems that were to surface later. Certainly something was causing Hugh Roy Cullen to change his mind; and Bill Kemmerer had reason to believe that James A. Elkins, Sr., not only had little enthusiasm for advancing the acting president to full title and authority, but was able to raise doubts about the proposed promotion time and time again.[26]

Acting President Kemmerer was also running a poor win-and-loss record with Corbin Robertson on the athletics scene. He had gone to the minute book to point out that the original Board of Regents resolution of November 20, 1945, authorizing an intercollegiate athletics program and acceptance of an invitation to join the Lone Star Conference, stipulated that the athletics program "was to be strictly subordinate to the academic purposes of the University, shall be kept free of any vestige of subsidized athletics, and shall be subject to the jurisdiction of the faculty and administrative officials of the University."[27]

When Dr. Kemmerer discovered that the 1951-1952 budget for athletics at the University would surpass that of the Rice Owls (who had begun the previous year with a victory in the Cotton Bowl), he made one last plea for cutbacks. This fell on deaf ears, and was totally forgotten in the euphoria over the brilliant 8-2 season in 1952, even though the acting president, as he described it to me, "waded in gently but firmly, insisted in seeing and conferring on athletic budgets . . . urged reductions in expenditures."

After the 28-6 upset of Baylor University on November 15, 1952, the Cougars were ranked among the Top Twenty teams for the first time, and went on to capture the Missouri Valley Conference title, their first football championship. Athletic fever was understandably high. And Bill Kemmerer, facing reality, finally gave up his one-man crusade against deficit budgets in the department of athletics, but not before he had incurred lasting high-level enmities in the process.

Hugh Roy Cullen was a kind man, in spite of his toughness, and he must have been distressed over the fact that Dr. Kemmerer had been led on at least three separate occasions to believe that he was being measured for his inaugural robes. There were complex and, to Mr. Cullen, justified reasons for the delay, bearing on minority but highly respected opinion within the Board of Regents; nevertheless, the chairman of the board attempted in the second year of Dr. Kemmerer's acting presidency (from May of 1951 until the following April) to "make things up to him." The $1,500 raise to the acting president fell in this expiatory category, as did the approval of a long list of new campus buildings, emergency appropriations for the library, and the tentative acceptance of new, innovative courses and projects.

The approval of new campus buildings meant a great deal to Dr. Kemmerer, and to the faculty and student body, as the broadening role and scope of the institution began to emerge. Actually, this was nothing more than affirmation of a 1946 motion to construct an Engineering Building, the Main Junior College Building, a Fine Arts Building, a gymnasium and a swimming pool, and the new Student Union.

There was no firm financial commitment to any of these structures, except for the swimming pool, which would be built from Frontier Fiesta income and from $30,000 raised from the student body over several years for "SABUH," the Student Union which was abandoned in 1954. It would be March 19, 1957, before the Cullen Foundation was able to commit $4.7 million for the Engineering Building; the Junior College Division would have to be housed in an old Army barracks, which burned down in 1953; and the other projects were not to be in place until the 1960's. Dr. Kemmerer would be especially disappointed when plans for the Student Union did not go forward, although the lack of progress on all the buildings continued to trouble and frustrate him; he had seen the Student Union as a project honoring Mr. and Mrs. Cullen, but one to be financed entirely apart from their traditionally generous support.

The emergency bolstering of library funds for the purchase of additional books came about when Mrs. Ruth Wikoff pointed out that in spite of heroic efforts since the early 1940's (when a special report by Dean Naason K. Dupre showed that the collections totalled barely 12,000 volumes "against a minimum requirement of 50,000 for any institution calling itself a university"), the new M.D. Anderson Library would probably have less than a third of its capacity of 120,000 volumes on opening day unless additional purchases, in quantity, were made almost immediately.

In the crisis, the bibliophile, raconteur, and all-round citizen Leopold Leopold Meyer organized the Friends of the Library, Mr. Cullen pitched in some money anonymously, and 56,000 books were under the roof, if not completely processed, when Dr. Earl Bigelow of Columbia University gave the dedicatory address for the Anderson Library on April 1, 1951. He was introduced by John H. Freeman, for whom a new wing of the library, bringing its capacity to almost two million volumes, was named in 1977.

With at least tacit encouragement from the Board of Regents, Dr. Kemmerer began to move again in mid-1951 toward the establishment of additional programs and activities or the expansion of those already in motion.[28]

Two new fields—radio-television and nursing—were doubly attractive for their innovation and strong overtones of public service; unfortunately, they were booby-trapped in terms of original and ongoing financing, appealing though they seemed on first inspection.

Dr. Kemmerer had jumped feet first into radio as early as 1947, sensing the significance of this new medium in a post-war world attuned to far more emphasis on news coverage. He obtained one of the first stations licensed to a university, and KUHF-FM went on the air from its luxurious quarters in the Ezekiel W. Cullen Building on November 6, 1950, as the nucleus of an extensive sequence of courses in the overall field of radio communications.

Dr. Kemmerer told me that he was in New York City in the summer of 1951, idly watching the Estes Kefauver hearings in his hotel lobby, "when the potential of television as an educational medium hit me like a bolt of lightning." As soon as he was back in Houston, he began to plan how the University of Houston might be able to obtain one of the very first of the proposed licenses for educational television stations, but this initial concept soon shifted to the idea of a channel licensed to the University, the HISD, Rice Institute, and the new St. Thomas College (chartered in 1947) as a joint operation.

In early discussions, it became apparent that the only concrete interest was at the University of Houston, and within the Board of Education. The trustees of the HISD elected to apply as sole licensees, and did so on October 8, 1951. This application was turned down, to some extent because Mrs. Frieda Hennock, one of the first members of the new Federal Communications Commission, was aware of Dr. Kemmerer's interest, and she thought that the public would be better served if the University and HISD were joint licensees. A joint application was sent forward on August 16,

1952, and the joint license was issued on December 31, 1956, temporary "construction permit" licenses being used in the interim. Thus the University of Houston became the first licensee of an educational television station, Walter W. Kemmerer again proved his prowess as an educational innovator of the first order, and another link was forged in the chain of circumstances that would lead to his sudden "resignation" less than a year later.

In the meantime, Dr. Kemmerer was considering other means of capitalizing on the burgeoning interest in television.[29]

He had been contacted by Channel 11 regarding the possibility of a joint tower for this station and Channel 8, and he envisioned a four-station television center on vacant University property between Wheeler Avenue and Brays Bayou, off Cullen Boulevard. The concept, tied to estimated tuition revenue of $200,000 annually from students majoring in television, was tentatively approved by Mr. Cullen, Colonel Bates and James W. Rockwell for the Executive Committee, but it ran into a fusillade of criticism by Judge Elkins before the full Board of Regents. He maintained that Dr. Kemmerer was once again shooting from the hip, without adequate research, facts, discussion or authority. But after Dr. Kemmerer read from the minutes of the Cullen-Bates-Rockwell meeting granting him permission to negotiate on the proposed television center subject to later affirmation, Judge Elkins showed that he could be a good loser. He moved approval of the project, and Corbin Robertson not only seconded the motion but accepted chairmanship of the new Board of Regents subcommittee on radio-television.

The television center ran into delays and complexities, heightened by escalating costs in connection with the University's start-up expenses for KUHT-TV. The center was abandoned, and Dr. Kemmerer, ironically, was a lame duck president before Channel 8 began its test patterns on May 25, 1953, and actually went on the air June 8, 1953.

Meanwhile, the College of Nursing had become an aggravated problem, primarily because the original concept of a central unit operated by the University for five participating hospitals had fallen apart. Dr. Kemmerer still hoped to rescue the College from burgeoning losses with additional students, but there were more and more questions about the basic feasibility of this component and the growing threat of serious budget deficits it presented.

In spite of these accelerating quandaries, and other difficulties not so apparent, the University found itself in reasonably stable health as the second anniversary of Walter W. Kemmerer's appointment as acting president approached. Colonel Bates recalled that there were still qualms about elevating Dr. Kemmerer to the full presidency, but when Mr. Cullen had not articulated his own views, it was assumed among the other regents that the chairman of the board must be favorable to ending what had stretched into an inordinately long *ad interim* appointment with a promotion:

"Mr. Cullen was a good and kind man," the vice chairman told me, "but he liked to get to the point, even if he had to be blunt. He just didn't bring the matter of Dr. Kemmerer's future up with me or, as far as I know, with the other regents. We figured that if H.R. hadn't asked for a search committee, after almost two years of an acting presidency, he must have decided to go along with Dr. Kemmerer."

Ironically, there is evidence that Mr. Cullen, knowing of the earlier problems between Regents Elkins and Robertson and Dr. Kemmerer, but having heard no voiced complaints recently about the acting president, came to the conclusion that he must be generally satisfactory to his fellow regents. A few days before the meeting of April 15, 1952, he asked Colonel Bates to move that Dr. Kemmerer be made president.

Dr. Kemmerer recalled that he had been told so many times he was going to be made president that he had no reaction when Mr. Cullen called him with the news on the weekend preceding April 15. "I was just sort of numb," he said.

Nine of the regents were present at the April 15, 1952, meeting; absent were Mrs. Isaac Arnold (Mr. Cullen's daughter, Agnes), S.P. Farish, Mrs. James P. Houstoun, Simon Sakowitz, Judge Elkins and A.D. Simpson. Excerpts from the actual appointment of Dr. Kemmerer (Item VIII) are footnoted.[30]

One year and two days later, on Friday, April 17, 1953, Walter W. Kemmerer had a 7:00 a.m. call from an obviously troubled Hugh Roy Cullen, who asked that the president meet him in his City National Bank Building office at 9:00 a.m.

Dr. Kemmerer steadfastly maintained for the next 22 years that he resigned "for personal reasons" a few minutes after that April 17 meeting began. On August 11, 1975, he told a *Chronicle* reporter that he "resigned because he was asked to, by Mr. Cullen." In 1976, he gave me the full details.

The moment that he was actually named president, Dr. Kemmerer became more vulnerable to some of the community pressures that had been building up steadily from the far right. Now he was truly the chief executive, clearly charged with responsibility as the officially designated legate for the Board of Regents.

One of the most active organizations in that 1953 heyday of McCarthyism[31] were the Minute Women, the vociferous, ultraconservative group headed by Mrs. Ross Biggers. Membership rolls were difficult to obtain, but it was known that the Minute Women had close ties with other right-wing extremists, and it was suspected that they had infiltrated the Women's Association at the University. Dr. Kemmerer had clashed with both the Minute Women and similar groups, and had bitterly excoriated John P. Rogge and some of his ultraconservative colleagues at a campus meeting. He had undoubtedly become a target.

Bill Kemmerer liked an occasional poker game, and he had dealt the cards until early on the Saturday morning of April 11, 1953, with a convivial group that included Harry Fouke, Myron "Bud" Swiss, Terrel Spencer, and others.

After only a few hours sleep, he was awakened by a call from what he described to me as "an aggressive and demanding female voice." "Why weren't you in the office yesterday afternoon when we called?" was the immediate question. Dr. Kemmerer must have realized later that he should probably have told the caller to go to hell, and resumed his sleep. Instead, he explained that he had been downtown on University business the previous afternoon, and was accustomed to meetings set by prior appointment. The loud and peremptory voice, now identified as belonging to Mrs. Biggers, continued: "Well, we're coming out to see you at ten this morning." Down slammed the receiver.

Saturday was a half-day for the administrative offices in 1953, and Dr. Kemmerer was in his office a little after nine a.m. "Promptly at ten," he recalled, "in marched Mrs. Biggers and two other women. The essence of their complaint was that one of the University professors had said in class that the Minute Women were subversive. Mrs. Biggers asked, in the tones of an absolute command, 'Will you go to her office right now, and make her apologize?' Well, nobody, including me, likes to be ordered around. I assured them that I would investigate, and if the teacher had made such a remark, I would ask her to apologize.

"I spent over an hour . . . trying to placate them, only to have all three literally stamp out. Of course, they reported to Mr. Cullen that I had thrown them out of the office."

The Minute Women, and affiliated groups, apparently decided to flood Mr. Cullen with letters, and did so. There were related campaigns: a columnist reported that KUHT-TV was in serious financial trouble, and would probably close; the members of the Farm and Ranch Club, who had made a $200,000 pledge to the University in return for an agreement to open a Department of Agriculture, which President Kemmerer felt was little needed, were contacted and urged to denounce him; a radio announcer sympathetic to the Minute Women urged his listeners to "help us get rid of those Commies out at the University of Houston."

Some of this persecution had its moments of high comedy. Charlie Hiller represented the University, and Mrs. Dallas Dyer the Board of Education, at a National Education Association seminar in Austin, organized by Governor Allan Shivers at the request of Dwight D. Eisenhower. The NEA had been under attack itself for some unfathomable reason, and the Austin meeting was described in the right-wing press as a left-wing plot, attended by Communist dupes and subversives. This set up howls of laughter among anyone who knew Charles F. Hiller, Dallas Dyer, Allan Shivers or President Eisenhower.

As the anti-Kemmerer hate mail piled up higher and higher in Mr. Cullen's office, the chairman of the board felt that he had to consult with Colonel Bates and the other regents on the matter. A meeting was held in Mr. Cullen's home on Thursday, April 16, and the situation was thoroughly discussed. The cascade of letters was regarded as a serious matter, but it seemed to serve more as a stimulus to further criticism of President Kemmerer. The principal charges were existing or anticipated losses in the nursing and television projects (and it was revealed that Mr. Cullen had personally paid some sizeable bills in both areas); what Colonel Bates later termed a propensity for " '*ex post facto*' planning and budgeting—telling us about it too late to do anything but go along"; and the related matter of President Kemmerer's "failure to prepare and present new projects in a manner satisfactory to the Board of Regents."

A consensus soon formed; it was clear that Dr. Kemmerer would have to go. He always thought that there were 14 votes against him, but there is no hard evidence that an actual vote was ever taken. The one thing I would wager is that the president failed to receive support from Regents Elkins and Robertson.

Colonel Bates was the only other person present at the traumatic April 17 meeting with Mr. Cullen, and he showed a marked reluctance to discuss the relatively brief session with me at any of our many visits 20 years later. It is obvious that the meeting was painful to all concerned.

As Dr. Kemmerer remembered it 23 years after what he termed "the crucial moments of my life," he thought at first that there had been another charge against one of his faculty members. Then Mr. Cullen showed him large open boxes filled with letters, and said, "We decided we have to look for another president, or something to that effect." Dr. Kemmerer also remembered specifically being told that "the regents don't approve of the way you present things, especially new projects."

President Kemmerer was then asked by Mr. Cullen to resign, "for reasons of health," effective September 1, 1953. Dr. Kemmerer replied that his health was fine, but he would resign if he had lost the confidence of the Board of Regents. He would state that he was stepping down "for personal reasons."

It was explained that Dr. Kemmerer would be given a year's salary, to August 31, 1954. Seizing the moment, the Pennsylvania Dutchman quickly asked, "Why not two years?" This was agreed. Dr. Kemmerer told me that he was also told a campus building would be named for him.

As to timing and details, the resignation would be announced to the press the following Monday, and accepted by the Board of Regents at the next regular meeting, on Tuesday, April 28. Dr. Kemmerer said that he would prepare a statement to be read to the faculty and student body on Monday, April 27. The statement was to be checked in advance with both Mr. Cullen and Colonel Bates.

The climatic meeting was over, and with it the remainder of a complete era. "My life's work, my dreams were . . . come to naught," Dr. Kemmerer wrote of it later. "I knew it was hopeless. I knew that I would not oppose Cullen."

The "resignation" and its aftermath were headlined for a week. Dr. Kemmerer rode in the now-traditional downtown Frontier Fiesta parade on Tuesday, April 21, realizing the irony of how his stepping down coincided with what seemed destined to be the largest and most successful of the "FF's" since he had organized the carnival thirteen years before.

The student body, on spring holiday until the following Monday, was up in arms within hours after the "resignation" was made known. Dozens of placards supporting "our president" and "Doc Kemmerer," some denouncing the regents, were carried in the parade. Delegations awaited President Kemmerer every day at his home, with representatives of dozens of student organizations, the presidents of the fraternities and sororities, Varsity Venuses, veterans' groups, delegations from the University Village—all the panorama of the complex extracurricular life that he had helped to bring back to the campus after World War II—begging him to "stay in there and fight."[32]

The students proposed a gigantic blockage downtown on April 28 to prevent the scheduled meeting of the Board of Regents. Another plan involved a "complete campus strike until all 15 regents resign."

Dr. Kemmerer pleaded with the students to react "responsibly, not with mob psychology." He then prepared his statement in advance, submitted it to Mr. Cullen and Colonel Bates, who made only minor suggestions for changes, and advanced his meeting with students and faculty from Monday to the previous Thursday.

The statement, delivered to an emotional, packed audience in Cullen Auditorium, defused any lingering ideas of student violence. Excerpts reveal the dignity and skillful conciliation, coupled with positive predictions for the future of the University, in Dr. Kemmerer's valedictory; an accompanying statement from the faculty indicates the genuine regard his colleagues held for the president.[33]

Dr. Kemmerer's three vice-presidents found the electrifying news of his ouster difficult to comprehend, even though the wise and canny Acadian, Charles F. McElhinney, always close to the key regents, must have had some Scotsman's foreboding of what might be afoot. Charlie Hiller, who had been planning a trip abroad for some time, postponed this until the situation stabilized. Terrel Spencer had far less seniority than his colleagues at the vice-presidential level, and was occupied day and night by remaining reverberations in the student body (although there was never a serious threat of a student strike after a tense

48 hours immediately following news of President Kemmerer's removal from office, in spite of downtown editorials against violence).

The media speculated immediately on a successor for Dr. Kemmerer. Dr. Oberholtzer, whom President Kemmerer had very generously honored at the dedication of Oberholtzer Hall on May 26, 1951, and at the 1952 Commencement exercises, was mentioned briefly as an *ad interim* appointee, but this was impossible on several scores, particularly since the founding president's health was failing rapidly. President Francis P. Gaines of Washington and Lee, and President Blake R. Van Leer of Georgia Institute of Technology, both of whom had been on campus recently, were listed as prime candidates.

It was obvious, however, that the Board of Regents would prefer another acting president, preferably a stable man of high competence and low controversy, well and favorably known to the University community and to the regents alike. Such an appointment had one drawback: it placed the institution again under a chief executive without full firepower; but it had many advantages, particularly that of a peaceful hiatus during which the wounds left by the precipitate, mysterious and disturbing dismissal of President Kemmerer could heal a bit, and the governing board could take a leisurely look around for new long-range leadership.

There was an obvious choice for such a skilled caretaker president in C.F. McElhinney, who could probably have been named to the full presidency had he been willing to maneuver the situation in which he found himself. A native of Truro, Nova Scotia, Charles Flemming McElhinney took the baccalaureate at Acadia University when he was only 18, in 1926, and taught in public schools in Canada before coming to Columbia University for graduate work in education. Here, it will be recalled, he was a tutor in statistics for Dr. Oberholtzer, and made a lasting impression on the older educator.

After completing the master of arts at Columbia, "Mac" taught at Troy (Alabama) State Teachers College, at Mississippi State College for Women, and at summer sessions of the University of Alabama. When President Oberholtzer invited him to join the HISD staff in 1934 as assistant director of curriculum and research under Dr. Kemmerer, he also accepted an appointment as an instructor of education at the infant University of Houston, thus beginning a four-decade association with the institution. In 1939, Mr. McElhinney became director of research for HISD and a staff assistant to Dr. Oberholtzer. He became the first full-time business manager of the University and had been elevated to the post of vice-president and business manager in June, 1950.

A member of the faculty for many years, sponsor of key student activities and projects, and erstwhile ice hockey coach, Vice President McElhinney took no sides in perennial campus feuding, had no discernible enemies, and soon became the advisor and confidante of both Dr. Oberholtzer and Dr. Kemmerer, after both men saw the necessity for bringing him to the campus from downtown in 1945. He became as familiar with the crucial aspects of financial flow and management of funds as he was with the billiards table in the Faculty Lounge, had the thorough respect of the instructional as well as the administrative staff, and was regarded as the best source of reliable information on virtually any aspect of the University's operations by Mr. Cullen, Colonel Bates and other key members of the Board of Regents.

I asked Dr. Kemmerer if he had any doubts about who should succeed him on September 1, 1953, and his reply was, "None whatsoever; it was obviously McElhinney." This view was as indicated echoed by the regents, probably all the more because Mr. McElhinney agreed to serve only as an acting president, with the clear understanding that he would return to his vice-presidential post on September 1, 1954. This would permit the indicated advantage of a grace period in which to carry out a deliberate search for a full-time replacement.

"Mac" ran a stable ship for the agreed term of 365 days, and he stepped ashore having made no changes of any consequence. This was his concept of his duty and responsibility, although I suspect that he saw more than one area in which he was tempted to clear away a little brush; but it was very substantially the University Bill Kemmerer had turned over to him on September 1, 1953 (driving away in his new Cadillac, given to him by students, faculty and staff) that he turned over to his successor a year later.

In his thoughtful and perceptive address to the faculty, an early valedictory of another time entitled "The Past Is Prologue," "Mac" McElhinney states a most profound truth about the Oberholtzer-Kemmerer era which had lasted 26 years (more than half the

University's age in 1977), when President Kemmerer turned the reins over to him. The first two presidents were good men and true, he found, due great and everlasting credit; but they were essentially public school men, out of place, finally, in a true university setting.

Now the University of Houston would move slowly, and sometimes painfully, to its proper role and scope—sometimes hindered, sometimes helped, by its antecedent history and the first two presidents who had shaped it. The man destined to bring the institution through the first seven years of this new era had been singled out by his old companion in arms, Colonel Bates, halfway through the McElhinney *interregnum.* He was Andrew Davis Bruce, Lieutenant General, Retired, United States Army, who would literally doff his uniform one morning and report immediately, in *mufti,* as the third president of the University of Houston.

Notes to Chapter Five

[1]Janus, the Roman god of inaugurals (beginnings) who gave us the name of our first month, had two faces and could peer into the past as well as the future.

[2]The noted geologist J. Brian Eby has written of his first meeting with Professor Eby. Having heard of the historian, he called on him once in Austin, and sent in a card marked "Dr. Eby to see Dr. Eby." He was immediately received, and found that Dr. Eby was not only a historian but a cousin and a genealogist who had traced the family to sixteenth-century Switzerland.

[3]Remembering perhaps that Gounod, although far better known for his opera, *Faust*, organized the Royal Choral Society during a five-year sojourn in London and spent the last years of his life composing and conducting oratorios.

[4]Hubert Roussel was a knowledgeable and elegant gentleman of polished writing skills whose reviews graced the pages of the *Post* for a generation. He distinguished himself in hundreds of scholarly, honest and witty columns over the years, and usually knew more about what was going on in the principal arts groups at a given time

than did their directors. Mr. Roussel's brilliant criticism even included an appraisal of his talented daughter Stephanie's performance with the Red Masque Players; but his masterpiece may have been a plea to those who determinedly come to concerts with a hacking, cacophonous cough. Rather than compete with the soloist, and even with the kettle drums, as you spew a fine and infectious mist for yards about you, he counseled, stay home. Or have yourself admitted to hospital.

[5]"Board of Control" is apparently used as a synonym for "Board of Regents," a mistake that no purchasing agent or business manager in a state agency would ever make. The "Board of Control" is just that. It controls state purchasing policies and procedures, tightly and efficiently, from its Austin headquarters.

[6]Mr. Cullen told reporters at the meeting in the Music Hall that he and Mrs. Cullen "had lawyers drawing up papers" which would establish the Cullen Foundation and fund it with production from some 11,000 acres estimated to have recoverable reserves worth about $80 million. When a delegation consisting of almost the entire directorate of the Houston Chamber of Commerce called on him in his new offices in the City National Bank Building a few days later to express their appreciation, he announced that "we've decided to double the ante with 8,000 more acres."

[7]Warren S. Bellows, Sr, general contractor on the new Cullen Building, told me that he met regularly with Mr. Cullen when the final details of finishing inside construction on the giant facility were proceeding. The two men were on the second floor, Mr. Bellows recalled, in the area outside the main administration suite. Plans called for marble walls to the ceiling, but the exact type of marble had not yet been specified. Mr. Bellows explained this to Mr. Cullen. "Well," said the donor, "we don't want just common old garden variety marble here. What do you recommend?" "How about Carrara, from Italy?" "Anything better?" "Well, yes; we could get marble with naturally matching patterns." "Good; get that."

[8]Some of the lesser structures did not meet the test of time. C.F. McElhinney once recalled the saga of "Robbels Hall," for example. Heinz Robbels, a chief petty officer in the World War I German Navy, was hired in 1944 for his abilities as a jack-of-all-trades and a superb scrounger; he was given the almost impossible task of finding lumber and other materials for desperately needed temporary classrooms, and of getting these structures in place as soon as possible. Robbels made some inquiries and began frequenting the beer joints where truck drivers for a group of jack-leg sawmills could be found. Soon the University had plenty of wood, all of it green. By the time Robbels and his questionable crew of apprentice carpenters had sawed and nailed the stuff together, there was not a square corner in the 22 resulting classrooms, and even less parallel surfaces. This im-

posing edifice served its purpose for a time, but fortunately burned to the ground.

[9]Colonel Bates recognized the fundamental importance of the professional schools, but he told me that "the College of Nursing was Kemmerer's idea, and a bad one, when all the cards were out on the table." He also said that "Dr. Oberholtzer sort of hinted once that perhaps we should look into a medical school, and I told him right off to forget that one. Earl Hankamer and Ray Dudley had told me enough horror stories about bringing Baylor Medical down here from Dallas, and keeping it alive in that old Sears & Roebuck warehouse on Buffalo Drive (Allen Parkway) until Mr. Cullen went in with them and others to move Baylor over to the Texas Medical Center. And of course I've had a little experience of my own looking at budgets in the Medical Center."

[10]Dr. Ferguson, an expert on South American drugs, including herbal laxatives among other things, will celebrate his seventieth birthday on December 20, 1977, in his new career at the Universidad Autonoma de Guadalajara, where he shows no indication of wearing down, or of learning more than three words of Spanish. Responsible for the sound foundations on which his successor, Joseph P. Buckley, is now building one of the preeminent colleges of pharmacy (including a five-story facility within the Texas Medical Center), Dean Ferguson would do almost anything to keep his component under way. This included teaching organic chemistry himself to students who could barely keep up with the formulae he covered the blackboards with from five minutes before, to five minutes after, the classroom gong; and energetic fund-raising. Ralph E. Frede (then director of development) and I went out recruiting team captains once with the dean. One especially appealing candidate begged off the assignment, pointing to the backlog of prescriptions in front of him. Dean Ferguson showed him his current license, which he kept in miniature version in his wallet, and pointed to the door. He then rolled pills two hours while Frede and I took the regular pharmacist out to call on prospects.

[11]Both deans qualify as "non-flappables." I was instructed to tell Charlie Stewart in 1957 that unless we could get the freshman class up from 12 to 15 students over the weekend, the College might have to close. He had four applicants on hand at 8 a.m. Monday. I also had to tell Chet Pheiffer in 1972 that in spite of favorable prospects earlier on, we were not going to get a $4.5 million grant for a new College of Optometry. He immediately wanted to know the deadline for submission of 1973 proposals, and prepared one which obtained a record $5 million grant.

[12]Shortly after his demotion at the University, Dean Dupre had returned to the HISD to accept the important assignment of assistant superintendent in charge of elementary education. He soon fell

victim to the eternal divisions on the Board of Education, and resigned November 15, 1949, with a statement that he "could no longer work under conditions as they are." He also commented on his own worsening health. Dr. Daily paid a deserved tribute to Superintendent Dupre: "I regret this resignation extremely. He has done a brilliant job, dealing with tangled post-war problems of inadequate buildings, huge enrollments and myriad administrative headaches. He revised our elementary supervisory plan, broadened in-service training, and constantly advocated needed improvement in teacher standards."

[13]The University of Houston has conferred only three honorary degrees in its fifty-year history. Mr. and Mrs. Cullen were awarded doctor of laws degrees at the May 29, 1947, Commencement exercises; and because Mr. Cullen admired the remarkable job he was doing with the huge post-war ROTC unit at the University, Colonel Michael H. Zwicker, professor of military science and tactics, was given the same honor.

[14]The dinner was to have been held on April 30, the sixteenth anniversary of the day on which the University became a four-year institution, but this fell on a Sunday and was deemed inappropriate. It was set instead two days after Founder's Day, and four days before Dr. Oberholtzer's seventieth birthday, at Ye Olde College Inn. The site was indicative of the importance attached to the occasion, since the faculty and administration in those days ran more to the thirty-cent blue plate at the "Rec" Building cafeteria. Ernest Coker set a $2.50 steak before you at the College Inn that was unmatched except at the little-known Ritz Cafe (Hebert's). The Ritz, an outgrowth of what had been Clifford Herbert's lunch wagon, closed if the proprietor was unable to get his shipment of aged Omaha prime beef. The cafe carried a unique advertisement from time to time in the local press. This warned against "eating second-class meat," and pointed out the difference between first-class "prime" and second-class "choice" under confusing government nomenclature.

[15]"Few men have been privileged as have you, Dr. Oberholtzer, to have dreamed the dream, to have seen the vision of a great educational institution, and then to have seen the dream come true, the vision converted into fact. That, tonight, must be your greatest reward. That you have the best wishes of your friends, particularly those who have helped to bring the dream to reality, is your just due. Generations to come will be thankful to you as the man who had the vision of the University of Houston, and they will be thankful, too, that you could fire the enthusiasm of those necessary to bring into being this great institution dedicated to education and good citizenship in our community." *Mrs. Ray L. Dudley*

[16]Final figures that became available after a 1950 audit showed that almost 33,000 persons were enrolled in the University's industrial training units during World War II, a total considerably higher than earlier estimates.

[17]Shasta is the traditional name for the cougar which has served as University of Houston mascot since 1947, when the service organization Alpha Phi Omega (APO) purchased Shasta I. The name was selected in a contest to raise funds for the mountain lion, and comes from the doggerel verse submitted by Joe Randol, a student, that won the contest: Shasta have a cage, Shasta have a keeper, Shasta have a winning ball club, Shasta have the best. Runner-up names among 225 entries were Spiritana and Raguoc. Shasta III retired in December 1976, at almost exactly the time Shasta IV was born in Florida. The new cub is now in training, and will be kept in an enlarged facility with Shasta III. Funds for the expanded cage and related areas were provided by an anonymous donor.

[18]Dr. Kemmerer had already located an extremely able director of placement services who would serve the University until her retirement almost 25 years later. This was Lily Lou Russell, an ex-teacher of Latin and USO executive who established and maintained sound relationships between the University of Houston and dozens of local and national corporations.

[19]Johnny Goyen, the first director of the Ex-Students' Association, his successor Jack Wilson, and alumni kingpins including Tom Menefee, Jack Valenti and Roger Jeffery, were good friends of President Kemmerer and, in some ways, a valuable tie to Mr. Cullen, who had begun avoiding meetings of the Board of Regents in late 1950 and on into 1951. He had become embarrassed over a campaign, in which the philanthropist wanted and had no part whatsoever, to rename the University after him. Goyen and his pals staged some rip-roaring Homecoming programs at this time that added greatly to school spirit. These began on Wednesday night with a downtown torchlight parade, and concluded Saturday after another parade featuring beautifully decorated floats, various campus events, including floating on rubber rafts in the Reflection Pool, a football game and a final dance.

In 1951, the Homecoming festivities coincided with "Cullen Day" and a historic football game against Baylor University in Rice Stadium. It was decided that Mr. and Mrs. Cullen might enjoy a Friday afternoon pep rally in Cullen Auditorium at which they were to be the guests of honor. The invitation was extended in person by Goyen, between busy telephone calls in Mr. Cullen's office, and was accepted. Mr. Cullen asked how many people would be at "this Homecoming thing," and Goyen replied, "about two or three thousand, as many as we can get in (Cullen Auditorium)." There was a momentary hesitation, but Mr. Cullen said, "Fine," and went back to his telephone calls. A few days before the pep rally, one of Mr. Cullen's secretaries called Goyen. "Mr. Cullen," she began, "was wondering if you had any closer estimate on the alumni group coming out to his home. We don't know whether to prepare for two thousand, or three thousand." The invitation to the Cullens was explained in more detail, and some caterer lost a really big piece of business, for Mr. Cullen had been certain that the Homecoming meant coming home to his palatial residence at 1620 River Oaks Boulevard.

[20]This probably resulted from confusion with Earl James McGrath, who served as United States commissioner of education from 1949-1953, and was later chancellor of the University of Kansas City and president of Eisenhower College. General Dwight D. Eisenhower, whom Mr. Cullen greatly admired, and brought to the campus with other Republican luminaries including Minority Leader Joseph Martin, is known to have mentioned Earl James McGrath, later a faculty member at Columbia University under General Eisenhower, in favorable terms to Mr. Cullen.

[21]The *Cougar*, in a special edition, correctly termed "the Zeke" a "a massive miracle of architecture," with its 180,000 square feet of space, 46 classrooms, 94 offices, 14 studios, 1668-seat plush auditorium and 122 "other rooms". It also pointed out that the building had usurped the site of the University's largest and more centrally located parking lot, where the 1948 Frontier Fiesta had been staged.

The various areas of the huge structure were equipped and furnished at bargain basement rates, in comparison to prices today. The fifth floor was fitted up for KUHF-FM (which began broadcasting six days later, on November 6) at a total cost of $20,000, including intricate soundproofing and complex features that few radio stations in the South had at the time. The faculty lounge on the fourth floor was furnished in lavish style for $10,000, and the large three-level Cullen Auditorium for $79,000, including complex acoustical installations and specially designed seats covered in "sea foam velour." Contracts totalling $205,000 covered all offices and classroom equipment. The *Cougar* concluded that the building was "unbelievably magnificent."

[22]This was probably Francis P. Gaines, Jr., the son and namesake of President Gaines of Washington and Lee College, who was appointed director of development at the University of Houston in December 1950, soon after completing his doctorate at the University of Virginia. A member of Phi Beta Kappa, the younger Gaines had attended Washington and Lee, Duke University, and the University of Arizona before serving as a military intelligence officer during World War II. Dr. Gaines left the University a few months after his appointment, to become dean of men at Southern Methodist Univer-

sity. He was later president of Wofford College, and has been dean of continuing education at the University of Arizona since 1959.

[23]Dear Colonel Bates:

"I am happy that Mr. Cullen has suggested that I present a statement concerning my part in the building of the University of Houston as an evaluation of my fitness for the position of top leadership. In doing so, I am presenting the record of my accomplishment since the founding of the University in 1934.

"As the school grew from a few hundred students to 13,624, it was my privilege to direct the formulation and installation of program after program which built the present extensive offering, and for six years (I) served as comptroller of the University. Every program started has been and is successful educationally and is self-supporting or is planned to be after the necessary initial years.

"While I feel confident of my ability to continue developing the University of Houston into one of the greatest universities, and I am not without just pride, I do not desire the position for personal glory. I was largely responsible for the ideas and policies which made the University so successful, and I have a deep and burning desire to see the philosophy and objectives continued which enabled this University to accomplish in so short a time what no other school has accomplished over a period of centuries. I want to see realized the vision held by myself and so many of our 350 faculty members.

"In order to succeed, a president must have the respect and confidence of his faculty. I would welcome the Board's investigating the extent to which the present faculty has such confidence and respect in me.

"Statements attached expressed in the first person are not intended to detract from the cooperative efforts of the entire staff. They are presented as the ideas in the promulgating and developing of which I played a leading role. The field of service of the University of Houston has not been to follow the pattern of traditional colleges, but to provide a complete educational program for all citizens. I have been at least in part responsible for this philosophy and desire to continue carrying out the policies which have been so eminently successful.

"I am presenting attached a brief record of my part in the development of the University. I would welcome the opportunity of appearing before the Board to answer any questions and explain further my qualifications, accomplishments and plans for the University of Houston."

Respectfully submitted,
W. W. Kemmerer
Assistant to the President

[24]Dr. Kemmerer listed in the first "Summary Record" 19 "major items which I initiated and for the development of which I was chiefly responsible. Of course," he added, "it is to be understood that I was working at the direction of the President and that all these activities were carried on with his full knowledge and approval." Many of the items have been mentioned in varying detail, but it is interesting to list most of them as shown in the "Summary":

Led in the development of the staff's spirit of unselfish devotion to the cause of the University; developed educational programs and financial formula for self-support; recommended salary increases in excess of 50 percent during the past five years, and adjusted program to support these increases; operated the University until 1944 on less than three percent for administrative cost, (which figure) has since increased to 10.5 percent; was chief operating executive from 1934 to 1944, while President (Oberholtzer) was superintendent of schools; started first program of daytime classes and carried on five-year (General College) experiment; established first budgetary and accounting system; directed the planning of the (1938) campaign to raise funds; secured National Youth Administration project for first campus improvements; organized and developed policies of the Graduate School; directed the construction of the Vocational (Industrial) Building and the Student Recreation Building; made unusual adjustments to provide for rapid influx of veterans; organized and developed the vocational and terminal courses; established the Downtown School (and) Extension Service; . . . and was primarily responsible for selecting of the University's administrative staff and faculty.

Similarly, the thirteen items in "Summary of My Ideas and Suggestions" provide a unique insight into the future of the institution, as Dr. Kemmerer perceived it in the beginning weeks of 1950:

With the approval of the Board of Regents, and with the incorporation of their suggestions, as President of the University of Houston, I would: continue and intensify my past policies which won (the) respect of the community and achieved the outstanding growth and progress of the University; develop more completely the Community Service (Junior College) Division; separate administratively the Community Service Division from the advanced and professional schools so that the vocational work will not lower the standing of the professional schools; expand the student service program so that all students may benefit by adequate educational, vocational, personal, health and financial guidance; this program alone, I believe, will achieve national recognition within a few years; develop a strong program of general and civic education for all; continue, improve and expand the terminal vocational program; build the advanced and professional schools to achieve national recognition for excellence; devise with Board sanction the University's specific plan for the future, and take necessary steps to accomplish this plan; establish a proper administrative set-up delineating duties, responsibilities and titles of staff members; improve faculty personnel procedures to stimulate greater use of existing talent; maintain always a balanced budget but at the same time increase faculty salaries, and establish a satisfactory retirement plan; make annual and interim reports of progress to the Board; and intensify our public relations program to secure all possible good will for the University and sponsors for specific projects.

"Exhibit A," dealing with Dr. Kemmerer's accomplishments at the University from 1934-1950, was largely an expansion of the 19 "major items" mentioned above. Two brief sections, however, presented interpretative material of value:

The Development of the "Spirit" of the University of Houston: Any institution reflects the spirit of its leadership. From 1934 to 1944 it was my privilege to be the chief operating official in the University. From nothing the University was "poor-boyed" to its present respectable position. I am now firmly convinced that with proper leadership the University of Houston can achieve recognition as the best school of its type in the nation.

The University is strong because we had to work and fight to make it what it is. In this struggle to build a school to serve all students with respect for their individuality, and with recognition of their differing abilities, we have developed and acquired a staff with an unselfish spirit of devotion. By precept and example I have been able to instill this spirit in others who flatteringly have followed my example. It is this spirit which is essentially "The University."

Why the University is Self-Supporting: The University has been able to operate on its earned income because (1) of the spirit of unselfish service held by the faculty; (2) the program constantly expanding to meet needs; (3) the University's offering is sufficiently attractive so that students buy its educational service; and (4) sound fiscal policies are being followed. Many of the key faculty members have received other offers of positions at higher salaries. On such occasions they came to my office and it was my privilege to transmit repeatedly the spirit of the University and my faith in its future, and as a result, they rejected such offers. In the past five years on my recommendation salaries have been increased over fifty percent. Few know how this was made possible. Tuition was raised 20 percent and class size raised 25 percent, and the balance met by reducing net earnings. I planned each course or program to be self-supporting on the simple formula that the gross income must be at least twice the teacher's salary.

"Exhibit B" delineates institutional objectives, and "desirable" administrative policies:

The Basic Objectives: By continuing the policies, philosophy and objectives which have made it large, successful and highly respected, the University of Houston should within the next ten years receive recognition as the best school of its type in the country. In a democratic society, each citizen must be allowed to rise to the extent of his ability and his willingness to exert himself. I believe, therefore, (1) that the University must continue to expand its services to give everyone who desires to continue his education an opportunity to do so; (2) that each program must be of the highest possible quality so that each student is fully qualified to do the work for which his program is planned; (3) that each student must be helped to find the field of work for which he has ability and aptitude, and in which he has a reasonable chance for success; and (4) that each student must receive a good general education in order that he may get the greatest possible satisfaction out of life and at the same time make the greatest possible contribution to our American way of life as an effective, intelligent citizen.

Administrative Policies Desirable if the University is to Achieve Highest Recognition: Pointing out that "up to the present time we have grown and operated without plan in a rather opportunistic manner," Dr. Kemmerer proposed the following: (1) a 10-year future plan covering educational goals, plant needs and policies governing the financing of the entire program . . . "a blueprint of the University's future"; (2) "an administrative organization plan" spelling out duties, responsibilities, rules and regulations in accordance with best business and administrative practice; (3) clearly defined personnel policies which spell out such important areas as job descriptions, salary administration and fringe benefits; (4) proper stimulation and recognition of "latent talent in the faculty (that) is dormant and unused"; (5) an annual report by the president including reports by deans, directors and heads of special divisions; (6) interim reports by various administrators at the regular meetings of the Board of Regents; and (7) "expanded and intensified" public relations activities.

Dr. Kemmerer also recommended that the overall salary schedule, "at present about 25 percent lower than that of the University of Texas," be increased along with the adoption of a "supplementary retirement plan." This would be funded from earned income in the Junior College Division and College of Arts and Sciences, but additional funding would be required in the professional schools to provide such a plan, "but only if the Board decides that these professional schools shall achieve top ranking."

Dr. Kemmerer concluded this remarkable communication to Colonel Bates (and to Mr. Cullen) with a thoroughly optimistic note: "In summary, I have complete faith that, by operating the University democratically with full respect and recognition of the contribution of each employee, the University of Houston will become an institution so honored that each Board member will claim, as his major distinction, that of having helped build "The University of Houston."

[25]Mr. Gilbert said, "I will do everything I can to encourage . . . required study of American history." Judge Townes stated, "I am surprised that the University of Houston and Rice Institute do not require (American history). They certainly should." Dr. Kemmerer said: "One American history course doesn't make a person a patriotic citizen . . . persons who raise such a furor about Americanism apparently believe that everyone will be patriotic if they take a course in American history. I am certainly not against history, but this is not the entire answer. Most University of Houston students take American history, but it is not required, as are a year of American government and two years of English. They can escape history if they try, but it would be difficult."

[26]The following sequence can be reconstructed from a written memorandum that Dr. Kemmerer gave me: "March 6, 1951: Mr. Cullen telephoned; he will recommend me for the presidency at the March 20 meeting of the Board of Regents. March 12: Mr. Cullen telephoned; he is not yet ready to make the recommendation. April 10: Mr. Cullen visited the campus in a happy and enthusiastic mood; he assured me that I would be made president at the April 17 meeting. April 16: Mr. Cullen called to say that he had changed his mind and would have to postpone the recommendation. May 21: Mr. Cullen telephoned; he will recommend me for the presidency at the meeting of the Board of Regents tomorrow."

But on May 22, there was a long agenda and continued discussion of a recommendation by Dr. Kemmerer to retain Donald Barthelme to carry out a comprehensive study for future campus planning, and to prepare preliminary plans for the Student Union Building. The recommendation, by Dr. Kemmerer, had been previously approved by both Mr. Cullen and Colonel Bates, but was "completely torn to pieces by Judge Elkins," who was also critical of a plan to purchase vacant lots and some residences along Wheeler Avenue for what Dr. Kemmerer termed "the logical location for a fraternity row." Both proposals, Judge Elkins claimed, had not been sufficiently examined. They were tabled, and when Dr. Kemmerer asked Mr. Cullen in an aside about the matter of his being named president, the chairman of the board "shook his head gruffly, in obvious annoyance." Once again, it was still Acting President Kemmerer, but he was given a $1,500 "annual increment" at the end of the spring semester of 1951.

[27]This unique stipulation made little impression on Regent Robertson and the other members of the governing board, the faculty, student body or alumni. Many of the current and former students, thirsting for recognition, would have campaigned to rescind the resolution had they known of it.

The University began to relish its first real successes in intercollegiate athletics between 1946 and 1951, after primordial memories of a dozen men practicing football between 9:30 p.m. and midnight, ice hockey games at the Polar Wave skating rink, basketball games with the W.T. Grant Department Store five, and a time when Sam Houston State Teachers College was an archrival, complete with offsetting campus "raids" and ceremonial shaving of the heads of captives. Guy Lewis, now one of the nation's most successful basketball coaches, and Willie C. Wells of the famous "leap shot" and jersey 32, now a prominent labor official and a regent of the University, led the basketball team to Lone Star Conference championships in the first two years of competition for Alden Pasche's Cougars, who once practiced with total inventory of two basketballs left behind by World War II campus Navy units, one of them with a slow leak. Both the 1945-1946 and 1946-1947 team made it to the National Association of Intercollegiate Athletics (NAIA) tournament in Kansas City, establishing a precedent for the great fives of the 1960's and 1970's and basketball's all-time game of games against the University of California at Los Angeles before 53,356 in the Astrodome on January 20, 1968.

Jason Morton, Glenn Hewitt and Don Napier (Hugh Sweeney was a squad member) won conference championships for Coach John E. Hoff in tennis, Morton being a champion in three separate conferences; the baseball team was getting under way, but awaited the arrival of Glenn "Pappy" Bond and the infant daughters who gave him his nickname; Jack Patterson was organizing the first track and field squads; and the football team was having occasional success under Head Coach Jewell Wallace, although it was still fielding light, inexperienced teams with questionable defenses.

With constant attention from Corbin Robertson, to whom Athletic Director Harry Fouke and the University must be forever grateful, the football situation changed dramatically for the better between 1949 and 1952. Football banquets were held at the Houston Club, with Mr. Cullen announcing the addition of major opponents to the schedule, and schoolboy football stars and their parents in the audience dining on the best porterhouse. Gene Shannon brought the Cougars from a 0-14 halftime deficit to a near-victory over William and Mary, in what was billed as the team's "big-time debut" on September 17, 1949. A capacity crowd saw the University lose to Baylor on Cullen Day in 1951, in Houston (Rice) Stadium. There was talk of the Cougar team having its own football stadium, after a cordial meeting between Mr. Cullen and the trustees of the Rice Institute indicated that the Owls would go their own separate way on stadium ownership.

Suddenly, in 1951 and 1952, Corbin Robertson's long and patient work with Harry Fouke and Head Coach Clyde Lee on the football front bore fruit. The 1951 eleven had a 5-5 record, and went on to defeat Dayton 26-21 in the Salad Bowl at Phoenix, where Gene Shannon gained 175 yards on 28 carries. It was hardly the Cotton Bowl, but the game brought a great deal of recognition, and set the stage for the ensuing season. In 1952, bolstered by the legendary All-American tackle J.D. Kimmel, the Cougars lost only to Texas A&M (13-21) and to mighty Mississippi (0-6). Among the victims were Arkansas (17-7, before a howling near-mob at Fayetteville), Texas Tech and Baylor, giving Coach Lee a 3-1 record against present-day Southwest Conference competition.

Corbin J. Robertson had carried the day, and the University of Houston was committed to major league intercollegiate athletic competition.

[28]This was the era during which the University earned the unjustified reputation of being ready "to set up a course in Chinese basket-weaving," as one of its critics once expressed it, "if three students enrolled for it." This was a wild exaggeration of Dr. Kemmerer's determination to broaden offerings to meet needs and demands, and not always within existing academic frameworks.

[29]Commercial television was brought to Houston by W. Albert Lee, whose various other interests included hotels, a laundry, and ranching. His KLEE-TV went on the air January 1, 1949, after a three-hour delay caused by technical difficulties in cooling the transmitter properly. Studios were in the Milby Hotel, and programs were broadcast to an estimated 2,000 sets in the city from a 537-foot tower next to a Quonset hut on Post Oak Road. Color television and the coaxial cable were in the research and discussion stage. KLEE-TV was sold to the Houston *Post* in 1950 and became KPRC-TV in an arrangement that Governor and Mrs. William Pettus Hobby would never have occasion to criticize.

[30]Colonel Bates asked Dr. Kemmerer to leave the room for a few minutes, saying he wished to take up an item in his absence.

Colonel Bates: "Dr. Kemmerer has been our acting president for the past two years, and I think we all agree he has done an excellent job out there, and that it is now time to change his title to president. . . . I would like to make the motion that Dr. Kemmerer be made president of the University of Houston."

(All regents present seconded the motion except F.M. Law, who appeared to be hesitant about the matter but actually wanted an opportunity to praise Dr. Kemmerer for his popularity with students, alumni and faculty, and for his civic activities. He concluded: "Dr. Kemmerer is a man of vision—a man who can plan and think fifty years in advance . . . it is my honest belief that Dr. Kemmerer is the best possible man in the whole country for this job. . . . I did want to say these things . . . before I voted for him; . . . and besides, I wanted him to be on needles and pins a little longer out there.")

Mr. Cullen: "He is the very best man we could get for the job, and if he had not been so unselfish and not spent so much time thinking about the other fellow, those faculty members and everybody out there, he could have been named the full president a year ago."

Mrs. Dudley: " . . . I really believe that the type of wife a college president has is a great factor in his success or failure, and I do want to say that I think Mrs. Kemmerer certainly deserves a great deal of credit in Dr. Kemmerer's being elected to the presidency."

Mr. Hutcheson: "I would also like to say that I think Dr. Kemmerer should be congratulated for continuing the "old regime" started by Dr. Oberholtzer. I think one of the reasons for Dr. Kemmerer's success is that he has had the privilege of working with Dr. Oberholtzer for so long and has kept the same associates with him that Dr. Oberholtzer had."

Mr. Cullen: "Yes, he has those three fine vice presidents. You know, Dr. Kemmerer delegates authority; he knew he needed somebody to help him, so the first thing he did was to ask us to appoint him some vice presidents, and I think that's mighty fine."

Mr. McElhinney: "I would like to say that I am sure the faculty, administration and students will all be delighted to learn the Board's action this afternoon."

Mr. Cullen: "That's an understatement if I ever heard one—I was afraid the whole bunch would go out on strike before we got this done. Well, I believe we've kept Dr. Kemmerer out long enough now, so I'll go get him."

. . . Mr. Cullen brought Dr. Kemmerer in, shook hands with him and said: "Well, Bill, you've just been made President, but Freddie here (Mrs. Dudley) has just given all the credit to your wife, so you can't get big-headed."

Dr. Kemmerer: "I can't express my feeling at the moment, nor can I tell you how humble I feel, but I do want to say that I recognize the responsibility and tremendous challenge of the job. I have said before that we have the finest Board imaginable, and with your continued support we will make the University of Houston one of the finest schools in the nation. I only pray for strength and courage to do the right thing and the wisdom to know what is right to do. We have the finest and most loyal staff of any school in the country to do the job."

[31]Dr. Kemmerer told me that Mr. Cullen once had Senator Joseph R. McCarthy as a house guest, partly out of curiosity to hear his views at first hand. The two men disagreed, almost violently, and Mr. Cullen, normally the soul of hospitality, asked that the great demagogue end his visit as soon as convenient.

[32]Neighbors near the Kemmerer home at 1915 Wentworth (which Dr. Kemmerer has maintained until now as an alternate residence and retirement home) had a rare opportunity to learn both the *Alma*

Mater and the Cougar Fight Song during almost a solid week of intermittent concerts outside the president's front door, by small bands, campus singing groups, and just harmonizing students. The *Alma Mater* was composed in 1942 when Bruce Spencer King (now an associate professor of music emeritus) gave his class in harmony a unique assignment. They were asked to write a song suitable as an official University *Alma Mater*, with both lyrics and music. Irwin T. Andrews, then only 18, wrote a violin melody which Professor King expanded into four-part harmony. The entire class then collaborated on lyrics, and their teacher arranged these for chorus. Both Arvin N. Donner and A.L. Kerbow of the education faculty urged that the new composition be sung at the 1942 Commencement; this was done, and, according to Professor King, "it just caught on." Irwin T. Andrews died March 26, 1977 in Houston, at the age of 53.

There have been at least two Cougar Fight Songs, and other so-called "pep songs," as at most institutions. The "official" version is by Forrest Fountain (lyrics) and Marion Ford (music), and was first popularized by Ed Gerlach's orchestra in the early 1950's (Ed Gerlach and his musicians, most of them University of Houston students, were so well thought of that the 1955 *Houstonian* was dedicated to the band leader).

Another popular Cougar Fight Song was composed by John Perry, a student who had a fine tenor voice and marked musical ability, although he was an accounting major. John Perry composed his version while a patient in the Jefferson Davis Hospital polio ward. The ex-GI had contracted the disease while living in University Village with his wife and three young children. He sang it many times in the polio ward, and it was popular enough to be introduced at the 1949 University of Houston football game with William and Mary, the Cougars' first try at big-time football competition.

[33]"The announcement of my resignation last Monday has been followed by so much consternation and so many questions that you are due an explanation. It was my intention to resign at next Tuesday's board meeting without fanfare, and quietly withdraw. Advance release of the information compelled me to state my intentions earlier.

"I DID NOT expect such overwhelming reaction and regret on the part of the faculty and students. Events moved too rapidly to permit me to appraise them properly. I can understand now that knowing my deep interest and attachment to the University, you would not let me fold my tent and quietly slip away without a reasonable explanation.

"I have dreamed, lived, and worked only for the University of Houston. Nothing will ever take its place in my affection. Let me assure and re-assure you—my faith in the University and my faith in you to carry it onward to greater achievement and service is greater than ever. I shall never desert the University in spirit and in fact, and I shall always do what I can to advance the cause of the University.

"I am forever grateful for the sentiments expressed by the faculty in their statement to me, as follows:

'Your recently expressed intention to resign as president of the University comes as a distinct surprise and shock to the members of the faculty.

'We are keenly appreciative of the highly harmonious relationship that has existed between you and the faculty under your administration.

'WE RECOGNIZE that the sterling leadership you have demonstrated and the unselfish service you have manifested are vital contributions to the progress of the University. In large measure, as a result of your vision and foresight, our school stands at the threshold of a brilliant future.

'We are aware of no facts which would warrant your proposed action, and we express to you our unqualified confidence in your ability and administration.'

"With all these expressions and many others from citizens not associated with the University, I feel amply rewarded for my 19 years' service in helping to build this great school.

"To the student body, so enthusiastic, loyal and ebullient, I say many, many thanks for your interest in me and your always loyal support. I appreciate your efforts to get me to reconsider my resignation. It hurts me deeply that I cannot do so.

"YOUR CONTINUED insistence, your abounding loyalty and your overwhelming support compels me to give you the explanation you are demanding. The easiest explanation is always the simple truth.

"To help you understand my decision, you need to know one of my basic principles. I have always avowed I would not want to work for an employer who did not desire my services, and I also acknowledge that the Board of Regents is a final authority. Consequently, when I was told last Friday by two members of the Board that my services were not desired by decision of 14 members, my resignation was practically automatic. Now you still wonder why. Let me assure you there is no criticism of the administration, faculty, educational program, or financial management.

"THE BOARD has always worked harmoniously with me, respected my wishes, and given me full authority to conduct the affairs of the University. The Board's most important obligation and duty is the selection and appointment of the President. The Board has given me to understand that they are not satisfied with my manner of developing and presenting new projects. I do not presume to speak for the Board. I respect the Board's wishes and want you to do likewise. There has been no quarrel or dissension, and to the best of my knowledge, the members of the Board are my friends, and it is their decision in carrying out their duties to get a new President.

"I assure you that Mr. Cullen has always supported me in everything during the three-year period of my administration. It has been a privilege to work with Mr. Cullen, and I count him today as one of my close friends.

"I HAVE submitted my resignation this morning, my friends, and under these conditions, I hope you will understand why my resignation cannot be reconsidered. You are wonderful friends, and a glorious team—students and faculty. Direct your tremendous potential energy to preserving the philosophy which built this school.

Together you will maintain the University of Houston as the leading democratic peoples University in the world.

Chapter Six

1954-1961

Colonel Bates and the FOTC provide a new president, General Andrew Davis Bruce . . . Clanton Ware Williams, colonel and academic administrator, accepts a key assignment and then a promotion . . . The "13" list becomes a blueprint for reorganization . . . Chancellor versus president; new competition for leadership . . . The providential arrival of Philip Guthrie Hoffman . . . Formation of the Board of Governors, and the Living Endowment Association . . . Remarkable progress by president and chancellor alike, in spite of rivalries . . . Hugh Roy Cullen dies, on the Day of Patriots . . . New contributions and new buildings, but the decision is for state support . . . President Williams completes a job well done and takes a leave of absence he might not have requested . . . A decisive victory with the TCOHE . . . The scene shifts to the State Capitol . . . Clear prospects of a disastrous legislative defeat . . . A one-vote breakthrough, filibuster, and desperately close triumph . . . General Bruce becomes chancellor emeritus and Hoffman the Builder is president

William Bartholomew Bates belonged to many organizations, and one in which he had been markedly active for 35 years, the First Officers' Training Camp (FOTC), would now provide the third president of the University of Houston by virtue of a vigorous recommendation from the Colonel to Mr. Cullen.[1]

Colonel Bates told me that he had maintained contact with General Bruce over the years, and how 20 years had run by in the post World War I Army before his old companion in arms was promoted to field grade (major) while stationed in the Canal Zone in 1936. He especially remembered a long visit with the General during the May 1947 FOTC convention at the Rice Hotel. General Bruce was en route at the time to his new post as deputy commander of the Fourth Army at Fort Sam Houston in San Antonio.

The General stayed on in Texas for three years. He was transferred from Fort Sam Houston to Fort Hood near Killeen, as commandant. This was familiar ground, since he had organized the Tank Destroyer Center at Fort Hood in 1941. The new assignment enabled him to maintain and reinforce closer ties with Colonel Bates and other FOTC colleagues, until he was sent to the Armed Forces Staff College in Norfolk, in 1950, as president (commandant). This appointment highlighted General Bruce's career-long emphasis on innovative methods of instruction and represented the assumption of responsibilities at least reminiscent of university administration. It was a potent factor in Colonel Bates' approaching Mr. Cullen early in 1954 about the possibility of Andrew Davis Bruce assuming the presidency of the University of Houston on September 1, 1954.

General Bruce was immediately a strong candidate with Mr. Cullen, who had been quick to express his profound admiration for both Dwight D. Eisenhower and Douglas A. MacArthur on many occasions and had demonstrated a high regard for the discipline, orderliness, and calculated progress of the military.[2]

Colonel Bates arranged for General Bruce to visit Houston twice in the winter and early spring of 1954, primarily to meet and to get acquainted with Mr. Cullen and the other regents, but also to renew the General's long-established ties with members of the FOTC and the numerous acquaintanceships he had made during almost 10 years of separate tours at Fort Hood.

A.D., as his close friends called him, and Roberta Bruce were a handsome, outgoing couple who made a strikingly positive impression on Houston. Over six feet tall, with an erect, military bearing, piercing eyes, and a full, leonine head of graying hair, the General drew attention and respect automatically. Instinctive good manners, reinforced by the punctilio of military protocol, constituted another major asset for General Bruce and his wife, a fine-looking, witty (sometimes trenchantly so) woman who complemented her husband in many ways. They had enjoyed an obviously happy marriage of almost 35 years, enduring together the slow promotions and low pay, the frequent changes in stations and the snubs sometimes accorded a non-West Point graduate in the regular Army, while enjoying the sense of duty properly discharged, the lasting friendships and the other compensations of the service. Since Pearl Harbor, and beginning even with the growing international tensions of the late 1930's, there had been a different life, with the deserved reward of increasingly high rank and assignments ranging from tours at Fort Hood through command of the 77th Infantry Division in the South Pacific, and a post-war appointment as military governor of Hokkaido, the northernmost of the four principal islands of Japan.

An immediate advantage for the Bruces on their visits to Houston in 1954 was the General's long residence in Texas, dating back to his father's purchase of land holdings during the earliest development of the Lower Rio Grande Valley, the removal of the family from St. Louis to Mercedes, and Andrew Davis' enrollment at Texas A&M College in the fall of 1912. He was virtually a native Texan, and a certified Aggie, rather than an infiltrating Yankee faced with still-lingering traces of xenophobia in a Houston that was not all that cosmopolitan back in 1954.

Another potent factor advancing General Bruce's candidacy was purely coincidental, but significant nevertheless: his sixtieth birthday, on which he was to retire from the Army after 37 years of active duty, was exactly one week before the end of Mr. McElhinney's agreed one-year term as acting president of the University of Houston, on August 31, 1954.

There was only the semblance of a "search committee," that modern day genuflection to democracy in university governance that can be so expensive in time and money invested, and so ineffectual in results. Mr. Cullen did ask five regents (Colonel Bates, Mrs. James P. Houstoun, F.M. Law, James W. Rockwell and Palmer Hutcheson) and Mrs. Bessie M. Ebaugh and Harper Beaty, representing the Faculty Assembly, to "help look for a new president"; but such meetings of the committee as there were seem to have been devoted to discovering further merits of Andrew Davis Bruce.

Early in the spring of 1954, Colonel Bates told Mr. Cullen that there seemed to be a clear consensus on General Bruce. This was communicated to the other regents, and Mr. Cullen called the General on June 12 to offer him the presidency of the University effective September 1, 1954. The call was not unanticipated; the candidate had received nothing but encouragement, and Colonel Bates had the telephone number for the General's direct line in his Norfolk office on file.

The candidate told Mr. Cullen that he was deeply honored, and asked for a few days to consider the situation. He had already determined that he would accept the presidency if it were offered; but an ingrained sense of decorum told him that a delay of a day or so might be indicated. Mr. Cullen told him to take his time; he pointed out, however, that the Board of Regents would be meeting three days later, on Tuesday, and often passed over the July as well as the August session.

On Monday morning, General Bruce telephoned his acceptance to Mr. Cullen, but not before telling his old *compadre*, Bill Bates, of his decision. The Board of Regents enthusiastically endorsed the appointment, after Colonel Bates had made a brief nominating speech in which the president-designate was described as "the top educator in the Armed Forces—unexcelled as an administrator." The vice-chairman of the governing board then telephoned the good news, and his congratulations, to the General. General Bruce thanked him and the other members of the governing board; but being completely honest, he also told Colonel Bates how clearly he recognized that retired generals had been singularly unsuccessful as university presidents, with a few glaring exceptions, such as Robert E. Lee at Washington College (later Washington and Lee University) and Dwight Eisenhower's brief yet creditable performance at Columbia University. He would be seeking early on, he confessed to his old friend, a man skilled in non-military academic administration—and he might have him in his gunsight already.

The University of Houston lost its first president just three days after A.D. Bruce agreed to become the institution's chief executive. Dr. Oberholtzer died June 18, 1954, in Memorial Hospital, where he had been hospitalized almost a month with increasingly grave circulatory disorders. Funeral services were held the next afternoon at the First Methodist Church, before an overflow gathering of those whose lives Edison Ellsworth Oberholtzer had touched. Bishop A. Frank Smith and Dr. W. Kenneth Pope officiated, with entombment in the Forest Park mausoleum.

The pallbearers included two former student leaders, Sherwood Crane and Richard (Racehorse) Haynes; two close friends from the faculty, Dean Arvin N. Donner and J. Chester Cochran of the College of Education; and C.F. McElhinney, his one-time tutor; W.E. Moreland, who had succeeded him as superintendent of schools; and his sometime nemesis but co-laborer in the educational vineyard during 21 years of the remarkable development of a school system and a university, H.L. Mills.

Editorials, long news stories and obituary notices paid tribute to Dr. Oberholtzer, his enormous contributions to education and the community overall, and his role as the founding father of the University; but he would have treasured more the innumerable former students, colleagues, and friends who came by the modest family home at 1709 West Alabama. There his two sons, Kenneth (himself a national figure in education, as superintendent of schools at Denver) and Edison Jr., and his daughter, Mrs. Esther M. Fuller, waited with their mother "Mame."

Among the endless line of callers were members of the first class at the old Houston Junior College who had followed Dr. Oberholtzer into education and now held key positions within the HISD: Miss Mabel Cassell, director of curriculum; Mrs. Jewell Askew, director of elementary education; four principals of elementary schools—Mrs. Louisa Eldredge (Jefferson), Mrs. Mabel T. Woods (Lantrip), Mrs. Esther Lawhon (Southmayd), and Miss Elsa Gehring (Grady).

"The Chief" was gone, but he would not be forgotten.

Andrew Davis Bruce rose early on the morning of Tuesday, August 31, 1954, as was his lifelong habit, and put on his uniform for his final day of active duty. His commander's plane landed at Ellington Air Force Base before noon; he thanked and dismissed the pilots, changed into civilian clothes in the nearby Officer's Club, and was driven to the President's Office at the University of Houston.

"Mr. Mac" and all the headquarters staff were waiting to greet and to welcome him; they had been flown up to Fort Hood just a week ago for his farewell retreat marking his sixtieth birthday, and he had met key members such as Leta Nutt and Marguerite Harris earlier.[3]

General Bruce tried out the chair in his private office, and resisted the temptation to place his three-star commandant's flag on immediate display (although it appeared later, as it should have, as a prime memento of 37 years of his life). He then betrayed his sensitivity on a crucial point that continued to bother him: equating high-level experience in Army education with the administration of a civilian university. "I am not bringing the drill field with me," he told reporters in an opening press conference. "I am going to use the same leadership that I employed in heading the Armed Forces Staff College at Norfolk."

Yet he began almost at once to share that leadership, by accelerating the hunt for a top academic administrator. The man General Bruce had in mind as vice-president and dean of faculties was Clanton Ware Williams, who had come to his attention a few days after he had told Mr. Cullen that he would accept the presidency of the University.

A professor at the University of Alabama since 1929, with time out for service in World War II and the Korean War, Dr. Williams had been recalled to active duty in the latter conflict because of his record in World War II, during which he rose from captain to colonel and became historian of the Air Force. As head of international studies for the Air War College of the Air University at Montgomery, Alabama, Colonel Williams was asked to lecture at the Armed Forces Staff College in the summer of 1954. For protocol, General Bruce was required to stage a dinner for the visiting Air University official; he told me once, "I would have done this anyhow for such a southern gentleman, but I changed the menu from chicken to steak when I saw Colonel Williams' biography." For here was a scholar with long experience in a major university who had also served in senior positions within the high echelons of Armed Forces educational institutions. Before Dr. Williams left Norfolk, General Bruce had confessed to him his uneasiness at transferring his experience at the Armed Forces Staff College and elsewhere to a civilian setting, and had suggested that he might visit the Air University official at his headquarters at Maxwell Air Force Base. Dr. Williams told him that he would be most welcome, but to hurry on down, as he was about to return to his academic duties at Tuscaloosa, site of the University of Alabama.

In a long letter written to me a few months before his untimely death in 1975, Clanton Williams recalled this episode: "General Bruce told me that he had just been offered the presidency of the University of Houston, and (that) he was scared to death; he had had no experience with civilian academic institutions and wondered whether or not he might stop by the Air University and chat with me some time. I, of course, was delighted (to receive him there)."

Andrew Davis Bruce hit the ground running, as some members of the staff adjusted their own schedules a bit when they noticed his blue Chrysler sedan arriving early from the small apartment he and "Miss Roberta" had taken at the dignified old Warwick Hotel. Shortly after taking office, he picked up the telephone and called Clanton Williams, who was back in Tuscaloosa as a senior professor of history. "Would you be interested in becoming my vice-president for academic affairs?" he asked.[4]

Dr. Williams had rather expected the offer, but it was sudden, and he paused for a moment. General Bruce, who had only partial hearing in one artillery-damaged ear, shouted, "Hello! Hello! Did you hear me?" Dr. Williams replied in the affirmative, and accepted the offer with thanks. He did not feel it appropriate to leave the University of Alabama until the end of the semester, in January, but he would arrange to come over to Houston for some visits in the interim.

Within a few weeks, General Bruce knew a great deal about the administrative staff, and some key changes were either initiated or actually made, sometimes at the General's suggestion or on his initiative, in other cases by the staff member involved. By the end of the academic year, Charlie Hiller had been shifted to a new post as dean of the Junior College, and Terrel Spencer was leaving for a new career in California. Mrs. Ebaugh became dean of women.

The General made only one move in the academic field, preferring to await the arrival of his new vice-president for academic affairs before advancing into unreconnoitered territory. No one could fault him for the action he took; it was in an area in which he had expert knowledge, and it was overdue. He recommended that the huge, 872-man ROTC unit of 11 companies plus a band and the Cullen Rifles be redesignated from its Quartermaster Corps specialty to General Military Science. This provided added flexibility for graduates of the unit, and it doubled the academic credit received. The recommendation was routinely approved by the Board of Regents.

Clanton Williams sent me an account of his arrival in Houston on January 21, 1955, after his appointment had been announced three weeks earlier. He included his impressions of many incidents during his six years with the University of Houston. Ironically, the University of Houston had attained its first major goal in the field of thoroughgoing academic respectability shortly before the new vice-president for academic affairs reported in for duty. The Southern Association of Colleges and

Secondary Schools had granted accreditation on December 2, 1954, at the annual meeting in Louisville, but only after a three-year wait from the time the petition was submitted, in 1951, and with some definitely negative comments by a visiting team whose members had combed the campus incessantly during a two-day visit the preceding October. The Grove of Academe was putting down deepening roots and spreading branches, but the new head gardener would need his pruning hook—and a sharp ax as well.

"I landed at Ellington Field," Dr. Williams recalled 20 years later, "and General Bruce was there to meet me. I could see that he was perturbed (about something). He had failed to instruct me not to wear my uniform. I told him not to worry, that I had civilian clothes in my grip. He took me to his apartment, where I changed.

"We went immediately to see Mr. Hugh Roy Cullen, chairman of the Board of Regents and then to see Colonel William B. Bates, vice-chairman. Mr. Cullen shook hands cordially when the General told him that I was the 'scholar' they had all agreed should be appointed to run 'academic things,' then turned to General Bruce and said, 'Now, A.D., we told you that internal matters were your own; that your staff was entirely your responsibility.' Turning to me, he said, 'Now, Dr. Williams, I'm glad to know you, sir.' Needless to say, I was delighted with this reception."

The new vice-president still managed to stub his toe a bit before he left Mr. Cullen's office. He asked Colonel Bates, "What outfit were you colonel of?"

Although General Bruce had confined his official academic surveillance to military science pending the arrival of Vice-President Williams, he had kept his eyes and ears open, and had not forgotten how to ask brief but penetrating questions. Soon after I joined his staff, on April 16, 1956, we were sitting in his inner office.[5] He handed me a list, pencilled in his distinctive handwriting and dated New Year's Day, 1955.

On the list, in this approximate order, were these words: deans, nursing, television, McElhinney speeches, faculty salaries plus, admissions, grading, Frontier Fiesta and credit, agriculture/demonstration farm, photography/19, modeling and charm, extension and Junior College. "What do you think of that list?"

General Bruce asked. "That's a troubleshooter's list if I ever saw one," I replied. "Everything on there I've heard about in negative or controversial terms, either on campus or around town—except for Mr. Mac's speeches to the faculty." The General smiled. "I included them," he said, "because they're such a good source of clues to other problems. Not much escapes Mr. Mac."

There was a moment of silence. He apparently expected me to reply further. "But you need another list," I went on, "a list of positive needs and goals. They're pretty obvious: buildings, faculty upgrading, a far better 'image' in the community as a foundation for better understanding and broader support, more school spirit, membership in a major athletic conference . . . " He nodded. "We have that list, too," General Bruce said, pointing to his head; "it's up here. And Mr. Mac and Dr. Williams and you had better have it up there too, thinking about it constantly. Each of you will have specific assignments on that positive list; but the only way we'll ever get it all done is as a team."

The General then asked me if I noticed anything else about the handwritten list. "Well, there are 13 items on it," I replied, and began to study the list intently. It was obviously a crucial piece of paper, and there were no indications that President Bruce was going to distribute copies. "I hadn't thought of that," he said. "That's an interesting point." And this time there was no smile. He continued to look at me, and I added: "Somehow, I predict that you and Dr. Williams are either well into every item on the list, or soon will be." The General said nothing more, but the semblance of a smile returned to his face. The interview was over.

I was correct about the list of 13 items. A week or so later, I was visiting Dr. Williams in his first floor office. "Have you seen the General's handwritten list he got up for me?" he asked. "Yes, it's a good list," I answered. "I assume that action is proceeding." He nodded, chewing on his pipe. "A little more cautiously than the General might want in some areas," he responded, "but proceeding." I did not volunteer the information that I had my own copy of the list, written down from memory the moment I returned to my office after having been shown the original by the author.

The civilian seldom understands that the military man spends a sizable portion of his career studying—either in a seemingly endless succession of schools or in the private scanning and analysis of books, reports, memoranda and the like. General Bruce made a disciplined habit of such reading, as his battered and misshapen briefcase attested. As the new president, he looked continually for information, and it took him little time to pounce upon a significant document delineating the condition of the University and the problems looming before it as his administration began. This was Acting-President McElhinney's September 11, 1953, address to the faculty. Mr. Mac first stated his concept of the role of an acting president: the duties to him were "best defined in terms of what (I) should *not* do. I conceive it to be my responsibility to provide impetus and coordination for the educational program which we already have under way. And although I have no intent to impose my personal philosophy or ideas," Mr. Mac continued, "I would nevertheless express to you some of my convictions in certain areas."

It was these "convictions," with one consequential change and some minor adjustments which Acting-President McElhinney expressed in a spring semester address to the faculty on January 28, 1954, that General Bruce studied intently before making up his list of 13 items. He had already ferreted out regency, faculty, staff and even some student opinion regarding Mr. Mac, and found that the Nova Scotian conservative was generally regarded as a prophet, had many friends, and was as dependable as the Rock of Gibraltar. He began next to assess his vice-president and business manager's analytical ability and foresight and he found that this also graded out in the superior range.

Mr. Mac's statements in strategic areas can be quickly summarized. He was never a man given to hyperbole:

Budget: After an almost unbroken tradition of operating in the black, the University had just closed the 1952-1953 fiscal year (on August 31) with either a tiny surplus, or a loss. Much of this deteriorating situation was traceable to losses on summer sessions (an estimated $150,000 in 1953 alone), complicated by decreasing enrollment and rising faculty salaries and operating costs. The summer sessions had to be reexamined, and all possible savings realized, especially if a projected schedule of ongoing faculty salary increases was to be maintained. Competitive bidding was to be closely enforced, and it was strongly recommended that any new faculty members be hired "at the lower limits of the salary schedule, wherever possible."

Cash Position: The University "has practically depleted its working capital." If the idea of a television center to incorporate commercial stations with Channel 8 was to continue as a viable project, its construction and operation had to be funded entirely from outside funds, preferably on an endowed basis.

Television: "Our television station has been variously pictured as a device which will bankrupt us and, on the contrary, as an instrument by which we may tremendously increase our educational services with economy both of physical plant and of personnel. I frankly do not pretend to know where, between these extremes, the actual truth will be found. I do urge that during this first year, which is necessarily experimental, we give the television staff our complete cooperation in their efforts to establish the most economical use of this medium. We have made our capital expenditures . . . it would be folly not to attempt the maximum efficient use of our facilities."

Tuition: Increased tuition would place a further burden on students, and freshmen and sophomores had to pay all tuition and fees by October 31 and wait for traditional "junior college" refunds from the State of Texas instead of paying only the difference at registration.

Overall Finances: " . . . tight, but not alarming."

Faculty Salaries: A proposed new salary schedule (reinforcing a tentative arrangement for somewhat modest but continuing escalation to a definitely better level of compensation) was in the hands of a Board of Regents committee, and reaction appeared positive.

Tenure and Promotion: The Board of Regents had just adopted, on September 2, 1953, "substantially the recommendations of a faculty committee" (after assurances that another faculty committee was hard at work on some internal housecleaning involving both higher standards for selection and promotion and enforcement of those standards).

Admission Standards: "This should be a place where any citizen, old or young, is enabled to pursue any type of training for which he is willing and able to pay. This does not, however, mean that everyone who attends long enough is entitled to some kind of degree. I believe in a most liberal policy for admission to this University, and in a more conservative policy for admission to candidacy for all degrees."

Grading: "There is entirely too much variation between departments and instructors. I invite the faculty to continue to study this problem and to suggest possible solutions."

General Education (actually the earlier concept of the General College, to which President Kemmerer had been returning in conjunction with his plan for a major Junior College Division): "I believe fully in a program of general education in the sense that there should be some minimum core of knowledge available to and required of candidates for all degrees. However, I am by no means convinced that the general, highly integrated course is the answer . . . (and) shall leave the decision on the development of additional such courses to the permanent president."

Acting-President McElhinney completed his address by warning that the first indications of interdepartmental jealousies and criticisms had appeared. There had been some fairly sharp backbiting, portions of it seeping out from campus to community, and he felt that, "Should any of us publicly condemn the work of our colleagues, we are surely and inexorably bringing discredit upon ourselves."

He also gave the faculty notice that he would have to delegate heavily to the vice-presidents and deans, especially since he would be operating two offices simultaneously. This would understandably cut down on his use of two highly effective communications vehicles that kept him abreast of what was going on across the campus: luncheon hour "eight ball" games in the billiards area of the Faculty Club and informal chats in his office. He did leave open consultation, upon invitation, with the Faculty Assembly and Executive Council,[6] and personal visits with individual members of the faculty and staff, "at the earliest moment my calendar will permit when you have a problem which really requires (this)."

The budget and cash position had improved dramatically by the time of Acting-President McElhinney's January 28 address, even though General Bruce would soon find that the patient had only rallied temporarily from grave and continuing fiscal ailments, and would soon be back for further diagnosis and treatment.

The miraculous though transitory alleviation of symptoms came about in a remarkable way. The Cougars, continuing their football successes, had smashed Baylor again, this time by 37-7, as little Kenny Stegall led a combined ground-air attack of 430 yards. A huge pep rally was arranged for the following Friday, November 20, and word spread that Mr. Cullen, enormously popular with the student body, would be the principal speaker. Cullen Auditorium was jammed, with hundreds of students milling around outside. The grapevine had reported that something definitely was up.

Mr. Cullen's address was brief, to the point, and electrifying: "Some years ago, I brought General Ike Eisenhower to this very auditorium, and from this platform he made a wonderful address and you students gave him a rousing welcome. He told me afterward that he had never seen a spirit which was finer on any campus, and I will say that the enthusiasm you students showed here this morning has not diminished.

"The great spirit and determination shown by the Cougars last Saturday in defeating Baylor fills me with enthusiasm and prompts me to do something for our great University.

"The commitments which the University has made and is now making . . . to enable us to get in the Southern Association of Colleges will put the University in the red $830,000. To help this situation I have decided to give the University $2,250,000 in oil payments."

The headlines bloomed across the nation, with various versions of the same erroneous message: *"Oil Tycoon Gives Millions For Football Victory."* Actually, as Mr. Cullen attempted to explain later, the gift had been under study for months with attorneys and other tax advisors, inspired at least in part by the gloomy picture that Mr. Mac had drawn concerning the budget and cash position.

"I just jumped the gun a little in announcing the gift," Mr. Cullen said. "I was feeling so good about the team." Taxicab drivers across the land would still be telling me fifteen years later, if they discovered that I was from Houston, "about the oilman who gave that college all those millions for winning a football game."

The Cougars lost disastrously to Texas Tech 41-21 the day after the new Cullen gift; but the University had its $2,250,000, payable over 10 years in equal installments. Without it, there would almost certainly have been some curtailment of programs.

General Bruce obviously had obtained a considerable number of his 13 items for priority attention from Acting-President

McElhinney's addresses to the faculty. The remainder he identified later in long conversations with Clanton Williams, through questioning other members of the staff, and from direct observation.

The General, oversensitive to his lack of civilian academic experience, remained somewhat isolated from the faculty for the first two or three years of his administration, although he and Mrs. Bruce quickly developed lasting friendships with some faculty members and were always treated with great respect. Until 1957, he depended heavily upon Dr. Williams for faculty contacts and reactions, as well as recommendations, not realizing that the vice-president for academic affairs was sometimes regarded with deep suspicion, especially by the small group of incompetents he was able to discover quickly through training and long experience in the Grove of Academe.

Dr. Williams combined his professional abilities with a warm, outgoing personality and convincing manner, however, and he gained added support from the faculty once rumors of a wholesale housecleaning subsided with the issuance of new contracts in the spring of 1956. The isolated weeding-out of the relatively small percentage of the marginally qualified (where tenure regulations permitted) was actually endorsed in the Faculty Club, although covertly, in hushed conversations.

"They began to realize that I was right more often than wrong," Dr. Williams told me. "An elderly lady of equine demeanor, for example, was really after me during a difficult session with a curriculum committee in her college. She was making the most caustic side comments imaginable, in a loud voice, knowing that I could hear her but would hardly respond. But she toned down more and more, and when the meeting was over, I heard her say to her companion, 'Well, he's not half the ogre I thought he was going to be.' I took that as a real compliment."

Dr. Williams said that soon after he arrived, the General remarked, "Colonel, some of your colonels (deans) are weak." Vice-President Williams had advance information on this, since a good friend of his was on the accrediting team from the Southern Association which had visited the University on October 13-14, 1953.

He agreed with General Bruce, and added, "I have already determined that a lot of housecleaning will have to be done."

Later, Dr. Williams told me, "One dean sat across from me and cried like a baby, while I explained that he must leave, and why; another went into deep depression."

Dr. Williams recalled for me that he and President Bruce also agreed on a plan of attack for the 13 identified trouble spots, "after I added a really crucial one, academic standards, and warned that the list would grow again." There was an understanding that totally different time phases might be involved in the resolution of the items, some being susceptible to reasonably quick settlement, others capable of becoming even more difficult over the years.

Both men would examine nursing, television, the McElhinney addresses, "Frontier Fiesta and credit," agriculture/demonstration farm, and the Junior College, since these areas had broader connotations as well as specific academic dimensions. The vice-president for academic affairs would concentrate separately on deans, "faculty salaries plus," admissions, academic standards, course offerings (with special attention to photography; beauty, modeling and charm; certain other unique catalogue listings; and extensive questions regarding the curricula in engineering and education), off-campus classes being offered as far away as Corpus Christi (plus related "correspondence courses," another trouble spot General Bruce had been unaware of) and "anything else of consequence he turned up."

Dr. Williams had to ask for a translation of the phrases "faculty salaries plus," and "photography/19," and for further information on just what aspects of the Junior College he was to examine. He found that by the "plus" added to "faculty salaries," General Bruce meant fringe benefits, which were sadly lacking at the University, and a growing problem in competing for academic stars; by "photography/19," the General meant that he had been amazed to find that the University offered 19 undergraduate (plus some graduate) courses in this subject, a hobby and favorite sub-area of communications for President Kemmerer. General Bruce had already asked the new provost to consider the Kemmerer concept of a Junior College Division tied closely to a General College approach emphasizing highly integrated courses; now he had discovered that Vice-President McElhinney was neutral on the subject, preferring to leave it for a specific decision by the new administration; on this basis, he wanted a definite recommendation by Dr. Williams as soon as possible.

Clanton Williams had wisely spent his first month at the University away from his office, prowling the campus by night and day, talking incessantly to faculty, students and staff. His first impression was that "admission standards were low, the faculty miserably paid and relatively unproductive. Even so," he added, "there are some who are proud of the school and ambitious for it." He found a fine spirit among the student body, "even though most of them work full time," and a dedicated, underpaid staff. Indeed, he found members of the maintenance crews being paid wages "on which they could hardly keep body and soul together," especially if they had large families to support.

Dr. Williams concurred in Mr. Mac's warnings about impending financial crisis, particularly when he found (in contrast to Vanderbilt University, where he had studied and taught before his years at Tuscaloosa) that the University of Houston had an extremely low endowment. As he recounted it to me many years later: " . . . this private school (without the usual comfort and protection of income from permanent endowment) was living off gifts, and tuition up to the hilt; but the gifts were going largely for buildings, and further tuition increases might easily turn away students."

The new vice-president saw a direct, and dangerous, connection between living off tuition hikes and gifts largely allocated to buildings, and admissions and academic standards that he found to be generally low. Somehow, he reasoned, both standards must be raised if he was to do a creditable job and the University of Houston was to emerge from what Mr. McElhinney and others had correctly identified as the "public school era"; but rising standards could easily accelerate decreases in enrollment, in a situation already complicated by the possibility of additional increases in tuition. Enrollment, he noted, was up slightly for 1955-1956 (from 13,066 to 13,330), but this was below totals of six years ago, and the level seemed to be stabilizing with the threat of a downward drift.

While he continued to struggle with these complex relationships, Dr. Williams decided that his first move would be a fundamental one: ". . . to eliminate all degree plans and course offerings which were not absolutely essential." This would require the direct interrogation of every dean, and every department chairman, in order to obtain fresh information, in depth and in broad, institution-wide perspective, upon which to base decisions.

The vice-president for academic affairs went to work. He described himself to me as "a devil's advocate, asking literally hundreds of questions." Some of the questions were deliberately framed to place the dean or departmental chairman on the defensive, others to invite confidential disclosures. "And I wanted answers immediately," Dr. Williams recalled. "I doubtlessly appeared to many as a bull in a china closet, taking orders from a lieutenant general of infantry. Even so, I was after those answers."

For a time, it seemed that the University of Houston again had a team of complementary top executives capable of addressing the internal as well as the external problems of the institution vigorously and successfully. After surmounting some initial criticism and mistrust born of suspicion and insecurity, General Bruce and Dr. Williams (sometimes called "Caesar and Napoleon" within the faculty ranks) made substantial progress.

They agreed early in 1956 on some of the more obvious problems in the "list of 13 items." Simultaneously, they began to move, with General Bruce providing the cutting edge in conjunction with Mr. Cullen, Colonel Bates and C.F. McElhinney, on such other fundamental difficulties as the need to continue to improve faculty salaries without turning away students by inordinate jumps in tuition. General Bruce also had to consider the escalating cry for new buildings, brought sharply into focus again by the long delay in projects announced in 1950 and 1951, the arrival of new and more demanding faculty members, the crowding of students into inadequate facilities, the growth of the professional schools and colleges, and a beginning emphasis upon research.

As Dr. Williams sharpened his pruning saw, the first component to go was the College of Nursing. He saw little or no academic justification for this unit; its remaining role could be taken over by a further expansion of the teaching hospitals (which had never accepted fully the concept of a "central" College of Nursing); and it was losing money hand-over-fist despite an energetic recruiting campaign. General Bruce sought the advice of close friends at the famed Scott and White Clinic at Temple, near Fort Hood, and the reactions of Houstonians within the medical profession and the Texas Medical Center. There was some concern over any move that might diminish the supply either of registered nurses or of licensed vocational nurses; but there was a strong consensus in favor of a shutdown. The College of Nursing was in effect phased out August 31, 1956, although several months were required to complete a few training cycles, the transfer of students, and final termination.

The television station, and with it the directly related instructional program in radio and television, was saved by several factors, paramount among them Mr. Mac's reasoning that it would be folly not to give this new and experimental component a fair trial, especially since major capital expenditures for it had already been made. Dr. Williams and General Bruce were also impressed by the articulate John C. Schwarzwalder, a veteran of the Office of Strategic Services (OSS), who could spin World War II stories with the best of them, and by the academic and technical strengths of the crew he had assembled to help him carry out his perilous assignment as first managing director for KUHT.[8]

Next on the list were the Frontier Fiesta "and credit," agricultural/demonstration farm, and the Junior College, with its overtones of the General College dating back to 1934. The "credit" mentioned in connection with the Fiesta was a curricular abberation that the General had stumbled on earlier. It was possible to earn academic credit in drama for working in the spring festival, a reasonably defensible matter until the complexities of variations in emphasis and approach arose. Who, for example, was really learning academically from such an experience, and who was concentrating instead on traditional Frontier Fiesta beach parties at Galveston and on dating the toothsome high school girls allowed to perform in the midway shows until they and all non-University participants were banned.

The question of academic credit went by the boards without debate, but both the General and his academic vice-president were aware that they were up against an entrenched Colossus in opposing the Fiesta itself. Among the proponents of the almost out-of-hand spectacle were Mr. Cullen himself, as files of photographs of the chairman of the board at Fiesta events over the years indicated, and growing thousands of alumni who were almost rabid on the subject of their memories of the Fiesta, and its centrality to school spirit. The Bruce-Williams team decided to move in stages on the Fiesta problem, first by raising questions with the faculty as to how much the carnival, including its full week of spring holidays, interfered with class attendance and assignments, and how much it could damage institutional image and incipient fund-raising if its negative aspects got out of hand.

In what he described as a "heart to heart talk," General Bruce told an assembly of the general faculty on January 28, 1955, that "one off-color remark" in the Frontier Fiesta or Varsity Varieties "could cost the University a $50,000 endowment." He had also initiated some private discussions with student life officials over the vast concentrations of can-can dancers, and their costuming and grooming, in the Top Five Shows of the Fiesta.

The opening *banderillas* had been placed, even though it would be the fall of 1958 before Dr. Williams could tell representatives of student organizations that the total time spent on the Fiesta must be limited to four weeks overall, that the maximum expenditure per show must be limited to $1,500,[9] and that anyone allowed to participate must be a full-time student with a minimum grade point average (GPA) of 2.0. This effectively placed a damper on the 1959 Frontier Fiesta; the 1960 event was cancelled in favor of a feasibility study for a 1961 Fiesta; and a feeble musical comedy imitation, the Cougar Capers, attempted to replace "The Greatest College Show In The World" with a three-day run March 16-18, 1961. The reviews for the Capers were mixed ("bad and worse," one disgruntled student said), and that was the end of both the Capers and the Frontier Fiesta tradition.

The next item, that of the department of agriculture and demonstration farm, involved some formidable complexities. Established through a $200,000 grant from the Houston Farm and Ranch Club which was being paid off in regular installments, the department and accompanying acreage represented a link to what one Houstonian called, "the sucker rod crowd." This alluded to the fact that the Club's members, just as the prime movers in the Houston Fat Stock Show, included some very prominent and prosperous oilmen and industrialists who operated plush ranches as a hobby. Some of these properties had fences made of aluminum sucker rods from the oilfields, kept immaculate with aluminum paint.

It was said of some of these weekend ranchers that they had their Luccehse handmade boots resoled if ever sullied by manure, but they were a fine and generous group whose members might have difficulty understanding why the University should want to rid itself of the department of agriculture and demonstration farm they had so generously provided.

Again, the solution was a gradual one. Dr. Williams failed to see how agriculture really fitted into the offerings of a struggling young urban university 93 miles southwest of one of the world's great centers of agricultural teaching and research, at College Station. General Bruce, both as an Aggie and as a university president confronted with worsening budgetary problems, had even stronger views on the matter, although he was quick to perceive the accompanying complexities.

As a first move, we turned to the demonstration farm, which had turned out to be amazingly expensive to operate and maintain in terms of the student credit hours involved. General Bruce sought preliminary conferences with acquaintances within the Farm and Ranch Club to determine how they might feel about giving the farm to a high school with courses in agriculture and strong student interest in Future Farmers of America programs. We had identified such interest at Pasadena in the general vicinity of the demonstration farm, an isolated holding once devoted to growing strawberries, a principal crop in Pasadena until Pearl Harbor, when the locals went over to petrochemicals. Farm and Ranch Club members were sympathetic once they understood the situation. I arranged a breakfast meeting in Oberholtzer Hall for representatives of the Pasadena School District, and there was immediate and substantial interest. A few weeks later we literally gave the farm away.

The department of agriculture remained, compounded by obligations to faculty members and to students. A particularly active, able and popular member of the instructional staff, Professor John Carter, was chairman, and his wife Evelyn, formerly secretary to Vice-President Terrel Spencer, was now on Mr. Cullen's secretarial staff. This latter coincidence was of course never mentioned by the Carters, and Mr. Cullen was as always careful to remain isolated from matters affecting individual members of the faculty or staff.

The solution, a compromise, came in 1957. At the April 1 meeting of the Board of Regents, a plan to convert the department of agriculture into a department of agricultural economics was approved. This allowed reasonable adjustments to be made, and agricultural economics was finally absorbed into the economics faculty. We had yielded the field to the Aggies, with a sigh of relief.

The Junior College matter, with the related question of whether or not to revert to highly integrated courses for freshmen and sophomores reminiscent of the General College, had, as indicated, concerned General Bruce because it was specifically referred to his administration by Mr. Mac.

Following his policy of awaiting action on academic decisions until his new provost could make a recommendation, the General bided his time until Dr. Williams could test the water; but as soon as he felt that he could, President Bruce asked for an opinion on Dr. Kemmerer's plan to resurrect the General College concept, along with an expanded Junior College Division.

Dr. Williams said that the president "told me about reassigning Charlie Hiller as dean of the Junior College and asked my opinion of Harvard Plan courses within that College. I told him that I would leave the Junior College as an administrative shell to pass out tuition rebates to our freshmen and sophomores, and hope to get rid of even the shell in time. Universities and junior colleges are two different leagues."

The General's response was, "So be it," although he continued to recognize the significance of the Junior College appropriations (which reached an annual level of $645,000 in the biennium ending August 31, 1958, and approached the $1 million mark before they ceased with the entrance of the University into the state stystem).

Before Clanton Williams turned to what he termed the "core problems" of deans, faculty salaries and fringe benefits, admissions, academic standards and curricula in engineering and education, he toned up a few other areas, even though some discontinued courses would not be phased out completely until as much as three years had elapsed. This took care of photography (with a very long termination period, to May 31, 1959), some of the more "esoteric" offerings Dr. Williams said he "had never heard of in any catalogue anywhere," all correspondence courses and, finally, 57 out of 58 extension courses, most of these in the College of Education.

After exhaustive interviews within the College of Engineering, which he noted with alarm would be due for a reaccreditation visit by representatives of the Engineers' Council for Professional Development (ECPD) within little more than a year, he recommended the elimination of about one-third of the courses currently listed and an expedited search for a new dean.

A promising candidate for this post was Frank M. Tiller, a 37-year-old chemical engineer with a doctorate from the highly respected University of Cincinnati, a long list of publications, teaching experience at his alma mater and at Vanderbilt University, and an established position in his sub-discipline of filtration research and in vector analysis. Dr. Tiller was marking time at Lamar State College of Technology, as dean of engineering and director of the research center, when he drew the attention of Houston executives, including a member of the Board of Regents, and noted the growing opportunities at the University of Houston. After a long interview with General Bruce and Dr. Williams, and dinner with them and their wives (to which he brought his own charming Ann, later a doctor of philosophy and professor), Dr. Tiller was named dean of the College of Engineering on March 14, 1955.

The new dean brought innovation, fresh energy, and accomplishment to his College almost immediately. Within weeks he had an agreement to install one of the first large-scale electronic digital computers (an IBM 650) on the campus for primary use within the College of Engineering. He was utilizing his knowledge of Spanish and Portuguese to launch the University into a series of international contracts in Ecuador, Brazil and elsewhere in Latin America. And he was adding faculty and curricular strength as he sought out weaknesses in preparation for the approach of the ECPD accreditation teams. Within the year, he was able to tell Dr. Williams and General Bruce that he was ready to go to Mr. Cullen with them to ask for a major grant with which to build a Cullen College of Engineering, estimated to cost about $5 million.

Clanton Williams' next stop was over at the College of Education, and he was quick to acknowledge to all concerned, "a natural suspicion of such colleges." He found, as he had feared, an over-proliferation of courses, a few mossbacks, and some fundamental attenuation of thrust and accomplishment.

The prescription was harsh: almost a third of the courses were to be abolished, and changes were recommended in the instructional and administrative staff. But Dean Arvin N. Donner, one of the landmarks of the campus with a well-established reputation in the region, accepted honest criticism in a constructive manner. The changes were made, without particular recriminations.

More than 20 years later, Dr. Williams wrote me: "I firmly believe that one of the finest things I ever did during half a century as an educator was to strengthen that (now) highly influential University of Houston College of Education."

The new provost was nearing the end of his review of the deans of the University as he ordered up a detailed study of the Graduate Division and turned his attention to the stewardship of H.J. Sawin, a brilliant, Harvard-trained paleontologist with limited experience in administration.

There was a heavy, unexpected loss in the College of Law, where the founding dean from 1947, the respected A.A. White, left on May 1, 1956 (although he would return later) to become general counsel for the Texas Gas Corporation. Newell H. Blakely, an able young professor with a demonstrated flair for administration, was named dean *ad interim*.

The downtown school, which Director James C. Taylor had brought from a beginning enrollment of less than 300 (in a crowded, dirty old building at Capitol and Fannin) to a student body of more than 1400, was Dr. Williams' next stop.[10]

The dean of faculties liked Director Taylor's enthusiastic, persistent approach, his dream of an eventual Continuing Education Center on the main campus, the unique and valuable role of the downtown school, the high regard in which the director was held by professional groups in real estate, accounting, insurance, distributive education and hotel management (for which the school had been conducting special courses almost since it was established in 1942), and the progress made in spite of major handicaps in facilities and equipment. He recommended that Director Taylor be promoted to dean, and this was done, effective September 1, 1956. He also expedited studies looking to a relocation of the downtown school in new leased quarters at Caroline and McKinney.

One other major change was in prospect on Dean's Row, but this would be delayed. It would finally involve the transfer of a senior administrator, and his replacement with a relatively new man, Alfred R. Neumann. But Dr. Neumann, a German scholar born in Frankfurt-am-Main who had come to Dr. Williams' attention as chairman of the Faculty Assembly, was still under trial in a new assignment as assistant to the vice-president for academic affairs.

Suddenly, as he neared the completion of his second full year at the University of Houston, there was a spreading rumor that Clanton Williams would be called back to the University of Alabama as president. I was already en route to a meeting in Milwaukee when I first heard this, and when I reached the hotel, delayed by a mid-November snowstorm blowing in from Lake Michigan, there was a call from General Bruce awaiting me.

"Clanton may leave us, to be president at Tuscaloosa," the General said, after I had apologized for calling him so late at his new home at 2121 Brentwood, "and just when he's doing such a good job with the deans and the faculty. What would you think of the regents making him president, and my becoming chancellor—and chief executive officer, of course?"

Some disastrous experiments involving the appointment of a chancellor and president on the same campus came immediately to mind, along with the immutable laws surrounding authority and responsibility; but I was speaking to a man many years my senior, a man I greatly respected and liked who had from the tone of his voice already made up his mind. Further, although I had already been promoted to Dr. Kemmerer's old post as assistant to the president, I was by far the junior member, in title, age and responsibilities, of the University's new quadumvirate. For just a moment, I remembered some of the best advice I had ever been given, by a distinguished Harvard professor who told our class as we left Cambridge for active duty, "You'll never get anywhere telling everyone 'yes' all the time; whatever you do, say 'no' if you think 'no.' Don't be a *jasager.*"[11]

In the idiom of today, however, I waffled completely, not issuing even the mildest of storm warnings or recommending a few discreet telephone calls to Alabama to check out the situation more completely. "General," I replied, "that should work out all right. I would certainly hate to lose Dr. Williams, not only because of what he is accomplishing as dean of faculties, but in terms of our gearing up for a fund drive." Having seen new budget projections through 1959 that clearly indicated the possibility of operating deficits at August 31 in each of the next three years, we were already testing the market and proposing key leaders from within the Board of Regents who might be particularly helpful in a special fund-raising effort.

Clanton Ware Williams was named president of the University of Houston at the regular meeting of the Board of Regents on Monday, December 10, 1956, and General Bruce was named chancellor and chief executive officer.

It all sounded so logical, in the statements I drafted for Mr. Cullen and for General Bruce. "These changes are being made," the chairman of the board said," to strengthen the top administrative organization of the University, in recognition of the increasingly complex problems the institution faces. The University needs both a president entrusted with internal affairs and a chancellor charged both with overall responsibility and external relationships. We are extremely fortunate in having in General Bruce and Dr. Williams two top men who are admirably suited for these posts."

Chancellor Bruce paid tribute to President Williams, in a short but gracious statement, and thanked the Board of Regents for their perceptive action freeing him for the proper development of future policies and programs of compelling significance to the progress of the University.

Dr. Williams liked to prepare his own speeches, releases and statements, even in first draft, writing on a legal brief pad in his sprawling but legible hand for transcription by his secretary, Eva Robertson. He also spoke well extemporaneously, if sometimes over-enthusiastically. I had recommended that there be a press conference following the dual appointments by the Board of Regents, realizing that the media would be anxious to question both the new chancellor and the new president, but principally the latter.

Little did I realize that this recommendation, readily accepted by all concerned, would signal before the Williams administration had barely begun, its inevitable and premature demise.

As expected, the media representatives moved in on President Williams, asking him a barrage of questions about his plans and prospective policies for the University. At first, his replies were fairly stereotyped, and they centered upon faculty-oriented matters, including the ongoing raising of admissions and academic standards. These were critical matters, but they had already been discussed in detail with General Bruce, approved and published in

Acta Diurna, the official University gazette. The replies showed the extent of the pivotal changes wrought by Dr. Williams in his opening two years at the University, and included the organization of the Deans' Conference as a replacement in part for the semi-moribund Executive Council,[12] the annual rotation of departmental chairmen, the seeking of a sharply higher percentage of faculty members with the doctorate, emphasis on scholarly publication or its equivalent, the overriding need for further improvement in faculty salaries and benefits, and some potentially catastrophic modifications for the non-diligent student. These included diagnostic testing for interest, aptitude, and achievement; new regulations on grade point average, academic warning, and suspension; non-credit remedial courses in English, mathematics, and science; and a major toughening of admission requirements for transfer students.

As he warmed to the task, however, the new president started to range far and wide in his direct answers to reporters at the press conference, and to add comments on everything from new buildings through long-range financing to the advisability of abandoning membership in the Missouri Valley Conference.

As the questioning, and President Williams' increasingly effusive comments continued, I began to watch General Bruce closely. While he had more of a hearing defect than most people realized, the General could hear rather well if he listened intently. He was listening very intently, and he did not like what he heard. As Dr. Williams ventured more and more into areas that might well be considered General Bruce's responsibility, I saw the General's head go back, his eyes narrow and his eyebrows shoot up. In a moment, he looked directly at me, and nodded toward the tiny notebook in front of him. As I watched, he took out his blue Scripto pencil, carefully adjusted the point, and wrote the following note, which he passed on to me: "Make certain that they understand that I am the Chief Executive Officer." The words "I" and "Chief Executive Officer" were heavily underscored.

I managed to shut down the press conference a few moments later, but the damage had been done. Andrew Davis Bruce and Clanton Ware Williams were gentlemen and friends, and colleagues together in a high cause. So they would remain. Yet from that afternoon of December 10, 1956, they were rivals for leadership in a situation that deteriorated slowly but steadily, until the fiasco of a chancellor-president relationship had to be terminated, and new leadership (fortunately available) finally installed.

There was no sudden cataclysm; rather, an inevitable erosion, as one proud and able man realized that he had maneuvered himself into an irredeemable situation in which elements of the faculty (and to some extent, large segments of the overall University community as well as of the general public) would never again identify him unmistakably as first consul and undisputed leader; and another man of equally fine character, marked ability, and good will saw that his efforts would now always be clouded or frustrated by the everpresent question of who was really running the show at the University of Houston.

Charles F. Hiller, Ph. D., whose crimson Harvard robes are sorely missed in the Commencement processions, once observed to me that conflict at the top characterized the opening 33 years of the University of Houston, and may be indispensable to the ongoing progress of an institution. In the turbulence and unrest typical of high-level rivalries, the challengers must gather their *sherpas* around them, leave the security of the Himalayan rest camp, and strike out for Annapurna, even in a snowstorm. Everyone on the expedition benefits from the excitement; the pure, rarified atmosphere; and the sense of heightened competition as the two contenders head for the peak. Instead of stasis, and gradual atrophy, there is constant movement—even though it may be agitated, erratic and sometimes retrograde.

So it was at the University of Houston, in the years between the appointment of Dr. Williams as president and the end of the Bruce administration on August 31, 1961. There was, in retrospect, remarkable progress despite the discord between chancellor and president. And much history was made. For between 1957 and 1961, both General Bruce and Dr. Williams made quantum jumps forward, with yeoman assistance from Mr. Mac and a new officer of the University, Philip Guthrie Hoffman.

As something of an orchestrator and facilitator, I was able to play a major role in many of the projects of this crucial four-year span that brought the University of Houston to the modern era—and I saw it all, either from the inner sanctum or from the 50-yard line.

Philip Guthrie Hoffman was born August 6, 1915, in the historic old Japanese city of Kobe at the eastern end of the Inland

Sea. The son and only child of Benjamin Philip and Florence Guthrie Hoffman,[13] he was five years old before he set foot on U.S. soil in 1920. His father had become a professor of religion at Pacific Union College, a small Seventh Day Adventist institution founded at Angwin, just north of San Francisco, in 1882. Here he took the baccalaureate in 1938, after two years at George Washington University in the nation's capital. There are suppressed stories of these days, concerning "Hot Lips" Hoffman's abilities as a trumpet soloist in the college band.

Although his primary field was history, Phil Hoffman had a strong minor in business administration, and he found a position as credit manager of the Harding Sanitarium at Worthington, Ohio (near Columbus) after graduation from Pacific Union. Here he met Mary Harding, niece of President Warren G. Harding and member of a prominent Ohio family with a tradition of producing skilled physicians and medical specialists. They were married on a day that Philip G. Hoffman would have occasion to remember, August 31, in 1939. The young couple decided that Phil's career lay in the academic world, and he resumed his studies soon after the marriage, this time at the University of Southern California. He graduated with the master of arts in history in 1942, just in time to serve almost three years at the Naval Intelligence branch on Nebraska Avenue in Washington, D.C.[14]

After the war, Phil Hoffman officially began his academic career, with an appointment as instructor in history at Ohio State University from 1946-1949. During this period he completed his doctorate, in a unique area of American history—the effects of the Revolutionary War on the founding of Australia. The terminal degree was awarded in 1948.

The next year, Dr. Hoffman became assistant professor of history and director of arts and sciences extension services at the University of Alabama; he was promoted to associate professor in 1951. At Tuscaloosa, he and Mary formed a close friendship with Clanton Williams and his attractive brunette wife Claudine, she of the marvelously liquid Alabama accent. Dr. Hoffman was growing more visible as an administrator, although he was also an able and popular professor and was named national president of Phi Alpha Theta, the honor society in history, in 1952.

After "Clancy" Williams, as he was called at Tuscaloosa, was recalled to active duty in the Korean War, Dr. Hoffman accepted a post on the other side of the continent, as vice-dean of the General Extension Division and associate professor of history in the Oregon state system of higher education. In 1955, Dr. Hoffman was promoted to dean of the General Extension Division, as he began to broaden his training and experience as an administrator substantially. A year later, he became dean of the faculty and professor of history at Portland State College.

Phil Hoffman had maintained contact with Clanton Williams, and Dr. Williams had specific interest in his former colleague as he saw that the University of Houston would need more administrative talent, both as replacement personnel and for new positions. When he was named president, on December 10, 1956, it was with the understanding that he would be allowed to recommend a new vice-president.

He thought immediately of Phil Hoffman, who now had 10 solid years of varying experience in academic administration and teaching.

President Williams next looked for a likely occasion and date, and Dr. Hoffman was asked to make the long flight in from Portland as principal speaker for the second Honors Day luncheon on March 15, 1957. Alfred R. Neumann, recently appointed assistant to the president, was master of ceremonies at the Oberholtzer Hall affair, and he and I helped usher the visitor around the campus later. The reaction was overwhelmingly positive. Phil Hoffman was perceived as an intelligent, pleasant and handsome man, obviously mature beyond his years, yet neither a greybeard nor a *wunderkind,* with a solid track record. Where I inquired, there was literally no one against him; many hoped he would exchange the Pacific Northwest for the Southwest as soon as possible.

What I immediately liked about Philip G. Hoffman, in addition to his personal qualities and ability to arm-wrestle successfully with the deans, key chairmen, and directors, was his reserved ambition—his peaceful but trenchant mien; Phil Hoffman was coasting a bit, and looking for larger things while he gained strength and experience. There was the look of quiet assurance and inner calm that one sees in someone with great potential. He seemed to comprehend quickly the myriad problems before us in development, to be willing to assist directly in community relations, image-building and fund-raising, while supporting these functions as an administrator. Finally, I was impressed by his interest in intercollegiate athletics. This was one of my chief concerns, since it had direct ties to overall development and to the personal interest of powerful members of the Board of Regents who were already making certain that I spent appropriate time with the Athletic Advisory Council.

When General Bruce and President Williams each asked me for my opinion on Dr. Hoffman, I told them both the same thing: "He looks like a winner." The conclusion was foregone. Dr. Williams knew that he had to have Dr. Hoffman, and General Bruce had already begun introducing and describing him as "my candidate."

Philip Guthrie Hoffman was named vice-president and dean of faculties on June 10, 1957, effective "as soon as possible in July." I was named vice-president for University development, effective immediately, at the same meeting of the Board of Regents. General Bruce (to whom I reported throughout the Williams presidency) asked if I would object to Dr. Hoffman's appointment being announced first. I told him that I would have no objection whatsoever, and that I was extremely pleased over both appointments.

Philip Hoffman arrived on time for the main events on the crowded 1957-1961 calendar at the University of Houston, though he missed some pivotal events that took place while in his final months at Portland State College. The most significant of these was a fundamental change in the outlook of Hugh Roy Cullen and the Board of Regents, and thereby in the fundamental philosophy and policies of the University. Mr. Cullen had become gradually aware that the University of Houston had outgrown his ability to support it almost singlehandedly. The institution would have to seek, and obtain, far wider community understanding and support, or else depart from its original role as the Mecca of opportunity for those who could not go elsewhere for an education. In this process there would have to be a conversion to what some of the regents and governors were to call the "Southern Methodist University pattern" of relatively high tuition and much smaller enrollments.

There were alternatives, of course, including tax support,[15] but this was still anathema to Mr. Cullen and to virtually all the regents.

Soon after I had joined General Bruce's staff, Colonel Bates asked me to stop by for a visit, "sometime soon when you are downtown." I found out from his always-knowledgeable secretary, Virginia Harris, that he was free for a time the next afternoon.

The Colonel wanted to know how I was getting along, but he also wanted, as usual, more specific reactions: How soon could we begin some actual fund-raising, and what were some of the preparatory steps the Board of Regents could help with? I told him that some kind of special fund-raising project might be feasible early in 1957. First, however, we must get away from the idea, widely held in the community, that the University of Houston was Mr. Cullen's responsibility[16]; proceed with a long-range program of image-building, stressing the many institutional strengths we were discovering; and reinforce even more that short-cut to recognition in U.S. higher education, intercollegiate athletics.

Being more specific, I told the Colonel also that the Board of Regents might consider naming advisory committees in different areas of the University in order to bring as many community leaders as possible to the campus and to involve them with the individual colleges and departments.

The Colonel was ahead of me. He agreed with the idea of advisory committees, and we subsequently formed more than 30 of these with the close cooperation of the deans and departmental chairmen, with an aggregate membership in excess of 400; but Colonel Bates wanted my thoughts about a major expansion of the Board of Regents wherein as many as 50 prominent citizens across the spectrum of the business, professional and cultural community would be added to the governing board. Legal questions would be surmounted by retaining the present regents as regents, and being certain that only regent-governors established quorums, made motions, and cast votes.

I was enthusiastic about this on several scores, especially because it was in effect a statement from Mr. Cullen that he and Mrs. Cullen and the Cullen Foundation would continue to provide major support for the University, but must now transfer part of an increasingly heavy burden elsewhere. And I saw the Board of Governors as the source of both manpower and influence in support of a broad-based fund drive.

The Board of Governors was organized during the late fall of 1956, through personal letters and telephone calls from Mr. Cullen himself. Its first meeting was held on January 21, 1957, in Oberholtzer Hall. The total of 71 persons who served on the Board of Governors from its inception until August 31, 1963 (when it was disbanded in favor of a "new" Board of Regents appointed by Governor John B. Connally, six of whose nine members had been on the Board of Governors) constituted with few exceptions a remarkable muster roll of the power structure of Houston 20 years ago.[17]

At the organizational meeting, it was obvious that Colonel Bates had kept development and fund-raising well in mind in his discussions with Mr. Cullen on the Board of Governors and how it should be oriented.

Two of the five committees announced by Mr. Cullen were Development Planning (DP) and Development Ways and Means (DW&M), both with able co-chairmen and members. One of the more active governors, T.C. (Bud) Evans, was already serving as president of the Athletic Advisory Council, a fund-raising operation administered through the Development Division. President Williams was given, as was appropriate, ample time for an able, but somewhat long presentation on the academic situation; General Bruce, Mr. Mac, and I were all on the program for summaries of fiscal and developmental problems.

At the conclusion of the opening session, bi-monthly meetings of the Board of Governors were calendared for the next year, it being understood that the Executive Committee was standing-by for more frequent sittings, as required. The University, especially with the addition of advisory committees which I was already organizing with assistance from the deans and departmental chairmen involved, was beginning an era of far wider interaction with the community.

In the consequential area of intercollegiate athletics, the Athletic Advisory Council provided the mechanism for emphasis that everyone agreed had to be kept on major sports. Under the energetic and effective presidency of T.C. Evans, the Council provided both the enthusiasm and the athletic scholarships underlying new successes in football, and saw unexpected dividends in golf, a sport in which the Cougars suddenly assumed national dominance.[18]

I turned immediately to the DP and DW&M Committees for leadership and support in fund-raising, and was never disappointed. W. Stewart Boyle, as chairman of DW&M, was a particularly resourceful and helpful member of the Board of Governors, and Mr. Cullen, Colonel Bates, Judge Elkins, Charles Fleetwood and others gave key assistance.

I got useful ideas from quick trips to Southern Methodist in Dallas, where an annual "Sustentation Drive" was staged, and to Northwestern University, which was conducting a uniquely successful campaign each fall for contributions from Chicago business and industry. Regents Robertson and Fleetwood flew me over to New Orleans one day for what was to be an hour's visit with Joseph M. Jones, an outstanding lawyer serving as chairman of the governing body of Tulane University, to discuss a community-wide campaign shaping up there. We found ourselves guests of honor at a luncheon for 50 civic leaders active in the Tulane fund-raising drive, at the Boston Club.

Stewart Boyle, Ralph Frede, and I decided that we would recommend a difficult type of fund-raising to cover estimated operating deficits until the University could build up the corpus, and thereby the income, of its endowment fund, and simultaneously effect operating economies. We felt that it was too soon for a more traditional campaign, but that there might be enough influence on the Board of Governors to make such an unusual approach successful. Our recommendation was accepted, and thus was born the Living Endowment Association (LEA), donors to which would contribute as a "living endowment" the estimated $1.8 million required to make up operating deficits through August 31, 1960.

The deficits, it was explained, were due to rising costs and the extremely small endowment fund at the University of Houston; the latter produced only a fraction of the percentage of total income which a private university must expect from endowment income.

As to operating economies, after the LEA campaign was launched the Cullen Foundation agreed to underwrite a management study by the nationally known firm of McCormick, Cresap and Paget. The study created a minor panic in faculty ranks until it was explained again and again that it would exclude course content, methods of instruction, and the evaluation of individual members of the instructional staff.

As organization of the LEA drive proceeded, a formal dinner was held at the Houston Club March 14, 1957. This honored Mr. and Mrs. Cullen, Mrs. Jesse H. Jones, the trustees of Houston Endowment, Inc., and the trustees of the M.D. Anderson Foundation. A secondary purpose for the dinner, in addition to paying tribute to major donors to the University, was to expose the power structure to the institution's need for additional support, and to some upper-echelon propaganda regarding the need for corporate contributions to higher education. The principal speaker was James H. Pipkin, a senior vice-president of the Texas Company with many close friends in the petroleum industry.

The dinner was pronounced a success, especially in comparison to a November 21, 1955, affair attempted in the Green Room of Oberholtzer Hall before a support group such as the Board of Governors was available. The one disappointment was that Mr. Cullen, already failing physically, could not attend. Leopold Meyer, the master of ceremonies, had hoped with the rest of us, until the dinner actually began, that the chairman of the board might still be able to attend, but this was not to be.

Mr. Cullen had effectively assured the success of the first LEA campaign by going down to Judge Elkins' office and asking him to serve as chairman.[19] The judge replied that he would do anything for Mr. Cullen, but to make him co-chairman and get another co-chairman to do the follow-up after he had made some telephone calls and sent out a few letters.

This is how Stewart Boyle (the other co-chairman) and I found ourselves in Judge Elkins' office on a Monday morning in May, 1957. We had arrived a little early, and Mr. Boyle remarked to me that the judge seemed to be in unusually good humor when he came in a few moments later and nodded to us as we sat in the anteroom.

We were ushered in and shown chairs. The judge's secretary was busily smoothing and stacking currency which he was pulling from both pockets, and we soon learned the reason for the judge's cheerful disposition. He had been on a traditional jaunt to the Kentucky Derby (the same expedition that had reportedly kept him from the May 1950 dinner honoring President Oberholtzer) with his friends J.S. Abercrombie and W.A. (Bill) Smith, and he had the winner.

After the cash was neatly sorted, Mr. Boyle thanked Judge Elkins for accepting the co-chairmanship of the LEA campaign, to get things started. "Well," said the judge, "Roy said you'd have a list." Mr. Boyle produced one, with the 10 prime prospects he felt the judge would be most likely to call, telephone numbers included. Judge Elkins looked it over a moment, checked three names, and handed the list to his secretary when she answered the buzzer. "See if I can talk to them," he asked. We started to leave but were signalled to sit down.

The first call came through. It was to a well-known and prosperous Houstonian, financed by the judge's bank and represented by his law firm. The deal was explained tersely: "Roy and Lillie can't keep that thing going out there all by themselves, and the town needs it more and more. Some of us are pitching in to help, and I thought I'd put you down for ten thousand."

There was a momentary silence at the other end, and some sort of mumbled comment. "That's fine," Judge Elkins replied, "and you understand, that's $10,000 a year for three years. We're doing this thing all at once, so we don't have to come around again in '58 and '59. Thanks. I know Roy Cullen will appreciate it." The judge hung up, and waited for the next call to be placed. The same day, he sent Hugh Roy Cullen a letter, pledging $150,000 from his law firm, payable at $15,000 annually through 1966. Mr. Cullen telephoned to thank him, and asked, "how about the bank?" Judge Elkins sent him a second letter, pledging the same amount under the same terms from the City National.

Just over a year later, on June 3, 1958, Colonel Bates presided at an LEA report luncheon at the Rice Hotel. Other sponsors of the event were Judge Elkins, Lamar Fleming, Jr., Mr. Boyle and Tom P. Walker of the Board of Governors, and Mrs. Oveta Culp Hobby. It was announced that $1.4 million of the three-year, $1.8 million goal had been raised in cash or in pledges. Chairman Jones of Tulane University congratulated Houston for its support of the University, and urged continuing assistance to the institution.[20]

The first LEA campaign, which went over the goal a few months later, was not as quickly or as simply accomplished as those telephone calls in Judge Elkins' office; but it was successful, and it became the pattern for many campaigns at the University of Houston since.

But there was a sad note at the Rice Hotel luncheon, as there had been so many other occasions since July 4, 1957, the day the University of Houston lost its greatest benefactor and friend, Hugh Roy Cullen. There had been an outpouring of sorrow, and tributes from every segment of the University community, repeated at campus meetings and ceremonies for almost a year. Yet there was the realization that if Hugh Roy Cullen's days on earth had to come to an end, how fitting that he went to his reward on Independence Day, the Day of Patriots, the day that John Adams and Thomas Jefferson, two men Mr. Cullen greatly admired, died within hours of one another.

Meanwhile, Vice-President Hoffman's arrival and quick, positive adjustment to the University was already proving the wisdom of his appointment.

Phil Hoffman almost immediately freed Clanton Williams from some routine yet vital administrative chores. This enabled Dr. Williams to get on with more essential matters, such as recruiting distinguished professors (a happy task made possible by a providential $1.5 million grant which Colonel Bates arranged in 1956 to establish six M.D. Anderson chairs); expediting the accreditation of additional colleges and other components; building up the library, still woefully small; increasing the percentage of Ph.D.'s in lesser faculty positions; battling for higher salary schedules and better fringe benefits for the instructional staff; determining the few areas in which it might be possible to add doctoral programs, in spite of financial stringencies; and countering stubborn opposition to the new, far tougher regulations affecting admissions and academic standards.

Dr. Hoffman was also an immediate comfort to General Bruce, both as a competent addition to the top command and in another and rather singular way: It did not occur to the chancellor that a new provost might free President Williams for excursions onto turf that the General regarded as his own. Instead, he reasoned, an able and active vice-president, dean of faculties might keep the president's energies in channels and functions well identified with internal, faculty-oriented business. That, at least, is how I interpreted what Chancellor Bruce said to me as we walked together to the fall 1957 meeting of the general faculty. "How is Dr. Hoffman getting along?" I asked. "Very well," the reply came, "and I hear that he keeps our new president plenty busy with faculty matters."

Whether this was wishful thinking or not, I detected almost from Dr. Hoffman's arrival on campus a tendency for General Bruce to withdraw from areas leading to confrontation with Clanton Williams. This averted, the chancellor zeroed in on some really pressing problems, both old and new, that were becoming more urgent every day. Among these were growing deficits, exacerbated by constantly higher costs and the threat of sharply lower enrollments (especially if almost inevitable increases in tuition were announced); his broader involvement with the much larger governing body represented by the new Board of Governors; the unmet need for new buildings, far more endowment and broad-based support; and what would soon surface as the central dilemma—a command decision on whether or not the University of Houston was to continue as a private institution. If not, there would be a fresh crisis and confrontation with the newly organized Texas Commission on Higher Education, and eventually, with the State Legislature.

The year 1956 had been a vintage one for gifts to endowment, in particular those that would help build faculty strength and morale. In addition to the $1.5 million grant to create the M.D. Anderson distinguished professorships, two anonymous donors increased an earlier contribution of Anderson, Clayton and Company stock from $250,000 to $600,000, and the Ford Foundation provided $695,000 (increased to $1,369,000 by a second installment of $674,000 in 1957).[21]

There was a provision in the Ford Foundation grant that it must be used for a minimum of 10 years to supplement faculty salaries. This was agreeable to the administration (and especially to President Williams) as well as the Board of Regents; it gained deserved approbation for the University from Ford Foundation officials, who perceived the Anderson professorships and the Fleming-Clayton gifts correctly as the exact type of local support for higher faculty compensation they hoped to stimulate.

Clanton Williams was a skilled and innovative recruiter, especially of top-flight professors at the zenith of their careers, or those facing mandatory retirement. He brought in Louis Brand, a distinguished mathematician from Cincinnati and Harvard as the first M. D. Anderson professor; then he added two top scholars already in residence, T. N. Hatfield in physics and Dwight A. Olds in law; he brought Charles I. Silin, an expert in the language and culture of France, with degrees from Harvard, Johns Hopkins, Lyons, and the Sorbonne and long teaching and research experience at Johns Hopkins and Tulane; and he enlisted Earl V. Moore, the grand old man of the famed School of Music at the University of Michigan, to form what he termed a "new concentration of excellence in teaching and research and scholarly activity." Nor was Dr. Williams disappointed in his significant additions to faculty strength. The Anderson professors at or beyond retirement age took fresh inspiration from their new posts and surroundings, bringing both new vigor and distinction to their departments. Younger men such as "Buddy" Hatfield and Dwight Olds, encouraged by deserved appointments, responded with higher levels of research activity, teaching excellence, and scholarly output that had corresponding benefits in the physical sciences and in the College of Law.

Next, President Williams brought back Americo Castro, the noted Hispanist who had joined the faculty in 1955 only to return temporarily to Princeton University; persuaded Andrea Radoslav Tsanoff, the noted philosopher retired by Rice Institute,[22] and William Prescott Webb, the great regional historian, to begin new careers at the University of Houston; and found to his amazement that Winifred E. Garrison, who had joined the faculty at the age of 77, was still a gifted teacher of philosophy and a prolific writer and editor in his eighties.

Dr. Williams had his successes in accreditation and in building up the library collections and budgets, too. Five departments within the College of Engineering, a potential trouble spot, were reaccredited, and new or continuing professional approvals were granted in law, pharmacy, and optometry. Music, psychology, and architecture were pronounced ready for visits by accrediting teams. Further, there were reassuring meetings with representatives of the Southern Association on certain criticisms raised before overall accreditation was first granted the University on December 2, 1954. Clanton Williams' long-established friendships and professional relationships within the academic world were obviously helpful in this encouraging progress.

On a brief August vacation in 1955, Clanton Williams attempted an early-morning visit to the Anderson Library on the very first day of the new academic year, to emphasize the consequence he placed upon this central component. To his horror, he found a sign on the front door:

CLOSED
STAY COMPLETELY AWAY
DANGEROUS CHEMICALS

The place was being fumigated for *Lasioderma serricorne* (tobacco beetle). But the library was making remarkable strides. At 56,000 volumes when the new facility opened in 1951, the collections reached 128,389 in 1954, and were up another 13 percent, to 145,379, a year later. Even more significant, the unbelievably low expenditures for the library which had plagued the institution into the early 1950's went to $191,917, and jumped another 26 percent to $241,060 in 1955.

Some of this progress was attributable to Leopold L. Meyer, who was inspired by the tradition of his fellow Galvestonian and bibliophile, Henry Rosenberg, to organize a Friends of the Library group for the University of Houston in 1940.[23] The Friends of the Library gave substantial assistance to the University for almost a decade before becoming inactive in 1949. Mr. Meyer reactivated the organization at the request of President A. D. Bruce in 1956, and it has become progressively stronger since, under Charles A. Saunders and others.

One of President Williams' most pronounced successes was in persuading young Ph.D.'s to throw in their lot with the University, as he began to restructure the instructional staff around existing strength. In his first year, 24 new faculty members with terminal degrees were placed under contract. This trend continued and accelerated: by mid-term of the 1957-1958 year, 47 percent of the faculty had the Ph.D. This was 12 percent above the average for 1,000 colleges and universities, and represented a gain of 24 percent in the number of Ph.D.'s at the University of Houston in only two years.

These data, reported to the faculty on February 20, 1957, met with a mixed response, especially when President Williams pointed out that the institution was 14 percent under the national average for Ph.D. members of the teaching staff when he arrived on the scene. The next week, eight members of the faculty applied for special leaves being granted in some cases for those still young enough, affluent enough, and motivated sufficiently to pursue a terminal degree.

At another meeting of the general faculty, on September 12, 1958, Dr. Williams noted that those hired since his arrival now outnumbered those on board when he assumed office four years earlier, 54 to 46 percent. "It's like the bloody Harvard Law School," one malcontent muttered aloud. "Look to your left, and then look to your right. One of the three of us will be gone next fall." But the able seemed to find the University, and to stay there, in Clanton Williams' time, along with the earlier settlers of established competency. It was the mediocre and the marginal, in the main, who moved on.

President Williams had reason to emphasize faculty salaries, which were still so low as to invite constant comparison and criticism. This was exacerbated by dramatic improvements at Rice Institute, where the industrialist George R. Brown had begun to enforce sharply higher salary schedules as a keystone achievement of his long and effective chairmanship of the Board of Trustees. The University of Houston administration was blamed even for a rise in the Social Security tax, from a now-minuscule two percent to 2¼ percent, and for a legislatively mandated increase in the contributions to the Texas Retirement System which became effective July 1, 1957.[24]

Clanton Williams would look back upon his hard-won victories to continue a modest advancement of faculty compensation, and of some fringe benefits, as perhaps his signal accomplishment—it added strength in both the recruiting and the retention of a competent teaching staff.

Meanwhile, he had other gains to contemplate: There was a continuing fray over new regulations on warning and suspension of academically marginal students, a "cheating policy," revisions in grading standards, and the institution of non-credit remedial courses in specific subjects; but there was enough acceptance to permit broad enforcement, and to plan even stronger measures which Dr. Hoffman would announce effective December 31, 1958. The Board of Regents had affirmed a policy of considerably more faculty promotions, to encourage the scholarly achievements President Williams wrote about in a regular column in *Acta Diurna*. There were 57 promotions for 1956-1957 alone, for example, against a dozen or less in earlier years. And the achievements continued.

Although a damper had been placed on some thriving, and expensive "Study Centers" in Mexico and Guatemala, the number of foreign students (I later insisted that the term be changed to "international" students, there being a certain amount of opprobrium in "foreign," and this designation fortunately stuck) grew to 188 from 53 countries in 1957, with most of these visitors coming from Canada and from the nations of Central and South America.[25]

The University began to attract important scholarly meetings. In 1956, the small but enterprising School of Architecture, for example, brought Professor Serge Chermayeff of Harvard University; Victor Gruen, pioneer in the design of shopping centers; Marcel Breuer, the noted disciple of Walter Gropius of Bauhaus fame; Finn Juhl, Finnish furniture designer; and John McLane Johansen, architectural writer, critic and expert on spatial problems. This was followed with an appearance by the iconoclast and genius, Frank Lloyd Wright.

Dr. Williams now saw Channel 8 as a possible means of preparing for what he described as "the coming student explosion of the 1960's." He worked with John C. Schwarzwalder, the gifted stormy petrel of Channel 8, but was unable to reconcile Dr. Schwarzwalder's dream of a College of Communications, built around a Radio-Television-Film Center (and headed by Dean Schwarzwalder), with the reality of ever-present budgetary restrictions. The matter was referred topside, where it met with a firm veto from General Bruce. Dr. Schwarzwalder left for icier climes, as general manager of a new educational television station for Minneapolis-St. Paul (where he remained almost 20 tumultuous but occasionally triumphant years.) Dr. Williams replaced Dr. Schwarzwalder with John W. Meaney, who had a Ph.D. in English and wide experience in television and film operations, and he made Roy E. Barthold program director, James J. Byrd chief engineer, James L. Bauer film operations director, and Patrick E. Welch chairman of the radio-television department, all effective January 23, 1957.

Finally, Dr. Williams named Joseph R. Crump, a talented engineer from Harvard, director of research, and he decided what to do about two other deanships that bothered him. He would not act precipitately, but in due course he would send H. J. Sawin, the graduate dean, back to the classroom, transfer R. Balfour Daniels from the deanship of the College of Arts and Sciences to Dr. Sawin's old post; and move up his able protégé Alfred R. Neumann (who was showing more promise all the while, including a few head-on collisions with obdurate departmental chairmen) to dean of arts and sciences, one of the most demanding assignments on campus. This change, he reckoned, would be helpful in many ways, including support for the delicate matter of adding doctoral programs for competent, ambitious, and restive faculties in chemistry, chemical engineering, and economics. The programs were overdue, but it was difficult to add them while other promising departments were being told about the dire fiscal situation.

The laudable progress in the academic field helped General Bruce, the development staff, Board of Governors,[26] and Living Endowment Association volunteers in their preoccupation with fund-raising, both to balance rising deficits and to provide new buildings. There were successes in this vital field as well, but Chancellor Bruce knew that the inescapable dilemma and approaching decision overshadowed everything: Was the University of Houston to remain a private institution, smaller, with progressively higher tuition and constricted role and scope and a differing mission? Or was it going over to the public sector, there to retain its broader mission and thrust through underlying tax support?

Just as the Board of Governors began to struggle with this enigma, Fate intervened to deal some cards of her own.

Farris Block called me about 11 p.m. on the evening of January 22, 1958. "Very bad news," he said, "General Bruce has had a heart attack on board an Eastern Air Lines plane. They had him on oxygen over Lake Charles 10 minutes ago, and he's expected on the ground here in about 20 minutes. There's an ambulance at the field, on standby."

"Does Mrs. Bruce know?" I asked. "She must be with him; no answer at the residence." I remembered that Mrs. Bruce had gone to Washington, D.C. with the General two days before. I asked my own physician, Dr. William K. Brown, to go on out to the airport, and as I was leaving for there myself, Farris Block called back. "It's President Williams," he said, "not General Bruce. I assumed it was the General because I knew that he was in the East, and coming back tonight or tomorrow; but Dr. Williams left suddenly last night on a surplus property negotiation, became ill, and booked this flight back. Eastern's first message reported only that it was the 'head of the University of Houston'."

The heart attack was a reasonably mild one, even though President Williams could not have visitors other than his wife and the two daughters, Pamela and Eleanor, for almost two weeks in hospital. And he had to convalesce until well into the spring at the new home that Clarence M. Malone had provided for the president of the University, at 2608 South Calumet.

Dr. Williams, of course, stayed closely in touch with his responsibilities at the University, as soon as Dr. Brown would allow him to. But by the time he was back in full harness, in September 1958, there had been subtle and irreversible changes that weakened his position on the campus and within the governing board. Not the least of these was a growing disposition on the part of Chancellor Bruce, the regents, and the faculty to look to Dr. Hoffman for academic leadership.

General Bruce had moved independently on such matters as obtaining an additional $500,000 from Houston Endowment, Inc., to complete the Fred J. Heyne Building, and the consummation of a $5 million grant from the Cullen Foundation for the long-delayed Engineering Building, first announced in March 1957. In President Williams' absence, however, the chancellor tended to involve himself considerably more in the details of the Heyne Building,[27] and in what was essentially academic planning for the new home of the College of Engineering (now renamed the Cullen College of Engineering).

Vice-President Hoffman, though meticulous about keeping President Williams informed, and in seeking his direction and approval when it could be sought, still found it necessary to discharge duties falling normally within the scope of the Office of the President, and was fully authorized to do so. Additionally, General Bruce had been in office four years when Clanton Williams returned to an approximation of his normal schedule in the fall of 1958. By this time, the General understandably felt far more comfortable in the academic arena, with individual members of the faculty, and with both academic and extracurricular matters concerning the student body.[28]

Thus, we saw Chancellor Bruce taking a prominent role in the fifth anniversary of the Honors Program for outstanding students, on May 20, 1958; at a reception in the Anderson Library at which Vassar Miller, the handicapped student poet already moving to deserved national recognition, gave a memorable reading of her work; at the fifth anniversary of KUHT, on May 23, 1958; and in planning sessions to honor the original faculty in 1959—all of these activities falling more normally within the absent President Williams' ken and function.[29]

General Bruce launched a unique fund-raising project in 1958, when he revived the idea of an expansive chapel and decided to raise $500,000 for an 18,500-square foot Religious Center with a central chapel, 16 offices for campus chaplains of the principal faiths, and conference rooms. The plan was to have major denominations accept quotas based on memberships among the student body. I sought an appointment with His Excellency Wendelin J. Nold, the Roman Catholic bishop of Galveston-Houston, through D. L. Connelly, a papal knight on the Board of Governors, with Mr. Connelly as spokesman.

The appointment was quickly granted. We explained the project, and Bishop Nold asked some searching questions. We gave the answers, and were told that we would be hearing from the diocese. After several weeks, I received a postal saver envelope mailed from Philadelphia, where Monsignor John J. Roach had been visiting his family. Inside was a check for $50,000, a contribution for our Roman Catholic students.

We found, however, that all denominations are not as efficiently organized as the Roman Catholics. In most cases it was necessary to go to individual congregations through campaign co-chairmen. The response was cordial, and in time, positive; but two years passed and the goal had not been reached. This brought about the only instance of reverse fund-raising in which I was ever involved.

In the fall of 1960, Monsignor Roach telephoned me to ask how the campaign was progressing. "It's solid, but slow," I replied.

"No contracts let yet?"

"No, monsignor; in the spring, perhaps."

"Well, then, do you suppose I could get our money back for awhile?" Monsignor Roach continued, "and you understand you can have it again when you need it."

I thought quickly, but there seemed to be no escape. "Why, ... I don't see why not, monsignor," was my reply.

"And God bless, could I get it today?" said the good monsignor.

So, I found myself down in my friend Mr. Mac's office (where I often went for guidance and counsel), asking for a $50,000 refund check. This was provided, and a year later the Diocese of Galveston-Houston not only replaced the $50,000, but added $28,000 because the number of Roman Catholic students at the University had increased substantially since 1958.

The Religious Center, now the A. D. Bruce Religion Center, was built through the close cooperation and help of Howard Tellef Tellepsen, who was willing to construct this beautiful and functional facility in stages, as Ralph Frede, Mrs. Ray L. Dudley and I were able to locate more funds with the assistance of campaign general chairman W. H. (Bill) Avery, General Bruce and others. Mr. Frede finally obtained an anonymous $85,000 gift from a gracious lady keenly interested in religious activities on campus. This paid all the bills and closed our first really unique campaign at the University.

By the fall of 1958, the Board of Governors was moving inexorably toward a decision on the question of private versus public aegis. The General told me early in the semester to prepare a position paper on another tuition increase, from data supplied by various administrative offices. The data indicated that a tuition jump of 40 percent (from an average of $500 per year to $700) would be necessary to stem further operating deficits; even this would cover only $1.35 million of an estimated $1.51 million loss for 1959-1960.

The governors, however, were highly sensitive to enrollment figures for the fall, 1959, semester; these had dropped alarmingly to 11,592, from a total of 13,030 the previous September. The Finance Committee recommended only a maximum tuition increase of 30 percent, and this was adopted, leaving a deficit in the $500,000 to $550,000 range. After the matter was resolved, General Bruce said to me privately: "The die is cast; we'll have to go public." This meant state support, a preliminary study having already shown how impractical it would be to seek municipal tax dollars. Why should the citizens of Houston pay twice for public higher education—once for components of the state system outside Houston, and again for their own municipal university?

It would be only a few weeks, on November 30, 1959, before the Board of Governors voted unanimously to "seek full state tax support, preferably as an independent unit in the state system of higher education."[30]

As General Bruce's attention was more and more forcefully directed to the engulfing need to find a safe and logical harbor within the state system of higher education, Clanton Williams had suffered another defeat in his attempt to resume full power and influence after the hiatus of heart attack, recuperation and return. The high thrust was toward Austin, yet there seemed to be no place of consequence for him in the battles shaping up around the Commission on Higher Education and in the Legislature itself. And in the specific field of academic affairs, where he had made substantial progress before his illness, General Bruce was turning more and more to Philip G. Hoffman for key information, day-by-day administration, and recommendations. So was the faculty, even though Vice-President Hoffman maintained both his scrupulous respect for decorum, and his warm friendship for his boss and colleague, Clanton Williams.

President Williams made an excellent address at the meeting of the General Faculty on September 12, 1958, an occasion that he hoped would signal his return to the full presidency. He emphasized the need to continue praiseworthy progress in the raising of academic standards, and presented data showing that the University was retaining a considerably higher percentage of students in spite of demanding much better performance from them in the classroom.

The faculty members present, however, were far more interested in what Chancellor Bruce had to say about the developing campaign for full state support. The chancellor had feared that a substantial number of the instructional staff might be opposed to joining the public sector, dreading the possibility of substantial losses in academic freedom, and various types of bureaucratic regimentation. He encouraged questions after his presentation, but there was only silence; finally, a hand went up in the back of Cullen Auditorium. "Sir," said a young assistant professor, "we're not concerned about becoming a state university—the sooner the better; has anyone looked into the possibility of becoming a *federal* university? That's where the real money is."

By the time the Board of Governors took its historic vote endorsing full state support, on November 30, 1959, Clanton Ware Williams saw that it would be difficult for him to get back fully into the power structure—to say nothing of the ascendancy.

General Bruce was cordial enough, except for one short, fearful row[31]; but he seemed always preoccupied with the overriding need to breach the high walls of the state system of higher education, a battle that President Williams would not be asked to join.

Taking the realistic view, Dr. Williams began to look around Capitol Hill on trips to Washington, where he was involved in negotiations with Health, Education and Welfare and the General Services Administration that led to the acquisition of Camp Wallace, a 1,603-acre surplus infantry base, as a research center. He had powerful friends in Congress, including Senator Lister Hill and

Congressman Carl Elliott of Alabama, the authors of the National Defense Education Act who had sought his advice on this and related matters.[32]

In the spring of 1960, he struck paydirt on a combination bet involving the Pentagon and the State Department. The Burmese were looking for a man with just his background to establish the War College of the Union of Burma. I almost stumbled on this fact myself when I ran into Dr. Williams in his colonel's uniform at the coffee bar for the "D" ring, second floor of the Pentagon. I recognized the man he was talking to as a liaison officer for the State Department, but thought nothing of it, since I knew that Dr. Williams (then pursuing the promotion to brigadier general he was never to get), as I, was sometimes at the Pentagon on special tours of duty and might have occasion to contact persons from State.

Dr. Williams loved the University of Houston, and he had helped it to move with far more confidence and prospect of success, on the road to academic excellence. Perhaps, he must have reasoned, General Bruce will wish to retire after a decision is reached in Austin. After all, the chancellor would be 67 soon after adjournment of the 1961 Legislature, and he, 10 years younger than General Bruce, would be a logical successor, as chief executive officer.

When President Williams checked further, however, he was unable to discover any considerable support for his own advancement. He and Claudine had one close friend among the regents, but the General had several, with regular exposure to regents and governors alike; and Andrew Davis Bruce might have been born in 1894, but he was in vigorous health, his energy level constantly contradicted his age, and he seemed to be in full command of the situation.

There was also Vice-President Hoffman, Dr. Williams' own protégé in a sense, no matter how much General Bruce now claimed him —a man at the ideal age of 44 as the 1959-1960 academic year got under way, with unquestionable and growing qualifications as a university president, manifest faculty support, and the approbation of key members of the governing board.

On balance, Clanton Williams decided to quietly continue pursuing the appointment in Burma, curiously akin to the Armed Forces Staff College post from which General Bruce had come to the University, while he carefully watched further developments. But it was obvious that weighty decisions were imminent.

As the showdown in the State Capitol approached, General Bruce considered how much simpler, and perhaps more effective, it would be for the University to return to the organizational chart in effect before Dr. Williams' promotion to the presidency. I saw him studying this at his desk before one of my directors joined us for a meeting. He seemed in the summer of 1960 to yearn to regain the powers of the presidency, delegate them to Vice-President Hoffmann except for certain stipulated areas, and then get on with his normal external relationships as chancellor, plus the surpassing new complexities facing him in Austin.

Rumors were flying in the last days of the 1959-1960 academic year, and on Thursday, August 11, 1960, I had an unusual call from General Bruce that would resolve some of them. He asked me to come down to his office and to be prepared to stay for some time if necessary. I cancelled an appointment, and went down. We chatted at first about some aspects of Senate Concurrent Resolution 64, which Senator Robert W. Baker had been successful in passing during a special session of the Legislature. This instructed the Texas Commission on Higher Education (TCOHE) to study the feasibility of the University becoming part of the state system of higher education, and to report back to the 1961 Legislature. SCR 64 was a beginning move in our developing strategy.

After a few moments, the General said abruptly, "Clanton is going on a leave of absence. He'll be leaving right away. I would like for you to prepare a news release on his background and accomplishments with us, stating in general terms that he wants to explore new career possibilities, needs time to look into this, etc. The leave is to be announced by Colonel Bates, as chairman of the Board of Governors (a post to which the Colonel had been elevated at the first meeting after the death of Mr. Cullen, with Lamar Fleming, Jr., succeeding him as vice-chairman). Could you draft something and come back fairly soon? I would appreciate it."

When I returned with a draft, I pointed out that it should obviously include comments by Dr. Williams, who was at a meeting in Asheville, North Carolina. The General nodded and reached for the draft; he quickly read it, and approved it with the tiny pencilled "B" that was his imprimatur.

General Bruce looked directly at me for a long moment. "Someone needs to talk to Dr. Williams," he said. There was no doubt in my mind as to who had been selected to bell the cat.

"Can Leta get him on the telephone?" I asked. President Williams was located at his Asheville hotel. I told him I was with General Bruce, who had asked me to read him a proposed news release concerning his leave of absence; I read it to him and indicated where I proposed to insert his comments. He made a few minor corrections, said that he would call me back with a brief statement, and did so later.[33]

To this day, I am not certain whether or not I gave Clanton Williams the first news that he was going on a leave of absence; on balance, I doubt that I did. In any event, he took the job of establishing the War College of Burma and went on to become chief educational advisor for the Agency for International Development in New Delhi from 1963-1967; he accepted a similar assignment from the Institute of International Education in East Pakistan (now Bangladesh) from 1967-1970 and returned home to complete his many-faceted career as the first executive director of the Alabama Commission on Higher Education, from which he retired as executive director emeritus in 1974. He wrote me once that the "emeritus" rank was one he did not reach at the University of Houston.

Clanton Ware Williams died on November 10, 1975, at the age of 72 at Montgomery Air Force Base Hospital, Montgomery, Alabama, full of honors, accomplishments, and memories. His friend and colleague Philip G. Hoffman was a pallbearer at his funeral.

Dr. Hoffman said of the University of Houston's fourth president: "Dr. Williams served the University with distinction as vice president and dean of faculties and as president. His outstanding contribution to the University came at a critical time in the institution's development and was most influential in stimulating sound academic progress during this period. The University is a better institution today because of the leadership and influence of Dr. Williams. His many friends at the University and in the city will share the great personal loss which I feel in his passing."

Although I had always assumed that I would be assigned a key role in the struggle for membership in the state system of higher education, it was not until very late in 1959 that I realized the full extent of my involvement. General Bruce had asked me to work directly with him on plans for the all-important first objective of our campaign, the April 11, 1960, hearing before the TCOHE. This was progressing well, as it had to; without TCOHE approval, the odds against legislative endorsement would be insurmountable. But now the General was looking ahead to the second stage: he had asked me to recommend "the best lobbyist in the state—the man who can put this thing across," to be retained by a special committee of the governing board. The necessary fee was already pledged by a regent.

There was no difficulty in identifying the best lobbyist in Texas. He was—and probably still is—Edward (Ed) Clark, later ambassador to Australia and counselor to President Lyndon B. Johnson. An East Texan of brilliant mind, courtly appearance and unfailing gentility, Mr. Clark's talents as a lobbyist were so widely recognized that he became the subject of an article in the *Readers' Digest*, a questionable honor that his numerous and puissant clients regretted, but overlooked.[34]

Ed Clark was not available to the University of Houston, however, for a number of reasons, not the least of them his close connections with the University of Texas, where he took a law degree after the baccalaureate at Tulane University. Thus, I found myself with General Bruce in mid-December, 1959, meeting with the man widely regarded as a close rival of Mr. Clark in terms of effectiveness as a lobbyist: Searcy Bracewell. A former state senator and an exceptionally able attorney, he represented leading corporations and trade associations, and had contacts in virtually every area of state government, plus staunch and valuable ties to such diverse groups as Baptist ministers and lay leaders, savings and loan depositors, Texas A&M alumni, and the conservative wing of the Democratic party.

Searcy Bracewell was generally familiar with the plan to seek full state support for the University of Houston, and he listened attentively as General Bruce briefed him on the current situation. It was soon apparent that the chancellor was determined to recruit him for the upcoming battle. As soon as he could, Mr. Bracewell said, "General, you have a good, strong case; this city, and this state, must have a tax-supported University of Houston. I'll do what I can to help, as a friend and as a Houstonian. But my commitments are such that I cannot take on another assignment—especially one as demanding as this will be.

"You have the man, however," he concluded. "He knows the University, the regents and the governors, the news media, the city that will have to support your campaign. And he's been in the middle of a half dozen political battles, including the one that put Ben Ramsey in as lieutenant governor and presiding officer of the Senate."

He pointed to me. Later that afternoon, after some hurried telephone calls to Colonel Bates, Warren Bellows, Corbin Robertson and Senator Baker, General Bruce asked me to his office. He told me that he wanted me "to clear (my) desk of everything but this state support business, to be responsible for planning and operations of the April 11 TCOHE hearing, and (to) be ready to take up temporary residence in Austin beginning January 10, 1961, the opening day of the 57th Legislature."

This meant reorganizing my own staff; establishing an effective *modus operandi* acceptable to the General and to the key regents and governors; and setting up for Austin, both in terms of the TCOHE hearing and of relationships with Senator Baker and the Harris County delegation in the House of Representatives.

Reorganizing was a simple matter; the Development Division was still relatively small in 1960, and had then, as now, a group of able, dedicated directors: Walter Williams, Farris Block and Ralph Frede, plus the capable Annie Laurie Fambrough and Margaret Graves. I told the directors that they would have to assume a great deal more autonomy, at least until June 1, 1961, while providing special support for Austin-oriented projects and for operations such as a second Living Endowment Association (LEA) campaign now assigned to Ralph Frede.

Then I converted the central Office of Information into a hub of intelligence gathering and communications regarding the 181 members of the State Legislature, with the capability to mount and sustain specially designed public relations and information projects for the media. The first two assignments in the latter category were basic: production of the "red book," a 20-page publication listing 12 fundamental reasons why the University of Houston should be admitted to the state system, and a revised film, "Center of Learning."

General Bruce and the key regents were exceptionally easy to work with, and their power base in Houston, with statewide connections, proved invaluable. The FOTC provided access to a prominent group of citizens ranging from Senator George (Cotton) Moffett of Chillicothe (who had guided the Midwestern University bill through the Legislature in 1959) to surviving associates of the late Governor

Beauford Jester. Many FOTC members were the entry point to regional concentrations of economic and political power across the state. Colonel Bates, Mr. Fleming, Judge Elkins, Warren S. Bellows and others constituted a literal storehouse of information, with direct and indirect ties to the key corporations and their skilled, agile lobbyists, the state agencies, the ranking state officials. From these and other sources such as lists of contributors to political campaigns, plus on-the-scene intelligence gathered in Austin (after sifting out inaccurate rumors), we started to build really useful and dependable files.

The TCOHE hearing was in effect a sub-orbital launch before the real blast-off aiming at the Legislature. After protracted study of the 15 members of the Commission, and personal visits with them, we lined up a battery of speakers for the April 11 hearing. These included representatives of the governing board, General Bruce and Mr. Mac, plus a careful selection of community leaders: Leon Jaworski, then president of the Chamber of Commerce; Superintendent of Schools John W. McFarland; Mayor Lewis Cutrer; Senator Baker; and Representative Criss Cole, who was to sponsor the University bill in the House of Representatives. Their topics were short, carefully-condensed versions of the principal points in the "red book."[35]

We had the detailed research, the borrowed private airplanes, the heavy emphasis on the media, the endless telephone calls—all the trappings and techniques that would come into play with the Legislature.

And we won handily before the TCOHE. It was reasonably clear on April 11 that we had the eight votes necessary for Commission approval, in spite of covert but formidable opposition from Executive Director Ralph Green, a Baylor University-trained economist. Chairman A. M. Muldrow of Brownfield explained that a formal vote would not be taken until the October 10 session of the TCOHE. In a showdown after midnight the evening before that meeting, Dr. Green was instructed to prepare a recommendation that the University of Houston become a member of the state system. The motion for the recommendation passed 10-1 at the public meeting some 10 hours later, with Dr. Green absent. On November 22, 1960, the Legislature was sent a recommendation "that the University of Houston be made a fully state-supported institution of higher education, and not a branch of the University of Texas," with course offering and degree programs "subject to the determination and approval of the TCOHE" (just as for the then 19 other state-supported institutions).

With the TCOHE behind us, we accelerated preparations for the opening of the 57th Legislature, now only eight weeks away. In the early summer, partly in preparation for bringing in groups of legislators on May 21 and again on September 16-17 (when they saw a disastrous 0-42 loss to Ole Miss in the Astrodome), I had prepared a position paper for General Bruce outlining the pluses and minuses of the situation as I saw them.

On the plus side, we had some real strengths: (1) Houston, then as even more now, was the center of a congeries of financial, legal, political, agricultural, manufacturing and industrial power that impacted every village, town and city from the Red River to the Cadillac Bar in Nuevo Laredo, and from the Arkansas line in Texarkana to El Paso del Norte. (2) The University of Houston's case was a fundamentally sound one—Why shouldn't the largest city in the state (and the South) have a public university for its burgeoning crop of college-age youngsters, many of whom (perhaps the children of the very same high school seniors who called upon Superintendent Oberholtzer in November, 1926, to plead for a Houston Junior College) could not leave the city either to continue their education? (3) The regents and governors of the University included at least a dozen men with superb connections to the inner workings of state politics. These were the *caciques* of business, industry and the professions, with a sophisticated knowledge and perception of legislative maneuvering—the men with the small fleets of private planes whose infrequent but consequential calls to the State Capitol were never unanswered. (4) As the University's man on the scene, I knew a number of key state officials, including Governor Price Daniel and Dr. James A. Turman, the speaker of the House of Representatives; I had been active in the last campaign of the presiding officer of the Senate (Ben Ramsey), a gentleman of the old school who forgot neither his friends nor his enemies; I was acquainted with many of the individual members of the Legislature; and I could get from the Capitol to the Driskill Hotel without getting lost.

The countervailing weaknesses of the University of Houston, on the other hand, were many: (1) The 1961 Legislature was still preponderantly rural in constituency, feeling, and reaction (Harris County had a single senator and eight representatives, against six and 23 in 1977). This fostered a basic animus against urban areas, eagerly encouraged by some major lobbyists who realized that the man from the boondocks was far more likely to support the poor-mouth, non-spending philosophy often demanded by their clients. (2) There were no three-billion-dollar surpluses, as in 1977, only the prospect of new needs, including our own, to be met with a highly controversial sales tax. (3) New institutions had recently been admitted into the state system of higher education, amid rising shouts of "never more," while yet others eyed their chances. (4) There was hidden, but enormous, opposition from the University of Texas, from Texas A & M College, from Texas Tech, and from a host of other state-supported normal schools and teachers' colleges. (5) The specter of redistricting—which always exacerbates frayed nerves and frustrates trade-outs in the closing weeks of the legislative session, when highly controversial measures are usually decided—hung heavily over both House and Senate.

Studying the position paper later, I realized just how difficult my assignment—to get the University of Houston in out of the fiscal cold and into the relative shelter of the statehouse—would be. Little did I know that we would be forced to create a major state controversy, throw the Senate into an extended filibuster, and utilize every shred of economic and political muscle that our regents, governors and other supporters of the University could muster before winning a bitter, protracted struggle by the single vote that brought our bill up in the Senate on April 17, 1961.

Meanwhile, there were important developments on the campus, where Vice-President Hoffman had been assigned more and more of the normal academic duties of the president and had assumed others because of General Bruce's almost total preoccupation with the drive for state support. The new Cullen College of Engineering was finally completed; Chester H. Pheiffer replaced Charles R. Stewart, the founding dean of the College of Optometry, who reentered private practice, to the University's loss; Donald W. Lee was named editor of *Forum*, the emerging literary quarterly founded in 1956, as Don Barthelme, Jr., the journal's founding editor and a future author of note, resigned to concentrate on his literary career; the Faculty Assembly, under John F. MacNaughton's leadership, began to reexamine its functions and structure; the first impact of massive new federal support programs was felt, with a sudden escalation of student loans to a semester record of $321,708, achieved mainly through the receipt of $253,711 for National Defense Student Loan Program funds; the College of Pharmacy achieved a goal of $127,913 in a historic fund-raising campaign that established this still-small component as a regional leader in such drives[36]; and a potentially disastrous trend toward lower enrollments was arrested, partly because of the University's successful appearance before the TCOHE (fall 1960 enrollment was 11,448, down only slightly from 11,592 the preceding September; it would grow to 12,187 in 1961, reach a new record level of 13,665 in 1962, and then balloon up to successive new highs every year for a decade).

But there were losses to report, as well. Mrs. E.E. Oberholtzer had died December 24, 1959, and Mrs. James P. Houstoun, secretary and a charter member of the Board of Regents, passed away May 22, 1960. *Le Bayou*, the internationally-known French literary journal edited for 20 years by Jules Vern, a long-time mainstay of the faculty before his death in 1956, was discontinued.

In retrospect, one of the most significant developments as the 1960's opened was the organizational meeting of the University of Houston Foundation, on July 22, 1960. I had asked General Bruce and several of the leaders of LEA to consider such a foundation, independent of the University but existing only for its benefit, as early as 1958. Lamar Fleming, Jr., was named founding chairman of the board; Frank C. Smith, president; Roy Henry Cullen, vice-president; General Bruce, secretary; and Mr. McElhinney, treasurer. The Foundation has since raised many millions of dollars for the University, and has growing holdings in endowment funds and real property. It is more important to the University of Houston with each passing year, and it is now one of the oldest such independent philanthropic organizations existing exclusively to benefit a public institution.

Suddenly, the 57th Legislature was opening within a week, and I made final preparations. The Harris County delegation sent the University a letter requesting the appointment of an officer of the institution to be readily available during the session, in view of the complexity and importance of pending legislation. Members of the Board of Governors had provided $8,750 as a special contribution to underwrite expenses of the campaign, and Mr. Mac was disbursing officer.

So, off to Austin I went.

Most bills of high controversy and real merit hew to a roughly predictable pattern in the Texas Legislature, or so they did in the early 1960's. They were introduced as early as possible with a relatively low number; then they were either buried in committee or heard there within about 30 days, and if heard, they were either approved, disapproved or referred to a subcommittee. The latter action could also be a form of burial; if not, action could be expected, or brought about by various means, within a period varying from a few minutes to several weeks. If it survived this stage, the bill was usually held while the sponsor(s) gathered strength by various techniques and strategies, especially to reach the two-thirds majority required to bring a measure up in the Senate. By now, the date being somewhere between March 15 and April 15, there was a tendency to have a run with the bill as soon as possible, since the proof is in the pudding. You don't really know until those little lights flash red or green in the House, or the Secretary of the Senate marks his tally sheet. And adjournment cometh.

On an actual vote, the fat was in the fire to some extent. A sound defeat usually meant that the bill was dead for the session; a narrow loss could sometimes be retrieved by amendments, negotiation or whatever, but it could also light the way to eventual catastrophe. Bills that survived a first test vote of course remained vulnerable. The further steps to final passage or defeat were boobytrapped with frustrating delays and maneuvering, with the complexities and dangers incident to technical rulings, joint conference committees, and the fact that the Legislature must adjourn after 140 days in session.

Looking over a journal that I kept from January 10 through May 12, 1961, one finds that both the Senate and House versions of the University of Houston bill had an elemental force and appeal, grounded in equity and need, that made it extremely difficult for either to be brought down. There would be countless times, however, when Senator Robert W. Baker, Representative Criss Cole and I were convinced that we could never overcome all the obstacles in our path.

Senator Baker was able to obtain an extremely low number for the Senate bill, which was introduced as SB 2 on January 23, 1961. In the House of Representatives, the Harris County delegation had nothing below #53 available, but Bob Eckhardt traded for #11. HR 11 was introduced on January 24, with almost 50 co-sponsors who signed the bill, and assurances from 32 other representatives that they could not co-sponsor, but favored the bill. [37].

We knew from the beginning that SB 2 was flawed, in terms of asking for entrance into the state system in 1961 instead of in 1963, thereby requiring an immediate appropriation, and in its failure to stipulate the role of the TCOHE in the approval of curricula; but there were strategic reasons for not accepting amendments too early, and Senator Baker and I were given wide-ranging authority to change the bill as necessary—hopefully in consultation with General Bruce and others, but immediately if necessary.

Lieutenant Governor Ben Ramsey, our staunchest ally throughout, asked me two questions at the first of the many meetings we were to hold on SB 2: What is the effective date? Is a supplementary appropriation required? When I answered, I could see him write on a note pad in front of him: 1963!

SB 2 was referred to the State Affairs Committee in the Senate and was voted out in a long hearing on February 13. We won a crucial vote from Senator Culp Krueger when the superintendent of schools in his home town of El Campo (George Thigpin) was a surprise witness for us. And we did have two votes next door, in reserve, at another committee meeting (our great friends throughout the campaign, Senators A. M. Aikin, Jr., and Grady Hazlewood).

HR 11 was heard later the same day, and was referred to what we regarded as a friendly subcommittee of Representatives W.H. (Bill) Pieratt (chairman), Sam Collins and H.G. Wells (of Tulia, Texas, not of London).

Early in February, Senator Baker and I had under way a series of non-ending counts, recounts and further checks on strength. I still have a list of the Senate that I used to study at long traffic lights.

Almost from the beginning, we had an unwavering nucleus of 15 senators with us, a core of nine seemingly unshakeable foes, and another seven of indeterminate persuasion [38].

The most amateur tactician could have devised the indicated strategy: you kept the original 15 men good and true carefully with you, watched for the outside chance of some unexpected convert among the nine pledged against you, and spent most of your time in proselytizing the seven still undecided.

Senator Baker and I, with the help of a blue ribbon steering committee of regents, governors and other prominent Houstonians, soon intensified our search for the center of the maze represented by each of the seven. Probing everywhere, we looked for campaign contributors, clients (if the prospect was a lawyer), old friends and classmates, business connections, fraternity and lodge associations, hobbies, ties to state agencies, favors done in the past—for almost anything translatable into support for our cause.

Bob Baker was in charge of a related operation that I termed the "swap shop." He, with most of the other members of the Senate, was on the lookout for colleagues with their own bills badly in need of a vote, whether on the floor or in the 11 committees with which Ben Ramsey had deliberately overburdened him—in order to increase the range of items available on the shelves of his politicking store.

The details you can turn up during energetic research is surprising. We learned, for instance, that John Crooker, Sr., had been a fellow Shriner and close friend of Galloway Calhoun's father for 40 years; that former Governor Dan Moody had little influence on his Yankee son-in-law Senator Hudson, but banking connections might make the senator talk to Lloyd M. Bentsen, Sr., or his holdings of Continental Oil stock make him susceptible to L. F. McCollum; that Senator Roberts had been on the National Youth Administration crew which surveyed the University of Houston campus back in 1938; that Senator Creighton knew my old Rice Institute roommate John A. Graves, III, and admired his *Goodbye To A River;* that Senator Owen really wanted to be a congressman-at-large; that LBJ forces had sent a special and potent envoy to the High Plains to defeat Senator Rogers, himself an ardent New Dealer; that Senator Herring might be split off from the opposition with data showing how often they opposed his University of Texas, openly or covertly, as "non-spenders."

By mid-March, Senator Baker felt that we must risk a test vote. HR 11 was temporarily stalled in the House, with internecine war between the liberal and conservative segments of our delegation compounding the situation. In the Senate, stasis brought the danger of attrition of support and intensified the need to know exactly where we stood.

On March 21, although Governor Ramsey counseled against it, Senator Baker made his move. We lost 14-15 and were an appalling six votes short of the necessary 2-1 margin to bring a bill up in the Senate in those days. Senator Ratliff was lost from the bedrock 15, and there was not a single convert from the seven "possibles," although Senator Crump took a gentlemanly walk and did not register another "Nay" in response to an offsetting courtesy by Bob Baker. We were especially dismayed to lose Senators Calhoun and Rogers, both of whom had been thought responsive.

It was bleak, but there were benefits from the March 21 setback. Ben Ramsey made a series of calls to Houston and told some of the most influential men in town that it was time to "either fish or cut bait." The proposed "1963" and review of curriculum amendments must be accepted, and the high chieftains must come to Austin in person, determined to switch votes. Otherwise, SB 2 was lost. I was on the telephone in another room, asking all three Houston newspapers for editorials pointing out that the temporary defeat had its positive aspects, praising Senator Baker (who was quite depressed), predicting eventual victory when the sales tax and other vexing problems had been resolved, and urging all possible support.

We rebuilt our strength progressively, gaining immediately by compromising on amendments, and then through the visits from men of ultimate power who were making the pilgrimage from Houston to Austin. At one time, we had Raybourne Thompson, Judge Elkins' personal emissary, inside Senator Colson's office reasoning with her, while outside, perched uncomfortably on waiting room chairs, were former Senator Ottis Lock, a ranking lobbyist; Colonel Bates, born and raised in Senator Colson's district; a senior officer of Humble Oil; and Warren S. Bellows, chairman of the Prison Board (the major state agency in the lady senator's district). As the ultimate tribute to our burgeoning campaign, Senator Weinert, then the dean of the Senate who seldom spoke to anyone other than Ed Clark, Dorsey Hardeman and former Governor Coke Stevenson, stopped me in the hall one day. "Young man," he said. "I admire your persistence, but tell them Senator Weinert doesn't want any more telephone calls from Houston."

Patient research finally paid off, however, when one of the junior yet most obdurate members of the opposition was revealed to have promised a client that he "had one call on him," in return for a personal favor of unremitting consequence. A "call" is as good as a man's word, and better than a promissory note, in Texas. Knowing this, the matter was thoroughly explored. The next Sunday a plane landed in a small city, a doorbell was rung, and the senator who answered it said, "Oh my God, it's that University of Houston bill." It was, and the senator involved would get up from a sickbed to honor his promise for "one call" on him.

By April 12, we had everything ready for the move that had to be made no later than the week of April 17-22 in order to be at all safe in terms of the dwindling days of the legislative session. We now had a 2-1 margin in prospect, desperately close though it was; the opposition knew nothing of the crucial switch of a single vote in their ranks, and had seemingly been lulled a bit by pessimistic articles planted in the Houston newspapers. Lest this be overdone, we were told that there would be a positive report from the Pieratt subcommittee in the House on HR 11, with its psychological lift throughout the lower chamber. But everything depended upon our being able to bring up SB 2 by 2-1 on Monday, April 17.

The showdown was at hand. The April 17 session was about to begin, and I could not locate Senator Krueger, who might be our margin; the other 30 senators were present, including our new convert who was honoring "one call" upon him. I caught Bob Baker's eye from the gallery, and said "Krueger" with a quizzical look. He shrugged his shoulders and pointed to the clock. It was now or never.

SB 2 hit the floor 20-10, as the opposition surrounded their apostate; he had kept a binding promise to a friend, one made long before he joined the cabal against the University of Houston; now he left with a raging fever and influenza. His vote had been crucial, but Bob Baker had also picked up four of the "undecideds," at least on agreements to bring SB 2 up for consideration. And Colonel Bates' remarkable memory had failed him for once. We did get a vote out of "that water lawyer" he had remembered back in Chapter Two. Senator Herring was one of the 20 "Ayes."

Senator Krueger, incidentally, had an understandable excuse. He had been detained by his duties as chairman of the reception committee for Chancellor Konrad Adenauer ("Der Alte"), the grand old man of West Germany. When he did come by for a moment to explain his absence, before the Senate adjourned to hear an address by Chancellor Adenauer, the filibuster against SB 2 had already begun.

For 11 days, the University of Houston was under constant attack as the filibuster proceeded, with Senators Lane, Moore and Hudson spelling one another with little assistance from our other opponents.

We kept our forces intact with everything from a small fleet of airplanes, both chartered and borrowed, on standby for quick emergency trips; to evening buffets, complete with bar, in Senator Parkhouse's office. Things remained in the gentlemanly tradition of the Senate in spite of occasional flare-ups on the floor; the opponents were welcome at our buffet-bar, and Senator Moore delighted in pouring himself a double of the best, toasting "good old Nicholson" with the admonition "not to believe all that stuff you hear on the floor."[39]

As the filibuster droned on, Ben Ramsey was extremely supportive; but he was reluctant to force a showdown, pointing out that with our minimum margin, a heavy gavel might end the filibuster but simultaneously kill any chance of a third reading and final passage, which still had to be preceded by a 2-1 vote.

The ice jam finally broke on the afternoon of Friday, April 28, after 11 days. The opposition was becoming physically exhausted, even though there had been far more recesses and interludes than in many filibusters; our forces were holding together; and dozens of bills were now piled up, endangering the political lives of most of the Senate and half of the Legislature.

Senator Willis agreed to move the previous question, thereby mandating rigorous enforcement of all procedural rules and in effect shutting off debate and forcing a vote on the pending question. This is done in the Senate under only the most unusual circumstances, with some members always refusing to have a part in such a parliamentary maneuver. The vote, however, was 11-11, after one opponent threw a rule book at Governor Ramsey while arguing a technical point, and several of our staunchest followers explained that they simply would not vote to close off debate.

Three hours of intrigue followed, as both sides tried desperately to bring in reinforcements who had gone home for the weekend. We flew in Senator Fuller from Port Arthur and ordered two more planes out for other absentees. The opposition managed to get Senator Lane airborne at Center, but he could not land in the dense fog at Austin and had to return home. Then, Senator Secrest changed his vote to "Aye," and we "put it on them" by a margin of 12-10.

About 10 p.m., Senator Baker, with the aid of Senators Schwartz and Kazen, worked out a compromise. The opponents, now bound by the strictest rules of procedure in which there could be neither recess nor adjournment unless we agreed to it (or even leaning against one's desk while in possession of the floor), were clearly approaching physical exhaustion. They feared we might get enough returning strength for a 2-1 vote on the spot, and final passage, since Bob Baker had spread the word that we had sent for every adherent, with a literal fleet of radar-equipped planes. The compromise was our accepting four minor amendments and two of major consequence (removing all graduate programs and restricting our right to finance campus improvements), in return for engrossing the bill and adjournment until Monday.[40]

Senator Baker motioned to me for the thousandth time to come down from the gallery, and we conferred while he watched the floor. "Can we ram it through?" I asked. "No. 15-9 is our high count, and they have Dies in his office now, resting" (Senator Dies, the most gentlemanly of foes who would admit on the floor that we had a deserving case but he could not vote for us, had been in a terrible automobile accident a few months earlier and was still recuperating).

"What does the Guv (Ben Ramsey) think?"

"He thinks buy the deal."

"How much time to think it over?"

"None."

I thought of a University of Houston pulled back to the baccalaureate level, of new difficulties in financing expansion of the campus; of the nagging little amendments on eminent domain, prior payment of bonded debt, etc. But I also remembered a recent statement by that most astute observer of politics and legislative maneuvering, Raybourne Thompson (managing partner of Judge Elkins' law firm). "Doctor," he had warned me, "you better get this animal through the Senate in any manner, shape or form you can. SB 2 is the most indigestible thing they've run across over there in many a year, and you may choke on it yet."

"Let's go," I told Bob Baker. "There's always another session to cure defects." And Senate Bill 2 was engrossed.

Now the opposition had time to reorganize, to plan new strategy, to try to win back at least one vote, because we still had to get our bill up again, 2-1, for final passage. There were endless delays as almost three more weeks spun out. We honored our bargain with the

Turman forces on redistricting, thus further strengthening our position in the House. The somewhat surprising passage of the first sales tax in Texas history improved both the appropriations situation and relations with Governor Price Daniel. But the question remained: How to get SB 2 out of the Senate and over to the House of Representatives, where our supporters now numbered in excess of 100 and every pressure possible was being exerted to add still more?

On May 12, we found that Senator Herring would be at a funeral until almost 11 a.m., that Senator Smith had to be absent in Lubbock, and that Senator Colson would continue a series of excused absences. We had a chance for a 17-8 vote, 18-8 if Senator Secrest could arrive in time from an early meeting in his home town of Temple. Should Senator Herring get back in time to vote, and Senator Secrest be late, we were dead, 17-9.

Senator Secrest arrived at the exact moment the Senate convened, at 10:31 a.m. I had been praying for a long invocation to allow him time to get there, and now suffered through one of the more protracted prayers of the entire session, expecting Senator Herring to walk in any moment. But Senator Herring was no where in sight, the vote, quickly taken, was 18-8, and SB 2 was on the floor for third reading. Senator Baker moved the previous question immediately to forestall another filibuster, and we won this test, 14-12. Our bill was finally passed a moment later, by voice vote, at 10:41 a.m. Bob Baker looked up at me in the gallery, and said aloud, "Dr. Nicholson, you look numb." I came down to congratulate him while he went over to the House of Representatives to report in person the passage of SB 2, and to receive an ovation.

I hurried to work on the media for maximum coverage, including editorials thanking our supporters in the Senate, and praising Senator Baker to the skies—but warning that SB 2 still had to emerge from the State Affairs Committee of the House, and to win final passage in the House itself.

Five days later, on May 17, we were in a new crisis. Our bill was stalled in State Affairs, where Chairman Bill Hollowell was under unremitting pressure to keep it as a means of whipsawing the Harris County delegation into line on final details of redistricting, and other still-pending matters. We were almost frantic to get the bill out of committee; State Affairs did not meet again until May 22, the first day of the last week of the session, when all manner of goblins begin to appear.

The chief Turman lieutenants reassured me, "Jimmy (Turman) says that SB 2 will come out, and it will pass." Yet when I went in to see the speaker late on the evening of May 17, he showed me a handwritten note just delivered by his most trusted floor manager. It read: "They just told me you could walk out there on your knees, but it won't pass tonight." And it was a long way from the speaker's office to the committee hearing table.

Late though it was, I placed three calls to Houston, to the loftiest level of wealth and power. Two of the men I contacted called Jimmy Turman back in minutes. The message was that if he had any ambitions to run for statewide office—and he did—they were riding on SB 2.

Speaker Turman, a staunch friend caught in a bind, did not walk out on his knees to the State Affairs Committee; nor was there any action on our bill that harrowing evening of May 17; but on May 22, at about 7:55 p.m., SB 2 was voted out of the Committee, unanimously.

Late the next morning, Representative Criss Cole, who had been presiding at the request of Speaker Turman as a final indication of the significance attaching to SB 2, was recognized on the floor of the House. SB 2 was immediately engrossed 111-29, and we next needed a four-fifths majority for suspension of the rules and immediate passage. As the speaker held the gavel for our floor leaders to round up every possible "Aye," and to persuade all the "Nays" they could to go look at the incomparable statuary on the Capitol grounds for a few minutes, we squeezed out a total verified at 118-23 to suspend the rules. A moment later, Criss Cole final-passed SB 2 107-35, made the customary motion to reconsider (so that this cannot be done later, in a less fortunate setting), with accompanying motion to table his original motion, and it was nailed down in history.

Speaker Turman: "Senator Baker also votes 'Aye'."

Representative Don Garrison: "Mr. Speaker, may we order oxygen for Senator Baker?"

"No sir; if I can't help him with this vote, oxygen won't help either!"

The great legislative adventure, the one development affecting the University of Houston more than anything to date, was over.

And in its immediate aftermath, Philip G. Hoffman became the sixth president of the University.

As the legislative campaign neared its final stages, the regents and governors realized more and more that the passage of SB 2 would open a completely new era for the University of Houston. General Bruce had brought the institution through crisis to victory, in what would always be regarded as a watershed triumph heralding this new age; but he was nearing his sixty-seventh birthday, and would be 69 before the University actually entered the state system on September 1, 1963.

The General sensed that the old order was changing, that there were compelling reasons for new leadership on September 1, 1961, and that Dr. Hoffman was his logical successor, in a simplified organizational structure returning to the concept of a president as chief executive officer. But he was human; he was in excellent health; he enjoyed his job; and in my judgment he would have welcomed an invitation to stay on until age 70, in the Oberholtzer pattern.

Instead, there were high-level discussions, principally with Colonel Bates and Warren Bellows (although Lamar Fleming, Jr., Corbin J. Robertson and a few other regents also participated) in which the General saw which way the wind was blowing. A selection committee was quickly appointed, primarily for window-dressing,[41] General Bruce requested retirement as of August 31, 1961, and Philip Guthrie Hoffman was the unanimous choice of the selection committee. This was announced on May 30, 1961, together with Dr. Hoffman's elevation to the presidency and General Bruce's appointment as chancellor emeritus, both effective September 1, 1961.

Since the meeting of the governing board affirming these historic changes on May 30 was set as usual for 2 p.m., the carefully guarded news fell on *Chronicle* time. I swore Emmet Walter, Everett Collier and Elmer Bertelsen to secrecy and worked out a detailed story, complete with a large front page color picture of the Hoffman family, (the new president and Mary; Philip Jr., 15; Mary Victoria, 14; Ruth Ann, 3; and Jeanne,2) for 2 p.m. release. The story and picture, a most attractive layout and compelling piece of publicity, hit the street about 1:30 p.m., just as the regents and governors were gathering for their meeting in the Houston Club to make all this news official. I brought a copy of the *Chronicle* with me from the parking garage, showing it quickly to Dr. Hoffman and then replacing it in my dispatch case. As I did, I tried to recall if any action of the Executive Committee, which had previously sanctioned the changes about to be revealed, had ever been overturned by the full governing board; but I dismissed this as paranoia.

Just as the meeting of the Board of Governors opened, in walked Palmer Hutcheson, Sr., returned that very morning from Europe and out of touch for several months. The governors proceeded at once to the principal business at hand, while Mr. Hutcheson looked for the first time at two agenda items which caught his eye immediately: Acceptance of request of Chancellor A. D. Bruce for retirement, and appointment of Philip G. Hoffman as president. "Well, now, what's going on here?" he asked. "Dr. Hoffman is a fine man, but why are we in such a hurry to accept A.D.'s retirement?"

Colonel Bates looked at his old friend for a long moment. His left hand, which always began a counter clockwise motion when he had made up his mind on a significant matter and was ready to proceed, was already tracing its circular design. "Now, Palmer," he said, "let's just go along with the agenda."

The vote was taken. I did not have to leave town hotly pursued by the top management of the *Chronicle*, and the era of Hoffman the Builder, now in its seventeenth year, had theoretically started.

Notes to Chapter Six

[1] The FOTC was organized soon after World War I by a group of outstanding men, many of them recent graduates of Texas University or Texas A&M College, who had been brought to Leon Springs (just northwest of San Antonio) for intensive training as "90-day wonders." They were sworn in as second lieutenants in front of the Alamo, and transferred to infantry training commands shaping up raw recruits for the 90th Infantry Division, a new National Guard "outfit." Colonel Bates (this military title came later, when he was appointed to the honorary staff of his friend Governor Dan Moody, although he returned from overseas as a wounded and decorated captain and company commander) formed lifelong friendships within the FOTC. These included

Governor Beauford Jester; Adjutant General Ike S. Ashburn; Robert Lee Bobbitt, speaker of the Texas House of Representatives, attorney general and justice of the Court of Civil Appeals; Railroad Commissioner Ernest Thompson; and Congressman Maury Maverick, among others. A favorite of Colonel Bates among the FOTCers was Andrew Davis Bruce, a 1916 graduate of Texas A&M who was to rise from second lieutenant to three-star general during a brilliant 37-year career as a professional soldier.

Houston members of the FOTC in 1954, who formed a strong group in support of General Bruce's selection as president of the University of Houston and gave him an immediate cadre of close friends in the city, included Major Ashburn, James A. Baker, Jr., Rex G. Baker; Albert M. Bowles, Lewis R. Bryan, Jr., W. T. Campbell, Francis G. Coates, Sam H. Davis, John K. Dorrance, Raymond P. Elledge, Sr., David Frame, Gillette Hill, Mike Hogg, George B. Journeay, Ardon B. Judd, Frank A. Liddell, E. L. Lorehn, Perry Moore, John E. Price, George E. B. Peddy, John T. Scott, Jr., Robert A. Shepherd, Micajah (Mike) S. Stude, Howard S. Warner, Ewing Werlein, and of course Colonel Bates himself.

[2] Mr. Cullen, hosting General Eisenhower in his River Oaks home early in 1951, became convinced that Ike was the only man capable of wresting the presidency from the Democrats in 1952. The General, then en route to Europe as commander of the North Atlantic Treaty Organization's western defenses, had pleased a capacity Cullen Auditorium audience earlier by warning that federal funds could mean the end of free speech and free universities. Mr. Cullen was also determined to bring General MacArthur (who, in addition to his other qualities, represented the epitome of opposition to Harry S. Truman) to Texas, to Houston, and to the University. This was a Herculean assignment: Douglas MacArthur was an international hero, surrounded by a formidable phalanx of aides skilled in isolating him from constant demands to accept speaking engagements.

But Hugh Roy Cullen had contacts, and he could be persistent. In late April of 1951 he telephoned General Robert E. Wood, a confidante of General MacArthur and a political ally of Mr. Cullen whose daughter Mary had married William Stamps Farish, Jr., and, after he was lost in World War II, Hugo V. Neuhaus, Jr. General Wood returned the call from the MacArthur penthouse atop the Waldorf-Astoria Towers. There was definite interest in a trip to Texas for General MacArthur (who was not without his own presidential aspirations), especially if high-level invitations, including a request to address the State Legislature were forthcoming.

Mr. Cullen quickly had telegrams sent by everyone who had ever amounted to anything in Houston, plus a thick overlay from key state officials in Austin. He did omit Mrs. Oveta Culp Hobby when someone told him that Mrs. Hobby had once sided with General George C. Marshall in a disagreement with General MacArthur. Negotiations continued for three weeks, and Mr. Cullen decided that he and Mrs. Cullen would spend one of their favorite weekends, semi-isolated at the ranch above Columbus, fishing for sun perch from a rowboat in the middle of a lake.

Before he left town on May 18, Mr. Cullen had a secretary call me and ask if I minded monitoring my home telephone over the weekend, since I was generally familiar with the situation, in the event that Major General Courtney Whitney, chief aide to General MacArthur, should happen to call. I made myself available, of course, and intricate instructions on how to complete any calls to Mr. Cullen were given.

Just before noon on Saturday, General Whitney called from the Waldorf-Astoria, expecting no doubt to be connected immediately with Mr. Cullen. Having served as an aide myself, although to an officer three stars down the ladder of rank, I made the appropriate replies, assured him of Mr. Cullen's consuming interest in the matter, and told him that Mr. Cullen would call back in exactly one hour. I then put our plan into motion. This involved ringing the home of the ranch manager in Columbus, who had been alerted. He drove to the lake, sounded his horn repeatedly, and waved a big Confederate flag he kept in his jeep. Mr. Cullen heard and saw the signal, rowed in, made the call, and General Douglas MacArthur gave a memorable address before a joint special session of the State Legislature on June 13, 1951, before speaking to a crowd estimated at 50,000 in Rice Stadium the next day. He learned while in Houston that Hugh Roy Cullen would back General Eisenhower for president in 1952, and wanted General MacArthur as Secretary of Defense. It was also revealed to him why Mr. Cullen was unable to agree to bring Douglas MacArthur to Austin on June 3, the day originally recommended: He had promised his granddaughter Mary Hugh Arnold that he and Mrs. Cullen would be at Dobbs Ferry that day for her graduation, and Dobbs Ferry, New York, it was.

[3] No one would soon forget the return trip from Killeen, where temperatures in excess of 100 degrees caused General Bruce to mercifully tear his prepared speech in pieces on the parade ground, and to speak briefly *ad lib*. The unpressurized aircraft in which the University guests were flying ran into severe late summer thunderstorms, and "pitched and bucked like a mustang," as one passenger described it.

General Bruce had toured the second floor of the Ezekiel W. Cullen Building a few weeks before. He must have been struck by the emphasis which C. F. McElhinney placed on resuming his post of vice president and business manager on September 1, 1954. Mr. Mac, whom the General immediately liked and trusted, let no one forget that he had agreed to serve exactly one year, and no longer, as acting president. He reinforced this clear understanding by functioning in effect as both vice-president and business manager, and president, during his 12 months as acting chief executive. He delegated management of the auxiliary enterprises (bookstore, cafeteria, residence halls and temporary housing) to Controller J. Treadway Brogdon, along with authority to transfer budgeted funds between accounts. Any net increase in a budget, however, went to C. F. McElhinney, as did alterations to buildings or any capital commitments. Mr. Mac spent mornings in the presidential suite, where Leta Nutt (Gilbert) was in charge. Four afternoons a week (Wednesday was his afternoon off, for recreation), he was in his vice-presidential office, working with Marguerite Harris and Fairy Havard on business and personnel matters.

It was a difficult year for Acting-President McElhinney, who was suffering from a temporary cardiovascular ailment that required a considerable amount of medication; but it was one that he carried out with characteristic attention to duty and effectiveness. When it was completed, and he was back in his vice-presidential quarters, panelled beautifully in "fiddleback" pecan, there was an important addition to the few things he had hanging on his handsome walls. Near a favorite sketch of his church, Trinity Episcopal on Holman at Main, was a signed testimonial from the Faculty Assembly, praising him for his steadfast leadership in a transitional year that could otherwise have been traumatic.

[4] General Bruce felt that the more usual title vice-president and dean of faculties might somehow be confusing. Deans to him were highly respected individuals, but they were a lower order of angels than vice-presidents.

[5] In June, 1955, General Bruce had named Douglas R. MacLaury of New York City assistant to the president for development and public relations. Former president of an obscure institution at Danville, Indiana (Canterbury College), Mr. MacLaury was an ordained Episcopalian minister who had been serving as a fund-raising consultant after leaving an earlier position with the Episcopal Diocese of Chicago. Mr. MacLaury attempted some development projects in late 1955 and early 1956, apparently without the necessary underpinning of community understanding and support of institutional role and scope, mission, and objectives. These were singularly unsuccessful, and he was dismissed by

General Bruce in February, 1956. Mr. MacLaury wore his clerical garb to the final interview.

A month or so later, James A. Clark, my partner in a consulting firm, and a historian of the oil industry, had told me that Colonel Bates "wanted to see me about something important." I assumed that this had to do with the Bank of the Southwest, which our firm represented, or with the impending move of former Congressman Lloyd M. Bentsen, Jr. (whose brother Kenneth was married to Mary Bates) to Houston. I had been in charge of media relations during Judge Bentsen's stirring bilingual campaign for the 15th Congressional District on the border, which depleted the Bentsen cattle herds for barbecue, but got the district a first-class representative and later U.S. senator.

But it was a different matter. Colonel Bates told me that he, Mr. Cullen, Charles Fleetwood (regional vice-president of the Prudential Insurance Company, and a regent of the University) and Corbin Robertson were "sort of a committee helping the General find someone who could help him with fund-raising and public relations," and he thought that I might be interested in the job. I replied that I had little or no direct experience in fund-raising, and was happy enough where I was, but certainly appreciated his interest. "Well," he replied, "you know the town, and you've had a fine education, and we all know you. You've been teaching out at the University, too. Go by and talk to Mr. Cullen and Corbin and Charlie Fleetwood about it."

I did this, and in the meantime, General Bruce called, asking me to come by his office. Dean Eugene H. Hughes of the College of Business Administration had heard that a recruiting operation was under way and had recommended me to the General through Vice-President Williams. Both men were present when I arrived in the presidential suite. There was some transparent pretext of soliciting my reaction to new courses in the Management Development Center, but I guessed correctly that the hidden agenda was the matter that Colonel Bates had already raised with me. I was being checked out.

We had a rather brief discussion, in which Clanton Williams seemed to be more interested in my knowledge of the community power structure than in my opinion of management curricula; then I was left alone with General Bruce. He talked for a few moments about some of his friends in the FOTC who knew me, and then asked directly if I might be interested in a position as executive director of development, adding that the post "was vacant, and needed filling in the worst way." I told him that I might well be interested, if I knew more about the position, and he and the other members of his immediate staff felt that I could help develop the obvious potential of the University. He showed me a fund-raising brochure, proposed earlier but left in the proof stage. I looked through it quickly and told him I would have to study it further, but on first blush it appeared to have some questionable copy. As he glanced with me at a page listing the Board of Regents, I almost unconsciously corrected Mrs. James P. Houstoun's name, which had been misspelled "Houston." This seemed to impress the General, who told me that he had difficulty (as did half the people who knew them) in remembering that William Vermillion Houston, the president of Rice Institute, spelled his name as the city but pronounced it "How-stun" and Mrs. Houstoun spelled and pronounced her name "How-stun."

I was asked back to see General Bruce a week or so later, having in the meantime sent him at his request a resume and various examples of reports, brochures, releases and other materials I had prepared, some of them for Mr. Cullen. "They tell me you have an interest in the labor movement, and a tradition of this in your family," the General said, there being the inference that this might not exactly be a 10-strike in my alley. For a moment, I could not imagine what he was talking about. Then, I recalled a short history of labor law in Texas that I had written at the request of the Texas Manufacturers' Association, almost 10 years before, and a monograph on pension funds prepared for some industrial client. And I realized that the General must also have heard somewhere that my cousin Martin Patrick Durkin (on the recommendation of Francis Cardinal Spellman to General Eisenhower, who was looking for a conservative Catholic labor leader to add to his cabinet) was Secretary of Labor. I explained these matters briefly, and President Bruce seemed relieved.

Three days later, General Bruce offered to name me executive director of development. He explained that another candidate for the post, Ralph E. Frede, had also been seriously considered. I asked to see a resume on Mr. Frede, as I had been told by Lloyd Gregory of the Houston *Post* that he was a skilled fund-raiser for Basil O'Connor's March of Dimes, an Austinite and former editor of the *Daily Texan* who wanted to return home from Saint Louis; and I knew also that General Bruce was preparing to replace the director of loans and scholarships. I suggested that if there were another vacancy in the development area, that he might offer this to Ralph Frede, as I would have to build an overall team. This was accomplished, fortunately, and Mr. Frede spent 14 years with me before my long-time acquaintance and sometime client, Leonard F. McCollum, then still chairman of the board of Continental Oil Company, hired him away after gentlemanly warnings of competition. Mr. McCollum, also chairman of the board of Baylor Medical College, installed Ralph Frede there, where he has continued the marked success that his professional abilities and personal characteristics merit.

I accepted General Bruce's offer but told him that, because of the low salary, even with some outside income I would have to continue one consulting arrangement and to retain a small company which I owned. This was agreed to, including a faculty appointment in the College of Business Administration which the General wrote into my new personnel file. I proposed to join his staff May 1, 1956, but he asked if I could move this up to April 16, which was arranged. When I reported in on April 16, I found Walter F. Williams, Jr., director of public relations; Farris F. Block, director of the News Service; Mrs. Annie Laurie Fambrough (now Lyon); and Mrs. Margaret Graves awaiting me in the present Office of Information. Mrs. Lyon had joined the University the year before as a research assistant in development. All four are still with me, after 21 years, plus James L. Bauer, then director of film operations at KUHT, and now general manager of the station. With Ralph E. Frede, who joined the group July 1, 1956, they became the nucleus of the expanding Development Division, which now has more than a dozen directors and a tradition of senior administrators of long experience, unequalled knowledge of the University and its manifold operations, and singular dedication and ability. The first thing I had to do upon meeting the original staff, incidentally, was to apologize to Farris Block. Elmer Bertelsen, the former *Cougar* editor and education specialist on the *Chronicle,* had somehow picked up a rumor that I was to join General Bruce's staff, called me at 5 a.m. that very day with proof that I could not deny (he had talked to a member of the Board of Regents) and scooped our own News Service.

[6] Both of these bodies dated from the Oberholtzer administration. The Faculty Assembly consisted of almost 100 representatives from the instructional departments and colleges, with the number of representatives varying from four to one, depending upon student enrollment within the component involved. The Assembly had an elected president and secretary, a 14-person Faculty Council with its own chairman, vice-chairman and representative to the Executive Council; and an eight-person Steering Committee. The Executive Council was composed of the president, the vice-presidents, the deans (who often sent alternates to meetings of the Council), the registrar, the comptroller and the elected representative of the Faculty Assembly.

[7] Dr. Williams apparently had knowledge not only of the overall findings and observations of the accrediting team, but of specific understandings with the University. These included agreements that a recognized scholar with an earned terminal degree would

be named dean of faculties, and that there would be substantial changes in the scope and character of extension offerings (which had mushroomed, particularly in the College of Education), or their abolition. There were some less specific agreements about the need for everything from a minor tune-up to a major overhaul in at least three colleges of the University. Disclosure of the fact that Dr. Williams had already agreed to accept appointment as vice-president and provost undoubtedly helped in obtaining membership for the University of Houston in the Southern Association, which was voted at the annual meeting held in Louisville on December 2, 1954.

[8] KUHT went on the air May 25, 1953, after several delays for the arrival of equipment, and was dedicated June 8, 1953, with Commissioner Frieda Hennock of the FCC as principal speaker. Among those on the original Schwarzwalder staff were film director Dr. John W. Meaney, former film director of KEYL-TV, San Antonio; George Arms and Patrick E. Welch, as associate professors charged with liaison between the station and the Radio-Television Department; Roy E. Barthold, program director; Bill Davis, chief engineer; George Collins, art director; and Helen Beth Potter, secretary.

The original 325-foot tower provided only limited coverage for the station, which was on the air in the beginning only from 5 p.m. to 9 p.m., five days a week, under a license jointly issued to the University and HISD, on October 20, 1952. In 1954, however, a new 658-foot tower allowed a step-up in power from 15,000 to 50,000 watts (prompting the design of a pistol-packing Cougar by Walt Disney Productions that embodied the concepts of a pioneer educational television station, the Frontier Fiesta, Shasta and the Old West, as the station symbol).

Dr. Williams was impressed by such pioneer programs as University Forum, which once featured Eleanor Roosevelt (and had as a regular guest Mrs. Joseph R. (Delia) Mares, a most well-read and knowledgable authority on international affairs and communism who was exactly 180 degrees from Mrs. Roosevelt in political orientation). He also liked the quick development of a widening range of well-produced telecourses and features such as "Doctors In Space"; a $37,500 grant from the prestigious Fund for Adult Education which permitted the establishment of a separate Film Division; and a four-year contract in 1955, with the Educational Radio and Television Center, for the production of a series of 52 films stimulated by the success of a biology telecourse, "The Nature of Life." The latter featured Dr. Burr Roney, who was to become KUHT's first local "star."

General Bruce also found many positive factors at Channel 8. He saw the station as a unique means of fostering community interest in the University, as well as internal support for his administration. He had Dr. Schwarzwalder organize a new program, "President's Television Assembly" on which he appeared with some regularity, and appointed a high-powered "Television Advisory Committee" in 1955. The members were John T. Jones, Jr., then president of the Houston *Chronicle* and of KTRK-TV; Jack Harris, vice-president of the Houston *Post* and general manager of KPRC-TV; Paul Taft, president and general manager of KGUL-TV (Channel 11); John Paul Goodwin of the Goodwin-Dannenbaum Advertising Agency; Roger Jeffery of Great Southern Life Insurance Company, alumni representative; and Corbin J. Robertson, representing the Board of Regents.

[9] The big shows such as Bella Union admitted spending $3,500, and the actual total was probably above $5,000 when donated materials and supplies were included. The average expenditure was calculated at $2,100 per show.

[10] I taught a sequence of management courses at the downtown school in the early 1950's and can attest to the pauperized look of the quarters in which it operated, much as Jim Taylor attempted to maintain things as well as he could. Shearn Moody, the grandson of the cotton, banking and insurance tycoon, came up to me during an intermission one night to request permission to be absent for two weeks because of "a family emergency." The emergency, it turned out, was that he "had to meet Mama in Paris at the Georges V." While I was mentally weighing just where this urgent matter should fall on the academic scale of values, I saw a huge rat emerge from a hole in the corner of the classroom. I had an eraser in my hand, and instinctively threw it at the intruder. Shearn ducked, thinking that I was aiming at him. I apologized, told him to read three extra chapters in a collateral text on the plane, and to submit a paper on the material as makeup. I also told him not to be confusing trips to Paris anymore with valid excuses for being absent from class.

[11] Literally, in German, a "yes-sayer."

[12] General Bruce had established Staff Conference, which immediately removed seven principals from the ranks of the Executive Council, in 1956. The earlier organization of the Deans' Conference, which Vice-President Williams got underway as soon as he could in 1955, had already siphoned off most of the other members of the Council.

[13] Mrs. Florence Hoffman is now one of the younger-looking octogenarians around, a small, alert and delightful woman who has her own apartment in Houston, where she keeps treasured mementos of her long and interesting life, and of the career of her only child. There are now two great-grandsons and four married grandchildren to keep up with between frequent calls and visits from her son, and daughter-in-law Mary, and granddaughter Ruth who lives nearby with her young husband, ophthalmologist Dr. Christopher Cabler.

[14] Curiously enough, Lieutenant (jg) Hoffman and I were both in the nation's capital at the same time, on related assignments, but did not ever meet, even though I saw liaison officers from Naval Intelligence every day at my "post of honor." (I ran into the legendary Senator Tom Connally on Capitol Hill during one of my days off, and we talked for a moment of one of his great favorites, Frank C. "Posh" Oltorf, my classmate at Rice Institute. "Tell me," said the senator, in his fustian yet marvelous manner, "where is your post of honor in this terrible conflict?" "Senator," I replied, "it's honorable enough, but not all that dangerous. It's just across the Potomac River, in an old girls' school." Our unit, which later became a nucleus of the Army Security Agency, had taken over Arlington Hall.

I had transferred from a Harvard University reserve unit to (Army) Military Intelligence following a depressing, snowy spring on maneuvers in the Virginia countryside, and found myself stationed in Washington, D.C. for the remainder of the war, as a Japanese language cryptanalyst. This was after intensive training at the Georgetown University School of Foreign Service by missionaries, a marvelous Korean (earlier assigned as a political assassin by his government), and by a master Finnish cryptographer.

Before I returned to civilian life at Harvard, the Army warned us of punishment ranging from hard labor at Fort Leavenworth to being drawn and quartered at a Fort Myer retreat if any of our World War II escapades were ever revealed; but this became moot after *Life* magazine told the entire story in detail a decade later.

You could understand the Army's concern over the unveiling of one of the war's best-kept secrets, although it would have inevitably surfaced, as in David Cahn's 1967 masterpiece, *The Codebreakers.* At one juncture of the conflict, our unit was decoding intercepted messages vitally affecting plans for the prospective assault on the Normandy beaches—almost before this so-called "diplomatic traffic" was available to the War Office in Tokyo. Our couriers were being flown to the Quebec conference of FDR and

Winston Churchill with the messages, which had become available in a most unusual way:

The Japanese, alarmed by the growing prospect of the Allies successfully invading Hitler's *Festung Europa,* had asked their ambassador in Berlin to discover the details of German defenses in the Trouville-Dieppe area. Der Fuhrer, enraged at such an inquiry, ordered the aging Field Marshal Gerd von Rundstedt himself to show the ambassador and party just how impregnable the defenses were, as Tokyo was advised in advance.

You can imagine our keen interest in such matters as the exact location of fortifications, depth of perimeter defenses at the beachheads, placement of minefields and artillery pieces, angle of machinegun fire, etc., all of which the Japanese observers busily noted and recorded for supposedly secret reports to their Imperial Headquarters—and the degree to which these reports helped in our planning for D-Day.

Our partnership in intelligence with the Navy also involved the Germans, who had emphasized to the Japanese the decisive importance of knowing the exact location of convoys on the high seas at all times. This led to an unbelievable piece of good luck, in which the Japanese ordered each convoy to radio its position at noon for the next 10 days (based on anticipated speed, weather and other variables) to the Admiralty as it left the great embarkation center at Moji. We treasured these messages, some of which were translated from clues in codes aboard a specially-equipped transport belonging to Admiral Isoroku Yamamoto, the five-star commander of the combined Japanese fleet who led the attack on Pearl Harbor. The transport was shot down off Bougainville in the Solomon Islands, by a Navy interceptor which appeared from nowhere after Naval Intelligence had deciphered a message revealing Admiral Yamamoto's itinerary. Divers then located codebooks in the Yamamoto plane, photographed the books, and carefully replaced them for the desperate Japanese search that followed. These were the codebooks that made it possible for a smaller, out-gunned U.S. fleet to defeat the Japanese warships at the climactic Battle of Midway.

The "noon position" messages were decoded and processed by a unit headed by Professor Edwin Oldfather Reischauer of Harvard, later a brilliantly effective ambassador to Japan. The messages went on to the Navy, and finally to some submarine commander, who proceeded to an indicated position and lurked about until the quarry came in sight. A few days later, we would translate another message, this time concerning the loss of another Japanese transport or merchant ship, often with a heavy loss of life and badly needed provisions for the South Pacific garrisons.

By mid-1944, two-thirds of the Japanese merchant marine was at the bottom of the ocean.

[15] E. A. Calvin, secretary of the Taxpayers' Association, uttered some prophetic words as early as 1936, while opposing the proposed donation of 150 acres of Memorial Park to the infant University of Houston: "It is inevitable that a university of the proposed magnitude of the Houston University (as the institution was often called in those days) must eventually become a tax-supported institution."

[16] Ralph Frede and I called on a former donor as soon as we could reorganize the Office of Loans and Scholarships (in 1956) to determine why he was no longer contributing badly needed scholarships. He pulled a letter out of his desk drawer and showed it to us. The letter was from Mr. Cullen. It was courteous, and it expressed gratitude for the scholarships provided earlier; but it could also be interpreted as saying, "Well, thanks; but I sort of take care of the University of Houston's needs myself."

[17] Governors of the University (asterisk indicates regent) were W. Leland Anderson, *Isaac Arnold, *Mrs. Isaac Arnold, Fred Ayers, *Colonel W. B. Bates, *Warren S. Bellows, Sr., Ben C. Belt, Karl R. Bendetsen, Mrs. John H. Blaffer, Robert L. Boggs, *W. Stewart Boyle, George R. Bryant, Mrs. George A. Butler, Marvin K. Collie, D. L. Connelly, *Hugh Roy Cullen, Roy Henry Cullen, Naurice G. Cummings, Mrs. John de Menil, Joe T. Dickerson, *Mrs. Ray L. Dudley, H. J. Ehlers, *Judge J. A. Elkins, Sr., James A. Elkins, Jr., T. C. Evans, A. J. Farfel, *Stephen P. Farish, *William G. Farrington, John C. Flanagan, *Lamar Fleming, Jr., *Charles Green Fleetwood, Claud B. Hamill, Earl C. Hankamer, General Maurice Hirsch, Harrison C. Hobart, *Sterling T. Hogan, Sr., *Mrs. James P. Houstoun, *Palmer Hutcheson, Sr., Russell L. Jolley, John T. Jones, Jr., Mrs. R. C. Kuldell, Alfred W. Lasher, Jr., *F. M. Law, Mrs. Max Levine, John F. Maher, Mrs. Douglas Marshall, Harris McAshan, A. G. McNeese, Jr., Leopold L. Meyer, Harry J. Mosser, Travis E. Parish, Charles A. Perlitz, Jr., Charles F. Reed, Jr., *Corbin J. Robertson, *James W. Rockwell, *Simon Sakowitz, Charles A. Saunders, Jr., Stanley W. Shipnes, *A. Dee Simpson, Curtis M. Smith, *Frank C. Smith, R. E. (Bob) Smith, Ross Stewart, John R. Suman, H. Gardiner Symonds, Howard T. Tellepsen, *Milton R. Underwood, Jack J. Valenti, Tom P. Walker, Mrs. Gus S. Wortham and Andrew Jackson Wray.

The Executive Committee was composed of Colonel Bates, Hugh Roy Cullen, Mr. Bellows, Mrs. Dudley, Mr. Elkins, Jr., Mr. Flanagan, Mr. Fleming, Mr. Hogan, Mrs. Levine, Mr. Robertson, Mr. Sakowitz, Frank C. Smith, and Mr. Underwood.

[18]The 1956 football season opened after a downtown campaign to sell season tickets, with what has become a traditional pre-opening-game cocktail buffet. The 1956 event was at the River Oaks Country Club, with Mr. Cullen as host. I complimented him on the party halfway through it, and asked if I could do anything for him. "Well," he replied, "could we get the cat here? She would add a real touch. And after all, we're playing the (Mississippi State) Tigers." It took me a moment to understand that he meant Shasta. I motioned to Captain Tom Sawyer, the Houston Police Department ambassador to River Oaks, who was standing nearby. A few moments later, he located "the cat," en route to the game with her Cougar Guard escort. Shasta was detoured through the River Oaks Country Club ballroom, where she was a sensation, providing a picture for a *Life* magazine photographer covering a Texas football weekend (and our first Band Day, with 6,000 high school performers playing as one massed band) that he must have remembered awhile. The Cougars went on in 1956 to defeat Mississippi State 18-7, to tie Texas A&M's first-ranked Cadets before 67,009 fans in Rice Stadium, and to lose Head Coach Bill Meek, who was lured away to Southern Methodist University and thence to relative obscurity. They also won the first of 12 National Collegiate Athletic Association (NCAA) golf championships to date under Coach Dave G. Williams, a title they took five years in a row from 1956 through 1960, and made Guy V. Lewis head basketball coach. He has responded so far by making the Cougars a national power, and by winning an even 400 victories, although he lost a chance to go on to 401 and thereby to win the National Invitational Tournament in a bitter 91-94 defeat on March 20, 1977, in Madison Square Garden. It was still, as we had to point out to the inconsolable Guy, the finest season since 1967-1968, when the Cougars defeated UCLA 71-69 on January 20, 1968, before 53,693 in the Astrodome (the largest crowd in basketball history), ranked number one in the polls and finished with a record of 30 wins, 2 losses.

[19]The fiscal details are difficult to comprehend, in terms of today's budgets. Campaign literature estimated that the University would spend $17.7 million between September 1, 1956 and August 31, 1959, 71 percent of this on faculty salaries, 13 percent on maintenance and operation of the physical plant, 15 percent on administrative and general expenses, and the remaining one percent on other costs. Income for the triennium was estimated at $15.9 million, 74 percent of this coming from tuition and fees, 14 percent from Junior College appropriations (which were in effect passed on to eligible students, and could be argued to be additional tuition income), seven percent from other income, primarily auxiliary enterprises and gifts and five percent from endowment.

Thus, $17.7 million, less $15.9 million, left the deficit, and campaign goal, of $1.8 million.

[20] Joseph M. Jones, surely among the most able volunteer leaders for higher education in the nation, was to die tragically with his wife in a heroic attempt to rescue her during a fire at their new residence—a major blow to Tulane University and to civic leadership in New Orleans.

[21] The donors were Regent Lamar Fleming, Jr., to whom I am indebted for guidance and assistance in my early days at the University, and his partner Will Clayton, who conceived many of the economic breakthroughs underlying the Marshall Plan. The last time I saw these great Houstonians together, I had gone by the Management Development Center one evening to retrieve some lecture notes, and thought I spied Mr. Fleming in an adjacent classroom where a practice debate on international affairs was under way. It was Lamar Fleming, all right, and with him was Mr. Clayton, paying tribute to student interest in an area they realized was vital to universities and nations alike.

[22] Dr. Tsanoff, an expert on the nature of evil, came to Rice from Cornell University with the original faculty, chopped wood for exercise, and was physically a man of 50 when he was placed on the inactive list under a new policy enforcing mandatory retirement at age 65. This was modified a year later, and the philosopher returned to Rice as the first Distinguished Trustee Professor, to remain until he was almost 80. He died at 89 in 1976. Professor Garrison, however, was the longevity champion who really placed mandatory retirement in question. Joining the University of Houston faculty when he was already 12 years past 65, he stayed on 12 more years, during which he served more than a decade as departmental chairman, wrote a dozen more books and went around the world on sabbatical. Professor Garrison requested retirement when he was 89; the request was reluctantly granted, and he lived on five more years.

Dr. Tsanoff attempted to teach me philosophy at Rice and once told me that much of his energy and longevity was attributable to Mrs. (Corinne) Tsanoff, his wife of more than a half-century, "who keeps us both so active and interested in things." Mrs. Tsanoff had a remarkable career of her own as an invaluable director or trustee of a variety of social service agencies. Their daughter, Katherine Tsanoff Brown, continues the family tradition of scholarship and community service.

[23] Mr. Meyer recalls his invaluable work on behalf of the University of Houston libraries in his own reminiscences, *The Days of My Years*. He remembers the opening 1940 campaign, when the entire

holdings at the University amounted to 12,290 volumes and were augmented by a $2,000 check presented to Librarian Ruth S. Wikoff. The 1940 Friends of the Library committee included Isaac Arnold, William T. Carter, III, Dr. Ray K. Daily (who originally asked Mr. Meyer to accept the chairmanship), Judge Roy Hofheinz, Palmer Hutcheson, Jr., Ernest Langston, Foster W. Montgomery, Henry Oliver and H. R. Safford, Jr. "Lep" Meyer was inspired to some extent originally by Jesse Ziegler, an 84-year-old historian and lover of classical literature who was helping the University of Houston libraries in the late 1930's when he wrote that he must "slow down a bit and let the younger generation take up the torch." Mr. Ziegler uncovered excerpts from Sam Houston's will of August 17, 1863, in which General Houston ordered that his sons "should receive a solid and useful education (with) no portion devoted to the study of abstract sciences . . . (should) possess a thorough knowledge of the English language . . . Latin . . . Holy Scriptures, and next to these, geography and history." Jesse Ziegler approved of this 1,000 percent.

[24] Social Security, then optional, had been approved, effective July 1, 1955, in an election of all 762 University employees, 560 to 108, with 94 not voting. The tenacious opposition, whose members equated Social Security with milder forms of communism, predicted that the supporting tax would "get as high as three percent, or even 3½, in a bureaucratic world gone mad." Little did they know that six percent, matched to total 12 percent, was a far more accurate estimate, and in little more than 20 years.

[25] The first Latin American students included Jose Ramon Garcia and Eloy Jaen of Panama, Antonio More of Cuba and Francisco de Javier Sanchez of Colombia, who graduated in 1946 and was one of the few international students to remain at the University throughout World War II. Edward K. T. Chen, whose family had emigrated to Galveston from China, and Keigo Matsumoto, a Japanese-American, were named outstanding students in 1941 and 1942, respectively, indicating perhaps the high degree of acceptance that has always existed for international students on the University of Houston campus. Edward Chen had a promising diplomatic career, but he died suddenly in 1957.

[26] Russell L. Jolley was typical of members of the Board of Governors with long experience in Community Chest (United Fund) campaigns who were invaluable in the Living Endowment Association drive. I wrote of Mr. Jolley in a professional journal, and parts of the paper were picked up in a book, then translated in a foreign edition.

[27] For months, General Bruce had sought an appointment with Jesse H. Jones, to ask him for an estimated $1 million for a

desperately needed building for the expanding College of Business Administration. The great day arrived, and the General, ever punctual, arrived five minutes early at the Bankers' Mortgage Building, grey Homburg, FOTC cufflinks and all. He was ushered in, and Mr. Jones rose from his desk to greet him. As he did, a look of acute distress came over the great financier's face. "General," he said, "I'm sorry, but you'll have to see me another time. You must excuse me."

General Bruce, mystified, said something or other as Mr. Jones disappeared out a side door. The General was both puzzled and downcast, thinking that he must somehow have offended Mr. Jones. He left early the next morning for a short vacation in Monterrey, and had just settled in at the Gran Ancira when Leta Gilbert called.

Over the formidable obstacles of Spanish-speaking operators, the General's partial deafness and the Mexican telephone system, she explained that Jesse Jones had called in his regards and further apologies, and wanted to know if it would be possible to see "Mr. Bruce" the following afternoon. General Bruce came back, Mr. Jones explained that he had suffered "a sudden bellyache," and it was agreed that he and Mrs. Jones and Houston Endowment, Inc., would give a building. There was one condition: the University was to name the building for "my friend and close associate of 47 years, Fred J. Heyne," and to engrave in the walls of the lobby a tribute from Mr. Jones to Mr. Heyne (the trusted and able chief lieutenant for the Jones Interests before, during and after Mr. Jones' extended absence in Washington, D.C. as Secretary of Commerce and as head of the Reconstruction Finance Corporation).

General Bruce agreed with thanks. A specific price was never set on the Heyne Building, and even after economies that included the omission of a traditional red tile roof, the expanded facility ran almost to $1.5 million. The extra sum was graciously provided after Mr. Jones' death in 1956, and the Heyne Building has been a keystone of the University of Houston's growing reputation in many phases of business administration and management from the day it was dedicated, September 28, 1958.

There was actually a little pre-dedication ceremony for "the Heyne." A few moments before everything was ready, John T. Jones, Jr., signalled to me, and I went over to him. There was a quick and whispered conference. Jesse Jones, II, his little son, had an urgent need to dedicate some of the plumbing in advance of the main ceremony. He trotted down the hall with me for a few minutes while the assembled notables waited.

[28] General Bruce had moved freely and comfortably in University Village, with its trailers and "shacks," or tiny apartments, because

virtually all the students living there were veterans. He asked that the Village be shut down as soon as possible, in recommendations made to the Board of Regents soon after his arrival in the fall of 1954; but he recognized that the 320 surplus trailers (some of them purchased for as little as $10, and then set on concrete block foundations) and the 351 "apartments" converted from 38 old barracks buildings, were home for ex-GI's struggling to complete their education. Where could you find even a tent, at prices ranging from $30 per month for a one-bedroom, to $37.50 for a three-bedroom unit, communal toilet and bathing facilities, plus utilities, thrown in?

There was, therefore, no sudden condemnation and padlocking in University Village, dreadful and unsafe though the area admittedly was; as the Korean War veterans and some holdovers from World War II were graduated, their units were either moved off or were not rented again. By 1956, the entire University Village, one of the greatest potential fire traps and health hazards in the history of campus housing, was no more. Everyone concerned, especially Ray Stidham, then in charge of Village maintenance, breathed a sigh of relief as the area, located in the eastern half of what is now parking lot 2-B of the Bates College of Law, was finally shut down.

Calhoun Road, then a narrow, shell-topped street, would never be the same. The entrepreneurs who had provided for a University Village population of almost 2,000 students and members of their families moved on. "Cannonball" Baker and his Saratoga Cafe at 4769 Calhoun had closed down early as the exodus from the Village started. Soon even Keno Garcia (Keno's Barber Shop and Liquor Store at 4619 Calhoun, a favorite hangout), was gone; so was Roy Brennan's branch of the Quality Laundry.

Raymond B. Allen's Bar S Cafe hung on. The former cowpoke featured 15-cent schooners of draft beer and barbecue sandwiches, plus advice. "I talk over their problems with them," Cowpoke Allen recalled. "If they're broke, they just sign the book. The highest bill ever run up was $17.90, by an ex-sergeant from Charleston, South Carolina. He left suddenly, but he sent me a money order for $18 a year later."

One of the "Calhoun Strip" businesses still survives. This is the Frat Club (Beer-Pool) at 4615 Calhoun, which Grace Hunsaker opened in 1950. The original name, Grace's Lounge, is still displayed on the south wall of the Frat Club after 27 years dating back to the last days of the Oberholtzer administration, and was recently added to the front as history came to the fore.

[29] The University dated its establishment from 1934 (when it was expanded to a four-year institution) until 1963. The founding date was moved back to 1927 when it was noted that virtually

every college and university was claiming the most antiquity possible, from Harvard University's 1636 [(when it consisted of one "master" in a tiny frame house at New Towne (Cambridge)] to Texas institutions which traced honorable but specious connections to one or more predecessors. The Rice Institute, in a project for which Howard S. Thompson had me doing volunteer research and writing as an alumnus, provided a correct and appropriate local model by changing both its name (to Rice University) and its founding date (from 1912, when classes began, back to 1891, when the charter of the Rice Institute was granted).

The "Silver Anniversary" of 1959, in which General Bruce took a considerable role, honored both the original faculty, dating back to 1927, and those who had completed 25 years of service since 1934: Bessie M. Ebaugh, Charles F. Hiller, Louis Kestenberg, C. F. McElhinney, L. Standlee Mitchell, E. Warren Rees, Mrs. Lillian Warren, Joseph S. Werlin, Ruth S. Wikoff, Zelda Osborne, and Alva Kerbow, who was retired in a special ceremony. He had been the first faculty member hired, in 1927.

A highlight of the Silver Anniversary was a scholarly and prophetic symposium on "The Next 100 Years of the Petroleum Industry," which I suggested to officials of the Texas Mid-Continent Oil & Gas Association when it appeared that the national observance of the industry centennial might fall into the hands of press agents who actually proposed a parade in Titusville, Pennsylvania with chorus girls sitting in the lap of a giant *papier mache* Colonel Edwin L. Drake (who discovered the first producing well near Titusville, in 1859). Chancellor Carey Croneis of Rice Institute presided in Cullen Auditorium, and meaningful papers were read in a half-dozen fields of marked significance. These included one of the first presentations on the possibility of ethical problems confronting the petroleum industry in future years, and one of Michel T. Halbouty's early, correct and unheeded predictions of potentially catastrophic energy shortages; see *Ahead of His Time,* a collection of Halbouty's speeches, published by Gulf Publishing Co., Houston.

[30] Translation: "We want in, and must get in, hopefully on our own, but we would consider joining the University of Texas System if it came to that, the odds on making it alone being so high." As recounted earlier, the University of Texas was not applying for adoption papers in 1961, even though the orphan had both hidden and visible strength, and enormous potential.

[31] Dr. Williams was extremely interested in football and had been known to lead cheers with vast enthusiasm at pep rallies. In the fall of 1959, after it had been announced that the Cougars were

leaving the Missouri Valley Conference to become an independent, there was continual discussion of the possibility of the University of Houston joining either the Southwest or the Southeast Conference. General Bruce regarded even discussion of this vital matter as something strictly reserved to himself, the Board of Governors and the Athletic Advisory Council. Dr. Williams was not really aware of this conviction on the part of the chancellor, but he had a strong personal preference for the Southeast Conference, which was quite understandable in terms of his background.

When a media representative called President Williams for comment on the situation, he told him of his predisposition toward the Southeast, added praise for the Crimson Tide of Alabama and the general level of competition in the Southeast, and suggested a press conference. The writer involved wasn't too keen on this, since he already had his story, but a conference was arranged nevertheless through the Office of Information.

At this point, General Bruce found out what was going on, called Dr. Williams in immediately, dressed him down properly, and cancelled the press conference. Clanton Williams was so furious, and crestfallen, that he walked the campus alone for an hour, to regain his composure.

[32] One interesting aspect of Clanton Williams' wide-ranging career little known in Houston was his experience as a news commentator on WJRD (Tuscaloosa) in the mid- and later 1930's. Using his detailed knowledge of history and geography, Dr. Williams originated a program he called "The Background of the News" to establish what amounted to his own regional network presentation. Through the program, reinforced by his ebullient personality, he met many of Alabama's long-established political leaders, and formed friendships that were maintained for decades.

[33] The text of President Williams' statement follows:

"When I first came to the University of Houston in 1955, the institution faced three problems of primary importance in the academic field. One was the need for an extensive self-study. A second problem was building a strong faculty on the excellent foundations provided by previous administrations. Third, there was the need for a revision of academic standards.

"While serving first as academic vice-president, and then as president, I have been able to see excellent progress toward resolving all of these problems, through the fine cooperation of my colleagues on the faculty and in the administration, and the strong and constant support of the governing board. Further accomplishments must now await the full state support which the University has requested, and so thoroughly deserves.

"Recently, I have been asked to consider other challenging opportunities. With very much of what I wished to achieve at the University now accomplished, The Board of Governors saw fit to grant me a leave of absence to consider the situation. I will begin a time away from the University on September 1, 1960.

"Whatever the future brings, I am certain of the continued progress of this fine institution, and of the great community which it serves."

It was a graceful statement, and a factual one, even though it did stretch a bit on the degree of progress made toward a self-study. There had been some discussions of this project, and very minor progress. But it would be 1964 before an actual self-study was launched as part of the 10-year reaccreditation requirements of the Southern Association.

General Bruce did not make a formal statement concerning President Williams. He did authorize the following for *Acta Diurna* and as part of the overall news release on the leave of absence: "(He) praised Dr. Williams' dedication to the institution, and his energetic work in uplifting academic standards. He emphasized the high regard in which Dr. Williams is held by his faculty and administration colleagues."

In a separate statement for *Acta Diurna,* the General pointed out that the organization can now be visualized, " . . . by simply showing the lines (which did run) to the president as (running) to the chancellor instead."

[34] I once stood near Ed Clark as he waited for the Senate to adjourn, often the signal for a convivial luncheon and some poker in his Driskill Hotel suite for Old Guard regulars within the upper chamber. Out strode Dorsey Hardeman, a conservative senator of considerable impact, seniority and sophistication, heading straight for his luncheon host; but as he walked toward Ed Clark, an elderly lady stepped in front of Mr. Clark for some reason, and announced in a loud voice: "That's Dorsey Hardeman; he's a senator." "I see," the lobbyist replied gravely in his St. Augustine drawl, bending over the woman as if she were the Queen Mother, while he signalled Dorsey Hardeman to walk on by him. "He looks like a senator, madam; I can believe it." As he spoke, he twirled a gold-headed walking cane, beautifully engraved with the signatures of Mr. Hardeman and his fellow lions of the Senate, as a token of appreciation to their host of so many legislative sessions. But Ed Clark, always the gentleman, was not willing to ignore or to risk embarrassing an old woman by indicating in any way that he knew Senator Hardeman.

[35] The "red book" was entitled "The University of Houston and Full State Tax Support." In addition to a dozen cogent reasons

for such support, this brochure had terse summaries and charts, graphs and pictures reproduced on a heavy, coarse paper that could be printed with color backgrounds that did not convey a "slick," expensive look (even though the back cover proclaimed that the publication was financed entirely by a special gift). I entered the brochure in a national competition, and it won first prize, which subjected me to much good-natured taunting from my friends in the private sector of higher education (which the publication would hopefully assist us to depart for fiscally more dependable shores). After returning from the conference at which the "red book" was awarded first prize, I received a telegram from my friend, colleague and chief heckler, Vice-Chancellor Edgar B. Cale of the University of Buffalo: "AIRMAIL IMMEDIATELY REPEAT IMMEDIATELY THREE COPIES PRIZEWINNING RED BOOK." The University of Buffalo, through a leading private institution in the East for generations, made safe harbor in public waters even before the University of Houston, and is now the State University of New York (SUNY) at Buffalo.

[36] The leaders of this campaign, which became something of a model for such projects in the component colleges, were Robert Balfanz of the Heights Pharmacy, chairman; W. Groce Lallier, president, Mading's Drug Company, co-chairman; C. H. Perkes, district manager, Walgreen Drug Company; Walter Kuntz, executive vice-president, Southwestern Drug Corporation; and L. A. Woods, district manager, McKesson & Robbins. Ralph Frede managed the drive for the University (and almost choked on his pipe tobacco one day when one of the volunteer leaders, awaiting a conference with him, noted that a large tin of his tobacco had been purchased from a highly competitive discount drug store near one of his own outlets).

[37] Co-sponsoring a bill can be tricky business. Maco Stewart, Jr., was once sitting at his desk, preoccupied with other matters, when a colleague came by with a bill for signature. It seemed complex, but upon being assured that it was a local bill, Representative Stewart signed it and thought nothing more about it. About a year later, the University's great friend and supporter A. R. (Babe) Schwartz found his Senate seat being challenged by Maco Stewart. Doing routine research, he came upon this local bill. It involved the right of nuns to teach in the public schools of certain German language areas, as had long been their custom. Maco Stewart thought that the bill protected this custom. Senator Schwartz found that it was the other way around. He ran off thousands of copies of the bill, with Maco Stewart's signature circled, and distributed them at the dozens of Catholic churches in his district. He then took a copy to the most influential monsignor in Galveston, who immediately summoned the unsus-

pecting Maco Stewart to a conference. Senator Schwartz was reelected.

[38] The charter, or early-on, supporters were Senators A. M. Aikin, Robert W. Baker, Jep S. Fuller, Henry B. Gonzalez, Grady Hazlewood, Abraham Kazen, Jr., Culp Krueger, George Moffett, George Parkhouse, William N. Patman, David W. Ratliff, Bruce A. Reagan, A. R. Schwartz, Jarrard Secrest and Doyle Willis. The seemingly unshakeable nine were Mrs. Neveille H. Colson, Tom Creighton, Martin Dies, Jr., Dorsey Hardeman, Hubert R. Hudson, Wardlow Lane, William T. Moore, Preston Smith and Rudolph A. Weinert. Those of indeterminate persuasions were Galloway Calhoun, Jr., a gentleman enamored of the introductory phrase, "Now, I'm gonna be frank with you;" Louis Crump, Charles F. Herring, Crawford C. Martin, who had told Bob Baker, "How can I be against you, when you voted for my John Tarleton College deal in 1959," but subsequently abandoned the cause; Frank Owen, III; Ray Roberts and Andy Rogers.

[39] A typical Moore-Lane colloquy during the filibuster: Moore—"I'll ask the senator from Shelby (County), when they start a branch of Oxford University in your district, because this state seems bound and determined to have one university per county, you going to locate yours in Teneha, or Bobo, or Blair?" Lane—"I'm studying that, senator; we might apply for one each."

[40] In Middle English, the literal meaning of "engrossed" was "written large"; in the legislative sense, "engrossing" is preparing the final text of a bill for third reading and, presumably, final passage—although an engrossed bill can be, and often is, amended.

[41] The members of the selection committee were Deans Noel Ferguson and Eugene H. Hughes; faculty members Corinne Weston and Thornton C. Sinclair; and Mr. Fleming, W. G. Farrington, Jack Valenti and Roy Henry Cullen of the Board of Governors, the latter two men being alumni.

Chapter Seven

1961-1971

A far larger canvas...Three roadblocks are removed, two by HB 291 and another at the TCOHE...Philip Guthrie Hoffman is inaugurated...Huge increases in enrollment, faculty, physical plant, library holdings and other critical areas...The Excellence Campaign takes over for LEA...A reorganized and augmented staff...The 1964 self-study...A new master plan...First steps toward the University of Houston System... Marked expansion internationally...Admission requirements of far-reaching impact...KUHT goes full power...Student unrest finally erupts...The new Alumni Federation...A golden era for intercollegiate athletics...General Bruce is buried with the storied dead of the armies

Now we must telescope our history.

Almost one-third of the institution's first 50 years remain to be chronicled, but the canvas suddenly becomes a mural—one is so close to the work that a broad, comprehensive perspective is difficult. You sense the need for related histories in specific fields (and they are already in preparation)[1]; for a perspective which will allow archivists and future historians to understand the overwhelming transformation of the University of Houston between 1961 and 1971, and on through 1977.

Another factor mandating a compression of our history after 1961 is the atmosphere of relative stability in which the Board of Regents and Phil Hoffman have led the University through 16 years of noteworthy progress—without the kaleidoscopic shifts, changes and rivalries of earlier administrations. Charles F. Hiller's theory of conflict at the top being indispensable to progress (see Chapter Six) has been eclipsed, at least temporarily, at the University of Houston, even though there have been and will be skirmishes (including brush fires between the Office of the President and a minority within the Faculty Senate) as the Hoffman administration confronts complex issues in the late 1970's.

A clear pattern for the advancement so evident throughout his presidency emerged in Phil Hoffman's first decade at the helm. These fundamental statistics tell the story, one of striking progress:

	1961	*1971*
Enrollment	12,187	26,475
Graduate Students	1,046	3,100
Faculty	675	1,450
Full-time	375	800
Part-time	300	650
Budget	$ 9,660,607	$ 29,395,460
Value of Physical Plant	$26,000,000	+$100,000,000
Library Volumes	262,765	664,469
Research Funds	$ 505,000	$ 7,131,000
Terminal Degrees Offered	8	24
Graduates/Degrees	1,345	3,891
Baccalaureate	1,116	3,011
Master's	194	597
Doctoral	35	283
Gifts (excluding federal grants)	$ 1,012,468	$ 2,851,878

Among other accomplishments in the decade 1961-1971 were:

1. The reorganization and augmentation of the administrative staff, including major shifts within the ranks of the academic deans;

2. Conducting an exacting, institution-wide self-study;

3. Completing a new master plan for campus development;

4. Taking substantial first steps toward the formation of a University of Houston System;

5. A marked augmentation of programs in the field of international affairs;

6. The institution of new admission requirements;

7. Converting KUHT from a low-power, black-and-white station to full power and color transmission—thereby expanding its capabilities, mission and services geometrically;

8. New scope and direction for the Faculty Senate;

9. Meeting the inevitable challenge of student unrest with firmness tempered with concern for just resolution of genuine issues and the preservation of traditional freedoms and values;

10. Reorganizing the Alumni Association into an Alumni Federation; and

11. Phenomenal achievements in the field of intercollegiate athletics.

But all of this laudable advancement had to await the removal of three massive roadblocks to further progress. These were the completely illogical ban (via Senate Bill 2) against state support for courses above the baccalaureate level, the further requirement of thorough curricular review and approval by the TCOHE, and the lack of a statutory means of financing additional buildings, desperately needed for a now predictably huge influx of students, with tuition dropping from approximately $700 to $100 on September 1, 1963, the day that the University entered the state system of higher education.

As it turned out, the galling 1961 provision against graduate work at the University of Houston was a blessing in disguise. From the moment we began framing corrective legislation for submission to the 1963 Legislature, it was agreed that the measure would be styled, “a bill to restore graduate work” at the University. How, we concluded, could anyone effectively oppose such a reasonable proposition? And why not, in curing this defect, do something about a statutory base for financing new buildings?

Thus, as we shall see, House Bill (HR) 291 of the 58th Legislature was not the Red Cross ambulance it appeared to be, but an armored tank in disguise. The guns cleared away two of the three roadblocks impeding the University’s inevitable advance, leaving the third vital matter of TCOHE sanction of courses, degrees, and related academic proposals.

Late in 1961, we launched an intensive review of the TCOHE, which had five new members and an extremely competent new director, Dr. Jack K. Williams, now president of Texas A&M University. President Hoffman undertook to visit each member of the Commission in home or office, after we had obtained detailed information on the background, connections, interests and likely reactions of the individual commissioners. Simultaneously, Dr. Williams and his staff were provided with comprehensive information on every aspect of the University of Houston operation within the purview of the TCOHE, with ample opportunity to react with and to question University representatives.

We decided from the outset that we would neither attempt to protect *every* curricular offering nor fail to defend any degree, program or course for which we felt there was a genuine need. Basic to this fundamental policy were the concepts of *unnecessary* duplication, marginal demand and appropriate role and scope.

The principle of unnecessary duplication (which was to assist the University mightily in later battles to extend doctoral programs), had strong underpinning in our long-established tradition of evening classes, in the distance to other state-supported institutions with comparable and available offerings, and in the growing differential between private and public tuition. In chemistry and chemical engineering, for example, our courses duplicated those at Rice University or Texas A&M; but even if a student were able to enter Rice, he would find no evening classes enabling him to work during the day; nor could he commute 93 miles to College Station. Similarly, law courses were available at South Texas College of Law, at increasingly high tuition, or 162 miles away at the University of Texas; but the College of Law of the University of Houston was not unnecessarily duplicative.

Dr. Hoffman had kept Clanton Williams' pruning shears well sharpened, although he snipped away carefully. By 1961, curricular offerings were in a fairly lean state of health. Nevertheless, there were remaining areas where either marginal demand or considerations of appropriate role and scope dictated further cutting back or downright removal of programs. The department of agricultural economics had been withering steadily away with smaller and smaller enrollments, and had reached a stage where it had to be abolished completely, with remaining instructional staff transferred to the economics staff (although virtually all chose to go elsewhere). This was accomplished quickly, with a stretch-out to May 31, 1963, for degrees in process. There were other deletions, most of them affecting relatively small numbers of students or faculty members.

Role and scope became an issue within several components of the University, especially in the College of Technology. Here there was a long tradition of vocational offerings (tied to the earliest institutional statements of purpose), though the College was already exhibiting the national and international leadership for which it is now known in the controlling field of technology.

The decision was that vocational courses were essentially more suited to a junior college or high school setting, and were not appropriate to the role and scope of a university. President Hoffman announced November 1, 1961, that only programs for training engineering technicians, accredited by the Engineers' Council for Professional Development (ECPD), would be retained in the College of Technology. Six vocational programs were deleted: auto mechanics, auto upholstery and trim, furniture upholstery, machine shop, radio and television servicing, and welding. Programs in air conditioning and refrigeration mechanics, applied electricity, and applied electronics were adapted to ECPD models and retained, along with civil, diesel and drafting technology. This actually affected only 71 of 816 students in the College of Technology and was a powerful impetus in further accelerating the striking progress of this component since 1961.

There were other course deletions as the University of Houston approached the crucial TCOHE meeting of April 9, 1962, at which the Commission would review the institution's curricular offerings, degrees and academic organization. All remedial courses were terminated; even though there remained a sound need for many of these, the State of Texas would not allow the use of appropriated dollars to support them. Telecourses were also unfunded, under a prohibitive rider to the general appropriations bill; it was decided, however, that some of these offerings would continue, at least for two years, while alternative support was pursued.

We felt the University had a strong case for submission to the TCOHE, reinforced by the cooperative attitude of the staff and of most members of the Commission. This attitude persisted after President Hoffman's brief but able presentation to the formal hearing of April 9, and was confirmed when the administration and key members of the faculty were invited back to meet with TCOHE members and staff on June 5, 1962, when most determinations regarding our role and scope would be announced.

The extremely favorable decisions then handed down can be best evaluated in Dr. Hoffman's own words at a subsequent press conference: "The decisions of the Texas Commission on Higher Education on the role and scope of the University of Houston," he said, "definitely establish this institution as a new major unit within the state system of higher education. The TCOHE established the fundamental principle of doctoral programs at the University by giving firm approval to Ph.D. degrees in chemistry, chemical engineering, physics and psychology. The Commission also approved 37 master's degree programs, and virtually our entire undergraduate program, as carefully revised by our staff and faculty in consultation with the TCOHE."

Dr. Hoffman spoke with unusual emphasis because there had been widespread pessimism and misunderstanding of TCOHE action in postponing final action on the crucial doctorate in education (Ed.D.), and on Ph.D.'s in mechanical and electrical engineering, which remained under study until at least July 9, 1962.

He pointed out that the doctorate in education, offered since 1947, pre-dated all of the professional degrees except pharmacy, approved by the TCOHE in a somewhat routine procedure on January 8, 1962, and all of the Ph.D. offerings affirmed thus far. The Doubting Thomases on campus countered by stressing the central importance of the Ed.D. and the fact that the Commission had agreed to consider studying the possibility of consolidating University of Houston programs in pharmacy and law with those at Texas Southern University. This question had been raised by one member of the TCOHE, to the consternation of both institutions involved.

Let us turn now to the inauguration of Philip G. Hoffman, on April 27, 1962, the first such event at the institution in 17 years, the second ever, and the last since 1962.[2]

Vice President McElhinney was chairman for the inaugural proceedings, which included a concert in Cullen Auditorium the preceding evening (all performers were members of our excellent music faculty); the inauguration itself, also in Cullen Auditorium; a luncheon at the Rice Hotel; and an evening reception at the Houston Club.

More than 300 delegates from colleges, universities, educational organizations and learned societies marched in the academic procession, which featured an "Academic March" composed especially for the occasion by Professor Elmer Schoettle and another original work by Professor Merrills Lewis. The inaugural address was by President Harlan Hatcher of the University of Michigan (President Hoffman's dean years before at Ohio State University), who praised the emergence of new institutions in an era when "education is the key that unlocks the door to greatness, and universities are the generative and focal center of the creative force of a nation."

President Hoffman paid tribute to Colonel Bates, Hugh Roy Cullen and others instrumental in bringing the University of Houston to its current level of accomplishment and potential. He made special mention of the presidents who had preceded him, of principal donors, and of the Board of Governors. He praised the Harris County delegation for its dedicated and successful work in bringing the University into the state system.

Referring to a difficult period of transition in which the institution had been "subjected to more than its usual quota of stress and strain," with extensive administrative reorganization and a redefinition of role and scope, President Hoffman pointed to the stable and mature manner in which the faculty had moved through what could have been a traumatic time.

"Realistically," Dr. Hoffman continued, "this will become a large university. This dictates a high priority for new buildings, for a more selective admissions process, for other reasonable controls on size. We do not prize size itself, other than as a possible index of public service. We do, however, prize quality."

President Hoffman concluded with excerpts from a 1959 report on "What Makes A University Great," by a committee headed by Professor T.N. Hatfield. The integrity of a university, he affirmed, requires constant re-evaluation of its aims, functions and curricula; an atmosphere which is at all times conducive to free enterprise in ideas; leading, not following; and "not lightly claiming greatness."[3]

"The University of Houston," Dr. Hoffman summarized, "is not a great university. We believe, however, that it is a good university which has very much within its total situation the basic ingredients of greatness."

It was an excellent address, well received, and a memorable day for the University and for Philip Guthrie Hoffman. But his finest moment came two hours later at the inaugural luncheon. One of the speakers (a Houstonian, at that) had the effrontery and poor taste to use the occasion to challenge the University's position in requesting TCOHE approbation of its College of Law and various doctoral programs.

After a moment of shocked silence from the audience, President Hoffman met his first post-inaugural crisis with the correct balance of justified counterattack, and good manners. He proceeded to cut the offender politely to ribbons with a few carefully chosen but pointed remarks that brought loud applause.

Dr. Hoffman's faith in the further determinations of the TCOHE was justified on July 9, 1962, even though the University of Houston did not carry the entire field at the moment. The doctorate in education, a 15-year old program of vast significance to the College of Education (which has traditionally prepared more than half of the teachers for the entire Gulf Coast region) was approved without qualification. At the same time, the TCOHE "endorsed in principle" the doctoral degree (Ph.D.) in electrical engineering and mechanical engineering, requesting a re-submission when adequacy in necessary library, laboratory and other research facilities could be clearly demonstrated, and agreed to hear a proposal for the Ph.D. in biophysics within three months.

On the same day, the Commission also announced that any study of consolidating University of Houston and Texas Southern University programs in pharmacy and law had been "postponed." This was further cause for rejoicing, especially when the question failed to resurface.

By the end of the 1964-1965 academic year, the TCOHE had approved the terminal degrees in electrical and mechanical engineering, economics, mathematics, biology, and biophysical sciences; and there was a steady progression to the 24 terminal offerings of 1971. Another most significant date in this regard was February 24, 1966, when the Coordinating Board, Texas College and University System (successor to the TCOHE) voted to limit the Ph.D. degree to the University of Houston, University of Texas, Texas A&M University, Texas Technological University, and to long-established programs at North Texas State University and Texas Women's University; to limit colleges or schools of law to the University of Houston, Texas and Texas Tech (with a phase-out of the Texas Southern University School of Law by September 1, 1968 subsequently rescinded); to limit schools or colleges of architecture to the University of Houston, Texas, Texas A&M and Texas Tech; and to continue to study pharmacy offerings at the University of Houston, Texas and Texas Southern.

Our successes with the TCOHE/Coordinating Board helped the situation on Austin's Capitol Hill as we prepared for the opening of the 58th Legislature on January 18, 1963; but there was lingering bitterness, and jealousy, engendered by the growing realization that the state system of higher education had a new, sharply competitive member with large and justifiable needs.

No longer did I have the redoubtable Ben Ramsey and the dependable, comforting presence of Senator Robert W. Baker in the Senate. Criss Cole, however, had been promoted to the upper chamber, and Representative Wallace H. Miller, a strong ally throughout the legislative struggle in 1961, was ready to manage our new bill in the House. He would have staunch support from Bill T. Swanson and other members of the Harris County delegation.[4]

To correct the shortcomings of SB 2, we drafted late in 1962 a doublebarreled measure which became HB 291. Ostensibly, this bill was almost exclusively directed to the restoration of graduate instruction at the University, with the usual other minor corrections. One section, however, based upon a variation of a seldom-used statute, authorized the Board of Regents to issue revenue bonds against academic building use fees. The fee was set initially at $10 per student per semester; at several times that amount it would still be a boon and a bargain to students paying only $100 a year in tuition but handicapped more and more by the greatest shortage of instructional facilities at any major university in the nation.

We had already located an expert on revenue bond issues through my gin rummy partner at the Houston Country Club, C. C. McClung of the firm of McClung & Knickerbocker. They were standing by with the best attorneys and other specialists available, awaiting passage of HB 291 and the statutory authority to proceed.

I was told that the provision for building use fees (BUF) would never pass, "that everyone in the Legislature would ask questions about it." Three of the 181 legislators did ask. I told them all the same thing: "That section will save the University of Houston (and thereby the State of Texas) money. It will allow us to borrow funds for some buildings we need at a lower rate." And it would, since our tax-exempt bonds were to have the added security and lower interest provided by statutory authorization—if we could pass HB 291.

There was another drawn-out legislative struggle, with the climax coming in the Senate only two weeks before adjournment. HB 291 had finally been guided through the House of Representatives by Wallace Miller, after some anxious moments with Speaker Byron M. Tunnell; but we simply could not get it out of committee in the Senate. As the days dwindled down, Lieutenant Governor Preston Smith's telephone lines became jammed with calls from Harris County campaign contributors he could not ignore. There was an agreement to have HB 291 quietly referred to a second committee where we enjoyed a comfortable margin. The motion, which had to be on the floor of the Senate, would be by the popular Senator Criss Cole, HB 291's sponsor in the upper chamber.

This delicate operation had to be accomplished in a moment or two of a routine afternoon session, with enough of the opposition absent. The fact that Senator Cole is blind complicated things somewhat, but our great friends Senators A. R. (Babe) Schwartz and Jim Bates were capable floor managers.

The moment arrived, the motion was made, and we had a safe margin to re-refer our bill to friendly hands—if there were no delay to allow the opposition to hurry reinforcements to the floor. At this moment, our long-time ally George Parkhouse, the lion-hearted senator from Dallas whose bellows of surprise or indignation could be heard throughout the Capitol, awoke from his postprandial nap. As he started to get to his feet and demand an explanation, Babe Schwartz rushed over and clamped his hand over his colleague's mouth. In a fierce whisper I could hear from my gallery station next to the Senate clock,[5] Senator Schwartz said, "Shut up, George; it's Criss' University of Houston bill."

HB 291 was thus sent to a committee having absolutely nothing to do with higher education, and it moved quickly toward final passage with a minor amendment limiting eminent domain to Harris County and adjacent counties.

But there was one more hurdle for HB 291. President Hoffman had come over for final passage, and he and I went to the Senate early on the agreed day to thank Preston Smith for his assistance. He came out on the floor to greet us, but with a grim and unhappy look. "Your bill can't come up today," he told me. Some of those House members of yours are blocking that movie bill we sent over."

I thought for a moment that Phil Hoffman was going through the handsome roof of the Senate chamber. He started to ask the obvious question: What did a "movie bill" have to do with the University of Houston? I knew the answer and was able to signal him to let me reply to the lieutenant governor, who happened to be a motion picture theater owner. "I'm sorry if some of our guys got mixed up on that," I told Governor Smith. "I'll try to have a report for you before the Senate convenes."

Some of our House members had indeed blocked the "movie bill" as part of the never-ending parade of trades, swap-outs and pressure tactics in the waning days of the session; but Wallace Miller and others were able to persuade them to change their minds quickly. HB 291 passed the Senate later that day, just after L. Gordon Cooper, Jr., had splashed down in Atlas 9, his Mercury program spacecraft for 34 hours, 19 minutes and 45 seconds aloft—the first long space flight by an American.

It was May 16, 1963, and the University of Houston had its corrected, basic legislation, including the authority to issue revenue bonds essential to a construction program that would exceed $100 million. Back at the Driskill Hotel, Dr. Hoffman and I sent a cablegram to Mr. Mac, who was on the high seas on a long-planned vacation: "Bill passed. Get off those pecan balls." (Vice-President McElhinney had developed a minor addiction to a Headliners Club specialty, plenty of vanilla ice cream covered with pecan halves and gobs of chocolate sauce.)

We then drank to the University, to Criss Cole, Wallace Miller and the other members of the Harris County delegation, and finally, to Gordie Cooper.

Astronaut Cooper had just splashed down; the University of Houston was finally in orbit.

The earlier summary of President Hoffman's accomplishments during his first 10 years as chief executive demonstrates clearly that if we label him Hoffman the Builder, it is in recognition of his building far more than a beautiful and functional physical plant for the University.

Remarkable gains in enrollment were to underlie much of the progress from 1961 to 1971.[6] A 131 percent jump in the student body fueled the machine, necessitating constant pressure for a priority construction program, doubling the faculty, almost tripling library holdings, escalating budgets that ran up 72 per cent in 10 years, similar gains in graduates and gifts—and an unbelievable 14-fold increase (from $505,000 to $7,131,000) in research funds.

Phil Hoffman knew from the moment he was chosen to succeed General Bruce in 1961 that the lack of anything even approaching an adequate physical plant was a crucial problem. Drastic overcrowding could literally engulf the University in a succession of difficulties unless this rudimentary problem was attacked quickly, relentlessly, and successfully. And if he could provide at least enough additional facilities to meet the first years of crisis, President Hoffman could buy time for a more adequate solution.

Studies, and common sense, told the new president that he had two years before the first precipitate jump in enrollment, immediately after state support became available on September 1, 1963. From that moment, no one really knew what pressures there would be for admission; but some new buildings would have to be on line as soon as possible after 1963, and then in steadily expanding number for at least 10 to 15 years.

Early in 1962 the Executive Committee of the Board of Governors was given a tentative list of the highest priority construction projects. These were a building for chemistry and pharmacy ($3.7 million), an addition to the M.D. Anderson Library ($3.3 million), a general classroom building ($3.8 million), and the $600,000 Religion Center, on which ground was about to be broken even though less than $400,000 was actually in hand from contributing religious denominations.

The "greatest need" projects were atop a longer list of urgent requirements which President Hoffman announced September 12, 1962, with the approval and complete support of the Board of Governors. The additional facilities were the University Center, a Fine Arts Building, the first phase of an eventual Law Center, a new home for the College of Engineering, a major addition to the College of Technology, a field house and sports arena/physical education center, a Student Services Building, a new dormitory complex, and a center for general services.

These requirements ran to $29 million, a staggering sum 15 years ago—especially before the passage of HB 291, with its authorization of building use fees (BUF's) and a constitutional amendment of November 2, 1965. The latter would provide a limited amount of construction funds through doubling an old five cents per $100 valuation tax (originally enacted for the support of widows of Confederate veterans) and adding the University of Houston and other new members of the state system of higher education to the list of beneficiaries.

We probably would have thrown in the towel had we known that the 1962 estimate of $29 million in building needs would quadruple with the spectacular gains in enrollment, the broadening of the University's role and scope, including a constant escalation in research and public service activities; and with the rampant inflation that would exceed one percent *per month* in construction and equipment costs.

Instead, we got a massive building program under way with key private gifts, accelerated it mightily with BUF dollars matched with federal grants, added three other large gifts totalling $4 million at a critical juncture, and turned what is now the Central Campus into a gallery of handsome and extremely functional buildings.

The facility that started things moving was the Lamar Fleming, Jr., Building for chemistry and pharmacy, the first major addition to the physical plant in five years. Another $1.5 million gift from the M.D. Anderson Foundation brought this long-delayed project from the drawing board to reality. After the untimely death of Regent Fleming on July 5, 1964, it was decided to name the building for him, and this stimulated additional contributions totaling more than another $1.5 million from Will Clayton, the Clayton Fund, the Cullen Foundation, the Brown Foundation, the estate of Mrs. Lamar Fleming, Jr., and from Mrs. Walter W. Fondren, Sr., Milton R. Underwood, Mr. and Mrs. J.M. Johnson, and C. Emmett Waddell.

The University kept up the momentum for this unprecedented building program. This was done through several innovative procedures, some of them involving elements of justifiable risk. Sensing that major construction grants under the revolutionary Higher Education Facilities Act (HEFA) would go to those institutions with (1) clearly demonstrated needs, (2) a ready source of matching funds, (3) completed architectural plans and specifications, and (4) political clout, President Hoffman and the governing board led the way in assuring that these elements were at hand as early as possible.

There was simply no problem in demonstrating a need, and a desperate one, for adding to physical plant—especially after the fall registration of 1963. A total of 12,870 former students and 4,740 freshmen jammed registration lines in the old "Rec" Building from morning until Registrar Ramon A. Vitulli's exhausted workers had to lock the doors late at night; enrollment was up 28 percent in a single year, 55 percent over 1959. The campus was as crowded as the sidewalks of New York City the day Charles A. Lindbergh returned home in a ticker tape parade.

The ready source of matching funds became available when Governor John B. Connally signed HB 291 into law on May 31, 1963, though the Board of Regents would have to set the amount of the BUF's authorized by the new statute, and C.C. McClung and his revenue bond experts would have to carry out complex legal and banking operations culminating in our receiving millions of dollars.[7]

The governing board adopted BUF resolutions as soon as possible after an organizational meeting held on September 18, 1963. The regents failed to realize, however, the impact of additional building needs coupled with rising inflation. The original fee of $10 per semester, described as "modest," was modest indeed. For by 1966 the shortfall on a building program expanded to $51.5 million was in excess of $30 million, and successive increases in the BUF, plus a separate fee charged for the University Center (not an academic building), had to be implemented. The BUF now stands at $80 per semester, still little enough when you consider what it has provided for the student body, and the extremely low tuition in effect in the Texas system of higher education.

Obtaining completed architectural plans and specifications in the volume required to keep such a massive construction program under full steam would have required several millions of dollars in advance or ongoing payments. The solution lay in an American Institute of Architects provision allowing members to prepare plans on a contingency basis differing from the normal contractual arrangements. The University, under such a contract, had to agree that when and if the project became a reality, it would be built from the plans prepared in hope of a future commission. The architects involved reasoned that they were dealing with a substantial client, with every reason to expect a commission, and agreed to these special agreements that were so helpful to the University and to those it served.

The University of Houston was extremely fortunate in the appointments to the Board of Regents announced by Governor John B. Connally on August 7, 1963. Six of the regents were members of the Board of Governors and prominent Houstonians with an intimate knowledge of the community and the University: Colonel Bates, James A. Elkins, Jr., Aaron J. Farfel, Corbin J. Robertson, Jack J. Valenti, and Mrs. Gus S. Wortham. The other three appointees were experienced executives with valuable ties in Austin, their own areas of the state, and elsewhere in Texas: George S. Hawn, the oilman and investor of Corpus Christi, an alumnus; James T. Duke, a rancher from LBJ's home town of Johnson City, retired from the Brown & Root organization after a long career as principal fiscal officer; and Edward D. Manion, a Beaumont businessman whose wife was a member of one of the families participating in the historic Spindletop discovery in 1901.

The economic and political impact of this group was significant from the outset of the University's priority construction program, as it was (and has been with succeeding governing boards) in the overall development of the institution.

The following summary shows how well Hoffman the Builder and the regents, with the cooperation of faculty and staff, worked together to resolve much of the central dilemma of lack of physical plant between 1965 and 1971—although the problem of adequate space continues to plague the University of Houston today:

Project	*Date Completed*	*Cost ($)*
A.D. Bruce Religion Center	1965	600,000
Lamar Fleming, Jr., Building	1966	3,700,000
University Center	1967	5,000,000
M.D. Anderson Library (Addition)	1967	3,300,000
Cullen College of Engineering[8]	1967	4,600,000
Agnes Arnold Hall[8]	1967	3,800,000
Underground Computer Center	1967	400,000
Student Life Building	1968	1,600,000
Science and Research Center	1969	7,300,000
1967 Additions to Utility Tunnels	1969	900,000
Bates College of Law[8]	1969	4,000,000
Central Power Plant (Addition)	1969	900,000
Hofheinz Pavilion and Men's Gymnasium[8]	1970	6,000,000
Moody Towers[8]	1970	10,400,000
Melcher Gymnasium[8]	1970	1,600,000
General Services Building	1970	1,800,000
Isabel C. Cameron Building[8]	1970	1,000,000
Roy G. Cullen Building (Remodeling)	1970	500,000
Science Building (Remodeling)	1970	300,000
Cullen College of Engineering (Addition)	1970	200,000
1968 Additions to Utility Tunnels	1970	600,000
World Affairs (Geology) Building (Remodeling)	1970	40,000
Architecture Building (Remodeling)	1970	77,000
Coastal Environmental Laboratory[8]	1970	65,000
Information Center	1970	21,000
College of Education	1970	4,000,000
New Electric Service	1970	300,000
1969 Additions to Tunnels (North Loop)	1970	900,000
McElhinney Hall[8]	1971	2,300,000
Clear Lake Graduate Center	1971	1,600,000
Maintenance Building (Remodeling)	1971	240,000
TOTAL		68,043,000

Even more noteworthy is the fact that all but two of these 31 projects were completed in the four years between 1967 and 1971, when much of the campus resembled a gigantic construction site, with towering cranes, barricades, warning signs, torn-up streets, flooded, muddy walkways...and dozens of workers, leering and whistling at the leggy co-eds ambling by in their miniskirts.

One of President Hoffman's basic strengths from the day of his arrival on campus in 1957 had been an ability to relate quickly and positively to the deans and key members of the faculty. He identified those of established ability and clear potential, and assisted them as he could to improve their performance; at the same time, he did not hesitate to transfer, demote or terminate when necessary. The latter procedures were accomplished with tact and consideration, and almost invariably through some face-saving device if the position being vacated was a highly visible one. Those decapitated nevertheless knew that they had been weighed in the balance and found wanting. They were told the particulars.

When the Hoffman administration began, in 1961, there was a solid core of teaching and administrative strength dating back to the 1940's and, in a few cases, to the first decade of the institution. This had been reinforced substantially by Clanton Williams' highly selective pruning, transfers, and recruiting. Nontheless, the avalanche of students expected each semester since 1963 would make it necessary to more than double the faculty by 1971, with attendant increases in academic and non-academic administrators alike; the new president seized this opportunity to shore up the entire operation with the best reinforcements available, even though he was hampered by thin salary budgets and mediocre fringe benefits (such as a maximum annual state contribution of $504 to the Teachers' Retirement System). Emphasis would be upon younger instructors and assistant professors from leading institutions, particularly those exhibiting prowess in research and other scholarly pursuits in addition to the basic ability to teach. There would also be an infusion of senior professors at the top, for seasoning and balance. To accomplish this, Phil Hoffman realized that he must find a talented replacement for the vice-president, dean of faculties position he had vacated to assume the presidency. He would continue to devote time and energy to selection and administration of the teaching staff, and to continuing the shifts within the ranks of the academic deans initiated by President Williams; but he knew he would have to delegate authority in considerable degree in order to stay on top of other pressing matters outside the purely academic arena.

For the central appointment affecting the faculty, Dr. Hoffman chose a brilliant young nuclear physicist, John C. Allred, not yet 35, who had come to the University in 1956 from Los Alamos and the University of Texas. Dr. Allred had been named associate dean of the College of Arts and Sciences in 1959, charged with breathing fire into the science departments of this component, semi-dormant under a policy of little or no research. Dr. Hoffman appointed him assistant to the president in 1961, and vice-president, dean of faculties a year later.

John Allred quickly assumed a central role in faculty selection and administration, and in the pivotal changes involving deans, although President Hoffman retained ultimate control.

The first shift in deans was a major one in every respect. Eugene H. Hughes, first and only head of the College of Business Administration since 1947, announced April 1, 1964, that he would resign to become a professor within the new Office of International Affairs, effective September 1. Jerome M. Peschke was named acting dean then, and served until June 1, 1965, when Ted R. Brannen replaced Dean Hughes.

Ted Brannen was "a new kind of cat in the dean business," said one member of the eventual parade of business administration faculty who came by to complain to me about him. Handsome, dapper and highly articulate, he came from Oklahoma State University, where he had been chairman of the general business department, after a varied career that had included earning the doctorate in economics and anthropology at the University of Texas; an administrative post with the Graduate Center of the Southwest in Dallas; consulting posts in Saudi Arabia; and the vice-chancellorship of the University of Kansas City.

Dean Brannen installed a strikingly different curriculum. "The College of Business Administration," he announced, "is now oriented toward value theory. Business has a social responsibility; the ultimate goal of this curriculum is to teach that principle, through quantitative and behavioral science plus specific (and more traditional) tasks and skills."

The Brannen curriculum prevailed, but something well over one-half of the faculty he inherited did not. They scattered to the four winds, while prophets of the new curriculum arrived. Today, fifteen years later, the College of Business Administration is one of the strongest components within the University, and Ted Brannen, who left to become dean of business administration at the University of Southern California, has gone back to classroom teaching there.

Another notable change within the ranks of the deans was Arvin N. Donner's retirement on August 31, 1966, after a long and distinguished career at the helm of the College of Education. He was replaced by Robert B. Howsam, associate dean of graduate studies at the University of Rochester. An innovative and highly competent educator and administrator, Dean Howsam had reorganized the College by 1970, led his strengthened faculty in planning an extremely flexible and functional "open space" building that is an architectural triumph, and had pushed through the concept of competency-based teaching.

There were other important changes in the leadership of the colleges of the University, some of them of lasting significance: Hugh E. McCallick replaced A. Ray Sims as dean of the College of Technology, after the latter's death from a brain tumor. Dean McCallick took office September 1, 1964, and has since brought his component to a position of international eminence by building on the foundations of his predecessor. John B. Neibel became dean of the Bates College of Law on September 1, 1965, after Dean Newell Blakely asked to return to teaching following a successful administration marked by constant growth in enrollment and recognition accorded the College. On the same date, Charles V. Kirkpatrick succeeded Frank M. Tiller as dean of the Cullen College of Engineering. Dean Tiller, involved in a highly successful program in the newly established Office of International Affairs, asked to be appointed as director of this component. He had accomplished much during his 10 years of leadership at the College, and was to continue this tradition of progress in his new position, where sizable contracts were to be signed early in 1966.

There were two additional appointments of consequence on September 1, 1967. Walter E. George replaced Richard W. Lilliott, long-time director (and then dean) of the College of Architecture. Dean Lilliott, an art historian and a capable administrator, was not an architect, and as his College continued a steady expansion it was felt that a practitioner was required as dean. He returned to a long and successful career in the classroom, but continued as a key member of the faculty and as an advisor until his retirement in 1977. Richard Lilliott was particularly helpful after Dean George resigned unexpectedly in 1969. W. R. Jenkins was named acting dean for two years, accepting full appointment in 1971; it was during this *ad interim* period that Dick Lilliott's experience and judgment were so valuable again to the College of Architecture.

Daniel E. O'Keefe became the first director (later dean) of the Graduate School of Social Work on September 1, 1967.[9] Nationally known in his field, Dean O'Keefe had made a fine start in establishing his new school (particularly in terms of vital relationships with the more than 60 social agencies in the city) when he became critically ill and died in 1971. He was succeeded by Gary Lloyd, formerly of Tulane University.

Two final changes in deanships were the naming of James C. Taylor as dean of continuing education (in addition to his post as dean of the Downtown School, on December 7, 1966) and R. Balfour Daniel's decision to retire as dean of the Graduate School (a post that was abolished later), effective August 31, 1968. Dean Daniels had previously served as dean of the College of Arts and Sciences from 1952 to 1959.

The appointment of Vice-President Allred, and the related reorganization and augmentation of the presidential staff, gave Dr. Hoffman the opportunity to concentrate on some of the less academic aspects of his new responsibilities—particularly, a workable *modus operandi* with the Board of Regents, and fund-raising. He saw immediately the need to propose an actual Manual of the Board of Regents, and this was prepared under the chairmanship of Regent George S. Hawn. As a result, the governing board fully discussed and adopted positions regarding the general functions of the regents, the principles of Board operation (plus how to put those principles into action), and reports to be made to the Board of Regents.[10]

In retrospect, the principles enunciated in the Manual of the Board have been fundamental to President Hoffman's ability to work so smoothly and effectively with the governing board, and to the mutual trust between him, the members of his administration, and the regents of the University.

Phil Hoffman told me that one of his first impressions of the University of Houston was the inevitability of it becoming a public institution. At the same time, he knew that it would have to have the "leverage" of gift dollars enriching appropriated dollars if it was to excel. He therefore turned as soon as possible to fund-raising, with its overtones of community relations, understanding and support.

On February 8, 1963, Dr. Hoffman spoke at a Houston Club luncheon where J.W. McLean (president of the Texas National Bank) was presiding as chairman of the new Excellence Campaign of the University of Houston Foundation. The other principals for the campaign, which was to replace the Living Endowment Association (LEA) drives, were J.K. Jamieson, executive vice-president, Humble Oil & Refining Company (and since, the chief executive of Standard Oil of New Jersey); Ross Stewart, chairman of the board, C. Jim Stewart and Stevenson; John H. Wimberly, president, Houston Natural Gas Company; Lloyd M. Bentsen, Jr., my friend of border politics and 3 a.m. *bailes* at Edcouch-Elsa followed by 100 miles per hour runs back to campaign headquarters (then president, Lincoln Liberty Life Insuarance Company, now a U.S. senator); and W.L. Lindholm, regional manager, Southwestern Bell Telephone Company, now president of the American Telephone and Telegraph Company. As one observer of the February 8 luncheon stated it, the group had clout *and* class.

President Hoffman said, "The University of Houston will now travel one of two roads: to mediocrity, or to a high level of performance with the potential for greatness." He told the chief executives of 31 "patternmaker" companies that the University could take the high road if contributions received yearly since 1957 were still forthcoming; these could now be placed atop the subsistence level of state appropriations to furnish the far more nourishing diet of tax support plus local enrichment.

To illustrate the point for the luncheon audience, and television viewers later in the day, I helped J.W. McLean and Ken Jamieson pour cream in the top of a partly empty quart of skim milk. We then shook up the bottle and had a far more palatable and nutritious drink. The point was made, and before the corporate decision-makers of the town. As a result the Excellence Campaign was a success, bringing in almost the previous year's total in 1964 after we had joined the state system. It has increased steadily since that time, providing a solid base of assistance.[11]

The success of the Excellence Campaigns helped somewhat in faculty recruiting, but the rising level of ability and accomplishment within the teaching staff had far more impact upon the campaign, and on fund-raising in general. As hundreds of volunteer workers combed the industrial and overall community for contributions, they and their companies began to realize the true value of the University as a source of trained manpower and, increasingly, of research ability and potential, consultants, and a spectrum of specialized services. The chief executive of one major corporation, based elsewhere, showed little interest in the Excellence Campaign until he was handed a report listing more than 600 of his employees, their spouses, children or parents as University of Houston students. He called the chairman of the company contributions committee and suggested a review of the University's request.

Dramatic increases in the caliber and accomplishments of the instructional staff were seen throughout the 1960's and thereafter. Noteworthy developments included the appointment of Ernst Bayer of the University of Tuebingen as first incumbent of a chair in chemistry, endowed by the Robert A. Welch Foundation at $1 million; Richard I. Evans' feat of videotaping four hours of interviews with the legendary Carl Gustav Jung at his residence near Zurich[12]; the temporary location of NASA's computing facilities on campus; selection of the cosmochemist John Oro to study both organic and inorganic samples from the moon, preceded and followed by other consequential grants to him; the decision to place one of the "THEMIS" projects in the department of chemical engineering. Some of these "breakthrough" developments brought a spectacular increase in research awards and helped tone the academic muscle throughout the University.

In retrospect, the remarkable gains in library holdings begat other forward strides in the first decade of the Hoffman administration. Within the institution, this permitted far more successful recruiting and greatly helped in the steady approval of additional doctoral offerings. It also attracted some notable acquisitions of private collections: the William B. Bates Collection of Texana and Western Americana; the Franzheim Memorial Collection in Architecture[13]; special holdings provided by Henry Rockwell, the Rockwell Brothers Endowment, Inc., and the Rockwell Fund, Inc.; the George Fuermann City of Houston Collection; a marvelous Spanish, French and Italian library located in Mexico City by Professor Harvey L. Johnson; and the papers of Israel Shreve, a Revolutionary War officer who served under George Washington at Valley Forge, donated by his direct descendant, Mrs. Joseph W. (Emily Scott) Evans. In terms of assisting research and scholarship, Mrs. Evans and her daughter, Alice Evans Pratt, provided perhaps the most noteworthy addition to the library: the J.W. Evans Collection in Bibliography, named for their husband and father, who had been so active in the early days of the University.

Much of the progress of the libraries in the first decade of the Hoffman administration could be credited to Edward G. Holley, the dynamic director of libraries who had replaced Howard S. McGaw in 1962, and to Marian Mackey Orgain, curator of special collections. Dr. Holley departed these shores in 1971 to become dean of library science at North Carolina University, but Mrs. Orgain, happily, remains.

The reorganization and expansion of the administrative staff undergirded much of the progress of the Hoffman administration in the 1960's, and has dramatically affected the manner in which the institution continues to develop. Even before the pivotal appointment of John Allred as provost, Dr. Hoffman named Alan W. Johnson dean of students, created the Office of the Dean of Students, and charged Dr. Johnson with reorganizing it along functional lines.

William A. Yardley accepted the post of associate dean of students in 1964 and succeeded Dr. Johnson in 1966. Under his guidance there were sound, innovative changes within what became the Student Life Division in 1968, with Dr. Yardley as its first vice-president. Bill Yardley made lasting contributions in his field before he resigned in 1970 to become a consultant. His replacement, Roger T. Nudd, was succeeded by W. Harry Sharp, the present incumbent, in 1973.

Mr. Mac became senior vice-president and treasurer in the first few weeks of the Hoffman administration, and he saw continuous expansion of the Business and Financial Division, with major reorganizations in 1963 and again in 1969. When he retired in 1973, an era had ended; the Board of Regents responded to nearly 40 years' dedicated service by accepting President Hoffman's recommendation that the handsome Graduate Studies Building be named McElhinney Hall.

In a change of consequence within the Business and Financial Division, the skilled veteran controller of the University, J. Treadway Brogdon, was appointed budget director effective January 1, 1964, and was succeeded later by another long-time employee, Harold W. Scott. This readjustment placed a senior fiscal official in a vital new position carrying responsibility for the preparation and administration of state budgets.

A future administrator arrived on campus in the fall of 1960, when Douglas G. Mac Lean was named director of personnel services. He came from the consulting firm of Cresap, McCormick and Paget. Mr. Mac Lean was named assistant to the president in 1962, and vice-president for staff services three years later. While continuing to expand the Personnel Services Office, he organized the Office of Institutional Studies to undertake specialized projects the University required. These included the development of a management information system in support of long range planning and analytical studies needed for decision-making or to investigate and apply new administrative concepts. After Mr. McElhinney's retirement, Vice-President Mac Lean assumed additional responsibilities with his new title of vice-president for financial and management services.

Another administrative shift of special consequence came in 1968, when it was decided to organize a Division of Facilities Planning and Construction, under a vice-president, to supervise with a staff of professionals what had obviously become a complex, massive building program. Coulson Tough, who was responsible for the planning and construction of the vast new University of California campus at Irvine, was chosen to head the new division. Mr. Tough was immediately drawn into a maelstrom, his duties enlarged still further with the development of what was to become our Clear Lake City campus. I found him extremely able, and most cooperative; he gave me immediate help as a member of the President's Committee on Art Acquisitions, which I had been asked to organize in 1967.

The President's Committee on Art Acquisitions (PCAA) interlocked with the Landscape Committee (headed by Vice-President Tough), which was charged with providing a series of plazas important to the overall development of the campus. The plazas usually involved outdoor sculpture, and our division soon had an additional source of common interest with Facilities Planning and Construction which was to grow in significance.

Under a policy adopted by the regents in December 1966, one percent of all future building contracts was escrowed by the PCAA for the purchase of art objects, especially outdoor sculpture by artists of international renown to be installed in the new plazas designed to tie together major additions to the physical plant. Since 1967, Regents Aaron J. Farfel and Leonard Rauch have worked with me, Professor Peter W. Guenther, Coulson Tough, Clifton C.

Miller, until his untimely death on February 18, 1977, and a series of student representatives, on PCAA acquisitions.

The University now owns Gerhardt Marcks' "Albertus Magnus" (Bates College of Law) and "Orpheus" (Fine Arts Building); Clement Meadmore's "Split Level" (Continuing Education Center); Lee Kelly's "Waterfall, Stele and River" (Cullen Family Center); Menashe Kadishman's "On 1969" (Entrance #6 Mall); Peter Forakis' "Tower of the Cheyenne" (Library Plaza); Francisco Zuniga's "Woman with Shawl" (McElhinney Hall) and other pieces under this unique program, which has drawn wide critical acclaim. The newest addition, installed by the artist Pablo Serrano in April 1977, is his striking "Spiritus Mundi," at the UH/CLC's main entrance.

Bob Fowler's abstract figure in the University Center preceded the "one percent program," and the copy of Rodin's "The Thinker" on Central Campus from 1973-1976 was on loan from the Cantor-Fitzgerald Foundation.

John Allred decided to return to the classroom and the laboratory on September 1, 1968. He had the usual scars of a provost after six years of dealing with a collection of generally competent but sometimes intransigent deans — complicated at times by a lack of communications skills and some understandable intransigence of his own.

But Vice-President Allred had accomplished much in a sensitive, highly vulnerable position during an absolutely crucial era of accelerated change. He took a key role in opening important new departments and higher components; saw the number of doctoral degrees doubled; and was instrumental in extensive reorganization throughout the academic departments.

Now President Hoffman had the challenging task of finding another vice-president, dean of faculties. After a long search, the choice was Emmett B. Fields, dean of arts and sciences at Vanderbilt University and president-elect of the Southern Association of Colleges and Schools. He took office July 1, 1969, the most experienced academic administrator ever to join the University of Houston, in terms of a proven track record in higher education at time of appointment.

I was given responsibility for the Radio-Television-Film Center in 1963 as an additional assignment, plus the post of executive director of the University of Houston Foundation which I inherited when Ralph Frede left in 1970. For a time in 1964, I considered leaving the

University for either a presidency or a position at my *alma mater,* Rice University. I was asked to accept nomination for several presidencies while president-elect of the American College Public Relations Association (ACPRA), but had no real interest in the opportunities since they meant leaving Houston. J. Newton Rayzor, a distinguished admiralty lawyer and trustee of Rice University, had inquired about my interest in another presidential nomination, which I declined with thanks; but a week later, he sent Willoughby Williams, a long-time friend and executive of the American General Companies who was president of the Rice Alumni Association, around to see me with a different proposition. He and a small group of ex-students were prepared to offer me what was then an enormous salary to reorganize and administer the Rice development program. I pondered this for some time, but decided in the end that I could probably make a greater overall contribution over the years where I was.

Another factor was an informal agreement I reached with Phil Hoffman at his old home on Valerie Street in Bellaire. The agreement was that I would take the development portfolio in his administration, under what we both understood would be a long-term arrangement.

Other accomplishments of the first decade of the Hoffman administration, mentioned briefly earlier, were formidable indeed, though they are not reported in any considerable detail.

The 1964 self-study was conducted by a seven-man team headed by Dewayne A. Stonebarger, director of the Management Development Center. Other members were Dr. Allred; Max F. Carman, Jr., professor of geology; A. E. Dukler, professor of chemical engineering; Vice-President Mac Lean; Dean Neibel; and Charles I. Silin, M. D. Anderson Professor of French. The principal findings were that "in a dramatic new context of challenge and response," the University is engaged in a meaningful effort toward excellence; the emphasis upon improvement of teaching and research permeates every area of University operation; and the benefits that the University now enjoys as a member of the state system of higher education are clear incentives to progress. The University's purpose, role and scope — rather than being restricted, are advancing.

The self-study was accepted by the Southern Association as a required decennial report, and the University was reaccredited early in 1966.

The new master plan of 1966 envisioned a quite different, pedestrian-oriented campus with Cullen Boulevard closed and Wheeler Street curved to the south and west. There would be substantial additions to acreage, including Jeppesen Stadium, (an absolutely essential acquisition to the immediate west for which we would finally have to pay the incredible sum of $6.8 million in cash), and room for 30,000 students. An overriding principle was a unified campus deriving from the institution's organization and goals, and speaking to a need for carefully scheduled classes and maximum "interdisciplinary discourse." As we shall see, the master plan of 1966, while already updated, has been rather closely followed to date.

A University of Houston System was inevitable, given the dynamic energy of the Houston metroplex and the possibility of requests for educational services in areas historically and economically linked to the city. The official beginning, however, stems from a May 29, 1968, meeting of the Coordinating Board in San Antonio at which the staff recommended two branch campuses for the University. The first, to the south, was first conceived as a four-year plus masters degree operation to be authorized by the 1969 Legislature, opened in 1973, and projected to reach a maximum enrollment of 9,500 students by 1980. The second campus, to be generally north of the city, was to be an upper-level operation, authorized in 1971, opened in 1977, and reaching a capacity of 4,800 students, also in 1980. As we shall see, the first recommendation was changed to specify an upper-level campus, now the University of Houston at Clear Lake City; the second campus has a handsome, functional and valuable site in The Woodlands, some 30 miles north of downtown, but has not yet been authorized. The May 29, 1968, meeting also recommended a 30,000 enrollment ceiling on the original University of Houston campus, along with limits for the remainder of the state system.

Legislative approval was obtained for the University of Houston at Clear Lake City (UH/CLC) in 1971, under the guidance of Allen Commander, who had come from the Office of International Affairs and a temporary assignment in Washington, D.C., to assume the key role in handling legislative affairs under President Hoffman.

Dr. Commander, who was to become vice-president for public affairs after his splendid work in bringing the UH/CLC through to victory, replaced me in Austin, although I continued to have special assignments there. This became advisable as my other duties expanded, but particularly when I went into the bill-killing business after the 1963 session. I was forced to take a direct role in opposing our friend John B. Connally's ill-advised campaign to place the University of Houston under the University of Texas System in 1965, and in killing legislative moves to establish an independent "Bayport College" in the Clear Lake City area in opposition to UH/CLC, and to found a duplicative college of law for Texas A&M University in downtown Houston, in 1967 and 1969. (I told my Aggie friends that I realized they would open a college of fortune-telling in order to get a foothold in the urban setting of Houston, but to back off our turf).

In another significant development, the Coordinating Board approved in 1971 a request by a group of the leading citizens of Victoria that the University be allowed to operate an upper-level institution there in quarters leased from Victoria College, to serve the only remaining large area of the state without a degree-granting college or university. This followed a surprise visit from our friend over the years, President J. D. Moore of Victoria College, and a series of conferences in Victoria. These began with a meeting with a select few of the ranching, industrial, banking and political tycoons of that unusual, power-packed and attractive city at which Dr. Hoffman and I represented the University.

International programs at the University, where the total of students from other countries had been growing spectacularly toward the present total of more than 2,500, suddenly became of major consequence in 1964. In that year, we began operating a $150,000 program for the Agency for International Development (AID) in India; this provided specially trained instructors for faculty members of India's 230 polytechnical institutes, at Chandrigara in the north, Madras in the south, Jadavpur in the east and Ahmedabad in the west, under the College of Technology. Simultaneously, Dean Tiller launched his series of programs to bring rectors from various Latin-American universities to the campus for on-site training; an $800,000 AID project to assist Ecuador in training engineers and business administrators at the University of Guayaquil;[14] and another AID program, this involving a grant of $633,000 atop an original agreement for $137,000 in 1963, to provide graduate engineering instruction in Rio de Janeiro.

Requiring the College Entrance Board Examination of entering freshmen beginning with the fall of 1962 had a striking impact on the make-up of the Class of 1966 and subsequent classes. Instead of a relatively smooth distribution of students from the four quartiles of their high school graduating classes, the University found itself with half of those entering from the top quarter, over 80 percent from the top half, and less than three percent from the bottom quarter of high school rankings. With this happy result, the College of Law moved to require the Law School Admittance Test, and other components began to establish their own special standards for admission.

KUHT was in dire trouble from the moment the University entered the state system, since specific riders to the general appropriations bill forbade the use of appropriated funds to support educational television. It was decided that we would struggle along on very limited private funds for another biennium, hoping for either some legislative relief or a new means of funding Channel 8. By mid-1964, it was obvious that we would get nowhere in Austin. We therefore summarily discontinued all telecourses effective September 1, 1965, and began an intensive search for other means of financial support.

The best approach seemed to be broadcasting to school districts within an 80-mile range, and being compensated for actual operational costs. We obtained a $20,000 grant from the University to organize Gulf Region Educational Television Affiliates (GRETA), centering upon the gigantic Houston Independent School District, once our partner in KUHT. The idea was favorably received, but it was contingent upon our going from a weak 46 kilowatts to full power, at 316.

We stumbled upon the solution when Willard E. Walbridge urged me to visit James C. Richdale, vice-president of Channel 11, on the rumor that this station was moving to a new tower, and abandoning their installation three miles from Alvin. The rumor was true, and Jim Richdale was most sympathetic; but when I mentioned the possibility of a tax write-off and gift, he said that this would have to go "all the way to the top of Corinthian Broadcasting." The top happened to be C. Wrede Petersmeyer, who was in the class ahead of me at the Harvard Business School.

We were given an 1,171-foot tower, with newly harnessed antennae, 18 acres of land, and a $40,000 transmitter building, contingent upon the gift being matched by the Department of Health, Education & Welfare under Public Law 87-447. With help from the ill but still hard-working Congressman Albert Thomas, and his colleague

Bob Casey, the HEW grant in the amount of $294,996 was approved August 26, 1964. The grant and gift gave KUHT new life, and allowed us to launch GRETA; it also helped us enormously when we went back in 1970 for a second grant that provided full color. Having met both goals of 316 kilowatts of power and color transmission, we could move on the next objective for the world's first educational television station: an active, effective citizen support group.

The Faculty Senate, encouraged by improvements in salaries as well as in fringe benefits, began at the very start of the Hoffman administration to reorganize itself under the chairmanship of my old classmate at Rice Institute, Edmund Pincoffs. New committees formed the basis for the reorganization; they included a Committee on University Committees, headed by Elmer Schoettle; Student Life (Sara Huggins); Educational Policy (A. E. Dukler); and Faculty Affairs, including direct compensation, fringe benefits, role in governance and the preparation of an official faculty handbook (C. V. Kirkpatrick). Although the committees were to change, their establishment seemed to mark a new and more positive era in the Senate and in its relationships with the administration.

The wave of student unrest on campuses throughout the nation finally surfaced at the University of Houston in 1969 and 1970, and then subsided rather quickly. When it did emerge, six years after the malady first appeared at the University of California in Berkeley, the unrest was tempered by the fact that some 75 percent of our students were employed, almost 45 percent were 24 years of age or older, and 40 percent were married.

The continuing controversy centered for months around 10 "demands" presented by the Afro-Americans for Black Liberation (AABL) on February 10, 1969. President Hoffman and his staff, in a series of emergency sessions, analyzed and responded to the AABL, and organized a task force, an information team, and a human relations committee charged with finding feasible solutions to "demands" that were not illogical or patently impossible (as a mandate that 35 percent of the class entering in 1969, and succeeding classes, had to be black).

When there was continuing disturbance and a series of minor incidents coupled with threats of real violence, the president issued a "law and order" statement widely acclaimed in the *Post* and *Chronicle*. The statement pointed out that the University would not accept any major disruption of the normal educational processes, or threats to life and property, and would take any appropriate action required to deal with acts of disruption, destruction or other violence, including threats. The statement, first appearing on February 19, was reissued and widely publicized on March 10, for those who had not seen it originally, and those "of reluctant comprehension."

The situation moved rapidly toward some type of resolution, with tendencies toward violence exacerbated by members of a minuscule campus branch of the Students for a Democratic Society (SDS) and imported SDS agitators. A "mini-riot" occurred on March 17 (St. Patrick's Day, of all days) after Eugene Locke, an AABL leader, asserted that he had been attacked by white students. Damage to the University Center and to the Bookstore within this facility was estimated at $2,000. The University made an exhaustive report of the incident to the district attorney, after detailed investigation by campus security forces, and three students were subsequently charged and tried for their role in the disturbance.

In a related incident, the SDS leader Mark Rudd spoke on campus March 20, 1969, even though he had been refused permission to do so. An injunction was obtained against Mark Rudd and an SDS agitator named Marjorie Ellen Davis Haile (who had been dubbed "Old Foul Mouth" by opposing students from the Young Americans for Freedom).

A five-day "tree controversy" erupted April 24, 1970, when students (including a large proportion of high school youngsters out for a spring lark) camped out in trees overlooking the site for the new Fine Arts Building. Amply supplied with food, beer and guitars, they claimed that they would remain until the University shifted the location of the new building (carefully selected after months of study in terms of the location of underground utility tunnels, related facilities and the preservation of a maximum number of healthy trees).

The confrontation was controlled at all times by the incomparable Larry W. Fultz, the University security chief who was an attorney, a sociologist and a retired veteran of 23 years on the Houston police force, where he attained the lofty rank of inspector. After five days, the fun and games had to stop, and an official warning to leave the site or be arrested at 6:00 p.m. was issued. There was a delay of a few minutes while Mr. Fultz helped find a contact lens lost by one of the demonstrators, and those wishing to escape arrest shinnied down their tree with the assistance of campus officers.

The paddy wagons were then loaded up with 70 assorted University and high school students who had kept telling one another that they would never be arrested. A former University employee with emotional problems triggered by the incident was taken separately to a hospital. Downtown, the miscreants were lectured by one of the sternest of the district judges, who explained the intricacies of injunction and contempt citations. They were then allowed to sign "honesty bonds" and went back to catch up on their homework and missed classes.

Among other incidents was one not without its humor. Governor Preston Smith came to the campus on his 1970 campaign for re-election, and I met him in President Hoffman's absence. After some pleasantries, and recollections of the old days in the Senate, we proceeded to the University Center, where a group including a persistent troublemaker named Randy Chapman (whose chief complaint seemed to be the fact that his father was an admiral) had a little group assembled. They carried signs protesting the hefty sentence given one Lee Otis Johnson on a marijuana violation. A chant began: "Free Lee Otis, Free Lee Otis, Free Lee Otis." I marched Governor Smith smartly along, and we were almost at the entrance of the University Center when he turned to me with a puzzled look: "Godamighty," he said, "whadda they got against *frijoles* (freeleeotis)?"

Inside, the pesky Mr. Chapman and his cohorts were shouting again as I prepared to introduce the governor, young Chapman orchestrating things with a broom. Governor Smith looked the situation over, turned to me and said, "there's nothing for me here; let's get out of this place." I escorted him back to his waiting limousine, to the glowering looks of his own Department of Public Safety officers, apologized profusely, and watched him drive off. Later that day, I saw that Randy Chapman was charged by Student Court, where I took considerable pleasure in testifying against him. I always thought that the incident aroused a great deal of sympathy for Preston Smith, and was a ten strike in his favor. Some of his campaign managers agreed, after his landslide victory, and one of the more sophisticated accused me of having rigged the whole thing.

The reorganization of the Alumni Association into an Alumni Federation of nine interlocking entities followed the resignation of several executive directors after the departure of the dedicated Ted R. Hendricks, who wrestled mightily with the problems of the ex-student group for five years before leaving for a position in industry in 1962. It was thought that obtaining the services in 1969 of Dick Proctor, long-time administrator of the huge Downtown Rotary Club, would finally set the new Federation on permanent high ground. Mr. Proctor returned to Rotaryland, however, in spite of the importunings of a long line of alumni presidents headed by John Van Ness, and including Harry Hedges, John Toomey, John C. O'Leary and Walter Rainey, Jr. The work of these men, their predecessors and those who have followed them, as we will see, finally appears to be bearing fruit in the mid- and late 1970's, under the experienced and effective David M. Rockoff, executive director for the past three years.

The 1960's, which started so auspiciously with the appointment of William A. (Bill) Yeoman as head football coach on December 14, 1961, became a true golden era for intercollegiate athletics at the University of Houston, although 1977 may still surpass the legendary year of 1967-1968. In that 12-month span:

Guy Lewis' basketball team finished third in the NCAA championships after ranking first at the end of the regular season on a celebrated 71-69 victory over UCLA before 53,356 fans in the Astrodome;

Lovette Hill's baseball nine made it to the finals of the College World Series;

Dave G. Williams' astounding golfers won their tenth NCAA golf championship in 12 years;

Johnny Morriss' cross-country team finished in the top 10 in the NCAA;

Bill Yeoman's footballers began years of dominating offensive statistics with the devastating new "Houston Veer" formation. They shocked Duffy Daughtery's Michigan State Spartans 37-7 in the 1967 season opener, climbed to second ranking in the polls, and led the nation in total offense.[16]

A major reward for the historic successes of 1967-1968, and for remarkable overall progress in an intercollegiate athletics program initiated only in 1946, came in 1971. The Cougars, with vital support from hometown Rice University and Darrell Royal and the University of Texas, were voted into the Southwest Conference. Full competition including football would begin in 1976. It was a moment of deserved triumph for Harry Fouke, the University's first and only athletic director, for his coaches and players over the years, for key regents such as Corbin Robertson and Charles Fleetwood who had supported the program so strongly and effectively for so long— and for President Hoffman, one of the most dedicated of Cougar fans for 14 years.

As the first decade of his presidency came to an end, Dr. Hoffman and the University of Houston suffered a grievous loss. Leta Gilbert called me early on Sunday morning, July 27, 1969. She had just talked to Mrs. Bruce. Chancellor Emeritus Andrew Davis Bruce was dead at their retirement home in Southern Pines, North Carolina, in the 75th year of a vigorous, eventful and successful life. He was buried in the beautiful national cemetery at Arlington, Virginia, with the storied dead of our armies, after a traditional ceremony beginning at Fort Myer across the winding Potomac.

There had been a succession of deaths since 1962 among key figures in the earlier history of the institution: J. Chester Cochran, 78, with the University from 1941-1956, on August 10, 1962; Joseph S. Werlin, 63, with continuous service since 1934, on May 30, 1964; Roy A. Crouch, 72, who organized the Department of Psychology in 1939 and had retired in 1961, on February 24, 1965; Mrs. Pearl C. Bender, 85, dean of women for 15 years, on April 30, 1966; Frederic Browne, 89, and still teaching part-time after 35 years on the faculty, on August 13, 1966; N. K. Dupre, 72, the dean of the beginning years who came with the old HJC in 1927, left the University in 1945 and the HISD in 1949, and managed his farms in West Texas until 1964, when he finally retired to Lubbock, where he passed away on October 27, 1967; and the incredible Winifred E. Garrison.

Professor Garrison had come to the University in 1952 at the age of 77, remaining until he was 89, and requested retirement, in 1964. He died February 6, 1969, at the age of 94.[17]

Three other deaths under unusually tragic circumstances touched the heart of the campus in these years. Howard M. Daniel, professor of accounting, his wife Eleanor and daughter Diane were killed in an automobile accident on August 10, 1962; Charles Bacarisse, professor of (Texas) history, was somehow swept overboard in a boating accident in Galveston Bay on June 22, 1969; and John E. Hoff, professor of civil engineering, tennis coach, and friend of all, died of a malignancy on December 2, 1966.

There were notable retirements during the decade. Lily Lou Russell, one of the most successful placement directors in the world of higher education, stepped down August 31, 1967; Ruth S. Wikoff, with the library 34 years including a 1961-1962 term as acting director, on May 31, 1967; and Roy E. Barthold, the grand old man of KUHT, on August 31, 1969, when James L. Bauer succeeded him as general manager of the station.

It had been a decade of rare accomplishment, bringing unprecedented new advances in decisive areas, and the resolution of formidable problems. But as Philip G. Hoffman celebrated the first 10 years of his presidency with members of Staff Conference on August 31, 1971, the challenges and complexities ahead already overshadowed the past.

Emmett Fields had barely begun the thorough review of academic planning, administration, and the intricacies of interlocking components necessary to his new responsibilities when he was confronted with a host of new problems including preparation for the decennial self-study required by the Southern Association.

I saw a constant need for raising the sights of our ongoing Excellence Campaign, of finding some means of stable support for KUHT, of myriad problems in development including preliminary planning for our 50th anniversary in 1977.

Doug Mac Lean, looking forward already to assuming broader responsibilities, could feel the increased financial pressures upon the University, gnawing demands for more budgetary detail and increased accountability at the Legislature, calls for many more special studies, and the perplexing difficulties precipitated by federal personnel requirements. Harry Sharp would ponder new complications in the field of student life centering upon demands for a meaningful role in institutional governance; plus additional problems in counseling and guidance, medical services, overall student government and special help for the handicapped. Allen Commander could perceive an entire range of complexities with the Legislature, budget offices and specialized committees, aside from the difficulties of passing a new bill to authorize an additional campus at The Woodlands, in the booming northwest quadrant of the metroplex.

And Phil Hoffman, looking out at the humid, late summer night, was ultimately responsible for the myriad difficulties outlined above, in addition to those he alone could confront. But he was to be equal to the mushrooming demands upon him, in a fresh decade of progress.

Notes to Chapter Seven

[1]David P. Bell has submitted an account of the "historical development of the University of Houston,...with..."particular attention to the curricular ramifications of institutional development" as part of a doctoral dissertation at Stanford University. Jerry Wizig is preparing a history of intercollegiate athletics at the University for publication in 1978. Future plans include the addition of a full-time archivist-historian for the University of Houston, probably on the staff of the Anderson Library, an amplification which will undoubtedly stimulate detailed study of separate aspects of the institution's remarkable unfolding since 1961.

[2]President Oberholtzer was inaugurated in 1945 after 18 years in office. President Kemmerer's inaugural ceremony was well along in planning when he "resigned." C. F. McElhinney had one or two hints from faculty members that he, although definitely an acting president, should consent to some type of installation; he simply did not bother to reply. General Bruce showed no enthusiasm for his own inauguration as president, and even less for that of Clanton Williams.

[3]The "Hatfield Report" also contained a statement that would have drawn fire from President Oberholtzer, and even more from his successor, President Kemmerer: "A great university is not one which teaches anything the customers are willing to pay for, but one which channels its resources and activities into the fields which its own expert and experienced management believes to be those of greatest value in relation to the total educational needs of society at large and its own constituency in particular." President Hoffman quoted the statement *verbatim*, and added: "We believe that the doctrine 'the customer is always right' has no application in the field of education."

[4]One of the regents telephoned me in July 1961 and asked that I arrange a small testimonial luncheon for Lieutenant Governor Ben Ramsey at the Houston Club. This was done, and on the appointed day I flew to San Augustine, picked up the Governor and his wife and little daughters, and brought them down. When the luncheon was over, without the customary award of a gift, I escorted the Ramseys to the garage and handed him a parking stub. The stub, prepaid, went with a new automobile, a remembrance from our generous and appreciative regent. Senator Baker's gift was a trip to Europe for him and his wife Iris, who must have summoned him to the telephone at least 100 times for early morning and late evening conferences while we were dug in at the battle of Capitol Hill.

We attempted to get both Governor Ramsey and Senator Baker over for a party at the Petroleum Club on the evening of August 31, 1963, when the members of Staff Conference rang out 37 years as a private institution and rang in the public sector era just at midnight. Neither could attend, but Senator Baker, still a campus hero as the author of SB 2, was on hand the next morning to help enroll Donna Aquilina, a 17-year-old graduate of St. Pius High School in Houston, as our first state system student. She was a freshman majoring in music education.

[5]H. J. (Doc) Blanchard, the new senator from Lubbock who had replaced Preston Smith, claimed that he had "never looked up to the gallery that he didn't see old Nicholson draped around our clock to get a better view of something on the floor." In the last days of the 1963 session, he handed me an official-looking but spurious bill for "irreparable damage to one clock, tugged and hauled out of shape."

[6]The enrollment figures tell their own story of a turnaround in 1961, a staggering increase in 1963, and a new level and steady march forward beginning in 1965: 1961, 12,187; 1962, 13,665; 1963, 17,430; 1964, 17,874; 1965, 19,558; 1966, 19,986; 1967, 21,770; 1968, 23,713; 1969, 24,383; 1970, 25,582; and 1971, 26,475.

[7]There are two reasons for the odd expression on Representative Wallace H. Miller's face at the signing of HB 291 (see picture section): his incredulity at the bill's actually having made it through the legislative maze, and the fact that Toni, Senator Criss Cole's Seeing Eye dog, had just clamped warning teeth on his ankle when he inadvertently moved too close to Toni's master.

[8]The Cullen College of Engineering was named for Mr. and Mrs. Hugh Roy Cullen in 1967, in recognition of their gifts toward this new component and earlier homes of the College. The Classroom, or Liberal Arts, Building was named for Agnes Cullen (Mrs. Isaac) Arnold, a Cullen daughter who served as a regent from 1950 to 1960. The College of Law was named for Colonel Bates after its completion in 1969. Hofheinz Pavilion was named for Judge Roy M. Hofheinz, alumnus; Moody Towers, for W.L. and Libbie Shearn Moody; the Men's Gymnasium for LeRoy Melcher, alumnus; and the Cameron Building for Mrs. Harry S. (Isabel C.) Cameron. Gifts aggregating almost $3.5 million were made by Judge Hofheinz, the Moody Foundation, Mr. Melcher, and the Cameron Foundation. The former Graduate Studies Building was named for Charles F. McElhinney in recognition of his four decades of service to the University, including more than a quarter-century as vice-president and senior vice-president. The Coastal Environmental Laboratory, some 900 acres of which were given to the University by the federal government for use in unique research projects, is located on the 1603-acre former Camp Wallace.

[9]The University had been asked many times in the mid-1960's to consider the establishment of a Graduate School of Social Work, especially by a

group headed by Monsignor John J. Roach and William P. Hobby, Jr. The possibility of an Institute of Urban Studies was also under intensive study, in an era when the problems of the inner city were attracting constant attention. Similar components were being examined at the new University of Texas at Arlington, and Senator Don Kennard of Fort Worth came to me in 1965 with a proposal to join forces for legislation to establish both these usnits at UT/Arlington and at the University of Houston. After further study, President Hoffman recommended this to the Board of Regents, and appropriate bills were framed. It was later determined that only the Institute of Urban Studies required actual statutory authorization, which was obtained. The Graduate School of Social Work was established at the University of Houston under institutional role and scope.

[10]Some of these general functions of the Board of Regents, the principles of Board operation, and how to put those principles into operation, are worth listing:

General functions: To bear legal responsibility and authority for all aspects of the University's operations. To represent the citizens of the State and to interpret their thinking in terms of University policies, facilities and programs. To actively support plans for securing necessary financial support. To determine major objectives and goals of the University and to approve major implementing policy. To select a chief executive officer for the University and to act upon the recommendations and reports of the chief executive officer.

Principles of Board Operation: The Board is a legislative body and not an executive agency (A Board that begins to dabble in executive matters creates an intolerable situation for the responsible executive officer). The Board should exercise its control over the University through the President. Representation of the professional point of view and authority over professional matters are best delegated to the President and, through him, to the faculty and administrative staff. Except as it is delegated to the President, authority resides only in the Board as a whole and not in its individual members. Board decisions and actions should be recorded in writing.

Principles in Practice: The normal contacts between the Board of Regents and the institution are maintained through the President. The President is delegated full authority for executive control of the University. The Board will deal directly with other members of the staff and faculty only with the President's prior knowledge and consent. Under normal conditions, the Board will take action only upon the President's recommendation. With the exception of matters relating to the President himself, the Board shall not initiate any formal action regarding the personnel of the institution. The President shall determine the administrative and organizational relationships best suited to the staff and faculty under his jurisdiction. The President is normally the spokesman for the University. The Board should look to the

President to be most knowledgeable about the institution and its current programs, as well as about the image presented by the institution to the public.

[11]Among other honors, the Excellence Campaign won the Silver Anvil Award of the Public Relations Society of America in competition against 273 other entries, for its success in maintaining and expanding community support after the shift to the public sector.

[12]Richard Evans, one of the most talented and prolific investigators and authors in psychology, had long cherished a project which would videotape the leading figures in his field. He convinced me in minutes of the worth of a plan to interview the legendary Carl Gustav Jung at his home near Zurich. This was done in four one-hour segments finally edited by the Bollingen Press. The great master fell ill within a year after the Evans project was completed, and the videotapes, ironically, had to be used by the Jung Institute for teaching purposes. Dick Evans also involved me in one of the more unique undertakings of my career at the University. I was named coordinator of one of the first large community action grants, with Dr. Evans as chief investigator under a joint grant to the University of Houston and the Community Council. This turned into a bureaucratic nightmare in which we formed Greater Houston Action for Youth, Inc., with General Robert M. Ives, Maurice J. Dannenbaum and myself as principal officers. The project accomplished much in the relatively new field of community action grants, but had its nightmarish aspects. I found myself, for example, at a store front headquarters on North Main one midnight, debating with opponents on the GHAFY directorate the merits of various applicants for key appointments. When Hartsell Gray, former Episcopalian minister and roughneck (now a highly controversial county treasurer) proposed a new candidate, I asked for a rundown on him. "Dr. Nicholson," replied Mr. Gray, "the hour is late. I'll save time by just saying that the man I propose would be against anything you're for." I thanked Mr. Gray for his consideration, and voted against his man.

[13]The University was extremely fortunate to obtain the nucleus of the Franzheim Collection after the death of the elegant and accomplished Kenneth Franzheim, Sr., who designed many of Houston's principal buildings a generation ago.

When I worked with Mr. Franzheim on the Allied Arts Council, I had often expressed admiration for his library. He told me that if a distant relative in the East did not want the library, he might leave it to the University of Houston. This was accomplished, and after a proper interval I sought an opening to thank Kenneth II again in person for the collection, and if he showed interest, to suggest how the nucleus might be expanded into a major holding. Finally, I stood with the younger Franzheim one perfect day in November, sipping champagne by the swimming pool while the string section of the Houston Symphony played for the baptismal festivities of his infant daughter. He was definitely interested in expanding his father's collection, but a bevy of dowagers hovered nearby waiting to congratulate him on the occasion. Finally, one of them looked directly at me, zoomed in, placed her hand firmly on our host's shoulder and hauled him away. As he departed, he turned and said to me, "How much?" "50K," I responded, "50 will do it." A few weeks later, I received the stock rights to a little over $50,000 worth of Xerox common stock from Ambassador-to-be Franzheim, mailed from some airport. The certificates followed in due course, and we had a superb new collection which has been steadily augmented by the continuing generosity of Mr. and Mrs. Franzheim.

[14]I went to Guayaquil and on to Quito to pay a courtesy call on the U.S. embassy and to see how the Ecuadoran project was, while at a medical congress in Lima. A few hours after I landed in Quito, someone blew up the Czech embassy. They took a hard look at me the next morning at the embassy, having noted in *Who's Who* that I was a Republican and a major in the Intelligence Corps reserve attached to a Pentagon headquarters.

There were other personal involvements for me in the burgeoning international program, especially at the Autonomous University of Guadalajara. I went here first in 1963 to help inaugurate a significant new project, Ford Foundation-sponsored, on development programs for Latin-American institutions. Since I have been back several times to visit my great friends Rector Luis Garibay and his wife Rita, and the Leaño family—notably when President Hoffman was given the *doctor honoris causa* in a resplendent ceremony in 1976. And our joint programs with the Autonoma continue to expand, especially in the College of Education.

Earlier, I headed a State Department-sponsored seminar in Caracas, to meet each morning for a week with a different minister of the Venezuelan government on problems arising from the nationalization of U. S. petroleum interests in that nation. A month later, I was the host for a Venezuelan delegation sent to Houston, after extending an invitation to President Rafael Caldera at the Casa Rosada, his official residence in Caracas.

[15]One of the best summaries of student unrest at the University is contained in an excerpt from the President's Message in the biennial report of 1967-1969: "The University of Houston maintained both essential institutional stability and energetic forward progress during the biennium ending August 31, 1969—a time of turbulence, constructive doubt and continuing reexamination for the world of higher education. Across the nation, the ubiquitous phenomenon of student unrest was reflected in a wide spectrum of attitudes and reactions. These varied from healthy reaction against long-term inertia and lack of educational imagination to deliberate obstructionism or worse. At the University

of Houston, student unrest was characteristically related to the activities of a small percentage of the total enrollment, plus some nonstudent activists. Protests, at times over-publicized, had their genesis and development both in (1) a well-motivated constructive desire to examine various aspects of the University and (2) in other contrasting "demands" identified with illogic and rhetoric. The response to unrest here was based primarily upon objective study and reasoned dialogue representing various elements of the campus community. Resulting decisions, accepted in the main as being quite reasonable, were clearly enunciated and fairly but firmly enforced."

[16]My host James "Spike" Denison of Michigan State took me up to the incredibly large Spartan press box before the kickoff. There a wit from the Chicago press corps demanded to know "where (Coach) Duffy (Daugherty) gets these intramural opponents from the boondocks of football—Howstun, Hewestun or however you pronounce it." We met the wit again in the third quarter after the Cougars were leading 23-7 on long runs by Warren McVea and other shifty backs slanting away from the beefy MSU linemen. "I want to confess my sins," he now announced to the assembled newsmen. "You pronounce it Houston, and they have just proved that speed beats fat."

[17]When we were planning a memorial service for the slain John F. Kennedy on November 25, 1963, we had an obvious choice for the faculty member to give the invocation. Winifred E. Garrison had the same sad but honorable assignment in 1901 at services for the assassinated President William McKinley. He was a 26-year-old assistant professor of philosophy at the time.

Chapter Eight

1971-1977

An attenuated perspective... Executive changes at a dizzying pace... The study commissions of 1972 and 1973... $214 million in physical plant... Colonel Bates, the builder Oake, dies at 85... The UHS expands again... Many more books, budget dollars, research grants and gifts... Sarah Campbell Blaffer and her gallery... ACT for 8... The 1974-1976 self-study... A birthday and the UH 50 Fund... On to 2027!

Our perspective is now grievously shortened, and the present is heavily upon us. History is difficult to write when it is just unfolding, as in such developments as the self-study of 1974-1976 (portions of which are still under analysis and consideration), almost bewildering changes in pivotal assignments, and temporary delays in the inevitable growth of the University of Houston System (UHS).

We can, however, report many of the principal objective developments of the past six years, speculate upon their significance, and begin to peer myopically into the future—the lack of perspective notwithstanding.

Eight areas have dominated the University's most recent history: executive resignations and appointments, the presidential study commissions of 1972 and 1973, continual additions to physical plant, the burgeoning of the UHS, the uninterrupted expansion of library holdings, budgets, research grants and gifts; the establishment or growth of important ancillary operations such as the Sarah Campbell Blaffer Gallery and KUHT; the 1974-1976 self-study; and the Fiftieth Anniversary observance and related UH 50 Fund.

One event must be chronicled separately as this last segment of our history begins: the death of Colonel W.B. Bates, in his eighty-fifth year, on April 17, 1974. In retrospect, he may have had more effect upon the University of Houston than anyone, over a period of 43 years from 1928 to 1971, when he asked not to be considered for another six-year term "because I'd be pushing 90 when I finished it," and was succeeded by Aaron J. Farfel as chairman of the Board of Regents, with James A. Elkins, Jr., moving up to the post of vice-chairman. It is warming to remember one paragraph from his memorial resolution, adopted by the Board of Regents, June 3, 1974:

> "...interment (was) in the family plot at Oak Grove Cemetery in Nacogdoches. One was reminded of Edmund Spenser's lines in *The Faerie Queen:* 'The builder Oake, sole king of the forests all,' as the brief but meaningful final service proceeded under stately old live oak trees; for William B. Bates was a builder, and an oak among men."

Executive appointments through August 31, 1973 (not previously noted) included Alfred R. Neumann, dean, College of Arts and Sciences, to chancellor UH/CLC; D. Reginald Traylor, professor of mathematics, to director (later chancellor), Victoria Center; Chas. F. Jones, former president, Humble Oil & Refining Company, to dean, College of Business Administration; Stephen R. Salmon, former president, Xerox Bibliographics, to director of libraries; Ronald F. Bunn, dean of the Graduate School (also) to interim dean, College of Arts and Sciences; and Joseph P. Buckley, formerly of the University of Pittsburgh, dean of pharmacy.

In the following biennium, there were changes of even more significance, and sometimes baffling complication, precipitated by Emmett Fields' decision to resign as of July 1, 1975, and accept the presidency of the State University of New York (SUNY) at Albany. Promoted to executive vice-president in 1971 (in a move that Senior Vice-President McIlhinney accepted and understood, but hardly applauded), Dr. Fields knew that he had accomplished much in his six years at the University, though much remained to be done. Further, a man of his ability and experience must have perceived almost limitless challenges ahead. At the same time, I surmise that he had become familiar with Phil Hoffman's negative views on having a chancellor and president on the same campus; and just as any provost worth his salt, he had been in office long enough to bear noticeable wounds, while another dean or two adjusted the periscope on the high-powered rifle. On balance, at the career-critical age of 51, he decided to accept the presidency at SUNY/Albany.

Roger Singleton, a brilliant young professor of accounting and computer science expert whose rise in administrative ranks at the University was unprecedented (assistant dean, College of Business Administration, 1969; acting dean, 1972, replacing Dr. Jones, who had resigned; assistant dean of faculties, 1973; associate dean of faculties, 1974) was named acting vice-president and dean of faculties on July 1, 1975. Four months later, he was the first incumbent of the powerful new post of vice-president for academic affairs, UHS, assigned to the coordination of the four campuses of the growing system and designated chief consul to President Hoffman.

This left Dr. Fields' former office vacant, and as the game of musical chairs proceeded, Dr. Bunn was named to this position *ad interim*, though he remained only a semester before resigning to accept a similar assignment at SUNY/Buffalo. The darting about all ended when Barry Munitz of the University of Illinois System, another young administrator of exceptional accomplishment, ability, and potential, became vice-president, dean of faculties on July 1, 1976.[1]

Meanwhile, three deans were named for the new colleges resulting from the dissection of the huge College of Arts and Sciences: David Gottlieb, professor of sociology, Social Sciences; R. Hugh Walker, professor of physics, Natural Sciences and Mathematics; and John C. Guilds, formerly of the University of South Carolina, Humanities and Fine Arts. A.A. White returned as dean of the Bates College of Law, when John C. Neibel became a special assistant to the president after 10 years of remarkable progress as dean of that component. John Jay Douglass, commandant of the Judge Advocate General School, U.S. Army, was appointed dean of the new National College of District Attorneys, and John Ackerman became associate dean of the National College of Criminal Defense Lawyers and Public Defenders (these being new and prestigious components attached to the law complex). Fannie S. Howard, professor of French, was named director of the Open University;[2] and Joseph P. Kimble of SUNY/Stony Brook replaced Larry W. Fultz, suddenly dead from leukemia in a bitter loss to the University and community in 1974, as director of security.

The presidential study (reorganization) committee of 1972 was succeeded by that of 1973, a unique body convened to examine the 1972 findings before they had been presented in final form. Both grew from a feeling in the Faculty Senate, and among the deans, that "the third floor" (office of the dean of faculties) tended to bog down in paperwork. There were three principal findings and recommendations by these committees: (1) to split the 27-department College of Arts and Sciences into the three colleges indicated earlier; (2) to name three "provosts" and two assistants for the third floor, by academic area; and (3) to scuttle the Office of the Graduate Dean, since authority over graduate programs had actually come to reside in the colleges and departments.

The first and third recommendations were adopted; the second met harsh criticism from many who claimed that the last thing they needed was another stratum of bureaucracy, and was disapproved.

The expansion of the physical plant moved on apace in spite of the loss of Coulson Tough, who was replaced by Clifton C. Miller (also from the California system of higher education). Vice-President Tough, now the president of our Alumni Organization, joined the Mitchell Energy and Development Corporation staff in 1973. Projects completed since 1971 (and those under construction, with estimated date of completion) follow:

Project	*Completion Date*	*Cost ($)*
Fine Arts Building	1972	$ 5,100,000
University Center Addition	1973	2,800,000
University Center Satellite	1973	1,900,000
Continuing Education Center	1973	7,000,000
Classroom and Office Building	1974	4,700,000
Child Care Center	1975	450,000
Bates College of Law, Phase II	1975	3,300,000
Computing Center	1976	1,600,000
Optometry Building	1976	10,000,000
College of Technology Addition	1977	5,500,000
Humanities Building & Lyndall Wortham Theater	1977	5,000,000
M. D. Anderson Library, Phase I	1977	10,000,000
Science & Research II	1977	9,500,000
	TOTAL	$66,850,000

It would be difficult to overestimate the significance of any of these additional facilities, each of which adds its own meaningful impetus to the overall thrust of the University. There are unique facets, however, to the Fine Arts Building, with its Fredrica Gross Dudley Recital Hall and Sarah Campbell Blaffer Gallery; the Continuing Education Center, which sometimes houses 25 or more meetings in a single day, in an era increasingly dedicated to lifelong education[3]; the Optometry Building, with facilities and equipment moving this College to a certain place in the front ranks of optometric education, research and clinical service; the new College of

Technology, rounding out a $12 million plant for this ever-expanding component; and the library addition, part of a three-phase plan to bring holdings above 2,500,000 volumes by 1985.

With the additional expenditure of $40 million at UH/CLC, virtually all of this on the revolutionary and extremely functional and attractive megastructure called the Bayou Building,[4] the value of the University of Houston physical plant was estimated on June 1, 1977 at $214 million. Some $188 million, or 88 percent of total value, was added since 1961 under the administration of Hoffman the Builder.

The evolvement of the University of Houston System (UHS) may be perceived in time as one of the foremost developments of the Hoffman era. Following the passage of legislation authorizing UH/CLC in 1971, BUF financing to a maximum of $40 million was approved, and the institution opened a year ahead of schedule in 1973, utilizing existing facilities of the Clear Lake Graduate Center. With the Bayou Building complete, more than 4,000 students are now enrolled at the upper-level institution between the ultimate technology of the LBJ Manned Spacecraft Center and the pristine quiet of Armand Bayou.

UH/CLC, with two main thrusts, (1) goal-directed professional training to a high level of skill and (2) liberal education designed to produce graduates with a broad appreciation and grasp of man's heritage and of contemporary society, has been extremely successful to date. Its three components (Schools of Sciences and Technologies, Sciences and Humanities, and Professional Studies) have attracted outstanding professors in an atmosphere constantly emphasizing dedicated teaching. Chancellor Neumann has recruited effective administrators and other staff members to match.

A most significant addition to the UHS evolved in a period of several weeks during the summer of 1974. In late June, I had a call from one of the city's prime movers and shakers, advising me that a letter would be issued that day telling officials of South Texas Junior College (STJC) that the HISD was not interested in the possible purchase of this long-established private institution. The University had shown some interest in acquiring the vast 613,000-square foot STJC property at One Main Plaza in the heart of downtown, as a new location for its Downtown School, which was losing its lease; but we had backed off because we did not want to compete with HISD and had no hard financial data on STJC and its home, the old

Merchants and Manufacturers (M&M) building at the foot of Main Street.

Now I was told that one impediment to further exploration had been removed, and that powerful interests in the core of the city felt it imperative that we move our Downtown School to the STJC location, especially since STJC would begin to lose its financial stability soon. Enrollment was still at 2,800, but dropping steadily against our far lower tuition.

When I reported this to President Hoffman, he asked me to discuss it with no one else. He would ask Doug Mac Lean to get the financial data together, while I found out whatever else I could. Within 48 hours, Dr. Hoffman had met with R.A. (Al) Parker, chairman of the STJC trustees, and he and I with Mr. Parker, Eddy Scurlock and Elliott A. Johnson, the highest ranking other STJC officials, and the STJC president, W. I. Dykes.

It was a complicated matter, with legal and technical ramifications, and the need to make some decision as early in August as possible, in order to get STJC enrollment into our base for the next biennial appropriations. There could be no drawn-out discussions, and no referrals to tortoise-like academic committees. The advantages, however, were many: a continuing University presence in the immediate downtown area, where we had been for 32 years; an open admissions campus, where clamoring students unable to meet the standards on Central Campus could enter with a high school diploma or its equivalent; opportunity for expanding service to the community; and the acquisition of a potentially most valuable property. On August 6, 1974, the acquisition was completed, while we watched a driving rainstorm from Baker & Botts' 30th floor conference room, surrounded by our attorney, Frank M. Wozencraft, STJC's counselor, E.E. Townes, Jr., and a bevy of certified public accountants. Final details were wrapped up a week or so later, and Doug Mac Lean brought me down a note: "Pat (C. Pat Bailey, our staff counsel) has the papers, Al (A.L. Haggard, director of internal audits) has the money; and the president has himself a Downtown College." I had suggested this name early on, since the institution was a continuation of our Downtown School in expanded form.

President Hoffman did indeed have a Downtown College, in record time. And the UHS had an extremely important new component. Today, the Downtown College (UH/DC), under Chancellor J.

Don Boney, has an enrollment in excess of 4,500 students and much potential for the future.

The Victoria Campus (VC) continues to expand steadily, although more slowly than UH/CLC and UH/DC. The lack of state support for varied offerings in engineering remains a negative factor, and other arrangements involving the Central Campus are under study. With the loyal support of the prosperous Victoria community, and the massive industrial installations of Du Pont, Union Carbide and Alcoa nearby, however, we see accelerated growth for this component as well.

The proposed Woodlands Campus, a vital link in the UHS, did not receive Coordinating Board approval in the latest review, on January 26, 1977, even though recommendations concerning this component that go back to 1968 have been affirmed. UHS expansion in this area of the metroplex, which will have more people than Dallas County by 1990, appears inevitable.

The University of Houston System took a notable step forward on April 27, 1977, when Representative Craig Washington's HB 188 passed the Senate, thus formally establishing UHS by statute, and funding its operation with state monies specified for that purpose.

Library holdings, budgets, research grants and gifts continued to expand from 1971 to 1977, sometimes at a spectacular rate. There were 664,469 volumes in 1971, but the millionth book was added in an impressive ceremony on January 28, 1977, during the dedication of the John H. Freeman Wing of the Anderson Library (as the remarkable nonagenarian Mr. Freeman participated fully and enjoyably). The millionth volume, appropriately given by Kenneth Franzheim, was a priceless work by Albrecht Dürer. President Hoffman pointed out, in the opening event of our Fiftieth Anniversary celebration, that the Anderson Library had only 56,000 volumes when it was dedicated on April 1, 1951, just 26 years earlier.

Budgets, at $29,395,460 in 1971, reached $56,008,875 in 1977, and are expected to cross the $100 million mark when finally determined by the current Legislature for the next biennium. Research seemed destined to cross the magic $10 million mark by August 31, 1977, having climbed almost 30 percent (from $7,131,000) since 1971.

Gifts have continued a steady enlargement since 1971, both in terms of the Excellence Campaign (now bringing in more than $2 million annually, although almost 90 percent of this is earmarked for specific purposes within the colleges and departments of Central Campus), and special grants. Among these were a magnificent contribution of $1,670,000 from the Cullen Foundation, enabling us to buy Jeppesen Stadium from HISD for $6.8 million; the completion of payments on separate $1.5 million grants from Roy Hofheinz and Conrad N. Hilton; and a large gift to endowment from Mrs. Stephen Power Farish, honoring the naming of the College of Education Building for her husband, the pioneer regent who accomplished much for the University in its earlier days. The dedication of Farish Hall in 1975 was a memorable occasion, with the ceremony beginning at sunset in the Office of the President overlooking the Cullen Family Plaza's lighted sculpture and fountains, and continuing in Farish Hall across from Cullen Plaza.

In the mid-1960's, I had been asked by the remarkable Sarah Campbell Blaffer, widow of R. Lee Blaffer, philanthropist, iconoclast and art connoisseur, to consider the establishment of a teaching collection for the Art Department at the University, a project in which her daughter Cecil Amelia (Titi) Blaffer Hudson, now the Princess Furstenberg, other members of her family, and the Blaffer Foundation would share.[5]

President Hoffman told me of course to proceed, and great benefit to the University, to the community, the area and the state resulted. The Board of Regents named the gallery in the new Fine Arts Building the Sarah Campbell Blaffer Gallery on May 4, 1971, and four years later, when Mrs. Blaffer died at 91 (on May 11, 1975), she and Mrs. Hudson had given the University or the University of Houston Foundation 15 paintings, and placed another 19 on loan at the University. Many of these works were choice examples of various schools and eras in painting.[6]

The Sarah Campbell Blaffer Gallery was dedicated March 13, 1973, with a strong opening show drawn from what are now termed the Blaffer Collections of the University. Under William A. Robinson, Gallery director, and Professor Peter W. Guenther, with major assistance and support from the trustees of the Blaffer Foundation, "the Blaffer" has become a small jewel among the nation's galleries, not only mounting its own significant exhibitions, but bringing in outstanding shows from other sources.

A noteworthy exhibition of the works of Edvard Munch, which I had promised Mrs. Blaffer we would organize, opened April 12, 1976, with six works of the Norwegian genius owned by members of the Blaffer family, others loaned from the Munch Museum in Oslo, and a superb group of Munch graphics from the collection of Mr. and Mrs. Lionel Epstein of Washington, D.C. The exhibition, a memorial to Mrs. Blaffer and her husband, Robert Lee Blaffer, drew wide critical acclaim. The 256-page catalogue, by Professor Guenther, is a masterpiece, as is the opening statement by Mrs. Owen concerning her mother's perception of Munch and his work.

KUHT has progressed famously since 1971, due in large part to the dedicated efforts of General Manager James L. Bauer and his staff in cooperation with the extraordinary citizen support group, the Association for Community Television (ACT).[7]

The 1975-1976 Mission Self-Study was the 10-year evaluation required by the Southern Association in unique format. It bore from the beginning the stamp of a group of able and ambitious younger faculty members, many of them from outstanding institutions. They were apparently concerned by a number of things, among them: (1) the "strong president" tradition of the University, which they felt gave them minimum input in crucial decisions; (2) an inability to recruit exceptional students; (3) the budgetary threat represented by new UHS components; (4) the unsupported thesis that vibrant, prosperous Houston would provide limitless gifts, if only asked (one committeeman asked me, "Why don't you just go raise $200 million?" I replied, "Why not $300 million?"); and (5) generalized insecurity over budgetary cuts in many states and the threat of "steady state" enrollments everywhere.

The study was superbly organized by Professor Wallace I. Honeywell in nine task forces, examining either goals or resources, under a steering committee which included President Hoffman and Executive Vice-President Fields. Principal recommendations of the final report submitted on December 12, 1976, were that the Central Campus become a "flagship" campus, holding its overall enrollment at 30,000 but reducing undergraduates from 24,000 to 20,000 and substantially stepping up research; that the University emulate nationally known institutions, to some extent by major augmentation of both appropriated and private funds; and that programs be identified as "eminent," "strong," "average," or subject to elimination or removal to another campus.

The visiting committee from the Southern Association did not take too kindly to various sections of the report; its members cautioned the University to keep high-flown ambitions tempered with reality, in terms of the real strength of faculty, students and staff, and actual availability of resources. Why a watered-down MIT, Illinois, or University of Southern California instead of a vigorous, independent-minded institution reflecting the unique needs, challenges, strengths and opportunities of Houston itself?

Immediate and strident howls went up from those opposing the unfortunate "flagship" concept, with its ominous overtones of more selective admission standards and "a Ph.D. factory"; and from departments facing the "average" classification or, far worse, transfer or the guillotine.

On March 8, 1976, President Hoffman recommended to the regents in open meeting that they accept the self-study, in a carefully worded statement which adopted certain proposals but retained others for further examination. The key paragraph of his statement follows:

> "...future implementation...will require (1) Board of Regents approval of major policy and degree program changes; (2) the University's being financially capable of carrying out any such changes; and (3) assurance of protecting and extending our long-standing commitment to the range of responsibilities of this major public institution."

The longest, most expensive and probably most significant academic exercise in the history had ended, at least for a time. Now, we continue to assess its impact and future results, as perspective develops.

On December 7, 1976, President Hoffman began a project he is particularly determined to bring to a successful conclusion. This undertaking, as so many of the projects he has seen through to victory, has the potential for an especially deep and long-lasting effect upon the University of Houston.

He announced, at the Houston Country Club, the 50th Anniversary of the University, to run through calendar 1977, and the related UH 50 Fund which will attempt to raise a minimum of $23.5 million, and hopefully $32.5 million, for priority needs by 1981.

The president had the traditional support of the Cullen family, and of the Cullen Foundation behind him; the Foundation had pledged $3 million to endow nine distinguished professorships contingent upon the raising of another $6 million in matching funds.

Thus far the campaign has met with success, after many months of careful preparation and organization. I like to think that this and ongoing success were predictable, as was the tremendous Cougar

Cotton Bowl victory of New Year's Day, 1977, which Dr. Hoffman told his December 7 Houston Country Club audience would come about (reinforced now by our further 1977 successes in indoor track, basketball and golf).

The academic events of the half-century observance have been exceptional: the arts festival sent us by the French government; a series of consequential speakers, seminars and conferences; the German Expressionism art exhibition and lectures; a noteworthy symposium in conjunction with the dedication of the new College of Optometry; the dedication of the Freeman Wing.

Other events of exceptional promise are in prospect: the dedication of the Lyndall Wortham Theater and Science and Research II; ground-breaking for a Pharmacy Building and Cardiovascular Institute, our first facility in the Texas Medical Center; a symposium celebrating the twentieth anniversary of our literary quarterly, *FORUM*, and the tenth of William Lee Pryor's capable editorship.

As this is written, three major new gifts have just brought the UH 50 Fund to above $10 million. Surely that is a harbinger of a resoundingly successful report to be given by President Hoffman on December 6, 1977, when he points the way to final success in a crucial campaign that will determine much as the University of Houston launches its fifty-first year, looking forward to the centennial of A.D. 2027.

Notes to Chapter Eight

[1]There was, however, another administrative change of major consequence on June 10, 1977, when Dr. Singleton was named executive vice president, UHS, and Dr. Munitz, interim chancellor and dean of faculties, Central Campus. Dr. Fields was also on the move again in the summer of 1977, having accepted the presidency of his alma mater, Vanderbilt University.

[2]The University became interested in the Open University (OU) after President Hoffman had pursued the new British concept in meetings with its scintillating Scots vice-chancellor, Walter Perry, while on a sabbatical during 1970. We were subsequently chosen, with the University of Maryland and Rutgers University, to participate in an experiment

to determine the feasibility of utilizing OU concepts and materials (closely tied to educational television) on American campuses.

In the process, several University representatives, including myself, have become friends of Sir Walter (he was knighted in 1975) and members of the OU faculty and staff at Bletchley in Buckinghamshire (one train stop from the improbably named Leightons Buzzard). The OU program at the University has advanced steadily under the direction of Dr. Fannie Howard. She now has among her students the Princess Rima of Riyadh, who is being taught through OU procedures and female tutors from our Central Campus (they alone being allowed in the harem) in an experiment that drew a 600-word front page article in the New York *Times* after local media had ignored tips on the story.

[3]The Hilton School of Hotel and Restaurant Management, named for donor Conrad Nicholson Hilton, reached its capacity of 500 students two years after opening in the Continuing Education Center. A cherished dream of Dean James C. Taylor, the School with its 80-room model hotel seems destined to become what Eric Hilton predicted it would at the 1974 dedication of the Center — the finest such operation in the world.

[4]The concept of the "everything under one roof" megastructure at UH/CLC evolved after Chancellor Neumann and Vice-President Tough had discussed the project while waiting for a plane at O'Hare Field in Chicago. "Why not put everything under a single roof, like the Galleria?" Coulson Tough asked. "OK," Chancellor Neumann replied, "but no skating rink."

[5]Mrs. Blaffer and I had dozens of visits and conversations before and after her decision to place many of her art treasures, and later acquisitions, at the University. She was heavily influenced by her belief that art, "which is what it creates within you," can have an enormous impact upon the individual, especially the impressionable young student; and art to her had "a thousand eyes."

Thus she felt that paintings and sculpture of high quality had a vital function on a large campus, where they can have an impact on many thousands of students.

She was also piqued, and properly so, at James Johnson Sweeney, the charming, enormously knowledgeable, but outspoken director of the Museum of Fine Arts. They had had a disagreement regarding a Fragonard which she subsequently gave to the Fogg Museum at Harvard University. I visited the great critic and scholar later at his elegant 1798 French chateau near Westport in County Sligo, Ireland, hoping that he might volunteer some reaction to the possibility of a Blaffer teaching collection at the University (there were already rumors to this effect in Houston); but we talked only of the Bronze Age artifacts on his hill overlooking gorgeous Clew Bay, of his children with the marvelous Gaelic names (Tadhg and Siadhal), of how I could be three hours late driving up from the Shelburne Hotel, of a lawsuit I had pending in the High Court in Dublin against a rapscallion cousin by marriage.

The dispute with J.J. Sweeney, however, was only a minor factor in Mrs. Blaffer's fortunate decision (and that of her daughter Titi) to provide a teaching collection at the University. She was motivated strongly, and almost exclusively, by the conviction that her art belonged at the University, and that I could accomplish its being appropriately placed there.

One of our students, incidentally, was to have the invaluable opportunity to become a member of Mrs. Blaffer's household during her last two years of life. She called me early one Sunday to say that she had decided to have a student live in the big house at 6 Sunset Boulevard in old Shadyside, to share the life there with her, Jim Houston, her black servant of a half-century, and Maria the cook. She began to list the qualifications for such a student: Chinese, since they honored the old, but from Hong Kong, where every student speaks the King's English; a pre-medical major, so that she could discuss her ailments with him; employed, and preferably at the nearby Texas Medical Center, since working students were highly motivated; able to drive her Mercedes-Benz occasionally; and interested in politics, which she loved to discuss — conservative politics, of course.

"Anything else?" I asked, desperately taking notes. "Well," Mrs. Blaffer concluded, "he should be able to cook a little; Maria's off on Sunday evenings. And make sure he plays bridge."

The next day, Jack D. Burke, director of international student services, and our computers cranked out the name of Nelson Wong, a Hong Kong native who spoke the King's English. He was an honor pre-medical student working part-time in St. Luke's Hospital, Texas driver's license, and a conservative, amateur cook and bridge player. Four months later, Mrs. Blaffer flew over his sister Francis, a registered nurse who married a physician here, and brought over three younger Wong brothers, all gifted students and highly motivated. Nelson is now a second-year dental student, and wrote me last from Copenhagen after winning an international competition at Baylor College of Dentistry. Mrs. Blaffer had started a new dynasty, and brought this country some fine new future citizens.

[6]These paintings included de Ribera's *Portrait of Archimedes;* Mantegna's *Descent into Limbo (The Harrowing of Hell);* Pinturicchio's *Madonna and Child;* Corot's *Le Meditation;* di Casentino's *Madonna and Child;* Lucas Cranach the Elder's *Lucretia;* Bonnard's *Les Baigneuses dans un Parc;* Feininger's *Self-Portrait* and his *Zirchow I* (once ordered destroyed by Adolph Hitler, a disappointed artist who detested Cubism); Nolde's *Reiter und Tonfigur;* Lawrence's *Sarah Siddons;* Beckmann's *Woman with Mirror and Orchids;* Leger's *Etude pour les Beaux Danseuses;* de Kooning's *Seated Figure (Self-*

Portrait); Jan Fyt's *Hounds Resting from the Chase;* Kline's *Sabro;* Still's *1960-F;* and Munch's *Kneeling Female Nude* and *The Kiss.*

[7]In 1969, I asked John T. Jones, Jr., for help in organizing a support group for KUHT. He recruited Frank M. Wozencraft as founding chairman, and John Emmerich of the *Chronicle* as president. The next crucial appointment was that of Mrs. Max (Marty) Levine, as vice-president and chairman of a proposed teleauction. Frank Wozencraft and I persuaded other outstanding Houstonians to become ACT directors, and Mrs. Levine set out to discover all she could about teleauctions. I asked President Hoffman for a $10,000 loan from a presidential fund, against expenses, and when organization proceeded, I was back for another $10,000 advance. He looked at me just a little askance and asked, "This teleauction, PJ, will it fly?" I assured him that it would, and it did, bringing in $107,000 and a new tradition. In 1977, a vastly-expanded ACT organization will bring in an estimated $800,000 for Channel 8, $375,000 from Auction VII, and the remainder from memberships. Marty Levine is now chairman of the board, Harry Walker president, and Jim Dale top administrator of ACT. I wish that there were room to list every officer, director and member, including Robert U. (Bob) Haslanger, former president, his wife Ann, and the lady with first seniority at KUHT, Delia Mares.

Epilogue

What has it all meant: Dr. Oberholtzer's early dream; the inchoate years of struggle in borrowed, cramped quarters in a high school, leading, incredibly, to a system of four campuses enrolling 40,000 students, with the prospect of 25,000 more, taught by a faculty of 2,000 in a physical plant soon to be worth a quarter of a billion dollars?

Certainly, it has meant educational opportunity, economic advancement, and intellectual challenge for tens of thousands of young men and women — and increasingly, for adults of every age pursuing lifelong interests and training. It has meant, as well, a major, indispensable resource for a unique, still-burgeoning city that demanded a top-quality large public university, with broad-scope teaching, research and public service.

Putting the history of the University of Houston into perspective for myself, I recall many things, some imagined, but most from a storehouse of memories and the great good fortune of having known those who are gone now: Dr. Oberholtzer, Colonel Bates, Mr. Cullen, General Bruce, Clanton Williams; the innovative Dr. Kemmerer, who has lived on, after contributing to the University an ability and dedication either little known or misunderstood.

And I see those who remained to mold and shape the University of today and tomorrow: President Hoffman; Mr. Mac, sorely missed since his retirement, my fellow members of the Staff Conference, my own staff, and dozens of others now and over the years.

I imagine Dr. Oberholtzer arriving at Union Station in 1924, and I see him again, in my office at 1428 Commerce Building, telling me of his early plans and hopes, a little sad to be retired (even at 70), but proud of what he had accomplished. Colonel Bates I remember in a dozen settings—telling me at the Coronado Club of a hundred happenings that worked upon and sometimes transformed the institution; characteristically, in a jeep deep in the beautiful forests of south Montgomery County, his hand starting the circular pattern of decision as he indicated to George Mitchell the choice site he preferred for the Woodlands Campus (subsequently a $10 million gift from George and Cynthia Mitchell).

I see Mr. Cullen and Dr. Kemmerer together on that triumphant evening of October 31, 1950, at the opening of the Ezekiel W. Cullen Building, in their white ties and tails for the dedication ceremony; and there is Charles F. McElhinney, crawling under a barbed wire fence in his hunting clothes to survey the Settegast-Taub tract; I see him again, testifying so capably before legislative committees.

There are memories of General Bruce, and when he came to my home to thank me for assistance in what he was to describe as his "last campaign," the legislative victory of 1961; of him and Colonel Bates, the old FOTC comrades, marching along in a Commencement procession in the twilight of a late May evening (the Colonel limping a bit from his bad leg, the General ramrod straight, making a mental note of the dean up ahead with the temerity to be wearing only shirtsleeves under his academic robes). And I hear Clanton Williams announcing triumphantly that he had hired my old professor, Andrea Radoslav Tsanoff, and "a dozen other Ph.D.'s."

There are kaleidoscopic recollections of President Hoffman and our colleagues today, so much having happened since 1961, so much still crowding into the picture. And in the forefront of all this is the amazing transformation of the Central Campus, in a city of incredible dynamism, a city that has become a world center; and the advancing development of the University of Houston System, intensifying the impact of an institution destined, in time, for true greatness.

In a way, LBJ said it all 20 years ago, when I drove him over from the Shamrock Hilton to deliver the Commencement address of 1958, our arrival delayed 20 minutes while he read the text to his mother back at the ranch in Johnson City. We reminisced of Roy Hofheinz, and LBJ's Senate campaign of 1941. He asked me to carry a message of reconciliation to Judge Hofheinz; they were temporarily alienated. Then, for some reason, he spoke of the brief time he had taught public speaking at old Sam Houston High School.

"You born here?" he asked.

"Yes, in Montrose, on Mount Vernon."

"Don't ever leave," he advised. "Houston is a great city. It needs a great public university, and this will be it."

Appendix

The University of Houston Seal

The seal of the University of Houston, according to University traditions and records, is the coat-of-arms of General Sam Houston, who claimed descent from a Norman knight, Sir Hugh of Padavan, and adopted his heraldic crest. Although the facts are difficult to come by in London, Sir Hugh apparently came to England from the Caen region of France with William the Conqueror, duke of Normandy, in the invasion of October 1066, which led to the historic battle of Hastings.

The legend is that Sir Hugh fought well at Hastings, was in the royal party when William was crowned king on Christmas Day, 1066, and was given lands on the Scottish border for his services. The stronghold he built there was called Hughstown, and eventually, Houstoun, since the Lowlands natives could not pronounce Padavan. The spelling "Houstoun," incidentally, is always used in heraldic records, not "Houston."

Sir Hugh supposedly became enfeoffed to Malcolm III (Canmore), King of Scotland and son of Duncan I, murdered by Macbeth (who was not quite the scoundrel Shakespeare would have you believe, guilty though he was of dispatching his king).

Malcolm returned from exile to kill Macbeth in battle, avenge his father, and gain the Scottish throne in 1057. Years later, he began to mount raids across the border into England. On one such raid, Malcolm was hard pressed by opposing forces when Sir Hugh came to the rescue with a detachment of archers and mounted pikemen, just in time to save King Malcolm.

In return the king gave Sir Hugh a Scottish knighthood, and much more fertile lands in Renwickshire, just west of present-day Glasgow, on the River Clyde. More important, he gave permission for his rescuer, awarded a simple escutcheon bearing checkered chevrons (denoting nobility) and three ravens (strength and long life) by William the Conqueror, to embellish and change his coat-of-arms considerably. Above the shield a winged hourglass was added, and surmounting this, the motto, "In Tempore" (In Time). Rampant greyhounds were placed at the sides, the whole indicating the speed with which Sir Hugh had brought succour to his liege lord, in time to save his life. Martlets, gentle Lowlands birds symbolizing peace and deliverance, supplanted the ravens. A different version holds that the coat-of-arms from which the University of Houston seal derives resulted from a similar episode 600 years later. Descendants of Sir Hugh, the Houstoun clan, are said to have saved James II, the Catholic monarch of Scotland, through their timely arrival during a battle in 1686. The embellishments attributed to Sir Hugh were actually added to the family coat-of-arms 600 years later, according to this story. In any event, the seal of General Sam Houston had appeal to President E.E. Oberholtzer, to Hugh Roy Cullen, and to other prominent Houstonians 40 years ago, whether or not they realized how appropriate the motto "In Time" would become for a young institution aspiring to greatness.
institution aspiring to greatness.

The seal was adopted in 1938 in conjunction with the beginning of construction on the new campus, and the first official version was placed on the floor of the new Roy Gustav Cullen Building when it opened June 4, 1939. Freshmen were required to kneel around the seal during registration week, in a tradition that persisted until the early 1950's.

A redesigned version of the seal with such changes as "anatomically correct" greyhounds and the true date of the institution's founding (1927 instead of the 1934 originally shown) was adopted by the Board of Regents in 1969.

Appendix

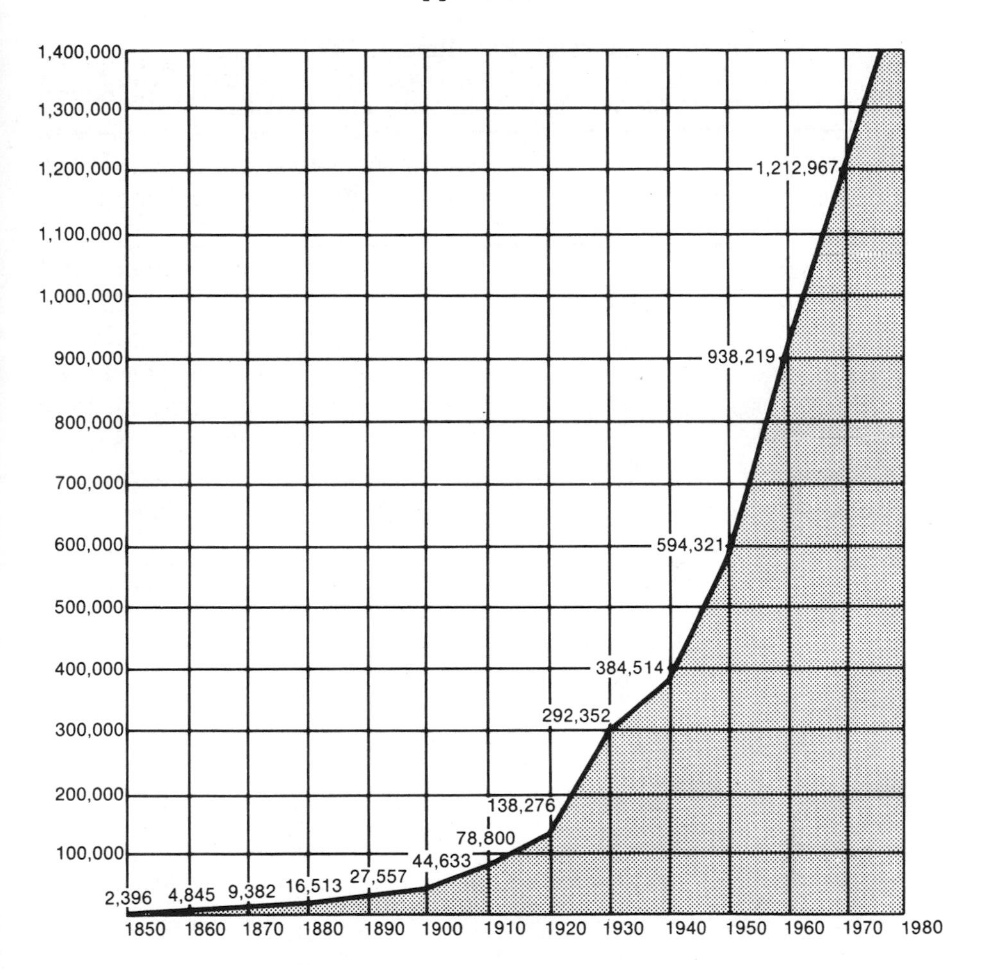

The population growth of Houston, 1850 to the present.

Appendix

University of Houston Enrollment, 1927—Present
Central Campus, Downtown School, Clear Lake Graduate Center, Victoria Campus, Correspondence, and Extension*

Academic Year	Fall	Spring	First Summer Semester and 12 Weeks	Second Summer Semester
1927			232	
1927-1928	461		242	
1928-1929	637		300	
1929-1930	730		383	
1930-1931	858		418	
1931-1932	743		231	
1932-1933	596		193	
1933-1934	624		504	
1934-1935	909	755	553	284
1935-1936	948	889	583	286
1936-1937	1249	1073	578	301
1937-1938	1285	1264	601	355
1938-1939	1563	1397	723	458
1939-1940	2067	1945	920	577
1940-1941	2488	2189	1109	619
1941-1942	2494	1829	943	617
1942-1943	1508	1224	557	231
1943-1944	1104	1015	542	382
1944-1945	2720	3780	2142	2119
1945-1946	5379	7302	4410	4256
1946-1947	10028	9479	5303	4659
1947-1948	10882	10125	5884	5060
1948-1949	11091	11649	6965	6349
1949-1950	13569	13557	7747	6725
1950-1951	13567	12947	7597	7763
1951-1952	13281	12374	5655	4625
1952-1953	12932	12193	5541	4495
1953-1954	12716	12221	5510	4686
1954-1955	13066	12520	5677	4683
1955-1956	13330	12239	5465	4582
1956-1957	13129	12156	5264	4452
1957-1958	13002	12237	5362	4674
1958-1959	13030	11773	5521	2605
1959-1960	11592	10730	4890	2323
1960-1961	11448	10771	5465	2640
1961-1962	12187	11676	5875	2875
1962-1963	13665	12960	6526	3353
1963-1964	17430	15855	8799	4257
1964-1965	17874	17038	9602	4661
1965-1966	19588	18465	10326	5211
1966-1967	19986	19291	10390	5632
1967-1968	21770	21170	11385	6772
1968-1969	23713	22636	11872	7195

Academic Year	Fall	Spring	First Summer Semester and 12 Weeks	Second Summer Semester
1969-1970	24383	23186	11569	7332
1970-1971	25582	24272	13150	8707
1971-1972	26475	24805	13193	8547
1972-1973	26473	25727	13376	8797
1973-1974	27552	26134	14179	9433
1974-1975	29996	29140	14347	9587
1975-1976	30465	28714	13092	8132

*The figures for the Summer Sessions of 1927 through 1934 were obtained from the *Statistical Report of Student Personnel* compiled in May, 1945, and on file in the Registrar's Office.

(Summer 1927 through Summer 1934)—The Fall figure indicates students enrolled for both Fall and Spring semesters and the 1st Summer figure indicates students enrolled for both summer sessions. A student was counted only once whether he was enrolled for one or two semesters or sessions.

(Fall 1934 through present)—A student is included in the registration total each semester that he registers during the academic year.

Clear Lake City Center opened First Summer 1965, changed to Clear Lake Graduate Center Spring 1972; Victoria Center opened Spring 1973; Clear Lake Graduate Center and the Downtown School closed the end of Spring 1974. Beginning Fall 1975 includes Central Campus only.

Excerpts from the Resolution Establishing a Junior College for the City of Houston

From the Minutes of the Board of Education
Houston Independent School District
March 7, 1927

Whereas, the Board of Trustees of the Houston Independent School District believes, after careful investigation of the matter, that there is a general demand and urgent need for a Junior College in the City of Houston, Texas, and

Whereas, said Board believes that the establishment of a Junior College in the City of Houston will make it possible for many young men and women to obtain the benefits of college training who could not otherwise do so, and

Whereas, said Board believes that a Junior College can be made to render a most valuable service to our public school system for providing training for teachers in and for our schools at a nominal cost and in a convenient manner and at a convenient time, and

Whereas, said Board also believes that a Junior College can be operated on a self-sustaining basis on a comparatively low tuition cost, and

Whereas, said Board feels as the representatives of the people, charged with the responsibility and duty of providing the best possible educational advantages for the city and that the establishment of a Junior College would be an advanced step in providing better educational opportunity . . . .

(The remainder of this somewhat lengthy document sets forth details concerning the organization of the Houston Junior College, and authorizes its immediate establishment).

CHARTER

OF THE

UNIVERSITY OF HOUSTON

WHEREAS, The Board of Education of the Houston Independent School District, at its regular adjourned meeting, held on April 30, 1934, did by certain resolutions authorize the establishment and define the authority of the UNIVERSITY OF HOUSTON, which resolutions are hereby affirmed, and

WHEREAS, It is now desirable for the Board of Education to give expression of the purposes motivating this undertaking;

Therefore, be it Resolved, That the Board of Education adopt the following as an expression of the purposes, social import, and fundamental principles and delegate to the UNIVERSITY OF HOUSTON the use of this charter in giving to the public an adequate understanding of its work:

ARTICLE I

We believe that continuance of democracy depends upon an organized public educational program which must become a continuous, lifelong educational process in co-operative study of the economic, political, social, and cultural realities of everyday life. Such an educational program is needed to provide a background for intelligent citizenship. The present greatly accelerated social and economic changes demand readjustments which in a democracy depend upon voluntary, concerted action; such voluntary co-operation can be secured only by an informed people. The education of our citizens to meet the issues of life must develop the qualities of open-mindedness, adaptability, and a willingness to work together for the common welfare. Although individual initiative must be maintained, citizens of a truly democratic society must become aware of the evils of selfishness and narrow individualism. They must be able to comprehend and to judge intelligently the plans of their leaders grappling with the common problems of life.

ARTICLE II

We believe that the responsibilities of the UNIVERSITY OF HOUSTON, shared with the citizens of the community, are:

1. To provide an educational program which will serve public welfare constructively.
2. To cultivate within individuals a better understanding of the richness of our physical, social, and spiritual inheritance, to the end that more intelligent leadership and co-operative effort may be assured.
3. To promote greater individual self-realization and personal satisfaction through a better adjustment of the individual to his work in some worthy service for the betterment of society.
4. To assist modern industry in obtaining more intelligent leaders and workers.
5. To encourage the constructive use of leisure time.
6. To promulgate social integration through open-minded inquiry and public discussion in order to prevent or to overcome apathy, prejudice, and selfish aggrandizement.

(Article III embodies the provisions of the enabling act to begin organization of the University of Houston.)

The foregoing resolution was readopted at a meeting of the Board of Education on the ninth day of June, 1934, to which the undersigned duly certify.

THE BOARD OF REGENTS
University of Houston
April, 1945

Index

Index

Index